Including Students
with Special Needs

Including Students with Special Needs

A Practical Guide for Classroom Teachers

FOURTH EDITION

Marilyn Friend
University of North Carolina at Greensboro

William D. Bursuck
University of North Carolina at Greensboro

PEARSON

Boston | New York | San Francisco
Mexico City | Montreal | Toronto | London | Madrid | Munich | Paris
Hong Kong | Singapore | Tokyo | Cape Town | Sydney

Executive Editor: Virginia Lanigan
Senior Development Editor: Sonny Regelman
Marketing Manager: Kris Ellis-Levy
Associate Development Editor: Adam Whitehurst
Editorial Assistant: Scott Blaszak
Editorial-Production Administrator: Janet Domingo
Editorial-Production Service: Susan McNally
Composition and Prepress Buyer: Andrew Turso
Manufacturing Buyer: Andrew Turso
Cover Administrator: Linda Knowles
Interior Designer: Carol Somberg
Photo Research: Larissa Tierney
Illustrations and Electronic Composition: Omegatype Typography, Inc.

Library of Congress Cataloging-in-Publication Data

Friend, Marilyn Penovich, 1953–
    Including students with special needs : a practical guide for classroom teachers/Marilyn
Friend, William D. Bursuck.—4th ed.
        p. cm.
    Includes bibliographical references (p.) and indexes.
    ISBN 0-321-31774-2
        1. Inclusive education—United States. 2. Mainstreaming in education—United States. 3.
Special education—United States. 4. Children with disabilities—Education—United States.
I. Bursuck, William D. II. Title.
LC1201.F75 2005
371.9'046—dc22

                                                                2005045914

Text and photo credits appear on page 562, which constitutes an extension of the copyright page.

Printed in the United States of America
10 9 8 7 6 5 4 3   WEB   10 09 08 07 06

To Beth and Bruce for their love, support, and infinite patience with our sometimes unkept promises—"Just one more weekend and I'll be done with this," and "I'll be right there"—and our obsessive concern about meeting (and missing) deadlines.

Brief Contents

Contents

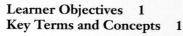

CHAPTER **4**   Assessing Student Needs   106

page 106

CHAPTER **5**

Planning Instruction by Analyzing Classroom and Student Needs   144

page 144

CHAPTER **6**

Students with Low-Incidence Disabilities   186

page 186

CHAPTER **7**

Students with High-Incidence Disabilities

232

page 232

CHAPTER **8**   Other Students with Special Needs   264

page 264

CHAPTER **9**   Instructional Adaptations   304

page 304

CHAPTER **10**   Strategies for Independent Learning   354

page 354

CHAPTER **11**   Evaluating Student Learning   396

page 396

CHAPTER **13** Building Social Relationships 470

page 470

Features at a Glance

(continued)

Technology Notes	Working Together	Special Emphasis On ...	Applications in Teaching Practice
• Using Computer Technology to Foster Cultural Awareness, 287 • Technology and Students at Risk, 299	Creating a School Environment for Collaborating with Parents, 291	Counselors and Students at Risk, 297	Diversity in a High School Class, 300
Supporting Student Journal Writing Using Word-Recognition and Speech-Synthesis Software, 318	Asking for Help, 311	Strategies for Teaching Science to English-Language Learners, 320	Developing a Repertoire of Instructional Adaptations, 350
Thinking Reader: The Textbook of the Future, 374	Fostering Team Communication and Self-Advocacy, 358	Getting Students to Study in Study Hall, 376	Designing Strategies for Independence, 393
Conducting Alternative Assessments Using Electronic Portfolios, 426	Communicating with Parents about Grades, 413	Testing English-Language Learners in Math-Problem Solving, 406	Adapting Evaluations for Students with Special Needs, 428
Help on the Web for Responding to Student Behavior, 459	When Differences of Opinion Occur, 455	Discipline in Related Arts Classes, 437	Developing Strategies for Responding to Individual Student Behavior, 466
• Using Technology to Build Positive Peer Relationships, 484 • Using Assistive Technology to Facilitate Cooperative Learning, 497	Collaborating with Families, 480	Fostering Social Skills in Drama Class, 499	Planning for Promoting Positive Peer Relations, 501

Preface

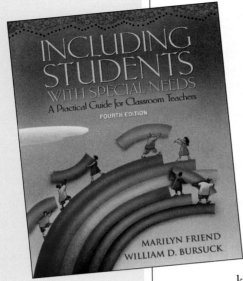

When the reauthorization of the Individuals with Disabilities Education Act was signed into law in December 2004, a critical piece of the future of education for students with disabilities was put into place. Combined with the provisions of the No Child Left Behind Act of 2001, a clear mandate has been given that nearly all students, whether or not they have disabilities or other special needs, should be educated in the same curriculum and, in most instances, in classrooms with their peers without disabilities. Like all students, those who struggle to learn because of intellectual, physical, sensory, emotional, communication, or learning disabilities or other special needs are to be taught using research-based practices, and they are expected to reach the same high standards as all students. Importantly, teachers, administrators, and other professionals are more accountable than ever before for ensuring that these lofty goals are accomplished.

The fourth edition of *Including Students with Special Needs: A Practical Guide for Classroom Teachers* reflects our continued strong commitment to inclusive practices, a commitment tempered by our knowledge and experience of the realities of day-to-day teaching. We know that inclusive practices are essential to meet the requirements of current legislation, and these practices are most likely to succeed with strong and sustained administrative support, extensive professional preparation for classroom teachers as well as special education staff, and a significant dollop of professional common sense regarding the necessity of tailoring educational programs to meet students' needs without assigning students indiscriminately to a single physical location. We have brought to this project our own backgrounds as teachers in the field and as teacher educators, researchers, and staff developers. We also bring our own diversity: Marilyn with expertise in elementary and secondary education, especially in urban settings, and in collaboration, inclusive practices, and co-teaching; Bill with expertise in secondary education, literacy, instructional strategies, assessment, and grading practices.

The organization of the book and the amount of space devoted to various topics and subtopics reflect our priorities for preparing general education teachers to instruct effectively the students they will encounter. These priorities are based on our own experiences in teaching undergraduate and graduate educators, our conversations with our colleagues across the country, and our analysis of the professional literature on preservice and inservice teacher preparation on inclusive practices. We also have listened carefully to the many teachers we have met who are facing the challenges of twenty-first-century classrooms. We hope that the results of all our discussions, our interactions with others, and our individual struggles to "get it right" have resulted in a book that is reader-friendly yet informative, and research-based yet readable. We hope that this text presents information and suggestions that are effective for teaching students with diverse needs and feasible for today's classroom teacher. Above all, we hope this fourth edition is responsive to the many issues confronting teachers as they attempt to help all their students succeed.

New to the Fourth Edition

- Chapter 1 includes updated information on the **No Child Left Behind Act** and **IDEA 2004.**
- Chapter 4, **Assessing Student Needs,** is presented earlier in order to underscore the importance of developing effective assessment practices to influence classroom

instruction. It includes new coverage of high-stakes testing of students with disabilities.

- Chapter 5 presents updated information about the concepts of **differentiated instruction** and **universal design** and how they apply to including students with special needs.

- Chapter 6 presents the most current information about **autism spectrum disorder.**

- Chapter 8 includes updated coverage of **attention deficit–hyperactivity disorder** and the best ways to accommodate students with ADHD in the general education classroom.

- Chapter 11 includes updated ideas on ways to make **grading adaptations** for students with disabilities.

- **INCLUDE** The new **INCLUDE** margin icon highlights text discussion in which the unique INCLUDE model is applied.

- The new **Working Together** boxed feature provides increased attention to teachers' **collaboration** with special education professionals, families, and paraprofessionals.

- **INTASC** **Council for Exceptional Children** The new **Working the Standards** feature includes information on INTASC and CEC standards and what classroom teachers should know about them.

Organization of the Book

The textbook is divided into four main sections. The **first section** provides fundamental background knowledge about the field of special education as well as current information on how students with disabilities are served within inclusive school environments. **Chapter 1** outlines key concepts for understanding special education, including new provisions of IDEA. **Chapter 2** introduces the people who specialize in working with students with disabilities and the procedures through which students may be identified to receive special education services. **Chapter 3** discusses the principles of collaboration and the school situations in which professionals are most likely to collaborate to meet the needs of students with disabilities.

The **second section** of the book provides a framework for thinking about effective instructional practices for students who struggle to learn. **Chapter 4** explores both formal and informal assessment strategies that help teachers contribute to the decision-making process for students with disabilities. **Chapter 5** introduces a step-by-step strategy for making instructional adjustments, called INCLUDE, that helps teachers accommodate students with special needs in a more deliberate way. This chapter also addresses the dimensions along which accommodations can occur.

The **third section** of the book introduces readers to students with specific disabilities and other special needs. **Chapters 6 and 7** address the various federally established categories of exceptionality and provide information about them essential for general education teachers in today's schools. **Chapter 8** considers students who may not receive special education but who nonetheless are at risk for school failure. However, the overall approach taken in these chapters (and in the text as a whole) is noncategorical. Even though students with disabilities or other special needs are unique, they share many physical, psychological, learning, and behavior characteristics, and they often benefit from similar instructional approaches.

The material in the **fourth section** of the text represents the heart of any course on inclusive practices: instructional approaches that emphasize teaching students effectively both in academic and in social and behavior areas, regardless of disability or special need. **Chapter 9** provides strategies for adapting curriculum materials, teacher instruction, and student practice activities for both basic skills and content-area instruction. The emphasis is on adaptations that are relatively easy to make. **Chapter 10** focuses on ways to help students with and without special needs become more independent learners by teaching them specific strategies. **Chapter 11** explores options for adapting classroom evaluations for diverse learners to ensure that the information gathered is accurate and helpful in guiding instruction. In **Chapter 12,** readers learn approaches for addressing a common teacher concern—student discipline, including procedures designed for mild through significant classroom behavior problems. Finally, **Chapter 13** explores several approaches for building positive relations among students with and without special needs.

Features of the Fourth Edition

Many of the popular features from the first three editions have been retained and enhanced in this fourth edition. These features have been designed to help readers learn more effectively, as well as to add to the general discussion in-depth information about topics such as teaching strategies, cultural diversity, and technology:

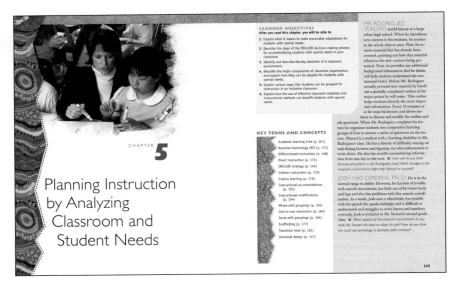

- **Learner Objectives** are listed at the start of each chapter as an organizational and study tool for readers.
- **Key Terms and Concepts** are listed at the start of each chapter and are highlighted throughout the text with boldface type. They are explained with easy-to-understand definitions provided both in context and in a glossary at the back of the book.
- **Chapter-opening vignettes** serve as introductory cases to help readers think about how the content of chapters relates to teachers and students. They conclude with critical-thinking questions. These cases serve as examples throughout the chapters and are revisited in the Working the Standards feature at the end of each chapter.
- **Professional Edge** features provide numerous research-validated, practical teaching applications related to each chapter's topics.

- **Case in Practice** features clarify key principles by providing brief case studies related to chapter concepts and teaching scripts as models.

- **Technology Notes** features illustrate the application of many types of technology available to support students with disabilities in inclusive schools.

- **Special Emphasis On . . .** features highlight topics related to nonacademic areas (for example, the arts, physical education, and counseling) that are frequently overlooked in other texts as well as provide up-to-date information on addressing the needs of students from diverse backgrounds and English-language learners.

- **New! Working Together** features present cases in which professional and family collaboration is needed and provide tips for optimizing collaborative efforts.

- **Marginal annotations** are designed to stimulate higher level thinking and provide additional information on cultural and linguistic diversity, research, and useful websites.

ANALYZE AND REFLECT

CONNECTIONS

DIMENSIONS OF DIVERSITY

WWW RESOURCES

RESEARCH NOTE

FYI

- **Chapter summaries** review key information covered in each chapter for easy synthesis and reference.

- **Applications in Teaching Practice** cases and activities at the end of each chapter are designed to encourage students to apply the text contents to real-life classroom situations.

- **New! Working the Standards** features list relevant INTASC Principles and CEC Content Standards for each chapter and revisit the chapter-opening vignettes to illustrate the application of those principles and standards. Questions and activities help provide context for understanding the standards. Additional information linking these principles and standards to the text contents is provided on the companion website (http://www.ablongman.com/friend4e).

- **New! Further Readings** features suggest carefully chosen books and journal articles related to chapter topics.

Supplements

For Instructors

- The **Instructor's Resource Manual** contains chapter overviews, outlines, activities, discussion questions, transparency and handout masters, and test items. The updated test item file, which also is available in computerized format for Windows and Macintosh operating systems, includes multiple-choice items, true–false items, performance-based items, and case-based application items. Answer feedback and guidelines are provided.

- *Professionals in Action: Teaching Students with Special Needs* **Videotape** (closed captioned, 120 minutes). This video contains five 15- to 30-minute modules presenting viewpoints and approaches to teaching students with various disabilities in general education classrooms, special education settings, and various combinations of the two. Each module explores its topic using actual classroom footage and interviews with general and special education teachers, parents, and students.

- The *Snapshots* **Video Series for Special Education** (all are closed captioned)

  Snapshots: Inclusion Video (22 minutes) profiles three students of differing ages and with various levels of disability in inclusive class settings. In each case, parents, classroom teachers, special education teachers, and school administrators talk about the steps they have taken to help the students succeed in inclusive settings.

  Snapshots 2: Video for Special Education (20–25 minutes) is a two-video set of six segments (covering traumatic brain injury, behavior disorders, learning disabilities, mental retardation, hearing loss, and visual impairments) designed specifically for use in college classrooms. Each segment profiles three individuals and their families, teachers, and experiences. These programs are of high interest to students; instructors who have used the tapes in their courses have found that they help in disabusing students of stereotypical views and put a "human face" on course material.

- **CourseCompass**™ Powered by Blackboard and hosted nationally, Allyn & Bacon's own course management system, **CourseCompass,** helps you manage all aspects of teaching your course. For colleges and universities with **WebCT**™ and **Blackboard**™ licenses, special course management packages are available in these formats as well.

- **PowerPoint Slides** are easily accessed by instructors from the home page of the Companion Website. More than 100 slides, organized by chapter, are ideal for use as lecture presentations and/or handouts for students.

- **Allyn & Bacon Transparencies for Special Education** (© 2005) include approximately 100 acetates, more than half of which are in full color.

- The **Allyn & Bacon Digital Media Archive (DMA) for Special Education** electronically provides charts, graphs, tables, figures, web links, and video clips on one cross-platform CD-ROM.

For Students

- The **Companion Website** with **Online Practice Tests** (http://www. ablongman.com/friend4e) features chapter learning objectives, activities, web links, cases, and practice tests for students.

- Available free when packaged with the textbook, the **Video Workshop for Special Education CD-ROM** contains 10 modules of 3- to 5-minute digitized video clips featuring real classroom settings. The VideoWorkshop CD comes with a **Student Study Guide** containing all the materials needed to help students get started. With questions for reflection before, during, and after viewing, this guide extends classroom discussion and allows for more in-class time spent on analysis of material. An **Instructor's Teaching Guide** also is available to provide ideas and exercises to assist faculty in incorporating this convenient supplement into course assignments and assessments. (Visit http://www.ablongman.com/videoworkshop for more details.)

- The **"What's Best for Matthew?" Interactive CD-ROM Case Study for Learning to Develop IEPs, Version 2.0** CD-ROM helps preservice and inservice teachers develop their understanding of IEP's and how they are written through the case study of Matthew, a 9-year-old boy with autism. It is sold separately and is also available at a reduced price as a "value package" with the textbook.

- **mylabschool** **MyLabSchool** is a collection of online tools designed to help prepare students for success in this course as well as in their teaching careers. Visit http://www.mylabschool.com to access the following:
  - video footage of real-life classrooms
  - help with research papers using Research Navigator
  - help with lesson planning
  - tools for planning a teaching career, including developing portfolios and preparing for licensure

- **Research Navigator™ (with ContentSelect Research Database)** (http://www.researchnavigator.com) is the easiest way for students to start a research assignment or research paper. Complete with extensive help on the research process and three exclusive online databases of credible and reliable source material, including EBSCO's ContentSelect™ Academic Journal Database, New York Times Search by Subject Archive, and "Best of the Web" Link Library, Research Navigator™ helps students quickly and efficiently make the most of their research time. Research Navigator™ is free when packaged with the textbook and requires an access code.

Acknowledgments

We know that we are very fortunate to be surrounded by people who are committed to helping us in our work. We are grateful to the many individuals who helped us during the preparation of the fourth edition of *Including Students with Special Needs*, for without their assistance and encouragement the project undoubtedly would have stalled. First and most important, we express our gratitude to our families. They have listened to us worry about how to meet the deadlines that sometimes seemed impossibly near, agonize over which new material to add and which existing material to delete, and obsess about the knowledge, skills, and dispositions that teachers must have to work with students with disabilities in this age of high standards and teacher accountability. They helped us sort through the conundrums, offered suggestions with the perspective of outsiders who deeply cared, and tolerated our need to hide in our offices as we wrote and rewrote. We cannot possibly say thank you in enough ways for their support.

We also thank the individuals who helped us with all the details that are necessary in writing a textbook. Graduate assistants Kazuko Matsuda, Kim Pope, and Erin Anderson confidently said "I can do that" when asked to find obscure bits of information, proofread, and check references. Lauri Susi helped with the Technology Notes. Sonia Martin, department administrative assistant at UNCG, not only assisted in checking the manuscript for accuracy and in ensuring that the project was well managed, but also completed the time-consuming task of obtaining all the permissions to reproduce others' work. We especially thank her for lending a sympathetic ear as we worked through many moments of deadline stress. Through it all, she kept the essential ingredient of humor in the mix of our work.

The professionals at Allyn & Bacon also have supported this effort with both words and actions. Executive editor Virginia Lanigan has steered this fourth edition through the many steps of its creation, offering guidance and encouragement with just the right touch of patience. Developmental editor Sonny Regelman was meticulous in her efforts to keep the book clear, responsive to the needs of the field, and on target with the correct number of pages!

Special thanks go to the reviewers for this edition: Opal Effie Laman, Texas Tech University; Susan L. O'Rourke, Carlow College; Gina Scala, East Stroudsburg University; Linda Domanski, Westminster College; Melisa A. Reed, Marshall University; Kalie R. Kossar, West Virginia University; Daniel P. Joseph, Coppin State College; Beth Day-Hairston, Winston-Salem State University; Philip Lanasa, Cameron University; Kimberly Bright, Shippensburg University; Judith Terpstra, University of Nevada–Las Vegas; Laura M. Frey, East Carolina University; and Paula W. Adams, Sam Houston State University. We were impressed with the care with which they reviewed the manuscript and the insightful suggestions they made. We freely admit that we sometimes questioned their opinions, but we know that they definitely helped us create a better textbook.

Finally, we continue to be grateful to all of our colleagues and students who influence our thinking about educating students with special needs in general education classrooms. Their questions about best practices, their challenges to our thinking, and their ideas for better communicating our message have been invaluable. We especially are appreciative of the individuals who have taken the time to correspond with us to share their impressions of the book, their concerns, and their ideas for what we might do the next time to improve our outcomes. We hope they see their influence in the current edition, and they can know with certainty that we continue to welcome their—and all readers'—input.

About the Authors

Marilyn Friend has worked in the field of education in a variety of roles for 30 years. In addition to teaching in both special education and general education, she has worked as a teacher educator and staff developer and currently is chairperson of the Department of Specialized Education Services at the University of North Carolina at Greensboro. Her particular areas of expertise—the focus of her research, teaching, writing, and work in the field—include inclusive schooling, co-teaching and other collaborative school practices, and family–school partnerships.

William Bursuck has been an educator for more than 35 years. During that time he has worked as both a general and special education teacher in the public schools as well as a university teacher educator. Although he has written numerous research articles and is a successful grant writer, Dr. Bursuck takes particular pleasure in providing classroom and future teachers with practical, evidence-based strategies to help students with special needs be more successful in school. He is professor in the Department of Specialized Education Services at the University of North Carolina at Greensboro.

The Foundation for Educating Students with Special Needs

LEARNER OBJECTIVES

After you read this chapter, you will be able to

1. Explain key terms and concepts that describe special education.

2. Trace the historical events that have shaped contemporary special education services.

3. Outline the laws that govern current practices for educating students with disabilities.

4. Analyze your beliefs related to inclusive practices as the basis for educating students with disabilities within the context of contemporary knowledge about effective instruction and educational access, and consider how your beliefs affect your approach to teaching and learning.

5. Describe the categories of disabilities addressed in federal law, and identify other special needs your students may have.

KEY TERMS AND CONCEPTS

Americans with Disabilities Act (ADA) (p. 10)

Brown v. Board of Education (p. 8)

Cross-categorical approach (p. 26)

High-incidence disabilities (p. 26)

Inclusive practices (p. 4)

Individuals with Disabilities Education Act (IDEA) (p. 10)

Integration (p. 8)

Least restrictive environment (LRE) (p. 3)

Low-incidence disabilities (p. 26)

Mainstreaming (p. 4)

No Child Left Behind Act of 2001 (NCLB) (p. 13)

P.L. 94-142 (p. 10)

Related services (p. 3)

Section 504 (p. 9)

Special education (p. 3)

THOMAS IS ONE of those students who makes his presence known very quickly. He announced on the first day in his seventh-grade social studies class that the color of the walls was *xantho-*(yellow). For several days later that fall, he came to school wearing only socks on his feet because, as his mother explained, he had completely outgrown his old shoes but would not wear new ones because he said they "had knots in the toes." That problem eventually was resolved. In all classes, Thomas tends to keep to himself and when group projects are assigned, he has difficulty knowing how to talk to his classmates about anything except the subjects he enjoys—French words commonly used in the English language and Alfred Hitchcock movies. When Thomas began elementary school, he was enrolled in a special education class for students with autism. However, most of his classmates had significant intellectual disabilities, and the teacher and Thomas's parents quickly realized that he needed to be challenged academically in a way that could not happen in that class. Since second grade, he has spent most of his time in general education classrooms. In some situations, a special education teacher worked in his classroom with the general education teacher, or a paraprofessional was present to assist the teacher and all the students. Now, though, such support is not necessary. Thomas meets with his special education teacher, Ms. Meyer, once each day with several other students who have learning and behavior disabilities and if an issue arises in class, Ms. Meyer works with the teacher to address it. Thomas would like to be a linguist when he grows up. ● *What is autism? Why is it so important for Thomas to access the same curriculum as his peers? What types of support might be needed to help Thomas succeed in school?*

TONYA IS A FIRST GRADER who loves school, has a wide circle of friends, and sometimes displays a stubborn streak. She also has many special needs: She uses a wheelchair, and she can use her arms, hands, and fingers only for very simple tasks. She has a significant cognitive disability, and she does not communicate

1

with words but usually can make her preferences known with her facial expressions. A paraprofessional is almost always available in Tonya's classroom to help her to use the computer and to facilitate her interactions with her classmates, but the paraprofessional also completes routine classroom tasks as the teacher directs and supports other students as needed. Tonya's parents are actively involved in her education, and they work closely with the teacher and specialists to set goals and to monitor progress in reaching them. Tonya's teacher recently made the comment, "I know Tonya is learning more than she can convey. I can tell by the twinkle in her eye." ● *How likely are you to teach a student like Tonya? What is a cognitive disability? What factors have led students like Tonya to be educated in typical classrooms instead of special education classrooms?*

AARON HAS A LEARNING DISABILITY that was identified when he was in second grade. He also takes medication for attention deficit–hyperactivity disorder (ADHD). Now in eleventh grade, Aaron continues to learn

how to compensate for the academic difficulties he experiences. Although he is a bright and personable young man, he reads at about a seventh-grade level. His writing is much like that of a student in second grade. He doesn't like to talk about his learning disabilities (LD); he doesn't want other students to make fun of him or treat him differently because he's "LD." He is even more sensitive when asked to talk about why he takes medication. In his U.S. history class, he is most successful on tests when he answers questions orally; he understands the concepts even if he sometimes cannot write his thoughts. Because he doesn't like to be singled out, however, he sometimes refuses to take tests or to get additional assistance during study period, so his grades are lower than they could be. Aaron is an excellent athlete, and on the basketball court he feels equal to his friends. However, his parents are concerned that his interest in sports is distracting him from schoolwork. ● *How often will you meet students like Aaron? What is a learning disability? What types of supports and services do students like Aaron need to succeed in school?*

Students like Thomas, Tonya, and Aaron are not unusual. They are among the 5.8 million school-age students in the United States who have disabilities that make them eligible for special education (U.S. Department of Education, 2002). But their disabilities do not tell you who they are: They are children or young adults and students first. Like all students, they have positive characteristics and negative ones, they have great days and some that are not so great, and they have likes and dislikes about school and learning.

As a teacher, you probably will instruct students like Thomas, Tonya, and Aaron along with other students with disabilities or different special needs. The purpose of this book is to help you understand students with disabilities and other special needs and learn strategies for addressing those needs. You can be the teacher who makes a profound positive difference in a student's life. With the knowledge and skills you learn for teaching exceptional learners, you will be prepared for both the challenges and the rewards of helping them achieve their potential.

What Key Terms and Concepts Define Special Education?

When professionals talk about students like Thomas, Tonya, and Aaron, they may use several key terms. For example, when teachers refer to students with *disabilities*, they mean students who are eligible to receive special education services according to federal and state guidelines. **Special education** is the specially designed instruction provided by the school district or other local education agency that meets the unique needs of students identified as disabled. Special education may include instruction in a general education or special education classroom, education in the community for students who need to learn life skills, and specialized assistance in areas such as physical education, speech/language, or vocational preparation. Students with disabilities also may receive **related services,** that is, assistance required to enable students to benefit from special education. Examples of related services include transportation to and from school in a specialized van or school bus and physical therapy. Additionally, students with disabilities are entitled to supplementary aids and services. In other words, they must receive supports such as preferential seating, access to computer technology, and instructional adjustments that enable them to be educated with their peers who do not have disabilities. All special education, related services, and supplementary aids and services are provided to students by public schools at no cost to parents.

DIMENSIONS
OF **DIVERSITY**

Issues related to race and culture continue to exist in special education. Even after more than 30 years of study, litigation, and other attention, African American students are still overrepresented in special education.

Least Restrictive Environment

As you read this textbook and complete the activities in your course, you will learn many important facts and skills related to working with students with disabilities. However, one of the most important concepts for you to understand as a general educator is **least restrictive environment (LRE),** a provision in the federal laws that have governed special education for three decades. LRE is a student's right to be educated in the setting most like the educational setting for peers without disabilities in which the student can be successful, with appropriate supports provided (Burnstein, Sears, Wilcoxen, Cabello, & Spagna, 2004; Karger, 2004; Pivik, McComas, & Laflamme, 2002). For many students, the least restrictive environment is full-time or nearly full-time participation in a general education classroom. In fact, in 1999–2000, approximately 47.3 percent of all school-age students with disabilities received 79 percent or more of their education in general education classrooms (U.S. Department of Education, 2002). This is true for Thomas, Tonya, and Aaron who were introduced at the beginning of this chapter. Thomas also receives instruction in a special education classroom once each day. Tonya leaves her classroom once a week for physical therapy only, a support best offered for her in a large space with specialized equipment. Aaron, who can succeed in social studies class when he gives test answers aloud, may leave his classroom for that purpose only. His LRE is a general education classroom; the test procedure is a supplementary service.

For some students—for example, those who have emotional or behavioral disabilities—being in a general education classroom nearly all day may be academically and emotionally inappropriate. For these students, the LRE may be a general education classroom for part of the day and a special education classroom, sometimes called a *resource room,* for the remainder of the day. Yet other students' LRE may be a special education setting for most of the day, sometimes referred to as a *self-contained class.* Students with significant behavior problems or students who require intensive supports may be educated in this way. Finally, just a few students with disabilities attend separate or residential schools, or learn in a home or hospital setting. These very restrictive options usually are necessary only for students with the most significant or most complex disabilities.

Identifying an LRE other than a general education setting is a serious decision usually made by a team of professionals and a student's parents only after intensive supports are provided in the general education classroom without success. Such supports can include alternative materials or curriculum, assistance from a paraprofessional (that is, a teaching assistant) or a special education teacher, adaptive equipment such as a computer, or consultative assistance from a psychologist or counselor. Alternatively, a few students' needs are so great that a setting outside general education is

ANALYZE
AND **REFLECT**

When you think about the concept of least restrictive environment, what factors do you think should be considered for a particular student? What does LRE imply for general education teachers?

the only one considered. Chapter 2 presents more detail about the range of LRE settings considered for students with disabilities. Here, the points to remember are that the LRE for most students with disabilities is general education and that, as a professional educator, you have a crucial role to play in these students' education.

Mainstreaming

When the LRE concept became part of special education laws during the 1970s, the LRE for most students with disabilities was a part-time or full-time special education class. When such students were permitted to participate in general education, it was called mainstreaming. **Mainstreaming** is the term for placing students with disabilities in general education settings only when they can meet traditional academic expectations with minimal assistance, or when those expectations are not relevant (for example, participation only in recess or school assemblies to access typical social interactions). In most locales, *mainstreaming* now is considered a dated term and has been replaced with the phrase *inclusive practices* that is explained next. However, as you participate in field experiences and speak to experienced educators, you may find that in some schools the vocabulary of inclusion is used but the practices implemented seem more like mainstreaming. That is, teachers may say that their school is inclusive but then explain that students like Aaron, featured in the beginning of the chapter, need to be in a separate class because of their reading levels. This practice is actually mainstreaming.

Inclusive Practices

ANALYZE AND REFLECT

Mainstreaming was an early interpretation of LRE. Schools now are emphasizing inclusive practices. How are these two concepts different? How might inclusive practices change the structure of schools and the roles of teachers, administrators, and even students and their families?

Over the past 2 decades, the entire structure of special education services has been undergoing significant change. Although federal law retains the range of educational environments previously described, many educators now seriously question the assumption that students who need more intensive services should routinely receive them in a restrictive setting such as a special education classroom (for example, Downing & Eichinger, 2003; Fitch, 2003; Hall, 2002; Simpson, deBoer-Ott, & Smith-Myles, 2003). They stress that in the past many students with disabilities were only temporary guests in general education classrooms and that few efforts were made to provide assistance so they could be successfully educated with their nondisabled peers. These educators contend that all or most supports for students with disabilities can be provided effectively in general education classrooms when teachers are prepared to work with such students and related concerns are addressed (McLeskey, Waldron, So, Swanson, & Loveland, 2001; Wolf & Hall, 2003). They further maintain that if students cannot meet traditional academic expectations, those expectations should be changed, not the setting. They reject the mainstreaming assumption that settings dictate the type and intensity of services, and they propose instead the concept of inclusive practices. **Inclusive practices** represent the belief or philosophy that students with disabilities should be fully integrated into general education classrooms and schools and that their instruction should be based on their abilities, not their disabilities. Inclusive practices have three dimensions:

1. They comprise *physical integration*, that is, placing students in the same classroom as nondisabled peers as a strong priority and removing them from that setting only when absolutely necessary.

2. They require *social integration*, that is, nurturing relationships between students with disabilities and their peers and adults.

3. They include *instructional integration*, or teaching most students in the same curriculum used for students without disabilities and helping students to succeed by adjusting how teaching and learning are designed and measured. For the few stu-

dents with significant intellectual disabilities, instructional integration means anchoring instruction in the standard curriculum but appropriately adjusting expectations.

Ultimately, inclusive practices imply that all learners are welcomed at their schools and that they are seen as the responsibility of all educators (Bateman & Bateman, 2002; Turnbull, Turnbull, Wehmeyer, & Park, 2003). In the Special Emphasis On . . . below, this responsibility is illustrated for music teachers, professionals who often instruct students with disabilities.

> Inclusive practices imply that all learners are welcomed at their schools and that they are seen as the responsibility of all educators.

Throughout this text, the phrase *inclusive practices* will refer to the belief that students with disabilities are full members of their school and classroom learning communities and that educators' strong preference is for them to be educated with their

Special EMPHASIS On . . .

Inclusive Practices for Choral Music

Are you planning to be a music teacher? Perhaps you are wondering how inclusive practices are likely to affect your instruction. Most music educators do teach students with disabilities, and this is true whether they work at the elementary, middle school, or high school level. In choral music classes in which the goal is a performance for parents and the community, teachers can arrange for success by using ideas such as these:

- *Write the rehearsal plan on the board.* This helps students who rely on visual cues, such as students who are deaf or hard of hearing.
- *Keep the rehearsal room neat.* This helps students who get disoriented or confused if things are not in their "proper places," including some students with autism, mental retardation, and attention deficit–hyperactivity disorder.
- *Be consistent with room setup.* This can create a sense of security in the students' surroundings and thus help them to feel in control of their situation. If permission sheets or fund-raising forms are always turned in at the same place, students who would normally have difficulty with such tasks can learn over time where to hand in their materials with minimal prompting.
- *Have a consistent seating arrangement.* This allows all students—including those with disabilities—to find their correct places within the ensemble without constant reminders from you. This also will give you time in advance to adapt the environment for students with physical disabilities.
- *Be aware that some students with special needs have a tendency to get up and roam about the room.* One solu-

tion that may minimize disruptions is to provide such a student with an alternative place to sit within the ensemble.

- *Use peer mentors to assist students with disabilities during rehearsals.* This strategy frees your time to manage the entire group while recognizing that some students may need assistance to participate.
- *Have a routine rehearsal structure so that rehearsals are as similar as possible.* For example, students who need to follow a routine will benefit if physical warm-ups start immediately at the beginning of class, followed by vocal warm-ups, and then the first piece of music, which is listed on the board.
- *Use modeling and rote singing to help students meet your expectations for quality.* You may need to demonstrate for students acceptable ways to sing as well as unacceptable ways.
- *Praise student efforts.* Students with disabilities may not be able to perform just like their classmates, but just like other students they need to hear positive words from you.
- *Be open to other preventive measures.* Nothing is guaranteed to work every day with every student. Keep this in mind, and think of other ways to prepare your classroom for all students. Staying in close touch with a special education teacher concerning student needs is also recommended.

SOURCE: From "Choral Mainstreaming: Tips for Success" (electronic version), by K. VanWeelden, 2001, *Music Education Journal, 88*(3), pp. 55–60.

peers without disabilities. We generally agree that this approach to education maximizes the potential of all students and protects their rights. We prefer the phrase *inclusive practices* to the term *inclusion* because the latter can imply that there is a single model or program that can serve students' needs, while the former more accurately conveys that inclusiveness is made up of many strategies and options. Later in this chapter, we address inclusive practices from the perspectives of teachers, administrators, parents, and students as well as the student outcomes that result.

You may find that teachers in your locale use words such as *LRE, mainstreaming,* and *inclusion* interchangeably, or they might have yet different terms to describe special education services. For example, teachers sometimes mention inclusive practices only when referring to students with physical or intellectual disabilities and use mainstreaming for students with learning disabilities. To assist you with the vocabulary of special education programs and instructional approaches, a glossary is provided at the back of this textbook. Keep in mind, though, that knowing the terms used in special education is not nearly as important as learning about your students, developing skills for addressing their needs, and celebrating your role in enabling them to achieve success.

How Did Today's Special Education Services Come to Exist?

Special education as it exists today has been influenced by a number of different factors. Although people with disabilities have been identified and treated for centuries, special education grew rapidly only in the 20th century (Kode, 2002; Rudd, 2002; Winzer, 1993). As special education has evolved, it has been shaped by federal law, the civil rights movement and related court cases, and changing social and political beliefs. Figure 1.1 illustrates some factors that have influenced the development of special education.

The Development of Education for Students with Disabilities

When compulsory public education began near the turn of the 20th century, almost no school programs existed for students with disabilities (Scheerenberger, 1983; Kode, 2002). Students with disabilities that were relatively mild, that is, learning or behavior problems or minor physical impairments, were educated along with other students because their needs were not considered extraordinary. Many children with significant intellectual or physical disabilities did not attend school at all, and others were educated by private agencies or lived in institutions. In fact, for the first half of the 20th century, many states explicitly legislated permission for school districts to prohibit some students with disabilities from attending (Yell, Rogers, & Rogers, 1998).

Special classes in public schools that began as compulsory education became widespread during the 1920s and 1930s. Schools were expected to be like efficient assembly lines, with each class of students moving from grade to grade and eventually graduating from high school as productive citizens prepared to enter the workforce (Patton, Payne, & Beirne-Smith, 1986; Scheerenberger, 1983). Special classes were developed as a place for students who could not keep up with their classmates. Because many students with disabilities still were not in school, most of the students sent to special classes probably had mild or moderate learning or cognitive disabilities. Educators at the time believed that such students would learn better in a protected setting and that the efficiency of the overall educational system would be preserved (Bennett, 1932; Pertsch, 1936).

By the 1950s, special education programs were available in many school districts, but some undesirable outcomes were becoming apparent. For example, students in

FIGURE 1.1 Influences on Current Special Education Practices

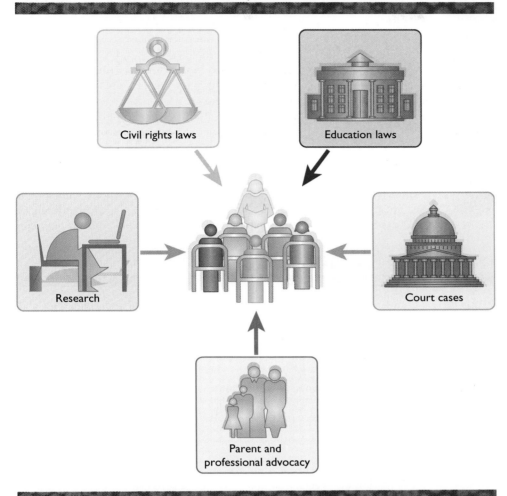

special classes often were considered incapable of learning academic skills. They spent their school time practicing "manual skills" such as weaving and bead stringing. Researchers began questioning this practice and conducted studies to explore the efficacy of special education. When they compared students with disabilities who were in special education classes to similar students who had remained in general education, they found the latter group often had learned more than the former (Blatt, 1958; Goldstein, Moss, & Jordan, 1965). Parents at this time also became active advocates for better educational opportunities for their children (Blatt, 1987). By the late 1960s, many authorities in the field agreed that segregated special classes were not the most appropriate educational setting for many students with disabilities (Blatt, 1958; Christopolos & Renz, 1969; Dunn, 1968; Hobbs, 1975; Lilly, 1971).

The Impact of the Civil Rights Movement on Special Education

During the 1950s and 1960s, another force began contributing to the development of new approaches for special education. The civil rights movement, although initially addressing the rights of African Americans, expanded and began to influence thinking about people with disabilities (Chaffin, 1975; Fleischer & Zames, 2001). In the

FYI

The Council for Exceptional Children (CEC), founded in 1922 by Elizabeth Farrell, is a professional organization for teachers, administrators, parents, and other advocates for the rights of students with disabilities.

How did the civil rights movement of the 1950s and 1960s also result in rights for people with disabilities? How are these groups similar in terms of education?

Brown v. Board of Education decision in 1954, the U.S. Supreme Court ruled that it was unlawful under the Fourteenth Amendment to discriminate arbitrarily against any group of people. The Court then applied this concept to the education of children, ruling that the state-mandated separate education for African American students could not be an equal education. This court decision introduced the concept of **integration** into public education, the notion that the only way to protect students' constitutional right to equal opportunity was to ensure that diverse student groups learned together. Soon, people with disabilities were recognized as another group whose rights often had been violated because of arbitrary discrimination. For children, the discrimination occurred when they were denied access to schools because of their disabilities. Beginning in the late 1960s and continuing through today, parents and others have used the court system to ensure that the civil and educational rights of children with disabilities are preserved. Figure 1.2 summarizes several of the most influential court cases that have helped shape special education concepts and services.

FIGURE 1.2 Court Cases Influencing Special Education

Matters relating to students with disabilities are addressed in federal and state laws. Issues concerning the interpretation of those laws often must be resolved through the courts. Since 1954, hundreds of legal decisions have clarified the rights of students with disabilities and the responsibilities of schools for educating them. The following cases have had a significant impact on special education.

Brown v. Board of Education (347 U.S. 483) **(1954)**

This U.S. Supreme Court case established the principle that school segregation denies students equal educational opportunity. Although the decision referred primarily to racial segregation, it has since become the cornerstone for ensuring equal rights for students with disabilities as well.

Pennsylvania Association for Retarded Children v. Commonwealth of Pennsylvania (343 F. Supp. 279) **(1972)**

In this suit, the U.S. District Court of the Eastern District of Pennsylvania ruled that schools may not refuse to educate students with mental retardation. The court ordered that a free public education was to be provided to *all* students.

Diana v. State Board of Education of California (No. C-70-37 RFP (N.D. Cal.)) **(1973)**

Diana was a Spanish-speaking student who scored poorly on an intelligence test administered in English and as a result was placed in a class for students with mental retardation. The U.S. District Court for the Northern District of Colorado ruled that students must be assessed in their native language.

Larry P. v. Wilson Riles (793 F. 2d 969) **(1986)**

U.S. District Court for the Northern District of California ruled that intelligence (IQ) tests could not be used to determine whether African American students had mental retardation because of the tests' racial and cultural bias. In 1986, the ruling was expanded to include IQ testing of these students for any disability.

Board of Education of Hendrick Hudson School District v. Rowley (632 F.2d 945) **(1982)**

The U.S. Supreme Court ruled that special education services must provide an appropriate education but that students with disabilities may not be entitled to optimum services. The parents of a student with a hearing impairment were denied an interpreter for their child in school because the child was achieving at grade level.

SOURCES: Adapted from "Reflections on the 25th Anniversary of the Individuals with Disabilities Education Act," by A. Katisyannis, M. L. Yell, and R. Bradley, 2001, *Remedial and Special Education, 22,* pp. 324–334; "The Least Restrictive Environment Mandate and the Courts: Judicial Activism or Judicial Restraint?" by M. L. Yell, 1995, *Exceptional Children, 61,* pp. 578–581; and "De Jure: Costly Lack of Accommodations," by P. A. Zirkel, 1994, *Phi Delta Kappan, 75,* pp. 652–653. "Medical Services: The Disrupted Related SErvice," by L. Bartlett, 2000, *Journal of Special Education, 33,* pp. 215–223; *Legal Issues in Special Educations,* by A. G. Osborne, 1996, Boston: Allyn and Bacon.

SECTION 504 ● One of the outcomes of the civil rights movement has been legislation designed to prevent discrimination against individuals with disabilities, whether they are children in schools or adults in the workforce. **Section 504** of the Vocational Rehabilitation Act of 1973 is a civil rights law that prevents discrimination against all individuals with disabilities in programs that receive federal funds, as do all public schools. For children of school age, Section 504 ensures equal opportunity for participation in the full range of school activities (Smith, 2002). Through Section 504, some students not eligible for services through special education may be entitled to receive specific types of assistance to help them succeed in school.

For example, Sondra is a student with a severe attention problem. She cannot follow a lesson for more than a few minutes at a time; she is distracted by every noise in the hallway and every car that goes by her classroom window. Her teacher describes her as a student who acts first and thinks later. Sondra does not have a disability as established in special education law, but she does need extra assistance and is disabled according to Section 504 because her significant attention problem negatively affects her ability to function in school. The professionals at her school are required to create and

Daniel R. R. v. State Board of Education (874 F.2d 1036) (1989)

This decision from the U.S. Court of Appeals for the Fifth Circuit established that the appropriate placement for students with disabilities depends on whether (a) a student can be satisfactorily educated in the general education setting with supplementary supports provided and (b) the student is mainstreamed to the maximum extent appropriate in cases in which the general education setting is not successful. For Daniel, a student with Down syndrome, the court ruled that the school district had not violated his rights when he was moved from general education after an unsuccessful attempt to include him.

Oberti v. Board of Education of Clementon School District (995 F.2d.204) (1993)

In this case, the U.S. Court of Appeals for the Third Circuit upheld a district court ruling that school districts must make available a full range of supports and services in the general education setting to accommodate students with disabilities, including the student with Down syndrome involved in the suit. The court further stipulated that just because a student learns differently from other students does not necessarily warrant exclusion from general education.

Doe v. Withers (20 IDELR 422, 426–27) (1993)

As Douglas Doe's history teacher, Michael Withers was responsible for making the oral testing accommodations needed by this student with learning disabilities. Although he was also a state legislator, Mr. Withers refused to provide the oral testing and Douglas failed this class, thus becoming athletically ineligible. The West Virginia Circuit Court awarded the family $5,000 in compensatory damages and $30,000 in punitive damages. This case illustrates the extent of general education teachers' responsibility to make good-faith efforts to provide required accommodations for students with disabilities.

Cedar Rapids Community School District v. Garret F. (119 S. Ct. 992) (1999)

In this case, Garrett, a 12-year-old with significant physical disabilities and above-average intellectual ability, required nursing assistance primarily because of the possibility that his ventilator might cease functioning at school. The parents requested that the school provide this service, but the school district refused this request. The U.S. Supreme Court ruled that the school must provide the service, acknowledging the cost of the service but noting that the law was intended to ensure that students like Garrett could attend school.

carry out a plan to help Sondra access education. Special education teachers may assist because they know techniques that will help Sondra, but Sondra does not receive special education services, and responsibility for the plan lies with the principal and teachers. Some of the other students who might receive assistance through Section 504 include those with health problems such as asthma or extreme allergies and those with physical disabilities who do not need special education.

AMERICANS WITH DISABILITIES ACT ● In July 1990, President George H. W. Bush signed into law the **Americans with Disabilities Act (ADA).** This civil rights law was based on the Vocational Rehabilitation Act of 1973, but it further extended the rights of individuals with disabilities. This law is the most significant disability legislation ever passed (Hinton, 2003; Smith, 2001). It protects all individuals with disabilities from discrimination, and it requires most employers to make reasonable accommodations for them. Although ADA does not deal directly with the education of students with disabilities, it does clarify the civil rights of all individuals with disabilities and thus has an impact on special education. This law also ensures that transportation, buildings, and many places open to the public are accessible to people with disabilities. If you are a teacher with a disability, you yourself might be influenced by ADA. For example, if your school is not accessible to wheelchairs and undergoes renovation, ramps, elevators, or wide entries with automatic doors probably will have to be installed. If you have a disability, this law also protects you from discrimination when you look for a teaching position.

ANALYZE AND REFLECT

Why are Section 504 and the ADA considered civil rights laws instead of education laws? What impact do they have on students, teachers, and schools?

The Legislative Basis for Contemporary Special Education

Influenced by researchers' growing doubts about the effectiveness of special education classes and by civil rights court cases, by the early 1970s many states had begun to address special education issues by passing laws to guarantee that students with disabilities would receive an appropriate education. Federal law soon mirrored this trend and continues to do so today.

THE FIRST FEDERAL SPECIAL EDUCATION LEGISLATION ● In 1975, Congress passed **P.L. 94-142,** the Education for the Handicapped Act (EHA), thereby setting federal guidelines for special education services. This law outlined the foundation on which current special education practice rests. It took into account many of the early court decisions that established the civil rights of students with disabilities, and it mandated the concept of least restrictive environment (LRE). For example, this law specifically described categories of disabilities that make students eligible to receive special education. It clarified the related services to which students might be entitled. It also set out procedures for identifying a student as needing special education and outlined the rights of parents who disapprove of the educational services offered to their children.

> In 1975, Congress passed P.L. 94-142, the Education for the Handicapped Act (EHA), thereby setting federal guidelines for special education services.

CURRENT SPECIAL EDUCATION LEGISLATION ● Since 1975, P.L. 94-142 has been reauthorized several times. As each reconsideration of the law has occurred, its core principles have been upheld. At the same time, the law has been extended and its provisions clarified. For example, in 1990 the name of the law was changed to the **Individuals with Disabilities Education Act (IDEA)** to reflect more contemporary "person-first" language. In addition, the term *handicapped* was removed from the law and the preferred term *disability* was substituted. This law also added significantly to the provisions for children from birth to age 5 with disabilities who had first been included in the law in 1986, the topic of the Professional Edge below. It also bolstered the provisions for supporting students with disabilities preparing to transition from school to work, postsecondary education, or other postschool options. One other important 1990 change in this law was the addition of two new categories of disability: autism and traumatic brain injury.

The Individuals with Disabilities Education Act was revised again in 1997. Perhaps most importantly for classroom teachers, this law recognized that most students with disabilities spend all or most of their school time in general education settings, and so it included a provision that a classroom teacher usually be a member of the team that writes each student's educational plan. Another important change occurred regarding assessment. Acknowledging that students with disabilities were often excluded from local or state assessments, the law added a requirement that all students with disabilities be assessed like other students, using either the same assessment instruments employed with typical learners or some type of alternative instrument. On December 3, 2004, President George W. Bush signed into law Public Law 108-446, the most recent reauthorization of IDEA. Given the short title of the Individuals with Disabilities Education Improvement Act (but still referred to by the acronym IDEA), this legislation mandated

FYI

In 1986, Congress passed P.L. 99-457. This law amended federal special education law to include programs and services for infants and toddlers with special needs with a strong focus on supporting their families. In IDEA, the section that addresses young children is referred to as Part C.

PROFESSIONAL EDGE

Special Education for Young Children with Disabilities

In 1986, Congress enacted P.L. 99-457. This law extended special education provisions to very young children, from birth through 5 years of age. These are some of the characteristics of early childhood special education:

- The focus for services is on the family, not just the child.

- Instead of an IEP, a young child has an Individualized Family Service Plan (IFSP) that spells out assistance needed by the child and the family.

- Parents usually do most of the direct teaching of their babies and toddlers so that they take advantage of natural learning opportunities. Professionals, sometimes called early interventionists, may model ways for parents to work with their young children.

- Children ages 3 to 5 may receive special education services in their homes, at centers providing services just to children with disabilities, or in inclusive settings such as private or public preschools.

- As is true for school-age students, inclusive practices are the current dominant philosophy for educating young children with disabilities. By interacting with peers without disabilities, young children encounter strong language and behavior models, and they participate in age-appropriate activities. Inclusive practices for young

One of the provisions of P.L. 99-457 focuses special education services for young children on the entire family.

children are preparation for inclusive practices during K–12 schooling.

During the 2000–2001 school year, a total of 230,853 children ages birth to 2 and 599,678 children ages 3 to 5 received services through IDEA (U.S. Department of Education, 2002).

yet further refinements in special education. For example, this legislation clarified the requirements for being licensed as a special education teacher, and it streamlined some procedures and paperwork. It also specified that all students with disabilities must participate in all assessment conducted by local school districts, but it also noted that needed supports can be provided. A provision that might be of particular interest to teachers is this: IDEA now permits school districts to use some of the funds allotted to special education to design strategies for prevention. That is, by providing intensive teaching, behavior interventions, and other supports, it will be possible to help some students avoid needing special education at all. The original principles of federal special education law and additional details on the provisions of P.L. 108-466 are summarized in Figure 1.3, and they are discussed further in Chapter 2.

FIGURE 1.3 Provisions of IDEA

Core Principles

- *Free appropriate public education (FAPE).*   Students with disabilities are entitled to attend public schools and to receive the educational services they need. This education is provided at no cost to parents.

- *Least restrictive environment (LRE).*   Students with disabilities must be educated in the least restrictive environment in which they can succeed with support. For most students, this environment is the general education classroom.

- *Individualized education.*   The instructional services and other assistance for students with disabilities must be tailored to meet their needs according to prepared individualized education programs (IEP) that are reviewed and updated annually. IEPs are discussed in detail in Chapter 2.

- *Nondiscriminatory evaluation.*   Students should be assessed using instruments that do not discriminate on the basis of race, culture, or disability. In considering eligibility for special education services, a student must be assessed by a multidisciplinary team in the native language using tests that are relevant to the area of concern. Eligibility cannot be decided on the basis of only one test.

- *Due process.*   If a disagreement occurs concerning a student's eligibility for special education placement or services, no changes can be made until the issue has been resolved by an impartial hearing and, if necessary, the appropriate court, a procedure referred to as due process. Likewise, if schools disagree with parents' requests for services for their children, they may also use due process procedures to resolve the disputes.

- *Zero reject–child find.*   No student may be excluded from public education because of a disability. Further, each state must take action to locate children who may be entitled to special education services.

Additional Major Provisions

- *Transition services.*   Transition services that prepare students for leaving school (for higher education, a vocational school, or a job) must be addressed in IEPs for students beginning at age 14. These service needs must include strategies to improve academic and functional achievement that will foster student success and must be based on student strengths. Transition plans must be updated annually, and they must become increasingly detailed as students reach age 16 and beyond. That is, they must include measurable goals for the postsecondary years.

- *General education teacher roles and responsibilities.*   At least one general education teacher must participate as a member of the team that writes a student's IEP unless school professionals and parents agree for some reason that this would not be beneficial to the student. In addition, the IEP must directly address student participation in general education and must justify placements that are not in general education.

- *Highly qualified special education teachers.*   After the 2005–2006 school year, special education teachers who teach core academic subjects must obtain two types of licensure. First, they must have a special education teaching credential. In addition, they must have an elementary or a secondary

SOURCE: Adapted from *Special Education: Contemporary Perspectives for School Professionals*, by M. Friend, 2005, Boston: Allyn and Bacon.

NO CHILD LEFT BEHIND ACT OF 2001 ● In January 2002, President George W. Bush signed the **No Child Left Behind Act of 2001 (NCLB)** (P.L. 107-110). This law, intended to raise academic standards and improve student achievement, has significantly influenced schooling, including approaches for educating students with disabilities. The law addresses four critical areas (Friend, 2005):

1. *Accountability for results.* All students are assessed yearly in grades 3 through 8 and once in high school to determine their progress and achievement, and the results of these efforts must be reported publicly.

2. *Budget flexibility.* Up to 50 percent of the federal funds for some education programs (but *not* funds allocated for IDEA) may be blended. This provision is

credential. In secondary schools, unless special education teachers work only with students with significant intellectual disabilities, they eventually must obtain a teaching credential in every core subject area in which they teach. However, if they work in general education classrooms, ensuring that students with disabilities receive their needed supports there, they are not obligated to obtain general education teacher credentials.

- *Parent participation.* Parents must be part of the decision-making team for determining eligibility for special education services as well as for determining the appropriate educational placement for their children. Further, schools now must report to parents on the progress of their children with disabilities at least as often as progress is reported for students without disabilities.

- *Evaluation and eligibility.* School districts generally have 60 days from the time a parent agrees that their child can be evaluated until a decision must be reached about eligibility for special education. Students are not eligible for special education simply because of poor math or reading instruction, or because of language differences. For some students the requirement that a complete reassessment be completed every 3 years can be modified. That is, already-existing information can be used in lieu of repeatedly administering standardized tests. Finally, the school district must take specific steps to ensure that students from minority groups are not over-identified as being eligible for special education services.

- *Assessment of students.* States are required to measure the academic progress of students who have IEPs, either by including them in the standardized assessments other students take or by using an alternative assessment process (requirements clarified in the No Child Left Behind Act). Students are entitled to appropriate adaptations (for example, extended time, large print) during assessment.

- *Discipline.* As needed, strategies for addressing students' behavior must be included as part of their IEPs. If a student is suspended or placed in an alternative interim placement, a behavior plan must be developed. In some cases (for example, when students bring weapons or drugs to school), schools may place students with disabilities in alternative interim placements for up to 45 days. Students must continue to receive special education services during this time.

- *Paraprofessionals.* Paraprofessionals, teaching assistants, and other similar personnel must be trained for their jobs and appropriately supervised.

- *Procedural safeguards.* States must make mediation available to parents as an early and informal strategy for resolving disagreements about the identification of, placement of, or services for students with disabilities. The cost of mediation is borne by the state. Parents are not obligated to mediate, and mediation may not delay a possible hearing. Unless waived with parent approval, the school district also must convene a dispute resolution session prior to a formal hearing regarding disagreements related to special education.

In addition to these essential provisions of IDEA, you will learn more about other requirements of the law as they pertain to the topics addressed throughout this textbook.

WWW
RESOURCES

The website article at
http://www.ed.gov titled
"Charting the Course:
States Decide Major Provisions under No Child Left
Behind" offers detailed information on NCLB and its
effect on students with
disabilities for students,
parents, and teachers.

intended to give state and local school officials more discretion in using funds as needed to maximize student achievement.

3. *Options for student success.* In high-poverty areas, students attending schools that consistently fail to raise achievement levels have the right to transfer to other schools in the district or to charter schools with better performance records. In addition, students in these schools are entitled to tutoring, summer school, and other programs to improve achievement.

4. *Research-based teaching methods.* One important NCLB goal is that every child be reading by the end of third grade. This part of the law, called "Reading First," funds the implementation of reading programs based on scientifically proven methods.

Other provisions of NCLB include requirements that all teachers be highly qualified and that English-language learners receive intensive language instruction so that they can meet the same high academic standards as other students. Have you learned about this law in your other courses? What are the major points that proponents and opponents of NCLB make to support their views?

As you consider NCLB and students with disabilities, you may realize that the most significant provision concerns accountability. In particular, NCLB requires that each school make adequate yearly progress (AYP) toward the goal of 100 percent student proficiency in reading and math by the year 2014, as explained in the Professional Edge on page 15, along with other accountability provisions. As you can surmise, NCLB is strongly influencing educators' thinking about raising expectations for students with disabilities, ensuring that these students access the same curriculum as other students, and implementing inclusive practices.

Special education has evolved on the basis of many factors. When special education began, essentially none of the services was offered in public schools. Today, comprehensive services in a wide variety of settings are supplied, and both very young children and young adults, as well as students in elementary and secondary schools, benefit from them. As the rights and needs of students with disabilities have been better understood and federal legislation has set higher standards for their education, classroom teachers have become increasingly involved in their education, a trend that surely will continue.

ANALYZE
AND REFLECT

Teaching students with disabilities has changed dramatically over the years.
How have IDEA and NCLB
altered the expectations
for students with disabilities? As an educator, what
are your responsibilities
for addressing the provisions of these two laws as
you work with all your
students?

What Are Current Perspectives on Inclusive Practices?

How do principals contribute to a school's support of inclusive practices? How do you think this benefits teachers and students?

Today's conversations about inclusive practices generally are not about whether inclusion should occur. Instead, professionals and parents debate the practical meaning of *inclusion;* the knowledge, skills, and attitudes that educators should possess; and the conditions in schools that are required for effective inclusive practices. In addition, they focus on the impact of inclusive practices on students and the roles of families and students with disabilities in making decisions about the least restrictive environment. As you read the following discussion, remember that your goal should be to become an informed professional who understands the multiple viewpoints on inclusive practices so that you can form your own opinions and foster student learning.

A Problem of Definition

One reason discussions about inclusive practices become complex and contentious is the lack of a clear and widely accepted definition for the term

PROFESSIONAL EDGE

Accountability Requirements of the No Child Left Behind Act of 2001

The No Child Left Behind Act of 2001 has brought sweeping changes to public education. For students with disabilities, the most significant changes deal with accountability for learning. Here are the requirements of the law:

- All states are required to administer assessments to all students attending public schools.

- Beginning in 2005–2006, students must be assessed in every grade from 3 through 8 in the areas of reading and mathematics. Students also must be assessed at least once across grades 10, 11, and 12. Each state is entitled to request a one-year extension in meeting this provision.

- Beginning with the 2007–2008 school year, students must be assessed in the area of science at least once within each of these grade spans: 3–5, 6–9, and 10–12.

- Assessment results must be reported in terms of proficiency levels, not just percentiles. Each state has developed a method for reporting proficiency, often using cutoff scores that rate students as having reached mastery or not.

- Assessments must measure higher order thinking skills.

- Assessments must include the reporting of individual student scores so that parents can be informed of their children's achievement.

- Students whose first language is not English must be assessed using tests written in English after they have received 3 consecutive years of instruction in U.S. schools.

A few students are entitled to an additional 2 years of instruction before this requirement is implemented.

- Each state must make adequate yearly progress (AYP) toward the goal of achievement at grade level for all students by 2014. Each state has set a baseline score for student achievement and has filed a plan for reaching this goal.

- The assessment scores of students with disabilities, those whose first language is not English, and other student subgroups must be disaggregated (that is, reported separately) from overall student achievement scores. Students in these subgroups also must show AYP.

- Schools in high-poverty areas (Title I schools) that fail for 2 years in a row to make AYP are subject to sanctions, including filing a plan for improvement and accepting technical assistance from the state. If student achievement does not improve after 4 years, students may be entitled to transfer to other schools, and additional sanctions may occur.

These requirements apply to students with disabilities in addition to all other students in public schools. What might be the impact of NCLB on students with disabilities?

SOURCE: From *Major Changes to ESEA in the No Child Left Behind Act,* by the Learning First Alliance, January 2003, Washington, DC: Author. Retrieved July 20, 2003, from http://www.nea.org/esea/images/ESEAsummary.pdf.

---

inclusion. Too often, research on inclusive practices and essays on their relative merits and drawbacks focus on where students are seated, that is, the amount of time they spend in general education classrooms (McGrath, Johns, & Mathur, 2004; Mock & Kauffman, 2002). As a result, some professionals argue that students with disabilities sometimes need small-group, highly structured environments that are difficult to create in general education classrooms (Kavale, 2002), and they conclude that inclusion—sometimes using the phrase *full inclusion*—is not sound educational practice.

Alternatively, in many school districts and among some authors (for example, Handler, 2003; Renzaglia, Karvonen, Drasgow, & Stoxen, 2003) inclusive practices are conceptualized as a belief system that emphasizes welcoming all students in a school learning community. Just as importantly, inclusiveness is not judged solely on the location of a student's education. In these schools, factors such as those in the inclusive practices checklist in the Professional Edge on page 16 are stressed. As you have learned, this broader view is the one taken in this textbook. In highly inclusive schools, professionals and parents sometimes realize that instruction must occur in a separate setting. However, their goal is to return the student to instruction with peers as soon

DIMENSIONS OF DIVERSITY

Linguistic differences and frequent family moves sometimes compound the already complex decision-making process for deciding on the educational supports needed by culturally and linguistically diverse learners (Overton, Fielding, & Simeonsson, 2004).

PROFESSIONAL EDGE

Checklist of Inclusive Practices

Are you wondering what types of activities schools undertake to become inclusive? The following are some of the key questions school professionals should ask. The more positive the responses educators make, the more likely it is that successful inclusive practices will be implemented.

- Does your school have a mission statement that expresses the belief that the professionals and other staff strive to meet the needs of all students? Is this mission statement discussed by staff and used to guide instructional practices?

- Have teachers and other staff members recognized that working toward an inclusive environment continues each year, that the process does not end?

- Have teachers had opportunities to discuss their concerns about student needs, and have steps been taken to address these concerns?

- Has planning to meet all students' needs included classroom teachers, special education teachers, other support staff, administrators, parents, and students?

- Have you clarified the expectations for students with special needs who are to be integrated into classrooms?

- Has shared planning time as well as possibly shared instructional time been arranged for teams of teachers?

- Have staff members received adequate professional development on pertinent topics (for example, collaboration, behavior supports, and curricular adaptations)?

- Have staff members become comfortable with working collaboratively?

- Has the plan for your inclusive school truly addressed the needs of *all* students?

- Have pilot programs been undertaken prior to full implementation?

- Have start-up resources been allocated for moving toward inclusive practices?

- Have steps been taken to ensure that teachers will be rewarded for experimentation and innovation, even if efforts are sometimes not successful?

- Have all teachers, even those who may not at first participate in teaching students who are more challenging learners, learned that they are integral to a schoolwide belief system?

- Have students had opportunities to learn about all types of diversity, including individuals with disabilities?

- Have parents and families of students with and without disabilities been involved in the development, implementation, and evaluation of the school's inclusive services?

- Has a plan been developed for carefully monitoring the impact of approaches for meeting student diversity? Does this plan include strategies for revision?

- Have teachers and other staff identified benchmarks, including student outcome data, so that they have attainable goals to celebrate after 1 year? 2 years? 3 years?

SOURCE: From *Special Education: Contemporary Perspectives for School Professionals,* by M. Friend, 2005, Boston: Allyn and Bacon.

as possible for as much time as possible. Further, they judge the effectiveness of inclusive practices on a student-by-student basis, monitoring student progress whether or not that progress looks similar to that of other students.

One additional problem related to the definition of inclusive practices concerns what occurs when students with disabilities participate in general education. Often, specific descriptions of the instruction delivered, the expectations set for students, and the strategies for making the curriculum accessible to all learners are missing from reports about inclusive schools. Without such information, you may find it difficult to judge the quality of the education the students receive.

Perceptions of School Professionals

The perceptions of teachers and administrators regarding inclusive practices represent a continuum (for example, Dore, Dion, Wagner, & Brunet, 2002; Paurit & Monda-Amaya, 2001; Rea, McLaughlin, & Walther-Thomas, 2002). Some professionals are strongly supportive of this educational approach, and they perceive that such practices have positive outcomes for students and themselves. Others express concern about the ability of many students with disabilities to succeed in fast-paced general education settings and the potential that other students' education may be harmed. Yet other professionals are ambivalent, recognizing the value of inclusive practices while doubting whether sufficient personnel and funding are available for implementation.

TEACHERS' PERCEPTIONS ● The range of teacher perceptions illustrates the complexity of professional thinking about inclusive practices. In some studies, general education teachers in elementary, middle, and high schools are found to believe strongly in inclusive practices based on high standards for students (King & Youngs, 2003; McLeskey et al., 2001). These teachers report making instructional accommodations to facilitate student learning and feeling positive about their work with students with disabilities. They also provide instruction to students that is in many ways as intensive as that offered in some special education classrooms (Helmstetter, Curry, Brennan, & Sampson-Saul, 1998).

At the same time, some teachers' perceptions of inclusive practices are mixed or negative. For example, one study of rural teachers in the Midwest found that the teachers preferred not having students with disabilities in their classrooms at all (Martin, Johnson, Ireland, & Claxton, 2003). Other teachers have indicated a lack of commitment to achieving educational goals for students with severe disabilities in their classrooms and some degree of rejection of students with mild disabilities (Cook, 2001). Of course, these negative perceptions of inclusive practices are likely to have a negative impact on students.

Another example of teachers' thinking about inclusive practices concerns their perceived levels of preparation to work with diverse groups of students. As you might expect, teachers report feeling prepared to work with students with learning disabilities but not students with behavior or emotional disabilities, mental retardation, or multiple disabilities (Cook, 2001). Do you agree with these teachers' perceptions? As you think about teaching students with disabilities and other special needs, what knowledge and skills do you anticipate needing? Among the items frequently mentioned are a commitment to inclusive practices and knowledge of effective instructional strategies (Stanovich & Jordan, 2002).

ADMINISTRATORS' PERCEPTIONS ● For a school to be inclusive, the principal must be a strong leader who keeps the vision focused, fosters among staff an understanding of inclusion, and nurtures the development of the skills and practices needed to implement these practices (Salisbury & McGregor, 2002). Generally, principals report positive attitudes toward inclusive practices (for example, Praisner, 2003). Interestingly, their attitudes are more positive than those of special education teachers (for example, Ward, Montague, & Linton, 2003) and general education teachers. Some professionals believe that this difference exists because of differences in their respective day-to-day realities: Principals can be supportive of inclusive practices at the overall school level, but teachers have to resolve the complexities in the immediate and demanding setting of each classroom. Principals do express concern that general education teachers may not have the skills to instruct students with disabilities in their classrooms (Cook, Semmel, & Gerber, 1999).

Perceptions of Parents

Parents generally are positive about special education services, and they usually prefer that their children be educated with peers in general education classrooms (Johnson & Duffett, 2002). They believe that inclusive practices are beneficial for academic achievement, but probably more so than educators, they also strongly believe that their

RESEARCH N O T E

Some teachers express concern about the time needed to work with students with disabilities in general education classrooms. Hollowood, Salisbury, Rainforth, and Palombaro (1995) found no evidence of a time problem in their study of students with severe disabilities.

FYI

As schools move toward more inclusive practices, special education teachers, speech therapists, occupational and physical therapists, counselors, and even remedial reading teachers may provide services to students with disabilities in the general education classroom.

children learn critical social skills when they spend most or all of the school day with their typical peers (Williams & Reisberg, 2003). For example, one parent commented that when her fourth-grade son who has autism was integrated into a general education classroom for most of the day, his behavior improved both at school and at home. She also noted that the other students in the class were clearly kind to her son, and she was grateful that they sought him out on the playground and chose him as a lunch partner.

When parents are uneasy about inclusive practices, their concerns usually relate to problems they have experienced or anticipate (for example, Hanline & Darley, 2002). For example, parents of children with physical disabilities have found that many teachers are poorly prepared to work with students with special needs and that these educators have not prepared students to have a classmate with a disability (Pivik et al., 2002). Some parents find that their children seem more comfortable in a special education classroom that has fewer students and more structure (Johnson & Duffett, 2002). For all parents, perceptions of inclusive practices are more positive when they are actively involved in the decision-making process concerning their children's educational services (Salend & Duhaney, 2002).

Student Outcomes

Any discussion of inclusive practices must consider the effect on student achievement. That is, if students with disabilities in inclusive settings do not make adequate progress, then inclusion is not in their best interest. At the same time, inclusive practices should not interfere with the achievement of other students. Generally, academic outcomes for students have been found to be positive. For example, in a statewide study, researchers found that students with disabilities who spent more time in general education passed the eighth-grade assessment at a higher rate than similar students with disabilities who were educated in special education settings, and they also graduated at a higher rate from high school with a standard diploma (Luster & Durrett, 2003). Another study found that students with mild mental retardation who were educated in general education classrooms generally made greater academic gains than their comparable peers in special education settings (Cole, Waldron, & Majd, 2004). Yet other researchers have found positive effects of inclusive practices on language development (Rafferty, Piscitelli, & Boettcher, 2003), problem-solving skills (Agran, Blanchard, Wehmeyer, & Hughes, 2002), and discipline referrals (Cawley, Hayden, Cade, & Baker-Kroczynski, 2002). Although only a few studies have been reported on the impact of inclusive practices on typical students, they suggest that these students' achievement is not hindered (for example, McDonnell et al., 2003).

WWW RESOURCES
One helpful online resource is the Internet Resources for Special Children (IRSC) website at http://www.irsc.org.

Over the next several years, a much clearer picture of the achievement of students with disabilities in inclusive schools is likely to emerge because of the adequate yearly progress (AYP) reporting requirement in NCLB. In many school districts, this group of students is not making the progress required by the law. What is unclear are the reasons for the problem: Are these students underachieving because they have in the past spent so much time in special education classrooms that they have missed large segments of the curriculum on which they are assessed? Or are these students failing to make adequate progress because they cannot be appropriately supported in general education? Questions such as these will continue to be central to debates about the appropriateness and effectiveness of placing students with disabilities in general education settings as part of inclusive practices.

Putting the Pieces Together

In some ways, perspectives on inclusive practices are like puzzle pieces. However, in today's schools some of the pieces may be missing and others difficult to fit into place (Pivik, McComas, & Laflamme, 2002). Even in your own course, classmates may have a wide range of opinions about inclusive practices, and they may come across studies that present contradictory results. In your field experiences, you are likely to discover that in some schools inclusive practices are the norm while in others very traditional approaches are still in place. You may find yourself struggling to reconcile all these views.

One way that you can put the puzzle together is to learn to teach in a way that is responsive to a wide range of student needs and to use collaboration with colleagues and parents, as described in the Working Together feature below, as a means for extending your expertise. As you will learn later in this text, much is known about effective ways to instruct students with disabilities, and many of those strategies help other students to learn as well (Kilgore, Griffin, Sindelar, & Webb, 2002; Vaughn, Gersten, & Chard, 2000). By welcoming all your students and making these strategies an integral part of your instruction, your part of the inclusive practices puzzle will fit right into place.

Finally, as you read about inclusive practices, you should keep in mind that the results researchers obtain and the viewpoints that authors present are influenced by many variables, including the abilities and disabilities, ages, and cultural backgrounds of students; the attitudes, knowledge, and skills of general and special education teachers; the commitment and participation of parents; the degree of support for inclusion from administrators, school policies, and school procedures; the type of outcomes measured; and even the predisposition of researchers and authors toward particular opinions about inclusive practices. As you develop your own understanding of inclusive practices, keep all these factors in mind to help you make sense of what you read. In this way, you will learn to be inclusive in your thinking but flexible in your approach to educating students with disabilities. Remember, there is not a single, guaranteed model or program for effective inclusive practices.

DIMENSIONS OF **DIVERSITY**

Beliefs and values related to disabilities vary as widely within cultures as they differ across cultures. Educators' responsibility is to be sensitive to cultural differences but not to stereotype based on culture.

WORKING **TOGETHER**

The Importance of Collaboration

As you read this textbook and learn about your responsibilities in educating students with disabilities, you will find that collaboration—working together with others—is the key to successful inclusive practices. Here are just a few examples of how you will collaborate on behalf of students:

- *Meeting with special education teachers.* You will meet frequently with special education teachers, both formally and informally. A special educator may contact you to see how a student is doing in your class, or you may contact a special educator to ask for new ideas for responding to a student's behavior. You and the special educator may share responsibility for meeting with parents during open houses or parent conferences.

- *Co-teaching.* Depending on local programs and services, you may co-teach with a special education teacher or a related services professional such as a speech/language pathologist. In co-teaching, you share teaching responsibilities, both educators working with all students. This topic is addressed in detail in Chapter 3.

- *Working with paraprofessionals.* If your class includes a student with a significant disability, the student may be accompanied by a paraprofessional. You will guide the work of that individual in your class and collaborate to ensure that student support is appropriately provided.

- *Meeting on teams.* In today's schools, many teams support inclusive practices. Your grade-level or middle or high school department team is likely to spend part of its time discussing students with disabilities and problem solving to address their needs. You also may be part of a team that tries to address student learning and behavior problems prior to any consideration of the need for special education. Further, if a student in your class is being assessed to determine whether special education is needed, you will be part of that team. The latter two teams are discussed in Chapter 2.

- *Interacting with parents.* Perhaps the most important part of collaborating on behalf of students with disabilities is working with parents. You may communicate with parents through notes sent home and through e-mail; meet with them occasionally as they express concerns about their children; confer with them at formal team meetings; and work with them as they volunteer at school, participate in field trips, and participate in other school activities and initiatives.

Who Receives Special Education and Other Special Services?

Throughout this chapter, we have used the phrase *students with disabilities*. At this point, we will introduce you to the specific types of disabilities that may entitle students to receive special education services, as well as other special needs that may require specialized assistance.

Categories of Disability in Federal Law

When we say that students have disabilities, we are referring to the specific categories of exceptionality prescribed by federal law. Each state has additional laws that clarify special education practices and procedures; the terms used to refer to disabilities in these state laws may differ from those found in federal law. Check with your instructor for the terms used in your state. According to IDEA, students with 1 or more of the following 13 disabilities that negatively affect their educational performance are eligible for special education services. These disabilities also are summarized in the Professional Edge on page 21.

LEARNING DISABILITIES ● Students with *learning disabilities (LD)* have dysfunctions in processing information typically found in language-based activities. They have average or above-average intelligence, but they often encounter significant problems learning how to read, write, and compute. They may not see letters and words in the way others do; they may not be able to pick out important features in a picture they are looking at; and they may take longer to process a question or comment directed to them. They also may have difficulty following directions, attending to tasks, organizing assignments, and managing time. Sometimes these students appear to be unmotivated or lazy when, in fact, they are trying to the best of their ability. Aaron, described at the beginning of this chapter, has a learning disability, but many types of learning disabilities exist, and no single description characterizes students who have one. Learning disabilities are by far the most common special need: Approximately 50 percent of all students receiving special education services in public schools in 2000–2001 had a learning disability (U.S. Department of Education, 2002).

SPEECH OR LANGUAGE IMPAIRMENTS ● When a student has extraordinary difficulties in communicating with others for reasons other than maturation, a *speech or language impairment* is involved. Students with this disability may have trouble with *articulation*, or the production of speech sounds. They may omit words or mispronounce common words when they speak. They may also experience difficulty in *fluency*, such as a significant stuttering problem. Some students have far-reaching speech or language disorders in which they have significant problems receiving and producing language. They may communicate through pictures or sign language. Some students' primary disability is a speech or language disorder, and they may receive services for this. For other students with disabilities, speech/language services supplement their educational services. For example, a student with a learning disability also might receive speech/language services, as might a student with autism or traumatic brain injury.

MENTAL RETARDATION ● Students with *mental retardation (MR)* have significant limitations in intellectual ability and adaptive behaviors. They learn at a far slower pace than do other students, and they may reach a point at which their learning levels off. Although federal listing of disability categories does not distinguish between students with mild mental retardation and those with moderate and severe mental retardation,

PROFESSIONAL EDGE

IDEA Disability Categories

Discussions about students with disabilities sometimes seem to be contradictory. As you read this textbook and learn from your instructor and classmates, you will hear again and again that the specific disability labels that students carry are not particularly important and that it is understanding students as unique individuals that will help you be successful in teaching them. At the same time, students are labeled according to the 13 federal disability categories. The former perspective is very true, but the latter is important, too. For example, federal special education currently provides funding for the costs of educating students with disabilities based on their identification within the 13 categories. Disability labels also ensure that students' civil rights are protected—rights that can extend throughout their lifetime. So, although you should not rely on labels to guide your perceptions of and decisions about students, labels currently have a function. Perhaps in the future, the benefits they provide will be made available and their often stigmatizing effects avoided. The categories of disabilities students must have in order to receive special education are summarized in the chart below.

Categories of Disability in Federal Special Education Law[1]

Federal Disability Term	Alternative Terms	Brief Description
Learning disability (LD)	Specific learning disability	A disorder related to processing information that leads to difficulties in reading, writing, and computing; the most common disability, accounting for half of all students receiving special education
Speech or language impairment	Communication disorder (CD)	A disorder related to accurately producing the sounds of language or meaningfully using language to communicate
Mental retardation (MR)	Intellectual disability, cognitive impairment	Significant limitations in cognitive ability and adaptive behavior; this disability occurs in a range of severity
Emotional disturbance (ED)	Behavior disorder (BD), emotional disability	Significant problems in the social-emotional area to a degree that learning is negatively affected
Autism	Autism spectrum disorder (ASD)	A disorder characterized by extraordinary difficulty in social responsiveness; this disability occurs in many different forms and may be mild or significant
Hearing impairment	Deaf, hard of hearing (DHH)	A partial or complete loss of hearing
Visual impairment	Low vision, blind	A partial or complete loss of vision
Deaf-blindness		A simultaneous significant hearing loss and significant vision loss
Orthopedic impairment (OI)	Physical disability	A significant physical limitation that impairs the ability to move or to complete motor activities
Traumatic brain injury (TBI)		A medical condition denoting a serious brain injury that occurs as a result of accident or injury; the impact of this disability varies widely but may affect learning, behavior, social skills, and language
Other health impairment (OHI)		A disease or health disorder so significant that it negatively affects learning; examples include cancer, sickle-cell anemia, and diabetes
Multiple disabilities		The simultaneous presence of two or more disabilities such that none can be identified as the primary disability; the most common example is the occurrence of mental retardation and physical disabilities
Developmental delay (DD)		A nonspecific disability category that states may choose to use as an alternative to specific disability labels for identifying students up to age 9 needing special education

[1]More complete definitions of each category of disability in federal special education law are presented in Chapters 6 and 7.

many state listings do. Despite the degree of mental retardation, most individuals with this disability can lead independent or semi-independent lives as adults and can hold appropriate jobs. The term *intellectual disability* sometimes is used instead of *mental retardation*. In this text, we use the two terms interchangeably.

EMOTIONAL DISTURBANCE ● When a student has significant difficulty in the social-emotional domain—serious enough to interfere with the student's learning—an *emotional disturbance (ED)*, also sometimes called an *emotional and behavior disorder (EBD)*, exists. Students with this disability may have difficulty with interpersonal relationships and may respond inappropriately in emotional situations; that is, they may have trouble making and keeping friends; they may get extremely angry when peers tease or play jokes on them; or they may show little or no emotion when it is expected, such as when family pets die. Some students with ED are depressed; others are aggressive. Students with ED display these impairments over a long period of time, across different settings, and to a degree significantly different from their peers. A student with an emotional disability is not just a student who is difficult to manage in a classroom; students with this disability have chronic and extremely serious emotional or behavioral problems.

> ❝ When a student has significant difficulty in the social-emotional domain—serious enough to interfere with the student's learning—an emotional disturbance (ED), also sometimes called an emotional and behavior disorder (EBD), exists. ❞

AUTISM ● Students with *autism* usually lack appropriate social responsiveness from a very early age. They generally avoid physical contact (for example, cuddling and holding), and they may not make eye contact. Problems with social interactions persist as these children grow; they appear unaware of others' feelings and may not seek interactions with peers or adults. They may have unusual language patterns, such as spoken language without intonation; echolalia, or repetition of others' speech; or little or no language. They may display repetitive body movements, such as rocking, and may need highly routinized behavior, such as a formalized procedure for putting on their clothes or eating their meals, to feel comfortable. Some students with autism have above-average intelligence; others have mental retardation. The causes of autism are not well understood, and the best approaches for working with students with autism are still under considerable debate. You may hear professionals refer to *autism spectrum disorder (ASD)*; this term is an acknowledgment that students with this disability vary tremendously in their abilities and needs. Thomas, one of the students you met at the beginning of the chapter, is identified as having autism. You can learn a little more about autism by reading the Case in Practice on page 23 in which teachers meet to problem solve regarding another student with this disability.

HEARING IMPAIRMENTS ● Disabilities that concern the inability or limited ability to receive auditory signals are called *hearing impairments (HI)*. When students are *hard of hearing*, they have a significant hearing loss but are able to capitalize on residual hearing by using hearing aids and other amplifying systems. Students who are *deaf* have little or no residual hearing and therefore do not benefit from traditional devices that aid hearing; however, they may be assisted through the use of advanced technology such as cochlear implants. Depending on the extent of the disability, students with hearing impairments may use sign language, speech reading, and other ways to help them communicate.

VISUAL IMPAIRMENTS ● Disabilities that concern the inability or limited ability to receive information visually are called *visual impairments (VI)*. Some students have *partial sight* and can learn successfully using magnification devices or other adaptive materials; students who are *blind* do not use vision as a means of learning and instead rely

FYI ▬▬▬▬▬

Depression is more common among children than previously thought. Up to 1.5 percent of children and up to 8.3 percent of adolescents in the United States have this serious disorder (National Institutes of Health, 2000). More information about depression can be found in Chapter 7.

FYI ▬▬▬▬▬

Students with a hearing loss (students who are deaf or hard of hearing) or visual impairment (students with low vision or who are blind) are referred to as *sensory impaired*. Students with these special needs are discussed in Chapter 6.

CASE IN PRACTICE

Problem Solving in Inclusive Schools: The Classroom Teacher's Role

At Highland Elementary School, staff members are meeting to discuss David, a third grader with autism. Ms. Dowley is David's teacher; Ms. Jackson is the special educator who provides needed support. Ms. Janes, the school psychologist, is also present.

Ms. Dowley: David is really a puzzle and a challenge. He is behaving much better in class than he was at the beginning of the year, but he still disrupts the entire class when he has a bad day. One of the parents called yesterday to complain about David taking time away from her daughter and the rest of the class. I'm starting to feel the same way. I hope we can come up with some ideas to improve the whole situation.

Ms. Jackson: What kinds of things seem to trigger the problems?

Ms. Dowley: That's part of my concerns. I'm still pretty new at teaching, and I have my hands full with the whole class. I don't even have time to think carefully about what's happening with David. I just deal with him when he does something inappropriate—bothering another student, refusing to come with the group—without really thinking about how it happened or how to avoid it, if that's possible.

Ms. Janes: You've mentioned problem behavior as one issue. Before we start

addressing that, are there any other issues we should be discussing, too?

Ms. Dowley: No. Right now, it's the behavior—and I want to be clear that I really can see all the other gains David has made. I *want* this to work for David and I know his parents do, too. They've been very helpful and always carry through with their part. I know David can be successful in my class—but it'll be much less stressful for all of us if we can work on his behavior.

Ms. Janes: It seems as though we need more information. One question I have is this: What happens with you and the other students when David does something inappropriate—talking in a loud voice, pushing books off the desk?

Ms. Dowley: Well, I try to ignore him, but that usually makes it worse. A few of the other students laugh, and that's not helping either.

Ms. Jackson: Maybe we should focus for a minute or two on when David doesn't have difficulty in class. What are the times of the day or the activities that David does without having behavior problems?

Ms. Dowley: Let's see. . . . He's usually fine and makes a good contribution when we're talking about science concepts. He loves science. When math is activity based, he's fine there, too.

Ms. Janes: Our meeting time is nearly up. I'd be happy to make time in my schedule to observe David, and perhaps Ms. Jackson could, too. I know you need answers right away, but I hope we can get a clearer sense of the pattern of David's behavior so we can find the right strategy for addressing it. If we can get in to observe this week, could we meet next Tuesday to try to generate some strategies?

Ms. Dowley: Sure. That would be great. Let's just work out the details on observing.

REFLECTIONS

Why was this meeting a positive example of teachers addressing a student problem in an inclusive school? What did they do that has set them up for success? If you were trying to understand David better, what other questions would you ask about him? What would you like others to observe in the classroom in relation to him? In relation to you as the teacher? What do you think will happen at the next meeting? On the basis of this case, how would you describe the role of classroom teachers in addressing the challenges of inclusion?

primarily on touch and hearing. Depending on need, students with visual impairments may use braille, specialized computers, and other aids to assist in learning. Some students need specialized training to help them learn to move around successfully in their environment.

DEAF-BLINDNESS ● Students who have both significant vision and hearing impairments sometimes are eligible for services as *deaf-blind*. These students are categorized separately because of the unique learning needs they have, particularly in the domain of communication, and because of the highly specialized services they require. The degree of the vision and hearing loss may vary from moderate to severe and may be accompanied by other disabilities. Students in this category are likely to receive special education services beginning at birth or very soon thereafter.

ORTHOPEDIC IMPAIRMENTS ● Students with *orthopedic impairments (OI)* have physical conditions that seriously impair their ability to move about or to complete motor activities. Students who have cerebral palsy are included in this group, as are those with other diseases that affect the skeleton or muscles. Students with physical limitations resulting from accidents also may be called orthopedically impaired. Some students with orthopedic impairments are unable to move about without a wheelchair and may need special transportation to get to school and a ramp to enter the school building. Others may lack the fine motor skills needed to write and may require extra time or adapted equipment to complete assignments.

TRAUMATIC BRAIN INJURY ● Students with *traumatic brain injury (TBI)* have a wide range of characteristics and special needs, including limited strength or alertness, developmental delays, short-term memory problems, hearing or vision losses that may be temporary, irritability, and sudden mood swings. Their characteristics and needs depend on the specific injuries they experienced, and their needs often change over time. Because TBI is a medical condition that affects education, diagnosis by a physician is required along with assessment of learning and adaptive behavior. Students who experience serious head trauma from automobile accidents, falls, or sports injuries are among those who might be eligible for services as TBI.

OTHER HEALTH IMPAIRMENTS ● Some students have a disease or disorder so significant that it affects their ability to learn in school; the category of disability addressing these needs is called *other health impairments (OHI)*. Students with severe asthma who require an adapted physical education program might be eligible for special education in this category, as might those who have chronic heart conditions necessitating frequent and prolonged absences from school. Students with diseases such as AIDS, sickle-cell anemia, and diabetes also may be categorized as having other health impairments, depending on the impact of their illnesses on learning. Also, some students with severe attention deficit–hyperactivity disorder (ADHD) receive special education services in this category.

MULTIPLE DISABILITIES ● The category used when students have two or more disabilities is called *multiple disabilities*. Students in this group often have mental retardation as well as a physical disability—as does Tonya, whose story you read in the chapter-opening cases—but this category may be used to describe any student with two or more disability types. However, this classification is used only when the student's disabilities are so serious and so interrelated that none can be identified as a primary disability. Students with multiple disabilities often benefit from assistive technology, that is, simple or complex devices that facilitate their learning, as explained in Technology Notes on page 25.

DEVELOPMENTAL DELAYS ● The category *developmental delays (DD)* is somewhat different than the other disabilities recognized in IDEA. It is an option that states may use for children from ages 3 through 9. This category includes youngsters who have significant delays in physical, cognitive, communication, social-emotional, or adaptive development but is applied instead of one of the more specific disability categories. Few states count children in this category, and those that do usually employ it as an alternative categorization for preschool children only. Is this term used in your state?

RESEARCH
N O T E

In a study by Taunt and Hastings (2002), parents of children with developmental disabilities reported a wide range of positive perceptions and experiences for themselves as well as their children's siblings and extended families.

> TECHNOLOGY NOTES

The Opportunities of Assistive Technology

Technology assists students with disabilities in many ways. Whether the students you teach have mild disabilities or significant disabilities, they may use technology to help them to communicate, to complete assignments, and to fully participate in school and community. *Assistive technology* is defined in a federal law that ensures that children and adults needing such assistance have access to it. The term refers to any device (that is, piece of equipment, product, or other item) that is used to increase, maintain, or improve the functional capabilities of an individual with disabilities.

Assistive technology sometimes is categorized according to its complexity. Here are examples of the levels of assistive technology students might use:

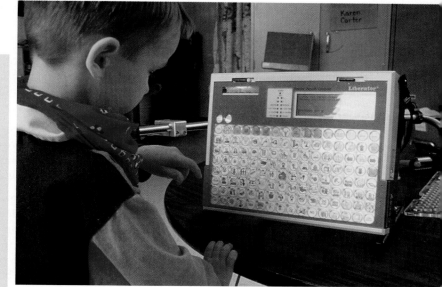

Electronic communication boards are an example of high-tech assistive technology that benefits students with communication disorders.

No Technology or Low Technology

No technology (no-tech), or *low technology (low-tech)*, refers to items that do not include any type of electronics. These are examples of low-tech devices:

- a rubber pencil grip that enables a student with a disability to better grasp a pencil or pen
- a nonslip placemat placed on a student's desk that makes it easier for the student to pick items up because it stops them from sliding
- a study carrel that helps a student pay closer attention to the schoolwork at hand

Mid-Technology

Devices in the *mid-technology (mid-tech)* category use simple electronics. Examples include the following:

- a tape recorder that a student uses to record lectures
- a calculator that assists a student in completing math computations
- a timer that lets a student know it is time to change from one activity to another

High Technology

The third level of assistive technology is referred to as *high technology (high-tech)*. Items in this category use complex technology, and they often are expensive compared to no-tech and mid-tech items. Examples include these:

- voice-recognition software that allows a student to dictate information that then appears in print on the computer
- electronic communication boards on which a student can touch a picture and a prerecorded voice communicates for the student. For example, a student touches a picture of himself, and a voice says, "Hello. My name is Danny. What is your name?"

Technology that used to be considered sophisticated (for example, talking watches and calculators, personal digital assistants) now is readily available and provides educational access for students with disabilities. As advances in technology continue, even more opportunities will become possible. As an educator, you should anticipate that assistive technology will be part of many students' tools for learning.

Cross-Categorical Approaches to Special Education

Federal and state education agencies and local school districts use the categories of disability described in the previous section for counting the number of students in special education and for allocating money to educate them. When you prepare to teach a student, however, you probably will find that the specific category of disability does not guide you in discovering that student's strengths and in devising appropriate

RESEARCH
N O T E

In a study by Blue-Banning, Turnbull, and Pereira (2002), Hispanic parents reported that their first wish for their children with special needs was general acceptance and respect from the extended family, neighborhood, and community.

ANALYZE
AND REFLECT

Which are the high-incidence disabilities? Which are the low-incidence disabilities? Why are these terms sometimes used instead of federal disability categories?

CONNECTIONS

The procedures for making decisions about placing students in special education programs are discussed in Chapter 2.

Why does the cross-categorical approach encourage teachers to identify strengths in all students? How does this help foster inclusive practices?

teaching strategies. Further, students in different categories often benefit from the same instructional adaptations. Therefore, throughout this book, students are sometimes discussed in terms of only two categories:

1. High-incidence disabilities are those that are most common, including learning disabilities, speech or language impairments, mild mental retardation, and emotional disturbance. Together, these disabilities account for more than 80 percent of the disabilities reported in 2000–2001 (U.S. Department of Education, 2002).

2. Low-incidence disabilities are those that are less common and include all the other categories: moderate to severe mental retardation, multiple disabilities, hearing impairments, orthopedic impairments, other health impairments, visual impairments, deaf-blindness, autism, traumatic brain injury, and developmental delays.

Consistent with a **cross-categorical approach**, characteristics of students with disabilities are discussed in more detail in Chapters 6 and 7, where more attention is paid to students' learning needs than to their labels. In addition, although some strategies specific to categorical groups (for example, the use of large-print books for students with visual impairments) are outlined in those chapters, most of the strategies presented throughout the text can be adapted for most students. If you adopt a cross-categorical approach in your own thinking about teaching students with disabilities, you will see that many options are available for helping all students succeed.

Other Students with Special Needs

Not all students who have special learning and behavior needs are addressed in special education laws. Many other students, described in the following sections, benefit from the ideas presented throughout this book.

STUDENTS WHO ARE GIFTED OR TALENTED ● Students who demonstrate ability far above average in one or several areas, including overall intellectual ability, leadership, specific academic subjects, creativity, athletics, or the visual or performing arts, are considered *gifted* or *talented*. Erin is included in this group; she seems to learn without effort, and she is also eager to learn about almost everything. Evan also is talented; still in elementary school, he has participated in state and national piano recitals, and his parents have requested that he have access to the music room during recess so he can practice. Students who are gifted or talented are not addressed in federal special education law. In the majority of states, separate laws exist that provide guidelines for identifying and educating students with special talents. Adequate funds are not always provided to implement these laws, however, and so the availability and scope of services for students with particular talents vary across the country and even within a particular state.

STUDENTS PROTECTED BY SECTION 504 ● Some students not eligible to receive special education services are entitled to protection through Section 504 and receive specialized assistance because of their functional disabilities, as described previously in this chapter. Among those likely to be included in this group are students with attention deficit–hyperactivity disorder (ADHD). These students have a medical condition often characterized by an inability to attend to complex tasks for long periods of time, excessive motor activity, and impulsivity. The impact of this disorder on students' schoolwork can be significant. Identification of ADHD requires input from a physician. Students with ADHD may take medication, such as Ritalin or Strattera, that helps them focus their attention. Many students with learning disabilities or emotional disturbance also have ADHD, but these students receive assistance through IDEA.

STUDENTS AT RISK ● Often, the general term *at risk* refers to students who have characteristics, live in an environment, or have experiences that make them more likely than others to fail in school. Students whose primary language is not English—sometimes referred to as *English-language learners (ELLs)*—sometimes are considered at risk, and they may need assistance in school learning. They may attend bilingual education programs or classes for English as a second language (ESL) for opportunities to learn English while also learning the standard curriculum, or they may receive assistance in their general education classrooms. Some ELLs also have disabilities; when this is the case, both English language instruction and special education are provided. Several points to keep in mind when considering the diversity of students you are likely to teach can be found in the Professional Edge below.

A second group of at-risk students includes *slow learners* whose educational progress is below average but who do not have a learning disability or mental retardation. These students are learning to the best of their ability, but they often cannot keep

CONNECTIONS

Students with special needs who are not necessarily eligible for special education (for example, students who are gifted and those with ADHD) are discussed in more detail in Chapter 8.

PROFESSIONAL EDGE

Myths of Multicultural Education

Most novice educators are aware of their responsibility for being sensitive to and respectful of the various cultural backgrounds of their students. However, myths such as the following sometimes prevent educators from making concepts of multicultural education a reality:

● *Multicultural education is primarily for white children because they lack exposure to other perspectives.* Minority children tend to grow up in homogeneous environments to the same extent that white children do. All students need to learn about other cultures.

● *The purpose of multicultural education is to learn about only one culture.* In some communities, one minority group is predominant. Teachers may presume that their goal is to educate students about that one culture—to the exclusion of others. Educators need to remember that the goal of multicultural education is to assist students to know their own culture yet at the same time to respect other cultures.

● *Multicultural understanding can be achieved through lessons about the food and festivals of minority groups.*

When professionals' approach to multicultural education is to focus only on foods and festivals, an approach sometimes referred to as *cultural tourism,* culture ends up being treated as an event and, in many ways, is trivialized. Information about culture should be integrated into student learning and should incorporate depth, including examining why biases exist against certain groups.

● *The sole purpose of multicultural education is to build a bridge between whites and nonwhites.* The population of the United States has become quite diverse; this country includes individuals from many racial and ethnic groups. Further, social and political tension sometimes causes deep divisions between minority groups. Multicultural education should be premised on an understanding that it addresses all groups.

SOURCE: From "Learning about the 'Other': Building a Case for Intercultural Understanding among Minority Children," by J. Pattnaik, 2003, *Childhood Education, 79,* pp. 204–211.

pace with the instruction in most general education classrooms without assistance. They are sometimes described as "falling between the cracks" of the educational system because most professionals agree they need special assistance but they are not eligible for special education. However, they sometimes receive assistance in remedial reading or tutorial programs.

Other students who might be considered at risk include those who are homeless or live in poverty, who are born to mothers abusing drugs or alcohol, who abuse drugs or alcohol themselves, and who are victims of physical or psychological abuse. Students in these groups are at risk for school failure because of the environments or circumstances in which they live.

You may find that students with special needs who do not have disabilities according to special education laws are particularly puzzling because no single group of professionals is responsible for educating them. As students with disabilities spend increasing amounts of time in general education classes, special education teachers and other special services providers often informally assist teachers in planning and adapting educational activities for these students. Thus, other students with special needs often benefit from the trend toward inclusive education for students with disabilities.

SUMMARY

Special education refers to the specialized instruction received by the millions of students in the United States who have disabilities and is guided by the concept of the least restrictive environment (LRE). Current special education practices have evolved from a combination of historical factors, including the inception of compulsory public education early in the 20th century, research questioning instructional practices for students with disabilities, the civil rights movement and related court cases, and a series of federal civil rights and education laws, including Section 504, ADA, IDEA, and NCLB.

The present trend in special education is toward inclusive practices, but implementing instructional practices to support them requires an understanding of their importance and a commitment to their realization. Teachers' perceptions of inclusion and their knowledge and skills for teaching in diverse classrooms affect the quality of many programs. Parents generally react favorably to inclusive practices in terms of social outcomes for their children, but they have concerns related to academic and functional outcomes. Data suggest that many students with high-incidence or low-incidence disabilities, but not all, can succeed in inclusive classrooms. Essential for inclusive practices is attention to systemic issues such as administrative leadership, personnel, time allocation, and cost.

Federal law identifies 13 categories of disability that may entitle students to special education services: learning disabilities, speech or language impairments, mental retardation, emotional disturbance, autism, hearing impairments, visual impairments, deaf-blindness, orthopedic impairments, traumatic brain injury, other health impairments, multiple disabilities, and developmental delays. However, many other students have special needs not addressed through special education, including those who are gifted or talented; who have ADHD; who are at risk, including English-language learners and slow learners; and whose life situations comprise high risk for school failure. Nearly all public school teachers are responsible for instructing students with disabilities and other special needs.

Applications in **Teaching Practice**

Understanding Contemporary Special Education Practices

It is a new school year—your first as a teacher in the Danville School District. You are excited about your new job but worried about following the district curriculum and making sure that your students succeed on the high-stakes test. Then you learn that you will be responsible for the following students, and you find that you need all the skills for reaching diverse groups of students that you learned in your professional preparation program:

- Cassie is a bright young woman who has a visual impairment. To read, she uses a computer that greatly magnifies her materials. She also needs to work in bright light, and she gets fatigued from the effort required to use what little vision she has.

- Ramon is a young man identified as having a learning disability. His reading ability is significantly below grade level. He also seems disorganized. He often forgets to bring materials and assignments to class, and he forgets to return permission forms for field trips he wants to participate in.

- Tory lives in a foster home. He was removed from his mother's home because of several incidents of abuse. Tory is an angry child. He often refuses to work, he sometimes loses his temper and throws a book or crumples a paper, and he misses school frequently.

QUESTIONS

1. What are the possible strengths that Cassie, Ramon, and Tory might bring to your classroom? How could their possible strengths be emphasized instead of their problems? What is the rationale for assigning these students to a general education classroom? How do the provisions of IDEA and NCLB affect these students' educational rights and responsibilities? What are appropriate goals you as a classroom teacher should accomplish with them? Discuss with your classmates how Cassie's, Ramon's, and Tory's special needs might be demonstrated in an elementary school, middle school, or high school classroom.

2. What are some of the benefits and opportunities of educating these students in your classroom? What positive outcomes should you expect? How can you ensure these positive outcomes?

3. What are some of the risks and concerns related to educating these students in your classroom? What types of systemic supports could prevent or significantly reduce these risks and concerns? How might your own beliefs be either a benefit or a risk for these students?

4. If you spoke with a parent of Cassie, Ramon, and Tory, what might you expect each to say? How might their views be influenced by their family cultures and experiences? What could you do to encourage parent participation for your students?

5. When you think about your responsibilities for educating students with disabilities and other special needs in your classroom—whether in kindergarten or in a senior-level content-area class—what are your concerns and questions? In what ways do you think you can make a contribution to your students' education? What types of supports might you need? If you write your responses to these questions, keep them with your text and use them as a basis for discussion as you learn more in later chapters.

WORKING THE **STANDARDS**

The Council for Exceptional Children (CEC) Special Education Content Standards consist of 10 narrative standards that must be mastered by all beginning *special education teachers*. These standards parallel the 10 Interstate New Teacher and Assessment Consortium (INTASC) principles that must be mastered by all beginning *general educators*. Together, these standards detail the knowledge and skills that *all educators* should possess in order to be effective teachers of students with disabilities. The Working the Standards feature in each chapter contains a list of the standards relevant to the chapter content.

INTASC PRINCIPLES REFLECTED IN THIS CHAPTER:

Principle #1 states that all teachers

- Have knowledge of the major principles and parameters of federal disabilities legislation. This includes knowledge of the Individuals with Disabilities Education Act (IDEA), Section 504 of the Rehabilitation Act of 1973, and the Americans with Disabilities Act (ADA) (Principle 1.04).

- Understand that students with disabilities may need accommodations, modifications, and/or adaptations to the general curriculum (Principle 1.03).

- Can access resources to gain information about state, district, and school policies and procedures relating to special education, including those regarding referral, assessment, eligibility, and services for students with disabilities (Principle 1.05).

Principle #9 states that all teachers continually challenge their beliefs about how students with disabilities learn and how to teach them effectively (Principle 9.02).

CEC STANDARDS REFLECTED IN THIS CHAPTER:

CEC Content Standard #1 states that special educators

- Understand the field as an evolving and changing discipline based on philosophies, evidence-based principles and theories, relevant laws and policies, diverse and historical points of view, and human issues that have historically influenced and continue to influence the field of special education and the education and treatment of individuals with exceptional needs both in school and society.

- Understand how the above factors influence professional practice, including assessment, instructional planning, implementation, and program evaluation.

CEC Content Standard #10 states that special educators

- Embrace their special role as advocate for individuals with exceptional learning needs (ELN).

- Promote and advocate the learning and well-being of individuals with ELN across a wide range of settings and a range of different learning experiences.

BACK TO THE CASES

The standards and principles just listed relate to the students described at the beginning of this chapter: Thomas, Tonya, and Aaron. The questions and activities that follow demonstrate how these standards and principles, along with other concepts that you have learned about in this chapter, connect to the everyday activities of all teachers.

Thomas

Thomas's story at the beginning of the chapter describes the inclusion of a student with autism. If you believe that inclusion has been successful for Thomas, explain what factors lead you to that conclusion and may contribute to successful inclusion with typically achieving peers. (See INTASC Principles 1.03 and 1.05, and CEC Standards 1 and 10.) If you believe that inclusion is problematic for Thomas, his teachers, or classmates, explain what factors lead you to that conclusion and may prevent successful inclusion with typically achieving peers.

Tonya

After you have read the description of Tonya's inclusion experiences at the beginning of the chapter, review the court cases provided in Figure 1.2. Each of these court cases had an impact on inclusive practices in public schools across the country. Which cases support the practices found in Tonya's case? (See INTASC Principles 1.05 and 9.02, and CEC Standard 1.) Offer specific examples to support your answer.

Aaron

Several of the assistive technologies mentioned in the Technology Notes on page 25 could provide support for Aaron's problems with attention and written tests. Select two or three of these that you would recommend to Aaron. (See INTASC Principle 1.03 and CEC Standard 10.) Remembering that Aaron does not want to stand out or be treated differently, what would you say to him that would help him accept these assistive supports?

 Visit the companion website (http://www.ablongman.com/friend4e) for a complete correlation of this chapter to the INTASC Principles and CEC Standards.

Further **Readings**

Donovan, M. S., & Cross, C. T. (Eds.). (2002). *Minority students in special and gifted education.* Washington, DC: National Academy Press.

This report from the National Research Council examines reasons why minority students sometimes are overrepresented in special education and underrepresented in programs for students who are gifted and talented. Also considered is the question of whether the benefits of special education programs, even if students are not appropriately placed in them, outweigh the potential problems.

Edyburn, D. L. (Ed.). (2003). Technology and special education [Special issue]. *Remedial and Special Education, 24,* 130–192.

This special journal issue addresses a variety of topics that are useful for educators, including the roles of assistive technology specialists, the use of technology in reading and writing instruction, the impact of technology in a ninth-grade language arts class, and technology for interdisciplinary units of instruction.

Klein, S., & Kemp, J. (2004). *Reflections from a different journey: What adults with disabilities wish all parents knew.* New York: McGraw-Hill.

This book is a set of essays and stories told by individuals with disabilities about what it was like growing up. Although the primary audience is parents, the book contains much information that is valuable to teachers and other educators for understanding students with disabilities.

O'Brien, R., & Smith, R. M. (2003). *Voices from the edge: Narratives about the Americans with Disabilities Act.* New York: Oxford University Press.

This book is a collection of stories about individuals with disabilities and their experiences in American society. The book aims to demonstrate that, in spite of federal legislation, people with disabilities still face many challenges in going about their daily lives.

CHAPTER 2

Special Education Procedures and Services

After you read this chapter, you will be able to

1. Explain the roles and responsibilities of the individuals who may participate in educating students with disabilities.

2. Describe the process through which a student may become eligible to receive special education services.

3. Name the components of individualized education programs (IEPs) and provide examples of them.

4. Describe the types of services that students with disabilities may receive and the settings in which they may receive them.

5. Discuss how parents participate in special education decision making and what occurs when parents and school district representatives disagree.

6. Outline the role of general education teachers in the procedures and services of special education, reflecting on their critical contributions to positive outcomes for students with disabilities.

KEY TERMS AND CONCEPTS

Annual review (p. 54)

Due process (p. 55)

Individualized education program (IEP) (p. 53)

Intervention assistance team (p. 49)

Mediation (p. 56)

Multidisciplinary team (MDT) (p. 50)

Self-determination (p. 42)

Three-year reevaluation (p. 55)

Transition plan (p. 60)

MR. VAZQUEZ IS CONCERNED. He teaches fifth grade, and one of his students, Marcus, is having increasing difficulty in the curriculum. Marcus reads at a beginning third-grade level, has learned just a few basic addition math facts, and increasingly is refusing to do any work at all. The other children are teasing him, and he reacts by using profanity and threatening to "get" them. Mr. Vazquez isn't sure what to do next; the strategies he has used in the past have no impact, and the difficulties Marcus is encountering are far beyond typical variations in learning rate and style. Mr. Vazquez has met with Marcus's mother and stepfather. They report they are having more and more difficulty getting Marcus to mind them. Marcus's parents are concerned that he doesn't seem to care about school and that he is spending much of his time hanging out with older boys. They are worried about gangs and drugs. ● *What steps should Mr. Vazquez take next? Whom might Mr. Vazquez contact to help him decide whether Marcus's difficulties are serious enough to consider assessing him for special education?*

MS. LEE, a high school English teacher, has just pulled from her mailbox something titled "Helping Your Students with Special Needs Succeed." As she glances through it, she realizes that it is a summary of the individualized education program (IEP) for Jennifer, one of her students. The summary includes a list of test accommodations Jennifer should receive, and it mentions steps being taken to help Jennifer prepare for a vocational program she'll attend after high school. Ms. Lee notes that the speech/language therapist, the transition specialist, and the social worker are mentioned, but the special education teacher is listed as the person to contact to answer questions. ● *What roles do classroom teachers play in writing and implementing IEPs? What is their responsibility for ensuring that IEP accommodations are available in the classroom? Who are the other service providers teachers may work with as they educate students with disabilities?*

MS. TURNER TEACHES SCIENCE

to seventh graders. Toward the end of the last school year, she was invited to become a member of her school's inclusive practices team. At a summer professional development seminar, she learned that many of the students in her school leave general education classes for a significant part of each day to receive special education services and that some students attend a different school. She worked with her colleagues to develop a plan to ex-amine whether the options available to students at her school encourage inclusive practices, to reconsider the types of services students should receive, and to enlist the assistance of administrators, parents, and teachers in refining the school's services.

● *What is meant by a continuum of placement option? How does it affect students with disabilities? How does it affect general education teachers and other school staff? How are decisions about placement made?*

A s a teacher, you will encounter students who are struggling in school. Some may appear to be doing everything they can *not* to learn. Others try their best but still are not successful. You might even have students who you suspect have a vision or hearing problem so serious that it prevents them from learning. You may find yourself wondering whether some of these students should be receiving special education services and who will provide them. This chapter introduces you to people who specialize in working with students with disabilities and procedures for deciding whether a student is eligible for special education services. You also will learn how students' individualized instructional programs are designed and monitored and which services students with disabilities use. You will discover that parents play a crucial role in special education procedures and that when they or students disagree with school professionals about special services, procedures exist to help them resolve these differences. Most important, you will learn about your role in working with other professionals and parents to determine student eligibility for special education, carrying out students' educational programs, and monitoring student learning.

> "You will learn about your role in working with other professionals and parents to determine student eligibility for special education, carrying out students' educational programs, and monitoring student learning."

Who Are the Professionals in Special Education?

Students with disabilities are entitled to a wide range of supports and services. Not surprisingly, many different individuals, sometimes collectively referred to as *special services staff members*, can be involved in the delivery of these services. You probably will interact with some of these professionals, such as special education teachers, almost every day. Others you might work with only occasionally. Some of these professionals serve students indirectly, or they work only with the few students who have the most challenging disabilities. Together, however, these educators create, implement, and evaluate the special education that students with disabilities receive.

General Education Teachers

As the *general education teacher*, you are the first professional discussed in this section because for many students with suspected or documented disabilities, you are the person who has the most detailed knowledge of students' day-to-day needs in your classroom. Your responsibilities span several areas. You are the person most likely to bring to the attention of other professionals a student who you suspect may have a disability. That is, you may encounter a student who is reading significantly and persistently below grade level, a student whose behavior is so different from other students' that you suspect an emotional disorder, or a student who has extraordinary difficulty focusing on learning. When you suspect a disability, you document the student's characteristics and behaviors that led to your concern by gathering samples of the student's work, compiling descriptions of the student's behavior, and keeping notes of how you have addressed the student's problem (Lane, Mahdavi, & Borthwick-Duffy, 2003). You work with special education colleagues and other professionals to systematically implement interventions in your classroom to clarify whether the student's problems need further exploration (Buck, Polloway, Smith-Thomas, & Cook, 2003; Knotek, 2003). If the student is referred for assessment for special education, you contribute information about academic and social functioning in your classroom, and you help identify the student's strengths, needs, and educational program components. For example, you might help others understand the curricular expectations in your classroom and the types of adaptations that may be necessary for the student to succeed there. If special education services are deemed necessary, you participate in deciding appropriate goals and, for some students, objectives. You also might assist special services staff members in updating parents on their child's quarterly and yearly progress. Most important, you are expected to work with special services staff to provide appropriate instruction within your classroom (Burstein, Sears, Wilcoxen, Cabello, & Spagna, 2004; DeBettencourt, 1999; Salend, Gordon, & Lopez-Vona, 2002). The responsibilities of a general education teacher are summarized in Figure 2.1.

Who are the professionals who support students with disabilities and their classroom teachers? What is the classroom teacher's role in identifying students with disabilities and providing their instruction?

FIGURE 2.1 General Education Teacher Responsibilities in Special Education

Member of pre-referral or intervention assistance team

Provider of day-to-day instruction

Identifier of students with possible special needs

Communication link with colleagues

Member of multidisciplinary team that writes the IEP

Liaison to parents

When all your responsibilities are listed, your role in planning and providing special services to students may seem overwhelming. However, studies of general education teachers typically indicate that they are able and willing to contribute to the education of students with disabilities as long as some conditions are met. The most important conditions include administrative leadership and staff preparation, sufficient time for teacher planning, and adequate funding and other resources for program support (Burstein et al., 2004; Taylor, Richards, Goldstein, & Schilit, 1997).

Special Education Teachers

Special education teachers are the professionals with whom you are most likely to have ongoing contact in teaching students with disabilities. They are responsible for managing and coordinating the services a student receives, including writing and implementing a student's individualized education program (IEP). They also typically provide direct and indirect instruction to students who are assigned to them (Wood, 1998). In addition, they may consult with you regarding a student suspected of having a disability and work with you to determine whether a referral for assessment for possible special education is warranted, a process explained later in this chapter.

Depending on the state in which you teach and the students in your classroom, you may work with different types of special education teachers. Sometimes, special education teachers are assigned to work with any of the students with disabilities in your class. For example, a special education teacher may support a student with learning disabilities and also work with a student with a moderate cognitive disability or a speech or language impairment. That professional works indirectly with other special education professionals to ensure that each student's educational plan is being implemented and monitored. In some locales, special education teachers work with a specific category of students. For example, your school may have a specific teacher for students with learning disabilities or emotional disabilities. Likewise, a teacher for students with visual or hearing impairments may be available if needed. In states that do not use categorical labels for students, some teachers work with students with high-incidence disabilities or low-incidence disabilities, or they may work with *any* student who has an IEP.

In other situations, special education teachers may be designated by the type of services they provide. For example, for some students with high-incidence disabilities in your class, you may work with a *consulting teacher* (Friend & Cook, 2003). This professional might meet with you regularly to monitor students' progress and address your concerns about the students but might not directly teach them. You also might work with a *resource teacher* who divides time between directly instructing students and working with teachers. In some high schools, special education teachers now are assigned to work with a particular department, attending department meetings and providing supports for all students with disabilities enrolled in that department's courses.

Yet another type of special education teacher designated by type of services is an *inclusion specialist* or *support facilitator* (for example, Klinger & Vaughn, 2002). In inclusive schools, inclusion specialists are responsible for providing some student instruction, for problem solving with teachers, and for coordinating the services a student receives. Often, they focus on ensuring that the needs of students with moderate, severe, or multiple disabilities are being met.

For some groups of students, the special educator with whom you interact might be an *itinerant teacher*. Itinerant teachers often have roles like the professionals just described, but they travel between two or more school sites to provide services to students. Teachers for students with vision or hearing disabilities often are itinerant. However, if you work in a school district where each school has only a few students with disabilities, even the special educator who specializes in working with students with high-incidence disabilities may deliver services this way.

One other type of special education teacher is a *transition specialist*. This professional typically works in a high school setting and helps prepare students to leave

RESEARCH NOTE

Wood (1998) studied teachers' perceptions of their roles in schools that included students with severe disabilities. She found that when inclusion was new, special education and general education kept clear role boundaries. As they worked together, however, those boundaries blurred and collaboration improved.

school for vocational training, employment, or postsecondary education (Field, Sarver, & Shaw, 2003). No matter what subject you teach in high school, you might work very closely with a transition specialist, but especially in business education, consumer sciences, industrial or other vocational arts, and similar areas. This professional also spends time working directly with students to assess their skills and interests related to life after school. A transition specialist works with community businesses to arrange student job sites and to resolve problems related to student workers (Cook, 2002). This professional also may serve as a *job coach*, accompanying a student to a job site and helping the student master the skills needed to do the job successfully.

As the nature of special education services changes, so do job responsibilities and titles of special educators. For example, you might find that the professionals in your school who used to be called special education teachers are now referred to as *special services teachers (SSTs)* or *intervention specialists (ISs)*. This change in title represents an effort to delabel teachers and parallels efforts to de-emphasize students' labels, that is, to stress student needs instead of the language of disability. As schools work to become more inclusive, the vocabulary related to teachers who work with students with special needs continues to evolve. More importantly, regardless of the type of special education teachers with whom you work, you will find that they are important instructional partners who are no longer relegated to teaching just in a special education classroom. They support students by creating adapted materials, teaching with you in the general education classroom, working directly and separately with students who have disabilities, and often serving as coordinators for all the services any single student may receive.

FYI

In some school districts, efforts are being made to decrease the labeling of not just students with disabilities but also their teachers. You might find that special educators sometimes are called *learning specialists* or *learning facilitators*.

Other Specialists and Related Service Providers

In addition to working with special education teachers, you will have contact with a variety of other service providers (Shapiro & Sayers, 2003). They, too, play important roles in educating students with disabilities.

SCHOOL PSYCHOLOGISTS ● School psychologists offer at least two types of expertise related to educating students with disabilities. First, *school psychologists* often have a major responsibility for determining a student's cognitive, academic, social, emotional, and/or behavioral functioning. They typically contribute a detailed written analysis of the student's strengths and areas of need; in many school districts, this document is referred to as a "psych report," that is, a psychological report. In a related role, school psychologists sometimes chair the multidisciplinary team that meets to decide whether a student has a disability and, if so, what types of services are needed.

> In addition to working with special education teachers, you will have contact with a variety of other service providers. They, too, play important roles in educating students with disabilities.

A second major task for school psychologists is designing strategies to address students' academic and social or behavior problems (National Association of School Psychologists, 2002). Sometimes, school psychologists serve as behavior consultants. Occasionally, they assist a teacher by working with an entire class group on social skills. They also might provide individual assistance to students with emotional or behavioral problems who are not eligible for special education. Unfortunately, many school districts can employ only enough school psychologists to complete required assessment duties; when this occurs, school psychologists may not be available to assist students or teachers directly (Giangreco, Prelock, Reid, Dennis, & Edelman, 2000).

COUNSELORS ● Although *counselors* most often advise high school students, they also work at other school levels and contribute to the education of students with disabilities (National Clearinghouse for Professions in Special Education, 2004). For example, counselors in some school districts assess students' social and emotional

WWW
R E S O U R C E S

You can explore career options related to working with students with disabilities at the website for the National Clearinghouse for Professions in Special Education, at http://www.special-ed-careers.org.

functioning, including areas such as self-concept; motivation; attitude toward school, peers, and teachers; and social skills. Counselors also can provide services to both teachers and students. For teachers, they might suggest ways to draw out a student who is excessively shy, to incorporate into day-to-day classroom instruction activities designed to enhance students' self-concept, and to create an emotionally safe classroom environment. For students, counselors might provide individual assistance to a student struggling to understand a parent's death or unexplained departure from the family or other stressful events, arrange group sessions with several students who share specific needs, or work with an entire class on how to interact with a peer who has a disability.

SPEECH/LANGUAGE THERAPISTS ●

Many students with disabilities have communication needs. Some have mild problems in pronouncing words or speaking clearly. Others have extremely limited vocabulary. Yet others can make only a few sounds and rely on alternative means of communication, such as communication boards. The professionals who specialize in meeting students' communication needs are *speech/language therapists*. They have a tremendously diverse range of school responsibilities. At the early elementary level, they might work with entire classes on language development or with individual students on pronouncing sounds. At the intermediate elementary level, they might work on vocabulary with a group of students and might also help a student with a moderate cognitive disability pronounce some words more clearly or to combine words into sentences. At the middle or high school level, they often focus on functional vocabulary and work mostly with students with low-incidence disabilities. For example, they might help a student with a cognitive disability learn to read common signs and complete tasks such as ordering in a restaurant or asking for assistance.

SOCIAL WORKERS ●

Social workers' expertise is similar to that of counselors in terms of being able to help teachers and students address social and emotional issues. Thus, they may serve as consultants to teachers and also may provide individual or group assistance to students. However, social workers have additional expertise. They often are liaisons between schools and families. For example, they can create a family history by interviewing parents and visiting a student's home; this information may be critical in determining whether a student needs special education services. Similarly, they may help other school professionals work with families on matters such as gaining access to community health services. The school social worker often follows up on teacher reports about the suspected abuse or neglect of students. In some school districts, both counselors and social workers are available to meet student needs. In others, only one of these professional groups is employed.

FYI

The term *gross motor skills* refers to students' ability to use their large muscles effectively for walking, hopping, running, skipping, and the like. The term *fine motor skills* refers to students' proficiency in using their small muscles for tasks such as writing, buttoning, and grasping.

PHYSICAL THERAPISTS AND OCCUPATIONAL THERAPISTS ●

In order for some students to benefit from education, they require assistance for problems with gross and fine motor skills, for example, skipping or tying their shoelaces. Physical and occupational therapists are the professionals who have expertise in these areas.

Physical therapists assess students' needs and provide interventions related to gross motor skills. They might participate on a multidisciplinary team by assessing areas such as the obviously awkward gait of a student suspected of having a disability. They also interpret information about a student's physical needs that has been provided by a physician. For students with identified disabilities, physical therapists might provide direct training in large-muscle movement and control. They also might monitor how students should be physically positioned, whether in a wheelchair, standing with assistance, or on the floor; how their physical needs are affecting their educational needs; and how classroom settings can be adapted to accommodate their needs.

Occupational therapists are concerned with fine motor skills; they often have the responsibility of assessing students' use of their hands and fingers and developing and implementing plans for improving related motor skills. For example, an occupational therapist may assess whether a student with a severe learning disability can appropriately grip and use a pencil. This professional might help younger students or those with more severe disabilities learn skills for feeding or dressing themselves. Occupational therapists are working increasingly with teachers to incorporate fine motor skills training into classroom routines.

ADAPTIVE PHYSICAL EDUCATORS ● When students have significant gross or fine motor problems, typical physical education programs in schools may not be appropriate given their needs. *Adaptive physical educators* assess students' motor needs and work with teachers, physical educators, and others to meet them, or they work directly with students. These professionals are experts in adapting traditional physical education activities for students with disabilities. For example, they might create a simplified form of a basketball drill so that a student who has difficulty running can participate in the activity. They also might create activities that help students develop such skills as balancing, skipping, running, and throwing.

NURSES ● A link between students' medical and educational needs is provided by *nurses*. They develop student medical histories as needed, and they may screen students for vision and hearing problems. They also provide the multidisciplinary team with information about specific medical conditions a student might have and the impact the student's medication could have on educational performance. Further, nurses assist other professionals in deciding whether a student's learning or behavior problem could have a medical basis and discussing such matters with parents. Nurses most often are responsible for ensuring day to day that students with disabilities take required medication and for providing first aid or other emergency treatment. They also work with teachers and families to monitor student medical needs (for example, whether a change in medication is causing drowsiness or hyperactivity).

ADMINISTRATORS ● The school principal, assistant principal, and sometimes a special education department chairperson or team leader are the *administrators* most likely to participate actively in the education of students with disabilities. Their role is to offer knowledge about the entire school community and provide perspective on school district policies regarding special education. Administrators assist the multidisciplinary team in determining students' eligibility for services and in exploring strategies for meeting their needs. They also play an important role in addressing parents' concerns. Every team that determines whether a student is eligible for special education must have administrative representation. For example, in one school, the mother of Marisha, a student with severe language delays, requested that her daughter receive speech/language therapy for 40 minutes daily. School professionals were in agreement that this amount of therapy was not appropriate. Dr. Wade, the principal, worked with the team and the parent to negotiate the amount of speech therapy needed to accomplish Marisha's goals.

In some locales, especially in large urban and suburban districts where it is difficult to ensure that all required special education procedures are followed, a *special services coordinator* is part of the district's administration. Special services coordinators specialize in understanding the sometimes complex procedures of special education. They help alleviate the pressure on school administrators to accurately interpret and follow guidelines. They also explain services and options to parents, problem solve with teachers when issues arise, and assist in monitoring to ensure that students with disabilities receive needed supports.

PARAPROFESSIONALS ● Individuals who assist teachers and others in the provision of services to students with disabilities are *paraprofessionals* (French, 1999a). These individuals usually have a certificate based on completing a community college or

CONNECTIONS

Additional information about working with paraprofessionals is included in the "Professional Edge" on page 41 and also in Chapter 3.

similar training program; some are even certified teachers. However, these service providers are considered a separate group from every professional group mentioned thus far. Specifically, their responsibilities for decision making about students are limited, and they complete their work by direction from teachers and other professional staff members. Paraprofessionals also might be called *instructional assistants*, *aides*, or other titles, depending on local practices.

School districts use paraprofessionals in many different ways (Trautman, 2004). Two of the most common are as follows. First, some paraprofessionals are assigned to specific students who need ongoing individual assistance. For example, students with no ability to move their arms may have paraprofessionals who take notes for them and complete other tasks such as feeding. A few students have medical conditions requiring that a specially trained paraprofessional be present to monitor their status. Paraprofessionals in this role may be referred to as *personal assistants*. They also may be called *one-to-one assistants*.

Second, and more common, are paraprofessionals who assist in the delivery of special services for many students. These paraprofessionals often work in both inclusive classrooms and special education classrooms as well as on the playground, at assemblies, and during bus duty. Their primary responsibility is to work with students with disabilities, but they sometimes also help other students and the teacher as the need arises and time permits. The Professional Edge on page 41 contains more information about working with paraprofessionals.

OTHER SPECIALISTS ● Depending on student needs and state and local practices, other professionals also may participate in the education of students with disabilities. For example, some school districts have *consultants* who are used only when a need exists in their specific areas of expertise (such as significant behavior problems, autism, or traumatic brain injury). If you work in a school district in which many students are non-native English speakers, you also may work with *bilingual teachers* or *bilingual special education* teachers. Bilingual teachers are not special educators, but they sometimes help in decision making related to students with disabilities who have limited English skills. Bilingual special education teachers are professionally trained both in special education and in bilingual education (Salend, Dorney, & Mazo, 1997).

Two other types of specialists may provide services to your students with disabilities. One is a *mobility specialist* whose job is to help students with visual impairments learn how to become familiar with their environments and how to travel from place to place safely. These specialists consult with classroom teachers regarding students with visual impairments. The other type of service provider is a *sign-language interpreter*. Interpreters are the communication link for students with significant hearing loss (National Clearinghouse for Professions in Special Education, 2004). Interpreters listen to the instruction in a classroom and relay it to students who are deaf or hard of hearing using sign language. Interpreters might accompany a student all day or might be needed only in specific academic subjects such as language arts.

Professionals from agencies outside the school also are part of the specialist group. If a student has been receiving services through a hospital or residential program, a physician, nurse, social worker, or other representative from that facility may work with school personnel to ensure that the student has a smooth transition back to school. Individuals from the medical community also might be involved when students are being assessed for attentional problems or when they have been injured or ill. Professionals from outside agencies also might be included when a student is receiving assistance from a community service organization or has contact with the juvenile justice system. In these instances, caseworkers may serve as liaisons to the school. Students who are transitioning from school to adult services may need services from a professional in vocational rehabilitation. Finally, parents may obtain an expert opinion from a specialist not associated with the school, and those individuals can attend multidisciplinary team meetings or submit written reports for team consideration.

PROFESSIONAL EDGE

Working with Paraprofessionals

No matter what grade level you teach, you are likely at some point to find yourself working closely with paraprofessionals, also called paraeducators. These individuals are employed by school districts to provide support to students with disabilities, either by working with a particular student one-to-one or by working in general or special education classrooms with several students.

Although paraprofessionals have been a part of special education services and supports for many years, only in the past decade has much attention been paid to their preparation for their roles and their responsibilities for students. Paraprofessionals do not have sole responsibility for any aspect of a student's educational program. Rather, they share responsibilities with teachers and other multidisciplinary team members, and they work under the direction of a special education teacher or another professional. If a paraprofessional is assigned to your classroom in order to support students with disabilities, you probably will be expected to direct his or her day-to-day activities there. The following is a list of some responsibilities paraprofessionals may carry out:

- Locate, arrange, or construct instructional materials.
- Assist students with eating, dressing, personal care, and bathroom use.
- Help to prepare the classroom for students and to keep work areas neat.
- Instruct special education students individually, in small or large groups, and/or with typical peers as specified in the IEP or by professionals on the service delivery team.
- Collect student data to contribute to professional team members regarding student progress toward goals.
- Score tests and certain papers using a key.
- Maintain files or records about students.
- Supervise playgrounds, halls, lunchrooms, busses, and loading zones.
- Provide specific health needs (for example, suction tracheotomy tubes, as assigned and trained by a school nurse).
- Assist and facilitate appropriate peer interactions.
- Assist students using adaptive equipment or devices (for example, a communication board).
- Support student behavior and social needs according to plans.
- Participate positively in evaluative or feedback sessions for the improvement of their skills.
- Participate in training and coaching sessions to improve their skills associated with all duties and tasks assigned.

- Communicate with professionals about their work and students' progress on assigned tasks.
- Move or accompany students from one place to another, assisting students with mobility and transition.
- Contribute to the effectiveness of the special education team by using appropriate communication, problem-solving, and conflict management strategies.

From the Research

As the list suggests, paraprofessionals offer many valuable services to students and to teachers in support of students. However, particularly when paraprofessionals are assigned to function as personal assistants to students with severe disabilities, problems can occur. Giangreco, Edelman, Luiselli, and MacFarland (1997) noticed the tendency of some assistants to hover around their charges in inclusive settings, and they decided to explore this topic systematically. Based on interview and observational data collected in 16 classrooms in 11 school districts, with students ranging in age from 4 through 20 who were served by a total of 134 team members, the researchers found that the following problems were caused by paraprofessionals' ongoing proximity to students:

- interference with general educators' sense of ownership for students and their sense of responsibility for those students
- separation of students from classmates
- students' dependence on adults
- negative impact on students' interactions with typical peers
- limitations on students' receiving competent instruction
- loss of students' personal control
- interference with instruction of typical learners

This research strongly suggests that paraprofessionals need clear instruction regarding their functioning in general education classrooms. It also indicates how important it is that you understand not just how paraprofessionals can assist students but how their actions can unintentionally interfere with students' education, too.

SOURCES: Adapted from "Paraeducators and Teachers: Shifting Roles," by N. French, 1999, *Teaching Exceptional Children, 32*(2), pp. 69–73; "Helping or Hovering? Effects of Instructional Assistant Proximity on Students with Disabilities," by M. F. Giangreco, S. W. Edelman, T. E. Luiselli, and S. Z. C. MacFarland, 1997, *Exceptional Children, 64*, pp. 7–18; and "Preparing and Managing Paraprofessionals," by M. L. Trautman, 2004, *Intervention in School and Clinic, 39*, pp. 131–138.

W W W
R E S O U R C E S

The Beach Center on Disability (http://www.beachcenter.org), affiliated with the University of Kansas, has as its goal helping families of individuals with disabilities and those individuals through research, teaching, technical assistance, and community service. The website has many resources to help you work effectively with families.

CONNECTIONS

The topics of student self-advocacy and student self-evaluation are addressed in depth in Chapter 10.

What is the role of parents or caregivers in their child's learning? How do parents or caretakers contribute on teams that decide whether a student needs special education services?

PARENTS, STUDENTS, AND ADVOCATES ● Whenever decisions are being made concerning a student with a suspected or documented disability, the best interests of the student and his or her family must be represented. Parents—or a person who is serving in the role of a parent, including a guardian or foster parent—have the right to participate in virtually all aspects of their child's educational program (Al-Hassan & Gardner, 2002; Dabkowski, 2004; Nelson, Summers, & Turnbull, 2004). Parents' involvement spans the following areas:

- requesting assessment for special services
- providing input on their child's strengths and needs
- bringing to the team independent professionals' opinions about their child's needs
- helping to decide whether their child has a disability and whether the child will receive special services
- assisting in writing goals and objectives for their child's educational program
- participating in delivering instruction to their child
- monitoring their child's progress
- seeking assistance in resolving disagreements with school professionals

Often, parents are strong allies for general education teachers. They can assist teachers by reviewing at home what is taught in school, rewarding their child for school accomplishments, and working with school professionals to resolve behavior and academic problems.

Whenever appropriate, students with disabilities also can be active participants in decision making about their own education. Increasingly, educators are involving students so they can directly state their needs and goals and can learn to advocate for themselves, a concept referred to as **self-determination** (Mason, Field, & Sawilowsky, 2004; National Center on Secondary Education and Transition [NCSET], 2002; Test, Mason, Hughes, Konrad, Neale, & Wood, 2004). The extent of student participation on the team depends on the age of the student, the type and impact of the disability, and professionals' and parents' commitment. In general, the older the student, the greater his or her ability to contribute, and the higher the value placed on student contribution, the greater the participation. Thus, first-grade students with disabilities usually are not expected to participate in very many decisions about their education. However, high school students with disabilities usually attend and participate in their team meetings, and their priorities and preferences are central to decision making. These students often have strong opinions about what they would like to do after high school, and they also take on more responsibility for monitoring their progress in reaching their goals (Gringel, Neubert, Moon, & Graham, 2003; Martin, Marshall, & Sale, 2004). You can learn more about student participation on teams in the Professional Edge on page 43.

A final team member is an *advocate*. Sometimes, parents sense that they are not knowledgeable enough about the policies and procedures that govern special education to represent themselves. In other instances, they are not sure school district personnel are acting in the best interests of their children. In yet other situations, parents may be uncomfortable interacting with school personnel because of language or cultural differences, or for other reasons. Parents have the right to bring an advocate to team and other school meetings concerning their children. This person serves as their advisor and sometimes their spokesperson. Although advocates do not have a direct role in implementing the education program for students with a disability, they might assist parents with their responsibilities. Advocates sometimes are professionals who are compensated by parents for their services. Alternatively, they may be volunteers provided through a professional organization or parent support group, or friends or relatives.

PROFESSIONAL EDGE

Self-Determination for Students with Disabilities

Think how you would react if other people constantly controlled your life, deciding what you should wear, where you should go, what career should be your goal, and the type of housing and roommates you should have. Beginning at a very young age, children typically begin to express their wishes, and they learn that they have a right to act on those wishes. (For example, have you ever tried to convince a three-year-old that the two articles of clothing she selected to wear do not match?) However, despite good intentions by professionals and parents, many students and adults with disabilities have been denied opportunities to make their own life decisions, and reversing this situation has become a goal for the field (for example, Eisenman, 2001; Gringel et al., 2003). One way self-determination can occur is for students to actively participate in or lead their IEP meetings and other planning activities.

Student-Led IEPs

When students lead their IEP meetings, they learn to think and advocate for themselves (Mason, McGahee-Kovac, & Johnson, 2004). They can learn to do this beginning at a very early age. For example, elementary students might have the role of introducing their parents to the team and describing to team members what they have been learning in school. Students in middle school might explain their disabilities and the impact of those disabilities, share their strengths, and discuss accommodations needed. In high school, students might lead the entire conference, working to ensure that the IEP and transition plan reflect their preferences and plans for the future. Specific student roles vary, and students need to be prepared for participating so that they know the process and ways they contribute to it. Further, general education teachers find that students who actively participate in their IEP meetings have better skills for interacting with adults, better understanding of their special needs, greater awareness of resources available to help them, and more willingness to accept responsibility for themselves (Test et al., 2004).

Person-Centered Planning

Another example of self-determination is called *person-centered planning*. This method was developed by profes-

sionals from both the United States and Canada and is usually related to IEP planning as a student with significant disabilities leaves the public school system. It emphasizes these dimensions:

- *Community presence.* Identify the community settings that the student uses and the ones that would benefit him or her. The intent is to incorporate these settings into the educational planning process.
- *Choice.* Identify decisions made *by* the student and decisions made *for* the student. The goal of person-centered planning is to transfer as many choices to the student as possible.
- *Competence.* Identify skills that best assist the student to participate fully in the school and community and strategies that are most effective for teaching those skills.
- *Respect.* Clarify roles the student has in the school and local community. The goal is to strengthen and expand those roles and decrease or eliminate student characteristics that might cause the student to be perceived by others in a stereotypical way.
- *Community participation.* Specify people with whom the student spends time at school and in other settings. The goal is to identify individuals who can advocate for the student and to foster friendships with age-appropriate peers.

A number of person-centered planning approaches have been developed, and you may find that one of these is used in your school district. They include Making Action Plans (MAPS), Planning Alternative Tomorrows with Hope (PATH), and Circle of Friends.

SOURCES: Adapted from *Person-Centered Practices: Building Personalized Supports That Respect the Dreams of People with Disabilities,* by REACH of Louisville, n.d. Retrieved September 15, 2004, from http://www.reachoflouisville.com/person-centered/Default.htm; and "How to Help Students Lead Their IEP Meetings," by C. Y. Mason, M. McGahee-Kovac, and L. Johnson, 2004, *Teaching Exceptional Children, 36*(3), pp. 18–25.

How Can You Decide Whether a Student Need Might Be a Disability?

> You will play a key role in deciding whether a student in your class should be evaluated for the presence of a disability.

You will play a key role in deciding whether a student in your class should be evaluated for the presence of a disability. Although youngsters with obvious cognitive, sensory, or physical impairments usually are identified when they are infants or toddlers, learning, language, attentional, and behavioral disabilities—such as those displayed by Marcus, introduced at the beginning of the chapter—may not be diagnosed until children start school. Because you are the professional in daily contact with the student, you are the person most likely to notice an unmet need. It is your judgment that often initiates a special education decision-making process.

Analyze Unmet Needs

As you teach, you sometimes will discover that you have a nagging concern about a student. This concern might begin early in the school year, or it might take several months to emerge. For example, when you review a student's records and your own impressions of the student and your concern, you may decide that the student's achievement is not within your classroom's typical range, given the standards of your school district, community expectations, and state achievement standards. Should you ask other professionals to assess the student for eligibility for special education? Perhaps. But first you need to ask yourself some questions. These questions are summarized in Figure 2.2.

FIGURE 2.2 Teacher Concerns about Student Needs

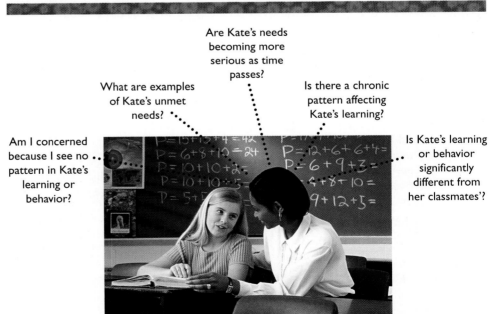

Are Kate's needs becoming more serious as time passes?

What are examples of Kate's unmet needs?

Is there a chronic pattern affecting Kate's learning?

Am I concerned because I see no pattern in Kate's learning or behavior?

Is Kate's learning or behavior significantly different from her classmates'?

WHAT ARE SPECIFIC EXAMPLES OF UNMET NEEDS? ● Having a nebulous worry about a student is far different from specifically stating what your concerns are. For example, sensing that a student is unmotivated is not a clear concern. What does the student do that leads you to conclude that motivation is a problem? Is it that the student doesn't make eye contact when speaking to you, or that the rewards and consequences that affect other students seem to have no effect—positive or negative—on this student? Vague concerns and hunches should be supported by specific information. Phrases such as "slow in learning," "poor attitude toward school," "doesn't pay attention," and "never gets work completed" might have very different meanings to different professionals. To prepare to share your concern with others, then, your first step is to ask yourself, "When I say the student . . . , what examples clarify what I mean?"

IS THERE A CHRONIC PATTERN NEGATIVELY AFFECTING LEARNING? ● Nearly all students go through periods when they struggle to learn, behave inappropriately, or otherwise cause you concern. Sometimes, a situation outside of school affects a student. For example, parents divorcing, families being evicted from their apartments, elderly grandparents moving in with the family, or a family member being injured or arrested might negatively affect student learning or behavior. However, the impact of these traumatic events should not be permanent, and the student should gradually return to previous levels of functioning.

Students with disabilities also may be affected by specific situations or events, but their learning and behavior needs form a chronic pattern. In other words, they struggle over a long period of time regardless of the circumstances. For example, Betsy, who has a learning disability, has difficulty remembering sight words no matter what level they are or how creatively they are introduced. Jared, a high school student with an emotional disability, is withdrawn whether sitting in a large class or interacting in a small group. Julianna, an eighth grader who had a severe head injury last year, usually seems to grasp abstract concepts as they are taught, but she struggles to describe or apply them after instruction.

ARE THE UNMET NEEDS BECOMING MORE SERIOUS AS TIME PASSES? ● Sometimes, a student's needs appear to become greater over time. For example, Ben, who seemed to see well at the beginning of the school year, now holds books closer and closer to his face, squints when he tries to read, and complains about headaches. Karen, who began the school year fairly close in achievement to her peers, is significantly behind by November. Indications that needs are increasing are a signal to ask for input from others.

IS THE STUDENT'S LEARNING OR BEHAVIOR SIGNIFICANTLY DIFFERENT FROM THAT OF CLASSMATES? ● As you think about your concerns about a student, you should ask yourself how the student compares to other students. For example, it has been demonstrated that students at risk for special education referral are achieving at a significantly lower level than other students and that they are more likely to have significant behavior problems (Hosp & Reschly, 2003). However, if you have eight students who are all struggling, the reason might be that the information or skills are beyond the reach of the entire group or that your teaching approach is not accomplishing what you had planned. Even though self-reflection is sometimes difficult, when many students are experiencing problems, it is important to analyze how the curriculum or teaching might be contributing to the situation. In such instances, you should make changes in those two areas before seeking other assistance.

Keep in mind that many students have needs that *do* signal the presence of disabilities. Perhaps you are an elementary teacher who cannot seem to find enough books at the right level for one student in your fourth-grade class who is almost a nonreader. Perhaps you are an eighth-grade industrial arts teacher who is worried about letting a student who gets extremely angry use equipment that could be dangerous, and

ANALYZE AND REFLECT

What might be the effect—on the student and on your perception of that student—of deciding prematurely that a student should be referred as possibly having a disability?

DIMENSIONS OF DIVERSITY

Teachers sometimes have biases they are not even aware of. For example, when middle school teachers were shown video samples of students displaying "traditional walking" or stylized "strolling," they concluded that the latter students had lower achievement, were more aggressive, and were more likely to need special education than the former students (Neal, McCray, Webb-Johnson, & Bridgest, 2003). The race of the student did not make a difference in the results.

this is the only student about whom you have this level of concern. Maybe you are an algebra teacher who finds that one student seems to lack many prerequisite skills for succeeding in the course. Students with disabilities have needs that are significantly different from those of most other students.

DO YOU DISCOVER THAT YOU CANNOT FIND A PATTERN? ● In some instances, the absence of a pattern to students' learning or behavior is as much an indicator that you should request assistance as is a distinct pattern. Perhaps Curtis has tremendous mood swings, and you arrive at school each day wondering whether it will be a good day or a bad day for him. However, you cannot find a way to predict which it will be. Or consider Becka, who learns science with ease but cannot seem to master even basic reading skills. You are not sure why her learning is so different in the two subjects. In a third example, in physical education, Tyrone some days seems to have average motor skills but on other days frequently stumbles and cannot participate fully in the learning stations you have created.

Communicate Your Observations and Try Your Own Interventions

CONNECTIONS

Additional information on parents' roles in working with teachers and other school professionals is included in Chapter 3. You also will find suggestions for working with parents in Chapters 6, 7, and 8.

Your analysis of your students' unmet needs is the basis for further action. Although ultimately you may decide to seek assistance from special education professionals for one of your students, part of your responsibility in attempting to help the student is gathering other information and trying to resolve the problem first.

CONTACT PARENTS ● One of your first strategies should be to contact a student's family (Smalley & Reyes-Blanes, 2001; Turnbull & Turnbull, 1997). Parents or other family members often can inform you about changes in the student's life that could be affecting school performance. Family members also can help you understand how the student's activities outside of school might influence schoolwork, including clubs, gang involvement, employment, and responsibilities at home. Further, by contacting the family, you might learn that what you perceive as a problem is mostly a reflection of a cultural difference. For example, a student whose family emigrated from Thailand is extremely quiet because silence signals respect in her native culture, not because she is unable to participate.

Parents also are your partners in working to resolve some student learning problems. They can assist you in monitoring whether homework is completed and returned to school, whether behavior problems are occurring on the walk home, or whether a physician is concerned about a child's medical condition. If you have students whose homes do not have telephones or e-mail access and whose parents do not have transportation to come to school, your social worker or principal can help you make needed contact.

> Especially as a new teacher, you will want to discuss your concerns with other professionals to gain additional perspectives on the student's needs.

CONTACT COLLEAGUES ● Especially as a new teacher, you will want to discuss your concerns with other professionals to gain additional perspectives on the student's needs. In many schools, a special education teacher or another professional can arrange to observe the student in your class and then to discuss the observation. If your school psychologist is available, you might ask for consultation assistance. In schools where grade-level teams or other types of teams meet, you can raise your concerns in that context. One hallmark of today's schools is an array of professionals who have expertise in many areas. With a little exploration, you are likely to find that your school has an in-house resource you can access to check your perceptions against a broader perspective.

TRY SIMPLE INTERVENTIONS ● Part of your responsibility as a teacher is to create a classroom where students can succeed. To cultivate such a setting, you can make adaptations part of your attempts to address a student's unmet needs. Here are some examples:

- Have you tried moving the student's seat?
- Have you incorporated teaching strategies that help the student to actively participate in lessons (for example, using choral responding)?
- Have you thought about ways to make your tests easier for the student to follow (for example, using more white space between items or sections)?
- Do you give the student only part of an assignment at one time because he becomes overwhelmed?
- Have you observed the student closely to determine whether helping her work one problem is enough to get her to work on the rest?

These are just a few alterations that many teachers make without even thinking of them as adaptations; many others are presented throughout this textbook. Sometimes, these small accommodations are sufficient to help a student learn. In any case, you should try common interventions before deciding a student might need special education.

DOCUMENT THE UNMET NEED ● If you anticipate requesting assistance for a student, you need to demonstrate the seriousness of your concern and your systematic attempts to help meet the student's needs. If you have implemented a plan to improve student behavior, you can keep a record of how effective it has been. If you have contacted parents several times, you can keep a log of your conversations. If you have tried to decrease the number of times the student misses your first-hour class, you can summarize your attendance data. Strategies to document student needs serve two main purposes. First, they help you do a reality check on whether the problem is as serious as you think it is. If you gather data from other students as a comparison, you can judge whether the unmet needs of one student are significantly different from those of typical students. Second, the information you collect helps you communicate with other professionals. Special service providers cannot possibly meet every need in every classroom. Their work is reserved in large part for extraordinary student needs, and your documentation helps in the decision about providing the assistance you seek.

How Do Students Obtain Special Services?

The majority of students who receive special education have high-incidence disabilities, such as learning disabilities, that you may be the first to recognize. If you teach at the elementary level, you probably will have students every year whom you refer for possible special services. If you teach in middle school, junior high, or high school, you will find that many students with disabilities already have been identified before they reach your class. However, there are exceptions; students may be found eligible for special education at any time during their school years. As a teacher, you always have the option of asking a team of professionals to decide whether one of your students needs special education.

Having a serious and documented concern about a student is only the first step in considering whether a disability may be present. Your concern brings the student to the attention of other school professionals so that further information can be gathered and decisions made. The specific, formal procedures that must be followed to determine student eligibility for special education services are designed to ensure that only students who truly need these services receive them. These procedures are described in the following sections and are summarized in Figure 2.3, which illustrates the flow of the procedures from beginning to end.

FIGURE 2.3 The Decision-Making Process for Special Education

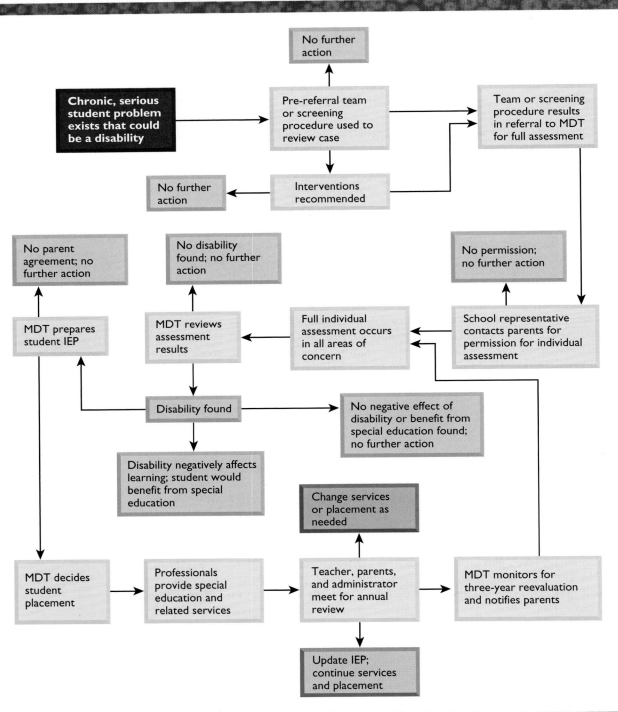

Initial Consideration of Student Problems

General education teachers, principals, special services personnel, parents, physicians, and social service agency personnel all may initiate the process of obtaining special education for a student. Most often, however, a general education teacher notices a pattern of academic underachievement, inconsistent learning, serious behavioral problems, difficulties in social skills, or a persistent physical or sensory problem. When such problems occur, the teacher brings the student to the attention of others who help decide whether special education is warranted.

INTERVENTION ASSISTANCE TEAM ● A common way to begin the process of helping a student suspected of having a disability is to bring the problem to the attention of a team (Bahr, Whitten, Dieker, Kocarek, & Manson, 1999; Friend & Cook, 2003). This pre-referral or **intervention assistance team** often includes general education teachers, special services personnel, and an administrator. Teachers wishing to "bring a student to the team" complete a referral form on which they describe the student's strengths and problems and describe efforts they have made to assist the student. The teacher then meets with the team to discuss the written information, consider alternative strategies for assisting the student, and determine whether the student should have a detailed assessment for potential special education services (Kovaleski, Gickling, Morrow, & Swank, 1999; Lane et al., 2003). The unifying characteristic of this type of team is an emphasis on problem solving among all members. The Case in Practice on page 50 illustrates how this type of team operates.

SCREENING ● Although most schools have teams to help make decisions about the need for assessment for special education, in a few schools the school psychologist, counselor, principal, or another professional has the responsibility of *screening* the referral, that is, meeting informally with a general education teacher about a student. This individual asks about the strategies the teacher has tried to assist the student and may make additional recommendations. If efforts remain unsuccessful and the presence of a disability is suspected, referral for a more comprehensive assessment follows. According to the provisions of IDEA, any initial special education referral procedure, whether through a team or another screening process, must include the review of existing data about the student. By using already-gathered data, school records, and other information, a more informed decision can be made concerning the need for a full assessment.

DIAGNOSTIC TEACHING ● *Diagnostic teaching* sometimes is part of screening. A special education teacher, another special services professional, or you may carry out sample lessons with a student, teaching different skills, using different teaching methods, and trying various ways of more effectively teaching the student. This approach helps the team working with you to determine the student's *response to intervention* suggests that the problem can be addressed through structured teaching approaches or whether it is more likely the result of a disability.

When a team initially discusses or screens a student, a parent is not required legally to be involved in the process. However, educators should notify parents of their concerns and enlist parental assistance in trying to solve the problem. In some schools, parents are invited to team meetings. Remember, parents should never be surprised that the possibility of special education is raised—they should have known of the existence of any serious problem.

The Special Education Referral and Assessment Process

If the decision as a result of team intervention or screening is that a full assessment of a student for possible special education placement should occur, the parents are contacted. Their written permission must be obtained prior to any individual assessment.

CASE IN PRACTICE

Participating in an Intervention Assistance Team Meeting

It is 3:15 p.m. and Ms. Jacob's students have just left. She gathers a stack of information from her desk and heads toward the conference room for an intervention assistance team meeting. Ms. Jacobs is the fifth-grade representative on the team this year. Along with two other classroom teachers (they just happen to be from the first and fourth grades this year), a special education teacher, and the assistant principal, Ms. Jacobs meets weekly to problem solve about students and to consider whether any of their needs are so great that a referral for individual assessment should be made.

The first student to be discussed today is third grader Toby. Reviewing her information sheets, Ms. Jacobs sees that Toby is chronically late to school, has what his teacher describes as a sullen attitude, is failing in math and language arts, and has a D in science. Toby's teacher, Mr. Petrovich, is worried that Toby is headed toward failure, especially as he faces the more intense reading load in the intermediate grades. According to Mr. Petrovich, reward systems have not been successful; Toby's dad seems cooperative but tends to forget to follow through on homework monitoring and other requests; and other teachers, including the art teacher and the music teacher, have expressed concern about Toby's future.

As the meeting begins and preliminaries are completed, Ms. Jacobs asks Mr. Petrovich several questions.

Ms. Jacobs: Mr. Petrovich, you've spent a great deal of extra time working with Toby this year. If you were to summarize your greatest concern for him, what would it be?

Mr. Petrovich: Probably his "I don't care and you can't make me" attitude. It seems to be getting worse as the year goes by. Toby is really a good kid; I don't know what's causing his problems—unless it's peer pressure—and I really want to get to the bottom of this.

Ms. Jacobs: Of all the things you've tried with Toby, what seems to have the biggest positive impact on him?

Mr. Petrovich: Right now, what's keeping him going is his interest in art and the computer lab. But Ms. Yancy says that if he doesn't improve his behavior and attitude during art, she feels she is going to have to take away some of his privileges there.

Ms. Jacobs: If you think about Toby's strengths, what might we start with to try to come up with some ideas for him?

Mr. Petrovich: I'd really like to see us work on something that takes advantage of Toby's computer skills. I know he likes art, but it seems like the computer area is one where we could tie in his academic needs. He'd work on the computer all day if I let him, and he's very skilled at finding information and creating art on it. He seems to like the structure and logic of the computer and the fact that it doesn't "get in his face."

Ms. Jacobs: It sounds as though you have an idea in mind.

Mr. Petrovich: I do. I'm hoping all of you can work with me to design some kind of very structured program that combines getting work done and getting to use computer equipment as a privilege. I think we have all the necessary components, we just need to put them together . . . and I think that's a concrete area to work in. I don't think a direct confrontation on attitude is going to have any effect.

The meeting continues with all the team members contributing. After 30 minutes, Mr. Petrovich leaves with a structured work-for-computer-privileges plan and an agreement to review its effectiveness in 3 weeks. Ms. Jacobs stays as the team discusses another student and recommends an individual assessment for this student.

REFLECTIONS

What is it that makes this team meeting constructive and productive? What purpose is served by including several general education teachers on the team? How does Mr. Petrovich help make the meeting a success? What other strategies might the team try in addition to the work-for-computer-privileges idea? What might happen when the team later reviews the intervention they have planned? Given what you have learned about students with exceptionalities, do you think Toby is the type of student who might be referred for an individual assessment?

At this point, a **multidisciplinary team (MDT),** including the parents, educators, and others as appropriate, assumes responsibility for determining how to assess the student and for deciding whether the student has a disability and is eligible for special education services.

COMPONENTS OF ASSESSMENT ● Assessment involves gathering information about a student's strengths and needs in all areas of concern. Typically, if the student has not had a vision and hearing screening and you have reason to suspect a sensory impairment, these tests precede other assessments. If sensory screening raises concerns, parents are notified of the need for a more complete assessment by a physician or appropriate specialist.

Assessments completed by school professionals may address any aspect of a student's educational functioning (Huefner, 2000). Often, for example, students' cognitive ability is assessed: An individual intelligence test (often referred to as an IQ test) is administered and scored by a school psychologist or another qualified school professional. Academic achievement usually is assessed, too: Students complete an individual achievement test administered by a psychologist, special education teacher, educational diagnostician, or other professional. A third area often evaluated is social and behavioral skills. This evaluation might involve a checklist that you and parents complete concerning a student's behavior, tests given by the school psychologist, or a series of questions asked of the student.

> ❝ Assessment involves gathering information about a student's strengths and needs in all areas of concern. ❞

Another domain for assessment is the student's social and developmental history. Often, a school social worker meets with the parents to learn about the student's family life and major events in the student's development that could be affecting education. For example, parents might be asked about their child's friends in the neighborhood and favorite out-of-school activities, their expectations for their child as an adult, and their child's strengths. Parents also might be asked whether their child has had any serious physical injuries, medical problems, or recurring social or behavioral problems.

As another assessment component, a psychologist, counselor, or special education teacher often observes the student in the classroom and other settings to learn how he or she responds to teachers and peers in various school settings. For example, a special education teacher may observe Chris, who usually plays with younger students during recess and gets confused when playground games are too complex. Chris also watches other students carefully and often seems to take cues for how to act from how they are acting. These observations all are helpful for understanding Chris.

If a potential need exists for speech therapy or occupational or physical therapy, another component is added to the assessment: The professionals in those areas complete assessments in their respective areas of expertise. A speech/language therapist might use a screening instrument that includes having the student use certain words, tell stories, and identify objects. The therapist also might check for atypical use of the muscles of the mouth, tongue, and throat that permit speech and for unusual speech habits such as breathiness in speaking or noticeable voice strain. Similarly, occupational or physical therapists might assess a student's gait, strength and agility, range of motion, or ability to perform fine motor tasks such as buttoning and lacing.

Throughout the entire assessment process, IDEA specifically gives parents the right to provide information to be used as part of the evaluation. In addition, as the general education teacher, you can provide details on the student's performance in class, patterns of behavior, and discrepancies between expectations and achievement. Your informal and formal observations play an important role in assessment.

ASSESSMENT PROCEDURES ● The exact procedures for assessing a student's needs vary according to the areas of concern that initiated the assessment process. The assessment must be completed by individuals trained to administer the tests and other assessment tools used; the instruments must be free of cultural bias; the student's performance must be evaluated in a way that takes into account the potential disability; and the assessment must provide data that are useful for deciding an appropriate education for the student. School professionals are responsible for ensuring that these obligations are met.

What areas of individual assessment are involved when a team is deciding whether a student is eligible for special education services? How is the information from these assessments used in decision making?

PARENTS' RIGHTS ● Throughout the assessment process, parents' rights to participate in their child's education must be respected as established in IDEA and reinforced in virtually all subsequent litigation (Rothstein, 1995). In addition to the rights already mentioned, parents have the right to be informed in a meaningful way about the procedures and processes of special education and the right to give permission before any individual assessment is completed. Parents also have the right to request information from a school district representative about how to get an independent evaluation for their child and the right to bring information from an independent evaluation to a meeting to discuss the educational needs of the student. In some cases, parents are entitled to be reimbursed for their expense in obtaining an independent evaluation. These and other parents' rights ensured through federal special education laws are outlined in Figure 2.4. Note that all rights must be communicated in the parents' language and in a manner they can understand. If you teach older students, you

FIGURE 2.4 Parent's Rights in Special Education

IDEA stipulates procedural safeguards to ensure that parents have the right to be active participants in their child's education. The following safeguards are some of the major ones provided to parents:

1. Parents are entitled to be members of any group that makes decisions about the educational placement of their child.

2. Parents are to be given written notice before the school initiates, changes, or refuses to initiate or change the identification or educational placement of their child.

3. Parents can participate directly in the determination of their child's eligibility for special education and in the development of the individualized educational program (IEP) and its periodic review, generally at least annually.

4. The school must obtain written, informed parental consent before conducting a formal evaluation and assessment and before initially placing a student in a program providing special education and related services. (*Note:* Written parental consent is required for initial evaluation and initial placement. Subsequent formal evaluation and placement actions require written notice, as described in Item 1.)

5. Parents can inspect and review any educational records maintained by the school district or other agency providing service under IDEA. Access to educational records will be granted to parents without unnecessary delay and before any meeting regarding an IEP or before a hearing relating to identification, evaluation, or placement of the child, and in no case more than 45 days after the request has been made.

6. Parents may request, and the school district must provide, information on where independent educational evaluations may be obtained. Parents have the right to an independent educational evaluation at public expense if they disagree with an evaluation obtained by the local school district or responsible public agency. However, the local school district or responsible public agency may initiate a due process hearing

to show that the original evaluation is appropriate. If the final decision is that the evaluation is appropriate, the parents still have the right to an independent educational evaluation, but not at public expense. The results of an independent evaluation obtained by the parents at private expense will be considered by the local school district in any decisions about the provisions of a free appropriate public education to the child. Such results may also be presented as evidence at a due process hearing.

7. Parents have the right to request mediation as a means to resolving conflicts with school districts concerning their child with a disability. Mediation must be available to parents prior to a due process hearing, but it may not delay a hearing. Information shared during mediation is confidential and may not be used as evidence at any subsequent due process hearing. The state, not the parents, bears the cost of mediation.

8. Parents have the right to request a hearing before an impartial hearing officer in cases in which they disagree with school district decisions regarding their child's education. Hearings may relate to any aspect of special education, including the fairness of the evaluation procedures used to determine the presence of a disability, the appropriateness of the disability label given the child, the adequacy of the services provided, and the suitability of proposed changes of placement. If parents fail to win a due process hearing at the local level, they may appeal the results of the hearing at the state department of education level. After this step, if parents are still dissatisfied with the outcome of the hearing, they may initiate court action.

9. Parents must be fully informed of their rights and the procedural safeguards related to special education. They initially should receive this information in a readily understandable manner when their child is referred for evaluation. They should also receive it prior to each IEP meeting and reevaluation, and when a complaint is registered.

SOURCES: Adapted from "Questions and Answers about IDEA," *NICHCY NewsDigest 21* (2nd ed.), January 2000, Washington, DC: National Information Center for Handicapped Children and Youth. Retrieved September 15, 2004, from http://nichcy.org/pubs/newsdig/nd21txt.htm; and "Parental Rights in Special Education," April 2004, Trenton: New Jersey Department of Education. Retrieved September 15, 2004, from http://www.state.nj.us.njded/parights/prise.pdf

also should know that, beginning at least one year before reaching 18 years of age, students also must be informed directly of their rights (NCSET, 2002).

Decision Making for Special Services

After a comprehensive assessment of the student has been completed, the multidisciplinary team meets to discuss its results and make several decisions (Dabkowski, 2004; Huefner, 2000; Miles-Bonart, 2002). The first decision the MDT must make is whether the student is eligible under the law to be categorized as having a disability. If the team members decide that a disability exists, they then determine whether the disability is affecting the student's education, and from that they decide whether the student is eligible to receive services through special education. Although not always the case, in most school districts these decisions are made at a single meeting. As outlined in Figure 2.4, parents must agree with the decisions being made or the student cannot receive special education services. Most school districts have specific guidelines to direct team decision making about the presence of a disability and the need for special education, but the decisions ultimately belong to the team, and the MDT may decide that the guidelines or descriptions do not exactly fit a particular case. For example, most states specify that students identified as having a mild intellectual disability should have an IQ less than 70 as measured on an individual intelligence test and should have serious limitations in adaptive behaviors. However, if a student's test scores are slightly above 70 and adaptive skills are particularly limited, a team can still decide that the student has a mild intellectual disability. Likewise, if a student has a measured IQ lower than 70 but seems to have many adaptive skills, the team might decide that the student does not have a disability.

If the MDT determines that the student has a disability affecting his or her education and that the student is eligible for services according to federal, state, and local guidelines, the stage is set for detailed planning of the student's education and related services. This planning is recorded in the student's **individualized education program, or IEP.** The IEP is the document that outlines all the special education services the student is to receive. Specific guidelines must be followed in developing an IEP; more details about IEPs and their preparation are provided later in this chapter.

The final decision made by the MDT concerns the student's placement. *Placement* refers to the location of the student's education. For most students, the placement is the general education classroom, often with some type of support offered. According to IDEA, when a placement is a location other than general education, justification must be provided for that decision. However, for a few students, the appropriate primary placement is a special education setting. Later in this chapter, special education services are discussed and placement options are outlined in more detail.

In your school district, the essentials of the procedures outlined in the preceding section must be followed, but the timelines used and the names for each part of the process may vary. However, all school district procedures are designed to ensure that students with disabilities are systematically assessed and that a deliberate and careful process is followed to provide for their education needs. Further, you are a critical participant in the entire process. A description of your rights as they relate to special education and students with disabilities is included in Figure 2.5.

Monitoring Special Education Services

In addition to specifying the procedures that must be followed to identify a student as needing special education services, federal and state laws also establish guidelines for monitoring student progress. The monitoring process is necessary to ensure that students' educational programs remain appropriate and that procedures exist for resolving disputes between school district personnel and parents.

ANALYZE AND REFLECT

As you think about yourself as a teacher—regardless of the level at which you plan to teach or the subject in which you are specializing—what are the unique contributions you could make to a team considering whether a student has a disability? Try to identify at least 10 contributions.

ANALYZE AND REFLECT

How can the differences in expertise among general education teachers, special education teachers, and related service professionals result in higher-quality education for students with disabilities?

FIGURE 2.5 General Education Teacher's Rights in Special Education

As a teacher, you play a crucial role in the design and delivery of special education services. The following is a set of rights that attorney and disability advocate Reed Martin has compiled to clarify what you can expect as you work with students with disabilities and other special needs:

- **The right to seek assistance for a student in a classroom who is not receiving benefit.** It is illegal under federal special education law to leave a child to fend for himself in a classroom designed for others. The student has a right to be referred for necessary assistance, and the teacher has a concomitant right to make the referral when assistance is needed. This is not a right to rid the classroom of that child but rather a right to bring additional information or assistance into the classroom.

- **The right to recognize the teacher as a child advocate.** The ADA recognizes teachers as advocates, and outlaws retaliation, or reprisals against, and intimidation of teachers who advocate for children.

- **The right to have a child fully evaluated.** The child has a right to be evaluated in every area that might adversely affect educational performance, and the teacher has a right to know everything educationally relevant to that child.

- **The right to receive any training needed under the Comprehensive System for Personnel Development.** If the key to serving a student appropriately is teacher training, then the teacher has a right to receive that training.

- **The right to participate in the IEP that develops the plan for a student in the teacher's class.** The statute includes "the child's teacher" as a participant in the IEP meeting. All questions a classroom teacher might have must be asked and answered before the child comes into the classroom. If the school's practice is simply to have "a representative of instruction" at the meeting, but that person does not repre-

sent the interests of the classroom teacher, the classroom teacher should ask to have the IEP meeting reconvened to ask and answer the questions that have not been addressed. If the classroom teacher advocates in this way, she is protected from reprisals of school administrators.

- **The right to receive the related services that should honestly be on the IEP.** If needed supplemental aids and services are not discussed at the IEP meeting, then the IEP violates the teacher's, student's, and parents' rights. If services are decided on at the meeting but are not provided in the classroom, the teacher's, student's, and parents' rights likewise are violated.

- **The right to be recognized as an advocate for all the children in the classroom.** A classroom teacher has a duty to all the children in the classroom. This duty is not antagonistic to a child with special needs. The cases on placing children in the least restrictive environment recognize that the interests of other children, and the ability of the teacher to teach the classroom, are balanced with the right of a child with special needs to be in that regular classroom.

- **The right to participate in assessing the effectiveness of the program.** When the IEP committee leaves the meeting, it must have an IEP that is reasonably calculated to confer benefit. Once the IEP is begun, the teacher must have a role in assessing whether the IEP is working. During the year, and at the next IEP meeting, the teacher's view is vital to determining whether that was an appropriate program and placement.

- **The right to be treated as a professional.** Teachers are not just subordinate employees expected to carry out orders without questions. They are professionals with rights to ask for referral, for evaluation, for reevaluation, for an IEP meeting, and for further refinements of an IEP.

SOURCE: From "Regular Teachers' Rights in Special Education," by R. Martin (n.d.). Retrieved Spetember 5, 2004, from http://www.reedmartin.com/teacherrights.htm. This information is educational and not intended to be legal advice.

FYI

IDEA includes a provision that allows some states to permit IEPs to cover up to a 3-year period. This option is an experiment related to reducing paperwork in special education.

ANNUAL REVIEWS ● The first strategy for monitoring special services is the **annual review.** At least once each year, a student's progress toward his or her annual goals must be reviewed, and the IEP changed or updated as needed. The purpose of this annual review is to see that the student's best interests are being protected. Not all multidisciplinary team members who participated in the initial decisions about the student's disability and educational needs are required to participate in annual reviews. However, a teacher instructing the student and an administrator or other professional representing the school district must meet with the student's parents to discuss whether goals and objectives (as required) have been met and what the next steps in the student's education should be. In practical terms, if your school district completes all annual reviews during a given month, you will find that the special education staff members with whom you work are unavailable because of their other responsibilities, such as meeting with parents. Depending on local practices, you are likely to be asked to attend annual reviews for some students. For many students, the general education teacher is the most knowledgeable about their day-to-day functioning. This concept was highlighted with the mandate in IDEA that a general education teacher participate in the development of each student's IEP, not necessarily by writing it but by contributing a classroom perspective.

THREE-YEAR REEVALUATIONS ● A second monitoring procedure required by law is the **three-year reevaluation.** At least every three years, and more often if deemed necessary by the MDT, students receiving special education services must be reassessed to determine whether their needs have changed. This safeguard is designed to prevent students with disabilities from remaining in services or programs that may no longer be appropriate for them. In some cases, the reevaluation includes administering all the tests and other instruments that were used initially to identify the student as needing special education. However, IDEA permits existing information to be used for reevaluation instead of requiring new assessments. In fact, with parent and team agreement, reevaluations may not involve any new assessment at all (Huefner, 2000; Yell & Shriner, 1997). On the basis of the three-year reevaluation, the MDT meets again to develop an appropriate IEP.

According to current law, parents are informed that it is time for a three-year reevaluation, but school districts are not required to obtain written permission for this monitoring procedure. This practice enables school districts to continue providing high-quality services to students without interruptions that could be caused if new permission had to be sought.

ADDITIONAL REVIEWS ● In addition to annual reviews and three-year reevaluations, IDEA specifically stipulates that IEPs must be revised whenever there is a lack of expected progress toward achieving goals noted, reevaluation information is gathered, or parents bring to the attention of the MDT information that affects the IEP. This suggests that IEPs may need to be revised more frequently than the once per year that the basic requirements of the law mandate.

Parents have one more formal mechanism for obtaining information about their child's learning. IDEA specifies that the parents of students with disabilities have the right to receive a progress report about their child as often as do parents of typical learners. In many school districts, this means that formal communication about student learning progress now occurs every 6 or 9 weeks during the school year, that is, at the end of each grading period.

DUE PROCESS ● Yet another strategy for monitoring students receiving special education services is **due process,** the set of procedures outlined in the law for resolving disagreements between school district personnel and parents regarding students with disabilities (Getty & Summy, 2004). Due process rights begin when a student is first brought to the attention of a team as potentially having a disability. Both school districts and parents are entitled to protection through due process, but parents typically exercise their due process rights when they fear that school districts may not be acting in the best interests of the child (Rothstein, 1995). For example, if parents have their child independently evaluated because they believe the assessment for special education did not accurately portray their child's needs, and if the school district does not agree with the findings of the independent evaluator, the parents may request a due process hearing. Or parents could request a hearing if they disagree with the goals and objectives listed on the IEP and with the way services are provided to meet those goals and objectives.

Due process hearings seldom address blatant errors on the part of schools or parents regarding special education; most often they reflect the fact that many decisions made about students with disabilities are judgment calls in which a best course of action is not always clear. For example, Mr. and Mrs. Schubat filed a due process complaint against their daughter's school district because they did not believe the programs offered were addressing their daughter Judy's needs. They wanted Judy to be more actively involved in general education activities despite her multiple disabilities. The school district personnel contended that the complexity of her needs prevented Judy from being reasonably accommodated in a classroom. They also indicated that she was part of a reverse tutoring program in which students without disabilities came to work

WWW RESOURCES

At the Wrightslaw website (http://www.wrightslaw.com/advoc/articles/iep_guidance.html), you can view a comprehensive guide to IEPs for parents, including general information, related case law, links to related sites, and examples of appropriate and inappropriate IEP goals and objectives.

FYI

Both elementary and secondary students can benefit from student-led IEP meetings. Young children learn age-appropriate skills such as introducing their parents and stating their preferences; middle and high school students identify their strengths and weaknesses, explain their need for accommodations, and discuss their plans for postschool education or employment (Barrie & McDonald, 2002).

in the special education setting. How do you think a hearing officer would decide this case? What information might be crucial for reaching an appropriate decision?

In practice, most school districts and parents want to avoid due process hearings, which tend to be adversarial and can damage parent–school working relationships to the detriment of the student. To foster a positive working relationship, IDEA requires that all states have a system in place to offer **mediation** to parents at no cost as an initial means for resolving conflicts with schools (Consortium for Appropriate Dispute Resolution in Special Education, 2001; Mills & Duff-Mallams, 2000). In mediation, a neutral professional skilled in conflict resolution meets with both parties to help them resolve their differences informally. Mediation, however, is not allowed to cause delay in the parents' right to a due process hearing. A hearing is preceded by mediation—a less formal dispute resolution strategy—unless parents decline this option. All hearings must now also be preceded by a dispute resolution session as well, a sort of last-chance for reaching agreement. If neither mediation nor a dispute resolution session is successful, the hearing is conducted by an independent and objective third party selected from a list provided by the state, but the school district bears the expense (D'Angelo, Lutz, & Zirkel, 2004). If either party disagrees with the outcome of a due process hearing, the decision can be appealed to a state-level review hearing officer. If disagreement still exists, either party can then take the matter to court.

Although school districts work closely with parents to avoid due process hearings, if one occurs concerning a student you teach, you may be called to testify at the hearing. In such a case, you would be asked to describe the student's level of functioning in your classroom, the supports you provided, and your efforts with other special service providers to ensure the student was successful. An administrator and an attorney might help you prepare for the hearing, and they would answer any questions you might have about your role.

DIMENSIONS OF **DIVERSITY**

Disproportionate representation in special education affects many groups of students. For example, American Indian and Native Alaskan students are overrepresented among students with learning disabilities, mild mental retardation, and emotional disabilities, while Hispanic and Asian/Pacific Islander students are underrepresented (Zhang & Katsiyannis, 2002).

What Is an Individualized Education Program?

As mentioned earlier, the document that the multidisciplinary team uses to decide the best placement for a student with an identified disability and that serves as a blueprint for a student's education is called an individualized education program. The IEP addresses all areas of student need, including accommodations to be made in a general education class and the services and supports to be provided there. The IEP also documents that services are being provided (Drasgow, Yell, & Robinson, 2001). Classroom teachers generally are involved as team participants in preparing an IEP if a student has any participation in the general education setting (Lytle & Bordin, 2001). Whether or not you are the teacher who serves in this role for particular students, if you have students with disabilities in your classroom, you will have opportunities to examine their IEPs or to meet with special educators to review highlights of these important plans, just as Ms. Lee, introduced at the beginning of the chapter, learned. Accessing IEPs and learning about your state's requirements for them have become very efficient practices with the increasing use of technology. Technology Notes on page 57 explains some of the electronic options related to IEPs and the procedures for developing them.

Required Components of an IEP

The essential components of the IEP were established by P.L. 94-142 in 1975, and they have been updated through the years. Although specific state requirements for

> TECHNOLOGY
NOTES

Using Technology for IEPs

The preparation of IEPs has changed significantly over the past several years. Although in some school districts IEPs are still written in longhand, increasingly these essential documents can be created on a computer using commercially available software or templates created at the state level. In addition, banks of goals and objectives (as needed) that align with state curriculum standards exist, and these can be inserted into IEPs, thus streamlining the IEP-writing process. A few of the options that exist are outlined here.

Computerized IEPs

A number of companies have produced IEP software that enables educators to write an IEP electronically, sometimes even incorporating information from a district database into the process so that basic demographic information already stored does not have to be entered separately on the forms. Examples of computerized IEP programs include IEPWriter (http://www.iepwriter.com), Special Education Automation Software (http://www.computerautomation.com), and e-IEP PRO (http://www.e-ieppro.com). These programs enable multiple educators to access IEPs from their computers, and they help professionals to generate the reports needed to report student progress.

State and Local IEP Policies and Forms

Every state and many school districts now make available online their policies and procedures related to special education as well as the forms that are needed for intervention assistance teams, special education referrals, IEPs, and other special education activities. A website for the State of Illinois is an example of how state information and forms are made available, at http://www.isbe.net/. You generally can find this type of information by using an Internet search engine, searching for the state's Department of Education or the school district, finding the home page for the office of special education, and then scanning to find policies and procedural information.

Information on Specific Issues Related to IEPs

When you are asked to attend an IEP meeting, you may have questions about particular aspects of a student's disability. Throughout this textbook, many websites that are mentioned fall into the category of specific information on special education issues, services, and disability types. One site that provides many links to information you may find useful is Special Education Resources on the Internet, at http://seriweb.com.

Questions and Activities

1. How might computerized IEPs make it easier for you to participate in the IEP-writing process? Ask an experienced professional to discuss computerized IEPs.
2. What is the web address for special education policies and procedures for your state? A large school district near you? In addition to forms and procedures, what additional helpful information can you find on those websites?
3. What aspects of special education are you particularly curious about? What websites can you find that address these issues?

IEPs vary somewhat, the federally required elements of IEPs are described in the following sections.

PRESENT LEVEL OF FUNCTIONING ● Information about a student's current level of academic achievement, social skills, behavior, communication skills, and other areas of concern must be included on an IEP. This information serves as a baseline and makes it possible to judge student progress from year to year. Often, highlights of the information collected from the individual assessment of the student are recorded on the IEP to partially meet this requirement. Individual achievement test scores, teacher ratings, and summary assessments by specialists such as speech therapists or occupational therapists can be used to report the present level of functioning. Another component of this assessment is information about how the student's disabilities affect involvement in the general education curriculum.

ANNUAL GOALS AND SHORT-TERM OBJECTIVES ● *Annual goals* are the MDT's estimate of what a student should be able to accomplish within a year, related to meeting his or her measured needs resulting from the disability. For some students,

RESEARCH
N O T E

General education teachers report that when they participate in IEP meetings, they talk more and include more discussion of student strengths and needs, sense they have a better idea about what to do next, and view meetings positively (Martin et al., 2004).

annual goals may refer primarily to academic areas and may include growth in reading, math problem solving, and other curricular areas. Specifically, a student with a learning disability might have an annual goal to read and comprehend books at a particular grade level or to demonstrate skills for finding and keeping a job. For other students, annual goals address desired changes in classroom behavior, social skills, or other adaptive skills. An annual goal for a student with a moderate intellectual disability, for example, may be to order a meal at a fast-food restaurant. A student with autism might have participating in conversation as a goal. Annual goals also may encompass speech therapy, occupational and physical therapy, and other areas in which a student has specialized needs. There is no "right" number of annual goals. Some students have as few as 2 or 3, others as many as 8 or 10. However, IDEA specifies that annual goals must be measurable, and increased emphasis is placed on annual goals that enable a student to progress in the general education curriculum.

Short-term objectives are descriptions of the steps needed to achieve an annual goal, and they generally are required only for the IEPs of students with significant intellectual disabilities. For example, for a student with a severe physical disability whose annual goal is to feed herself, short-term objectives might include grasping a spoon, picking up food with the spoon, and using the spoon to transport food from plate to mouth. The number of short-term objectives for each annual goal relates to the type and severity of the disability, its impact on student learning, and the complexity of the goal. For some students, only a few short-term objectives may be needed; for others, each annual goal may be divided into several smaller steps. Examples of IEP goals and objectives are included in the Professional Edge on page 59.

ANALYZE
AND **REFLECT**

How might the IEP goals for a student with a significant disability (for example, a student in middle school who reads at a second-grade level or a student with multiple disabilities) be implemented in a general education class? What factors might lead the MDT to decide that services should not be delivered there? What are the costs and benefits of such decisions?

EXTENT OF PARTICIPATION IN GENERAL EDUCATION ● In keeping with the trend toward inclusive practices, the IEP must include a clear statement of justification for placing a student anywhere but in a general education classroom for all or part of the school day. Even for extracurricular and other nonacademic activities, if the team excludes the student from the general class, an explanation of why that student cannot participate in such activities must be part of the IEP.

SERVICES AND MODIFICATIONS NEEDED ● The IEP contains a complete outline of the specialized services the student needs; that is, the document includes all the special education instruction to be provided and any other related services needed to ensure instructional success. Thus, a student receiving adaptive physical education has an IEP indicating that such a service is needed. A student's need for special transportation is noted on the IEP, too. A student who is entitled to transition or vocational assistance has an IEP that clarifies these services. Perhaps most importantly, the statement of services must include information about the modifications and supports to be provided so that the student can access and progress in the general education curriculum.

One additional element of this IEP component concerns assessment. IDEA stipulates that if a student needs accommodations (for example, extended time) on district or state assessments, including high-stakes assessments, these should be specified on the IEP. If a student is to be exempt from such assessments, the team must ensure that the student will complete an alternative assessment that takes into account her functioning levels and needs. Remember that the No Child Left Behind Act set specific limits on which students are exempt from high-stakes testing and eligible for alternative assessments, and these limits were confirmed and clarified in IDEA. Most of the students with disabilities whom you teach will be required to complete mandated assessments and their scores must be considered for measuring adequate year progress (AYP).

CONNECTIONS

Students' IEPs address not just academics but also behavior and social skills. These topics are addressed in Chapters 12 and 13.

Part of identifying services is indicating who is responsible for providing them. Any of the professionals introduced earlier in this chapter could be listed on the IEP to deliver special services. As a general education teacher, you probably will be included, too. For some students, you will be the teacher who completes most of the required instruction; for others, you will assist but will not be primarily responsible. For

PROFESSIONAL EDGE

Sample IEP Goals and Objectives

The goals and objectives on IEPs are related to assessed student needs, and they are written in a specific way (Lignugaris-Kraft, Marchand-Martella, & Martella, 2001). For example, they must be measurable, and they must specify the conditions under which the student should be able to carry out an activity (such as the reading level of print material or the people with whom a student should communicate). They also should indicate the level of mastery needed (such as a level of accuracy in an assignment).

Goals outline the progress expected for approximately one school year. They are supplemented by short-term objectives, or benchmarks, that measure progress toward achieving the annual goal. The following are sample IEP annual goals and objectives:

Students with Mild/Moderate Disabilities

- Goal: When assigned to write an essay of three paragraphs, Jerome will use capital letters and punctuation with 80 percent accuracy.

- Goal: Susan will complete at least 80 percent of her homework assignments in English, algebra, and U.S. history.
  - Objective: Susan will write down homework assignments 90 percent of the time with 90 percent accuracy.
  - Objective: Susan will have in her backpack at the end of the day all needed materials to do assignments 90 percent of the time.

Students with Significant Intellectual Disabilities*

- Goal: Maria will make eye contact when communicating with adults in school at least five out of six trials.
  - Objective: Maria will make eye contact with the speech/language therapist during individual sessions in five out of six interactions initiated by the therapist.
  - Objective: Maria will make eye contact when the special education teacher calls Maria's name and looks at her in at least five out of six interactions.
  - Objective: Maria will make eye contact when a classroom teacher calls Maria's name and looks at her in at least five out of six interactions.

You can find a complete sample IEP form on the website for this textbook (http://www.ablongman.com/friend4e). On that form, can you identify each of the components required in an IEP? Using a lesson you have created for another class or one provided by your instructor, try writing several goals and objectives for one of the students described at the beginning of this chapter.

*Remember that the IEPs for students with mild or moderate disabilities are not required to include objectives, unless requested by parents.

---

example, a student with a mild cognitive disability probably will be able to complete many class tasks with minor accommodations that you can make. However, if your student has significant cognitive and physical disabilities requiring an alternative curriculum, other professionals undoubtedly will help develop the materials you will use when the student is in your classroom.

BEHAVIOR INTERVENTION PLAN ● A critical aspect of the current regulations for educating students with disabilities concerns discipline and the need to respond to inappropriate behavior. Every student with significant behavior problems, not just those students labeled as having emotional disabilities, must have as part of the IEP an intervention plan based on a functional assessment of the student's behavior. This requirement reflects the increasing pressure for students to be supported in general education settings and the acknowledged difficulty of accomplishing that goal without fostering appropriate student behavior.

DATE OF INITIATION AND FREQUENCY AND DURATION OF SERVICE AND ANTICIPATED MODIFICATIONS ● Each IEP must include specific dates when specialized services and modifications begin, the frequency of the services and modifications, the types of modifications that are part of the services, and the period of time during which services and modifications are offered. Because the law generally requires that student progress in special education be monitored at least once each year, the most typical duration for a service is a maximum of one year. If during the year an MDT member sees a need to reconsider the student's educational plan, additional IEP meetings can be convened.

STRATEGIES FOR EVALUATION ● When a team develops an IEP, the members must clarify how to measure student progress toward achieving the annual goals and how to regularly inform parents about this progress. For example, when short-term objectives are written, the team indicates the criteria and the procedures to be used to judge whether the objective has been met. For the student learning to move around the school without assistance, the criteria might include specific point-to-point independent movement, and a checklist might be used to judge student progress toward reaching the goal. As with all aspects of special education, the evaluation criteria and procedures are individualized; they are as general or specific as needed to accomplish the student's educational goals.

TRANSITION PLAN ● For all students who are 14 years of age and older, part of the IEP is a description of strategies and services for ensuring that the student is prepared to leave school for adult life. This part of the IEP is called a **transition plan.** Students with disabilities who are college-bound might have transition plans that include improvement of their study skills, exploration of different universities and their services for students with disabilities, completion of high school course requirements necessary to obtain admission to a university, and preparation in life skills such as responsibly using credit cards and checking accounts. For students who plan to work immediately after graduation, the transition plan might include developing skills such as reading employment ads and filling out job applications, as well as developing important job skills such as punctuality, pleasant manners, and respect toward people in authority and customers. As with IEPs, there is no single correct way to write a transition plan. However, this plan must be tailored to match the assessed strengths and needs of the particular student. It is updated annually, with participation by professionals from agencies outside the school typically increasing as the student nears graduation or school departure at age 21.

In addition to the basic components, IEPs have several other requirements. For example, they are signed by the individuals who participate in their development, including the student's parent or guardian. They also list a justification for the placement recommended. For example, a decision that the student should receive some services in a pullout program might be justified on the basis of the student's need for one-to-one or small-group intensive instruction to succeed. In addition, if a student has specific types of needs, they must be addressed in the IEP. Examples of such needs are behavior, communication, braille (unless specifically excluded on the IEP), and assistive technology. In such cases, appropriate supports, services, and strategies must be specified (Drasgow et al., 2001).

The Value of IEPs

To some educators, IEPs represent paperwork that mostly consumes time and energy (Carlson, Chen, Schroll, & Klein, 2003). This is unfortunate because IEPs guide the education of students with disabilities. An IEP helps you clarify your expectations for a student and provides a means for you to understand the student's educational needs. The document also informs you about the types of services the student receives and when the student's educational plan will next be reviewed. Your job is to make a good-faith effort to accomplish the goals and/or short-term objectives on the IEP as they relate to your instruction. If you do that, you will have carried out your responsibility; if you do not do that, you could be held accountable. For example, suppose an IEP indicates that a student should learn the concept of freedom of speech. You can demonstrate that you are helping the student learn this by providing class discussion, role-play activities, and access to appropriate resources on the Internet, even if the student does not master this concept. If you state that the student is expected merely to read about the concept in the textbook chapter and you refuse to create opportunities for supported learning in this area, you may be violating the IEP.

Do you have additional questions about your role in the preferral, referral, or IEP process? Additional considerations are presented in the Working Together feature below.

WWW
R E S O U R C E S
Many statistics about students with disabilities and how they receive their education services come from the federally compiled annual reports to Congress on the implementation of IDEA. You can find copies of the reports from the past several years at http://www.ed.gov/about/reports/annual/osep/index.html.

What Services Do Students with Disabilities Receive?

The services that a student with disabilities can receive are comprehensive, limited only by the stipulation that they must be necessary as part of that student's education. These services are provided in a variety of placements. Both the services and placements are determined by the multidisciplinary team.

Special Education and Related Services

As noted in Chapter 1, the types of services students receive can be grouped into two categories: special education and related services. *Special education* refers to the specially

WORKING **TOGETHER**

Understanding the Intervention, Assessment, and Decision-Making Process

Even experienced teachers sometimes have questions about their roles and responsibilities in pre-referral or intervention assistance teams, in the eligibility process, and in designing special education services. Here are a few common questions and their answers:

● I work in a high school, and most students already have been identified by the time they get to this level. Do high school teachers still need to have intervention assistance teams?

Federal law does not specifically require that teams exist, but it does require that, across all levels of schools, a system be in place to identify students who might need special education. In one study of intervention assistance teams in an urban school district, researchers found that classroom teacher involvement on teams was essential for their success (Rubinson, 2002).

● Do all the teachers on a middle school team need to attend the pre-referral and/or IEP team meetings for their students who have been referred or assessed?

In most cases, expecting all the teachers on a middle school team to attend a meeting about a student with a suspected or identified disability is not reasonable. The composition of the prereferral team is a school's decision; in some cases, the middle school team might actually serve as the pre-referral team. When initial IEPs are written, in nearly all cases one general education teacher can provide a representative perspective for the team.

● Are general education teachers responsible for writing parts of the IEP?

Federal law requires participation of general education teachers in IEP meetings in most situations because they bring an important viewpoint to those discussions. However, those teachers generally do not write sections of the IEP. No matter what your role (for example, elementary, middle school, or high school teacher; related arts teacher; technology specialist), you are obligated to carry out any of the IEP provisions that pertain to you, including participating in services offered in the general education classroom and making adjustments to assignments and strategies as noted in the IEP.

designed instructional services students receive. These services may include adapted materials, alternative curriculum, access to a special education teacher qualified to teach students with a particular disability, and individualized instruction. When a student's special education teacher comes to the classroom and teaches with the general education teacher, that is special education. When a student leaves a classroom for 30 minutes three times each week for intensive tutoring, that is special education. When a middle school or high school offers a life skills class for students with disabilities, that is special education, too.

Related services refer to all the supports students may need in order to benefit from special education. Examples of related services are speech therapy, transportation, physical and occupational therapy, adapted physical education, rehabilitation counseling, psychological services, and social work. A student's need to ride a special bus equipped with a wheelchair lift is a related service need. A student's need for assistance with personal care such as toileting is a related service need.

As you might guess, the range of possibilities for special education and related services is immense. Some students, particularly those with high-incidence disabilities, receive a limited number of special education services and perhaps no related services at all. For example, Lucas, a high school student with a learning disability in math, attends a geometry class in which a special education teacher teams with a math teacher. Lucas's assignments are sometimes shortened, and he is allowed extra time to complete tests. He already is looking into colleges that are known to be supportive of students with his special needs. Students with more complex or severe disabilities may have a more highly specialized special education as well as numerous related services. For example, Charmon, a student with physical and cognitive disabilities, might receive the services of a physical and occupational therapist, speech/language therapist, and inclusion specialist, as well as a special education teacher.

Student Placement

Until recently, any discussion of special education services typically began with a discussion of the least restrictive environment (LRE) and rapidly moved to a detailed discussion of the place in which the services would occur. This was because many students spent some, most, or all of the school day in a special education classroom, where it was believed appropriate instruction could best be delivered. Now, views about placement are changing (McLeskey, Henry, & Axelrod, 1999). Some school districts still use special education classrooms, even for students with relatively mild disabilities, and these are sometimes an appropriate LRE. However, the high standards and accountability provisions of NCLB and the requirement that students with disabilities be taught by highly qualified teachers of IDEA are leading to schools becoming more inclusive (U.S. Department of Education, 2002). As in Ms. Turner's school that you read about at the beginning of the chapter, school professionals are considering how to support students more effectively in general education settings. Figure 2.6 shows the continuum of placements that must exist for students with disabilities and recent data on the percentage of students with disabilities in each of those placements. The decision about placement is made by the MDT and reviewed at least annually along with the IEP. Placements can be changed as often as appropriate, with parental permission. Generally, if parents and school district representatives disagree about placement, the student remains in the current placement until the disagreement is resolved. Exceptions to this occur when discipline issues arise. Administrators may unilaterally change a student's placement (for example, through suspension) for up to 10 days, provided such methods are used with other students, too. If students with disabilities bring a weapon or drugs to school, they can be placed in an alternative educational setting for up to 45

FYI

Students with disabilities who are enrolled in faith-based private schools are entitled to some benefits from IDEA. For example, although these students must be identified by the public school district in that locale, they may receive only limited services that do not have to be available at the private school—they may be available only at the public school (Eigenbrood, 2004).

ANALYZE AND REFLECT

Zigmond (2003) suggests that questions about *where* students with disabilities should be educated are misguided and that the more important questions concern *how* best to help each student learn. What are the implications of this thinking for teachers? What impact could this thinking have on the continuum-of-placements model?

FIGURE 2.6 IDEA Continuum of Placements for Students with Disabilities

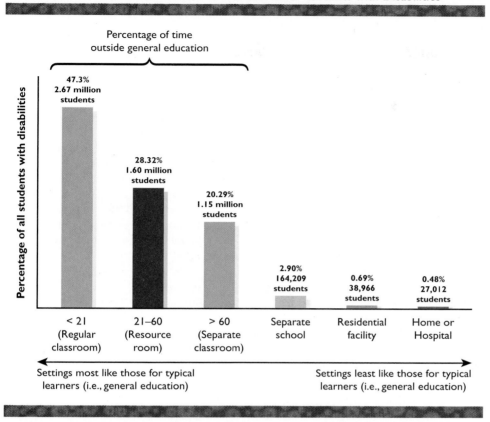

SOURCE: From *24th Annual Report to Congress on the Implementation of the Individuals with Disabilities Education Act,* 2002, Washington, DC: U.S. Department of Education.

school days while decisions are made concerning their long-term placement needs (Bear, Quinn, & Burkholder, 2001).

REGULAR (GENERAL EDUCATION) CLASS ● Nearly half of students with disabilities leave the general education setting for less than 21 percent of the day to receive special education services (U.S. Department of Education, 2002). Thus, these students spend the majority of their time in the general education classroom. For example, a student in kindergarten with a communication disorder might be served by a speech/language therapist who comes to the classroom and teaches language lessons with the general education teacher. For a student in middle school with cognitive and physical disabilities, an inclusion specialist might adapt a lesson on fractions by helping the student learn how to cut simple shapes into halves. For a student with a learning disability in high school biology, a paraprofessional might assist the student in carrying out lab directions and in recording and completing assignments. The student with LD might have one class period covering study skills and strategies assistance in a special education classroom.

RESOURCE PROGRAM ● Another group of students with disabilities attends school mostly in general education settings but also receives assistance in a special education

RESEARCH
N O T E

Research suggests that three factors other than race strongly influence the restrictiveness of the placement of a student with disabilities: the perceived severity of the student's problem, the presence of serious behavior problems, and a low level of family involvement (Hosp & Reschly, 2002).

classroom, often called a **resource room,** for 21–60 percent of the day (U.S. Department of Education, 2002) in what is called a *resource program*. In elementary schools, resource programs sometimes are organized by the skills being taught. For instance, from 10:00 a.m. until 10:45 a.m., basic math skills may be taught, and all the second-, third-, and fourth-grade students needing math assistance may come to the resource room at that time. Alternatively, some resource rooms are arranged by same-age groups. For example, in these programs all fifth graders with disabilities in resource room programs may go to the resource room together. In another approach, special education teachers negotiate with general education teachers about specific times students will attend.

In middle schools and high schools, students are scheduled to have resource classes in the same way that the rest of their classes are scheduled. For example, a student may attend a resource class that provides study strategies or reviews the curriculum being taught in general education classes. How a resource program is organized depends on many factors, including the number of students to be served and their ages, the nature and intensity of their needs, and local policies. One hallmark of resource services is that they are supplemental to the instruction in the general education classroom, that is, they are not in lieu of core academic classes.

FYI

In many school districts, students have the opportunity to make choices about the schools they attend. Many students with disabilities are entitled to choose their schools, too—including charter and magnet schools—although students needing highly specialized programs that are site-bound may be obligated to receive their education at specific schools (Ahearn, 2001).

SEPARATE CLASS ● Some students with disabilities attend *separate classes* for more than 60 percent of the school day (U.S. Department of Education, 2002). In this placement, a special education teacher has the primary instructional responsibility for the students who receive grades from the highly qualified special educator for the subjects taught there. However, a separate class placement does not mean that students do not interact with typical peers; they may attend a general education classroom for part of the day, and they also may participate in related arts and other school activities with peers. For example, although Kurt is in a separate class most of the day at his high school, he takes a shop class with students without disabilities. A paraprofessional accompanies him because he has limited ability to understand directions and needs close guidance from an adult to operate equipment. At Kyle's elementary school, 30 minutes each day is called "community time," during which students read and write together, share important events from their lives, and learn about their neighborhood and community. For community time, Kyle goes to Mr. Ballinger's fifth-grade class. The students are about Kyle's age and assist her with the community activities and learning. Kyle's special education teacher helps Mr. Ballinger plan appropriate activities for Kyle during that time.

If you teach in one of the related arts—for example, art, music, physical education, or drama—you are likely to instruct students with disabilities regardless of their specific placement. More information about your responsibilities in this regard is included in the Special Emphasis On . . . feature on page 65.

SEPARATE SCHOOL ● A small number of students with disabilities attend public or private *separate schools* (U.S. Department of Education, 2002). Some separate schools exist for students with moderate or severe cognitive and physical disabilities, although such schools are becoming obsolete. Other separate schools serve students with multiple disabilities who need high levels of specialized services. For example, in a small community near Chicago, approximately 25 students are educated at a separate school. These students all need the services of a physical and occupational therapist; most have complex medical problems that must be closely monitored; and most cannot move unless someone assists them. These students have opportunities for contact with typical peers who, through a special program, are brought to the separate school to function as "learning buddies."

Special EMPHASIS On …

The Arts

If you are an art, music, dance, or drama teacher, you might wonder what role you play in the education of students with disabilities. In fact, in many school districts you are the professional who is most likely to work with most, if not all, of the students with disabilities attending your school. In many cases, these students come to your class along with typical peers. In a few cases, a separate class has been arranged for them. Teachers in the arts often express the concern that little attention is paid to the support needs of students with disabilities in their classes, and few materials are available to prepare teachers in the arts for working with students with disabilities.

One website that you will find particularly helpful is VSA Arts (formerly Very Special Arts), at http://www.vsarts.org. Founded in 1974 by Jean Kennedy Smith, VSA Arts is an international organization that creates learning opportunities through the arts for children and adults with disabilities. The organization has affiliates across the United States and in 60 other countries.

VSA Arts includes an online gallery of works by individuals with disabilities, a showcase of recordings from recent awards for playwrights and musicians with disabilities, a link to frequently asked questions, a chronicle of the difference that the arts have made in the lives of individuals with disabilities and the programs serving them, and other information about the organization and its work. Educators can link to a VSA Arts site to search for information and websites on topics related to their teaching.

VSA Arts also distributes materials to assist educators in working with students with disabilities. One instructional program, Start with the Arts, is designed to foster literacy skills for young children in inclusive settings. Another resource is Express Diversity!, a set of five modules with art activities designed for fifth graders but adaptable for students in grades 1 through 7. The intent of the modules is to demonstrate that students with a wide range of abilities and disabilities share in the joy of arts. The modules include one simulation activity (with cautions about the shortcomings of this approach for trying to understand individuals with disabilities), a creative-writing exercise, an art mural activity, a performance arts activity, and a visual arts activity. The package of materials also includes letters (in Spanish as well as English) that can be sent home to explain the program to parents, bulletin board items, video biography cards about people with disabilities, and other support materials.

SOURCE: Adapted from "Publications and Resources for Educators and Parents," by VSA Arts, 2003. Retrieved September 15, 2004, from http://www.vsarts.org/x572.xml.

Some students with serious emotional disabilities also attend separate schools. These students might harm themselves or others. They might not be able to cope with the complexity and social stress of a typical school, and so the least restrictive environment for them is a school where their highly specialized needs, including therapeutic supports, can be addressed.

RESIDENTIAL FACILITY ● A few students have needs that cannot be met at a school that is in session only during the day. If students in separate settings have even greater needs, they might attend school as well as live in a public or private *residential facility*. Few students with disabilities are educated in this manner (U.S. Department of Education, 2002). The students for whom this placement is the LRE often are those with severe emotional problems or severe and multiple cognitive, sensory, and physical disabilities. In some states, students who are blind or deaf also might receive their instruction in a residential facility, an approach that is supported by some professionals and parents and opposed by others.

A somewhat different group of students also can be considered under the residential placement option. According to IDEA, children and young adults with disabilities who are incarcerated in the juvenile justice system must receive special education services. Further, children and young adults who are convicted of a crime and incarcerated as adults also are entitled to special education services unless the IEP team determines there is a compelling reason to discontinue services (Howell & Wolford, 2002). Finally, this group includes incarcerated adults who are 18 to 21 years of age but who were receiving special education services before their incarceration or before they dropped out of school and subsequently were convicted of a crime.

HOME OR HOSPITAL ● A very small number of students with disabilities receive their education in a home or hospital setting (U.S. Department of Education, 2002). This placement often is used for students who are medically fragile or who are undergoing surgeries or other medical treatments, or for students who have experienced an emotional crisis. For a few students with limited stamina, school comes to the home because the student does not have the strength to come to school; that is, a special education teacher comes to the home for a specified amount of time each week to deliver instruction there.

If parents and school representatives disagree about an appropriate educational placement, students sometimes are educated at home pending the outcome of a due process hearing. When students are educated at home or in a hospital, the amount of actual instruction often is limited. Home services might involve as little as 4 or 5 hours of teaching per week, delivered by an itinerant teacher. Hospital services range from a few hours of itinerant teaching to a full school program delivered by teachers who are assigned full time to work in that setting.

> " The appropriate educational setting for most students with disabilities is the same classroom they would attend if they did not have a disability. "

One more point should be made about placements. For some students, the team may decide that students' learning will suffer significantly if schooling stops during the summer. For these students, any of the services in any of the placements just described can be extended into school breaks and summer vacations through extended school year (ESY) programs.

As you can see, because of NCLB and IDEA separate classes and schools for placement are rapidly becoming less important than supporting the education of students with disabilities in general education classrooms and schools. When placement includes a specialized setting, often that alternative placement is appropriate for a specific skill or service for a specific and limited period of time. However, the appropriate and required educational setting for most students with disabilities is the same classroom they would attend if they did not have a disability. As a general education teacher, you play a major role in the education of students with disabilities, so it is important for you to understand the kinds of special services your students receive.

SUMMARY

Many individuals work to ensure that students with disabilities receive an appropriate education. These people include general education teachers; special education teachers; related service providers such as school psychologists, counselors, speech/language therapists, social workers, physical and occupational therapists, adaptive physical educators, nurses, administrators, paraprofessionals, and other specialists; and parents, students, and advocates. Depending on need, a student with a disability may receive instruction from just one or two of these professionals, or from several of them.

To determine whether special services are needed, general education teachers usually begin a process of deciding whether to request that a student be assessed for the presence of a disability. They carry out this process by analyzing the nature and extent of a student's unmet needs; clarifying those needs by describing them through examples; determining that the needs are chronic and possibly worsening over time; comparing the student's needs to those of others in the class; possibly recognizing that no pattern seems to exist for the student's performance; and intervening to address the unmet needs and documenting those efforts. Based on these early strategies, the student's needs may be assessed by an intervention assistance team or screening procedure, and then if warranted, a multidisciplinary team (MDT) follows federally established special education referral and assessment steps. This process includes completing an individualized assessment with parental permission, making decisions about the need

for special education, developing an individualized education program (IEP), and monitoring the special education services. If parents and personnel disagree on any aspect of a student's special education program or services and if the disagreement cannot be resolved informally, due process procedures, including mediation and dispute resolution sessions, are used to ensure that the student receives the appropriate education.

When an IEP is developed, it includes the student's present level of functioning, goals (and sometimes objectives), justification for any placement outside general education, needed services, the person(s) responsible for the services, beginning and ending dates for service delivery, and criteria for evaluation. It may also include a behavior intervention plan and a transition plan. The IEP generally must be reviewed at least annually, and the student must be reevaluated at least every 3 years. The services a student may receive, as outlined by the IEP, include special education and related services and a designation of the placement for the student: a general education classroom, resource program, or separate special education setting.

General education teachers play an integral role in the education of students with disabilities. They are involved in the early identification of students who seem to have special needs, contribute during the assessment and identification process, and implement IEP goals and, possibly, objectives as outlined by the multidisciplinary team.

Applications in **Teaching Practice**

A Visit to an MDT Meeting

Ms. Richards teaches science to sixth graders. Beginning in the fall, she and her team members will be working with Natasha, a student newly identified as having a learning disability. Natasha enjoys many friends and extracurricular activities, but she has extraordinary difficulties with reading fluency, comprehension, and written expression. She also has significant problems organizing her work and remembering to complete and turn in assignments. To help set appropriate goals for the coming year, Ms. Richards is participating in an MDT meeting to create an IEP for Natasha. Although it would be preferable for all the sixth-

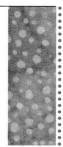

grade-team members to attend the meeting, this is not feasible, and so Ms. Richards is representing her colleagues as well.

General education (sixth-grade) science teacher: Ms. Richards

General education (fifth-grade) teacher: Mr. Tucker

Special education middle school teacher: Ms. Hill

Principal: Ms. Hubbert

Psychologist: Ms. Freund

Speech/language therapist: Mr. Colt

Parent: Ms. Wright

Ms. Hubbert: Our next task is to develop goals for Natasha. I'd like to suggest that we discuss academics first, then social areas, and wrap up with related services needed. Let's look at Natasha's strengths first—in all those areas.

Mr. Colt: Natasha has a very strong speaking vocabulary. She is considerably above average in that realm.

Ms. Freund: Along with that, Natasha's general knowledge is very good. She also is near grade level in basic math skills.

Mr. Tucker: It's not really academics, but one strength Natasha has that I see is her willingness to help classmates. She really wants to help everyone in class learn even when she herself is struggling. She also was very active in extracurricular activities this year— she participated in the service learning program, volunteered to read to the kindergarten class, and competed in the after-school sports program.

Ms. Hill: As we write academic goals, then, we need to remember that Natasha has strong vocabulary skills and general knowledge and that she does not need help in math. Perhaps we can use her social skills and other interests to help in the academic arena. Ms. Wright, what strengths do you see in Natasha?

Ms. Wright: Hmmm. She minds me, that's for sure. And she helps out around the house with chores. She likes to help me watch her baby brother.

Ms. Hill: Helping really seems to be Natasha's thing—let's keep that in mind.

Ms. Hubbert: Let's focus for a minute on academic areas of need.

Ms. Freund: Reading comprehension and written expression are by far the areas that need the most work. Natasha's comprehension is just at a beginning third-grade level and her written expression is below that.

Ms. Wright: She says she doesn't like reading because the other kids make fun of her when she can't read the words and they tease her when Mr. Tucker gives her a baby book.

Ms. Richards: In middle school, that could be even more of a problem. We need to be sure that she uses the same textbooks as the other students next year. I'm sure we can also arrange to get some supplemental materials for her to use at home. Let's be sure that before we finish today we talk about that some more.

Ms. Freund: Ms. Richards and Ms. Hill, given what you know and have heard about Natasha, what might be the priorities for next year?

Ms. Hill: I agree that comprehension is the key. I think a goal should be for her to improve her comprehension to a fourth-grade level on reading tasks that include stories, textbooks, and other materials such as children's magazines.

Ms. Hubbert: Ms. Wright, how does that sound to you? [*Ms. Wright nods.*]

[*The conversation continues . . .*]

Before the meeting ends, the MDT has generated the following additional goals in reading comprehension using materials at her instructional level: Natasha will identify the main characters and the problem and solution in literature that she reads at a third-grade level. She will comprehend 80 percent of both narrative and expository material she reads aloud and 80 percent on material she reads to herself.

QUESTIONS

1. What are the responsibilities of the professionals represented at the MDT meeting? Which of the professionals are required to attend? How would your responses be different if this were an annual review?
2. What role does Ms. Richards take at the meeting? Why is her presence helpful in creating an educational program for Natasha? How else might she contribute during this meeting?
3. What is the purpose in having both the fifth-grade teacher and a sixth-grade teacher attend the meeting? How might this improve the quality of the IEP? What problems might it cause?
4. What steps do you think occurred prior to this meeting? How did the general education teacher prepare? What other team responsibilities were met?
5. What part of the IEP is the team addressing? What other parts have to be completed before the meeting ends? What must occur for the IEP to be valid?
6. What would happen if Natasha's mother asked the school district for a separate class as Natasha's placement and the school district disagreed with this?

WORKING THE **STANDARDS**

 INTASC PRINCIPLES REFLECTED IN THIS CHAPTER:

Principle #1 states that all teachers

■ Understand key concepts such as special education and related services; disability definitions; free appropriate public education; least restrictive environment and continuum of services; due process and parent participation and rights; and nondiscriminatory assessment (Principle 1.04).

■ Understand the purpose and requirements of individualized education programs (IEPs), including transition plans, and individualized family support plans (IFSPs), both of which are specified in IDEA, and individual accommodations plans (IAPs), which are specified in Section 504, and their responsibility for implementing these plans (Principle 1.04).

■ Know about and can access resources to gain information about state, district, and school policies and procedures regarding special education, including those regarding referral, assessment, eligibility, and services for students with disabilities (Principle 1.05).

Principle #8 states that all teachers understand the purposes, strengths, and limitations of formal and informal assessment approaches for making eligibility, placement, and instructional decisions for students with disabilities (Principle 8.01).

Principle #10 states that all teachers

■ Understand the purposes of, and are effective members of, the different types of teams within the special education process (for example, child study and teacher assistance teams, multidisciplinary teams that focus on identification and placement, IEP/IFSP teams), including the role of the general education teacher in initial and ongoing assessment, and planning and instruction of students with disabilities (Principle 10.02).

■ Accept families as full partners in planning appropriate instruction and services for students with disabilities, and provide meaningful opportunities for them to participate as partners in their children's instructional programs and in the life of the school (Principle 10.04).

WORKING THE **STANDARDS** *(continued)*

CEC STANDARDS REFLECTED IN THIS CHAPTER:

CEC Content Standard #1 states that special educators understand the relationships of organizations of special education to the organizations and functions of schools, school systems, and other agencies, and use this knowledge as a ground upon which to construct their own personal understandings and philosophies of special education.

CEC Content Standard #7 states that special educators

- Develop long-range individualized instructional plans anchored in both general and special curricula.

- Systematically translate these individualized plans into carefully selected shorter-range goals and objectives, taking into consideration an individual's abilities and needs, the learning environment, and a myriad of cultural and linguistic factors.

CEC Content Standard #8 states that special educators

- Understand the legal policies and ethical principles of measurement and assessment related to referral, eligibility, program planning, instruction, and placement for individuals with exceptional learning needs.

- Collaborate with families and other colleagues to ensure unbiased, meaningful assessments and decision making.

BACK TO THE CASES

The standards and principles just listed relate to the teachers described at the beginning of this chapter: Mr. Vazquez, Ms. Lee, and Ms. Turner. The questions and activities that follow demonstrate how these standards and principles, along with other concepts that you have learned about in this chapter, connect to the everyday activities of all teachers.

Mr. Vazquez

Mr. Vazquez and Marcus's parents have tried several strategies to change Marcus's behavior and improve his academic

progress. However, they do not think there has been significant improvement and want to consult the school's instructional assistance team. (See INTASC Principles 1.05, 10.02, and 10.04; and CEC Standard 8.) What information should Mr. Vazquez provide to the team? Use specific examples from the case.

Ms. Lee

Ms. Lee is looking forward to working with the speech/language therapist, but she is unsure what to expect. Does she need to tell the therapist what to do? Should she be keeping records of Jennifer's language difficulties? (See INTASC Principle 1.04 and CEC Standard 8.) Using information from the chapter and the American Speech-Language-Hearing Association website (http://www.asha.org), outline how a speech/language therapist works with teachers and IEP teams, and explain what Ms. Lee should expect to happen in her classroom.

Ms. Turner

As Ms. Turner works with her school's inclusive practices team, she becomes concerned that student rights to an inclusive education may create unrealistic expectations for a general educator's ability to work with students who have exceptional learning needs. She has other concerns about the amount of paperwork and time required to meet the IDEA requirement that general education teachers participate in IEP meetings. (See INTASC Principles 1.04 and 10.02.) How would you assure her that she is a necessary participant in the process and address her concerns? In your answer, specifically address both Ms. Turner's responsibilities and her personal concerns.

> Visit the companion website (http://www.ablongman. com/friend4e) for a complete correlation of this chapter to the INTASC Principles and CEC Standards.

Further **Readings**

Malian, I., & Nevin, A. (Eds.). (2002). Impact of self-determination curricula [Special issue]. *Remedial and Special Education, 23*(2), 66–128.

This special issue of the journal considers several aspects of self-determination, including the implications of self-determination for classroom practice at all school levels, the importance of administrative support for self-determination, and students' views on this topic.

Pickett, A. L., & Gerlach, K. (Eds.). (2003). *Supervising paraeducators in educational settings: A team approach* (2nd ed.). Austin, TX: Pro-Ed.

This book provides practical and specific information on preparing para-educators for their roles, helping them to manage their roles and responsibilities, supervising them, and resolving issues that arise.

Stodden, R. A., Galloway, L. M., & Stodden, N. J. (2003). Secondary school curricula issues: Impact on post-secondary students with disabilities. *Exceptional Children, 70,* 9–26.

This article is a review of literature on the status of students with disabilities in high schools in the context of rigorous, standards-based curricula and high-stakes testing and other accountability practices. The authors clearly map out the dilemmas, but they devote much of their writing to exemplary practices that can help all high school teachers help their students with disabilities to succeed.

Ulrich, M. E., & Bauer, A. M. (2003). Levels of awareness: A closer look at communication between parents and professionals. *Teaching Exceptional Children, 35*(6), 20–25.

This teacher-friendly article outlines types of reactions and stages parents may go through when they learn that their child has a disability. The article can help teachers to better understand and respond appropriately to the parents of their students.

Building Partnerships
through
Collaboration

After you read this chapter, you will be able to

1. Explain what the term *collaboration* means, and describe how collaboration is part of providing services to students with disabilities.

2. Clarify how an emphasis on collaboration in schools shapes the roles and responsibilities that you have as a general education teacher.

3. Describe services for students with disabilities and other special needs in which collaboration is integral, including shared problem solving, co-teaching, teaming, and consulting.

4. Identify ways in which you can work effectively with parents to successfully educate students with special needs.

5. Outline your responsibilities in working with paraprofessionals, and describe ways in which you can enhance collaboration with them.

KEY TERMS AND CONCEPTS

Collaboration (p. 75)

Consultation (p. 92)

Co-teaching (p. 87)

Family-centered practices (p. 96)

Paraprofessionals (p. 100)

Shared problem solving (p. 81)

Teams (p. 90)

IN MS. GODINA'S biology class, 5 of her 36 students have IEPs. Natalie, who has a mild learning disability, does not need assistance in the course. James and Tyler, both receiving services for emotional disabilities, are capable of completing the work, but they need a great deal of structure and support. Carl, a student with an intellectual disability, does part of the course work, but he is not expected to master the extensive vocabulary or to write lengthy lab reports. Janet, who has a physical disability that requires her to use a motorized wheelchair and has limited stamina, often needs encouragement to keep up with the work. Four days a week, Ms. Godina is joined by Mr. MacLean, a special education teacher. During these class periods, the two teachers share teaching responsibilities and group the students for instruction in a variety of ways—by skill needs, interest, and random assignment, among others. On the day that Mr. MacLean is not in class, Ms. Hugo, a teaching assistant, is available to help Ms. Godina and individual students. ● *What happens when two teachers share instructional responsibilities in a classroom? What topics might Ms. Godina and Mr. MacLean need to discuss to ensure that their shared teaching is effective?*

THREE FOURTH-GRADE TEACHERS

are having a grade-level team meeting; Ms. Chiang, the special education teacher, also is present. They have discussed a curriculum issue related to social studies, and now the conversation has turned to a common problem. Mr. Balen states that his students with disabilities are taking a disproportionate amount of his time, especially in the morning. He explains that this group of students does not seem to be able to come into the classroom, put away their belongings, and settle into work without his close and constant supervision. Mrs. Dyer agrees but adds that many students without disabilities are having the same problem. After a few minutes of general conversation about this problem, the teachers begin generating ideas for dealing with it. Included in the list of ideas are letting students choose their own morning work, assigning all students a "morning study buddy," and reviewing expectations with all the classes. Even though Ms. Chiang does not teach fourth grade, she is so often in the classrooms to assist students, to observe, or to take part in lessons that she has several excellent ideas to contribute to the discussion. ● *What is Ms. Chiang's role on the team? How can the team ensure that all the members feel committed to the team and valued as team members?*

CHRIS'S PARENTS, Mr. and Mrs. Werner,

arrive promptly for their after-school meeting with Ms. MacDougal, the middle school inclusion facilitator, and Mr. Saunders, the seventh-grade team leader. Mrs. Werner begins by declaring that the school is discriminating against Chris because of her learning disability. Mr. Werner asserts that Chris should not be singled out in any way because of her special needs and that he was unhappy to learn that she has been receiving tutoring during a lunch-period study hall. He stresses that the family already provides tutoring for Chris so that this type of discrimination will not occur at school. Further, Mr. and Mrs. Werner show the teachers Chris's modified assignment sheets, another example of discrimination. When Mr. Saunders starts to explain that he is modifying Chris's work so she can learn more in his class, Mr. Werner cuts him off, stating that a teacher's poor instructional practice is no excuse to destroy a child's self-concept through public humiliation. ● *If you were Mr. Saunders, what type of assistance would you want from Ms. MacDougal during this difficult interaction? How can you prevent miscommunication in your work with parents of students with disabilities?*

In the past, becoming a teacher—whether in general education or in special education—meant entering a profession frequently characterized by isolation and sometimes loneliness (Little, 1993; Lortie, 1975; Mitchell, 1997). Teachers typically spent most of the day alone in a classroom with students. They learned that they were expected to have all the skills to manage student learning and discipline issues, and they rarely had opportunities to discuss their questions, concerns, and misgivings with anyone, especially their colleagues at school.

Over the past several years, that atmosphere of isolation has changed. Elementary school teachers are meeting on grade-level teams to share ideas and problem solve, and middle school and high school teachers are creating interdisciplinary teams to redesign curriculum and share instructional responsibility for smaller groups of students. School reform efforts also are characterized by partnerships. For example, professional development schools in which teacher trainees work with experienced educators and university instructors emphasize team approaches (Paese, 2003). Likewise, entire schools are stressing the need to build a collaborative learning community in order to meet the current expectations of accountability for student learning (Marchant, 2002; Noguera, 2002).

As the scenes that open this chapter illustrate, these emerging partnerships extend to special education and other support staff as well. Particularly as schools increase inclusive practices to meet the requirements of federal laws, the working relationships among all the adults involved in the education of students with disabilities become critical. For example, as a classroom teacher, you may find that you have questions about a student's behavior in class. A consultant might come to your class, observe the student and the overall classroom setting, and then meet with you to discuss how to address your concerns. Similarly, you might find that some of your students cannot complete the grade-level work you are accustomed to assigning. To assist you, a special education teacher might meet with you to design the necessary modifications.

At first glance, these interactions seem like logical and straightforward approaches to optimizing education. However, because of the strong education tradition of professionals working alone and the still-limited opportunities many teachers have had in preparing to work effectively with other adults, problems sometimes occur (Friend &

Cook, 2003). In some instances, support personnel are reluctant to make suggestions for fear that they may sound as if they are interfering with a classroom teacher's instruction. In other cases, a classroom teacher insists that no change in classroom activities is possible, even though a special education teacher is available for co-teaching. And often, when professionals in schools disagree, they are uncomfortable directly discussing the issues and struggle to find shared solutions.

Professionals in inclusive schools usually assert that collaboration is the key to their success in meeting the needs of all students (Friend & Cook, 2003; Hollingsworth, 2001; Keefe, Moore, & Duff, 2004). The purpose of this chapter is to introduce you to the principles of collaboration and the school situations in which professionals are most likely to collaborate to meet the needs of students with disabilities. You also will learn how to develop strong working relationships with parents, an essential part of every teacher's responsibilities and an especially important one when educating students with special needs. Finally, the special partnerships that are formed when teachers work with paraprofessionals also are considered.

WWW
RESOURCES
The Center for Effective Collaboration and Practice (http://cecp.air.org) is a federally funded organization designed to promote effective educational practices for students with emotional and behavior problems. It includes links for parents, teachers, and other professionals on topics related to working together on behalf of these students.

What Are the Basics of Collaboration?

As a teacher, you will hear colleagues refer to many of their activities as collaboration. Sometimes they will be referring to a team meeting to propose ideas to help a student; sometimes they will mean sharing a classroom to teach a particular subject; and sometimes they will even use the term as a synonym for inclusive practices. How can all these things be collaboration? Actually, they are not. Collaboration is how people work together, not what they do. As Friend and Cook (2003) have stated, **collaboration** is a style professionals choose in order to accomplish a goal they share. Professionals often use the term *collaboration* to describe any activity in which they work with someone else. But just the fact of working in the same room with another person does not ensure that collaboration occurs. For example, in some team meetings, one or two members tend to monopolize the conversation and subtly insist that others agree with their points of view. Although the team is in proximity, it is not collaborative. True collaboration exists only on teams when all members feel their contributions are valued and the goal is clear, where they share decision making, and where they sense they are respected. The same can be said of other activities that bring professionals into proximity: Merely being together is not collaboration—it is how the individuals work with each other that defines whether collaboration is occurring, a fact illustrated in the Professional Edge on page 76 that describes collaboration between general and special education teachers in secondary schools.

> " Collaboration is how people work together, not what they do. "

Characteristics of Collaboration

Collaboration in schools has a number of defining characteristics that clarify its requirements. Friend and Cook (2003) have outlined these key attributes.

COLLABORATION IS VOLUNTARY ● Teachers may be assigned to work in close proximity, but they cannot be forced to collaborate. They must make a personal choice to use this style. For example, your principal may tell you and another teacher that you are expected to be part of an intervention assistance team. You could choose to keep your ideas to yourself instead of readily participating. Or you could conclude that even though you did not plan on volunteering for this activity, as long as you are a team

PROFESSIONAL EDGE

Secondary Teachers and Collaboration

When middle and high school teachers in urban settings were asked to identify their expectations of their special education colleagues when they worked together in general education classrooms, as well as areas in which they themselves needed to improve, they mentioned the following items:

General Expectations for Special Educators

● Understand that students with disabilities are the priority but not the only responsibility.

● Get to know all of the students.

● If possible, provide a schedule of times in the classroom.

Planning Expectations for Special Educators

● Meet for planning at least two times per month.

● Discuss strategies for working with diverse learners.

● Provide some type of background information on each student with an IEP in the class.

● Look at long-range lesson plans and provide suggestions for how these plans can be carried out to benefit students with disabilities.

● Give suggestions for modifying tests and collaborate on grading decisions.

Expectations for Special Educators in Delivering Instruction

● If possible, share teaching responsibilities and present lessons.

● During class, walk around the room and provide assistance to students, monitor student work, and provide feedback regarding student performance.

● Provide more intensive support to students who need it.

Expectations for Special Educators in Classroom Management

● Consistently and actively reinforce standards for positive behavior.

● Take an active role in developing and implementing classroom routines.

● Consistently praise students.

● Feel free to intervene when behavioral problems arise during class.

● During conflict situations, either take over the class or leave class with the students involved in the conflict.

Things General Educators Say They Need to Work On

● Provide the special educator with resources related to content.

● Open avenues of communication by being receptive and taking risks.

● Try to prepare instruction at least two weeks in advance.

● Offer a time to meet to discuss activities.

● Create opportunities for the special educator to lead instruction.

● Share responsibility and power in the classroom.

● Make it clear to students that the teachers in the class are equals.

● Ask for and use the special educator's ideas, opinions, and creativity.

● Try to remember the importance and value of different perspectives.

● Create a work space in the classroom for the special education teacher.

SOURCE: Adapted from "Clarifying Collaborative Roles in Urban High Schools: General Educators' Perspectives," by C. Murray, (2004), *Teaching Exceptional Children, 36*(5), pp. 44–51.

member, you will contribute. Your principal assigned the activity; *you* decided to collaborate. Because collaboration is voluntary, teachers often form close but informal collaborative partnerships with colleagues whether or not collaboration is a school-wide ethic.

COLLABORATION IS BASED ON PARITY ● Teachers who collaborate must believe that all individual contributions are equally valued. The number and nature of particular professionals' contributions may vary greatly, but all participants need to recognize that what they offer is integral to the collaborative effort. If you are at a meeting concerning highly complex student needs, you might feel you have nothing to offer. However, you have important information about how the student responds in your class and the progress the student has made in developing peer relationships. The technical discussion of the student's disabilities is not your area of expertise, nor should it be; your ideas are valued because of your knowledge and skills related to teaching in your classroom. As you read Working Together below, think of how the concept of parity applies to your interactions with related services personnel such as speech/language therapists and physical therapists.

COLLABORATION REQUIRES A SHARED GOAL ● Teachers truly collaborate only when they share a goal. For example, if a fifth-grade teacher and a special educator want to design a behavior intervention to help support a student with an emotional disability, their goal is clear. They can pool their knowledge and resources and jointly plan the intervention. However, if one teacher wants the student to spend more time in a special education setting and the other opposes that solution, they are unlikely to work collaboratively on this issue. The teachers might even think at the outset that they share a goal—assisting the student—but that broad statement does not capture their differing views of how the student can best be assisted. They need to resolve this difference for collaboration to occur.

COLLABORATION INCLUDES SHARED RESPONSIBILITY FOR KEY DECISIONS ● Although teachers may divide the work necessary to complete a collaborative teaching or teaming project, they should share as equal partners the fundamental decision making about the activities they are undertaking. This shared responsibility reinforces the sense of parity that exists among the teachers. In the behavior intervention example, the teachers share decisions about what the key problems are, what strategies might work, the length of time for trying an intervention, and the impact of the intervention on the student. However, if they assign many tasks to just one person, they are not truly collaborating. Instead, one may ask the school psychologists for ideas, review a book of behavior intervention ideas, and talk to last year's teacher. The

ANALYZE
AND **REFLECT**

If you are required to work with special education teachers and other colleagues, how can collaboration be voluntary? Why is the concept of voluntariness so important as you think about your responsibilities as a teacher for creating partnerships with your colleagues?

DIMENSIONS
OF **DIVERSITY**

Think about cultural differences. How might these differences enhance or constrain collaboration? What can you do to ensure that multicultural collaboration is successful?

WORKING **TOGETHER**

Collaborating with Related Services Personnel

Although the professionals with whom you most often collaborate probably will be special education teachers, you also may work closely with related services personnel. The following are some points to keep in mind when working with speech/language therapists, physical therapists, adaptive physical educators, and other related services providers:

● Related services professionals often serve students in several schools and may have difficulty adhering to schedules. Be respectful of their time by preparing your questions and concerns prior to meetings and trying to keep within the time frame for the session.

● If a related services professional completes an observation in your classroom, try to arrange a short meeting afterward. Face-to-face communication often can be more ef-

fective and efficient than follow-up e-mail or other written communication.

● Some related services professionals may not have a complete grasp of the expectations you have for students in your general education classroom. Help them to understand what types of activities your students complete, whether students with disabilities are experiencing difficulty, and how they can assist you.

● If one of your students receives related services outside the classroom, ask for updates so that you can provide follow-up in the classroom and report any difficulties that you notice.

● In some situations, related services professionals who travel from school to school feel like they are not truly members of any school team. Help them feel welcome in your classroom and school.

other may call the parents to seek their input, interview the student, and prepare any needed materials, such as a behavior chart.

COLLABORATION INCLUDES SHARED ACCOUNTABILITY FOR OUT-COMES ● This characteristic of collaboration follows directly from shared responsibility; that is, if teachers share key decisions, they also must share accountability for the results of the decisions, whether those results are positive or negative. If both the teachers carry out their assigned tasks, the behavior intervention they design will have a high probability of success. If one fails to carry out a responsibility, valuable time is lost and their shared effort is less successful. If something happens that is just wonderful (for example, the student's behavior changes dramatically in a positive direction), the teachers share the success. If something happens that is not so wonderful (for example, the intervention appears to have no impact on the behaviors of concern), they share the need to change their plans.

COLLABORATION IS BASED ON SHARED RESOURCES ● Each teacher participating in a collaborative effort contributes some type of resource. This contribution increases commitment and reinforces each professional's sense of parity. Resources may include time, expertise, space, equipment, and other assets. The teachers working on the behavior intervention contribute the time needed to make necessary plans, but they also pool their knowledge of working with students with behavior difficulties, share information about other professionals who might assist them, and contribute student access to the computer and other rewards they design.

COLLABORATION IS EMERGENT ● Collaboration is based on a belief in the value of shared decision making, trust, and respect among participants. However, although these qualities are needed to some degree at the outset of collaborative activities, they are not mature in a new collaborative relationship. As teachers become more experienced at collaboration, their interactions become characterized by the trust and respect that grow within successful collaborative relationships. If the teachers described throughout this section have worked together for several years, they may share freely, including offering constructive criticism to each other. If this is their first collaborative effort, they are much more likely to be a bit guarded and polite because each is unsure how the other person will respond.

Prerequisites for Collaboration

Creating collaborative relationships requires effort on everyone's part. Most professionals who have close collaborative working relationships note that it is hard work to collaborate—but worth every minute of the effort. They also emphasize that collaboration gets better with experience; when colleagues are novices at co-teaching or working on teams, their work seems to take longer and everyone has to be especially careful to respect others' points of view. However, with additional collaboration, everyone's comfort level increases, honesty and trust grow, and a sense of community develops. Here are some essential ingredients that foster the growth of collaboration.

REFLECTING ON YOUR PERSONAL BELIEF SYSTEM ● The first ingredient for collaboration is your personal beliefs. How much do you value sharing ideas with others? Would you prefer to work with someone to complete a project, even if it takes more time that way, or do you prefer to work alone? If your professor in this course offered the option of a small-group exam, would you be willing to receive a shared grade with your classmates? If your responses to these questions suggest that you prefer working with others, you probably will find professional collaboration exciting and re-

ANALYZE
AND **REFLECT**

Think about a field experience in which you have participated or about your current teaching job. How does each of the characteristics of collaboration apply to it? When is it worth the time and effort to collaborate and when is it not?

warding. If your responses are just the opposite, you might find collaboration somewhat frustrating. For collaboration to occur, all people participating need to feel that their shared effort will result in an outcome that is better than could be accomplished by any one participant (Friend, 2000). They also must believe that a shared effort has value, even if the result is somewhat different from what each person envisioned at the outset (Friend, 2000; McLaughlin, 2002).

Part of examining your belief system also concerns your understanding of and respect for others' belief systems. This tolerance is especially important for your collaborative efforts with special educators in inclusive programs. For example, what are your beliefs about changing your teaching practices so that a student with disabilities can achieve the standards for your curriculum? You might at first say that changing your teaching practices is no problem, but when you reflect on the consequence of that belief, you might have second thoughts. For example, changing your practices means that you must give alternative assignments to students needing them, that you must deliberately change the way you present information and the way you expect students to learn that information, and that you must grade students with disabilities differently than other students. The special educators with whom you work are likely to believe strongly not only that alternative teaching practices are helpful in inclusive settings but that they are a requirement. How will you respond when you meet a colleague with this belief? Similarly, what if three teachers in your department are strongly opposed to alternative teaching practices for students with disabilities? Will you debate the matter with them and hold your beliefs, or will you feel pressured to compromise? Teachers everywhere have faced these issues. However, in schools in which collaboration is stressed, issues such as these tend to become more apparent and the need to resolve them more intense. Further, as collaboration becomes more integral to public schools, learning to value others' opinions and to disagree respectfully with them while maintaining a positive working relationship becomes more and more essential.

REFINING YOUR INTERACTION SKILLS ●

The second ingredient you can contribute to school collaboration is effective skills for interacting. In many ways, interaction skills are the fundamental building blocks on which collaboration is based because collaboration occurs through our interactions with others (Friend & Cook, 2004). There are two major types of interaction skills: communication skills and steps to productive interactions. You already may have learned about the first type, communication skills, in a public-speaking or communication course. These skills include listening, attending to nonverbal signals, and asking questions and making statements in clear and nonthreatening ways (Hollingsworth, 2001). They also include paralanguage, such as your tone of voice and your use of comments like "uh-huh" and "ok." Additional information about communication skills is included in the Professional Edge on page 80.

The other type of interaction skill comprises the steps that make interactions productive. Have you ever been in a meeting and thought that the same topic was being discussed repeatedly? Perhaps you wished someone would say, "I think we've covered this; let's move on." Or have you ever tried to problem solve with classmates or friends only to realize that every time someone generated an idea, someone else began explaining why the idea could not work? In both instances, the frustration occurred because of a problem in the interaction process, that is, the steps that characterize an interaction. The most needed interaction process for you as a teacher is shared problem solving (Knotek, 2003; Wallace, Anderson, & Bartholomay, 2002). Other interaction-process skills include conducting effective meetings, responding to resistance, resolving conflict, and persuading others.

You need both types of interaction skills for collaboration to occur. If you are highly skilled in communicating effectively but cannot contribute to get an interaction

Collaboration includes a shared goal, shared decision making, shared accountability, and parity. Why are these characteristics important?

CONNECTIONS

Students experience many of the elements of adult collaboration through cooperative learning, a topic discussed in Chapter 13. This chapter's focus is adult interactions.

PROFESSIONAL EDGE

Barriers to Effective Communication

Effective communication is essential for professional collaboration. Here are some barriers to communication that teachers and administrators must overcome. Which might apply to you?

- *Advice.* When you offer unsolicited advice to a colleague or parent, that person may be confused by your intent, may reject the advice and form an unfavorable opinion of you, or may feel obligated to follow it even if it seems inappropriate. In general, advice should be offered only when it is sought.

- *False reassurances.* If you offer parents or colleagues false reassurances about student achievement, behavior issues, or social skills, you are damaging your own credibility and setting the stage for additional future issues. Being truthful is the best strategy, even if you are concerned that a difficult situation may result.

- *Wandering interaction.* As another person communicates with you, it is sometimes easy to drift to peripheral topics that waste valuable time. For example, discussing a student's soccer team when the concern is academic performance is a distraction that may reflect avoidance of the key issues.

- *Interruptions.* When you interact with others, they are entitled to your full attention. When you are buzzed on the intercom or called to the door, you should politely decline until your interaction is concluded. During an interaction, it also is important to avoid interrupting others. Especially when the person speaking has a language pattern that is slower than yours, you may have to make a concerted effort to wait until the person finishes speaking before adding your contribution.

- *Being judgmental.* If you tend to speak in absolutes (for example, "The only way to resolve this is to . . . " or "I don't see any way for him to complete the work . . . "), you may be perceived as a professional who sees only one right answer. One outcome may be that others minimize their conversation with you because they view it as futile.

- *One-way communication.* Communication is most effective when it involves all participants. If one person monopolizes the interaction, the others' points of view are not represented and any decisions made are likely to be questioned later.

- *Fatigue.* If you are so tired that you cannot accurately follow the thread of a conversation, your communication will be impaired. You may misspeak or misunderstand others' messages. In such cases, it may be best to request that the interaction be rescheduled.

- *Hot words or phrases.* In some communities and in some schools, certain words are "hot." For example, even the word *inclusion* sometimes is considered controversial. For productive interactions, such words (or even suspected words or phrases) are best avoided.

Do any of these barriers sound familiar? What examples of each can you and your classmates generate relating to your own communication experiences in internships or field experiences? What could you do to decrease the likelihood that these barriers will occur in your interactions with colleagues and parents?

SOURCE: Adapted from "Communication in Interprofessional Collaboration" (Chap. 6, pp. 91–115), by M. P. Mostert, 1998, in *Interprofessional Collaboration in Schools,* Boston: Allyn and Bacon. Copyright 1998 by Allyn and Bacon. Adapted by permission.

from its beginning to its end, others will be frustrated. Likewise, even though you know the steps in shared problem solving, if you speak to others as though you know all the answers, they will withdraw from the interaction.

CONTRIBUTING TO A SUPPORTIVE ENVIRONMENT ● The third ingredient for successful collaboration is a supportive environment (Pugach & Johnson, 2002). As a teacher, you will contribute to this atmosphere through your personal belief system and interaction skills, but this environment includes other items as well. For example, most professionals working in schools that value collaboration comment on the importance of administrative support. Principals play an important role in fostering collaboration (da Costa, Marshall, & Riordan, 1998; DiPaola & Walther-Thomas, 2003; Sanders & Harvey, 2002).

> " Principals play an important role in fostering collaboration. "

They can raise staff awareness of collaboration by making it a school goal and distributing information about it to staff. They can reward teachers for their collaborative efforts. They can urge teachers who are uncomfortable with collaboration to learn more about it and to experiment in small-scale collaborative projects, and they can include collaboration as part of staff evaluation procedures. When principals do not actively nurture collaboration among staff, collaborative activities are more limited, more informal, and less a part of the school culture. If you work in this type of school, you may find that you collaborate with specific teachers but that your efforts are considered a luxury or a frill and are not rewarded or otherwise fostered.

Another component of a supportive environment is the availability of time for collaboration (Akins, Parkinson, & Reeder, 2002; Zimmerman & Grier, 2003). It is not enough that each teacher has a preparation period; shared planning time also needs to be arranged. In many middle schools, shared planning occurs as part of the middle school team planning period. In other schools, substitute teachers are employed periodically so that classroom teachers and special services staff can meet. In some school districts, "early-release" or "late-arrival" days are used; once each week or month, students are dismissed in the early afternoon or arrive later in the morning. Teachers use the time created to plan instructional units, confer about student problems, and attend professional development activities.

As a teacher, you will find that time is an important issue (Rose, 2001). The number of tasks you need to complete during available preparation time will be greater than the number of minutes available. The time before and after school will be filled with faculty meetings, meetings with parents, preparation, bus duty, and other assignments. You can help yourself maximize time for collaboration if you keep several things in mind. First, it may be tempting to spend the beginning of a shared planning time discussing the day's events or comparing notes on some school activity. But if you engage in lengthy social conversation, you are taking away time from your planning. A trick discovered by teachers in collaborative schools is to finish the business at hand first and then to chat about personal and school events if time is left. Second, because you never truly have enough time to accomplish all that you would like to as a teacher, you must learn to prioritize. You have to choose whether collaborating about a certain student or teaching a certain lesson is justified based on the needs of students and the time available. Not everything can be collaborative, but when collaboration seems appropriate, time should be allocated for it.

What Are Effective Applications of Collaboration in Schools That Foster Inclusion?

The basic principles of collaboration are your guides to many types of partnerships in schools. These partnerships may involve other classroom teachers, special education teachers, support staff such as speech therapists or counselors, paraprofessionals, parents, and others. Collaboration sometimes extends even beyond the classroom and becomes electronic, as illustrated in the Technology Notes on page 82. Four of the most common collaborative activities concerning students with disabilities are shared problem solving, co-teaching, teaming, and consultation.

Shared Problem Solving

Shared problem solving is the basis for many of the collaborative activities school professionals undertake on behalf of students with disabilities (Rubinson, 2002; Johnson &

> TECHNOLOGY NOTES

Electronic Collaboration

Collaboration traditionally has been thought of as the way in which professionals interact when they are face to face or perhaps on the phone. However, more and more collaboration is occurring on the Internet, enabling professionals from all over the country and other countries as well to share ideas, ask questions, and provide support to others.

One of the most comprehensive web resources for learning to use electronic tools to interact with other professionals is *Electronic Collaboration: A Practical Guide for Educators* (http://www.alliance.brown.edu/pubs/collab/elec-collab.pdf). Developed by the Northeast and Islands Regional Educational Laboratory at Brown University, (LAB), the National School Network, and the Teacher Enhancement Electronic Community Hall through a project funded by the U.S. Department of Education, the downloadable guide provides an explanation of what electronic collaboration is, a rationale for participating in electronic collaboration, sites with discussion groups, tools for electronic collaboration, and strategies for creating vehicles for electronic collaboration. For example, the guide discusses the use of videoconferencing as a means of collaborating, and it presents a range of websites for collaborating with other educators.

Other sites also foster electronic collaboration. The Partnership for Family Involvement in Education, at http://www.ed.gov/pubs/whoweare/index.html, a federally funded website for parents and families designed to help them get more involved in their children's education. The site directs parents to links for building partnerships, for seeking information about what is new in education, and for learning about publications and activities of the organization. The website is open to everyone interested in building family–school collaboration, and it includes many resources for using technology for collaboration.

Special Needs Opportunity Windows (SNOW), at http://snow.utoronto.ca, is a Canadian initiative to support teachers and others working with students with special needs. The site includes not only curriculum materials and other resources but also a discussion forum where ed-

Electronic Collaboration

A practical guide for educators.

ucators can meet and share concerns and ideas and bulletin boards for posting ideas.

At A to Z Teacher Stuff (http://forums.atozteacherstuff.com), you can join any of several discussion forums concerning students with special needs or issues related to them. For example, recent postings include advice on managing time, responding to the needs of students with autism, and dealing with back-to-school night. This website also includes a discussion forum for classroom discipline problems.

If you explore the Internet, you will undoubtedly find other sites that focus on electronic collaboration. These sites can give you fresh ideas, basic knowledge, and a broader understanding of how you and others can make a profound difference in the lives of students with disabilities. They also can help you to connect with colleagues from across the country and around the world who have similar interests and questions.

Pugach, 2002). Although shared problem solving sometimes occurs when a classroom teacher and a special education teacher meet to decide on appropriate modifications or other interventions for a student, it occurs in many other contexts, too. For example, as you read the applications that follow, you will find that some variation of shared problem solving exists in each. This happens because one way of thinking about co-teaching, teaming, and consultation is as specialized problem-solving approaches.

You might be wondering why problem solving is such a critical topic for professional partnerships. In fact, you may consider yourself already adept at problem solving, because it is an ongoing responsibility of educators. However, as many authors have noted (for example, Friend & Cook, 2003; Johnson & Pugach, 2002), when professionals problem solve together the process is much more complex than when educators problem solve alone because the needs, expectations, and ideas of each participant must be blended into shared understandings and mutually agreed-on solutions. Successful shared problem solving requires skilled participants.

DISCOVER A SHARED NEED ● The starting point for problem solving is discovering a shared need, which demonstrates the complexity of shared problem solving. If you face a problem that concerns only you, you try to resolve it by yourself. When you problem solve with colleagues and parents, all participants need to perceive that a problem exists. Further, it is important that all participants believe that they can have an impact on the problem, that they feel accountable for the results of problem solving, and that they can contribute constructively to resolving the problem. When these conditions exist, shared problem solving results in a high level of commitment, as might be the case when you collaborate with your school's library media specialist to find appropriate learning materials and activities for one of your students with disabilities, a topic discussed in the Special Emphasis On . . . feature below. When these

Special EMPHASIS On . . .

Collaboration between School Library Media Specialists and Teachers

If you are a preservice teacher, you will sometimes find that you are looking for new ideas for reaching students with disabilities and other special needs. If you are studying to be a school library media specialist, you may be thinking, "That's exactly what I can help to accomplish!" In fact, the collaboration that occurs between teachers and school library media specialists often can result in more appropriate materials and resources for all students and in better student outcomes. The following are some suggestions for media specialists to use to foster collaboration with teachers:

- Begin by establishing a relationship with just one teacher and developing effective collaborative projects. Successful examples of librarian–teacher collaboration can become contagious, creating a demand for other such experiences throughout the school. Success breeds success.
- Be open and friendly with teachers. Seek them out—they are not going to come looking for you. A proactive library media specialist is a critical prerequisite to successful collaboration.
- Volunteer to do staff development workshops on technology. This helps to establish your credibility as an instructor and your expertise in a valuable area for potential collaboration.
- Develop administrator support for flexible scheduling and collaborative planning. Administrator support can make a big difference in how hard or easy it is to create cooperative relationships with teachers.
- Sit in on team or grade-level meetings or other planning sessions.
- Study classroom and hallway bulletin boards; find out what is happening and think of ways you might collaborate.
- Offer to be in class the day a teacher assigns a research project, to give a research pep talk.

How might each of these suggestions help teachers to educate all the students in their classrooms, including those with disabilities and other special needs? If you have the opportunity, ask a media specialist about collaborating in an inclusive school.

SOURCE: Adapted from "Developing a Collaborative Culture," by R. V. Small (2004), *School Library Media Research*, Editor's Choice Resources, Best of ERIC. Retrieved September 30, 2004, from http://www.ala.org/ala/aasl/aaslpubsandjournals/slmrb/editorschoiceb/bestoferic/besteric.htm.

Effective teams can be found throughout society. How are teams such as this one similar to the teams of school professionals?

RESEARCH
N O T E

A recent study of parents' perceptions found that parents valued both the quantity and quality of communication from educators, a sense of educators' commitment to the welfare of their children as students, a feeling of equality in power, trust, and respect (Blue-Banning et al., 2004).

conditions do not exist, shared problem solving is not shared at all and may appear one-sided, with some participants trying to convince others to contribute. For example, many teachers report that they have been unable to enlist parents' help in resolving discipline problems. They then go on to describe meetings with parents in which school personnel describe the problem and the parents respond that they do not see such behavior occurring at home. Too often, instead of all parties working to come to a shared understanding of the problem behavior, this type of meeting ends with the parents superficially agreeing to assist in a problem they do not believe exists and the school professionals perceiving the parents as only marginally supportive. The dilemma can be avoided if more effort is made to identify a shared need to problem solve (Blue-Banning, Summers, Frankland, Nelson, & Beegle, 2004).

IDENTIFY THE PROBLEM ● Research on problem solving suggests that the most critical step in the process is problem identification (Rodgers-Rhyme & Volpiansky, 1991). However, when educators meet to share problem solving, they often feel pressured because of time constraints; hence, they rush through this essential stage. Experts suggest that up to half of the time available for problem solving should be devoted to this step (Bergan & Tombari, 1975; Friend & Cook, 2003). Problem identification includes gathering information, compiling it, analyzing it, and reaching consensus about the nature of a student's problem.

In a shared problem-solving situation, you can help emphasize the importance of problem identification by asking whether everyone has agreed on the problem, by asking someone else to restate the problem to check your understanding of it, and by encouraging participants who have not spoken to share their opinions. Consider the following situation, which shows what can happen when problem identification is not done correctly: A teacher in a shared problem-solving session says to the parent of a student whose attendance is irregular and who consistently comes to school without assignments or basic supplies, "We really need your help in making sure Rickie gets up when his alarm goes off so he can catch the bus. And we'd like to establish a system in which you sign off on his written assignments." The parent replies, "It's so hard. I work until midnight and I don't get up when it's time for the kids to go to school. I don't think he sees any point in the homework he's getting—that's why he doesn't bring it back." In this situation, the educator has identified the problem before the meeting has even started: Rickie needs to assume responsibility, and his parents need to provide more guidance for school activities. Furthermore, the teacher is proposing a solution to the problem and not exploring the problem itself. The parent's response suggests that the parent does not see the same problem; in fact, the parent is implying that perhaps the problem belongs not to Rickie at all but to the school staff.

Consider how this interaction could have been handled alternatively: The teacher says to the parent, "Ms. Trenton, thanks so much for taking time off work to meet with us. We appreciate your concern for Rickie. Lately, we've seen a problem with Rickie's attendance. We asked you to come to school so we can learn about your perspective on this situation and to let Rickie know that we're working together to help him." When the parent replies with the comment about her working hours and Rickie's perception of the homework, the teacher replies, "That's important information for us. We're hoping we can find ways to motivate Rickie to come to school—and that includes assigning homework that he sees as valuable." In this situation, the school professionals are working with the parent to identify the problem, not presenting the problem to her.

PROPOSE SOLUTIONS ● Once a problem has been clearly identified, the next step is to create a wide range of options for solving the problem. One of the most common ways to come up with solutions is to *brainstorm*. Brainstorming is based on two important principles. First, judgment is deferred; that is, to free the mind to be creative, people must suspend their predisposition to judge ideas. Second, quantity leads to quality; that is, the more ideas that are generated for solving a problem, the more likely it is that novel and effective solutions can be found. Brainstorming requires openness and creativity. The fourth-grade team you read about at the beginning of this chapter was engaged in proposing solutions. What other solutions might they have generated if they had stressed brainstorming principles?

EVALUATE IDEAS ● With a list of ideas, the next step in shared problem solving is to evaluate the ideas by considering whether they seem likely to resolve the problem and whether they are feasible. One way to evaluate ideas is to use a decision sheet like that illustrated in Figure 3.1. On this decision sheet, the participants listed the problem—encouraging Angela to work independently on classroom tasks—and generated

FIGURE 3.1 A Sample Decision-Making Sheet for Problem Solving

Problem Statement: How can we encourage Angela to work independently on assigned classroom tasks?

Ideas:

Tape-record instructions	~~Don't give independent work~~
Have an assigned "study buddy"	Let her choose the assignment
Make the work easier	~~Make her stay in from recess to~~
Use pictures for directions	~~complete work~~
Ask a parent volunteer to help	Give her frequent breaks

Decision Making: (3 = high, 2 = medium, 1 = low)

Criteria

Idea	Angela will work for at least 5 minutes	Time commitment is reasonable for teacher	Idea does not disrupt class routine	Total	Rank
1. Taped instructions	3	1	2	6	
2. Study buddy	3	3	3	9	1
3. Easier work	2	2	2	6	
4. Picture directions	3	2	3	8	2
5. Parent volunteer	1	3	2	6	
6. Choose assignment	1	2	1	4	
7. Frequent breaks	2	2	2	6	

ideas for achieving this goal. They then selected criteria by which to judge the merits of each idea. They considered the following:

- how well the idea would work for increasing the amount of time Angela spends on her independent assignments
- the extent to which the idea has a reasonable time cost
- the extent to which the idea preserves classroom routines

Ideas not seriously considered were crossed out, and the criteria for decision making were applied to those remaining, with each idea being rated against each criterion. In Figure 3.1, the two ideas with the highest rating were assigning a study buddy and using picture directions.

PLAN SPECIFICS ● Once one or two ideas are chosen using a process such as the one just described, more detailed planning needs to occur. For example, if you and others have decided that you would like to try having a high school service club provide volunteer tutoring in an after-school program, some of the tasks to assign include asking club members about their interests, arranging a place for the program, ensuring that needed supplies are available, obtaining permission to operate the program, establishing a schedule for students, determining who will provide adult supervision and scheduling it, advertising the program, and creating and conducting training sessions for the tutors.

Typically, at this step of shared problem solving, not only do participants list the major tasks that need to be completed to implement the solution, but they also decide who will take responsibility for each task. They also specify a timeline for completing all the tasks and usually decide how long to implement the solution before meeting to evaluate its effectiveness.

IMPLEMENT THE SOLUTION ● If all the steps in the shared problem-solving process have been carefully followed, implementing the selected idea(s) may be the most straightforward part of the process. When problem solving occurs concerning a student with a disability in an inclusive school, each team member may have some responsibility for implementing the solution. Occasionally, you will have much of the immediate responsibility. In other cases, parents will have a major role to play. Each person involved must do his or her part so that the solution has a high probability of success. During implementation, it is helpful to keep some type of record documenting your efforts and the impact of the intervention on the student.

> If all the steps in the shared problem-solving process have been carefully followed, implementing the selected idea may be the most straightforward part of the process.

EVALUATE OUTCOMES ● After a period of time—anywhere from just a few days to two or more weeks—the professionals who are implementing the solution meet to evaluate its effectiveness. At this time, three possibilities exist. First, if the solution has been especially effective, it may be judged a success. It then will be continued to maintain the results, discontinued if no longer needed, or gradually phased out. Second, if the solution seems to be having a positive effect but is not ideal for some other reason, it may be modified. For example, a behavior management plan may be helping a student attend class rather than skip it, but the classroom teacher notes that the system is too time-consuming. The problem-solving group then may try to streamline the plan to make it more feasible. Finally, even when the steps in problem solving are carefully completed, a solution occasionally is judged ineffective. The team then must decide what to do next: Should a different solution be selected from the list already generated? Should additional solutions be proposed? Is the problem accurately identified? The team needs to consider all these possibilities before additional problem solving occurs.

Professionals who regularly employ the strategies of shared problem solving are quick to acknowledge that the steps do not automatically lead to simple solutions that always work. However, they report that when they problem solve in this fashion, they perceive that their professional time is well spent and that the problem-solving process is truly a collaborative endeavor.

Co-Teaching

Co-teaching occurs when two or more educators—one a general education teacher and the other a special education teacher or other specialist—share the instruction for a single group of students, typically in a single classroom setting (Friend & Cook, 2003). Although any two teachers can teach together—and this sometimes occurs at elementary, middle, and high schools—we focus here on the unique arrangement of two professionals with potentially very different points of view working together on behalf of all the students in a class, the type of arrangement that Ms. Godina and Mr. MacLean, introduced at the beginning of the chapter, have in their classroom.

Co-teaching is becoming a very popular service delivery option in inclusive schools (Morocco & Aguilar, 2002; Murawski & Dieker, 2004). In a classroom with several students with disabilities, combining the strengths of the general education teacher and a special educator can create options for all students (Friend & Cook, 2003). Co-teaching typically occurs for a set period of time either every day (for example, every morning from 9:30 until 10:15) or on certain days of the week (for example, on Mondays and Wednesdays during third period or second block). Occasionally, especially in middle and high schools, a group of students with disabilities who used to attend a separate class for a specific subject might join a general education class permanently. In such cases, the special education teacher may be available every day. For example, if a school used to have a general science class for students with disabilities, the group of 6 students from that class and their teacher might become members of a general education biology class of 22 students. One other strategy for co-teaching is to have a special education teacher and a classroom teacher share instruction for a particular unit, often one that many students find difficult (for example, changing decimals to fractions). After the unit is completed, the co-teaching is stopped until another specific need arises.

Effective as co-teaching is when carefully implemented, it is not the answer for every student with a disability or for every classroom in an inclusive school. Co-teaching is only one option for meeting the needs of students (Friend & Cook, 2004). It should be reserved for situations when the number of students with disabilities in a class justifies the presence of two teachers, or the class is one in which all students with disabilities enroll (for example, a high school U.S. history class).

Many approaches are available to teachers who decide to co-teach (Dieker, 2001; Weiss & Lloyd, 2002, 2003). Friend and Cook (2003) have outlined some of the common ones, which are depicted in Figure 3.2.

ONE TEACH, ONE OBSERVE ● In this approach, one teacher leads the lesson and the other gathers data on students to understand them better and to make instructional decisions. For example, while Ms. Tran, the general education teacher, leads a lesson in which students work in cooperative groups to answer questions about a map, Ms. Firestone, the special education teacher, may systematically observe three students who are known to struggle with social skills. Ms. Firestone may note on a chart the number of times those students initiate an interaction with a peer, as well as how often other students direct comments or questions to them. How may this information be helpful to the teachers? Teachers can observe students' ability to pay attention, to work independently, to make productive use of spare time, and to seek assistance when they have questions. However this approach is used, it is essential that each educator sometimes take the primary teaching role in the class while the other observes. In this way, both

DIMENSIONS OF DIVERSITY

Co-teaching can enhance education for many students. For example, at the website of the Association for Supervision and Curriculum Development (http://www.ascd.org), you can read an article by Kathy Checkley about the increasing use of co-teaching to reach students who are English-language learners.

RESEARCH NOTE

In high school co-teaching, the role of the special educator varies considerably, from providing general support to students, to teaching all students part of the content being covered, to closely teaming with the general educator (Weiss & Lloyd, 2002).

FIGURE 3.2 Co-teaching Approaches

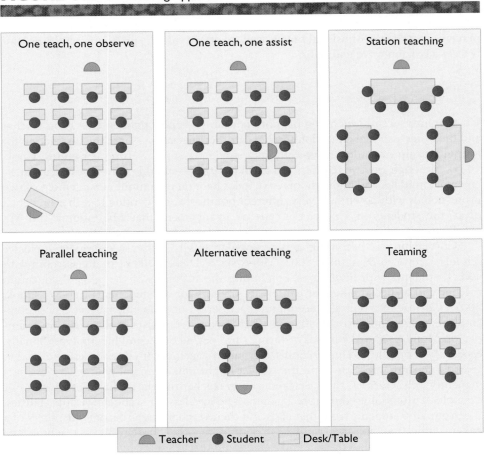

teachers have the opportunity to watch the class "in action," and both have credibility with students as a result of leading instruction.

ONE TEACH, ONE ASSIST ● Occasionally during instruction, one teacher can be appropriately leading the lesson while the other quietly assists individual students. For example, while the special education teacher leads a lesson on a test review, the classroom teacher helps students individually as they have questions about the vocabulary. Alternatively, while the classroom teacher leads a lesson on the causes of World War II, the special education teacher helps keep students on task, checks written work as it is being completed, and responds quietly to student questions. The key to using this approach successfully is to make it only one out of many approaches you use. With overuse, one of the teachers, often the special educator, may perceive that he or she has no legitimate role in the class and functions mostly like a teaching assistant. In addition, if this approach to co-teaching is used too frequently, students may become overdependent on the extra help that always seems to be available.

STATION TEACHING ● This approach is similar to the concept of stations found in many kindergarten and first-grade classes. In *station teaching*, curricular content is divided into two parts. One teacher teaches half the content to half the students while the other teaches the other half to the rest. The groups then switch, and each teacher repeats his or her part of the lesson. With classes of students who are able to work inde-

CONNECTIONS

In Chapters 8, 9, 10, and 11, you will be introduced to a wide variety of instructional strategies to use as you co-teach. Co-teaching requires two components: effective arrangement of teachers and students and effective instructional practices.

pendently, a third group may be formed in which students work alone or with learning partners who tutor each other on a review assignment. Alternatively, a parent volunteer may provide instruction at a third station. In elementary schools, an entire lesson based on stations may be completed in a single day; in secondary schools, a station may take an entire class period or more. For example, in a ninth-grade math class, some of the students are working with the general education teacher to learn one method for solving quadratic equations. A second group is meeting with the special education teacher to learn an alternative method. A third group of students is working in pairs on an assignment. Each station lasts an entire class period.

PARALLEL TEACHING ● Sometimes when two teachers are present, they find it advantageous simply to divide a heterogeneous class group and have each teacher instruct half the class separately. In this format, called *parallel teaching*, every student has twice as many opportunities to participate in a discussion or respond to teacher questions. A teacher particularly skilled in presenting information through pictures can use this approach while the other teacher emphasizes learning through listening. Students who prefer one method to the other can be placed with the appropriate teacher. In an elementary school classroom, this approach may be used to enable students to read different books based on their interests or possibly skill levels. In a secondary classroom, this approach may give students more opportunities to respond during a discussion of a current-events topic.

ALTERNATIVE TEACHING ● In many classrooms, having one teacher work with most of the class in one large group while the other teacher focuses attention on a small group is sometimes appropriate. This co-teaching option is referred to as *alternative teaching*. Traditionally, the small group has been used for remediation, but many other options are recommended. For example, some students may benefit from preteaching. In preteaching, one teacher works with a small group of students who may struggle to learn (whether or not they have IEPs), who are shy, or who are just learning to speak English. Information to be presented the next day or later in the same day or class is taught to these students so that when questions are asked or vocabulary introduced, the students have a "jump start" on learning.

Enrichment also works well in small groups. For example, as a unit of instruction on space exploration is concluding, several students may have a strong interest in the topic. As the other students review and complete assigned tasks, this group may meet to discuss career opportunities related to the space industry, write letters to obtain more information on current U.S. space efforts, or explore websites on related topics. The members in this group could include high-achieving students, students who have average academic achievement but a strong interest in space topics, a student with a behavior disorder who would benefit more from this activity than from the assigned work, and a student with a moderate intellectual disability for whom the written task is not appropriate.

Grouping students for remediation is appropriate, but only when it is one among many grouping options and used only occasionally. Otherwise, such an arrangement becomes the equivalent of running a special education program in the back of a general education classroom, an arrangement that completely undermines the purpose and principles of inclusive schooling.

TEAMING ● In the co-teaching option of *teaming*, the teachers share leadership in the classroom; both are equally engaged in the instructional activities. For example, one teacher may begin a lesson by introducing vocabulary while the other provides examples to place the words in context. Two teachers may role-play an important event from history or demonstrate how to complete a lab activity. Two teachers may model how to address conflict by staging a debate about a current event. One teacher may lecture while the other models note-taking strategies on the chalkboard. You reach the

ANALYZE
AND **REFLECT**

Co-teaching is an energizing but complex way of providing services to students in general education classrooms. As you think about yourself as a professional, what aspects of co-teaching would be easy for you? Which might be challenging? What is your responsibility to work out differences with colleagues so that co-teaching is a success?

Co-teaching is an exciting and effective way to provide special services to students with special needs. How can educators best use their collective expertise when they share instruction? What dilemmas might occur, and how can these be resolved?

66 In a co-taught class, students are heterogeneously grouped so that students with disabilities are integrated appropriately with their peers without disabilities. 99

limits of teaming only when you run out of exciting ideas for creating instruction with two teachers instead of one. Co-teachers who use this approach find it the most energizing of all the co-teaching options, but you should also be aware that you and a co-teacher might not be compatible enough in terms of teaching style to use this approach. If that is the case, using the other approaches might be more effective.

CO-TEACHING PRAGMATICS ● As you consider these co-teaching approaches, you might notice that several other factors need to be taken into account in addition to how the teachers arrange themselves and the students (Austin, 2001; Keefe et al., 2004). First, in a co-taught class, students are heterogeneously grouped so that students with disabilities are integrated appropriately with their peers without disabilities. Thus, in a station teaching arrangement, students with special needs are likely to be in each of the three station groups, and when alternative teaching occurs, the smaller group may or may not contain students with disabilities. Second, both teachers take on teaching and supportive roles. This principle is critical if students are to view both teachers as credible; without using it, the special education teacher may be seen as a helper who does not have teacher status. Third, the best approach to use depends on student needs, the subject being taught, the teachers' experience, and practical considerations such as space and time for planning. Novice co-teachers may prefer station teaching or parallel teaching over teaming, especially in a class that includes several students with attention problems who would benefit from a smaller group structure. We make this recommendation because the former approaches require less minute-to-minute coordination with another teacher. Finally, the type of curriculum sometimes dictates the approach. For example, curriculum that is sequential obviously cannot be taught in stations; it may be presented best in a format of one teach, one assist, followed by parallel-taught study groups.

Working on a Team

In Chapter 2, you learned that you have responsibility as a member of an intervention assistance team to problem solve about students before they are considered for special education (Slonski-Fowler & Truscott, 2004). You also learned you may be a member of the multidisciplinary team that determines whether a student is eligible to receive special education services and then writes the student's IEP (Lytle & Bordin, 2001). These teams rely on collaboration among members, and it is important that you understand the concepts and procedures that they and other school teams have that make them effective.

When you think about highly successful teams, what comes to mind? Your favorite athletic team? A surgical team? An orchestra? What is it about these teams that makes them noteworthy? **Teams** are formal work groups that have certain characteristics. They have clear goals, active and committed members, and leaders; they practice to achieve their results; and they do not let personal issues interfere with the accomplishment of their goals. Can you think of other characteristics of effective teams?

The teams you will be part of at school have many of the same characteristics as other kinds of teams (Fleming & Monda-Amaya, 2001; Ormsbee, 2001). Their success depends on the commitment of every member and the clarity of their goals (Hunt, Soto, Maier, & Doering, 2003; Welch, Brownell, & Sheridan, 1999). On effective school teams, members keep in mind why they are a team, setting aside personal differences to reach a goal, that often is to design the best educational strategies possible for students with disabilities or other special needs.

TEAM PARTICIPANT ROLES ● As a team member, you must assume multiple roles. First, you have a *professional role.* In your role as a classroom teacher, you bring a particular perspective to a team interaction, as do the special education teacher, counselor, adaptive physical educator, principal, and other team members (Shapiro & Sayer, 2003). You contribute an understanding of what students without disabilities are accomplishing in your grade or course, knowledge of curriculum and its pace, and a sense of the prerequisites of what you are teaching and the expectations for students likely to follow the next segment of instruction.

The second contribution you make is through your *personal role.* The characteristics that define you as a person shape this role. For example, are you an eternal optimist, a person who sees the positive aspects of almost any situation? If so, you will probably be the person who keeps up the team's morale. Are you a detail-oriented person who is skilled at organizing? If so, you will probably be the team member who ensures that all the tasks get completed and all the paperwork is filed.

Third, you have a *team role* to fulfill as well. You may be the individual who makes sure the agenda is being followed or who watches the time so that team meetings do not last too long. Or you may have the role of summarizing and clarifying others' comments or of suggesting ways to combine what seem to be contradictory points of view into integrated solutions to student problems. As an effective member, you will recognize your strengths and use them to enhance the team; you will also be vigilant so that your weaknesses do not interfere with the team's accomplishing its tasks. Common formal team roles include team facilitator, recorder, and timekeeper. These roles might rotate so that every team member has the opportunity to experience each one. Informal team roles include being a compromiser, an information seeker, and a reality checker. These informal roles are not usually assigned, but team members ensure that they are being fulfilled as the need arises.

TEAM GOALS ● One of the keys to effective teams is attention to goals (Friend & Cook, 2003). Being clear and explicit about goals is particularly important in educational settings because team goals are often assumed or too limited. For example, on some intervention assistance teams, teachers perceive the team goal to be to document interventions so that the special education assessment and identification procedures can begin. Others believe the team functions to help teachers problem solve so that the entire referral process can be avoided. Note how crucial this difference is! In the former case, a team may function as a sort of "confirmation-hearing" process for students with learning and behavior problems. In the latter case, it may be a resource and idea support group. Without clear and specific goals, teams often flounder.

Another aspect of team goals is especially important. The goals just discussed are commonly referred to as *task goals;* that is, they are the business of the team. But teams have another set of goals as well, called maintenance goals. *Maintenance goals* refer to the team's status and functioning as a team. Maintenance goals may include beginning and ending meetings on time, finishing all agenda items during a single meeting, taking time to check on team members' perceptions of team effectiveness, and improving team communication both during meetings and outside of them. These and other maintenance goals enable effective teams to accomplish the task goals they set.

One maintenance goal with which many teams struggle concerns how their meetings are scheduled, structured, and operated. Concerns frequently mentioned include some members' failure to arrive on time, the tendency of some members to wander off the topic, some members' habit of monopolizing the conversation while others seldom say anything, and a pattern of hurrying to finish meetings and in the process making hasty decisions. All these problems can be addressed and often alleviated through team attention to them.

The following example from an elementary school problem-solving meeting shows how each team member plays a vital role. The team included the principal, two general education teachers, a special education teacher, a speech/language therapist, a reading teacher, and a social worker. The reading teacher often spoke a great deal more

**RESEARCH
N O T E**

Each team member plays a crucial role. Knotek (2003) found that decisions about students who were referred to intervention assistance teams were influenced by the social status of team members, comments high-status members made about students, and the way they stated their comments.

W W W
R E S O U R C E S

The Center for Collaborative Organizations at the University of North Texas (http://www.workteams. unt.edu) provides a glimpse into the importance of teams in a wide variety of professions. At this website, you can link to exercises for team building, assessments of your qualities for working on a team, and information on teams operating in specialized contexts. How do these items relate to your profession?

than other team members, talking until others simply nodded their heads in agreement with whatever she wanted. At one team meeting, the reading teacher left early, just after the team had decided to assess a student for possible special education services. No sooner had the teacher left than the team members confronted the principal, explaining that they did not believe the referral for assessment was appropriate and asking the principal to make the reading teacher stop pushing through ideas other team members did not want. The principal made a wise reply. He said, "Wait a minute. If there's a problem, it's a team problem. If a poor decision was made, it was a team decision. It's not 'What am *I* going to do?'; it's 'What are *we* going to do?'"

In the conversation that followed, team members recognized that each of them had a responsibility to speak out when they disagreed with an idea that was presented. They also acknowledged that they were uncomfortable confronting the reading teacher about her interactions during team meetings. However, with the help of the principal, the team spent part of the next meeting talking about each team member's verbal contributions and establishing procedures for checking all team members' perceptions prior to making a decision. Although these actions did not completely change the reading teacher's style, they did bring the team closer together and dramatically increased its effectiveness.

The Case in Practice on page 93 lets you in on another team meeting, this time a problem-solving session that includes two teachers, a counselor, and a parent. Notice how each team member contributes to completing problem-solving steps using recommended communication skills. By doing so, the positive quality of their team effort comes through.

Consultation

In some cases, you may find that you do not have direct support for a student in your classroom. Perhaps the student does not have an identified disability, or perhaps the student's needs can be met with occasional supports. For example, you might have an outgoing student who suddenly begins acting very withdrawn. Or you may learn that for the next school year you will have a student who has a significant hearing impairment; you would like to know how to assist the student and whether you should enroll in a sign-language class. If you have a student with autism in your class, you might find that both you and the special education teacher need assistance from someone else to help the student learn the best ways to transition from activity to activity. These are the types of situations in which you might seek support through consultation (Denton, Hasbrouch, & Sekaquaptewa, 2003; Dole, 2004).

Consultation is a specialized problem-solving process in which one professional who has particular expertise assists another professional (or parent) who needs the benefit of that expertise (Dettmer, Thurston, & Dyck, 2005). For example, you may contact a behavior consultant for assistance when a student in your class is aggressive. You might meet with a vision or hearing consultant when students with those disabilities are included in your class. If you have a student who has received medical or other services outside of school, you may consult with someone from the agency that has been providing those services.

Although consultation is most effective when it is based on the principles of collaboration presented earlier in this chapter, it has a different purpose than collaboration (Schulte & Osborne, 2003). Even though the consultant working with you may learn from you and benefit from the interaction, the goal of the interaction is to help you resolve a problem or deal with a concern, not to foster shared problem solving in which both or all participants share the problem. In consulting, the assumption is that you are experiencing a problem and that the consultant's expertise will enable you to solve the problem more effectively.

The process of consulting generally begins when you as the teacher complete a request form or otherwise indicate that you have a concern about a student (Kampwirth, 2002). The consultant then contacts you to arrange an initial meeting. At that meeting,

CASE IN PRACTICE

A Problem-Solving Meeting

Travis has been experiencing a variety of difficulties in his ninth-grade English class. Although Travis states that he enjoys English, he has not been turning in his homework assignments, even though they are adapted for him. He also tends to be inattentive in class, watching other students and hallway traffic. Lately he has begun talking out whenever he feels like it. Ms. Biernat, the English teacher; Ms. Antovich, the special educator; Mrs. Spence, Travis's mother; and Mr. Crain, Travis's counselor are present at this meeting. They have completed introductions, they have sketched the overall situation, they have mentioned Travis's strengths, and they now are ready to directly address the problem.

Mr. Crain: Given what we've described, Mrs. Spence, I'm wondering what your reaction is.

Mrs. Spence: I don't know. I didn't realize there were all these problems.

Ms. Antovich: That's why we wanted to meet with you in person. This is just not like Travis. I'm sure there is a way to help Travis improve if we all put our heads together to come up with some ideas.

Ms. Biernat: It seems like we should start by looking at the most troublesome area. That's the homework not being turned in. This is affecting Travis's grades because of my grading system. I also know he can do the work. He sometimes comments that it's easy.

Ms. Antovich: I think looking more closely at homework is a good idea. Mrs. Spence, what do you think?

Mrs. Spence: Yes, I'd like to discuss that some more. Travis tells me he has not had homework, and I checked his assignment notebook and none is written in it.

Mr. Crain: So we know that Travis is not writing down assignments in addition to not turning them in. I wonder whether it's the writing down that is the real problem. Because he has such difficulty remembering details, if the assignments aren't written down, he won't remember what he is to do.

Ms. Biernat: I noticed that Travis isn't writing down assignments, but he refuses to accept assistance doing that.

Mr. Crain: I wonder whether we have something else going on here. Maybe this has become a matter of him being embarrassed with the classroom support he receives.

Ms. Antovich: Maybe we should check into a couple of things while we try to get to the bottom of this. I'll talk with Travis privately during his supervised study hall. He's usually pretty open with me. Then maybe we can develop an alternative way for him to get his assignments.

The meeting continues for a few more minutes. Group members generate the idea of giving Travis an inexpensive voice recorder so that he can record his assignments orally instead of writing them. They also consider the option of having another student write the assignments using carbon paper and giving one copy to Travis. Mrs. Spence is concerned that the issue is not the assignments at all but that Travis's new friends, who are somewhat older than he is, are a negative influence on him. They agree to meet again in 2 weeks to continue their conversation.

REFLECTIONS

1. What steps in a shared problem-solving process did this team complete? If you were asked to state succinctly the problem at hand, what would be your response? Is there more than one problem? If so, what are they?

2. Considering the topics that came up at the meeting, what additional information do you think the team needs to make decisions about Travis's work?

3. Travis was not present at this particular meeting. Why not? How could Travis's input be included anyway? How might the meeting have been different with Travis present?

4. What are indicators that the individuals in this interaction used effective communication skills?

5. Consider another problem mentioned that Travis is experiencing in English. Brainstorm ideas for addressing it. Create any additional details you need to complete this exercise (for example, Travis's friends, the time of day he has English).

the problem is further clarified, your expectations are discussed, and often, arrangements are made for the consultant to observe in your room. Once the observation phase has been completed, the consultant and you meet again to finalize your understanding of the problem, generate and select options for addressing it, and plan how to

FYI

Instructional consultation (Gravois, Knotek, & Babinski, 2002) is a specific model for helping classroom teachers to design and implement interventions for students struggling to learn. In this approach, a school psychologist or other professional works intensely with the teacher using recommendations of a team that includes teachers and other service providers, but the teacher is not expected to participate in team meetings.

implement whatever strategies seem needed. A timeline for putting the strategies into effect is also established. Typically, you then carry out the strategies. Following this phase, the consultant and you meet once again to determine whether the problem has been resolved. If it has, the strategy is either continued to maintain the success or eliminated as no longer needed. If the problem continues to exist, the consultant may suggest that you begin a new consulting process, or together you may decide that some other action is needed. When appropriate, the consultant "closes" the case.

For consulting to be effective, both the consultant and the consultee (that is, you as the teacher) need to participate responsibly. Your role includes preparing for meetings, being open to the consultant's suggestions, using the consultant's strategies systematically, and documenting the effectiveness of ideas you try.

How Can You Work Effectively with Parents?

The partnerships presented thus far in this chapter have focused primarily on your interactions with special education teachers and other professionals who will support you in meeting the needs of students with disabilities in your classroom. In this section, we emphasize your working relationship with parents.

The quality of your interactions with the parents of all your students is important, but it is vital with those of your students with disabilities (Blue-Banning et al., 2004). Parents may be able to help you better understand the strengths and needs of their child in your classroom. They also act as advocates for their child, so they can help you ensure that adequate supports are provided for the child's needs. Parents often see their child's experiences in your classroom in a way that you cannot; when they share this information, it helps both you and the student achieve more success. Finally, parents are your allies in educating students; when you enlist their assistance to practice skills at home, to reward a student for accomplishments at school, and to communicate to the child messages consistent with yours, then you and the parents are multiplying the student's educational opportunities and providing a consistency that is essential to maximize student learning.

Understanding the Perspective of Family Members

You might be tempted to assume that because you work with a student with a disability in your classroom on a daily basis, you understand what it would be like to be the student's parent. This assumption could not be further from the truth. For example,

When professionals interact with parents, they should follow the principles of family-centered practices. What does this mean? Why is it especially important for interactions with parents who are from nondominant cultures?

the parent of a high school student with a moderate cognitive disability as well as multiple physical disorders made this comment at a meeting of parents and teachers:

> You see my child in a wheelchair and worry about getting her around the building and keeping her changed. But remember, before you ever see her in the morning, I have gotten her out of bed, bathed her, cleaned her, washed her hair and fixed it, fed her, and dressed her. I have made sure that extra clothes are packed in case she has an accident, and I have written notes to teachers about her upcoming surgery. When she's at school, I worry about whether she is safe, about whether kids fighting in the hall will care for her or injure her, and whether they are kind. And when she comes home, I clean up the soiled clothes, work with her on all the skills she is still learning, make sure that she has companionship and things to do, and then help her get ready for bed. And I wonder what will be the best option for her when she graduates in 3 years. You can't possibly know what it's like to be the parent of a child like my daughter.

As a teacher, you need to realize what this parent so eloquently demonstrated: that you do not understand what it is like to be the parent of a child with a disability unless you too are the parent of a child with a disability. This means that you should strive to recognize that the range of interactions you have with parents is influenced in part by the stresses they are experiencing, their prior dealings with school personnel, and their own beliefs about their child and his or her future. Apply this concept to Chris's parents, Mr. and Mrs. Werner, who were introduced at the beginning of the chapter. What factors might be influencing their interactions with the school professionals? How would knowing about their reluctance to have Chris identified as needing special education and their concerns about the stigma of the learning disability label help the teachers respond appropriately to them?

Parents' Reactions to Their Child's Disability

Parents of children with disabilities have many reactions to their children's special needs, and these reactions may focus on positive or negative factors (Ferguson, 2002). Some parents go through several emotions roughly in a sequence; others may experience only one or several discrete reactions. For some, the reactions may be minor and their approach pragmatic. For others, their child's disability might affect their entire family structure and life. Part of your work with parents includes recognizing that the way parents respond to you may be influenced by any of the following responses to their children's disabilities (Ferguson, 2002):

> ❝ Parents of children with disabilities have many reactions to their children's special needs, and these reactions may focus on positive or negative factors. ❞

CONNECTIONS

In addition to the information in this chapter, ideas for working with parents of students with disabilities are integrated into nearly every chapter of this textbook. For example, to learn about parents of students with specific disabilities and other special needs, see Chapters 6, 7, and 8.

1. *Grief.* Some parents feel grief about their child's disability. Sometimes this is a sorrow for the pain or discomfort that their child may have to experience; sometimes it is sadness for themselves because of the added stress on the family when a child has a disability; and sometimes it is a sense of loss for what the child may not be able to become. Parents have a right to grieve about their child, a right educators should respect.

2. *Ambivalence.* Another reaction parents may have toward their child is ambivalence. This feeling may occur as parents attempt to confirm that the child's disability is not temporary or "fixable," as they try to determine what the best educational options are for their child, and as they ponder how their child will live as an adult. The decisions that parents of children with disabilities have to make are often difficult, and these decisions continue throughout childhood and adolescence, and sometimes through adulthood. Parents often attend meetings with school personnel at which tremendous amounts of information are shared with little time for explanation, and they often meet with representatives from many different disciplines. It is no wonder that they may feel ambivalent.

3. *Optimism.* One of our students was once interviewing the parent of a student with a mild cognitive disability. When asked what it was like having a child with a cognitive disability in the family, the parent replied, "Mary is my child. Just like any other child. I love her as my child. She is sometimes funny and sometimes clever and sometimes naughty. She can really get into trouble. She's just like my other children, except she's Mary." For this parent, her child's special needs are just part of the configuration of needs that the children in any family may have. In this family, the emphasis is on the person, not the disability. There are many families like this one. In these families, the special needs of the child are met without extraordinary reactions. Parents may work diligently to optimize their child's education, and they are hopeful about their child's future. They work closely with educators and others to ensure that the child's life, whatever it may be, is the best one possible.

How parents respond when they have a child with a disability depends on many factors. One is the intensity and complexity of the disability. The reaction of a parent whose child is diagnosed with a learning disability in third grade is likely to be somewhat different from that of parents who learned 2 months after their child was born that she could not see.

Another factor affecting the way parents respond is how the information about the disability is shared with them. When such information is presented in a coldly clinical manner, without adequate sensitivity to the parents' emotions, their response can be quite negative. This is true even for mild disabilities. When one parent was told about her son's learning disability, she said, "Wait a minute. Stop and let me think. Do you realize what you've just said? You've just unraveled my whole way of thinking about my son. What do you mean, a learning disability? What does that mean? Will it ever change? How can you sit there and keep talking as though it's no big thing?" A father related how he learned about his daughter's moderate cognitive disability: A physician simply said, "She's retarded. There's nothing we can do." The father left the office crying, partly because of the information and partly because of the insensitive way in which it had been communicated.

Yet another factor influencing a family's response to a child with a disability is culture (Harry, 2002). In some cultures, disability is a spiritual phenomenon that may reflect a loss of the soul or evidence of transgressions in a previous life. In other families, a child with a disability is considered a reflection on the entire family. In some families, a disability is accepted as just part of who the child is. In others, it is believed that a cure should be sought. It is important to listen to family members as they discuss their child to better understand their perspective on the child as well as their response to ideas and suggestions that you and the rest of the team make.

One other factor that affects parents' responses concerns resources, including financial support (Lott, 2003; Turnbull & Turnbull, 1997). If parents have the resources necessary to provide what they believe is the best set of support services for their child, they are less likely to experience negative emotions. However, when parents know that their child would benefit from some intervention, whether it is surgery, a piece of computer equipment, or tutoring, they are invariably frustrated if they cannot provide that needed support and have difficulty accessing it from school and community resources. Another important resource is personal. In large families, families with many supportive relatives living in the same community, or families with a strong network of neighbors and friends, the stresses of having a child with a disability are greatly reduced. When parents are isolated or when friends and family are uncomfortable with the child, the parents will likely experience far more difficulties.

Family-Centered Practices

The recommended approach for working with families of your students with disabilities is referred to as **family-centered practices** (Dunst, 2002). Family-centered practices are based on the notion that outcomes are best for students when their families' perspectives are respected, family input is sincerely sought, and school professionals view their jobs as helping families to gain information that can assist them to make the best decisions for their children. Do you agree with this approach? Most professionals do, but implementing it means setting aside preconceived notions about parents and families and sometimes respecting the fact that families' goals for their children may not be the ones that you would choose.

One of the most important factors that influences whether you can develop strong working relationships with parents and families is your sensitivity to the parents' point of view (Harry, 2002; Nelson, Summers, & Turnbull, 2004). Some parents find school an unpleasant or intimidating place. They may have had negative experiences when they were students, or, if they are from another country, they may be unfamiliar with expectations for involvement in U.S. public schools. If parents' primary language is not English, they may be uncomfortable because of the need for an interpreter, or they may misunderstand information communicated by school personnel, whether in face-to-face interactions or in writing. The unique problems that immigrant parents may face and ideas for addressing them are outlined in the Professional Edge below.

Some parents may not be visibly involved in their children's education because of pragmatic barriers. If a parent works at a job that is far from school, he or she may not

PROFESSIONAL EDGE

Involving Immigrant Parents of Students with Disabilities

Nearly all teachers and parents believe that they should form productive partnerships in order to best educate children. However, they also find that collaboration can be a challenge, especially if parents have only recently come to the United States. Here are some suggestions for fostering a positive working relationship:

- Try to understand the language needs of the family. If parents need information in a language other than English, they are entitled to receive it. If a translator is needed in meetings, this service should be provided. The translator often can be chosen by the parents or can be another parent of a child with a disability.

- Check to see whether English classes are offered to parents by your school district. In large districts, welcome centers or parent centers also may operate. If so, share this information with parents.

- Use icons (for example, happy faces and sad faces) to convey information. If you need to send essential information to the family, ask about having it translated.

- Avoid jargon. Provide specific examples to illustrate information that you are communicating.

- Verify with parents that your communication has been understood. Be aware that some parents may consider it rude to ask you to repeat information, so you should be alert to the possible need to restate information.

- Develop your own key vocabulary list in the parents' language (for example, key special education terms, greeting words, and action words) so that you can participate directly in some small way in communicating with them.

- Read about the family's culture. Ask parents who are bilingual to describe the education system in their native country.

- Welcome parents to your classroom and be respectful of the differences among cultures in willingness to share information.

- Recognize that nonverbal communication varies tremendously among cultures. Be careful not to misinterpret nonverbal signals, and ask for assistance in this area if you need it.

- Include cultural and religious holidays on school calendars.

- Visit families at home, if this practice is customary in your school district. However, remember that some families would prefer to meet you at a neutral location such as a library rather than in their homes.

- Encourage family members to become involved in their child's education. Try to connect families with other immigrant parents from their native country.

SOURCE: Adapted from "Involving Immigrant Parents of Students with Disabilities in the Educational Process," by S. Al-Ahssan and R. Gardner, 2002, *Teaching Exceptional Children, 34*(5), pp. 52–58.

be able to take time off to participate in activities at school and may not be able to afford the lost work time. For some parents, involvement is largely a matter of economics: The costs of child care and transportation may prevent them from being able to work with you. These parents, however, may be involved through their work with their child at home.

In general, your attitude toward parents and their perceptions of their children greatly affect how you interact with them. If you telegraph through your choice of words, through your question-asking skills, and through your body posture that parents should see their children as you do and should accept your input without question, you are violating the principles of family-centered practice, and you probably will find that parents do not communicate with you readily. However, if you make parents feel welcome in your classroom or by phone or e-mail; listen carefully to their perceptions and concerns; treat them as important; and work with them to address student needs, many benefits will ensue for the student, for the family, and for you (Ulrich & Bauer, 2003).

Collaborating with Parents

As a school professional, you can make family-centered practices a reality when you find ways to effectively collaborate with parents. Some examples of positive ways to partner with parents include home–school communication, parent conferences, parent volunteer programs, and parent education.

HOME–SCHOOL COMMUNICATION ● One simple way to build a positive working relationship with parents is by using informal and formal home–school communication strategies. For example, at the beginning of the school year, you can send home a letter to parents that introduces you and explains your classroom goals for the year. You can follow this up with a positive phone call to parents sometime during the first few weeks of the school year. A positive call is particularly important for parents of students with disabilities because they often hear from educators only when a problem exists.

You can continue a system of communication with parents throughout the school year. For example, some teachers send home weekly updates or newsletters to the parents of all their students. For a student who is struggling, you might exchange a notebook in which you briefly list accomplishments of the day and a parent writes back with information from home (Davern, 2004). A time-saving alternative is to have a checklist that describes the positive behaviors expected of your student (for example, raises hand to ask a question; comes to class with all needed materials). You can then check the items that were successfully completed for that day. For a student with severe disabilities in your class, a paraprofessional might assist by preparing under your direction daily communication to parents (Chopra, Sandoval-Lucero, Aragon, Bernal, De Balderas, & Carroll, 2004). Whenever you use a daily communication system, you should encourage parents to respond so that you are aware of their perspectives and concerns.

Some teachers are finding that electronic communication can be a useful tool. If the families of your students have access to e-mail, you can send a group communication or electronic newsletter on a weekly basis, and you can send information about a specific student more frequently as needed. Some teachers also use e-mail to ensure that communication about homework is clear (Salend, Duhaney, Anderson, & Gottschalk, 2004). Remember, though, that some families cannot readily access a computer, so you need to use an alternative means of communication with them.

PARENT CONFERENCES ● In addition to the informal, day-to-day communication in which you engage with parents, you also collaborate with them through conferences. Preparing for, conducting, and following up on parent conferences helps ensure that this communication vehicle is valuable for the parents of all your students, including students with disabilities. For example, before a conference you should clarify the purpose of the meeting. Is it to speak to a group of parents about your overall goals for the year? Is it to meet individually with parents to discuss their child's progress? You can help parents prepare for the latter type of meeting by sending home in advance a list of questions and suggestions. A sample of such a conference-preparation flyer is presented in Figure 3.3. As you prepare questions for parents, you also should think about the questions you wish to address with them and make a list. Finally, you will communicate more effectively if you have samples of student work, your grade and plan books, and other pertinent student records easily available.

During the conference, your goal is to create a two-way exchange of information. Whether meeting with parents by yourself or with a special educator, you can accomplish this goal when you greet parents positively, arrange to meet with them at a table instead of at your desk, set a purpose for the conference, and actively involve them in discussion. In addition, you should use language respectful of the parents, their child, and their culture. Avoid using jargon (for example, acronyms such as AYP or MDT). In addition, you should work to understand that parents might interpret the meaning of disability and educators' response to it in ways that differ from educators. For example, some African American parents may distrust school professionals and the decisions made about their children because of past segregation and discriminatory special education practices (Kalyanpur, Harry, & Skrtic, 2000).

After a parent conference, you should complete several tasks. First, you should write a few notes to remind yourself of the important points discussed. These notes will help you improve the accuracy of your recollections. Second, if you made any major decisions regarding strategies that you and the parents will implement, you might want to write a brief note to the parents to confirm the decisions you made. Third, if you agreed to any action (for example, sending information to parents or asking a counselor to call parents), it is best to carry it out as soon as possible. Finally, if the special education teacher did not attend the conference, he or she may appreciate a brief note from you with an update on the conference outcomes.

PARENT EDUCATION ● Another type of communication with parents occurs through a variety of parent education activities. Although you probably would not undertake this type of activity without your colleagues, sometimes parent programs can help to inform parents and give them an opportunity to discuss important matters concerning their children. For example, if your school decides to emphasize inclusive practices, an information session for parents of all students might be very helpful. One school invited the parent of a student with disabilities to present on this topic to other parents; the result was increased understanding and a positive start. Some schools offer parent

DIMENSIONS OF**DIVERSITY**

Many parents, especially those from minority groups, can find school an intimidating place. You can promote participation by encouraging parents to come to school meetings with a friend or another family member and by asking them positive questions early during meetings (for example, "What does your child say about school at home?").

FIGURE 3.3 Sample Set of Questions to Help Parents Prepare for Conferences

1. What is your child's favorite class activity?

2. Does your child have worries about any class activities? If so, what are they?

3. What are your priorities for your child's education this year?

4. What questions do you have about your child's education in my class this year?

5. How could we at school help make this the most successful year ever for your child?

6. Are there any topics you want to discuss at the conference for which I might need to prepare? If so, please let me know.

7. Would you like other individuals to participate in the conference? If so, please give me a list of their names so that I can invite them.

8. Would you like me to have particular school information available? If so, please let me know.

9. Do you have other questions about our upcoming conference? If so, you can reach me by phone between 7:30 and 8:10 a.m. and between 3:00 and 3:45 p.m. at _____. If you prefer, you also can reach me by e-mail at _____.

programs related to understanding children's behavior, preparing for transitions from one school level to the next, and other topics of common interest, including ADHD.

PARENT INVOLVEMENT ● One additional type of collaboration with parents occurs through their involvement in their children's schools. Some parents, especially at the elementary level, make time to volunteer at school, tutoring students, helping with clerical chores, and helping to supervise students on field trips. However, many parents cannot make such commitments. They might be willing, though, to help you design a newsletter by working at their convenience or to come to school on a Saturday to help you set up for a special event. Alternatively, some schools help parents get involved by making school facilities more available. For example, some schools regularly hold evening sessions during which parents can bring their children to school to work on computers, read, or participate in discussion groups. Some schools find space in the building for a parent center, a comfortable gathering place designed for and operated by parents, with books that can be borrowed and important school district and community information available there.

How Can You Work Effectively with Paraprofessionals?

Throughout this chapter, an assumption has been made that everyone involved in forming school partnerships has equal status; that is, a general education teacher has approximately the same level of authority and equivalent responsibilities as a special education teacher, speech/language therapist, school psychologist, reading teacher, and so on. In many school districts, individuals in these types of positions are referred to as *certified staff.*

One other partnership you may form involves another type of staff. As mentioned in Chapter 2, **paraprofessionals,** or *para-educators,* are staff members who are employed to assist certified staff in carrying out the educational programs and in otherwise helping in the instruction of students with disabilities. (Although some school districts also employ other types of paraprofessionals, for this discussion we refer only to paraprofessionals who are part of special education services.) Paraprofessionals usually have completed two years of college or have passed an examination related to their responsibilities, but they generally are not required to have a college degree. When students with disabilities are members of your class, a special educator may not have adequate time or opportunity to assist them frequently, or the students might not need the direct services of that professional. Instead, a paraprofessional might be assigned to you for a class period or subject or, depending on the intensity of student needs, for much of the school day (Giangreco, Edelman, & Broer, 2003; Trautman, 2004).

Understanding Your Working Relationship with Paraprofessionals

The partnerships you form with paraprofessionals are slightly different from those with certified staff because you have some supervisory responsibility for a paraprofessional's work, a situation that would not exist in your work with other colleagues (French, 2003). For example, you may be expected to prepare materials for the paraprofessional to use in working with a group of students, you may have the responsibility of assigning tasks to this person on a daily basis, and you may need to provide informal training to the paraprofessional regarding your classroom expectations.

Many classroom teachers have never been supervisors, and they worry about what types of tasks to assign to a paraprofessional and how to set expectations. Adding to the complexity is the fact that some paraprofessionals have extensive professional preparation, a teaching license, and years of classroom experience, which makes them prepared to do nearly everything you do; whereas others have only a high school diploma and little training or experience in working with students (Marks, Schrader, & Levine, 1999). In Chapter 2 you learned about the types of responsibilities paraprofessionals may have in your classroom. If you will be working with a paraprofessional, you probably will receive a written description of that person's job responsibilities that specifies the activities that individual is to complete. Also, you can arrange to meet with the special education teacher or other professional who has overall responsibility for the paraprofessional's job performance.

Two general guidelines for working effectively with paraprofessionals are these: First, paraprofessionals generally enjoy working with students and want to participate actively in that process, and they should have the opportunity to do so. However, they appropriately also are expected to help teachers accomplish some of the "chores" of teaching, such as record keeping and instructional preparation tasks. Second, paraprofessionals always complete their assignments under the direction of a teacher who either has already taught the information or has decided what basic work needs to be completed; that is, paraprofessionals should not engage in initial teaching, nor should they make instructional decisions without input from a certified staff member.

Clearly, you have a key role in setting the expectations for a paraprofessional who may work in your classroom, for ensuring that you and the paraprofessional are satisfied with your working relationship, and for resolving any problems that arise. At the beginning of the school year, you can orient the paraprofessional to your classroom by providing a place for him or her to keep personal belongings and instructional materials, explaining essential rules and policies for your classroom, clarifying where in the classroom you want him or her to work, and asking him or her to voice questions and concerns (French, 2003). It is particularly important to touch base with the paraprofessional frequently early in the school year to be certain that expectations are clear. The paraprofessional may be working in several classrooms and trying to remember several sets of directions from different teachers, all with their own styles. You might even find that discussing these topics is best accomplished in a meeting that includes the special education teacher, you, any other general education teachers involved, and the paraprofessional. Figure 3.4 outlines some guidelines for you to keep in mind throughout the school year as you work with paraprofessionals so that your experience is positive for you and your students as well as the paraprofessional.

To continue nurturing the working relationship you have with a paraprofessional, you should communicate clearly and directly all activities that you would like the paraprofessional to complete. Some paraprofessionals report that they enter teachers' classrooms only to find that the teacher is already working with students and expects the paraprofessional to know what lesson to review with the students with special needs, assuming that the special education teacher has provided this direction. Meanwhile, the special educator is assuming that the general education teacher is guiding the paraprofessional. Unfortunately, in this situation the paraprofessional may be left wondering how to proceed.

Although most paraprofessionals work diligently, have a tremendous commitment to working with students with disabilities, and manage their roles superbly, occasionally problems arise. If you teach older students, you might find that the paraprofessional does not have enough knowledge of the information being presented to reinforce student learning. A few paraprofessionals violate principles of confidentiality by discussing classroom or student matters away from school. Some paraprofessionals are disruptive in classrooms—for example, their speech is too loud or their movements are too noticeable. If problems such as these occur and cannot be resolved directly between you and the paraprofessional, you should request that the special educator with whom you work meet with you and the paraprofessional to problem solve. If further action is needed, an administrator such as a principal or special education coordinator can assist.

FYI

Some paraprofessionals are highly trained to work with students with specific disabilities. For example, a paraprofessional working with students who are deaf probably knows sign language. A paraprofessional working with a student with autism probably has been prepared to respond to the student's behaviors using specific strategies known to be effective.

FYI

Vocabulary related to paraprofessionals can be confusing. Accepted terms for these school staff members include *para-educator* and *teaching assistant*. In large districts, specially trained paraprofessionals might have a title related to their training, such as *behavior technician* or *personal* or *one-to-one assistant*. The term *aide* is considered an out-of-date title for these individuals.

FIGURE 3.4 Guidelines for Effective Teamwork with Paraprofessionals

- Consider the paraprofessional an important member of the instructional team. Be sure to include him or her in team meetings whenever possible.

- Treat the paraprofessional with dignity and respect. Provide support and backup.

- Discuss goals, priorities, and plans with the paraprofessional on a daily basis.

- Avoid interrupting the paraprofessional when he or she is engaged in an activity. Keep interruptions to a minimum.

- Coordinate activities with the paraprofessional so you both accomplish as much as possible.

- Provide as much lead time as you can. Avoid last-minute rush jobs for the paraprofessional.

- Discuss problems and ideas with the paraprofessional. Ask for his or her ideas, suggestions, and opinions.

- If you must leave the classroom temporarily, tell the paraprofessional where you are going, how you can be reached, and when you will return. Adhere to district policies concerning leaving paraprofessionals alone with groups of students.

- Keep the paraprofessional fully informed about what is happening in the school environment. Ask what he or she would like to know about your priorities.

- Expect the best. Include the paraprofessional in staff development opportunities whenever possible.

- If you are one of several teachers with whom a paraprofessional works, be alert for contradictory directions that may be given. Clarify expectations as needed.

- Ask the paraprofessional whether you are using his or her time wisely or somehow hindering his or her performance. Make changes based on the feedback you receive.

SOURCE: Adapted from *Strengthening the Partnership: Para-Educators and Teachers Working Together: Time Management for Teams* (p. 18), by K. Gerlach, 1994, Seattle: Pacific Training Associates.

Collaborating with Paraprofessionals

W W W
R E S O U R C E S

The National Resource Center for Paraprofessionals (NRCP) (http://www. nrcpara.org) was founded in 1979 to support paraprofessionals who work in schools. This site includes several discussion boards, including one for teachers and administrators who have questions about working with paraprofessionals.

An often-asked teacher question regarding paraprofessionals is this: Given the supervisory nature of teacher–paraprofessional work, is it possible to collaborate with this group of staff members? The answer is yes! Paraprofessionals can collaboratively participate in shared problem solving about student needs, in planning field trip details, and in making decisions regarding how best to adapt information for a specific student (Carroll, 2001; Riggs, 2004). Your responsibility as a teacher is to encourage this type of collaboration. At the same time, you should clearly inform the paraprofessional when a matter being discussed is not one in which the principles of collaboration are appropriate. It is also important that you tell paraprofessionals when they are meeting your expectations and that you promptly address any issues of concern as soon as you become aware of them. For example, some paraprofessionals tend to hover over students with disabilities, preventing them from establishing social relationships with peers and fostering dependence instead of independence (Giangreco & Doyle, 2002). You should discuss this well-intentioned but inappropriate activity with such paraprofessionals and give clear, alternative directions for their interactions with students. By offering encouragement and addressing concerns, you can establish an environment that will make your collaboration with paraprofessionals invaluable.

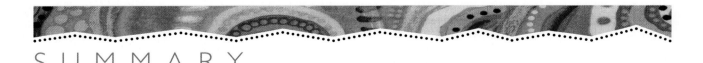

S U M M A R Y

Collaboration has become an important job responsibility for all educators and is especially important in educating students with special needs. Collaboration is a style professionals use in interacting with others, and it

involves key characteristics such as voluntary participation, parity, shared goals, shared responsibility for key decisions, shared accountability for outcomes, shared resources, and the emergence of a collaborative belief system, trust, and respect. You can help make your school's collaborative efforts more successful by identifying and clarifying your personal beliefs about collaboration, refining your interaction skills, and contributing to a supportive environment.

Collaboration can occur in many programs and services, but for students with special needs the most common ones are shared problem solving, co-teaching, working on a team, and consultation. Each of these applications has its own set of guidelines and its own use in educating students.

Another collaborative responsibility teachers have relates to parents. You need to understand parents' per-spectives on having a child with a disability; work collaboratively with parents on the basis of your respect for their perspective; communicate effectively with parents in conferences and in other ways; and respond professionally to parents in team meetings, annual reviews, and other interactions at which you and they are present. Collectively, this approach to working with parents is referred to as family-centered practice.

A final group with whom general education teachers collaborate is paraprofessionals. Understanding your roles and responsibilities and those of the paraprofessionals, and basing your collaboration on them, leads to positive working relationships with paraprofessionals.

Applications in **Teaching Practice**

Collaboration in the Washington School District

Although the administrators in the Washington School District would tell you that staff members have always worked together well, when increasing inclusive practices was made part of the district's strategic plan, it became clear that collaboration also needed to be a priority. Each principal was asked to work with staff members to incorporate collaboration into the school's improvement plan. Each school created a committee to study collaboration and its application in inclusive schools, set priorities, and plan staff development. Committee members also created a plan for evaluating the impact of increased collaboration on student outcomes.

In every elementary, middle, and high school, the teachers reviewed their school mission statement as a starting point for discussions of their beliefs about how students learn, how teachers teach, and how schools can be learning communities. In most of the schools, the teachers quickly realized that their mission statement did not explicitly say that teachers in the school were expected to work together to meet the needs of all their students. During after-school meetings, the mission statements were revised.

Next, teachers began to discuss various forms their collaboration might take. In one elementary school, Carole, a first-grade teacher anticipating a class group with many special needs, argued strongly for co-teaching. She stated that she needed someone to help her for at least a couple of hours each day. Peggy, another teacher, reminded her that with only two special education teachers and one paraprofessional available for everyone from kindergarten through fifth grade, she was asking for far too much, especially because these professionals also had other responsibilities. Jim, the special education teacher who works with students with moderate and severe disabilities, agreed. He noted that he had to reserve time to work individually with some of his students in a special education setting.

Co-teaching was a popular topic in other schools, too. In the middle school, one special education teacher was assigned to each team, and the teachers learned that they had the responsibility for deciding how to co-teach while making sure that students' IEP goals were addressed. Most teams decided that co-teaching should occur mostly in English and math classes. In the high school, the teachers approached their investigations with caution. First, they decided that special education teachers should be assigned to academic departments. Then they decided that co-teaching would occur only in English for the first year. Other services would remain the same while everyone became accustomed to working together. These teachers also decided that they wanted to learn more about collaboration skills, and they arranged with a local consultant for professional development as well as for observations of and feedback related to their interactions during meetings.

Principals made planning time a priority. They ensured that co-teaching teams could meet every week, but they also required that lesson plans be submitted after those meetings.

Principals also decided to survey teachers, paraprofessionals, and parents at the halfway point of the school year and again at the end of the year in order to gauge perceptions of these efforts to enhance collaboration.

With much excitement and a little anxiety, the district's administrators and teachers finished their detailed planning. They were a little concerned about new teachers who might be hired during the summer and how to help them become oriented quickly to the collaborative initiative. They also were concerned about whether they could demonstrate that working more closely improved student achievement, the ultimate goal. However, they felt they had worked closely to develop the plan and were eager to implement it.

QUESTIONS

1. Which characteristics of collaboration can you identify from the teachers' interactions and plans? Which are not evident?
2. How were the teachers working to ensure that their collaborative efforts would be successful? What is the role of the principal in fostering collaboration?
3. How would you respond to Carole? What do you recommend that she do? What do you recommend that her colleagues do in their interactions with her?
4. Why would it be important to incorporate a statement about collaboration into a school mission statement? Check the websites of your local schools. Are their mission statements posted? If so, do they address collaboration, either directly or indirectly?
5. How could the teachers communicate with parents about their plans? What reactions might they expect from parents? Why? How could they involve parents in their programs?
6. How might collaboration among professionals be similar and different in the elementary schools, middle schools, and high schools? What opportunities and constraints might exist for each group?

WORKING THE **STANDARDS**

INTASC

INTASC PRINCIPLES REFLECTED IN THIS CHAPTER:

Principle #7 states that all teachers contribute their expertise as members of a collaborative team to develop, monitor, and periodically revise individualized educational plans for students with disabilities, such as individualized education programs (IEPs), individualized family service plans (IFSPs), and individual accommodations plans (IAPs) (Section 504) (Principle 7.01).

Principle #10 states that the teacher fosters relationships with school colleagues, families, and agencies in the larger community to support students' learning and well-being. To accomplish this task, all teachers

- Share instructional responsibility for students with disabilities and work to develop well-functioning collaborative teaching relationships (Principle 10.01).
- Understand the roles and responsibilities of para-educators and other paraprofessionals, and collaborate with

these staff members to foster the safety, health, and academic and/or social learning of students with disabilities (Principle 10.03).

- Demonstrate sensitivity to differences in family structures and social, economic, and cultural backgrounds of students with disabilities (Principle 10.04).
- Communicate with families in ways that honor families' beliefs and practices, and seek to promote families' confidence and competence in furthering their children's development and learning (Principle 10.04).

CEC STANDARDS REFLECTED IN THIS CHAPTER:

Council for Exceptional Children

CEC Content Standard #5 states that special educators

- Help their general education colleagues integrate individuals with exceptional learning needs in regular environments and engage them in meaningful learning activities and interactions.

WORKING THE **STANDARDS** (continued)

- Coordinate all these efforts and provide guidance and direction to para-educators and others, such as classroom volunteers and tutors.

CEC Content Standard #10 states that special educators routinely and effectively collaborate with families, other educators, related service providers, and personnel from community agencies in culturally responsive ways.

BACK TO THE CASES

The standards and principles just listed relate to the case studies described at the beginning of this chapter. The questions and activities that follow demonstrate how these standards and principles, along with other concepts that you have learned about in this chapter, connect to the everyday activities of all teachers.

Ms. Godina's Biology Class

Briefly outline or describe two styles of co-teaching you might recommend to Ms. Godina and Mr. MacLean. Assume that you have chosen to teach this grade level and subject area. (See INTASC Principle 10.01 and CEC Standard 5.) For each of these two co-teaching styles, answer both of the following questions:

- Why would you select these two methods to teach this particular content?
- How does each of these styles meet the needs of each student with special needs in the class?

Fourth-Grade Team Meeting

Ms. Chiang is pleased to be part of this grade-level team. In addition, she is aware of the characteristics of collaboration that must be in place for the team to be successful. She sees herself as a *shared resource,* because she works with all of the teachers. She also knows that she should *share accountability for the outcomes* of the strategies the team has decided to use. (See INTASC Principles 7.01 and 10.01, and CEC Standards 5 and 10.) How can she help the team achieve success? Name specific actions she can take in the classrooms.

Werners' Parent–Teacher Conference

As Ms. MacDougal listens to the exchange between the Werners and Mr. Sanders, she determines that the meeting is not going to come to a productive end. She quickly decides to suggest that the participants enter into a shared problem-solving activity. (See INTASC Principle 10.04 and CEC Standard 10.) Do you think this is an appropriate strategy for this meeting? Provide reasons for your thinking.

> Visit the companion website (http://www.ablongman.com/friend4e) for a complete correlation of this chapter to the INTASC Principles and CEC Standards.

Further **Readings**

Friend, M., & Cook, L. (2003). *Interactions: Collaboration skills for school professionals* (4th ed.). Boston: Allyn and Bacon.

This book is designed to help all the professionals who work in schools to enhance their collaboration skills, including their communication, the collaborative services they provide to students, and their ability to address difficult or controversial situations.

Hanson, M. J., & Lynch, E. W. (2003). *Understanding families: Approaches to diversity, disability, and risk.* Baltimore: Brookes.

This book examines the impact of disability on families, combining information from recent research as well as practical ideas for working effectively with families, including families of young children with disabilities.

McLaughlin, M. J. (Ed.). (2002). Fostering collaboration between general and special education: Lessons from the "Bea-

cons of Excellence Projects" [Special issue]. *Journal of Educational and Psychological Consultation, 13,* 277–406.

This special journal issue presents knowledge about collaboration gained from research projects that were funded by the U.S. Department of Education. Topics addressed include teamwork, the development of collaborative cultures, and the importance of creating a sense of shared responsibility.

Peck, A. F., & Scarpati, S. (Eds.). (2004). Communication and collaboration [Special issue]. *Teaching Exceptional Children, 36*(5), 1–80.

In this journal, teachers are invited to learn about a variety of topics related to collaboration—from co-teaching to home–school communication to working with paraprofessionals and physical therapists.

Assessing Student Needs

MS. LYONS is concerned that Rob, a student in her second-grade class, is not keeping up with the rest of the class in math. She knows that he will be taking the state math test in third grade, and she is afraid that if he continues to fall behind, he won't meet state standards. Mr. Blair, the special education teacher, suggests that Ms. Lyons do some informal assessment herself before referring Rob for special education or other services. ● *What kinds of assessments can Ms. Lyons use to clarify Rob's problems in math? How might these assessments help her make changes in Rob's math instruction? Under what circumstances should she refer Rob for special education or other services?*

MR. BLOUNT TEACHES a high school U.S. history class. He has learned that three special education students will be in his class this fall. Mr. Blount was told that these students have some reading problems and may have trouble reading the textbook. He decides to make up a test to give at the beginning of the year to see how well all of his students are able to use the textbook. Using a section of a chapter from the text, he writes questions to test how well students can figure out the meaning of key vocabulary words, use parts of the book (for example, the table of contents, glossary, and index), read maps, and read for information (for example, note main ideas and draw conclusions). When Mr. Blount gives the test, he finds that the three identified students have trouble reading the text, but many other students also have difficulty. ● *How might he use the information from this assessment to differentiate instruction for his students?*

ROBERTO IS A STUDENT with moderate to severe disabilities who is in Ms. Benis's sixth-grade social studies class. As a result of Roberto's cerebral palsy, he has significant cognitive, language, and motor deficits. Roberto can read his name, as well as some high-frequency sight words. He uses a wheelchair, and he has trouble with fine motor movements such as cutting and handwriting. Roberto speaks with the aid of a communication board. ● *How can Roberto meet* *state standards for sixth grade in social studies? What kinds of assessments can Ms. Benis use to determine whether Roberto is meeting standards in social studies?*

As more and more students with disabilities are being served in general education classes, teachers need to make many important decisions that can greatly affect these students' success. This is particularly important in view of federal requirements in IDEA that all students with disabilities participate in district testing programs; and in No Child Left Behind, which requires that all students make adequate yearly progress as measured by high-stakes tests. For example, in the preceding vignettes, Ms. Lyons wanted to help Rob before he failed the state math test in grade 3. Mr. Blount wanted to find out whether his students could read the textbook for his history class, to help him decide which students would benefit from adapting the book. Ms. Benis needed to include Roberto, who had moderate to severe disabilities, in her social studies class but had to figure out how he would meet the state standards. To respond effectively in situations such as these, teachers need accurate, relevant information. Thus, they need to develop informal measures to help them make a number of instructional decisions as well as to participate in special education decision making. This chapter explores assessment strategies that help general education teachers contribute to the process of decision making for students with special needs. This involves determining matters such as whether a student needs special education services; when a student is ready to learn in inclusive settings; when an alternative to state testing is required; and what classroom accommodations and modifications to try, continue to use, or change.

How Do Your Student Assessments Contribute to Special Education Decisions?

As a classroom teacher, you make an important contribution to the process of identifying and meeting the needs of students with special needs. A major part of that contribution involves assessing student needs. **Assessment** has been defined as the process of gathering information to monitor progress and to make educational decisions when necessary (Overton, 2003). The two most common ways of collecting information are through standardized, commercially produced tests and through informal tests devised by the teacher. Much of the information in this chapter is about ways in which these measures can be used to make decisions about students with special needs. General education teachers contribute assessment information in six important decision-making areas for students with special needs: screening, diagnosis, program placement, curriculum placement, instructional evaluation, and program evaluation.

Screening

In Chapter 2 you learned that **screening** involves the decision about whether a student's performance differs enough from that of his or her peers to merit further, more in-depth assessments to determine the presence of a disability. For example, to clarify Rob's problems in math, Ms. Lyons from the chapter-opening vignettes examined the most recent group achievement test scores for her class in math and found that Rob's total math score was 1 to 2 years below grade level. Ms. Lyons then gave Rob and his classmates some minitests on various math computation skills she had taught to see

ANALYZE AND REFLECT

What questions are involved in making a screening decision? Under what circumstances might it be difficult to screen for a disability?

CONNECTIONS

Legal requirements for assessing students with disabilities are covered in Chapters 1 and 2.

Students' needs can be identified, addressed, and monitored through assessment based on observation, screening, diagnostic testing, program placement and evaluation, curriculum placement, and instructional evaluation. What role do general education teachers play in assessing students' special needs?

whether Rob was behind his peers in these skills. Using this information, Ms. Lyons found that a number of students were performing similarly to Rob. She therefore decided not to refer Rob for a more comprehensive evaluation until she first tried some adaptations in the classroom with Rob and several other students.

Diagnosis

The major decision related to **diagnosis** concerns eligibility for special education services, a decision you first learned about in Chapter 2. Does a student meet established federal guidelines for being classified as having a disability? If so, what are the nature and extent of the student's disability? For example, Paula was a student in Ms. Clark's class. In September, when Paula appeared to be struggling to keep up with the class in reading, Ms. Clark paired her up with a classmate for 15 minutes before reading each day to go over key words and vocabulary. When Paula's reading accuracy and fluency problems persisted even after four weeks of this extra help, Ms. Clark arranged for her to have 30 minutes more practice later in the day with the reading teacher. After a month of this extra help, Paula still showed no improvement. Ms. Clark suspected she had a learning disability and referred her for a case study evaluation. The school psychologist gave Paula a test on cognitive functioning, including a test of memory, attention, and organization, and an individual achievement test. She found that Paula was slow in processing visual information (that is, letters, numbers, and shapes) and that her achievement in reading was significantly lower than that of other students her age. However, her achievement in math was at grade level. Ms. Clark evaluated Paula's classroom reading performance by having her and five "average" students read orally and answer questions from a grade-level trade book that was part of the classroom literature program. Paula read slower and with less accuracy than her peers, and she was able to answer only 40 percent of the comprehension questions. In the end, Paula was declared eligible to receive services for learning disabilities, because she did not respond favorably to two levels of extra classroom help; she showed problems processing visual information quickly enough; and her achievement differed significantly from that of her classmates, as measured by both a standardized achievement test and informal classroom reading tests. Working Together on page 110 highlights effective ways to communicate results of diagnostic tests, as well as resulting decisions about placement, to parents.

ANALYZE
AND REFLECT

What questions are involved in diagnosing a student? What role can you as a general education teacher play in answering these questions?

WORKING **TOGETHER**

Communicating Effectively with Parents

Mrs. Perez has just attended a multidisciplinary committee meeting for her son Jorge and is distraught. First, being in the same room with all those professionals made Mrs. Perez nervous; she felt like an outsider who was there because she had done something wrong. Second, she was embarrassed that her English wasn't very good, so she was afraid to say anything. She had hoped the meeting would result in Jorge's getting extra help, but that was not what happened at all.

The school psychologist, Mr. Tanner, talked too fast and used a lot of technical words Mrs. Perez didn't understand, such as "performance-based," "verbal IQ," and "age and grade-level expectations." He said Jorge was in the slow learner range. Mrs. Perez was afraid that he meant her Jorge was stupid. She thought that Jorge was unable to understand tests because his English skills weren't very good, but she was afraid to say so.

When the special education teacher said that Jorge was two to three years below grade level in reading and writing and about one year below level in math, Mr. Tanner nodded, saying that that was about what could be expected for someone with Jorge's ability. Mrs. Perez wondered whether that meant there was no hope for Jorge. His teacher said that Jorge was having trouble keeping up in class and that last year he had failed to pass the state tests in reading and writing. Mrs. Perez wanted to hear more about what the class was doing and how Jorge was coping with the material, but she was afraid she would offend Jorge's teacher. Mr. Tanner finished by saying that Jorge was behind in his skills but achieving as expected given his scores on the IQ test. He said that Jorge wasn't eligible for special education services and asked Mrs. Perez if she had any questions.

Mrs. Perez knew that Jorge's English skills were holding him back, but now the committee members were telling her he couldn't get any extra help. Having a million questions but not knowing how to ask them, she nodded her head and left the meeting, afraid that there was no hope for her Jorge in school.

Chapter 3 presented communication barriers that can exist between parents and teachers. Here are some ideas that this team could have implemented to remove some of those barriers and improve communication with Mrs. Perez:

- It appears that few attempts were made to make Mrs. Perez feel comfortable. Taking time at the beginning of the meeting to introduce everyone present and to break the ice usually helps. Making sure that parents are not seated apart from the rest of the team also makes them feel more a part of the group.

- Mrs. Perez has difficulty speaking English. The team should have predetermined the extent of her English skills and provided supports such as a translator if needed. Even suggesting that Mrs. Perez bring an advocate with better English skills would have greatly facilitated the communication process.

- The team needed to explain the testing and eligibility process using nontechnical language that Mrs. Perez understood. Such communication should have started when parental consent for a case study evaluation was first attained. Clearly, Mrs. Perez had expectations that the process would lead to extra help for Jorge. The team needed to explain more carefully the criteria that eligibility is based on and the fact that it is not an automatic process.

- The standardized tests needed to be more carefully explained. Mrs. Perez appears to have had serious reservations about their validity.

- Given that persons from some other cultures often have difficulty asserting themselves with authority figures from the majority culture, more care needed to be taken to obtain Mrs. Perez's consent to the committee's decision. Simply asking whether she had any questions was not enough. Explaining the decision in concrete terms also would have helped—for example, "This means Jorge will not get extra help in special education. Do you understand that? Do you agree with this decision by the committee?"

- The team neglected Mrs. Perez's primary need: to get help for her son. Even if Jorge was not eligible for special education, the team should have described other options for help in the school, such as Title I reading programs or supports for English-language learners.

Program Placement

The major **program placement** decision involves the setting in which a student's special education services take place (for example, in a general education classroom, resource room, or full-time special education classroom). The IEP team must make this decision carefully. In the past, the tendency was to pull students out of general education classrooms without considering whether they could be supported within the general education program instead. In today's schools, the emphasis is on doing all that can be done within the general education class first, an approach consistent with guidelines for accessing the general education curriculum outlined in IDEA. Still, students have different needs, and some may require instruction in a specific area at a level of intensity that cannot be delivered in the general education classroom. That is why it is important to make placement decisions based on measures that accurately reflect student performance in class. For example, Carlos was eligible to receive services for learning disabilities in math. His IEP team needed to decide whether his learning needs could be met by adapting the math methods and materials in the general education classroom or whether he should be provided more intensive math instruction in a resource room setting. Carlos's classroom teacher gave Carlos and his classmates a series of informal math tests. She found that Carlos was significantly behind his peers on some but not all of the tests; his math-problem solving was very deficient compared to that of his classmates, but his math computational skills were fine. The IEP team decided to keep Carlos in his general education class and to support his instruction in problem solving by providing him extra teacher-guided practice whenever a new problem-solving skill was introduced. The team also decided to carefully monitor Carlos's problem-solving skills; if those skills showed little improvement, they would consider other options.

Curriculum Placement

Curriculum placement involves deciding at what level to begin instruction for students. For an elementary school teacher, such a decision may mean choosing which reading or math book a student should use. For example, Ms. Tolhurst has her students read orally and answer questions to find the appropriate trade books for them to read. That is, she determines the level of difficulty at which the books in her classroom reading program are neither too easy nor too hard for them. At the secondary level, curriculum placement decisions are likely to determine which class in a sequence of classes a student should take. For example, Mr. Nowicki, the guidance counselor, was trying to decide whether to place Scott in Algebra 1. He asked the math department to identify basic math skills that all students entering algebra should have. The department constructed a test based on those skills and gave it to Scott as well as other incoming ninth graders.

Of course, information about curriculum placement also provides teachers with a good measure of the extent to which students with disabilities are accessing the general education curriculum, an explicit goal of IDEA. In the examples just mentioned, a student with a disability in Ms. Tolhurst's class who can read only books that are two levels below grade level could be seen as having great difficulty accessing the general education reading curriculum. In contrast, a student who enters Mr. Nowicki's algebra class with all of the necessary prerequisite skills is fully accessing the district math curriculum.

> Information about curriculum placement provides teachers with a good indicator of the extent to which students with disabilities are accessing the general education curriculum, an explicit goal of IDEA.

Instructional Evaluation

Decisions in **instructional evaluation** involve whether to continue or change instructional procedures that have been initiated with students. For example, Ms. Bridgewater is starting a peer tutoring program to help Cecily, a student with severe cognitive disabilities, read her name and the names of her family members. Each week, Ms. Bridgewater tests Cecily to see how many of the names she has learned. She uses the results of the tests to find out whether the peer tutoring program is helping Cecily make progress. In another example, Mr. Jackson decides to accompany each of his history lectures

with a graphic organizer of the material. He gives weekly quizzes to find out whether the graphic organizer is helping his students better learn the material.

Program Evaluation

Program evaluation decisions involve whether a student's special education program should be terminated, continued as is, or modified. One consideration is whether or not the student is meeting standards as evidenced by reaching goals or attaining benchmark levels on assessments. For example, when Addie, a student with a reading disability, attained benchmark levels in reading fluency and comprehension for her grade level, her program was changed; she was integrated into the general education reading program and her performance was carefully monitored to ensure that her gains were maintained. Another way to evaluate the success of special education programming is by monitoring the attainment of IEP goals. For example, Amanda is receiving social work services twice per week. Her IEP goal is to decrease the number of times she has a verbal confrontation with Mr. Alvarez, her teacher. Mr. Alvarez is keeping track of the number of times daily that Amanda refuses to comply with his requests to see whether sessions with the social worker are improving Amanda's behavior.

ANALYZE
AND**REFLECT**

What questions are involved in evaluating the program of a student with special needs? Under what circumstances might a student with disabilities require more special education services? Require fewer services? Be ready to exit special education?

WWW
RESOURCES

The use of high-stakes testing is a controversial issue in today's schools. The website of the American Psychological Association (http://www.apa.org) is a good place to learn about all kinds of assessment, including high-stakes testing.

What Information Sources Are Used in Programming for Students with Special Needs?

A number of information sources are used in programming for students with special needs. The use of multiple assessment sources is consistent with the principle of nondiscriminatory testing, discussed in Chapter 2, which says that no single measure should be used to establish eligibility for special education services. The measures described in this section include high-stakes achievement tests, standardized achievement tests, individually administered tests, psychological tests, alternative assessments, and curriculum-based assessments.

High-Stakes Achievement Tests

A key requirement of IDEA is that students with disabilities have maximum access to the general education curriculum. Unlike in the past, however, access today is defined not as spending a certain amount of time in general education but as making meaningful progress toward meeting general curriculum goals (Nolet & McLaughlin, 2000). In general education today, that means meeting educational standards. Standards, which are set by individual states, comprise what students should be able to know or do as a result of their public education. For the past 3 decades, general dissatisfaction with public education has dramatically raised learning standards and has led to increased accountability for schools as they teach students to attain those standards.

As you learned in Chapter 1, **high-stakes tests** are assessments designed to measure whether students have attained learning standards. These tests are a type of assessment referred to as *criterion-referenced* because they involve comparing student performance to a specific level of performance, or benchmark, rather than to a norm, or average, as with traditional standardized achievement tests. Most states have created their own high-stakes tests based on an agreed-upon set of learning outcomes. For each identified outcome, standards or benchmarks are set that represent an acceptable level of knowledge or competence. Schools are then evaluated on the basis of the

ANALYZE
AND**REFLECT**

On what are high-stakes tests based? Are all students with disabilities required to take them? To what testing accommodations are students with disabilities entitled?

percentage of students meeting standards on each of the learning outcomes identified. For example, State A wanted all its fifth graders to be able to comprehend the key elements of short stories such as character, setting, problem identification, problem resolution, and moral. Reading experts were chosen by the state to create an item that would test student competence in comprehending short stories. The experts chose a short story written at the fifth-grade

How do high-stakes tests relate to students meeting educational standards? What are the implications for students with special needs?

level and developed a series of multiple-choice questions about the story elements. They then tried out the test on a diverse sample of students and through careful analysis determined that students who could answer at least 90 percent of the story-element questions were competent at identifying story elements. State A then tested all its fifth-grade students on this item to determine the percentage that could identify key elements in short stories.

IDEA requires that most students with disabilities take their states' high-stakes tests. This is how districts can show the degree of access to the general education curriculum attained by students with disabilities. These IDEA requirements were reinforced by the No Child Left Behind Act (NCLB), which requires that all children in each of grades 3–8 and at least once in grades 10 through 12 take high-stakes tests to show whether they are meeting state standards or making adequate progress toward them. NCLB requires that at least 95 percent of students with disabilities take high-stakes tests. Both IDEA and NCLB require that the results for students with disabilities be aggregated together with the results of the other students and reported publicly. Results for students with disabilities must also be disaggregated and reported separately; students with disabilities who are tested are held to the same standards and levels of adequate yearly progress as their classmates without disabilities.

> **IDEA requires that most students with disabilities take their states' high-stakes tests.**

To ensure that the scores obtained are accurate, students with disabilities are entitled to a range of accommodations while taking high-stakes tests. Common accommodations include changing the setting of the test (for example, allowing students to take tests in special education classrooms), changing the timing of the test (for example, providing extended time or more frequent breaks), changing the response format (for example, allowing students to mark responses in test books rather than on Scantron sheets), and changing the presentation format (for example, using a braille edition of a test or giving directions in sign language) (Roeber, 2002; Thurlow, Elliott, & Ysseldyke, 1998). A more complete description of the accommodations available is provided in the Professional Edge on page 114. The process for determining appropriate testing accommodations for individual students is explained in Chapter 11.

Students with significant cognitive disabilities are entitled to take alternate assessments geared to their individual needs as specified on their IEPs. Alternate assessments are described in more detail later in the chapter.

FYI

Rose (2000) suggests that traditional assessments are limited in accuracy because they involve only one questioning medium, print; allow limited means of expression, usually using fine motor skills; and involve a limited means of engagement (test taking) that is stressful and undermines performance. He proposes a system of *universally designed assessments* that, through the use of the latest technology, allow for greater testing accuracy through multiple means of engagement, expression, and representation of information. For more information, see http://www.cast.org.

PROFESSIONAL EDGE

Accommodations for Students with Disabilities on Standardized Tests

Under guidelines from IDEA and NCLB, most students with disabilities are required to take district and state standardized tests, including state high-stakes tests. A list of standard accommodations provided is shown here. Keep in mind that research on effective strategies for determining which students get which accommodations is still being done. Given the range of abilities within all disability groups, it is recommended that teachers avoid using students' labels to make these decisions and instead base them on individual student characteristics.

RESEARCH NOTE

Most, if not all, of your students with learning disabilities will take your state's high-stakes tests. Fuchs and Fuchs (2001) report a series of studies showing that not all students with disabilities benefit from the accommodations used with them. For example, only 23 percent of the students with learning disabilities benefited from extended time on a reading test, a common accommodation. When extended time was applied to math tests, just 10 percent benefited on computation items, and only 5 percent benefited on word problems. Equally disturbing, Fuchs and Fuchs report that teacher judgments about which accommodations to select for individual students with LD were generally inaccurate. The researchers found that although teachers provided accommodations in reading for 73 percent of students with LD, only 41 percent appeared to benefit. In addition, Fuchs and Fuchs found that students who were not eligible for accommodations by the teachers tended to benefit from accommodations when they were provided.

So, how should decisions about testing accommodations be made? They should be made with caution and on an individual basis. Fuchs and Fuchs have developed a measure called the Dynamic Assessment of Test Accommodations (DATA), which is technically adequate and can help match students with testing accommodations for grades 2–7. In this measure, students are administered a series of brief tests under different conditions to determine, before testing, how students benefit from common accommodations. A more general process for linking students with the appropriate accommodations is described in the "Professional Edge" in Chapter 11.

Why is the issue of high-stakes testing and students with disabilities important for you? The answer is that students with disabilities who are included in your classroom (except for those with significant intellectual challenges) are expected to meet the same standards as everyone else. And, under NCLB, there are consequences involved when students fail to meet expectations. The names of failing schools are posted publicly, children in failing schools are allowed to transfer to higher-performing schools, and failing schools can be required to provide extra tutoring for all students not making adequate yearly progress. Furthermore, in as many as 23 states, students need to pass an exam to receive a high school diploma, and at least 6 states require that students pass a test to be promoted to a certain grade (Thompson & Thurlow, 2003). Therefore, it is critical for you to carefully monitor the progress of your students with disabilities and, if needed, to provide extra supports or resources to ensure that the standards are met. Effective monitoring requires paying close attention to the results of high-stakes tests. More importantly, it requires you to keep track of student performance on a daily basis using assessments such as the ones described in this chapter.

Standardized Achievement Tests

Another common source of information for making educational decisions is **standardized achievement tests.** These tests are designed to measure academic progress,

Types of Testing Accommodations

Setting

- Provide special lighting.
- Provide adaptive or special furniture.
- Provide special acoustics.
- Administer the test to a small group in a separate location.
- Administer the test individually in a separate location.
- Administer the test in a location with minimal distractions.

Timing

- Allow a flexible schedule.
- Extend the time allotted to complete the test.
- Allow frequent breaks during testing.
- Provide frequent breaks on one subtest but not another.

Scheduling

- Administer the test in several sessions, specifying the duration of each session.
- Administer the test over several days, specifying the duration of each day's session.
- Allow subtests to be taken in a different order.
- Administer the test at a different time of the day.

Presentation

- Provide the test on audiotape.
- Increase spacing between items or reduce number of items per page or line.
- Increase size of answer spaces.
- Provide reading passages with one complete sentence per line.
- Highlight key words or phrases in directions.
- Provide cues (for example, arrows and stop signs) on answer forms.
- Secure papers to work area with tape or magnets.

Responding

- Allow marking of answers in booklet.
- Tape-record responses for later verbatim transcription.
- Allow the use of a scribe.
- Provide copying assistance between drafts.

Other

- Make special test preparations.
- Provide on-task/focusing prompts.
- Make any accommodation that a student needs that does not fit under the existing categories.
- Conduct an alternate assessment.

SOURCE: *Testing Students with Disabilities: Practical Strategies for Complying with District and State Requirements,* by M. L. Thurlow, J. L. Elliott, and J. F. Ysseldyke, 1998, Thousand Oaks, CA: Corwin.

or what students have retained from the curriculum. Unlike the high-stakes tests just described, standardized achievement tests are *norm-referenced*. In a norm-referenced test, the performance of one student is compared to the average performance of other students in the country who are the same age or grade level. Student performance is often summarized using grade equivalents and/or percentile ranks.

GROUP-ADMINISTERED TESTS ● Two major types of standardized achievement tests are group-administered and individually administered diagnostic tests. As the name implies, *group-administered standardized achievement tests* are completed by large groups of students at one time; this usually means that the general education teacher gives the test to the entire class. These tests assess skills across many areas of the curriculum, none in much depth. For this reason, they are intended to be used solely as screening measures. Nonetheless, caution is advised in using these scores, even if only for screening. As with any test, the general education teacher should be sure that students with disabilities receive appropriate accommodations when taking the test. Otherwise, the resulting score may be a measure more of the disability than of the ability. For example, Alicia has a learning disability in reading and has problems comprehending written directions. When Alicia obtained a low score on a social studies test, it was hard to determine whether her low score was due to a lack of knowledge or her inability to follow the directions.

WWW
RESOURCES

For more information on the topic of state and national testing policies, access the website of the National Center on Educational Outcomes (NCEO), at http://education.umn.edu/nceo.

Another potential problem with group-administered standardized achievement tests is that the norms used to interpret scores are of little use when evaluating students with disabilities; these students are often excluded from the norming group because they have taken the test with accommodations. Also, all students may be affected by the fact that the content of the test might not match what is taught in a particular classroom (Deno, 1985, 2003; Marston, 1989). For example, one teacher stressed problem solving in his science class, whereas the standardized achievement test given in his district stressed the memorization of facts. Therefore, the teacher had to give his own tests to determine whether students were learning the material. Finally, standardized achievement tests might be culturally biased and have led to the overrepresentation of minorities in special education classes (Artiles, Harry, Reschly, & Chinn, 2002; National Alliance of Black School Educators, 2002). For example, Bill comes from a single-parent home in the city. When he read a story on a standardized achievement test about an affluent two-parent family in the suburbs, he had difficulty predicting the outcome.

> 66 Standardized achievement tests might be culturally biased and have led to the overrepresentation of minorities in special education classes. 99

Whereas, in the past, group-administered standardized achievement tests were used to make administrative and policy decisions on a school district or even national level, it appears that high-stakes tests are being used more often for these purposes. Given the time and effort it takes to test an entire school, as well as the value of instructional time to children's learning, many schools have found it more prudent to use only their state's high-stakes test.

INDIVIDUALLY ADMINISTERED TESTS ● A special education teacher or the school psychologist usually gives **individually administered diagnostic tests** as part of a student's case study evaluation. Although these tests may screen student performance in several curricular areas, they tend to be more diagnostic in nature. For example, an individually administered diagnostic reading test may include test components in the areas of letter identification, word recognition, oral reading, comprehension, and phonetic skills; a diagnostic test in math might include math computation, fractions, geometry, word problems, measurement, and time. Because individually administered diagnostic tests provide information on a range of specific skills, they can be useful as an information source in making educational decisions. For example, Tamara scored 2 years below grade level on the comprehension subtest of an individually administered diagnostic test in reading. Yet in an oral reading sample taken from her fourth-grade reader, she read both fluently and accurately. On the basis of these two findings, her teacher placed her in a literature-based reading program that stressed skills in reading comprehension.

Although individually administered diagnostic tests may be more helpful than group-administered achievement tests, they are still subject to many of the same problems. Again, you should always verify findings from these tests using more informal measures based on the content you teach.

Psychological Tests

Psychological tests are used as part of the process of evaluating students with special needs, particularly to determine whether a student has cognitive or learning disabilities. Reports of the results of these tests are often written by school psychologists and consist of a summary of the findings and the implications for instruction. **Psychological tests** can include intelligence tests and tests related to learning disabilities (Overton, 2003; Salvia & Ysseldyke, 2004).

The overall purpose of psychological tests is to measure abilities that affect how efficiently students learn in an instructional situation. These abilities are inferred based on student responses to items that the test author believes represent that particular ability. For example, comprehension, an important learning ability, is often assessed on psychological tests (Salvia & Ysseldyke, 2004). To test their comprehension, students may be asked to read and answer questions about a series of directions or other tasks described in printed material. Student scores are then compared to a norm group of other same-age students, with an average score being 100. Other abilities commonly assessed by psychological tests include generalization (the ability to recognize similarities across objects, events, or vocabulary), general or background information, vocabulary, induction (the ability to figure out a rule or principle based on a series of situations), abstract reasoning, and memory (Salvia & Ysseldyke, 2004).

Psychological tests can be helpful if they clarify why students may not be learning in class and lead to effective changes in instruction. For example, the results of Tiffany's test showed that she had difficulty with visual memory. Her teacher, Ms. Fasbacher, felt that this was related to her poor performance in spelling. As a result, Ms. Fasbacher provided Tiffany with extra practice on her weekly spelling lists. Interpreting the results of psychological reports seems less daunting if you follow these five general guidelines:

1. Do not be intimidated by the sometimes generous quantity of technical terms and jargon. You have the right to expect that reports be translated into instructionally relevant language.

2. In the event of discrepancies between psychological reports and your experience, do not automatically discount your experience. The results of psychological tests are most valid when corroborated by classroom experience. Keep in mind that your impressions are the result of many more hours of classroom observation than are psychological evaluations, which are based on fewer samples of student behavior and on samples that represent behavior that takes place outside the classroom.

3. Be sure to check the technical adequacy of the psychological tests included in your report. You may be surprised to find that many of these tests are not acceptable.

4. Be sure to check for possible cultural bias. Psychological tests may discriminate against students from culturally diverse or disadvantaged backgrounds. The various ways in which psychological and other tests can be biased, along with suggestions for making them more fair, are presented in the Special Emphasis On . . . feature on page 118.

5. Keep in mind that the primary purpose of psychological tests is to establish possible explanations for particular learning, behavioral, or social and emotional problems. Such explanations should be springboards for helping students overcome these problems, not excuses for students' lack of achievement.

The Professional Edge on page 119 contains lists of standardized tests commonly used in special education decision making. These include standardized group and individual achievement tests, and psychological tests used to assess intelligence or cognitive functioning.

Alternate Assessments

As you have learned, IDEA and NCLB require states to include students with disabilities in statewide and districtwide educational assessments. Although most students with disabilities are able to participate when given appropriate accommodations, a small percentage of students are typically working on a more basic, functional curriculum and do not have to meet the same requirements as those students graduating with a standard diploma. In other words, they are required to meet the same broad standards as your other students, but they meet them in different, more basic ways in **alternate assessments.** For example, one of the standards in Ms. Barber's state is that students develop an appreciation for literature. One of the ways that Darrell, a student

Special EMPHASIS On …

Strategies for Fair Assessment of Diverse Students

Grossman (1995) reports that although today's teachers are much more knowledgeable about the presence of bias in assessing poor students and students from culturally diverse backgrounds, bias and discrimination continue to exist. The following two lists present areas that can be problematic when assessing diverse students and strategies for assessing and interpreting their performance more accurately, respectively.

Problem

1. Students may exhibit test anxiety due to lack of familiarity with the assessment process.
2. Students may lack motivation to perform well on tests because of differing cultural expectations.
3. Students may not respond to traditional motivators.
4. Students' test scores may be depressed because the assessor is unfamiliar or speaks a different language.
5. Students may have different communication styles; for example, they may not feel comfortable asking for help with directions or may respond using fewer words.
6. Students may be unwilling to take risks; for example, they may be reluctant to guess on a test even though it is to their benefit.
7. Students may be accustomed to working at a slower pace.
8. Students may lack exposure to test content.
9. Students may not be proficient in the language used for a test.
10. Students may speak with a dialect that differs from the assessor's.

Recommendation

1. Give students practice tests. Teach test-taking skills.
2. Qualify test performance with class performance.
3. Individualize reinforcers; use individualistic, competitive, and cooperative goal structures.
4. Allow more time to establish rapport and gain trust.
5. Check for understanding of directions; avoid automatically penalizing students for not saying enough or not giving details.
6. Teach students strategies for when and how to make a best guess on a test.
7. Extend test-taking time to accommodate students' pace.
8. Eliminate unfamiliar content or don't give the test.
9. Assess students using both English and students' native language.
10. Do not count dialectical differences as errors; examine your attitudes about nonstandard dialects for potential bias.

Research Note

Abedi, Hofstetter, and Lord (2004) reviewed the research literature on the effectiveness of testing accommodations for English-language learners in the content areas of math, science, and social studies. The accommodations studied included assessing in the students' native language, modifying the level of English in questions, providing extra time, providing dictionaries and glossaries, and oral administration. In general, the researchers found evidence for the effectiveness of only two accommodations: modifying the language (but not the content) of the test items by reducing low-frequency vocabulary and complex language structures; and providing students with definitions or simple paraphrases of potentially unfamiliar or difficult words on the test. Not surprisingly, the authors found that these accommodations helped all students, not just English-language learners. Research shows that curriculum-based assessments also work well with English-language learners, whether the assessments are in their native language or not (Deno, 2003).

---

with a significant intellectual disability, meets that standard is by watching a video of *Oliver Twist* and answering a few basic questions using his communication board.

The use of alternative assessments is still relatively new. Although districts in some states such as Kentucky and Vermont began using them earlier, most school districts began using alternate assessments in 2002, the year required for implementation by IDEA. This means that guidelines for conducting alternate assessments are still evolving. A recent survey of state special education directors found that most states have

PROFESSIONAL EDGE

Standardized Tests Commonly Used in Special Education Decision Making

You can choose from many standardized tests to help you make decisions for special education assessment. When selecting an instrument, make sure it is appropriate for the student being tested. If you have questions about the suitability of a particular test, consult your school psychologist or special education teacher. The following lists provide the names and sources of commonly used standardized tests for special education decision making.

Standardized Achievement and Diagnostic Tests

Woodcock-Johnson Revised Tests of Achievement (Chicago: Riverside)

Peabody Individual Achievement Test–Revised/Normative Update (Circle Pines, MN: American Guidance Service)

Kaufman Test of Educational Achievement/Normative Update: (Circle Pines, MN: American Guidance Service)

KeyMath Diagnostic Arithmetic Test–Revised/Normative Update (Circle Pines, MN: American Guidance Service)

Woodcock Reading Mastery Tests–Revised/Normative Update (Circle Pines, MN: American Guidance Service)

Wechsler Individual Achievement Test II (San Antonio, TX: Psychological Corporation)

Test of Written Language–3 (Austin, TX: PRO-ED)

Test of Written Spelling–4 (Austin, TX: PRO-ED)

Test of Reading Comprehension–3 (Austin, TX: PRO-ED)

Gray Oral Reading Test–4 (Austin, TX: PRO-ED)

Intelligence Tests and Tests of Cognitive Functioning

Wechsler Intelligence Scale for Children–IV (San Antonio, TX: Psychological Corporation)

Woodcock-Johnson Revised Tests of Cognitive Abilities (Chicago: Riverside)

Stanford-Binet V (Chicago: Riverside)

Kaufman Assessment Battery for Children, Second Edition (Los Angeles: Western Psychological Services)

---

chosen to compile a body of evidence to demonstrate that a student has met standards rather than using paper-and-pencil tests (Thompson & Thurlow, 2003). This body of evidence is usually in the form of a portfolio containing classroom observations, skills checklists, and reviews of records, such as an analysis of the student's IEP.

The system of alternate assessment used by the state of Kentucky is a good example of a portfolio system (Kleinert, Kearns, & Kennedy, 1997). In Kentucky, all

CONNECTIONS

Portfolio assessments can be difficult to develop and score. Chapter 11 provides information about how you can use portfolios effectively.

Students with more severe disabilities participate in alternate assessments that stress authentic skills and experiences in real-life environments. What skills do you think are being assessed here?

These teachers are using information from assessment probes to make decisions about their students with special needs. How can you use assessment probes to make decisions in your area of teaching?

FYI

As of this writing, NCLB has set a 0.5 percent level of students who may be alternatively assessed (Roeber, 2002).

**RESEARCH
N O T E**

In a recent study, special education directors nationwide listed more positive than negative outcomes when asked about their alternate assessment programs (Thompson & Thurlow, 2003). On the positive side, 96 percent saw increased inclusion for students with disabilities in their state's accountability system; 88 percent saw an increase in academic expectations for students with disabilities; and 82 percent said students with disabilities now had greater access to their state's learning standards. The most frequently mentioned negative outcomes were fears that students with disabilities would not be able to meet state standards (48 percent); and high stress levels among students taking the tests (40 percent).

students, regardless of disability, are required to meet standards in a range of areas, including using patterns to understand past and present events and to predict future events; using technology effectively; demonstrating knowledge, skills, and values that have lifetime implications for involvement in physical activity; and completing a postsecondary opportunities search (Kearns, Kleinert, Clayton, Burdge, & Williams, 1998). Although the portfolios reflect the same set of outcomes for all students, students with significant intellectual disabilities meet them in different ways. For example, Damon met the standard of completing a search for postsecondary opportunities by compiling a list of his work preferences and specific jobs aligned with his preferences. Sibilie demonstrated her effective use of technology by using an augmentative communication device across a range of school and community settings. Carolyn, a student with multiple disabilities, demonstrated achievement in skills and values related to physical activity by participating in a volleyball game in physical education class. Linus demonstrated his ability to use patterns to understand events by recognizing that on days when his paraprofessional wasn't in school he had less time to get ready for recess.

Here are eight questions to consider about alternate assessments when you have a student in your classroom with severe disabilities:

1. *What are the district's eligibility requirements for alternate assessments?* Keep in mind that only a small number of students have disabilities so severe that they are eligible. The decision to give an alternate assessment should not be based on whether the student is expected to do poorly on the general education assessment.

2. *Is the focus of the assessment on authentic skills and on assessing experiences in community or real-life environments?* For a younger child the community might mean the school, playground, or home; for a high school senior the community might mean the store, bank, or other commercial or public sites.

3. *Is the assessment aligned with state standards?* The skills assessed need to be functional, but they also should have a meaningful relationship to content areas covered by the standards, such as reading and math. For example, one of Clifford's IEP goals in language is to communicate by pointing to pictures on a communication board. This skill is both functional and aligned with standards in language arts. Chatrice is learning to give correct coins to the bus driver. This skill is functional and aligned clearly with math standards involving money. As the general education teacher who is responsible for his or her students' meeting the regular state standards, you may be in the best position to answer this question of standards alignment.

4. *Is the assessment tied to ongoing classroom instruction and data collection?* If alternate assessments are truly to help students with significant intellectual challenges meet state standards, then they must help a teacher guide instruction on a daily basis, as opposed to relying on a checklist of skills or a one-time observation of performance. For instance, Everett's teacher took weekly video clips of Everett eating lunch and had another teacher rate his competence in feeding himself. These weekly clips were used by Everett's teacher to gradually reduce the level of teacher assistance given to him while working toward his goal of completely feeding himself.

5. *Is the assessment closely linked to the IEP so that expectations between home and school are consistent?* Tying alternate assessments to the IEP assures appropriate parent and student involvement in the assessment/teaching process. Studies show that parent and student involvement in the alternate assessment process is positively related to student outcomes on alternate assessments (Kampfer, Horvath, Kleinert, & Kearns, 2001).

6. *Are the measured skills integrated across many areas?* Personal and social skills, for example, should be assessed right along with academic and functional literacy skills, rather than separately. For example, Ms. Halpern assesses Thomas's literacy *and* social skills when he is ordering food at a fast-food restaurant.

7. *Are there clear scoring guidelines, and have staff been adequately trained to consistently apply these guidelines when evaluating student performance?* Recent studies (for example, Johnson & Arnold, 2004) show that this issue can be a problem when evaluating student portfolios. In some cases, scoring problems have actually prevented states from releasing results to students and parents. Check the scoring guidelines for your students performing alternate assessments. When possible, you might want to get involved in the assessment training. Although you will usually not be responsible for scoring your students' alternate assessments, becoming familiar with them will ensure that the help you provide will be focused and relevant to your students' IEP goals.

8. *Are scores on the assessment used to continually monitor the extent to which it leads to better outcomes for students?* Alternate assessments should inform the need for services, which, in turn, should lead to more productive, independent lives for students with severe disabilities in school and the community. For example, Eduardo's teacher, Ms. Bland, noticed that Eduardo was able to ask for help more effectively in class than in the community. She decided to observe the two settings and look for differences. She noticed that Eduardo was receiving too much help from his paraprofessional in class and that this was discouraging Eduardo's independence when he was out of class. Ms. Bland's observation led to more careful monitoring of Eduardo's paraprofessional to ensure that the level of support she was providing was eventually reduced.

Curriculum-Based Assessments

Because of the limited utility of standard achievement tests and psychological reports for making day-to-day instructional decisions, you need other tools in order to be a partner in the evaluation process. **Curriculum-based assessment (CBA)** is an effective option that in many instances can be an alternative to standardized tests. CBA has been defined as a method of measuring students' level of achievement in terms of what they are taught in the classroom (for example, Deno, 2003; Hosp & Hosp, 2003; Tucker, 1985). In CBA, student performance is also measured repeatedly over time, and the results are used to guide instruction (Hosp & Hosp, 2003; Tucker, 1985). CBA has a number of attractive features:

- When using CBA, you select the skills that are assessed, based on what you teach in class, thus ensuring a match between what is taught and what is tested. This match makes CBA measures accurate as indicators of student access to the general education curriculum, and ideal for use in pre-referral intervention systems.

WWW RESOURCES

Learn about the National Assessment of Educational Progress (NAEP), the only ongoing national test of academic progress, at http://www.nagb.org.

FYI

Curriculum-based measurement (CBM) is a particular kind of curriculum-based assessment. CBM is characterized by a research base establishing its technical adequacy, as well as standardized measurement tasks and scoring procedures that are brief and fluency-based (Deno, 2003). The DIBELS measures described in the Professional Edge on page 126 are examples of CBM.

■ CBA compares students within a class, school, or district, not with national norms, to show learning differences (Deno, Reschly-Anderson, Lembke, Zorka, & Callender, 2002; Marston, Muyskens, Lau, & Canter, 2003), thus ensuring that a student referred for special education services is performing significantly differently from his or her peers (Bursuck & Lessen, 1987; Marston et al., 2003). For example, in the chapter-opening vignettes, before referring Rob to special education, Ms. Lyons gave him some curriculum-based assessments in math to determine the specific kinds of problems he was having. She then implemented a peer tutoring program and used these same tests to measure its effectiveness. Mr. Blount used an informal reading assessment based on his U.S. history textbook to see how well his students were able to read the text.

> *Research shows that when teachers use CBA to evaluate student progress and adjust their instruction accordingly, student achievement increases significantly.*

■ Research shows that when teachers use CBA to evaluate student progress and adjust their instruction accordingly, student achievement increases significantly (Deno, 2003; Fuchs, Fuchs, Hamlett, & Stecker, 1991; Shinn, Collins, & Gallagher, 1998).

ANALYZE
AND REFLECT

Why is it harder to design probes for higher level thinking skills such as math-problem solving? What can teachers do to make sure that probes of higher level skills provide useful, accurate information?

What Kinds of Curriculum-Based Assessments Can You Create for Your Students?

Two major kinds of CBAs are commonly used: probes of basic academic skills (for example, reading, math, and writing) and probes of content-area knowledge and learning strategies (for example, vocabulary knowledge, prerequisite skills, textbook reading, and note taking). Although probes of basic academic skills relate more directly to elementary school teachers and probes of content-area knowledge and learning strategies to middle and high school teachers, each of these measures is relevant for both groups. For example, high school students need to perform basic skills fluently if they are to have ready access to curriculum content; elementary school students need early training in learning strategies to make the difficult transition to middle and high school instruction easier.

Probes of Basic Academic Skills

www
RESOURCES

You can find more information about curriculum-based assessments, including various samples, at the websites of the National Center on Accessing the General Curriculum (http://www.cast.org/publications/ncac/ncac_curriculumbe.html), Jim Wright Online (http://www.jimwrightonline.com/pdfdocs/cbaManual.pdf), Intervention Central (http://www.interventioncentral.org/interventions/cbmwarehouse.shtml), AIMSweb (http://www.aimsweb.com), and McGraw-Hill Digital Learning (http://www.mhdigitallearning.com).

Probes are quick and easy measures of student performance in the basic skill areas of reading, math, and written expression. They consist of timed samples of academic behaviors and are designed to assess skill accuracy and fluency.

Probes can sample a range of skills in a particular area, as in a mixed probe of fifth-grade math computation problems in addition, subtraction, multiplication, and division; or they can sample one skill area, such as letter identification or writing lowercase manuscript letters.

Typically, students work on probe sheets for 1 minute. The teacher then records the rate of correct and incorrect responses as well as any error patterns. Student performance rates have been shown to be useful for making many of the important evaluation decisions described earlier in the chapter: screening, diagnosis, program placement, curriculum placement, instructional evaluation, and program evaluation (Deno, 2003; Shinn et al., 1998; Tindal & Marston, 1990). The Professional Edge on page 123 describes the importance of considering both student accuracy and student fluency when assessing basic academic skills.

Probes are classified according to how students take in task information (for example, seeing or hearing) and how they respond (for example, writing or speaking).

PROFESSIONAL EDGE

Assessing Student Rates on Basic Academic Skills

When basic skills or other academic content is assessed informally in the classroom, *student accuracy* is usually stressed. For example, we say that Jill formed 85 percent of her cursive letters correctly, John was 90 percent accurate on his addition facts, or Al identified key pieces of lab equipment with 100 percent accuracy. Although accuracy is important, because it tells us whether a student has acquired a skill or section of content, accuracy is not the only useful index of pupil performance. *Student fluency,* or how quickly a student is able to perform a skill or recall academic material, is also relevant. Before you consider the reasons for assessing student fluency provided here, consider this: If your car needed service and you had your choice between two mechanics, both of whom did accurate work and charged $35 an hour but one of whom worked twice as fast as the other, which mechanic would you choose?

The Rate Rationale

1. Students who are proficient in a skill are more likely to remember the skill, even if they do not need to use it very often. If they forget the skill, they need less time to relearn it.

2. Students who are proficient in a basic skill are better able to master more advanced skills. For example, students who can perform addition problems fluently often acquire advanced multiplication skills more easily.

3. Performance of basic skills at an "automatic" level frees students to perform higher level skills more readily. For example, students who can read fluently with understanding are more likely to be successful in high school classes that require reading lengthy textbook assignments in little time. Students who know their math facts without counting on their fingers can solve word problems more efficiently.

4. Students with special needs are often so labeled because they work more slowly than their peers. Fluency scores allow teachers to compare these students directly with their classmates on this important dimension of speed; they also provide a useful index of student progress, including, for some students, readiness for inclusion in general education classes.

USING THE RESEARCH

If you are interested in learning how your students' oral reading rates compare to national norms, Hasbrouck and Tindal (1992) have compiled national norms based on student oral reading fluency scores from multiple school districts across the country. These norms are shown in Table 4.1. Notice that separate norms are presented for fall, winter, and spring, to account for student growth during the year. So, if Simone is reading 80 words correct per minute in February of second grade, she is reading at just above the 50th percentile for winter of grade 2.

TABLE 4.1 National Norms for Student Oral Reading Fluency

Grade	Percentile	Fall (August–December) WCPM*	Winter (January–March) WCPM	Spring (April–June) WCPM
	75	82	106	124
2	50	53	78	94
	25	23	46	65
	75	107	123	142
3	50	79	93	114
	25	65	70	87
	75	125	133	143
4	50	99	112	118
	25	72	89	92
	75	126	143	151
5	50	105	118	128
	25	77	93	100

*WCPM = words correct per minute

SOURCE: From "Curriculum-Based Oral Reading Fluency Norms for Students in Grades 2–5," by J. E. Hasbrouck and G. Tindal, 1992, *Teaching Exceptional Children, 24*(3), pp. 41–44.

They include four major types: see-say, see-write, hear-write, and think-write (Bursuck & Lessen, 1987). For example, when reading orally from a textbook, students *see* the text and *say* the words. Hence, oral reading is referred to as a see-say probe. Similarly, in a spelling probe, students *hear* the teacher dictate words and *write* the words as they are dictated. This is a hear-write probe.

RESEARCH
N O T E

Tindal, McDonald, Tedesco, Glasgow, Almond, Crawford, and Hollenbeck (2003) developed a series of curriculum-based measures in reading and math for use in alternate assessment programs. Their research showed that effective measures were brief and easy to give and provided information that was of potential use to teachers.

RESEARCH
N O T E

Good (2002) studied the relationship between the oral reading performance of third-grade students and their performance on the Oregon Statewide Assessment Test (OSAT), Oregon's high-stakes test. He found that, of 91 students who met benchmark levels of 110 words correct per minute in oral reading fluency in May of grade 3, 90 students, or 90 percent, met standards on the OSAT. Of the 23 students scoring below the benchmark of 70 words per minute, only 4 students, or 17 percent, met state standards.

RESEARCH
N O T E

Allinder, Bolling, Oats, and Gagnon (2000) found that students of teachers who regularly asked themselves the following questions when giving curriculum-based measures made more academic progress in math computation: On what skills has the student done well during the last 2 weeks? What skills should be targeted for the next 2 weeks? How will I attempt to improve student performance on the targeted skills?

As you develop CBAs, keep in mind the following three suggestions:

1. Identify academic skills that are essential in your particular room or grade. In the elementary grades, include skills in handwriting, spelling, written expression, reading (for example, letter identification, letter sounds, oral reading accuracy, and comprehension), and math (for example, number identification, computation, problem solving, time, and money).

2. Select skills representing a *sample* of skills that are taught, not necessarily every skill. Performance on these skills then acts as a checkpoint for identifying students in trouble or measuring student progress. For example, in assessing reading performance, having students read a passage aloud from their reading or literature books and then answer comprehension questions may not represent all reading skills you have taught (such as words in isolation), but it does include a representative sample of many of these skills.

3. Even though CBAs are considered informal assessments, their utility in helping to make instructional decisions depends on the teacher's keeping the difficulty level of the assessment items, as well as the administration and scoring procedures, consistent over time (Deno, 2003). For example, Ms. Solomon was monitoring the progress of three of her students with special needs in oral reading fluency. Every 2 weeks she conducted one-minute timings using passages from their third-grade reading book. To make sure the information she was getting was accurate, she conducted her timings the same way each time, and made sure that the passages selected for the timings were roughly equivalent in difficulty.

PROBES OF READING SKILLS ● The critical reading skills in the elementary years include phonemic awareness, letter sounds, word recognition, vocabulary, and comprehension. Phonemic awareness can be measured using a hear-say probe. See the Professional Edge on pages 126–127 for specific examples of how to assess phonemic awareness. Student ability to identify letter names and sounds can be assessed using a see-say probe. Word recognition and comprehension can be assessed using a see-say oral passage reading probe, such as the one in Figure 4.1.

Although the easiest method for assessing comprehension is to use the questions that accompany most classroom reading series, if you are having your students read trade books, you may need to design your own questions, which can be a difficult task. Carnine, Silbert, Kameenui, and Tarver (2004) have suggested one practical model for designing comprehension questions, based on story grammar. *Story grammar* is simply the description of the typical elements found frequently in stories. These include theme, setting, character, initiating events, attempts at resolution, resolution, and reactions. These elements can be used to create comprehension questions that may be more appropriate than traditional main idea and detail questions, because story grammar describes the organization of most stories that elementary school students are likely to read. The Case in Practice on page 128 shows how a teacher uses story grammar with one of her second-grade students.

At times, you might not wish to ask questions about a story. Specific questions can give students clues to the answers, and they especially help students identify the information you think is important to remember or the way you organize this information. One way to solve this problem is to have students retell stories after they read them. Students themselves then must organize the information they think is important, and you can evaluate the completeness of their recall. Such a situation has two requirements for effective evaluation to occur: a standard set of criteria to evaluate the completeness of the retelling, and the opportunity to evaluate each student's retelling individually. The Professional Edge on page 126 offers additional means of assessing students' reading skills. The Professional Edge on page 123 shows how curriculum-based probes can be used to make eligibility decisions for special education.

FIGURE 4.1 See-Say Probe: Oral Passage Reading

Time	1 minute
Materials	*Student*—Stimulus passage
	Examiner—Duplicate copy of stimulus passage, pencil, timer
Directions to Student	"When I say 'Please begin,' read this story out loud to me. Start here [examiner points] and read as quickly and carefully as you can. Try to say each word. Ready? Please begin."
Scoring	Place a slash (/) on your copy of the materials where the student started reading. As the student reads, place a mark (X) on your copy over any errors (mispronunciations, words skipped, and words given). (If student hesitates for 2–3 seconds, give him or her the word and mark it as an error.) If student inserts words, self-corrects, sounds out, or repeats, do not count as errors. When the student has read for 1 minute, place a slash (/) on your copy to indicate how far the student read in 1 minute. (It is usually good practice to let students finish the paragraph or page they are reading rather than stopping them immediately when 1 minute is over.) Count the total number of words read during the 1 minute sample (the total number of words between the two slashes). Tally the total number of errors (words mispronounced, words skipped, and words given) made during the sample. Subtract the total number of errors from the total words covered to get number correct (total words – errors = correct words).

If students complete the passage before the minute is up, compute student rate using this formula:

$$\frac{\text{\# Correct words}}{\text{Seconds}} \times \frac{60}{1} = \text{Correct words per minute}$$

Note	Probe is administered individually. If you use the optional comprehension questions, be sure to have students finish the passage first.

Billy decided to go down by the river and	(9)
demonstrate his fishing ability. He always could deceive	(17)
the fish with his special secret lure. He had his best	(28)
luck in his own place, a wooded shady spot downstream	(38)
that no one knew about. Today he was going to try	(49)
to catch a catfish all the boys called Old Gray. Old Gray	(61)
was a legend in this town, because even though many boys	(72)
had hooked him, he always managed to get away.	(81)
This time Billy knew that if he sat long enough, he could	(93)
catch his dream fish!	(97)

1. Who is the main character in this story?
2. Where does the story take place?
3. What problem is Billy trying to solve?
4. How is Billy going to try to solve the problem?
5. What do you think is going to happen?

SOURCE: From *Curriculum-Based Assessment and Instructional Design,* by E. Lessen, M. Sommers, and W. D. Bursuck, 1987, DeKalb, IL: DeKalb County Special Education Association. Used with permission.

PROBES OF WRITTEN EXPRESSION ● Written expression can be assessed using a think-write probe. In this probe, the teacher reads the students a story starter. The students then have 1 minute to plan a story and 3 minutes to write it. This probe is scored according to the number of intelligible words the student is able to write per minute. Intelligible words are those that make sense in the story. This way of scoring is useful for screening students for serious writing difficulty (Shinn & Hubbard, 1992). If you are interested in other diagnostic information, such as grammar usage, spelling,

PROFESSIONAL EDGE

Using DIBELS Probes to Identify Children at Risk for Reading Problems

The problem with identifying children who are experiencing reading difficulties is that, by the time they are identified, they are already so far behind that catching them up is often a losing proposition. That is why the current emphasis in reading instruction is on preventing reading problems before they become insurmountable. To do this, children who are at risk of having reading problems need to be identified early. Fortunately, more than 3 decades of research show that two early language skills are highly predictive of reading success in school: letter-naming fluency and phonemic segmentation (Good, Gruba, & Kaminski, 2002). Good and his colleagues at the University of Oregon have developed a series of measures that can be used to measure these and other early literacy skills, called the Dynamic Indicators of Basic Early Literacy Skills, or DIBELS (frequently referred to as "dibbles") (Kaminski & Good, 1996). A hallmark of the DIBELS assessments is efficiency, with each measure taking less than 5 minutes to give. DIBELS measures are also well researched; benchmarks

helpful in identifying children at risk have been identified for each of the measures. The DIBELS measures of phonemic segmentation and rapid letter naming have been used successfully to identify children at risk from the middle of kindergarten to the middle of grade 1.

The ability to identify or retrieve from memory letters of the alphabet already learned is a good early indicator of reading fluency. Ultimately, children who can read accurately and fluently are much more likely to understand what they are reading (Fuchs & Fuchs, 2001). The DIBELS Letter Naming Fluency measure gives students a one-minute see-say letter-naming probe using guidelines discussed in this chapter. Shown below are benchmarks that can be used to identify children who are at risk in kindergarten. As not all kindergartners come to school knowing their letters, some schools delay giving this measure until the middle or even the end of kindergarten. Note that DIBELS assessments measure fluency, so benchmarks reflect the number of letters identified correctly per minute.

Benchmarks for DIBELS Letter Naming Fluency Assessment

	Beginning of Kindergarten	Middle of Kindergarten	End of Kindergarten	Beginning of Grade 1
At Risk	Less than 2	Less than 15	Less than 29	Less than 25
Some Risk	2–7	15–26	29–39	25–36
Low Risk	8 or more	27 or more	40 or more	37 or more

FYI

King-Sears, Burgess, and Lawson (1999) suggest using the following steps, abbreviated as the mnemonic APPLY when using CBAs in your classroom: Analyze the curriculum, prepare items to meet curriculum objectives, probe frequently, load data using a graph format, and yield to results for making revisions and decisions.

CONNECTIONS

Using probes of prerequisite skills is a good way to measure student access to the general education curriculum, a requirement of IDEA.

handwriting, punctuation, vocabulary, or ideas, you can score this probe differently or give another probe designed to measure these areas specifically (see Choate, Enright, Miller, Poteet, & Rakes, 1995; Ellis & Colvert, 1996; Howell & Morehead, 1993; and Mercer & Mercer, 2001, for sample informal assessments in these areas).

PROBES OF MATH SKILLS ● Teachers in the primary grades need to measure student identification of numbers, coins, and geometric figures. This assessment can be done as a see-say probe using numbers and symbols. Computation and problem-solving skills can be assessed using see-write probes (for example, see Howell & Morehead, 1993).

Content-Area Assessments

Although content-area teachers can use CBA probes to test student knowledge of subject matter (see Figure 4.2), they may need to take a somewhat different approach to student assessment. Content-area classrooms are characterized by increased curricular demands with fewer opportunities for individualization; students are expected to learn more material and to take responsibility for learning much of it on their own. While IDEA and NCLB clearly state that the curricular expectations for most students with

Phonemic segmentation involves the understanding that speech is composed of individual sounds (Bursuck & Damer, 2006; Chard & Dickson, 1999). Phonemic segmentation is the ability to say the individual sounds in words that are presented orally. In giving the DIBELS Phoneme Segmentation Fluency measure, the teacher presents a series of words orally, and the student says the sounds in each word.

For example, the teacher says *sad,* and the student says *ssss . . . aaaa . . . dddd.* The teacher continues to present words for 1 minute, and then the total number of phonemes or sounds identified correctly in a minute is scored. Shown below are benchmarks for the DIBELS Phoneme Segmentation Fluency measure from the middle of kindergarten through the middle of grade 1.

Benchmarks for DIBELS Phoneme Segmentation Fluency Assessment

	Middle of Kindergarten		End of Kindergarten–Middle of Grade 1
At Risk	Less than 7	*At Risk*	Less than 10
Some Risk	7–17	*Some Risk*	10–34
Low Risk	18 or more	*Low Risk*	35 or more

All of the DIBELS measures, including videos of persons administering them, are available free of charge at the DIBELS website, http://dibels.uoregon.edu. For more information on how to teach phonemic awareness, including phonemic segmentation, see Bursuck and Damer (2006), and Carnine, Silbert, Kameenui, and Tarver (2004).

SOURCE: *Summary of Decision Rules for Intensive, Strategic, and Benchmark Instruction Recommendations in Kindergarten through Third Grade* (Technical Report No. 11), by R. H. Good, D. Simmons, E. A. Kame'enui, and J. Wallin, 2002, Eugene: University of Oregon, Department of School Psychology.

disabilities are the same as for their classmates without disabilities, students who enter a class significantly behind their classmates either in background knowledge or independent learning skills are likely to struggle. Thus, it is important to identify these students

FIGURE 4.2 Using Curriculum-Based Assessment (CBA) Probes in Content Areas

Content Area	CBA Probe Examples
Geography	Identify each state's location on a map by writing the correct state abbreviation. Match the terrain of an area to corresponding industries and products. Compare and contrast regions so that two similarities and two differences are provided.
Science	Given science terms to define, write the correct definitions. Identify steps in the scientific process, and describe how to apply each step to a given hypothesis. Describe the human body systems so that each system's function and relationship to other systems is stated.

SOURCE: From "Applying Curriculum-Based Assessment in Inclusive Settings," by M. King-Sears, M. Burgess, and T. Lawson, 1999, *Teaching Exceptional Children, 32*(1), pp. 30–38.

CASE IN PRACTICE

Using Story Grammars

Ms. Padilla's second-grade students have just read the story *The Funny Farola*, by Ann Miranda and Maria Guerrero. The story is about a girl and her family participating in an ethnic festival in their city. The girl, Dora, makes a farola, which is a type of lantern people carry while marching in a parade. Dora's family laughs at her farola, because it is in the shape of a frog. However, her unusual farola saves the day when it helps Dora and her parents find Dora's lost brother and sister.

Ms. Padilla is assessing Chantille's comprehension of the story using the story grammar retelling format.

Ms. Padilla: Chantille, you have just read *The Funny Farola*. Would you tell me in your own words what the story is about?

Chantille: The story is about a girl named Dora who made this funny frog that she carried in a parade. You see, her brother and sister got lost at the parade 'cause they were having such a good time, but they got found again 'cause they could see Dora's frog.

Ms. Padilla: Chantille, where does this story take place?

Chantille: It took place in a city and the people were having a big festival.

That's why they were having the parade.

Ms. Padilla: Chantille, what was the problem with Dora's frog?

Chantille: Well, it was called a farola, which is a kind of lantern. Everyone was making them for the parade. Dora's family laughed at her farola 'cause they had never seen a frog farola before.

Ms. Padilla: You said that Dora's sister and brother got lost. What did they do to solve that problem?

Chantille: Well, they saw Dora's frog, so they knew where to find them.

Ms. Padilla: How did you feel at the end of the story?

Chantille: I felt happy.

Ms. Padilla: Why did you feel happy?

Chantille: Well, 'cause Dora's brother and sister found their mom and dad.

Ms. Padilla: Chantille, what lesson do you think this story teaches us?

Chantille: Not to get lost from your mom and dad.

A score sheet that Ms. Padilla completed for Chantille is shown in Figure 4.3. A plus (+) means that Chantille responded accurately to that element without any prompting or questioning; a check mark (✓)

means that Chantille mentioned the element after she was questioned or prompted; a minus (−) means that she failed to refer to the element even after questioning or prompts.

Look at Chantille's scores. As you can see, she had a good idea of who the main characters were and received a + for this component (Characters). Chantille named two problems in the story: Dora making a farola that her family laughed at and Dora's brother and sister getting lost. Chantille identified the problem of the lost kids without being prompted, and the problem of the funny farola with prompts; thus, a + and a ✓ were scored for Goal/Problem. It was unclear from Chantille's response exactly how the characters tried to solve their problem, so she received a − for Attempts. Chantille did say the problem was solved when Dora's brother and sister saw the frog; she received a + for this element of Resolution. However, she did not say how this resolved the problem of her family laughing at the farola, so she received a −. Chantille's reaction to the story was appropriate, so a + was scored. For Setting, Chantille received a ✓; she identified the setting after Ms. Padilla prompted her. Finally, Chantille received a − for Theme. This re-

---

early so that they can be better prepared when they enter a content-area class. For example, at the beginning of this chapter, Mr. Blount assessed his history students' ability to read the class textbook independently because students in his class were expected to read much of the material on their own.

PROBES OF PREREQUISITE SKILLS ● The decision to place a particular student in a given middle school or high school class depends on identifying which skills or content are prerequisite. For example, the English department at a high school developed a test of prerequisite skills for ninth-grade English. Clarise, a student with a learning disability, was given this test at the end of eighth grade to find out whether this class was appropriate for her. For skill-oriented classes such as math and English, prerequi-

FIGURE 4.3 Story Grammar Retelling Checklist

Student Name	Story Elements Evaluated												
	Theme		Setting		Characters		Goal/ Problem		Attempts		Resolution		Reactions
Chantille	–		✓		+		+	✓	–		+	–	+	

+   Responded correctly without prompting
✓   Responded correctly after prompting
–   Did not identify relevant story component

sponse was lacking, even after prompting.

Notice that Ms. Padilla's prompts included explicit references to the various story grammar components. For example, she asked, "You said that Dora's sister and brother got lost. What did they do to solve that problem?" as opposed to asking a more general question, such as, "What happened to Dora's sister and brother?" This use of specific language makes the story grammar components more clear, a necessary structure for younger, more naïve learners.

REFLECTIONS

How could story retellings be incorporated into a classroom literature-based program? How do you think these results will be helpful to Ms. Padilla?

site skills are those covered in elementary school or previously taught courses, such as computation skills for algebra and sentence writing for English. For classes that stress content rather than basic skills (for example, science), having the necessary background information to understand the new material is also vital.

Unfortunately, the process of determining whether students have necessary prerequisite skills can be problematic. A key problem involves identifying these skills. Teachers' choices of prerequisite skills often include skills that a student can bypass while still retaining access to course content, such as reading in a history class (which can be bypassed by using an oral text) or written expression in a science class (which can be bypassed by using oral tests and reports). When testing for prerequisite skills, you must be careful not to inadvertently exclude students with special needs, many of whom are capable of passing content classes despite their problems in certain basic skill areas.

Such problems suggest the need for a fair way of making placement decisions for students with special needs at the high school level. A potentially useful method is for teachers to develop probes to evaluate student performance on critical prerequisite skills. The probe-development process, which is similar to the process of developing curriculum-based assessments described previously in this chapter, consists of the following six steps:

1. Identify critical content learning or skills for your class.

2. Identify entry-level content or skills needed. Be certain these are not skills for which a bypass strategy would be possible.

3. Develop a probe to measure the identified skills.

4. Administer the probe to current classes to make sure that students passing the class are able to pass the probe.

5. Set a minimum score necessary for student course entry based on the results of the preceding step. You may want to use an acceptable range rather than a single score, particularly during the initial stages of this process.

6. As with all educational decisions, no one score should be the sole basis for a decision. Other factors, such as student motivation and level of supportive assistance, need to be considered.

MEASURES OF INDEPENDENT LEARNING SKILLS ● When students enter high school, they find an environment often not as supportive as the smaller elementary and junior high or middle school environments they left. The student body is often larger and more diverse. Daily routines change and curriculum is more difficult (Sabornie & deBettencourt, 2004). High schools also demand a much higher level of student independence through the application of a range of independent learning skills. These skills, often referred to as *learning strategies* or *study skills*, include note taking, textbook reading, test taking, written expression, and time management. Student ability to perform these various skills independently can make the difference between passing or failing a class. For example, at the beginning of the chapter, Mr. Blount decided to assess textbook-reading skills because these were important for success in his class. A sample instrument to measure textbook-reading skills, which was originally developed by Voix (1968) and later adapted by Lessen, Sommers, and Bursuck (1987), is shown in Figure 4.4. Notice that the reading tasks for this measure are taken directly from the students' history and science textbooks. Doing this ensures that the results are relevant for the particular classroom situation. Note also that this textbook-reading assessment can be given to the entire classroom at once, enabling the assessment of many students who have trouble reading their textbooks, not just students with special needs.

As with the basic and prerequisite skills mentioned previously, probes can be developed to assess independent learning. A key consideration is that the tasks used for assessment should parallel the tasks students are faced with in your classroom: If you are evaluating textbook reading, the reading task should come from the textbook you are using in class; if you are measuring a student's ability to take

FYI

The maze (Shin, Deno, & Espin, 2000) is a curriculum-based measure for assessing reading comprehension that can be given either in groups or using a computer. To give the maze, select a passage at the student's grade or instructional level, then delete every seventh word. In place of each deleted word, insert three choices. One of the choices is the correct choice, and the other two are distracters. Students read the passage silently and circle the answers they think are correct. Unlike most CBMs, the maze is not timed. The number or percentage of correct responses is scored. Research has shown that the maze is an effective, time-saving way to measure regularly student growth in reading comprehension (Shin et al., 2000).

What curriculum goals might a physical education teacher observing this class be assessing?

FIGURE 4.4 Evaluating Content-Area Textbook-Reading Skills

Suggestions for specific types of questions are included here. The information in parentheses explains or offers additional information about a particular item.

Using Parts of the Book

1. On what page would you find the chapter called _____? (Tests ability to use table of contents.)
2. Of what value to you are the questions listed at the end of each chapter? (Tests understanding of a specific study aid.)
3. How are the chapters arranged or grouped? (Tests knowledge of text organization.)
4. What part of the book would you use to find the page reference for the topic _____? (Tests knowledge of index.)
5. On what page would you find the answer to each of the following questions? (Tests ability to use index.)

Using Source Materials

1. What library aid tells you the library number of a book so that you are able to find the book on the shelves? (Tests knowledge of functions of card catalog and computerized cataloging systems.)
2. What is a biography? (Tests knowledge of a type of reference book.)
3. Explain the difference between science fiction and factual science materials. (Tests knowledge of important types of science materials.)

Comprehension

These questions would be based on a three- or four-page selection from the textbook.

Vocabulary

1. Turn to page _____. How does the author define the word _____? (Tests ability to use context clues and the aids the author uses to convey the meaning of a word.)
2. Define _____.
3. What is a _____?
4. *Vocabulary in context:* From the paragraph on page 584 beginning "In Poland, the Soviet Union . . . ," write an appropriate and brief definition of each of the following words: _____, _____, and _____.

Noting Main Ideas

These questions would ask for main points of information, such as the main ideas of longer, important paragraphs of a chapter or the summary of an experiment. (*Examples:* What are atoms composed of? What reason was given for the conservation of human resources? What is the result of the photosynthetic process?)

Noting Details

These questions would ask for specific bits of information, such as an aspect of a process, the application of a law, the principal steps in an experiment, a life cycle, or incidents in the life of a scientist. (*Examples:* Describe the photosynthetic process. What are the different stages in the cycle of precipitation and evaporation? List the major incidents in the life of Marie Curie.)

Drawing Conclusions

Ask questions about the significance or value of a finding, the implication of a description of some species or natural phenomenon, causes and effect, or a comparison of two or more types of organisms. The questions should call for answers that are not stated in the text. (*Examples:* Illustrate the term *balance of life*. What conclusion can you draw from the importance of the photosynthetic process? What is the principal difference between mitosis and meiosis?)

continued

FIGURE 4.4 *Continued*

Applying Theoretical Information

These questions would ask for examples of practical uses of scientific law and principles. (*Examples:* Explain the relationship of photosynthesis to the conservation of plant life. Explain the idea that air confined in a small area exerts pressure in all directions, in relation to the action of air in a football.)

Following Directions

These questions would ask learners to show the sequence of steps or ideas for solving a problem or performing an experiment, or the sequence of a chain of events. (*Examples:* What is the second step of the experiment? What should you do after you have placed the flask over the burner?)

Understanding Formulas and Symbols

These questions test student understanding of how symbols and formulas are used with scientific data. (*Examples:* What does the H refer to in the symbol H_2O? What does 40# mean?)

Maps and Graphs

Use questions that require knowledge of map and graph symbols and how to use them. (*Examples:* Use the graph on page 602 to answer these questions: By 1925, how many millions of people inhabited Earth? How many times over will the world population have increased from 2000 to 2050? Use the map on page 174 to answer these questions: Who ruled Gascony in the 12th century? Who governed the major portion of Flanders after 1550?)

Study Reading

Directions: Read pages 584–586. Take notes. Then, close your book and keep it closed. However, you may use the notes you made to help you answer the following questions. (Have questions on a separate sheet for distribution after notes have been made.) *Note:* Ask detail, main idea, and inference questions.

SOURCE: Adapted from *Evaluating Reading and Study Skills in the Secondary Classroom: A Guide for Content Teachers,* by R. G. Voix, 1968, Newark, DE: International Reading Association.

CONNECTIONS

Sample direct observation checklists can be found in Chapter 11.

DIMENSIONS OF DIVERSITY

Student-centered assessment strategies such as self-evaluation are an important part of empowering students through multicultural education.

lecture notes, the task should involve elements similar to a typical lecture delivered in your class.

Once the task has been selected, decide what kind of measure to use. Three possible choices are direct observation checklists, analysis of student products, and student self-evaluation. With direct observation checklists, the teacher develops a list of observable steps necessary to perform a given strategy. Next, the teacher has a student perform a classroom task that requires him or her to use the strategy and records on the checklist which behaviors the student performed.

Although direct observation of student behavior can provide much more useful information, it is time-consuming, particularly when you are a high school teacher who teaches many students each day. For most students, you can use analysis of student products or student self-evaluations. Nonetheless, if you have the luxury of a free moment with an individual student, such as before or after school or during a study hall, the time spent directly observing a student perform a task is very worthwhile.

Analysis of student products involves looking at student notebooks, tests, papers, and other assignments or written activities to find evidence of effective or ineffective strategy performance. In most cases, you can evaluate your whole classroom at once, and you do not have to score the products while you are teaching.

In student self-evaluations, students perform a task such as taking a test, are given a checklist of strategy steps, and are then asked to tell which of these steps they used (Mercer & Mercer, 2001; Miller, 1996). Student self-reports are useful for several reasons. They can provide information about strategy behaviors that cannot be directly observed. Student evaluations also stimulate student self-monitoring, a behavior critical for independent learning. Self-report measures can also include interview questions that further clarify strategy usage. For example, one teacher asked, "What was the first thing you did when you received your test?" As with all measures, student self-evaluations need to be corroborated by information from other sources (for example, direct observation checklists and student products). Such corroboration may be particularly important for students with special needs, many of whom have difficulty evaluating their own behavior.

CONNECTIONS

Examples of student self-evaluations are shown in Chapter 10.

How Are Curriculum-Based Probes Used to Make Special Education Decisions?

Academic probes can help teachers make many of the assessment decisions discussed previously in this chapter. Several examples are discussed in the following sections.

Peer Comparison in Screening

The key question involved in screening is whether a student is different enough from his or her peers on important skills in a given academic area (or areas) to indicate that some form of classroom accommodation is necessary. If the difference between a student and his or her peers continues or worsens despite repeated attempts in the classroom to remediate, a referral to special education and a more comprehensive assessment may be necessary.

When used for screening, probes are first selected in the area(s) of suspected difficulty. Next, the probes are given to the entire class or a representative subsample of the class (for example, five "average" performers) (Deno, 1985, 1989). Figure 4.5 shows probe results for oral reading fluency in context. The scores are ranked from high to low, and then the class median is determined. The median, or middlemost score, is used

CONNECTIONS

The national norms for oral reading in Table 4.1 on page 123 can also be used to screen students with reading problems. Students who score below the 25th percentile are generally considered to be at risk.

FIGURE 4.5 Classroom Performance on Academic Skill Probe in Reading

Reading Orally in Context

Number of correct words per minute read orally

190	136	103
189	128	99
172	125	97
160	123	96
159	120	94
151	119	90
139	119	50*
136	117	

Median   123

Median/2   61.5

*Denotes score of Median/2 or lower

RESEARCH
N O T E

Deno and colleagues (2002) used the bottom 20 percent on a CBM probe of reading comprehension to successfully identify students considered to be highly at risk and in need of more frequent progress monitoring.

to summarize the scores because it is affected less by extreme scores than the mean, or average, which could over- or underestimate the performance of the group as a whole.

Figure 4.5 also gives a score equal to one-half of the median. This score can be used as a cutoff for identifying students who are having trouble with that particular skill (Shinn & Hubbard, 1992). Such a cutoff point typically identifies 6 to 12 percent of a class or grade level that may be experiencing difficulty with a particular skill (Bursuck & Lessen, 1987; Marston, Tindal, & Deno, 1984). Some probes may identify more students in trouble. For example, we would expect a higher percentage of third graders to be discrepant on basic multiplication facts in the fall than in the spring, because in the fall these facts have not yet been covered in class. Similarly, many first graders score low on probes given during the first half of the year, because many of the skills assessed are being presented for the first time.

> TECHNOLOGY NOTES

Computerized Curriculum-Based Measurement

You may be wondering how you are going to assess your students systematically and still have time to prepare and teach your lessons. Researchers have developed a product that may help you (Fuchs, Fuchs, Hamlett, Philips, & Bentz, 1994). They have developed software that makes scoring and interpreting curriculum-based measures in math much easier. In the Fuchs et al. system, students take a weekly probe test that measures required math operations for a given grade level. Students then are taught to enter their own data into a computer program that scores their test and summarizes the results.

The software program summarizes student performance using a display like the one shown in Figure 4.6. The graph shows the student's rate and accuracy on weekly math tests over time. This student (Sheila Hemmer) went from a score of 10 digits correct per minute at the beginning of October to a score of more than 30 digits correct per minute in March. The skills profile chart shows which skills (A1 = first skill in addition; S2 = second skill in subtraction) have been mastered and which may require more instruction.

FIGURE 4.6 Individual Student Performance

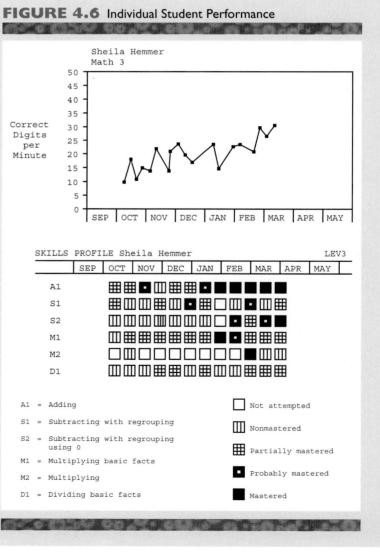

To see how these scores are used to make decisions about screening, look again at Figure 4.5. Oral reading in context represents the number of correct words read orally from a grade-level passage in the classroom reading program. As shown, the class scores range from a high of 190 words read correctly per minute to a low of 50 words read correctly per minute. The median, or middlemost, score for the class is 123 words read correctly per minute. A score of 61.5 words read correctly per minute is half of the median. One student scores below this point. Although this student may be in need of extra support from the classroom teacher or even a referral to special education, other factors should also be considered, including how the student performs across other academic skills assessed and whether other students in the class are having similar problems. The Technology Notes starting on page 134 illustrates a way you can use software to help you assess your students.

Teachers also receive a display like the one in Figure 4.7. The graph shows the teacher, Mr. Martin, how his students progressed from October through March. The top line indicates scores at the 75th percentile; the middle line, scores at the 50th percentile; and the bottom line, scores at the 25th percentile. The lists below the graph provide information about which students should be watched, or monitored; areas in which the class has improved or not changed; and recommendations for skills that could be covered in whole-group instruction (most of the class needs instruction) or small-group instruction (only one or two students).

FIGURE 4.7 Summary of Class Performance

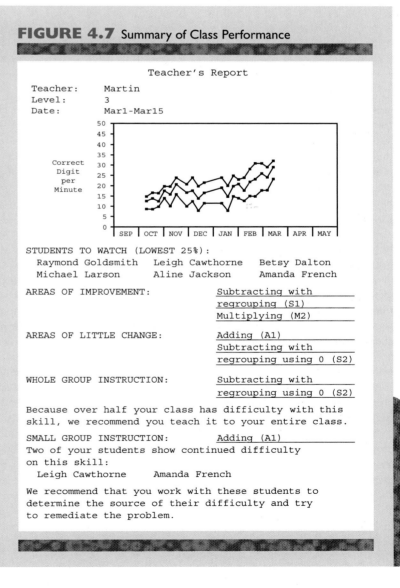

Teacher's Report

Teacher: Martin
Level: 3
Date: Mar1-Mar15

STUDENTS TO WATCH (LOWEST 25%):
  Raymond Goldsmith   Leigh Cawthorne   Betsy Dalton
  Michael Larson   Aline Jackson   Amanda French

AREAS OF IMPROVEMENT: Subtracting with
                                 regrouping (S1)
                                 Multiplying (M2)

AREAS OF LITTLE CHANGE: Adding (A1)
                                 Subtracting with
                                 regrouping using 0 (S2)

WHOLE GROUP INSTRUCTION: Subtracting with
                                 regrouping using 0 (S2)

Because over half your class has difficulty with this skill, we recommend you teach it to your entire class.

SMALL GROUP INSTRUCTION: Adding (A1)
Two of your students show continued difficulty on this skill:
  Leigh Cawthorne   Amanda French

We recommend that you work with these students to determine the source of their difficulty and try to remediate the problem.

Fluency and Accuracy in Diagnosis

**ANALYZE
AND REFLECT**

What kinds of diagnostic information can you learn by checking both student fluency and accuracy that you would be unable to learn from checking accuracy alone?

CBA probes also can help teachers diagnose specific skills deficits. For example, a student who performs poorly on a math facts probe may not know the math facts or may simply be unable to write numbers fast enough. You can figure out which situation exists by examining the student's rate, or *fluency*, of think-write number writing. Likewise, keeping track of the number of errors per minute, or *accuracy*, in oral reading can help you detect a particular student's reading problem. Figure 4.8 shows the results of an oral reading probe for two third-grade students. The correct-reading rate for both students is 53. However, Student 1 seems to have a problem with reading fluency. What she reads, she reads accurately; the problem is that 53 words correct per minute is slow for a third-grade student. Student 2, moreover, is less accurage in her reading than Student 1; she is making many word identification errors and needs to be further assessed to ascertain whether these errors are part of a pattern or are due to carelessness. The Case in Practice below gives an example of how collaborative problem solving using CBAs can help identify students in need of additional support.

CASE IN PRACTICE

Using a Classroom-Based Problem-Solving Model

At the beginning of the last school year, Ms. Henning, a fourth-grade teacher, discovered that Yun, a transfer student, was far behind the rest of the class in reading fluency. Whereas most students in the class were reading at least 100 words correct per minute, Yun was reading about 40 words correct per minute.

Yun's school was using a problem-solving model (Marston et al., 2003) to identify students who might have disabilities. The idea behind this model is that if children can be identified and differentiated instruction provided in the general education classroom, many students may not need special education, and those who do will be the ones truly in need. With this in mind, Ms. Henning approached the problem-solving team for help with Yun.

The problem-solving team used progress graphs such as the one shown on page 137 developed by Deno (2003) to help make decisions about students' instruction. Note that Yun's progress was being monitored in terms of words read correctly and

incorrectly per minute on a classroom reading assessment. Note also the presence of an aim line represented by the solid black line. The aim line starts at Yun's current level of performance in September of 40 words per minute, and extends to the goal set for the end of the year, in this case the expected level of Yun's classmates or 120 words per minute with 2 or fewer errors per minute.

Yun's progress graph is divided into 3 parts, labeled Stage 1, Stage 2, and Stage 3. In *Stage 1, Classroom Intervention*, Ms. Henning tried an intervention on her own; she paired Yun up with a classmate and had them read to each other from books of their own choosing for 30 minutes, three times per week. After 4 weeks, as shown in the graph, Yun's scores remained about the same, so Ms. Henning moved to *Stage 2, Problem-Solving Team Intervention*. For this stage, Ms. Henning went to the team for advice on what to do. The team suggested that Ms. Henning increase the time allotment for paired reading to 5 times per week, and use books at

the students' instructional level. Ms. Henning added that she was going to monitor more carefully the paired reading to make sure the students were carrying it out faithfully. After these changes were made, Yun's performance improved at first, but around Week 11 she began to fall below the aim line, and the team was afraid she wouldn't meet her end-of-year goal unless something else was done. During *Stage 3, Special Education Referral and Initiation of Due Process*, Ms. Henning continued to work on fluency with Yun in the general education classroom, alternating paired reading with several other research-based strategies she learned in a teacher workshop to help Yun read with expression. Permission was also obtained to conduct a case study evaluation. After several standardized assessments were given, Yun was declared eligible for learning disabilities services and received 45 minutes of intensive instruction daily from the special education teacher. As you can see, this final intervention was quite

FIGURE 4.8 Reading Fluency Information for Two Students

Student 1		Student 2	
Number of words correct per minute	Number of words incorrect per minute	Number of words correct per minute	Number of words incorrect per minute
53	2	53	16

The fact that CBA probes measure fluency as well as accuracy adds an important diagnostic dimension. For example, if the reading performance of the two students in Figure 4.8 were reported solely as a percentage of accuracy, the results would look like those shown in Figure 4.9. Using percentages alone, Student 1 does not appear to have

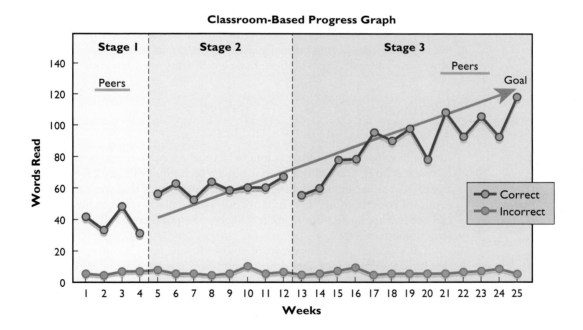

Classroom-Based Progress Graph

successful; after 25 weeks, Yun met her goal of reading 120 words per minute in grade-level material.

For more information about issues related to this method, see Chapter 3, as well as the discussion in Chapter 2 about pre-referral interventions.

REFLECTIONS

In what ways did both Ms. Henning and the problem-solving team contribute to the process of helping Yun? What were some features of this problem-solving model that made it

effective? Can you think of any problems that might occur when using this approach? How might those problems be overcome?

FIGURE 4.9 Percentage of Accuracy in Passage Reading for Two Students

Student 1	Student 2
Percentage of accuracy	Percentage of accuracy
96	70

a problem at all. However, as previously shown, she is reading much more slowly than Student 2.

Skill Mastery and Curriculum Placement

Inclusive education involves the use of a variety of instructional grouping arrangements. Sometimes students are grouped together based on their skill levels; other times a broader range of student skills is desired in a group. Students with special needs benefit from both types of instructional arrangements. You can use CBA probes to group your students by rank ordering and then visually inspecting your students' probe scores. For example, Mr. Glass wanted to form cooperative groups in math. He used scores on a problem-solving task probe, picking one lower performer, two middle performers, and one higher performer for each group. Ms. Robins, in contrast, found that three of her students were having difficulty with capitalization but the rest of the class was not. She formed a small group of those having difficulty, to review capitalization rules.

Monitoring Student Progress and Instructional Evaluation

Although education has come a long way in terms of researching what constitutes effective teaching, predicting whether a given technique will work for a given student in a particular situation is still difficult. It is thus important that you carefully monitor the results of your teaching. This monitoring is particularly relevant for students with special needs who, by definition, are less likely to respond favorably to commonly used instructional methods.

CBA probes, because they are time-efficient, easy to give, and match what is taught in the classroom, are ideal for monitoring student progress in class. For example, Mr. Harris was interested in whether Maria, a student with learning disabilities, was retaining any of the words featured on weekly spelling lists. She had scored 90 and above on her weekly tests, but Mr. Harris was unsure whether she was remembering the words from week to week. He developed a spelling probe using words from previous spelling lists. He gave the probe to his entire class and found that Maria and 10 other students were retaining only 20 percent of the words. As a result, he started a peer tutoring program to help students review their words. Mr. Harris also set up group competitions and awards for groups scoring the highest on the review probes. Implementing these two activities improved Maria's and the other students' retention significantly.

A final example of a CBA probe is worthy of mention. Mr. Rock's school recently switched its reading program from a literature-based program to a more structured basal program. Mr. Rock wanted to make sure that the new series was meeting the

ANALYZE AND **REFLECT**

How could the information from student progress-monitoring probes be used to establish eligibility for special education services?

W W W R E S O U R C E S

For the latest research on student testing, curriculum, and achievement, go to the website of the National Institute on Student Achievement, Curriculum, and Assessment at http://www.ed.gov/offices/OERI/SAI/index.html.

needs of both his higher- and lower-performing students. He randomly selected one representative 300-word passage from a story that the students had recently read and had each student read it orally, recording the number of words read correctly per minute. He also asked the students several questions about what they had read. Mr. Rock found that one of his students read at a rate much slower than his classmates. Mr. Rock decided to provide him with extra reading practice with a peer tutor three times a week. Mr. Rock also found that two other students read much more fluently than the rest of the class while still understanding what they had read. He decided to place them in a group reading at a higher grade level. Teaching approaches, no matter how well they are carried out, can affect students differently. By monitoring the progress of all of his students using CBA probes, Mr. Rock was able to meet their individual needs.

> Teaching approaches, no matter how well they are carried out, can affect students differently.

SUMMARY

General education teachers can make assessments that contribute to six decision-making areas of special education: screening, diagnosis, program placement, curriculum placement, instructional evaluation, and program evaluation. General education teachers can go to a number of information sources to make these decisions for students with special needs. High-stakes tests and group-administered standardized achievement tests can be used to screen students having difficulty, but they have serious drawbacks for making other types of decisions. Individually administered diagnostic tests provide more specific information but are susceptible to many of the same problems as group-administered tests. Psychological tests, such as tests of intelligence and tests related to learning disabilities, measure abilities that affect how efficiently students learn in an instructional situation. A small percentage of students who are typically

working on a more functional curriculum do not have to meet the same requirements as those students graduating with a standard diploma. These students are eligible for alternative assessments based on their more functional curriculum. Curriculum-based assessments (CBAs) measure student achievement in terms of what they are taught in the classroom. There are two major kinds of CBAs: probes of basic academic skills and probes of content-area knowledge and strategies. CBAs are helpful in making a range of special education decisions, particularly those involving day-to-day instruction. A peer comparison method can help screen students who are having academic difficulty. Probes can also be used to help teachers diagnose specific skill deficits to help form instructional groups, and allow teachers to monitor the progress of students in class by measuring student performance over time.

Applications in **Teaching Practice**

Collecting and Using Assessment Information

It is October 1, and you are concerned about two students in your reading program. The students' parents have commented that they have not seen improvement in their children's reading at home. You have also noticed that both of these students pick books during independent reading that are too hard for them and repeatedly guess at words without approaching them systematically. You wonder whether you should make some changes in their reading program.

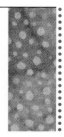

QUESTIONS

1. What areas of reading do you want to assess here? Why?
2. How will you assess each area using the curriculum-based assessment procedures described in this chapter? What probes will you give? What will your probes look like? How will you score them?
3. What additional assessment information (for example, standardized tests, psychological tests) will you collect?
4. How will you use the information you obtained in Questions 2 and 3? Under what circumstances will you decide to accommodate the students in the current program? To use an alternative program? To advocate for intensive instruction from a special education teacher?
5. What will you do to evaluate the changes suggested in Question 4? What measures will you give? How often? What kinds of decisions will you be making?

Yolanda is a student with a learning disability in your class who has been receiving indirect support in one area. You are interested in knowing how she is doing in relation to the rest of the class. Select the subject area in which Yolanda has been receiving indirect support (reading, math, or written expression). Then, select a particular skill in that subject matter that you have been working on in your class (for example, in reading: sight-word reading, passage reading, comprehension, letter or letter–sound identification; in math: any math computation skill, word problems, money, geometry; in written expression: writing mechanics, writing productivity, quality of ideas). Next, describe a curriculum-based assessment strategy you would use to judge how well Yolanda is doing on that skill as compared with her classmates. Respond to the following questions in your description.

QUESTIONS

1. How will you use peer comparisons to measure the extent of Yolanda's problem?
2. What additional information will you collect to clarify Yolanda's problem?
3. How will you use probe information to measure the effectiveness of classroom supports for Yolanda?
4. How will you use probe information to help you instruct the rest of the class?

The high school resource room teacher has suggested that Antoine, who has a learning disability, be included in your second semester class. The teacher has asked you to help collect some information to assist him in deciding what support service (if any) Antoine should receive. Assuming you are a math teacher, describe a strategy for determining whether Antoine has the prerequisite skills for your class. Your strategy should respond to the following questions.

QUESTIONS

1. What skills will you include on your probe and why?
2. Are all these skills essential, or could some of them be bypassed?
3. How will you design, administer, and score your probe?
4. How will you determine whether Antoine is experiencing academic difficulty?
5. How will you use the information collected to determine needed support services for Antoine?
6. How might the information collected help you in teaching the rest of the class?

If you are teaching a class for which the ability to read the textbook is an important skill, select a sample textbook from your content area. Then, develop a probe of content-area reading skills using the model shown in Figure 4.4 on pages 131–132.

QUESTIONS

1. How did you select the skills to be included on your probe?
2. How could you use the information collected to determine the nature and extent of classroom support needed for students with disabilities? For the rest of the class?

Design a 1- or 2-day lesson in the content area of your choice, describing briefly all the instructional activities involved. Be sure to specify objectives for as many of the following student outcome areas as possible: using patterns to understand past and present events and to predict future events; using technology effectively; demonstrating skills and values for physical activity; and completing a postsecondary opportunities search. Tell how you would use an alternate assessment to measure the progress of Darrell, a student with a severe cognitive disability who is in your class.

QUESTIONS

1. What outcomes would you expect for your students without disabilities?
2. What outcomes would you expect for Darrell?
3. Describe how you would assess the outcomes for Darrell using alternate assessment devices. Include evaluation criteria for each of the assessments described.

WORKING THE **STANDARDS**

INTASC PRINCIPLES REFLECTED IN THIS CHAPTER:

Principle #4 states that all teachers provide a variety of ways for students with disabilities to demonstrate their learning (Principle 4.05).

Principle #7 states that all teachers monitor student progress and incorporate knowledge of student performance across settings (for example, home, after-school programs, and neighborhood) into the instructional planning process, using information provided by parents and others in those settings (Principle 7.05).

Principle #8 states that the teacher understands and uses formal and informal assessment strategies to evaluate and ensure the continuous intellectual, social, and physical development of the learner. In addition, this standard requires that all teachers

- Understand the purposes, strengths, and limitations of formal and informal assessment approaches for making eligibility, placement, and instructional decisions for students with disabilities (Principle 8.01).

- Use a variety of assessment procedures to document students' learning, behavior, and growth within multiple

environments appropriate to the students' age, interests, and learning (for example, home, child-care settings, preschool, school, community, work). This information is used initially to consider eligibility for special education services, and later to construct and modify individualized education programs (IEPs), individualized family service plans (IFSPs), and individual accommodation plans (IAPs). Subsequently, information from the general education teacher is used to monitor the progress of students in the general education classroom toward achieving those students' learning goals, and for making decisions about appropriate instruction (Principle 8.02).

- Collaborate with others to incorporate accommodations and alternative assessments into the ongoing assessment process of students with disabilities when appropriate (Principle 8.03).

- Engage all students, including students with disabilities, in assessing and understanding their own learning and behavior (Principle 8.04).

- Understand that students with disabilities are expected to participate in district and statewide assessments and that accommodations or alternative assessments may be

WORKING THE **STANDARDS** *(continued)*

required when appropriate. They collaborate with the special education teacher to facilitate the participation of students with disabilities and provide appropriate accommodations or alternative assessments when needed (Principle 8.05).

CEC STANDARDS REFLECTED IN THIS CHAPTER:

CEC Content Standard #8 states that special educators

- Use the results of assessments to help identify exceptional learning needs and to develop and implement individualized instructional programs, as well as to adjust instruction in response to ongoing learning progress.

- Conduct formal and informal assessments of behavior, learning, achievement, and environments to design learning experiences that support the growth and development of individuals with exceptional learning needs.

- Understand the appropriate use and limitations of various types of assessments.

- Use assessment information to identify supports and adaptations required for individuals with exceptional learning needs to access the general curriculum and to participate in school system and statewide assessment programs.

- Regularly monitor the progress of individuals with exceptional learning needs in general and special curricula.

BACK TO THE CASES

The standards and principles just listed relate to the cases described at the beginning of this chapter: Rob, Mr. Blount, and Roberto. The questions and activities that follow demonstrate how these standards and principles, along with other concepts that you have learned about in this chapter, connect to the everyday activities of all teachers.

Rob

Ms. Lyons has determined that Rob's needs should be discussed with the school's instructional assistance team. In addition to presenting information outlining his specific problem areas in mathematics, she will need to describe what teaching methods, strategies, and/or accommodations she has used to support Rob's learning and how he has responded to them. This is an informal assessment technique often referred to as *response to treatment.* (See INTASC Principle 8.03 and CEC Standard 8.) How might Ms. Lyons document the instructional strategies she has tried with Rob and the results of these? Provide a rationale for your choices.

Mr. Blount

Mr. Blount has been proactive in assessing how well his students can use the assigned text in his class and has used the data from those assessments to teach the prerequisite skills needed to learn from text. However, he is aware that if his special education students have difficulty reading textbooks, they may also have difficulty reading the text of high-stakes end-of-grade tests required in his school system. He wants to use appropriate accommodations during these tests. (See INTASC Principles 8.01 and 8.05, and CEC Standard 8.) How should he determine which accommodations to use? Further, how might he prepare students to use these accommodations?

Roberto

Most likely, Roberto will have difficulty participating in the standardized assessments given in his state. Ms. Benis and Roberto's special education teacher met after school yesterday to discuss what assessment methods they will use to demonstrate Roberto's progress toward meeting state standards. At this meeting, the two teachers reviewed the full range of options available to them and prepared a list of pros and cons for each option. (See INTASC Principles 4.05, 8.02, 8.03, and 8.05; and CEC Standard 8.) What would be on your list of options? As you prepare your list, include the pros and cons of each option based on what you know about Roberto.

> Visit the companion website (http://www.ablongman.com/friend4e) for a complete correlation of this chapter to the INTASC Principles and CEC Standards.

Further **Readings**

Bryant, D. P., & Bryant, B. R. (Eds.). (2004). Reading assessment [Special issue]. *Assessment for Effective Intervention, 29*(4), 3–76.

This special issue contains valuable information about issues and practices in all aspects of reading instruction for students with special needs.

Hosp, M. K., & Hosp, J. L. (2003). Curriculum-based measurement for reading, spelling, and math: How to do it and why. *Preventing School Failure, 48*(1), 10–17.

This article presents clear, nontechnical guidelines for monitoring student progress using curriculum-based measurements in reading, spelling, and math.

Kleinert, H., Green, P., Hurte, M., Clayton, J., & Oetinger, C. (2002). Creating and using meaningful alternate assessments. *Teaching Exceptional Children, 34*(4), 40–47.

This very practical article contains a wealth of examples of alternate assessments for students with significant cognitive disabilities.

Salvia, J., & Ysseldyke, J. E. (2004). *Assessment in special and inclusive education* (9th ed.). Boston: Houghton Mifflin.

This classic text is an excellent reference for finding out about standardized tests used in special education.

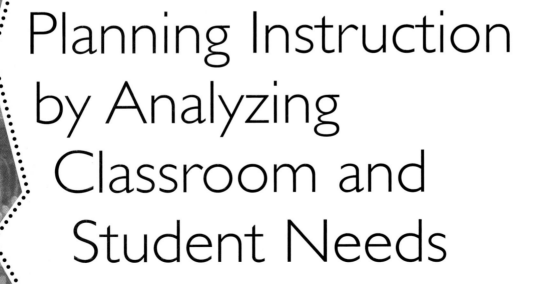

CHAPTER 5

Planning Instruction by Analyzing Classroom and Student Needs

After you read this chapter, you will be able to

1. Explain what it means to make reasonable adaptations for students with special needs.

2. Describe the steps of the INCLUDE decision-making process for accommodating students with special needs in your classroom.

3. Identify and describe the key elements of a classroom environment.

4. Describe the major components of classroom organization, and explain how they can be adapted for students with special needs.

5. Explain various ways that students can be grouped for instruction in an inclusive classroom.

6. Explain how the use of effective classroom materials and instructional methods can benefit students with special needs.

KEY TERMS AND CONCEPTS

Academic learning time (p. 161)

Assistive technology (AT) (p. 171)

Differentiated instruction (p. 148)

Direct instruction (p. 173)

INCLUDE strategy (p. 146)

Indirect instruction (p. 176)

Inquiry learning (p. 176)

Instructional accommodations (p. 152)

Instructional modifications (p. 154)

Mixed-skill groupings (p. 164)

One-to-one instruction (p. 164)

Same-skill groupings (p. 164)

Scaffolding (p. 177)

Transition time (p. 161)

Universal design (p. 147)

MR. RODRIGUEZ TEACHES world history at a large urban high school. When he introduces new content to his students, he teaches to the whole class at once. First, he reviews material that has already been covered, pointing out how that material relates to the new content being presented. Next, he provides any additional background information that he thinks will help students understand the new material better. Before Mr. Rodriguez actually presents new material he hands out a partially completed outline of the major points he will make. This outline helps students identify the most important information. Every 10 minutes or so he stops his lecture and allows students to discuss and modify the outline and ask questions. When Mr. Rodriguez completes his lecture he organizes students into cooperative learning groups of four to answer a series of questions on the lecture. Manuel is a student with a learning disability in Mr. Rodriguez's class. He has a history of difficulty staying on task during lectures and figuring out what information to write down. He also has trouble remembering information from one day to the next. ● *How well do you think Manuel will perform in Mr. Rodriguez's class? What changes in the classroom environment might help Manuel to succeed?*

JOSH HAS CEREBRAL PALSY. He is in the normal range in ability. However, he has lots of trouble with muscle movements, has little use of his lower body and legs and also has problems with fine muscle coordination. As a result, Josh uses a wheelchair, has trouble with his speech (he speaks haltingly and is difficult to understand) and struggles to write letters and numbers correctly. Josh is included in Ms. Stewart's second-grade class. ● *What aspects of the classroom environment do you think Ms. Stewart will need to adapt for Josh? How do you think she could use technology to facilitate Josh's inclusion?*

Disabilities and other special needs arise when characteristics of individual students and various features of students' home and school environments interact. Effective teachers analyze their classroom environment in relation to students' academic and social needs and make adaptations to ensure student success in the classroom. For example, Manuel has difficulty staying on task and retaining new information. However, features of Mr. Rodriguez's class make it easier for Manuel to function. The partially completed lecture outlines help Manuel focus his attention on specific information as he tries to listen and stay on task; the pauses help him catch any lecture information he might have missed. The review sessions are intended to help Manuel retain information by giving him a mechanism for rehearsing newly learned material. In another case, Josh has some serious motor problems, but he may be able to function quite independently if Ms. Stewart makes her classroom accessible to a wheelchair and works with special educators to use assistive technology to meet Josh's needs in handwriting and oral communication.

This chapter introduces you to a systematic approach to helping all students with special needs gain access to the general education curriculum, a requirement of IDEA. Part of that approach is for you to be the best teacher you can be so that fewer of your students require individualized instruction in the first place. Despite your best efforts, however, there will always be students who require a more individualized approach. The **INCLUDE** strategy is provided for these students. Although there are other ways to adapt instruction for students with special needs, INCLUDE gives teachers a systematic process for making adaptations for students based on their individual needs and the classroom demands on or expectations of the teacher. The rest of the text—especially Chapters 8 through 13, in which specific strategies are presented—expands and elaborates on this approach. Later chapters also present a more in-depth look at the relationship between your classroom environment and the diverse needs of learners. An important assumption throughout the text is that the more effective your classroom structure is, the greater the diversity you will be able to accommodate and the fewer individualized classroom changes you will need to make.

> **INCLUDE gives teachers a systematic process for making adaptations for students based on their individual needs and the classroom demands on or expectations of the teacher.**

How Can the INCLUDE Strategy Help You Make Reasonable Adaptations for Students with Special Needs?

At a recent conference presentation that included both classroom teachers and special education teachers, one of the authors of this text asked the audience how many of those present worked with students with disabilities. A music teacher at the back of the room called out, "Everyone in schools works with students with disabilities!" He is right. As you have learned in the previous chapters, IDEA entitles students with disabilities to "access," "participation," and "progress" in the general education curriculum. These entitlements were reinforced by the No Child Left Behind Act of 2001 (NCLB), which requires that most students with disabilities meet the same standards as their classmates without disabilities. Therefore, although the professionals who specialize in meeting the needs of students with disabilities are valuable and provide critical instructional and support systems for students, ultimately, you and your peers will be the primary teachers for many students with disabilities and other special needs, and you will form partnerships with special educators to meet the needs of others. That makes it critical for you to feel comfortable making adaptations for students in order for them to have fair access to your curriculum.

The INCLUDE strategy is based on two key assumptions. First, student performance in school is the result of an interaction between the student and the instructional environment (Pisha & Coyne, 2001; Smith, 2004). Consequently, what happens in a classroom can either minimize the impact of students' special needs on their learning or magnify it, making adaptations necessary. In the first chapter-opening example, Mr. Rodriguez engaged in a number of teaching practices that minimized the impact of Manuel's learning disability, such as starting each class with a review of material covered the day before, providing the students with lecture outlines to help them identify important ideas, and engaging his students in regular discussions of the material presented. Nevertheless, if part of Manuel's learning disability is in reading and the classroom text used in Mr. Rodriguez's class is too difficult for Manuel to read independently, Mr. Rodriguez will need to make an individualized adaptation for Manuel as well.

The second key assumption of INCLUDE is that by carefully analyzing students' learning needs and the specific demands of the classroom environment, teachers can reasonably accommodate most students with special needs in their classrooms. You can maximize student success without taking a disproportionate amount of teacher time or diminishing the education of the other students in the class. For example, with the help of the special education teacher, Mr. Rodriguez provided Manuel with a digital text with a built-in speech-to-print component and study guide. Soon, Mr. Rodriguez discovered that other students in the class could also benefit from using the digital text and made it available to them. In this way, reasonable adaptations often assist many students in the class.

The INCLUDE strategy contains elements of both universal design and differentiated instruction, two widely recognized approaches to addressing classroom diversity in general, and inclusion in particular. The idea of **universal design** originated in the field of architecture, where it was learned that designing buildings for persons with diverse needs from the beginning makes them more accessible and saves money spent on costly retrofits of ramps and automatic doors. As applied to classrooms, the idea is that instructional materials, methods, and assessments designed with built-in supports are more likely to be compatible with learners with special needs than those without such supports (Curry, 2003; Hitchcock, Meyer, Rose, & Jackson, 2002; Pisha & Coyne, 2001), and they minimize the need for labor-intensive adaptations later on. For example, print alternatives such as graphics, video, and digital text allow students with

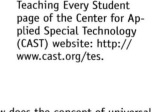

WWW
RESOURCES

For more information on universal design, go to the Teaching Every Student page of the Center for Applied Special Technology (CAST) website: http://www.cast.org/tes.

How does the concept of universal design relate from architecture to teaching? How does this concept simplify the job of a general education teacher?

reading problems to more readily access subject content. The use of templates with partially filled-in sections and links to more information can help students construct a better essay. The INCLUDE assumption that a well-designed classroom requires fewer adaptations for students with special needs is consistent with the universal design approach.

The idea behind **differentiated instruction** is that a variety of teaching and learning strategies are necessary to meet the range of needs evident in any given classroom. According to Tomlinson (2000), students' diverse needs can be met by providing materials and tasks at varied levels of difficulty, with varying degrees of support, through the use of multiple grouping arrangements and with time variations. The INCLUDE process of determining student supports based on student needs and classroom demands is an ideal vehicle for implementing differentiated instruction in your classroom. See the Professional Edge in Chapter 9 on page 314 for an example of differentiated instruction as it applies to beginning reading instruction for students with special needs.

The INCLUDE strategy for accommodating students with special needs in the general education classroom follows seven steps:

Step 1 **I**: **I**dentify environmental, curricular, and instructional classroom demands.

Step 2 **N**: **N**ote student learning strengths and needs.

Step 3 **C**: **C**heck for potential areas of student success.

Step 4 **L**: **L**ook for potential problem areas.

Step 5 **U**: **U**se information gathered to brainstorm instructional adaptations.

Step 6 **D**: **D**ecide which adaptations to implement.

Step 7 **E**: **E**valuate student progress.

These steps are designed to apply to a broad range of special needs and classroom environments. Throughout this text, this icon will denote suggestions for accommodations according to this strategy, with an emphasis on the appropriate step.

Step 1: Identify Classroom Demands

Because the classroom environment significantly influences what students learn, identifying and analyzing classroom requirements allows teachers to anticipate or explain problems a given student might experience. Then, by modifying the environment, teachers can solve or reduce the impact of these learning problems. Common classroom demands relate to classroom organization, classroom grouping, instructional materials, and instructional methods.

CLASSROOM ORGANIZATION ● The ways in which a teacher establishes and maintains order in a classroom are referred to as *classroom organization* (Doyle, 1986). Classroom organization includes a number of factors:

■ *Physical organization*, such as the use of wall and floor space and lighting

■ *Classroom routines* for academic and nonacademic activities

■ *Classroom climate*, or attitudes toward individual differences

■ *Behavior management*, such as classroom rules and monitoring

■ *The use of time* for instructional and noninstructional activities

Classroom organization strategies can have real benefits for students with special needs. For example, LaVerna is a student who needs adaptations in physical organization; she uses a wheelchair and requires wide aisles in the classroom and a ramp for the step leading to her classroom. Shawn has behavioral difficulties and thus would bene-fit from a behavior management system; he might go to his next class prior to the end of each period to eliminate potential opportunities to fight with classmates. He would also benefit from an efficient use of time; minimizing transition times or the amount of time between activities would eliminate further opportunities for inappropriate in-teractions with his classmates.

CLASSROOM GROUPING ● Teachers use a variety of *classroom grouping* arrange-ments. Sometimes they teach the whole class at once, as when they lecture in a content area such as social studies. Other times teachers may employ small-group or one-to-one instruction. For example, they may teach a small group of students who have sim-ilar instructional needs, such as a group of students who all require extra help on multiplication facts, or an individual student who needs extra help with an English as-signment. Teachers may also group students of differing interests and abilities in an ef-fort to foster cooperative problem solving and/or peer tutoring. Students respond differently to these types of groupings. For example, Mike needs adaptations in class-room grouping in order to succeed; he might do better in a small group in which other students read assignments aloud so that he can participate in responding to them.

INSTRUCTIONAL MATERIALS ● The types of *instruc-tional materials* teachers use can have a major impact on the academic success of students with special needs. Although many teachers are choosing to develop or collect their own materials, published textbooks are most commonly used. Pub-lished textbooks include basic skills texts called basals, often used in reading and mathematics, and texts that stress academic content in areas such as history and science. Other materials commonly used by teachers include concrete representational items such as manipulatives and technological devices, includ-ing audiovisual aids, telecommunication systems, and comput-ers. Roberta's use of large-print materials to assist her in seeing her work and Carmen's use of a study guide to help her identify important information in her history text are both examples of adaptations in instructional materials.

> " The types of instructional materials teachers use can have a major impact on the academic success of students with special needs. "

INSTRUCTIONAL METHODS ● The ways in which teachers present content or skills to students and evaluate whether learning has occurred are the essence of teach-ing and are crucial for accommodating students with special needs. These are their *in-structional methods.* Teachers use a number of different approaches to teach content and skills. Sometimes they teach skills directly, whereas other times they assume the role of a facilitator and encourage students to learn on their own. Instructional methods also involve student practice that occurs either in class, through independent seatwork ac-tivities, or out of class, through homework. Ms. Correli's decision to use a PowerPoint presentation in class and then give Lon a copy of the slides to help his learning is an ex-ample of adapting the presentation of subject matter. Using a paraprofessional to write a student's words is an example of adapting student practice.

Student evaluation, or determining the extent to which students have mastered aca-demic skills or instructional content, is an important aspect of instructional methods. Grades are frequently used to communicate student evaluation. For some students, grading is an appropriate evaluation strategy. But for others, such as Anita, a fifth-grade student who has a moderate intellectual disability and is learning to recognize her name, a narrative report might be a better evaluation tool.

When evaluating students with disabilities, teachers must focus on measuring what a student knows rather than the extent of his or her disability. For example, Alex, who has a severe learning disability in writing, may need to answer test questions orally to convey all he knows; if he gives written answers, you may be measuring only his writing disability.

Step 2: Note Student Learning Strengths and Needs

CONNECTIONS

A variety of assessment strategies for determining student strengths and needs in academics were described in Chapter 4. Ways to assess social-emotional development are described in Chapter 12.

Once instructional demands are specified, the N step of INCLUDE calls for noting student strengths and needs. Remember that students with disabilities are a very heterogeneous group; a disability label cannot communicate a student's complete learning profile. For example, some students with cognitive disabilities can learn many life skills and live independently, whereas others continually need daily assistance. Also, keep in mind that students with disabilities are more like their peers without disabilities than different from them. Like their nondisabled peers, they have patterns of learning strengths and weaknesses. Focusing on strengths is essential (Epstein, 2004; Epstein, Rudolph, & Epstein, 2000; Shaywitz, 2003). Three areas describe student learning strengths and needs: academics, social-emotional development, and physical development. Problems in any one of these areas may prevent students from meeting classroom requirements, resulting in a need for adaptations.

ACADEMICS ● The first part of academics is basic skills, including reading, math, and oral and written language. Although these skills might sometimes be bypassed (for example, through the use of a calculator in math), their importance in both elementary and secondary education suggests you should consider them carefully. For example, a student with a severe reading problem is likely to have trouble in any subject area that requires reading, including math, social studies, and science, and on any assignment with written directions.

Cognitive and learning strategies make up the second part of academics. These strategies involve "learning how to learn" skills, such as memorization, textbook reading, note taking, test taking, and general problem solving. Such skills give students independence that helps them in adult life. Students with problems in these areas experience increasing difficulty as they proceed through the grades. For example, students who have difficulty memorizing basic facts have trouble learning to multiply fractions, and students who cannot take notes could fall behind in a history course based on a lecture format.

Survival skills, the third area of academics, are skills practiced by successful students, such as attending school regularly, being organized, completing tasks in and out of school, being independent, taking an interest in school, and displaying positive interpersonal skills (Brown, Kerr, Zigmond, & Harris, 1984; Vallecorsa, deBettencourt, & Zigmond, 2000). Students lacking in these areas usually have difficulty at school. For example, disorganized students are not likely to have work done on time, nor are they likely to deliver parent permission forms for field trips to their parents or return them to school. Survival skills also help some students compensate for their other problems. For example, given two students with identical reading problems, teachers sometimes offer more help to the student who has good attendance and tries hard.

SOCIAL-EMOTIONAL DEVELOPMENT ● Students' social-emotional development involves classroom conduct, interpersonal skills, and personal-psychological adjustment. Classroom conduct problems include a number of aggressive or disruptive behaviors, such as hitting, fighting, teasing, hyperactivity, yelling, refusing to comply with requests, crying, and destructiveness. Although most of these behaviors may be exhibited by all children at one time or another, students with special needs may engage in them more frequently and with greater intensity. Conduct problems seriously interfere with student learning and can lead to problems in interpersonal relations and personal-psychological adjustment. For example, students who are disruptive in class are less likely to learn academic skills and content; their outbursts also may be resented by their peers and may lead to peer rejection, social isolation, and a poor self-image.

Interpersonal skills include but are not limited to initiating and carrying on conversations, coping with conflict, and establishing and maintaining friendships. Although these skills are not ordinarily part of the explicit school curriculum, their overall impact on school adjustment makes them important. For example, students lacking in peer support may have difficulty completing group projects (an example of student practice) or finding someone to help with a difficult assignment (an example of homework).

Personal-psychological adjustment involves the key motivational areas of self-image, frustration tolerance, and proactive learning. For example, students with a poor self-image and low tolerance for frustration may do poorly on tests (an example of student evaluation); students who are inactive learners may have difficulty pursuing an independent science project (an example of student practice).

> ❝ Conduct problems seriously interfere with student learning and can lead to problems in interpersonal relations and personal-psychological adjustment. ❞

PHYSICAL DEVELOPMENT ● Physical development includes vision and hearing levels, motor skills, and neurological functioning. Students with vision problems need adapted educational materials. Students with poor fine motor skills may need a computer to do their homework, an adaptation for student practice. Finally, students with attention deficits may need a wider range of approaches for instruction, including lecture, discussion, small-group work, and independent work.

Step 3: Check for Potential Areas of Student Success

The next INCLUDE step is *C*, analyzing student strengths in view of the instructional demands identified in Step 1 and checking for activities or tasks students can do successfully. Success enhances student self-image and motivation. Look for strengths in both academic and social-emotional areas. Reading the "Current Levels of Performance" section of the IEP is a good way to begin identifying a student's strengths. For example, Jerry doesn't read but can draw skillfully. In social studies, his teacher asks him to be the class cartographer, drawing maps for each region of the world as it is studied. Kurt has a moderate intellectual disability and learns very slowly, but he always comes to school on time. His second-grade teacher appoints him attendance monitor. Dwayne has attention deficit–hyperactivity disorder, is failing all his classes in school, and is beginning to become difficult to handle at home. His parents and teachers have noticed, however, that he is able to identify personal strengths, has a good sense of humor, and can enjoy a hobby. They support Dwayne's positive interests by enrolling him in the school band.

Step 4: Look for Potential Problem Areas

In the *L* step of the INCLUDE strategy, student learning needs are reviewed within a particular instructional context, and potential mismatches are identified. For example, Susan has a learning need in the area of expressive writing; she is unable to identify spelling errors in her work. This is an academic learning need. When evaluating students' work her history teacher, who believes that writing skills should be reinforced in every class, deducts one letter grade from papers that contain one or more spelling errors. For Susan to succeed in history class, this mismatch needs to be addressed. Similarly, Sam has a severe problem that prevents him from speaking fluently. This physical problem creates a learning need. His fourth-grade teacher requires that students present book reports to the class. Again, a potential mismatch exists that could prevent Sam from succeeding. Mismatches such as those experienced by Susan and Sam are resolved by making adaptations, the topic of the next two INCLUDE steps.

Step 5: Use Information to Brainstorm Adaptations

Once potential mismatches have been identified, the *U* step of INCLUDE is to use this information to identify possible ways to eliminate or minimize their effects. IDEA stipulates that two types of adaptations may need to be made for students with disabilities: accommodations and modifications. The Professional Edge below summarizes points to keep in mind when making instructional adaptations for students.

ACCOMMODATIONS ● **Instructional accommodations** are typically defined as services or supports provided to help students gain full access to class content and instruction, and to demonstrate accurately what they know (Nolet & McLaughlin, 2000). It is important to remember that with accommodations, school expectations that students meet learning standards remain unchanged. This means that students with disabilities receiving accommodations are expected to learn everything their classmates

PROFESSIONAL EDGE

Selecting Appropriate Instructional Adaptations

The following list of general guidelines can help you make reasonable adaptations in instruction.

● Employ an adaptation only when a mismatch occurs. Your time and energy as a teacher are limited; make changes only when necessary.

● Be certain that the student's problems are not physical in origin before you make any adaptations. This concern relates particularly to students with no obvious physical or sensory needs. Prior to adapting your class for a student with an attentional problem, be sure that the problem is not the result of a hearing loss, seizure disorder, or other physical problem.

● Determine whether you are dealing with a "can't" or a "won't" problem. Blankenship and Lilly (1981) describe a "can't" problem as one in which the student, no matter how highly motivated, is unable to do what is expected. A "won't" problem implies that the student could do what is expected but is not motivated to do so. Each type of problem may require a different adaptation.

A student unable to do what is expected might need a bypass strategy; a student unwilling to do the work might need a behavior management strategy. This distinction can also save you time. For example, if a student fails a test because she doesn't feel like working on the day of the test, a teacher's attempt to provide extra tutorial as-

sistance is likely to be wasted effort. The "can't" and "won't" problems are particularly relevant for adolescents, who are often less likely than younger students to work to please their teachers.

● Keep adaptations as simple as possible. A good rule of thumb is to try the intervention that requires the least time and effort on your part and is likely to affect the student positively. Try a more involved adaptation only when needed.

FROM THE RESEARCH

A number of recent studies show that students with disabilities have definite preferences for certain adaptations in the areas of homework (Nelson, Epstein, Bursuck, Jayanthi, & Sawyer, 1998), testing (Nelson, Jayanthi, Epstein, & Bursuck, 2000), and grading (Bursuck, Munk, & Olson, 1999) and that student acceptance of an adaptation can affect its implementation and effectiveness (Reimers, Wacker, & Koeppl, 1987). Further, students believe that particular adaptations can affect their emotional well-being, their interactions with teachers and peers, their success in school, and their desire to learn in ways suitable to them (Nelson et al., 1998). Therefore, we suggest that you actively seek student input when choosing adaptations for your students.

without disabilities are supposed to learn (Nolet & McLaughlin, 2000). Examples of accommodations include bypassing students' learning needs by allowing them to employ compensatory learning strategies, making an adjustment in classroom teaching or organization, and teaching students basic or independent learning skills.

Bypass or *compensatory strategies* allow students to gain access to or demonstrate mastery of the school curriculum in alternative ways. For example, a bypass strategy for Susan, the student with a serious problem with spelling, would be a computerized spell-checker. Alternatively, a peer could help her proofread her work. However, bypassing cannot be used in a primary area of instruction. In other words, Susan cannot spell-check her spelling test, but she can spell-check her history homework. Also, bypassing a skill does not necessarily mean that the skill should not be remediated. Susan may need spelling instruction as part of her English class. Finally, bypass strategies should encourage student independence. For example, Susan might be better off learning to use a spell-checker rather than relying on a peer proofreader.

Teachers can also provide accommodations in their classroom teaching and organization to help students succeed. For example, if Ramos has attention problems, he might be seated near the front of the room, and he might benefit from a special system of rewards and consequences as well as a classroom from which "busy" bulletin board displays are removed. All these are classroom organization adaptations. A change in classroom instruction would be to call on Ramos frequently during class discussions and to allow him to earn points toward his grade for appropriate participation.

A third option for accommodating students with special needs is to provide intensive instruction on basic skills and learning strategies. Often, a special education teacher carries out this instruction in a resource room. This approach assumes that basic skills and learning strategies are prerequisites for successful general education experiences. It also assumes that some children require instruction delivered with a greater degree of intensity than can reasonably be provided by a general educator responsible for 20–30 students (Bursuck, Smith, Munk, Darmer, Mehlig, & Perry, 2004). Unfortunately, the results of research on whether skills taught in pullout programs transfer to the general education class are mixed (Kavale & Forness, 2000); some studies show positive results (Freeman & Alkin, 2000; Marston, 1996; Snider, 1997), whereas others show minimal effects (Baker & Zigmond, 1995; Wang, Reynolds, & Walberg, 1988). Studies do suggest that teachers play an important role in determining whether skills taught in a separate setting transfer to their classrooms (Bursuck et al., 2004; Ellis, Lenz, & Sabornie, 1987a, 1987b). For example, Ms. Henry had Jamie in her English literature class; Jamie was receiving pullout services on taking effective lecture notes. First, Ms. Henry found out from the special education teacher what strategy for note taking Jamie was learning. Then she reminded Jamie to perform the strategy before she delivered a lecture, and sometimes even during a lecture. Finally, Ms. Henry collected Jamie's notes on a weekly basis to see whether she was performing the strategy correctly, giving specific feedback to her as needed and reporting her progress to the special education teacher.

An alternative is for the general education teacher to provide this type of instruction. This option is feasible when many students have similar instructional needs and when the teacher can easily monitor skill development. For example, Mr. Higgins, a seventh-grade science teacher, lectures frequently. As a result, students need to be proficient note takers. At the beginning of the school year, Mr. Higgins noticed during a routine check of student notebooks that many students were not taking adequate notes. With assistance from the special education teacher, he taught note taking as part of science. Three students for whom note taking was especially difficult handed in their notes each day so Mr. Higgins could monitor their progress. Working Together on page 154 discusses a co-teaching situation in which the general education teacher is developing a strategy to provide accommodations in her classroom with the help of the special educator.

What classroom demands might this student have difficulty meeting? What bypass strategies or adaptations might help him demonstrate that he has learned his assignment as well as his classmates have?

WORKING TOGETHER

The Reluctant Co-Teacher

Juanita Kirk, math teacher, initially was excited about co-teaching with Susan Harris, the special educator assigned to the seventh-grade team. Now, though, she is disillusioned. Although offered paid planning time during the summer, Susan declined to participate, explaining that she had made her family the focus of her summers and that she would not make professional commitments during that time. Juanita could understand that, but then, at their first meeting in the fall, Susan explained to Juanita that she had always disliked math and had not studied it since she was in high school. She said that she would be most comfortable adjusting to co-teaching by spending the first semester taking notes for students, learning the curriculum, and then helping individual students after instruction had occurred. She stated clearly that she did not have much time for preparing outside of class given all her other responsibilities, and she also made it clear that she did not consider it her responsibility to grade student work.

Juanita was surprised. This was not at all what she expected co-teaching to be. She envisioned a partnership where she and her colleague not only could make instruction more intensive but also could energize math instruction by using various grouping arrangements and brainstorming new ways to reach their students. Now 6 weeks into the school year, she is beginning to think that co-teaching is more like having an assistant in the classroom—an assistant who is highly paid for not doing very much work. She wonders if this is how co-teaching looks in English, the other seventh-grade course to which Susan is assigned. If you were Juanita, how would you address this situation?

Addressing the Dilemma

These are some ideas that Juanita could use to make the co-teaching situation with Susan more productive:

● First, Juanita should find a quiet time and a private place to discuss the situation with Susan. She should directly relate to Susan that she is disappointed in how co-teaching has occurred thus far and then wait to see what Susan has to say.

● If Juanita suspects that Susan lacks confidence in her ability to teach math, she might try to get at this topic using a comment such as this: "You've mentioned that you haven't had math since high school. What a change it must be to be assigned to this class! I think we need to talk about topics we're teaching this year that are most familiar to you so that I don't inadvertently ask you to lead instruction in an area you haven't even thought about for years." This type of statement might prompt Susan to more fully describe what she could do in the classroom.

● As an alternative, Juanita might try being more proactive. For example, she might plan a co-taught set of lessons that call for students to be in three groups, one group having the purpose of reviewing previously taught information (for example, basic problem solving, fractions). She could explain to Susan that after more than a month of adjusting to having a two-teacher classroom, she was ready to try something new, and then describe the plan, offering Susan the review group to lead. If Susan expressed reluctance, Juanita could request that they try this for one week and then review the plan's success.

MODIFICATIONS ● **Instructional** or curricular **modifications** are made when the content expectations are altered and the performance outcomes expected of students change (Nolet & McLaughlin, 2000). Typically, students who receive modifications have behavioral and/or intellectual challenges that are so severe that the curricular expectations in general education are inappropriate. These are usually the same students described in Chapter 4 as being eligible for alternate assessments. Instructional modifications are generally of two types: teaching less content and teaching different content (Nolet & McLaughlin, 2000). For example, in order to meet district grade-level science standards, Ms. Lamb's class was learning to label the parts of the human digestive system and state the purpose for each. Manny, a student with a severe intellectual disability included in Ms. Lamb's class, met the same learning standard by pointing to his stomach when asked where food goes when it is eaten. This is an example of teaching less content. In contrast, teaching different content means that the curricular outcomes are different from those of the rest of the

> " Students who receive modifications have behavioral and/or intellectual challenges that are so severe that the curricular expectations in general education are inappropriate. "

class. For example, an instructional goal for Tony, a student with autism, is to remain calm when there is a change in the classroom schedule.

It is important to reserve instructional modifications for students with only the most significant disabilities. Otherwise, instructional modifications reduce a student's opportunity to learn critical knowledge, skills, and concepts in a given subject, leaving gaps in learning that can interfere with meeting school standards and that can be a disadvantage in later school years and beyond. For example, when one class was learning four reasons for the worldwide spread of AIDS, Steven, a student with a learning disability, was required to learn only two reasons, because he had difficulty remembering information. However, when Steven was required to take the state high-stakes science test, he was held responsible for learning the same information about AIDS as everyone else. It would have been more effective for the school to help Steven better remember science content by using mnemonic devices rather than reducing the amount of information. In short, reducing or simplifying content inappropriately can lead to watering down the curriculum.

Step 6: Decide Which Adaptations to Implement

After you have brainstormed possible accommodations or modifications you can implement the *D* step in INCLUDE, which involves selecting strategies to try. A number of guidelines are suggested here to help you decide which adaptations best suit your students' needs.

SELECT AGE-APPROPRIATE ADAPTATIONS ● Students' adaptations should match their age. For example, using a third-grade book as a supplement for an eighth-grade science student who reads at the third-grade level would embarrass the student. In such a situation, a bypass strategy such as a taped textbook would be preferable if the student has the necessary background and cognitive skills to listen to the book with understanding. A good rule of thumb is to remember that no students, whether in first or twelfth grade and regardless of their special needs, want to use what they perceive as "baby" books or materials.

SELECT THE EASIEST ADAPTATIONS FIRST ● Adaptations need to be feasible for the general education teacher. Although making adaptations often means some additional work for you, it should not require so much time and effort that it interferes with teaching the entire class. For instance, it is easier to circle the 6 out of 12 math problems you want Maria to complete than to create a separate worksheet just for her.

SELECT ADAPTATIONS YOU AGREE WITH ● You are more likely to implement an approach successfully if you believe in it (Polloway, Bursuck, Jayanthi, Epstein, & Nelson, 1996), especially in the area of behavior management. For example, in selecting rewards for good behavior, if you are uncomfortable with giving candy try giving time for desirable activities such as time on the computer. However, adaptations should not be considered only in light of teacher beliefs. IDEA is clear that the unique needs of students take precedence over the convenience of schools. With imagination and some input from special educators, you will undoubtedly find strategies that match your teaching approach while maximizing your students' learning.

SELECT ADAPTATIONS WITH DEMONSTRATED EFFECTIVENESS ● Over the past 30 years, a massive body of professional literature on effective teaching practices has accumulated. This research can help you avoid fads and other unvalidated practices. The strategies suggested throughout this text are based on research and form a starting point for your understanding of validated practices. Such an understanding has always been important, but it is particularly important in view of the recent

CONNECTIONS

Alternate assessments are described in Chapter 4.

ANALYZE
AND REFLECT

What is the difference between instructional accommodations and modifications? Describe situations when each would be appropriate. What problems might arise when deciding whether accommodations or modifications are most appropriate for a given student? Can you think of a situation in which both kinds of adaptations might be used?

ANALYZE
AND REFLECT

Why is age appropriateness a key concept for thinking about students with special needs in general education classes? Can you think of situations when age appropriateness might be less important?

emphasis placed on evidence-based practices in NCLB. Another means of staying professionally current is to read relevant professional journals.

Step 7: Evaluate Student Progress

Although many effective teaching practices exist, it is difficult to predict which will be effective for a given student. As a result, once an adaptation is implemented, the *E* step of INCLUDE is essential: evaluate strategy effectiveness. You can track effectiveness through grades; observations; analysis of student work; portfolios; performance assessments; and teacher, parent, and student ratings. Evaluating this information helps you decide whether to continue, change, or discontinue an intervention.

In the next section the relationship between your classroom and the diverse needs of learners is examined. As you have read, the use of effective practices allows teachers to accommodate more diversity in their classrooms while at the same time reducing the need for making more individualized adaptations. The key aspects of classroom environments are shown in Figure 5.1. These features include classroom organization, classroom grouping, instructional materials, and instructional methods.

How Is an Inclusive Classroom Organized?

Your classroom organization involves physical organization, routines for classroom business, classroom climate, behavior management systems including classroom rules and monitoring, and the use of time. You may need to use the INCLUDE strategy to make reasonable adaptations for students with special needs in all these areas.

Physical Organization

Although the direct effects of physical organization on student academic performance are open to interpretation (Doyle, 2002), the way a classroom is physically organized can affect student learning and behavior in a number of areas (Kerr & Nelson, 1998). Carefully arranged classrooms can decrease noise and disruption, improve the level and quality of student interactions, and increase the percentage of time that students spend on academic tasks (Paine, Radicchi, Rosellini, Deutchman, & Darch, 1983). Classroom organization influences learning conditions for all students, as well as the accessibility of instructional presentations and materials for students with sensory and physical disabilities. Physical organization includes the appearance of the classroom and the use of space, including wall areas, lighting, floor space, and storage.

Wall areas can be used for decorating, posting rules, displaying student work, and reinforcing class content, sometimes through the use of bulletin boards. For example, one teacher taught a note-taking strategy and posted the steps on a bulletin board to help her students remember them. In using wall space, keep in mind two possible problems. First, wall displays may divert students with attention problems from concentrating on your instruction. Place these students where they are least likely to be distracted by displays. Second, students may not notice that important information appears on a display, and you may need to direct their attention to it. For example, Ms. Huerta posted a display showing graphic representations of the basic fractions. She reminded her students to look at these fractions while they were doing their independent math work.

Lighting, either from windows or ceiling lights, also can affect students with special needs. Students with hearing impairments might need adequate light to speech-

ANALYZE
AND **REFLECT**

What impact would the use of universal design have on teacher implementation of the INCLUDE strategy?

ANALYZE
AND **REFLECT**

What are the similarities and differences between INCLUDE and differentiated instruction?

FYI

The rest of this chapter aims to help you answer two questions: How can I teach my whole class so that students' individual difficulties are minimized? What adaptations of the instructional environment might I still need to make to meet individual students' special needs?

FIGURE 5.1 Overview of Classroom Environments.

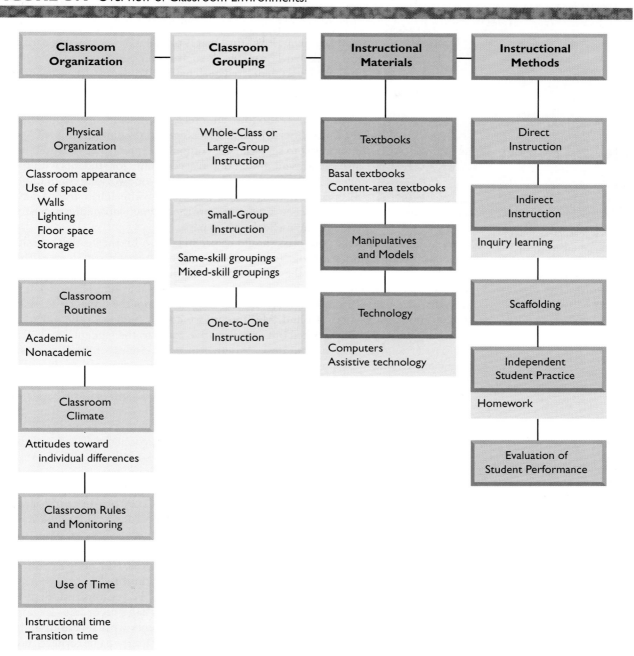

read; they also are likely to have problems with glare in areas where the light source comes from behind the speaker. Students with visual impairments also have difficulty working in areas that are not glare-free and well lighted. Occasionally, students with learning disabilities or emotional disturbances may be sensitive to and respond negatively to certain types of light. In most cases, problems with lighting can be remedied easily by seating students away from the glare caused by sunshine coming through the classroom windows.

This is a teacher-centered grouping arrangement for large-group instruction. What are some advantages and disadvantages of this strategy for students with special needs? What other ways of grouping students should be part of a teacher's instructional repertoire?

> " The arrangement of student desks, whether in rows, circles, or small groups, can have considerable impact on students with special needs. "

The organization of floor space and the kinds and placement of furniture used also need to be considered. For example, floors that do not have a nonslip surface can make wheelchair and other travel difficult. Furniture that is placed in lanes can block access to the chalkboard or materials such as computers and make mobility difficult for students in wheelchairs or students with visual impairments. Tables, pencil sharpeners, and chalkboards that are too high may prove inaccessible to students who use wheelchairs. Desks that are too low can interfere with students who have prostheses (artificial limbs). Placement and configuration of special equipment in science labs, computer centers, and vocational areas also can present difficulties in accessibility for students with special needs. For example, the lathe in the woodworking room might be positioned too high for a person in a wheelchair to operate; the space between work areas in the science lab might not be wide enough for a wheelchair to pass.

The arrangement of your class should be predictable. This means that you should not make major changes without first considering their impact on students with special needs and then informing these students so they have time to adapt. For example, Mr. Tate decided to move one of the bookshelves in his classroom. He noticed, however, that the new location would block the passageway from the door to the desk of a student in his class who was blind. Mr. Tate informed the student of the move in advance, and together they worked out an alternative route to the student's desk.

The arrangement of student desks, whether in rows, circles, or small groups, can have considerable impact on students with special needs. For example, traditional row configurations, which provide students with an immediate, unobstructed view of the teacher, have been shown to help students with attention disorders focus better when the teacher is instructing the whole group at one time. However, the placement of desks into clusters of four works better when you are using mixed-ability, cooperative learning groups to help integrate a student who is socially withdrawn. Another important consideration about floor space concerns student monitoring: Teachers should be able to see all parts of the classroom at all times, whether they are teaching large or small groups or are working at their desks. Designing such visual access means that all specially designated areas in the classroom, such as learning/interest centers, computer stations, small-group instructional areas, and study carrels, need to be positioned so they can be monitored.

An additional area of physical organization is storage. For example, students with visual disabilities may need to store equipment such as tape recorders, large-print books, braille books, and magnifying devices. For students with severe disabilities, space might be needed to store book holders, paper holders, page turners, braces, crutches, and communication boards.

Routines for Classroom Business

Establishing clear routines in both academic and nonacademic areas is important for two reasons. First, routines that are carefully structured (that is, clear to students and used consistently) reduce nonacademic time and increase learning time. Second, you can prevent many discipline problems by having predictable classroom routines.

Most students, especially those with special needs, find stability in knowing that classroom activities will be similar each day. In the absence of this stability, misbehavior often follows. You can find many examples of misbehavior related to breaks in school routines. On the day of a field trip, elementary school students are more likely to hit or push, to delay beginning assignments, and to do poor work. In middle schools and high schools, teachers often dread shortened schedules for assemblies and other school programs because of increased student behavior problems.

You can create daily classroom routines that help students learn. For example, you might expect fourth graders to enter your classroom each morning, begin their morning work, and read quietly if they finish before instruction begins. Having routines for sharing time, for setting up science experiments, for preparing to go to physical education, for moving to the computer lab, and so on helps students meet your expectations. Routines are especially helpful to students who need a strong sense of structure in classroom life. In secondary schools, routines might include having specific lab procedures, starting each class with a 5-minute review, or scheduling a particular activity on the same day every week. For example, in a geometry class, students who complete their assignments might choose to begin the day's homework, complete a Math Challenger worksheet from the activity file, or work on research papers or other long-term projects.

Classroom Climate

A number of authors have noted that classroom climate contributes significantly to the number and seriousness of classroom behavior problems (Jones & Jones, 1990; Morse, 1987). The classroom climate concerns the overall atmosphere in the classroom—whether it is friendly or unfriendly, pleasant or unpleasant, and so on. Climate is influenced by the attitudes of the teacher and students toward individual differences. For instance, is the classroom characterized by a cooperative or a competitive atmosphere? Is the classroom a safe place for all students to take risks? Are skills for interacting positively with children and adults actively supported in the classroom?

Teachers who communicate respect and trust to their students are more successful in creating positive classroom environments in which fewer behavior problems occur (Arends, 2004). For example, Mr. Elliott reprimanded a student who talked out of turn by saying, "I know you have a question about your work, and I'm glad you care enough to ask for help; but I need to have you raise your hand because I can only help people one at a time." Mr. Elliott showed respect for the student and built the student's trust by not putting her down. Yet Mr. Elliott stuck to his rule about not speaking before being called on and explained why it was important. Similarly, Ms. Belson asked Harriet to define the word *diffident*. Harriet gave an incorrect definition, saying it meant "being bored." Ms. Belson said, "Harriet, I can see how you might think the meaning is 'bored' because *diffident* looks a lot like *indifferent*. The word actually means 'lacking in confidence.' "

You can build the overall quality of your communication with your students in many small ways. For example, finding the time each week to speak privately with students lets them know that you care about them as individuals. Asking older students sincere questions about their friends, out-of-school activities, or part-time jobs also conveys your interest in them. Taking the time to write positive comments on papers lets students know that you appreciate their strengths and do not focus only on their needs. When you encourage each student to achieve his or her own potential, without continually comparing students to one another, you are communicating the idea that each class member has a valuable contribution to make. Teachers who fail to take these small steps toward positive communication with students, or who publicly embarrass a student or punish a group because of the behavior of a few, soon may create a negative classroom climate that thwarts appropriate and effective learning.

DIMENSIONS OF DIVERSITY

Kleinfeld, in her research on Athabascan Eskimo and Indian children, found that the most effective teachers demonstrated personal caring and concern for students while at the same time demanding and facilitating high academic performance (1974, 1975, as cited in Gay, 2002). Foster (1995, 1997) and Ladson-Billings (1994) observed similar traits among effective teachers of African American students.

> Teachers who communicate respect and trust to their students are more successful in creating positive classroom environments in which fewer behavior problems occur.

RESEARCH
N O T E

Research suggests that the most effective classroom rules are ones that students develop themselves and express with teacher guidance (Bullara, 1993).

DIMENSIONS
OF DIVERSITY

If your classroom includes students who are not native English speakers, you need to make sure that they understand classroom expectations. You may need to explain in concrete terms in a one-to-one situation what you expect, with the possible help of a translator, a student's parents, or both.

Classroom Rules

What rules do you intend to establish in your classroom? Rules help create a sense of order and expectations for a classroom, and they form a significant first step in setting up a learning environment based on preventive classroom management. Teachers who are effective classroom managers have well-defined rules for their classrooms (for example, Olson & Platt, 2004; Ornstein & Lasley, 2004).

Effective classroom rules share three key characteristics: they are brief and specific, positively worded, and clearly understood by students (Alberto & Trautman, 2002; Doyle, 1990) and accommodate students from different cultures (Grossman, 1995). First, rules should be few in number but as specific as possible. For example, a list of 10 or 12 general rules that urge students to be fair, kind, and respectful is not as useful as 3 or 5 specific rules such as "Speak one at a time," "Keep your hands to yourself," and "Be prepared to start class when the bell rings by having all your learning materials ready."

Second, rules should be worded in a positive way (Arends, 2004; Olson & Platt, 2004). In some classrooms, rules sound punitive because they are too negative. Consider the difference between a rule that states, "Don't call out answers," and one that says, "Raise your hand to speak." If students assist in making classroom rules, you can encourage positive wording by rephrasing any rules that students have inappropriately worded. Keep in mind that students who participate in rule making might be more motivated to obey rules.

Third, rules should be explained carefully to your students so that they are understood. Post rules during the first weeks of school, explain and discuss them, and model them for students. Violations of the rules should be pointed out and corrected immediately. For example, after you and your students have established and reviewed classroom rules, explain their use, congratulate students for following them, and ask students whom you reprimand to explain why their behavior violated the rules. Younger students could draw pictures about their classroom rules and procedures. Older students could write about the necessity for rules. This early attention to setting your classroom expectations has a yearlong payoff. By rehearsing them and focusing student attention on them, you make the rules part of students' understanding of their classroom interactions. If you do not take this time to teach the rules, too often they become merely a bulletin board display, ignored by teachers and students alike.

Finally, you need to be sure that your rules accommodate students from different cultures. For example, rules about respecting other students' property may be puzzling for Latino students, for whom sharing one's belongings is a highly valued activity. Similarly, rules related to aggressive behavior may need to be enforced with care for students whose parents expect them to stand up for themselves, especially when someone says something derogatory about a student's family (Grossman, 1995). It is important to note that taking cultural differences into account does not necessarily mean that the rules need to be changed, only that the rules may need to be more carefully explained and enforced.

Monitoring

CONNECTIONS

Strategies for effective classroom management programs are presented in more detail in Chapter 12.

In addition to having clear expectations, you also need to monitor student classroom behaviors frequently. For example, scan the room to check that students are following the rules. To do this, you always need to have a clear view of the entire class, regardless of the activity in which you or the class are engaged. When student behavior is not carefully monitored, students choose not to follow the rules consistently. For example, Charmaine was a student in Ms. Patrick's fifth-grade class who had behavior problems. Ms. Patrick had a rule that students needed to complete all their independent work before they could go to the computer station to play a problem-solving game. Ms. Patrick did not have time to monitor Charmaine's behavior. One day, she saw Charmaine at the computer station and asked her whether she had completed her assignments. Not only had Charmaine not completed her assignments on that day, but she hadn't done any work for the past 3 days. Thereafter, Ms. Patrick was careful to monitor the work progress of all her students.

The Use of Time

The way teachers use time in the classroom is one of the most important aspects of classroom organization. Effectively using instructional time and managing transition time constitute two particularly important tasks.

USING INSTRUCTIONAL TIME ● The amount of time that students are meaningfully and successfully engaged in academic activities in school is referred to as **academic learning time** (Arends, 2004). Research has shown that more academic learning time in a classroom results in increased student learning (Fisher, Berliner, Filby, Marliare, Cahan, & Dishaw, 1980). Time usage is particularly important for students with special needs, who may need more time to learn than their peers.

Paine and colleagues (1983) suggest several ways in which teachers can maximize academic learning time. One way is to minimize the time spent on organizational activities such as lunch counts, opening activities, getting drinks, sharpening pencils, cleaning out desks, and going to the bathroom. For example, teach students how to perform organizational tasks efficiently and how to hold them to a firm time schedule when carrying them out. Another way is to select activities that have the greatest teaching potential and that contribute most to students' achieving the core school curriculum. Although learning activities can be fun, they should ultimately be selected for the purpose of teaching students something important. Finally, the strategies described in this chapter and throughout this book for organizing your classroom, grouping your students, and adapting your methods and materials also help ensure the productive use of your students' time. One specific technique to increase the academic learning time of your students is described in the Professional Edge on page 162.

MANAGING TRANSITION TIME ● Just as important as the amount of time spent in academic activities is the management of transition time. **Transition time** is the time it takes to change from one activity to another. Transition time occurs when students remain at their seats and change from one subject to another, move from their seats to an activity in another part of the classroom, move from somewhere else in the classroom back to their seats, leave the classroom to go outside or to another part of the school building, or come back into the classroom from outside or from another part of the building (Paine et al., 1983).

Research studies show that teachers sometimes waste academic learning time by not managing transitions carefully (Ornstein, 2004). Paine and colleagues (1983, p. 85) suggest that you have rules devoted specifically to transitions and that you teach these rules directly to students. The following are among the rules they suggest:

1. Move quietly.
2. Put your books away and get what you need for the next activity. (You may need to state what that activity is and what materials students need for it.)
3. Move your chairs quietly. (In some classes with small-group instruction, students carry their desk chairs to the group for seating there.)
4. Keep your hands and feet to yourself.

As with all rules, those for transitions need to be consistently monitored and reinforced.

The way you organize classroom materials also can affect the management of transitions. For example, you need to have all materials ready for each subject and activity. In addition, materials should be organized so that they are easily accessible. No matter how well organized your transitions are, you still may need to adapt them for some

W W W
R E S O U R C E S
Ideas to make teaching easier, including a variety of classroom management and other teaching tips, can be found at Classroom Connect, http://corporate.classroom.com.

PROFESSIONAL EDGE

Using "Sponges" to Increase Academic Learning Time

You almost always have times during the day when you have a minute or two before a scheduled academic activity or before the class goes to lunch, an assembly, or recess. You can fill that extra time with productive activities by using "sponges." Sponges are activities that fit into brief periods of time and that give students practice or review on skills and content you have already covered in class. The following lists of sponges can help you "soak up" that extra classroom time.

Lower-Grade Sponges

1. Tell children to be ready to state one playground rule.
2. Tell children to be ready to list the names of children in the class that begin with *J* or *M*, and so on.
3. Tell children to be ready to draw something that is drawn only with circles.
4. Tell children to be ready to think of a good health habit.
5. Flash fingers—have children tell how many fingers you hold up.
6. Say numbers, days of the week, months—and have children tell what comes next.
7. Ask what number comes between two numbers: for example, 31–33, 45–47.
8. Ask children what number comes before or after 46, 52, 13, and so on.

9. Write a word on the board. Have children make a list of words that rhyme with it.
10. Count to 100 by 2s, 5s, 10s, and so on, either orally or in writing.
11. Think of animals that live on a farm, in the jungle, in water, and so forth.
12. Name fruits, vegetables, meats, and the like.
13. List things you can touch, things you can smell, and so on.

Dismissal Sponges

1. "I Spy"—ask children to find something in the room that starts with *M, P,* and so on.
2. Ask children to find something in the room that has the sound of short *a,* long *a,* and so forth.
3. Number rows or tables. Signal the number of the table with fingers, and allow children to leave accordingly.
4. Count in order or by 2s, 5s, and so on.
5. Say the days of the week, the months of the year.
6. Ask what day it is, what month it is, what the date is, what the year is. Ask how many months are in a year, how many days are in a week, and so on.
7. Use reward activities:

    "We have had a good day! Who helped it to be a good day for all of us? Betty, you brought flowers to brighten

students with special needs. Students with physical disabilities may need more time to take out or put away their books. Students with physical and visual disabilities may have mobility problems that cause them to take more time with such transitional activities as getting into instructional groups or moving from room to room. Furthermore, you may need an individualized system of rewards or other consequences to guide students with attention deficit–hyperactivity disorder or behavior disorders through transition times.

How Can You Group All Your Students for Instruction in Inclusive Classrooms?

Students with special needs benefit from a variety of classroom grouping arrangements, including large- and small-group instruction, mixed- and same-skill groupings, and teacher-centered or peer-mediated group instruction. Remember that the partic-

our room. You may leave. John, you remembered to rinse your hands, good for you. You may leave. Ellen showed us that she could be quiet coming into the room today. You may leave, Ellen. Bob remembered his library book all by himself. Dawn walked all the way to the playground—she remembered our safety rules. Lori brought things to share with us. Tom surprised us with a perfect paper—he must have practiced. . . . "

Students' good deeds can be grouped together to speed up dismissal. The teacher can finish with, "You're all learning to be very thoughtful. I'm very proud of all of you and you should be very proud of yourselves."

8. Use flashcards. A first correct answer earns dismissal.

9. Review the four basic shapes. Each child names an object in the room in the shape of a triangle, circle, square, or rectangle.

Upper-Grade Sponges

1. List the continents.

2. Name as many gems or precious stones as you can.

3. List as many states as you can.

4. Write an abbreviation, a roman numeral, a trademark, a proper name (biological), or a proper name (geographical).

5. Name as many countries and their capitals as you can.

6. List the names of five parts of the body above the neck that are spelled with three letters.

7. List one manufactured item for each letter of the alphabet.

8. List as many nouns in the room as you can.

9. List one proper noun for each letter of the alphabet.

10. Name as many parts of a car as you can.

11. List as many kinds of trees as you can.

12. List as many personal pronouns as you can.

13. Name as many politicians as you can.

How many sponges can you think of for your grade or subject area? Additional ideas for sponges can be found at the Busy Teachers' Web Site K–12: http://www.ceismc.gatech.edu/busyt.

FROM THE RESEARCH

The effectiveness of sponges shows how important it is to use school time wisely. A study by Muyskens and Ysseldyke (1998) shows that the way teachers structure school time is even more important for student learning than time of day. For example, children are often thought to be more receptive to learning in the morning, when they are fresh. Because of this belief, many teachers schedule more important subjects such as reading in the morning. Muyskens and Ysseldyke observed 122 students with and without disabilities in 10 urban and suburban school districts. They found that when classrooms were appropriately structured, learning occurred, regardless of the time of day during which the instruction was delivered.

SOURCE: From "Effective Teaching for Higher Achievement," by D. Sparks and G. M. Sparks, 1984, *Educational Leadership, 49*(7).

ular arrangement you choose depends on your instructional objectives as well as your students' particular needs.

Whole-Class or Large-Group Instruction

Students with special needs benefit from both whole-class (or large-group) and small-group instruction. One advantage of whole-class instruction is that students spend the entire time with the teacher. In small-group instruction, students spend part of the time with the teacher and also spend time working independently while the teacher works with other small groups. Research shows that the more time students spend with the teacher, the more they learn (Rosenshine & Stevens, 1986). This increase in learning may be because students are more likely to go off task when they are working on their own, particularly when they have learning or behavior problems. Whatever grouping arrangements you use, try to make sure that students spend as much time as possible working with you.

Another advantage of whole-group instruction is that it does not single out students with special needs as being different from their peers. However, you may need to adapt whole-group instruction for students with special needs. For example, students in

An advantage of co-teaching (see Chapter 3) is that it gives teachers more grouping options and students more time with the teacher.

Forming same-skill groupings across grade levels, sometimes referred to as the *Joplin Plan,* gives teachers more options for meeting the specific skill needs of students.

Mr. Nichols's fourth-grade class was reading *Charlotte's Web* as a large-group instructional activity. Simone read more slowly than the rest of the class. To help her keep up, Mr. Nichols provided a book on tape. He also gave Simone more time to answer comprehension questions about the story in class because it took her longer to look up some of the answers. In another example, before his lectures, a high school science teacher identified technical words he was going to use and then worked before school with a small group of students with vocabulary problems to help them learn the words.

Small-Group Instruction

You may encounter situations in which small-group instruction is more appropriate for students with special needs. You can use same-skill groupings, mixed-skill groupings, or one-to-one instruction in setting up your groups.

Same-skill groupings are helpful when some but not all students are having trouble mastering a particular skill and need more instruction and practice. For example, Ms. Rodgers was showing her students how to divide fractions that have a common denominator. She gave her class a quiz to see who had learned how to do the problems. She found that all but five students had mastered the skill. The next day, Ms. Rodgers worked with these five students while the rest of the class did an application activity. Small-group instruction is not only for special education or remedial students; most students benefit from extra help in a small group at one time or another. In fact, many times students with special needs do not need extra instruction.

Small same-skill groups have also proven effective in basic skill areas when students are performing well below most of the class (Bursuck et al., 2004; Mosteller, Light, & Sachs, 1996). For example, Lori is in Ms. Hubbard's fourth-grade class and is reading at the second-grade level. Lori is learning decoding and vocabulary skills in a small group with other students who read at her level. Because the group is small and homogeneous, Ms. Hubbard is able to proceed in small steps, present many examples, and allow students to master skills before they move on. Lori is making progress and feels good about herself because she is becoming a better reader.

Clearly, some students do require instruction that is more individualized and intensive than can be provided in the large group (Bursuck et al., 2004). However, small same-skill groups should be used only when attempts to adapt instruction in the large group have been unsuccessful. Same-skill groups tend to become permanent and take on a life of their own. Thus, the ultimate goal of any small group should be its eventual dissolution. Also, on many days students can benefit from instruction with the rest of the class. For example, Lori's group participates in large-group reading when the teacher is reading a story and the class is working on listening comprehension. Another potential problem in using same-skill groupings is the danger that students in a low-achieving group in one area will be placed in low-achieving groups in other areas even though their skill levels do not justify it. For example, just because Lori is in the lowest-level reading group does not automatically mean she needs to be in low-achieving groups in other areas such as math.

The major advantage of **mixed-skill groupings** is that they provide students with special needs a range of positive models for both academic and social behavior. In mixed-skill groupings students often help each other, so such groups can also be a vehicle for providing direct instruction to individual students, something for which classroom teachers often do not have the time. In addition, mixed-skill groups, like large groups, tend not to single out students with special needs.

One-to-One Instruction

Providing **one-to-one instruction** for students with special needs can be very effective under some circumstances. In this grouping arrangement students work with a teacher, a paraprofessional, or a computer on well-sequenced, self-paced materials that are

---

DIMENSIONS OF DIVERSITY

Research suggests that students can sometimes benefit from working in same-sex groups. The achievement scores of girls grouped together for science instruction are generally higher than for girls grouped with boys (Moody & Gifford, 1990).

RESEARCH NOTE

Fuchs and colleagues (2000) found that students in academic difficulty were more productive when working collaboratively on complex tasks in pairs as opposed to small groups. Working in pairs, these students had a higher level of participation, helpfulness, and collaboration and co-operation. Work quality of pairs on application, conceptual, and problem-solving tasks was also superior.

geared to their specific level. For example, Waldo is having trouble with addition and subtraction facts. For 15 minutes each day, he works at the classroom computer station on an individualized drill-and-practice program. Right now he is working on addition facts through 10. When he masters these, the software automatically provides more difficult problems. Shamika, a student with a moderate to severe intellectual disability, works with a paraprofessional on selecting food items for a balanced lunch while the rest of the class listens to a presentation on the process of performing a nutritional analysis.

Although one-to-one instruction may be appropriate in some circumstances it is not necessarily the grouping arrangement of choice in either general or special education. First, it is inefficient; when it is carried out by the classroom teacher the extensive use of one-to-one instruction will result in less instructional time for everyone. Second, the logistics of one-to-one instruction sometimes require that students complete much independent work while the teacher moves from student to student. This can lead to high levels of off-task behavior, a problem many students with special needs experience (Hardman, Drew, Egan, & Winston, 2002; Mercer & Pullen, 2005). Third, the lack of peer models in one-to-one instruction makes it more difficult to motivate students, a problem particularly relevant at the high school level (Ellis & Sabornie, 1990). Sometimes, habitual use of one-to-one instruction can exclude students from critical social interactions. Finally, when a student requires this type of instruction for extended periods of time, further analysis of his or her needs and instructional setting is needed.

How Can You Evaluate Instructional Materials for Inclusive Classrooms?

The nature of the instructional materials you use is another very important consideration in accommodating students with special needs in your classroom. Classroom instructional materials include textbooks, manipulatives and models, and technology.

Textbooks

Basal textbooks (often called *basals*) are books used for instruction in any subject area that contain all the key components of the curriculum being taught for that subject. The careful evaluation of basals is vital because the selection of well-designed textbooks that require few adaptations for students with special needs can save you much time and energy. For example, a math basal that contains plenty of practice activities does not need to be adapted for students who require lots of practice to master a skill. Similarly, a history textbook that highlights critical vocabulary and includes clear context cues to help students figure out the words on their own may make it unnecessary for teachers to prepare extensive vocabulary study guides.

Fortunately, over the past 20 years, guidelines for distinguishing well-designed texts have been developed (Armbruster & Anderson, 1988; Kameenui et al., 2002; King-Sears, 2001). A set of questions to help you evaluate basals and other basic skills materials is included in the Professional Edge on page 166. Carefully evaluating basals helps alert you to any adaptations you may need to make. For example, a spelling basal with little provision for review can be troublesome for students who have problems retaining information. For example, you may want to develop review activities for every three lessons rather than every five as is done in a given book.

Many teachers are choosing to develop or collect their own materials rather than depending on published basal series. For example, some teachers have their students read trade books instead of traditional reading books; others have their students engage in the actual writing process rather than, or in addition to, answering questions in a book. Still others involve their students in real-life math-problem solving rather than

RESEARCH
N O T E

Vaughn and colleagues (2003) compared the effectiveness of three group sizes for providing supplemental instruction to struggling readers: 1:1 (1 teacher with 1 student); 1:3 (1 teacher with 3 students); and 1:10 (1 teacher and 10 students). Both the 1:1 and 1:3 grouping sizes were highly effective, and they were significantly more effective in improving reading comprehension than the 1:10 grouping size.

C O N N E C T I O N S

The grouping strategies in this chapter are all teacher-centered. Strategies for using groupings that are peer-mediated, such as peer tutoring and cooperative grouping, are covered in Chapter 13.

RESEARCH
N O T E

Elbaum, Moody, and Schumm (1999) asked 53 third-grade students, 27 of whom had learning disabilities, what they thought of mixed-skill grouping in reading. Students were concerned that small-group work was often noisy, encouraged disruptive students, and made it harder to get individual help from the teacher. Children who had lower reading skills, including some children with learning disabilities, were often anxious when working in small mixed-skill groups, because the grouping made their problems more obvious. Some children who were high-achieving felt that working with struggling readers hindered their progress.

PROFESSIONAL EDGE

Guidelines for Evaluating Basals and Other Basic Skills Curricula

Before evaluating any material, read the evaluative questions and place an asterisk next to those that are critical for the type of material you are examining. Answer each question with yes or no. Examine all your responses in a single area, paying special attention to the questions you designated as critical. Rate each area inadequate (1), adequate (2), or excellent (3). If the area is inadequate, designate whether the features can be easily modified (M).

Rating Scale: **Inadequate**   **Adequate**   **Excellent**   **Easily modified**
                         1   2   3   M

1 2 3 M   Effectiveness of Material

Yes No   Is information provided that indicates successful field testing or class testing of the material?
Yes No   Has the material been successfully field-tested with students similar to the target population?
Yes No   Are testimonials and publisher claims clearly differentiated from research findings?

1 2 3 M   Prerequisite Skills

Yes No   Are the prerequisite student skills and abilities needed to work with ease in the material specified?
Yes No   Are the prerequisite student skills and abilities compatible with the objectives of the material?
Yes No   Are the prerequisite student skills and abilities compatible with the target population?

1 2 3 M   Content

Yes No   Are students provided with specific strategies rather than a series of skills in isolation?
Yes No   Does the selection of subject matter, facts, and skills adequately represent the content area?
Yes No   Is the content consistent with the stated objectives?
Yes No   Is the information presented in the material accurate?
Yes No   Is the information presented in the material current?
Yes No   Are various points of view, including treatment of cultural diversity, individuals with disabilities, ideologies, social values, gender roles, and socioeconomic status, represented objectively?
Yes No   Are the content and the topic of the material relevant to the needs of students with disabilities?

1 2 3 M   Sequence of Instruction

Yes No   Is the scope and sequence of the material clearly specified?
Yes No   Are facts, concepts, and skills ordered logically?
Yes No   Does the sequence of instruction proceed from simple to complex?
Yes No   Does the sequence proceed in small, easily attainable steps?

1 2 3 M   Behavioral Objectives

Yes No   Are objectives or outcomes for the material clearly stated?
Yes No   Are the objectives or outcomes consistent with the goals for the target population?
Yes No   Are the objectives or outcomes stated in behavioral terms, including the desired behavior, the conditions for measurement of the behavior, and the desired standard of performance?

use basal math books. Even if your school does not use basals, the guidelines discussed here for teaching basic skills apply.

Content-area textbooks, which are books used for instruction in subject areas such as science or social studies, also need to be evaluated. In secondary schools, students are often expected to read their textbooks to access curriculum content (Sabornie & de-

Rating Scale:	Inadequate	Adequate	Excellent	Easily modified
	1	2	3	M

1 2 3 M   **Initial Assessment and Placement**

Yes No   Does the material provide a method to determine initial student placement in the curriculum?

Yes No   Does the initial assessment for placement contain enough items to place the learner accurately?

1 2 3 M   **Ongoing Assessment and Evaluation**

Yes No   Does the material provide evaluation procedures for measuring progress and mastery of objectives?

Yes No   Are there enough evaluative items to measure learner progress accurately?

Yes No   Are procedures and/or materials for ongoing record keeping provided?

1 2 3 M   **Instructional Input (Teaching Procedures)**

Yes No   Are instructional procedures for each lesson either clearly specified or self-evident?

Yes No   Does the instruction provide for active student involvement and responses?

Yes No   Are the lessons adaptable to small-group and individualized instruction?

Yes No   Are a variety of cueing and prompting techniques used to gain correct student responses?

Yes No   When using verbal instruction, does the instruction proceed clearly and logically?

Yes No   Does the material use teacher modeling and demonstration when appropriate to the skills being taught?

Yes No   Does the material specify correction and feedback procedures for use during instruction?

1 2 3 M   **Practice and Review**

Yes No   Does the material contain appropriate practice activities that contribute to mastery of the skills and concepts?

Yes No   Do practice activities relate directly to the desired outcome behaviors?

Yes No   Does the material provide enough practice for students with learning problems?

Yes No   Are skills systematically and cumulatively reviewed throughout the curriculum?

FROM THE RESEARCH

Guidelines such as those shown here have been confirmed in numerous reviews of effective teaching practices (Forness, Kavale, Blum, & Lloyd, 1997; Kameenui et al., 2002). Overall, programs that employed many of these features have shown large gains for both general and special education students, in both elementary and secondary classes. These gains occur in a variety of subject areas, when measured using norm-referenced or criterion-referenced measures, and last up to one year or more.

SOURCE: From *Instructional Materials for the Mildly Handicapped: Selection, Utilization, and Modification,* by A. Archer, 1977, Eugene: University of Oregon, Northwest Learning Resources System. Used by permission of the author.

Bettencourt, 2004; Mercer & Pullen, 2005). Because students are required to read and understand their texts, often without previous instruction, the texts should be written at a level at which students can easily understand them. Armbruster and Anderson (1988) refer to readable textbooks as "considerate." Considerate textbooks are easier for students to use independently and require fewer teacher adaptations. The following

FYI

Workbooks are commonly used to practice skills taught in basals. Information about practice activities in this chapter and in Chapter 9 applies to workbooks as well.

CONNECTIONS

Ways to adapt content-area texts are described in Chapter 9. Student strategies for reading texts are covered in Chapter 10.

WWW RESOURCES

When your textbooks lack clarity, incorporate alternative presentations of information into your lesson plans using library and media resources. The Internet School Library Media Center provides a massive index to Internet lesson plan sites for K–12 educators at http://falcon.jmu.edu/~ramseyil/index.html. The Equal Access to Software and Information (EASI) site has a page specifically devoted to library accessibility issues, including a collection of useful links: see http://bpm.nlb-online.org.

FYI

Taped textbooks can be helpful for students with reading problems. Ellis (1996) suggests that you tape only key sections of texts and that you highlight the main points in the text to help students focus on the most critical information. The Technology Notes feature for Chapter 10 on page 374 describes a strategic reader that has many technological supports for students to make reading their textbooks easier.

guidelines refer to aspects of considerate textbooks involving content, organization, and quality of writing.

CHECK THE CONTENT COVERED IN THE TEXT TO SEE WHETHER IT STRESSES "BIG IDEAS" RATHER THAN FACTS IN ISOLATION ● Big ideas are important principles that enable learners to understand the connections among facts and concepts they learn (Kameenui et al., 2002). For example, in a text that stressed facts in isolation, students learned that Rosa Parks was an important figure because she led the Montgomery bus boycott in 1955. In a text that stressed big ideas, students learned that the bus boycott, led by Rosa Parks in 1955, was carried out in response to the problem of segregation in the South in the early 1950s and that the boycott was the first in a series of civil rights protests eventually leading to the Civil Rights Act of 1965.

CHECK TO SEE WHETHER SUPPORT IS PROVIDED FOR STUDENT COMPREHENSION ● Support for student comprehension can be detected in the following three ways:

1. Check the organization of the headings and subheadings. Make an outline of the headings and subheadings in a few chapters. How reasonable is the structure revealed? Is it consistent with your knowledge of the subject matter?

2. Check the consistency of organization in discussions of similar topics. For example, in a science chapter on vertebrates, information about the different groups of vertebrates should be similarly organized; that is, if the section on amphibians discusses structure, body covering, subgroups, and reproduction, the section on reptiles should discuss the same topics, in the same order.

3. Look for clear signaling of the structure. A well-designed text includes information headings and subheadings. The most helpful headings are those that are the most specific about the content in the upcoming section. For example, the heading "Chemical Weathering" is a more helpful content clue than the heading "Another Kind of Weathering." A well-signaled text also includes format clues to organization. Page layouts, paragraphing, marginal notations, graphic aids, and the use of boldface, italics, and/or underlining can all serve to highlight or reinforce the structure. For example, a discussion of the four stages in the life cycle of butterflies could be signaled by using a separate, numbered paragraph for each state (that is, 1. Egg; 2. Larva; 3. Pupa; 4. Adult) and by including a picture for each stage. Finally, look for signal words and phrases that designate particular patterns of organization. For example, the phrases *in contrast* and *on the other hand* signal a compare-and-contrast organization, whereas the words *first*, *second*, and *third* indicate an enumeration or list pattern.

CHECK TO SEE THAT IMPORTANT BACKGROUND KNOWLEDGE IS ACTIVATED ● Despite the importance of background knowledge for comprehension (Beck & McKeown, 2002), many textbooks assume unrealistic levels of students' background knowledge (Gersten, Fuchs, Williams, & Baker, 2001). A failure to activate important background knowledge may be especially problematic for students with special needs, who are more likely to lack this information (Hallahan et al., 2005; Lerner, 2003). A number of textbook features indicate adequate attention to background knowledge. For example, social studies texts often activate background knowledge by providing definitions for important vocabulary content, displaying geographical information on maps, and featuring timelines delineating when key events took place (Kameenui et al., 2002).

CHECK FOR QUALITY OF WRITING ● The quality and clarity of writing can also affect student comprehension. Quality of writing can be evaluated in five ways.

1. Look for explicit or obvious connectives, or conjunctions. The absence of connectives can be particularly troublesome when the connective is a causal one (for example, *because, since, therefore*), which is frequently the case in content-area textbooks. Therefore, look especially for causal connectives. For example, the sentence *Because the guard cells relax, the openings close* is a better explanation than the sentences *The guard cells relax. The openings close.*

2. **Check for clear references.** Another problem to watch for is confusing pronoun references when more than one noun is used. For example, consider the following: *Both the stem of the plant and the leaf produce chloroform, but in different ways. For one, the sun hits it, and then . . .* Here, the pronouns *one* and *it* could be referring to either the stem or the leaf. Also, look out for vague quantifiers, those that do not modify the noun being quantified (for example, *some, many, few*). For example, the sentence *Some whales have become extinct* is clearer than *Some have become extinct*. In addition, check for definite pronouns without a clear referent (for example, *She saw him*, where the identity of *him* is not specified).

3. **Look for transition statements.** Transitions help the reader move easily from idea to idea. Given that a text covers many topics, make sure that the topic shifts are smooth. For example, in a biology chapter on the respiratory system, the text signals the transition from naming the parts of the respiratory system to describing the actual respiratory process by stating, *Next, the role each of these parts of the body plays in the respiratory process will be described.*

4. **Make sure the chronological sequences are easy to follow.** In a discussion of a sequence of events, the order of presentation in the text should generally proceed from first to last; any alteration of the order could cause confusion if not clearly signaled.

5. **Make sure graphic aids are clearly related to the text.** Graphic aids should contribute to understanding the material rather than simply provide decoration or fill space; should be easy to read and interpret; and should be clearly titled and labeled, and referenced in the text so the reader knows when to look at them.

Manipulatives and Models

Manipulatives and models can help students make connections between the abstractions often presented in school and the real-life products and situations these abstractions represent. *Manipulatives* are concrete objects or representational items, such as blocks and counters (for example, base-10 blocks for math), used as part of instruction. *Models* are also tangible objects; they provide a physical representation of an abstraction (for example, a scale model of the solar system). Strategies to help students make these connections have great potential benefit for students with special needs, who may lack the background knowledge and reasoning skills to understand abstractions (Cass, Cates, Smith, & Jackson, 2003; Smith, 2004). Still, manipulatives and models should be used carefully, because their use with students with special needs has not been heavily researched (Stein, Silbert, & Carnine, 1997; Cass et al., 2003). When using these tools, consider the following seven guidelines (Marzola, 1987; Ross & Kurtz, 1993).

1. **Select materials that suit the concept and the developmental stage of the students.** When you are first introducing a concept, materials should be easy to comprehend. Generally, the order in which you introduce materials should follow the same order as students' understanding: from the concrete to the pictorial to the abstract. However, not all students need to start at the same level. For example, in a biology lesson on the heart, many students benefit from viewing a three-dimensional model of a human heart, whereas other students are able to understand how a heart works just by seeing a picture of one.

2. **Use a variety of materials.** Students with special needs may have trouble transferring their understanding of a concept from one form to another. For example, Curtis's teacher always demonstrated place value using base-10 blocks. When Curtis was given

DIMENSIONS OF DIVERSITY

Fennema and colleagues (1998) and Carr and Jessup (1997) found that girls in grades 1–3 tended to use concrete strategies and boys tended to use abstract strategies when solving multidigit addition and subtraction problems. Armbrose (2002) makes these suggestions for encouraging girls to use mental math: (a) let them know that efforts to do math "in their heads" are valued; (b) create a spirit of risk taking by encouraging students to try new things, and send the message to students that they don't have to be perfect; (c) give students easy problems when they have no access to manipulatives, to foster the habit of trying mental math; and (d) keep a close eye on girls so that you can catch them in the act of using mental math, and celebrate these attempts. Give students opportunities to verbalize and reflect on their attempts.

WWW RESOURCES

Learn about ways to improve your teaching through technology by contacting Florida's Instructional Technology Resource Center at http://www.itrc.ucf.edu.

a place-value problem using coffee stirrers, he was unable to do it. Curtis's teacher could have prevented this problem in the first place by demonstrating place value using a range of manipulative materials, such as coffee stirrers, paper clips, and so on.

3. Use verbal explanations whenever possible to accompany object manipulation. Models and manipulative demonstrations should be preceded and accompanied by verbal explanations of the concept or skill being demonstrated. Verbal explanations are valuable because students may not be able to identify the important features of the model on their own. For example, Ms. Balou put a model of a two-digit-by-two-digit multiplication problem on the board. She verbally explained to her students all the steps in computing the problem and wrote each step on the chalkboard as it was completed.

4. Encourage active interaction. It is not enough just to have the teacher demonstrate with manipulatives or models as students observe. Allow your students to interact actively with models and manipulatives. Hands-on experience helps them construct their own meaning from the materials.

5. Elicit student explanations of their manipulations or use of models. Encourage your students to verbalize what they are doing as they work with models and manipulatives. This is a good way for you to assess whether they really understand the concept or skill. For example, Ms. Conway had her students name the main parts of the human heart using a model. Mr. Abeles had his students explain out loud how they would subtract 43 from 52 using base-10 blocks. Although explanations can help you evaluate how your students process information, students with special needs may not be able to articulate concepts right away because of language problems or a lack of reasoning skills. These students may require frequent demonstrations of how to articulate what they are doing.

6. Present clear guidelines for handling manipulatives to prevent management problems. Although manipulatives can be helpful instructional tools, they also can create management problems, particularly in larger groups when your physical access to students is limited. For example, Ms. Leifheit wanted her students to manipulate blocks to show the sounds in words. Each child received three blocks. When the children heard a word such as *man*, they were to move a block as they said each sound: *m-a-n*. Ms. Leifheit had trouble getting students' attention at the beginning of the lesson because they were busy handling the blocks. She also found that students were not listening to her say the words, again because they were playing with the blocks. Ms. Leifheit decided to break the class into smaller groups so she could more carefully monitor student use of the blocks. She also established a simple rule: When the teacher is talking, students are not to touch their blocks.

7. Move your students beyond the concrete level when they are ready. Some students with special needs may have trouble moving from one learning stage to another. One effective way to help students make the transition from the concrete to the abstract is to pair concrete tasks with paper-and-pencil tasks. For example, Ms. Conway had her students label a picture of a human heart after they had observed and discussed a physical model. Mr. Abeles had his second graders solve subtraction problems using manipulatives and then record their answers on a traditional worksheet. However, Marsh and Cooke (1996) found that students with learning disabilities who were taught to solve story problems using manipulatives were able to solve similar problems at an abstract level without having to go through the representational stage.

Technology

Teachers today have available to them a broad array of technology to enhance the presentation of material to their students. As mentioned in Chapter 1, technologies range from low- to high-tech options. One common use of computers in inclusive classrooms is to provide instruction to students through drill-and-practice programs, tutorials, and simulations. In general, *drill-and-practice programs* are used most often with students with special needs. Drill-and-practice programs have been shown to be effective for students with special needs largely because they allow students to learn in small steps, provide systematic feedback, and allow for lots of practice to mastery. Still, not all drill-and-practice programs are created equal (Arends, 2004; Okolo, 1993). Some guidelines for what to look for and what to avoid in these programs are given in the Professional Edge on page 172.

Computers can also provide initial, sequenced instruction for students, using tutorials in problem solving, decision making, and risk taking, and using simulations. Each of these forms of computer-assisted instruction has potential advantages and disadvantages (Roblyer, Edwards, & Havriluk, 2004). For example, *tutorials* can present instruction to mastery in small, sequential steps, an instructional approach shown to be effective with students with special needs. Tutorials can also provide one-to-one instruction at varying levels of difficulty, something teachers usually do not have time to do. Still, you need to check to be sure that students have the necessary prerequisite skills to benefit from the tutorials. In addition, tutorials may not provide sufficient review for students, and students may not be motivated enough to work through them independently (Roblyer et al., 2004). *Simulations* are of great potential benefit in teaching students to be active learners by confronting real-life situations. However, simulations may be difficult to integrate with academic curriculum, may require much teacher assistance, and can be time-consuming (Roblyer et al., 2004).

Assistive technology (AT) is an important part of an inclusive classroom. An assistive-technology device is any piece of equipment that is used to increase, maintain, or improve the functional capabilities of a child with a disability. An assistive-technology service is any service that directly assists a child in the selection, acquisition, or use of an assistive-technology device, according to the Technology-Related Assistance for Individuals with Disabilities Act of 1998. A range of high- to low-tech AT is available to enable students with disabilities to communicate or to access information by allowing them to bypass their disability. Students with physical disabilities such as Josh from the chapter-opening vignette can operate computers with a single key or switch rather than through a regular keyboard. Students with physical disabilities can use voice-command systems to enter information into a computer verbally. Students with deafness can communicate with hearing students or other deaf students using computer-assisted telecommunication devices such as those described in Chapter 6. Computer-generated large print, braille translations, and synthesized speech can assist students with visual disabilities in communicating. Students with communication problems can benefit from augmentative communication devices, which are computers equipped with speech synthesizers that can type text and produce speech heard by everyone. These devices can also be programmed with words and phrases for particular situations. Students with learning disabilities can compensate for poor handwriting, spelling, and grammatical skills using word-processing equipment. Ways to use INCLUDE to determine the AT needs of students with disabilities are described in the Technology Notes on pages 176–177.

Assistive technology promises to revolutionize education in U.S. schools. In what ways might technology serve as a "great equalizer" in inclusive classrooms?

WWW
RESOURCES

The National Center to Improve Practice in Special Education through Technology, Media and Materials has gathered and synthesized information about technology, disabilities, and instructional practices through a broad range of resources. This site also provides opportunities for teachers to exchange information, build knowledge, and practice through collaborative dialogue: http://www2.edc.org/ncip.

WWW
RESOURCES

For more information about direct instruction, consult the Association for Direct Instruction at http://www.adihome.org.

CONNECTIONS

Presenting new content also involves using strategies for activating students' prior knowledge. These strategies are explored further in Chapter 9.

How Can You Analyze Instructional Methods in Relation to Student Needs?

Teachers use a number of instructional methods in class, including direct instruction, indirect methods of instruction, scaffolding, independent student practice, and evaluation of student performance. Each of these methods should be analyzed in relation to student needs and then used and/or adapted as needed.

PROFESSIONAL EDGE

Features of Effective Drill-and-Practice Software

The introduction of technology in the classroom has given teachers a new array of tools to use in presenting material to students. Students with special needs can especially benefit from using drill-and-practice software, which allows them to learn at their own pace. Keep in mind the following guidelines when choosing an effective drill-and-practice program for your students who have special needs.

What to Look For	What to Avoid	Rationale
Programs that provide high rates of responding relevant to the skill being learned	Programs that take too much time to load and run or that contain too many activities unrelated to the skill being learned	The more time students spend on task, the more they learn.
Programs in which animation and graphics support the skill or concept being practiced	Programs with animation or graphics that are unrelated to the program's instructional objective	Although animation and graphics may facilitate student interest in an activity, they may also distract students, interfere with skill mastery, and reduce practice time.
Programs in which reinforcement is clearly related to task completion or mastery	Programs in which the events that occur when students are incorrect (for example, an explosion) are more reinforcing than the events that occur when the student is correct (for example, a smiling face)	Some programs may inadvertently encourage students to practice the incorrect response to view an event they find more interesting.
Programs in which feedback helps students locate and correct their mistakes	Programs in which students are told merely whether they are right or wrong or instructed to try again	Without feedback that informs them of the correct answer after a reasonable number of attempts, students may become frustrated and make random guesses.
Programs that store information about student performance or progress that can be accessed later by the teacher	Programs without record-keeping features	Students may encounter difficulties with the skills covered by a program that requires teacher intervention. However, teachers often find it difficult to monitor students as they work at the computer. Access to records of student performance enables the teacher to determine whether a program is benefiting a student and whether the student needs additional assistance.
Programs with options for controlling features such as speed of problem presentation, type of feedback, problem difficulty, and number of practice trials	Programs that must be used in the same way with every student	Options are cost-effective; they enable the same program to be used with a broad range of students. Furthermore, they permit a teacher to provide more appropriate individualized instruction.

FROM THE RESEARCH

Sands and Buchholz (1997) report numerous studies showing the effective use of well-designed drill-and-practice software to teach reading to persons with severe reading disabilities, such as dyslexia. These students benefit from repeated activities that are multisensory (visual, auditory, motoric) in nature.

SOURCE: From "Features of Effective Instructional Software," by C. M. Okolo, 2000, in *Technology and Exceptional Individuals*, 3rd ed., edited by J. Lindsey. Austin, TX: PRO-ED.

Elements of Direct Instruction

Several decades of research in teaching effectiveness have shown that many students learn skills and subject matter more readily when it is presented explicitly in what is often referred to as **direct instruction** (Marchand-Martella, Slocum, & Martella, 2004; Rosenshine & Stevens, 1986; Stronge, 2002). Direct instruction consists of six key elements.

1. Review and check the previous day's work (and reteach if necessary). This aspect of direct instruction may include establishing routines for checking homework and reviewing relevant past learning and prerequisite skills. These procedures are important because students with special needs might not retain past learning and/or know how to apply it to new material. For example, on Thursday Ms. Guzik taught her students how to round to the nearest whole number. On Friday she gave her class a story problem to solve that required rounding. Before the students solved the problem, she pointed to a chart in the front of the room that displayed a model of how to round numbers and suggested that they refer to this chart as they solved the problem.

2. Present new content or skills. When content or skills are presented, teachers begin the lesson with a short statement of the objectives and a brief overview of what they are going to present and why. Material is presented in small steps, using careful demonstrations that incorporate illustrations and concrete examples to highlight key points. Included within the demonstrations are periodic questions to check for understanding.

3. Provide guided student practice (and check for understanding). At first, student practice takes place under the direct guidance of the teacher, who frequently questions all students on material directly related to the new content or skill. You can involve all students in questioning by using unison oral responses or by having students answer questions by holding up answer cards, raising their hands when they think an answer is correct, or holding up a number to show which answer they think is right. For example, when asking a yes-or-no question, tell your students to hold up a 1 when they think the answer is yes and a 2 when they think the answer is no. This approach can be used with spelling, too. Have your students spell words on an index card and then hold up their answers. Unison responses not only give students more practice but also allow you to monitor student learning more readily. Prompts and additional explanations or demonstrations are provided during guided practice when appropriate. Effective guided practice continues until students meet the lesson objective. For example, Mr. Hayes was teaching his students how to add *es* to words that end in *y*. After modeling two examples at the board, he did several more examples with the students, guiding them as they applied the rule to change the *y* to *i* before they added *es*. Next, Mr. Hayes had students do a word on their own. Students wrote their answers on an index card and held up the card when directed by Mr. Hayes. Mr. Hayes noticed that five students did not apply the rule correctly. He called these students up to his desk for additional instruction and had the rest of the students work independently, adding *es* to a list of words on a worksheet.

4. Provide feedback and correction (and reteach when necessary). When students answer quickly and confidently, the teacher asks another question or provides a short acknowledgment of correctness (for example, "That's right"). Hesitant but correct responses might be followed by process feedback (for example, "Yes, Yolanda, that's right because . . ."). When students respond incorrectly, the teacher uses corrections to draw out an improved student response. Corrections can include sustaining feedback (that is, simplifying the question, giving clues), explaining or reviewing steps, giving process feedback ("The reason we need to regroup in this subtraction problem is that the top number is smaller than the bottom number"), or reteaching last steps

RESEARCH NOTE

Research shows that students are usually more attentive to varied, fast-paced presentations than to other kinds (Darch & Gersten, 1985). The key to providing a fast-paced presentation is to begin the directions for the next question (or for correction of the current question) immediately after the students make a response to the first question. It also helps to limit your own talk, to give your students as many opportunities to respond as possible.

FYI

Whole language represents an indirect, constructivistic approach.

RESEARCH NOTE

Kroesbergen, Van Luit, and Maas (2004) compared the effects of explicit and constructivistic instruction on the basic multiplication performance of two groups of students ages 8–11 who were low-achieving. The results showed that both groups of students performed better than a control group, but that the explicit instruction group outperformed the constructivistic group in problem solving. The groups did not differ in their fluency and accuracy in multiplication computation. These findings show not only that systematic, explicit instruction is effective for lower level skills but that it can be used successfully to teach your students with special needs higher level problem-solving skills as well.

> TECHNOLOGY NOTES

Using INCLUDE to Determine Assistive-Technology Needs

According to IDEA, the IEP team must consider whether a child needs assistive-technology devices and services as part of his or her plan for an appropriate education. We believe that the steps in the INCLUDE strategy can assist greatly in helping the team make this decision. What follows is a series of questions related to assistive technology (AT) that teams may want to incorporate into the INCLUDE process. These questions were adapted from ones originally suggested by Beigel (2000) and Pedrotty-Bryant, Bryant, and Raskind (1998).

Identify Classroom Demands

1. How do you present information? For example, teachers who use a lot of classroom discussions place a particular demand on children's speaking abilities; teachers who lecture frequently place a strain on students' writing and organizational skills.

2. What types of grouping arrangements do you use? For example, an emphasis on cooperative learning places a burden on student communication skills.

3. What types of assignments do you make? For example, a project-driven class requires students to find and organize resource materials and then present them to the class in a clear, orderly way.

4. What are the primary ways you assess and evaluate your students? For example, oral assessments can place a strain on student verbal communication skills; written assessments place demands on written language skills such as handwriting, spelling, and sentence and paragraph construction.

5. How comfortable are you with having a learner who uses AT in the classroom? Your role in this process is very important. Without your support for learning to use AT and then continuing its use, a student may abandon his or her device.

6. What is the physical structure of your classroom and school? Issues such as whether there are adequate electrical outlets or tables large enough to accommodate a computer and various peripherals need to be considered.

Note Learner Strengths and Needs and Check for Potential Success and Problem Areas

1. What purposeful motoric movement does the student have? A purposeful movement is one that the learner controls in a conscious, consistent manner (Beigel, 2000, p. 240). Examples of purposeful motoric movement include raising an eyebrow, moving the fingers of one hand in a motion similar to that of typing, and using a pen or pencil to write or draw.

2. How willing is the student to try new activities or tasks? Using AT requires a willingness to change on the part of the student. Your knowledge of the student in this area can help determine the nature of the equipment selected (for example, easy to use or hard to use) as well as the amount of time needed to achieve independent usage.

3. What does the student desire from the use of AT? The personal goals of the learner can greatly influence AT usage. Relevance of the material is an important factor in learning to perform any skill. For example, Tamra had an expressed desire to write poetry and was quite receptive to learning to use a laptop with a large keyboard especially designed for her.

4. What emotional and psychological supports does the student need when learning to use the device? Some students may require considerable emotional and psychological support as they learn to use an AT device. You or other staff working with the student should provide such support when it is needed, or students are not likely to use the device. It is important to remember that students cannot be forced to use AT; they can only be encouraged and supported whenever using the device.

5. What level of training do the student and others who interact with the student need? You, the student, and other staff working with the student need to be given the opportunity to see how the various devices work and to see who needs training and in what areas.

6. What impact, if any, do the student's socioeconomic status and cultural background have on the use of AT? Students who live in poverty, as well as their parents, are less likely to have previous experience with technology and may need more extensive training. There is also the question of the impact of culture on the acceptance of AT by students and their families.

Brainstorm and Then Decide on Adaptations

You need to consider the features of the technical devices as well as the extent to which they help students meet identified IEP goals.

1. How durable is the device? All devices that are used in schools should be able to withstand minimal bumps and jars common in schools.
2. What setup and maintenance issues must be addressed? How easy is the device to update and repair? Do compatibility issues with other technology already in the classroom exist that must be addressed? Devices that are difficult to maintain, take a long time to repair, are not easily upgraded, or are incompatible with other technology should be avoided, because eventually they are abandoned.
3. How willing is the vendor of the device to provide a trial or loaner period of use for the student? You often need to try several devices in the school environment before a final AT decision can be made.
4. What is the reputation of the company in terms of construction, service, training, and reliability? These questions can be answered by consulting publications that deal with AT (*Team Rehab, TAM Connector*), contacting organizations (Council for Exceptional Children, Center for Applied Special Technology), and asking others who use AT. A number of websites that also may be helpful are listed at the end of this feature.
5. Does the student have the psychomotor skills needed to use the device in a functional manner? This question should be answered during student assessment. Many devices can be adapted for students with limited motoric control; if this device is not, then it is unrealistic to expect that the device will be used.
6. Is the device aesthetically acceptable to the student? Some students may prefer a certain color or type of mouse; others may prefer a brightly colored exterior as opposed to the typical colors of blue, black, and beige; still others may want to decorate their equipment (as long as this doesn't interfere with its function). If students' aesthetic needs are not addressed, they may feel the device doesn't fit into their social milieu and are not likely to use it.
7. Does the device meet the student's needs in a way that is easily understood by others? Students should be able to use their devices without causing a distraction. In addition, the device should not be so complex that only the vendor is able to program the device or explain how it can be used.
8. How portable is the device? For AT to be useful, the student or support person must be able to move the device from one class to another—from an elementary classroom to a special class such as art or physical education or between various academic classes in a middle or high school environment.

Evaluate Student Progress

The ultimate goal of AT is to enable students to more readily meet their IEP goals. Pedrotty-Bryant, Bryant, and Raskind (1998, p. 55) suggest that teachers ask the following questions when determining whether the assistive technology selected is an appropriate match for the student.

To what extent does the AT assist the student in compensating for the disability?

To what degree does the technology promote student independence?

What is the student's opinion of the technology adaptation?

What is the family's opinion of the AT?

Is the AT efficient and easy for the student to use?

Does the device promote meeting IEP goals and objectives in the least restrictive environment?

For additional information on assistive technology, consult the following websites.

ABLEDATA
http://www.abledata.com

The Alliance for Technology Access
http://www.ataccess.org

Apple Disability Resources
http://www.apple.com/accessibility

Closing the Gap
http://www.closingthegap.com

DREAMMS for Kids
http://www.dreamms.org

Microsoft Accessibility
http://www.microsoft.com/enable

("Remember, at the end of this experiment you need to tell whether the hypothesis was accepted or rejected. Let me show you what I mean"). Corrections continue until students have met the lesson objective, with praise used in moderation. Specific praise ("I'm impressed by how you drew a picture of that story problem!") is more effective than general praise ("Good boy, Leon").

5. Provide independent student practice. Students practice independently on tasks directly related to the skills taught until they achieve a high correct rate. Practice activities are actively supervised and students are held accountable for their work.

6. Review frequently. Systematic review of previously learned material is provided, including the incorporation of review into homework and tests. Material missed in homework or tests is retaught (Rosenshine & Stevens, 1986).

It is important to note that for older students or for those who have more subject-matter knowledge or skills, these six steps can be modified, such as by presenting more material at one time or spending less time on guided practice. For example, when a second-grade teacher presented a unit on nutrition, she spent a whole week defining and showing examples of complex carbohydrates, fats, sugar, and protein. In an eighth-grade health class, this material was covered in one day, largely because students already had much background information on this topic. Moreover, each of the direct instruction steps is not required for every lesson you teach, although they are particularly helpful to students with learning and behavior problems, who have been shown to benefit greatly from a high level of classroom structure (Hallahan et al., 2005; Mercer & Pullen, 2005; Swanson & Deshler, 2003). The Case in Practice on page 177 presents an example of a direct instruction lesson.

Indirect Methods of Instruction

CONNECTIONS

Ways to use scaffolding to teach students study skills are described in the discussion of learning strategies in Chapter 10.

FYI

Scaffolding is a helpful strategy for teaching basic skills in addition to problem-solving skills.

Indirect instruction is based on the belief that children are naturally active learners and that given the appropriate instructional environment, they actively construct knowledge and solve problems in developmentally appropriate ways (Knight, 2002). This type of teaching is often referred to as *constructivistic* because of the belief that students are capable of constructing meaning on their own, in most cases without explicit instruction from the teacher (Knight, 2002; Hallahan et al., 2005). Indirect instruction is used by classroom teachers for both basic skills and content areas.

A common indirect method is called **inquiry learning,** or *discovery learning* (Maroney, Finson, Beaver, & Jensen, 2003; National Research Council, 1996; Jarolimek, Foster, & Kellough, 2004). Unlike direct instruction, which is very teacher-centered, in the inquiry approach the teacher's role is that of a facilitator who guides learners' inquiry by helping them identify questions and problems. (Jarolimek et al., 2004; Knight, 2002). The learners, therefore, are placed in situations that require considerable initiative and background knowledge in finding things out for themselves. In this way students are actively involved in their own learning (Jarolimek et al., 2004).

You can see these elements of inquiry learning in a social studies lesson on Inuit or native Alaskan people developed by Lindquist (1995). The goal of the lesson was for students to "realize that there are many different groups of Inuit people, each having unique customs and traditions, but whose culture has been shaped by the Far North" (Lindquist, 1995, p. 54). First, the teacher gave the students 5 minutes to list everything they knew about the Inuit people. The teacher then had some students share their lists with the class. Student sharing of their background knowledge was followed by a short film on the Inuit people. After the film, the students were asked to cross out anything on their lists that the film caused them to change their minds about. When the children had revised their lists, the teacher divided the class into pairs; each pair was asked to research a different Inuit tribe. They were to gather information about food, shelter, clothing, and language. Each pair of students recorded information about their

CASE IN PRACTICE

A Direct Instruction Lesson

This direct instruction lesson is designed to help students use pronouns clearly. Notice that Mr. Francisco first reviews the preskill of what a pronoun is. Then he guides students through the skill of substituting pronouns for nouns.

Mr. Francisco: Remember, yesterday we said that for every noun, there's a more general word called a *pronoun*. So, for the word *boys*, the pronoun is *they*. For the word *car*, the pronoun is *it*. What's the pronoun for the word *James?*

Students: He.

Mr. Francisco: Right. You're going to rewrite sentences so they have no nouns, only pronouns. Here's the first sentence: *Elephants eat grass.* What's the noun in the subject?

Students: Elephants.

Mr. Francisco: What's the pronoun that replaces *elephants?*

Students: They.

Mr. Francisco: What's the noun in the predicate?

Students: Grass.

Mr. Francisco: What's the pronoun that replaces *grass?*

Students: It.

Mr. Francisco: What is the entire sentence with pronouns?

Students: They eat it.

Mr. Francisco: Right. Look at the pronouns written on the board: *he, she, it, they, him, her, them.* You're going to use these words to rewrite sentences so they won't have any nouns, just pronouns. Here's sentence 1: *George is watching birds.* What noun is the subject?

Students: George.

Mr. Francisco: What's the noun in the predicate?

Students: Birds.

Mr. Francisco: What's the sentence with pronouns in place?

Students: He is watching them.

Mr. Francisco: Good. Look at the next sentence: *Fred and Carlos build houses.* You are going to write it with pronouns in place of the nouns. [Teacher observes students and gives feedback.]

Mr. Francisco: Here's the sentence you should have: *They build them.*

[*Teacher repeats with two more examples.*]

REFLECTIONS

What direct instruction steps did Mr. Francisco use here? Why do you think direct instruction is particularly effective for students with learning and behavior needs? Can you think of some situations in which you would *not* want to use direct instruction?

SOURCE: Adapted from *Reasoning and Writing: A Direct Instruction Program,* by S. Engelmann and B. Grossen, 2001, Columbus, OH: SRA/McGraw-Hill.

---

particular tribe on a data sheet and reported their information to the class. As each group reported, the teacher synthesized the information on an overhead chart, creating a graphic display for comparing and contrasting similarities and differences among the various tribes.

Maroney and colleagues (2003) recently compiled a list of skills required for success in an inquiry-based approach to teaching science. A range of competencies was listed in the areas of classroom behavior skills, social skills, group coping skills, basic academic skills, science process skills, and inquiry skills (see Table 5.1).

As you can see in the table, the sheer number of skills listed is daunting when applied to all children, let alone to children who are likely to have problems in many of these areas. Clearly, for an inquiry approach to be effective for students with special needs, you will need to provide them with extensive supports such as the use of scaffolds described in the next section.

Scaffolding

Scaffolding is an approach that has been used successfully to support students as they develop problem-solving skills (Dickson, Chard, & Simmons, 1993; Larkin, 2001).

ANALYZE AND **REFLECT**

Give an example of how scaffolding can be used to make indirect instruction more effective for students with special needs. What risks are involved in using scaffolds? How do you know when students are ready to have their scaffolds removed?

TABLE 5.1 Student Skills Required for Success in Inquiry-Based Learning

Classroom Behavior Skills	Basic Academic Skills
• Listens quietly to directions and instruction	• Can read and comprehend required materials
• Follows classroom rules	• Has necessary writing skills
• Follows directions accurately	• Can understand information presented
• Is prepared with needed materials	• Has required math and measurement skills
• Begins work promptly	• Knows basic necessary science concepts
• Works quietly	• Understands necessary vocabulary
• Asks for help when needed	• Can use equipment and materials
• Completes assignments on time	• Has skills needed to succeed in a given activity
• Completes work at acceptable level of accuracy	
• Accepts criticism and corrections	

Social Skills	Science Process Skills
• Interacts appropriately with others	• Gathers information through observation
• Has acceptable conversation skills	• Communicates observations and findings
• Thinks before acting	• Makes an educated guess/hypothesis
• Shows a friendly attitude	• Uses experimentation to solve a problem
• Uses language appropriately	• Uses measurement to record results
	• Uses graphs and diagrams effectively
	• Uses classification skills
	• Forms generalizations
	• Makes reasonable predictions based on data

Group Coping Skills	Inquiry Skills
• Works cooperatively in a group	• Understands the problem
• Contributes to group work	• Generates simple questions
• Expresses opinions	• Generates complex questions
• Disagrees politely	• Uses previously learned information to solve problems
• Listens to others	• Is motivated by inquiry
• Negotiates and compromises	• Can accept more than one answer
• Accepts criticism	• Displays confidence in own ideas

SOURCE: Adapted from "Preparing for Successful Inquiry in Inclusive Science Classrooms," by S. A. Maroney, K. D. Finson, J. B. Beaver, and M. M. Jensen, 2003, *Teaching Exceptional Children, 36*(1), 18–25.

Scaffolds are "forms of support provided by the teacher (or another student) to help students bridge the gap between their current abilities and the intended goal" (Rosenshine & Meister, 1992, p. 26).

Before using scaffolding, you need to find out whether students have the necessary background ability to learn a cognitive strategy (Rosenshine & Meister, 1992). For example, a strategy for helping a student read a physics textbook is not useful if the student lacks basic knowledge of mathematics and physical properties. Similarly, teaching

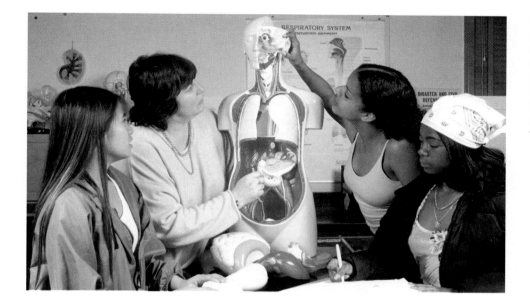

With the appropriate support, nondirect instruction can be effective for students with special needs. What steps should this teacher take to ensure effective instruction using scaffolding?

a strategy for solving math word problems cannot succeed if the student does not have basic math computation skills. Using scaffolding to teach higher order cognitive strategies consists of six stages:

1. **Present the new cognitive strategy.** In this stage, the teacher introduces the strategy concretely, using a list of strategy steps. The teacher then models the strategy, including all "thinking" and "doing" steps. For example, Mr. Bridges is teaching his history class how geographic features and natural resources affect the growth and location of cities. First, he introduces the problem-solving strategy to his students: (a) define the problem, (b) propose hypotheses to explain the problem, (c) collect data to evaluate your hypotheses, (d) evaluate the evidence, and (e) make a conclusion. These steps are posted on the chalkboard for easy reference. Mr. Bridges then models the strategy by showing students a map of the state of Illinois and thinking out loud as he applies the steps. For example, he explains how he would sort through many pieces of information in determining which factors led to the development of Chicago (for example, being on Lake Michigan) and which did not (for example, cold climate).

2. **Regulate difficulty during guided practice.** At this stage, students begin practicing the new strategy using simplified materials so they can concentrate on learning the strategy. First, the strategy is introduced one step at a time. Students are guided carefully through the steps, with the teacher anticipating particularly difficult steps and completing these difficult parts of the task as necessary. Before tackling difficult problems, such as the geography of Chicago, Mr. Bridges has his students use the problem-solving steps to solve simpler problems on topics familiar to them. For example, he has them solve problems such as why the cookies someone made were dry, why a hypothetical student is late for school every day, or why the school lunches taste awful. He also helps students brainstorm ideas for how to collect data, a step that can be difficult. Mr. Bridges does this by compiling an initial list of data collection procedures for each problem. For the problem of why the cookies were dry, Mr. Bridges gives his students a list of possible data collection procedures, such as identifying the ingredients, finding out how long the cookies were baked, and figuring out how old the cookies were.

3. **Provide varying contexts for student practice.** Students practice the strategy on actual classroom tasks under the teacher's direction. The teacher starts out leading the practice, but the students eventually carry out the practice sessions in small

RESEARCH NOTE

The use of repeated student practice is often negatively referred to as "drill and kill." Burns (2004) wanted to find out the impact of student drill on student achievement. She analyzed and summarized 13 articles that looked at this issue and found that a drill task is more effective when the task involves new learning. She also found that drill is most effective when at least 50 percent of the practice items are known. Péladeau, Forget, and Gagné (2003), in a study of college students enrolled in a statistics class, found a positive relationship between the amount of practice and student attitudes toward the course, subject matter, and the practice activities themselves. In our experience, drill can "thrill" when practice is lively and geared to student needs on skills leading to important outcomes.

cooperative groups. In Mr. Bridges's class, students practice the problem-solving strategy using examples from their history textbooks.

4. Provide feedback. The teacher provides corrective feedback to students using evaluative checklists based on models of expert problem solving carefully explained to the students. Students are encouraged to evaluate their performance using these checklists. For example, each time Mr. Bridges's students use the problem-solving strategy, they evaluate their performance by asking themselves questions such as, Did we clearly state the problem? Did we state a complete list of hypotheses? How thorough were our data collection procedures? Were we able to evaluate all the hypotheses using the information collected? Did we interpret the results accurately? Were our conclusions consistent with our results?

>  Student independence is encouraged by removing elements of the scaffold. "

5. Increase student responsibility. Next, the teacher begins to require students to practice putting all the steps together on their own. Student independence is encouraged by removing elements of the scaffold. For example, prompts and models are diminished, the complexity and difficulty of the materials are increased, and peer support is decreased. The teacher checks for student mastery before going to the last step, independent practice.

6. Provide independent practice. Finally, the teacher provides the students with extensive practice and helps them apply what they have learned to new situations. For example, Mr. Bridges shows his students how problem solving can be used in other subjects, such as science.

Independent Student Practice

The major purpose of practice is to help students refine or strengthen their skills in various areas. Consider the following seven guidelines for using practice activities effectively in your classroom:

1. Students should practice only skills or content they have already learned. This guideline is particularly important in order for students to be able to perform practice activities independently. Tasks that are too difficult can lead to high levels of off-task behavior.

2. Practice is more effective when students have a desire to learn what they are practicing. Whenever possible, point out to students situations in which they can use the skill in other phases of learning. For example, you may explain to your students that if they learn to read more quickly, they will be able to finish their homework in less time.

3. Practice should be individualized. Exercises should be organized so that each student can work independently.

4. Practice should be specific and systematic. Practice should be directly related to skills and objectives you are working on in class. This guideline is particularly important for students with special needs, who require more practice to master academic skills.

5. Students should have much practice on a few skills rather than little practice on many skills. Focusing on one or two skills at a time is less confusing and gives students more practice on each skill.

6. Practice should be organized so that students achieve high levels of success. Correct answers reinforce students and encourage them to do more. Most students

CONNECTIONS

Strategies for adapting seatwork, independent practice activities, and homework for students with special needs are presented in Chapter 9.

CONNECTIONS

Chapter 11 explores strategies for adapting classroom tests and report-card grades for students with special needs. It also covers potentially valuable additions to testing and grading, such as performance-based assessments and portfolios.

need at least 90 percent accuracy when doing practice activities, though higher-achieving students can tolerate a 70 percent rate as long as the teacher is present to assist them (Good & Brophy, 1986).

7. Practice should be organized so that students and teacher have immediate feedback. You need to know how students are progressing so you can decide whether to move to the next skill. Students need to know how they are doing so they can make meaningful corrections to their work (Ornstein & Lasley, 2004).

For students with special needs, consider these additional questions: What are the response demands of the activity? Do students have to answer orally or in writing? How extensive a response is required? Do the students have enough time to finish the activity? Response demands are important because students who are unable to meet them will not be able to do the practice activity independently. For example, Mr. Edwards is having his class practice weekly vocabulary words by orally stating their definitions. Ross stutters and is unable to answer out loud. Mr. Edwards allows Ross to submit a written list of definitions. Ms. Osborne is having her students complete short-answer questions in their history books. Clarice has a physical disability and is unable to write her answers independently. She uses an adapted classroom computer to prepare her answers. Mr. Nusbaum has asked his students to write a paragraph summarizing the reasons for the stock market crash of 1929. Maurice cannot write a coherent paragraph but can answer orally into a tape recorder. Amanda writes very slowly, so Mr. Nusbaum gives her more time to complete the activity. Ways in which direct instruction and scaffolding can be used to teach vocabulary to English-language learners are in the Special Emphasis On . . . feature on pages 182–183.

Perhaps the most common form of practice used by teachers is homework. Research shows that homework can have a positive effect on student achievement when it is properly assigned (Cooper, 1989, 2001).

Homework is often a challenge for students with special needs. For example, most teachers expect homework to be completed independently, and students must have the sensory, academic, and organizational skills to do so. A student with a severe reading disability might be unable to read a chapter in a history book and answer the questions without some form of adaptation such as a peer reader or taped text. Similarly, a student with fine motor difficulties might be unable to answer the questions unless allowed to do so orally or with an adapted word processor. In addition, you may need to provide this same student more time or to assign fewer questions. Therefore, it is important that you carefully examine your own particular homework requirements and adapt them to ensure full participation by all your students.

Evaluation of Student Performance

The major purpose of student evaluation is to determine the extent to which students have mastered academic skills or instructional content. Chapter 4 discussed formal and informal assessments that can be used to evaluate student progress. Student evaluations are also communicated through grades, which are determined in a number of ways, including classroom tests and assignments. Because student evaluation is so important, you need to consider how classroom tests and assignments may interact with student learning needs. Most critical is that the method of evaluation measures skill or content mastery, not a student's disability. For example, Carson, a student who has an attention deficit, should be given tests in small segments to ensure that the tests measure his knowledge, not his attention span. Similarly, Riesa, a student with a severe learning disability in writing, needs to take an oral essay test in history if the test is to be a valid measure of her history knowledge rather than her writing disability. The type of report-card grade used as well as the system used to arrive at that grade might also need

Special **EMPHASIS** On . . .

Teaching Vocabulary to English-Language Learners with Learning Disabilities

Content-area instruction requires teaching new vocabulary words, many of which can be technical. Gersten, Baker, and Marks (1998) suggest the following research-based strategies when teaching vocabulary to your English-language learners who have learning difficulties.

Focus Vocabulary Instruction on a Small Number of Critical Words.

Providing extensive drill on lengthy word lists is ineffective for students with learning difficulties. Instead, focus on several critical words at a time and emphasize these for several days. Enhance understanding of vocabulary by showing how the words are used in a variety of contexts, including below-grade-level books in the same subject area, texts in different content areas, and personal writing projects.

Provide Multiple Exposures.

You need to expose students to the word in a variety of contexts before they begin to develop a deeper understanding of the meaning of the word and to use the word as part of their expressive vocabulary. Multiple exposures can include how the words are used in below-grade-level books in the same subject area, texts in different content areas, and personal writing projects.

Introduce New Words before They Are Encountered in Reading.

The introduction of vocabulary should be done explicitly during a short segment of class time, usually around 5 minutes (Echevarria, 1998). During these 5 minutes, say the vocabulary word, write it on the board, ask students to say and write it, and then define the word using pictures, demonstrations, and examples familiar to students. (See "Teaching Vocabulary through Modeling Examples, Synonyms, and Definitions" in Chapter 9.)

Practice with New Words.

Give your students many opportunities to practice the new words they are learning. Gersten and colleagues (1998) report an example of teaching the word *audience* in *Mr. Popper's Penguins*. After teaching the definition of *audience,* the teacher discussed other kinds of audiences with the class, such as an audience at a Roots concert, an audience at a *Harry Potter* movie, an audience at a football game, and an audience with the pope. It is critical that English-language learners have lots of practice so they can go from a basic understanding of a word to actually being able to use the word in classroom conversation.

to be adapted for some students. For example, Hal was discouraged about always getting a C in English no matter how hard he tried. His teacher decided to supplement his grade with an A for effort to encourage Hal to keep trying. Mr. Henning encouraged his students to come to class on time by giving them credit for punctuality.

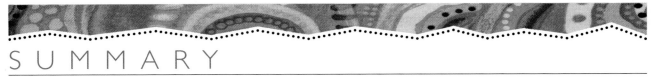

S U M M A R Y

Various aspects of classroom environments can affect the learning of all students, including those with special needs. Fewer individualized accommodations for students with special needs are required in classrooms that are well structured and organized. However, even in the best situations, some adaptations are needed.

The INCLUDE strategy is a decision-making process to help teachers make reasonable adaptations

Focus on Idioms.

Idioms may be hard for English-language learners to understand, because their overall meaning can be quite different from their individual parts. Still, idioms can be used effectively to focus students' attention on important differences between standard and contextual definitions of words, as well as to increase student comprehension. For example, in a history class devoted to the rise of labor unions, a union leader was quoted as using the idiom "hit them in the pocketbook where it hurts." The teacher explained carefully that this expression was not to be taken literally and that it simply meant the unions wanted to hurt managers by causing them to lose money.

Develop Word Banks.

A word bank is a place where key vocabulary is stored and posted for students' reference throughout a teaching unit or beyond. Selection of words for word banks should be based on their relevance for understanding key concepts, high frequency of use, and relevance for students' lives. For example, in a unit on the topic of the greenhouse effect, explaining what the ozone layer is would be more important than presenting the definition of fluorocarbons. Word banks can be created by groups of students or by students individually. They can also be visually displayed. For example, as a word is introduced, its meaning and key attributes can be written on chart paper and posted in the room. The displays can then become reference points for students, can help students remember definitions and relationships among words, and can provide guides for correct spelling. Word banks can also be dynamic; as students learn more about words, this new information can be added to existing definitions. For example, the class that was learning the word *audience* came across the term *audience share* in an article students read about a current television show. The class added this use of *audience* to its visual display.

Use Visual Organizers.

Visual organizers can help students access and understand vocabulary that they could not understand if presented only verbally. Examples of using visual organizers to teach vocabulary are described in Chapter 9.

From the Research

Carlo et al. (2004) significantly improved the depth of vocabulary knowledge, understanding of multiple meanings, and reading comprehension of the fifth-grade English-language learners who were integrated in classrooms with English-speaking students. The strategies of presenting vocabulary words in meaningful contexts, providing access to word meanings in students' primary languages, and presenting vocabulary in multiple contexts worked well for both groups of students.

for students with special needs. Reasonable adaptations are those that maximize student success without taking a disproportionate amount of time or diminishing the education of the other students in the class. The steps in INCLUDE are as follows: identify environmental, curricular, and instructional classroom demands; note student learning strengths and needs; check for potential areas of student success; look for potential problem areas; use information gathered to brainstorm instructional adaptations; decide which adaptations to implement; and evaluate student progress.

An important part of the INCLUDE strategy is analyzing classroom demands. Demands covering four major areas should be analyzed: classroom organization, classroom grouping, instructional materials, and instructional methods. Classroom organization includes physical organization, classroom routines, classroom climate, behavior management including classroom rules and monitoring, and the use of time. Key aspects of classroom grouping involve the use of whole-class and small instructional groups, same-skill and mixed-skill groups, and one-to-one instruction. Instructional materials that need to be considered are basal textbooks, content-area textbooks, manipulatives and models, and instructional and assistive technology. With regard to teaching demands, two common instructional models used in schools are direct and indirect instruction. Sometimes students with special needs may require support in the form of scaffolds when participating in indirect teaching. Also, consider the demands of your student practice activities, and follow guidelines for using practice effectively. Finally take into account how student learning needs may interact with your classroom evaluation system including tests and grading.

Applications in **Teaching Practice**

Planning Adaptations in the Instructional Environment

Consider the following two scenarios:

- Verna is a student with a learning disability in Ms. Chang's fourth-grade class. Ms. Chang uses whole-group instruction in math. This method is sometimes hard for Verna, who is behind her peers in math; Verna is slow to answer math facts, has trouble keeping numbers straight in columns, and sometimes forgets a step or two when she is computing a problem that requires several steps.

- Mr. Howard wants to teach the following textbook-reading strategy to his ninth-grade history students (Bartelt, Marchio, & Reynolds, 1994):
  R *Review* headings and subheadings.
  E *Examine* boldface words.
  A *Ask*, "What do I expect to learn?"
  D *Do* it: Read!
  S *Summarize* in your own words.

QUESTIONS

1. How can Ms. Chang use the INCLUDE strategy to help Verna succeed in the large group?
2. How can Ms. Chang use direct instruction to teach students to round numbers to the nearest 10? Design such a lesson.
3. How can Mr. Howard use scaffolding to teach his history students the READS strategy?
4. Find a drill-and-practice computer program for elementary or high school students and evaluate it. Does it meet the criteria discussed in this chapter?

WORKING THE **STANDARDS**

INTASC PRINCIPLES REFLECTED IN THIS CHAPTER:

Principle #1 states that all teachers understand that students with disabilities may need accommodations, modifications, and/or adaptations to the general curriculum depending on their learning strengths and needs (Principle 1.03).

Principle #4 states that all teachers understand that it is particularly important to provide multiple ways for students with disabilities to participate in learning activities (Principle 4.04).

Principle #5 states that all teachers

- Identify the interests and preferences of students with disabilities, and use this information to design activities

that encourage students with disabilities to make positive contributions to the learning community (Principle 5.01).

- Take deliberate action to promote positive social relationships among students with disabilities and their age-appropriate peers in the learning community. Thus, teachers may group students and construct learning tasks to help students with and without disabilities recognize the differential contributions that each student can make to the learning experience (Principle 5.03).

- Recognize factors and situations that are likely to promote (or diminish) intrinsic motivation, and create learning environments that encourage engagement and self-motivation of students with disabilities (Principle 5.04).

WORKING THE **STANDARDS** *(continued)*

CEC STANDARDS REFLECTED IN THIS CHAPTER:

Council for Exceptional Children

CEC Content Standard #5 states that special educators

- Foster environments in which diversity is valued and individuals are taught to live harmoniously and productively in a culturally diverse world.

- Shape environments to encourage the independence, self-motivation, self-direction, personal empowerment, and self-advocacy of individuals with exceptional learning needs.

CEC Content Standard #7 states that special educators facilitate instructional planning in a collaborative context, including the individuals with exceptionalities, families, professional colleagues, and personnel from other agencies as appropriate.

BACK TO THE CASES

The standards and principles just listed relate to the cases described at the beginning of this chapter: Mr. Rodriguez and Josh. The questions and activities that follow demonstrate how these standards and principles, along with other concepts that you have learned about in this chapter, connect to the everyday activities of all teachers.

Mr. Rodriguez

Mr. Rodriguez has provided a digital copy of the text and, a daily review of previously presented content, outlines of lectures, and small-group discussions to support Manuel's learning of content. Step 7 of the INCLUDE strategy asks teachers to evaluate student progress. (See INTASC Principles 1.03 and 4.04.) Using information in this chapter and Chapter 4, suggest two assessment methods that Mr. Rodriguez might use to assess Manuel's progress. Explain why you selected these two methods.

Josh

Josh's peers may have difficulty adjusting to his speech. As a result, they may shy from interactions with him. Based on information provided in this chapter, name two ways in which Ms. Stewart can use routines, classroom organization, instructional materials, or specific teaching methods to support Josh's interactions with peers. (See INTASC Principles 5.01 and 5.03, and CEC Standard 5.) Explain why you believe these methods would be helpful for Josh.

Visit the companion website (http://www.ablongman.com/friend4e) for a complete correlation of this chapter to the INTASC Principles and CEC Standards.

Further **Readings**

Arends, R. I. (2004). *Learning to teach* (6th ed.). New York: McGraw-Hill.

An invaluable resource for teachers that provides models and strategies for teaching all subject areas at all levels.

Curry, C. (2003). Universal design: Accessibility for all learners. *Educational Leadership, 61*(2), 55–60.

Provides an excellent overview of applications for universal design to all aspects of the classroom.

Kameenui, E. J., & Darch, C. (1995). *Instructional classroom management: A proactive approach to behavior management.* White Plains, NY: Longmont.

Describes a wealth of practical strategies for preventing behavioral problems through carefully planned instruction.

Marchand-Martella, N. E., Slocum, T. A., & Martella, R. C. (2004). *Introduction to direct instruction.* Boston: Allyn and Bacon.

An indispensable guide to published direct instruction programs.

Students with Low-Incidence Disabilities

LEARNER OBJECTIVES

After you read this chapter, you will be able to

1. Describe what it means to say that a student has a low-incidence disability, and apply the INCLUDE strategy to effectively instruct these students in your classroom.

2. Describe the characteristics of students with moderate, severe, and multiple disabilities, including mental retardation, and deaf-blindness, and the accommodations general educators can make for them.

3. Explain the characteristics of students with sensory impairments (that is, vision or hearing loss) and the accommodations general educators can make for them.

4. Explain the characteristics of students with physical, medical, and health impairments and the accommodations general educators can make for them.

5. Outline the characteristics of students with autism spectrum disorder and the accommodations general educators can make for them.

6. Critically analyze your own beliefs about and skills for implementing inclusive practices for students with low-incidence disabilities.

KEY TERMS AND CONCEPTS

Acquired immune deficiency syndrome (AIDS) (p. 217)

Asperger syndrome (p. 224)

Augmentative and alternative communication (AAC) (p. 198)

Autism (p. 222)

Autism spectrum disorder (ASD) (p. 222)

Down syndrome (p. 194)

Functional curriculum (p. 194)

Hearing impairments (p. 201)

Low-incidence disabilities (p. 188)

Orthopedic impairments (OI) (p. 213)

Other health impairments (OHI) (p. 213)

Traumatic brain injury (TBI) (p. 213)

Visual impairments (p. 201)

KYLIE IS A first-grade student with a moderate intellectual disability. She is described by her teachers and her mother as a "bundle of energy," and she is enthusiastic about school and all the activities that occur in her classroom. Although Kylie is just learning to recognize colors and identify shapes and is a prereader, she receives nearly all her instruction in the first-grade classroom. Because Ms. Wilson often uses cutouts, puppets, or other concrete strategies to illustrate the literature being read, Kylie follows along without much difficulty. When other students work on writing or editing, Kylie works with a computer program, either practicing shapes and colors or learning to recognize her name. ● *What are the learning characteristics and needs of students like Kylie? What are appropriate expectations for Kylie's teacher to have for her this year? What accommodations does Kylie need to succeed in first grade? If Ms. Wilson has a question about Kylie, how can she find an answer?*

JULIAN IS A fifth-grade student who was diagnosed last year with cancer. According to federal guidelines, he is eligible to receive special education as other health impaired. Julian underwent chemotherapy and experienced many side effects, including hair loss, lack of appetite, and tendency to bruise. Now more chemotherapy is needed, and a bone marrow transplant is being considered. Julian often misses one or more days of school after treatment because of side effects such as nausea and fatigue. He also was hospitalized twice when he developed a dangerously high fever. Despite Julian's illness, he is enthusiastic about finishing elementary school and moving on to middle school. His teachers prepare work for him when he will be absent for several days, and his special education teacher monitors him closely to ensure that he does not fall significantly behind in his studies. Julian's mom reports that he relies on the e-mails he receives from classmates and the personal notes from his teachers to see him through difficult times. "School," she explains, "gives Julian an anchor in the normal activities of a child. It reminds him that his illness is not all there is to his life." ● *What types of accommodations is Julian likely to need? What is your responsibility as an educator to help Julian not only keep up academically but also remain a true classroom community member?*

CARTER IS AN eighth-grade student diagnosed with an autism spectrum disorder (ASD) who has some remarkable skills. His math achievement is far above grade level, and he has a prodigious ability to remember facts and figures, particularly about his favorite subjects—currently, presidents of the United States and South American countries. However, his reading and written language skills are somewhat below grade level. Carter also has many routines that he insists on following in school. For example, before he leaves the classroom, he counts the books in his backpack, reties his shoes, and says as he leaves the room, "Who's your daddy?" Any change in the schedule of the day or interference with his personal rou-

tines can lead to disruptive behavior. ● *What is autism spectrum disorder? What should Carter's teachers do to help him learn? What accommodations might Carter need now, in middle school, and later, in high school?*

ALYSSA IS A senior this year. She plans to become a special education teacher someday, and she is studying hard to improve her chances of succeeding in college. As the result of a very high fever, Alyssa has had a profound hearing loss since she was 3 months old. Alyssa did not learn a lot of sign language until she began high school. She now prefers signing to oral language as a communication approach, and she has an interpreter who accompanies her to core academic classes. Alyssa's most difficult subject is English. She has problems writing down her ideas logically and elaborating on them. ● *How does a hearing loss or deafness affect learning for students like Alyssa? What are Alyssa's responsibilities for self-advocacy? What can her teachers do to help her prepare for college?*

Students like Kylie, Julian, Carter, and Alyssa have the same rights as other students to be part of a classroom community with nondisabled peers. For Kylie and other young children with significant disabilities, attending first grade with peers prepares them for the demands of school and also creates the expectation that they can fully participate in typical educational environments and live as valued and contributing members of communities after their school years. For Carter and Alyssa, success in college depends on receiving the strong academic background available in general education classes. However, because of their disabilities these and other students in inclusive schools might need specialized equipment, instruction, or other assistance.

In this chapter, you will learn about the characteristics and needs of students with **low-incidence disabilities,** which encompass moderate, severe, and multiple disabilities; sensory impairments; physical, medical, and health disabilities; and autism. The federal terms for these disabilities and the number of students with these disabilities served through IDEA are summarized in Table 6.1. You also will explore accommodations specific to the unique needs of these students that general education teachers and other professionals can make to enable them to learn.

CONNECTIONS

Chapter 1 lists all the categories of disability and explains the concept of high- and low-incidence disabilities.

What Are Low-Incidence Disabilities?

When you work with students with low-incidence disabilities, you will notice immediately the diversity of their abilities and needs, the range of educational services they access, and the variety of specialists who ensure they receive an appropriate education.

TABLE 6.1 School-Age Students with Low-Incidence Disabilities Receiving Special Education Services in 2000–2001[a]

Federal Disability Category	Defining Characteristics	Total Number of Students	Percentage of All Students Receiving IDEA Services	Percentage of All Students Ages 6–21
Mental retardation	Significant below-average general intellectual functioning with deficits in adaptive behavior	612,978	10.6[b]	.92
	Identified between birth and 18 years of age			
	Adversely affect educational performance			
Multiple disabilities	Two or more disabilities so interwoven that none can be identified as the primary disability	122,559	2.1	.19
	Adversely affect educational performance			
Hearing impairments	Hearing loss is permanent or fluctuating, mild to profound in nature, in one or both ears	70,767	1.2	.11
	Loss may be referred to as *hard of hearing* or *deaf*			
	Adversely affect educational performance			
Orthopedic impairments	Physically disabling conditions that affect locomotion or motor functions	73,057	1.3	.11
	May be the result of a congenital anomaly, a disease, an accident, or other causes			
	Adversely affect educational performance			
Other health impairments	Conditions resulting in limited strength, vitality, or alertness and caused by chronic or acute health problems	291,850	5.1	.44
	Adversely affect educational performance			
Visual impairments	Vision loss in which student cannot successfully use vision as a primary channel for learning or has such reduced acuity or visual field that processing information visually is significantly inhibited and specialized materials or modifications are needed	25,975	0.5	.04
	Adversely affect educational performance			
Deaf-blindness	Presence of both a vision loss and a hearing disability that causes severe communication and related problems	1,320	0.02	.00
	Adversely affects educational performance			
Autism	Developmental disability characterized by impairments in communication, learning, and reciprocal social interactions	78,749	1.4	.12
	Usually identified in infancy or early childhood			
	Adversely affects educational performance			
Traumatic brain injury	Impairment manifested by limited strength, vitality, alertness, or other impaired development resulting from a traumatic brain injury	14,844	0.3	.02
	Adversely affects educational performance			

[a]Students ages 6–21 receiving services through IDEA, Part B (U.S. Department of Education, 2002). Approximately 28,683 additional students received services categorized as having developmental delays, and some of these students have low-incidence disabilities.

[b]Because federal categories of disability do not distinguish among students with various degrees of mental retardation, it is difficult to provide a precise estimate of the number of students with moderate or severe cognitive disabilities. However, approximately one-third of the students in this category have moderate or severe cognitive disabilities.

SOURCE: From *Twenty-Fourth Annual Report to Congress on the Implementation of the Individuals with Disabilities Education Act,* 2002, Washington, DC: U.S. Department of Education.

FYI

If you work with children who are under 9 years of age, you may hear the term *developmentally delayed*. States have the option of using this broader, possibly less stigmatizing term to refer to young students who have disabilities, including those who have mental retardation and other disabilities discussed in this chapter.

ANALYZE
AND REFLECT

Why is collaboration so important when you teach students with low-incidence disabilities? With whom do you anticipate you will need to collaborate? What might be some of the opportunities and problems that could occur as part of this collaboration?

The following points can help you keep in perspective these students' uniqueness and your role in their education.

First, students with low-incidence disabilities together make up only about 10 percent of all the students with disabilities in schools. That means that you are unlikely to teach these students every year unless your school houses a program that brings together students with these disabilities from across your school district, sometimes referred to as a *cluster program* or a *district class*. Otherwise, you may encounter a student with a low-incidence disability only a few times in your career.

Second, students with low-incidence disabilities often have received some type of special education services from birth or shortly thereafter. They might come to kindergarten already having attended an infant program or a preschool program in a daycare, inclusive preschool, or special education setting in which their special needs were addressed. You also may find that many supports and extensive technical assistance are available for students with low-incidence disabilities.

Third, students with low-incidence disabilities need the same type of attention from you that other students do. If you are unsure about a student need, it is nearly always best to rely on the same professional judgment you use in working with other students. If you encounter difficulty, you can access the technical support that special education professionals offer. Students with certain disabilities, especially significant or complex ones, often are accompanied by paraprofessionals or personal assistants who might work with them for several years. Such an individual may be able to offer insight about responding to a given student, but the responsibility for ensuring the student's success is yours.

You may have many concerns about meeting the needs of a student with a low-incidence disability in your classroom. The Professional Edge on page 191 features questions you can ask to prepare for a student with a low-incidence disability to join your class. The questions address the student's strengths and potential, learning and social needs, and physical or health needs. They also cover domains in which accommodations might be needed, including the physical arrangement of the classroom. What other questions would you add to these lists?

If you look ahead in this textbook, you will find that this chapter as well as Chapter 7, on high-incidence disabilities, address students with intellectual disabilities. This dual consideration occurs because the federal category of mental retardation is used for all students with intellectual disabilities, whether mild, moderate, or severe. This chapter addresses only students with moderate or severe intellectual disabilities. Students with mild intellectual disabilities have characteristics and needs more similar to those of students with learning and behavioral disabilities, and they are discussed with those groups in Chapter 7.

What Accommodations Can You Make for Students with Moderate, Severe, or Multiple Disabilities?

Students with moderate, severe, or multiple disabilities include those whose intellectual impairments and adaptive behavior deficits are so significant and pervasive that considerable support is needed for them to learn. This group also includes students with multiple disabilities, that is, students who have two or more disabilities that significantly affect their learning. Both groups of students typically have a curriculum that differs somewhat from that of other students in your class, but many students with such significant disabilities can still learn in a general education setting, partially accessing the general curriculum. They also can benefit from social interactions with classmates who do not have disabilities.

PROFESSIONAL EDGE

Questions to Ask When Working with Students with Low-Incidence Disabilities

When you teach a student with low-incidence disabilities, you probably will have concerns about the student's needs and your responsibilities for helping him or her succeed. In your conversations with special educators, related services personnel, and administrators, these are key questions that you might ask about such a student:

Student Strengths and Needs

1. What are the student's greatest strengths?

2. What activities and rewards does the student most enjoy?

3. What are the student's needs in these domains: academic, social, emotional, behavioral, other?

4. Does the student have physical or health needs that require my attention? For example, does the student need to take medication? Is the student likely to have a reaction to medication? Does the student tire easily? Does the student need assistance in moving from place to place?

5. What additional information should I know regarding this student's strengths and needs?

Student Goals

1. What are the three or four most important instructional goals for this student in my class? What are the academic, social, behavioral, emotional, and other goals?

2. What are the goals for this student in each subject (for elementary teachers)? How do the goals for this student interface with the instructional goals of this course (for secondary teachers)?

3. What are the goals that this student is working on throughout the day? Which of those are emphasized during different periods of the day?

Student Supports and Accommodations

1. If I have a question about the student, who is my primary contact person? How do I reach that person?

2. Does the student have a paraprofessional or interpreter? If a paraprofessional is assigned, what responsibilities should that person carry out? Are there activities that the student and not the paraprofessional should be responsible for? To what extent may the paraprofessional help other students in the class as well?

3. What other services (for example, speech/language services) will the student access? How often? Who will be in touch to help arrange these services? Will they be delivered in the classroom or in another location?

4. Do I need to adapt the physical environment for this student? If so, how?

5. Do I need to adapt my expectations for this student because of physical or health needs? If so, how? Are there restrictions on this student's participation in any class activities?

6. What are the most important ways that I can adjust my teaching in order to accommodate the student's needs?

Students with Moderate to Severe Intellectual Disabilities

Students with moderate to severe intellectual disabilities have ongoing needs for supports during their school years and into adult life. Some students are able to learn the academic, social, and vocational skills that enable them to live independently or semi-independently as productive adult citizens. Others' learning will be more limited, and they may need intensive services throughout their lives. In many school districts, students with moderate or severe disabilities are integrated into general education classrooms, most often at the elementary school level but sometimes at the middle school and high school levels. One class in which these and many other students with disabilities commonly participate is physical education, the topic of the Special Emphasis On . . . feature on page 192.

Most states use scores on intelligence tests and adaptive behavior scales to determine the presence of an intellectual disability. Although intelligence tests must be

CONNECTIONS

In Chapter 2, you learned about a variety of strategies for communicating with parents of students with disabilities. Such strategies can foster a positive educational experience for students with low-incidence disabilities.

Special EMPHASIS On …

Physical Education

Whether in elementary, middle, or high school, physical education often is the first area considered for the inclusion of students with low-incidence disabilities. In many schools, physical education teachers work with all students attending the school, both those with disabilities and those without.

No one would disagree with the fact that students with low-incidence disabilities need as much as any student to participate in physical activities. Evidence supports inclusive approaches. Lorenzi, Horvat, and Pellegrini (2000) studied typical elementary students and those with mental retardation as they shared unsupervised recess time. They found that for both groups, boys tended to have a higher level of activity and to raise their heart rates more than girls, but they also found that both boys and girls with intellectual disabilities raised their heart rates more than their classmates. The authors concluded that inclusive recess settings fostered healthy habits for students with disabilities.

Strategies and Approaches

The key to successfully including students with low-incidence disabilities in physical education classes is careful planning with the students' IEP teams using the INCLUDE strategy. Here are some guidelines for accommodating students:

Evidence supports the success of inclusive approaches in physical education for students with low-incidence disabilities.

INCLUDE
- Whenever possible, allow time for students to gain independence in the activities.
- Focus on student abilities, not disabilities. Use student and parent information to give yourself greater understanding of what students are capable of learning and doing.
- Encourage students to choose and adapt activities.
- Maintain activity integrity, but make enough changes so that students can participate successfully.
- Emphasize cooperative games. One example is a relay race in which the objective is to "beat the clock," that is, improve personal performance.
- Avoid elimination games. Students who most need to participate often are the first eliminated.
- Maintain students' right to take risks. Be careful about assuming that certain activities are not suitable for certain students.
- When introducing activities, keep explanations simple, demonstrate, use multisensory approaches, check for understanding, break instruction into small pieces, and ensure students understand any safety issues.

- Check the physical environment to be sure it is appropriate—for example, ensure the space is large enough to accommodate wheelchairs, shortened distances for students with stamina problems, and consistency for students with visual impairments.
- Adapt equipment as needed—for example, change the weight, color, or size of balls or targets.
- Modify student roles when appropriate, for example, by having students stay on base while another student runs, by simplifying the type of movement required, or by changing scoring to foster student success.
- Modify rules to enhance successful participation, for example, by adapting time given for an activity.
- Use peers without disabilities to assist students with disabilities by having them share roles, tutor or coach, or assist students during class activities.

SOURCE: Adapted from "Inclusion of a Diverse Population" (electronic version), by S. L. Sutherland and S. R. Hodge, 2001, *Teaching Elementary Physical Education, 12*(2), 16. © 2001 by Human Kinetics. Adapted with permission from Human Kinetics (Champaign, IL).

interpreted carefully and are not helpful in designing instruction for students, an over-all IQ score of less than 70 with significant difficulty in the area of adaptive behaviors (for example, ordering a meal in a restaurant) leads to eligibility for special education in the category of mental retardation. Students with moderate or severe intellectual disabilities generally have IQ scores of approximately 55 or below. Leaders in the field argue that a more appropriate strategy for identifying individuals with intellectual disabilities is to define the disability by adding other key factors, including social participation, health, and individual functioning within the broader context of school, home, and community (American Association on Mental Retardation, 2002). Kylie, whom you learned about at the beginning of the chapter, is a student with a moderate intellectual disability. As you read the following sections, think about how she might learn in your classroom.

LEARNING NEEDS AND RATE ● Generally, students with moderate or severe intellectual disabilities have several noticeable characteristics. First, the amount of information they can learn may be limited, and the rate at which they learn may be slow. These two factors suggest that considerable repetition of skills essential for adult functioning is needed. For example, Destiny, a middle school student with a severe intellectual disability, is working to learn to communicate her needs to others. She has a communication device that enables her to indicate that she needs a drink of water, that she needs to use the bathroom, and that she is hungry. Her paraprofessional sometimes works with her on this skill, but her classmates also ask her questions related to these needs. Jordan, an elementary student with a moderate intellectual disability, is learning a variety of preacademic skills within his general education classroom, including telling a story from a picture book, recognizing his name and address, and understanding directional prepositions such as *up, down, inside,* and *outside.* He rehearses these as opportunities arise during general instruction, and when other students are completing individual assignments that are beyond his capability, he works on his skills on the computer, sometimes with a peer assistant.

Students with moderate or severe intellectual disabilities need to learn many other essential skills. One example is social skills. Several IEP goals and objectives may relate to participating in one-to-one or small-group interactions with peers, responding to questions asked by others, and sharing toys, games, or materials. These students also may need to learn how to participate appropriately in nonacademic and extracurricular activities such as field trips and after-school programs (Wagner, Cadwallader, Garza, & Cameto, 2004). Without direct assistance from teachers implementing inclusive practices, these students may have difficulty making friends throughout their school careers (Doré, Dion, Wagner, & Brunet, 2002; Geisthardt, Brotherson, & Cook, 2002; Turnbull, Pereira, & Blue-Banning, 2000).

MAINTENANCE OF LEARNED SKILLS ● A second characteristic of individuals with moderate or severe intellectual disabilities is that they may have difficulty maintaining their skills; without ongoing practice, they are likely to forget what they once learned. In the classroom, you may find that this means that it is not necessary to provide new activities each day. For example, Jordan, the student mentioned previously who is learning to recognize his name and address, will need computer practice on that skill for many days. In addition, once he has identified the information, he should practice printing it on cards, writing it on the chalkboard, and saying it aloud. Extensive practice on a single skill using many approaches is usually appropriate.

GENERALIZATION OF LEARNING ● A third characteristic of students in this group is that they may have difficulty generalizing skills learned in one setting or situation to another setting or situation. It is thus critical that they learn as many skills as possible in context. For example, rather than having these students practice buttoning and unbuttoning out of context, as part of a segregated classroom exercise, they can

DIMENSIONS OF DIVERSITY

Children with low-incidence disabilities who live in rural areas have advantages and disadvantages. Because of a strong sense of community, they are likely to be welcomed in classrooms and in their communities. However, specialized services such as special transportation and advanced technology options may be difficult to arrange, and families may feel isolated when no other family has a child with complex needs.

www RESOURCES

The Arc, an organization dedicated to including children and adults with intellectual disabilities in everyday life, has a website filled with resources for understanding students with intellectual disabilities. You can access it at http://thearc.org.

apply this skill in the morning and afternoon as they enter and leave school wearing coats or sweaters. Older students need to learn how to greet classmates and teachers appropriately, for example, with a handshake or by just saying hello instead of shouting or tightly hugging them. This skill is most easily taught as students meet and greet people throughout the school, not in a special education classroom.

WWW
R E S O U R C E S
One valuable source of information about students with Down syndrome is the website of the National Association for Down Syndrome, at http://www.nads.org. This site includes resources, news, and information about this relatively common syndrome.

SKILL COMBINATION ● One additional characteristic of students with moderate to severe intellectual disabilities is difficulty combining a series of small skills into a larger one. For example, a student may be taught each step involved in making a sandwich, but unless the steps are taught in an integrated way, the student probably is going to have difficulty carrying them out in a logical sequence. Some older students are learning to use personal digital assistants (PDAs) to help them remember sequences of skills (Davies, Stock, & Wehmeyer, 2002). How might this student characteristic affect your instruction of them?

Crystal is a young woman with **Down syndrome,** a condition that often includes a moderate intellectual disability. Her story is typical for such a student in a school district committed to inclusive education. She attended elementary school with her peers even though she did not always learn the same things they were learning. Her teachers expected her to behave appropriately, and her peers helped her when she got confused by the teacher's directions or otherwise needed support in the classroom. As she moved to middle school, she participated with peers in co-taught science and social studies classes and in elective classes such as foods and computers, and she received some of her reading and math instruction in a special education classroom. In high school, she took several classes, including choir, U.S. history, home economics, career exploration, and family living. She also entered a vocational preparation program so she would be ready to get a job after high school. At 21, Crystal graduated from high school. She now works in a local medical office. Her job includes duplicating medical records, doing simple filing tasks, running errands, and helping get mail ready to send. Crystal's success as an adult is in large part a result of learning many skills fostered while in inclusive schools.

INSTRUCTIONAL PRINCIPLES ● Three principles usually guide instruction for students with moderate or severe intellectual disabilities (Hickson, Blackman, & Reis, 1995):

1. *Functional curriculum.* In a **functional curriculum,** the goals for students are based on the real-life skills they need to succeed. For example, a student might benefit more from learning to make purchases than learning to write a story because most adults make purchases regularly but not all must have story-writing skills. The most important job skills Crystal learned during her school career were punctuality, following multiple-step directions, and keeping her voice appropriately low.

> In a functional curriculum, the goals for students are based on the real-life skills they need to succeed.

2. *Community-based education.* Most students, but especially those with significant intellectual disabilities, benefit from applying skills learned in school to real-life settings and activities (Burcroff, Radogna, & Wright, 2003). Community-based education might include applying money and counting skills at a restaurant, interacting with people who live in a retirement center, and exploring job possibilities in hotels, assisted living centers, and other businesses.

3. *Age appropriateness.* Individuals with disabilities, even very significant disabilities, should use materials that look appropriate for their age and should learn skills or variations of skills that typical learners their age are acquiring. For example, students with significant intellectual disabilities in high schools should not be using materials designed for young children. Similarly, life skills appropriate for young children include taking turns, sharing, and following directions, skills that can be learned in the school setting with other children. Specific vocational skills such as operating a cash register or stocking shelves should be reserved for older students who are chronologically much closer to using such skills.

Accommodations for Students with Moderate to Severe Intellectual Disabilities

Attending school as members of general education classrooms is beneficial for many students with moderate or severe intellectual disabilities. In one review of 36 studies on including students with intellectual disabilities in general education settings, the authors found that students did better both academically and socially than comparable students in self-contained special education classrooms (Freeman & Alkin, 2000). In fact, many of the adaptations and general school conditions needed by students with moderate and severe disabilities are the same ones that make learning more successful for all students. Added to those are a few unique strategies designed for the abilities and special needs of each individual student (Downing, 2002) and instructional principles such as those described next.

MATCH EXPECTATIONS TO INSTRUCTION ● The INCLUDE strategy can help you, working with colleagues, effectively teach students with moderate or severe intellectual disabilities. For example, in a social studies class, the goal for most students might be to understand detailed topographical maps. At the same time, a student with a moderate intellectual disability might work to locate on a map states where relatives live, and a student with severe mental retardation might work to identify photos of businesses in the community. Your plan should be to use the principles of universal design for learning (UDL) that were introduced in Chapter 5 to ensure that assignments appropriate for a student draw from the standard curriculum, or as close to it as possible (Wehmeyer, Lattin, Lapp-Rincker, & Agran, 2003). Table 6.2 provides additional examples of how the skills on a student's IEP can be mapped onto classroom instruction.

IDENTIFY OPTIMAL TIMES FOR SPECIALIZED INSTRUCTION ● Students with moderate or severe disabilities sometimes need to learn skills that are unlikely to arise as part of the traditional school curriculum, but these activities should nevertheless be integrated into instruction. For example, students might complete activities such as gathering homework, handing out materials, working on key vocabulary related to the topic being studied, or helping the teacher to call on students. How could each of these activities relate to a student's IEP goals and objectives? Why might activities such as these represent appropriate instruction for some students?

INCLUDE

FYI

Even when students with significant intellectual disabilities cannot learn exactly the same curriculum as other students, they benefit from *partial participation,* that is, learning appropriate skills that are based on the general education curriculum. Examples include pouring during a science experiment, choosing between two or three items during a consumer science course, and recognizing one name during reading.

Why do instructional adaptations and strategies for including students with moderate to severe cognitive disabilities benefit all students in a classroom? What does this indicate about focusing on student similarities, rather than their differences?

TABLE 6.2 Sample Communication Skills Mapped onto Elementary School Subjects

Communicative Skills	Daily Oral Language (DOL)	Social Studies	Math	Spelling
	Subjects			
Rejecting	Says no to the activity	Rejects one topic for another	Rejects certain manipulatives for others	Rejects one picture for another
	Rejects certain pictures to illustrate a sentence	Rejects the offer of help from a peer	Rejects the offer of help from a peer	Rejects the offer of help from a peer
Social interaction skills	Exchanges visual glances	Exchanges visual glances	Exchanges visual glances	Exchanges visual glances
	Smiles in response to a comment	Smiles in response to a comment	Smiles in response to a comment	Smiles in response to a comment
	Teases others between activities	Teases others between activities	Teases others between activities	Teases others between activities
	Asks others to come talk	Asks others to come talk	Asks others to come talk	Asks others to come talk
Making comments	Decides on what picture goes best with a DOL sentence	Makes comments about the topic of study	States whether it is fun to do math	Decides which picture/item goes with each spelling word
	States whether a sentence is funny	Responds to direct questions from teachers/peers	Makes comments at beginning and end of school day	States whether a sentence using word and written by peer is OK or not
Greetings/ departures	Beginning and end of school day	Beginning and end of school day	Beginning and end of each class (secondary)	Beginning and end of school day
	Beginning and end of each class (secondary)	Beginning and end of each class (secondary)	As new people enter a room	Beginning and end of each class (secondary)
	As new people enter a room	As new people enter a room	Errands to the office	As new people enter a room
	Errands to the office	Errands to the office		Errands to the office
Requesting activity/items/ information	Asks for help during an activity	Chooses to do one activity over another	Asks for help to solve problems	Requests that spelling end or continue
	Asks for certain paper, pen, or pictures to do an assignment	Requests different writing materials	Asks for manipulatives to do math	Asks for another spelling word
		Asks for help or more information	Asks whether problems are correct	Asks for a specific partner to work with
			Asks for a calculator	

SOURCE: Adapted from "Analyzing the Communication Environment" (p. 59), by J. E. Downing, 1999, in *Teaching Communication Skills to Students with Severe Disabilities,* Baltimore: Paul H. Brookes Publishing Co. Reprinted with permission.

ENLIST NATURAL SUPPORT SYSTEMS ● Peers, older students, parent volunteers, student teachers, interns, and other individuals at school all can assist a student with a moderate or severe disability (Ryndak & Alper, 2003). Peers often can answer simple questions or respond to basic requests without adult intervention. They sometimes also can make needed adjustments in equipment, retrieve dropped articles, and get needed instructional materials for the student. Older students can serve as peer tutors or special buddies, both for instruction and for the development of appropriate social skills. Parents, student teachers, interns, and others all can assume part of the responsibility for supporting students. For example, an administrative intern who reads a story to the class releases the classroom teacher to observe or work with a student with a moderate or severe intellectual disability. A student teacher can work with a small instructional group that includes both typical learners and a student with mental retardation.

CREATE A COLLABORATIVE EFFORT WITH FAMILIES ● As with your other students, when you teach a student with a moderate or severe disability, you should communicate regularly with the student's parents. Families know their children better than school professionals do, and parents can provide valuable information about teaching them. Parents might also have questions about how to reinforce at home skills learned at school. One strategy for drawing on parent, family, and peer knowledge about a student with a low-incidence disability in order to plan an effective education is included in Working Together below. Occasionally, you may encounter a family that does not want to be actively involved in the education of their child. In these cases, it is your responsibility to accept their decision without judging it.

As with all parents, it is also essential to remember that the responses of parents of students with moderate or severe disabilities to their children are based on many

ANALYZE
AND**REFLECT**

What are some of the strategies implemented in meeting the needs of students with moderate or severe disabilities that are beneficial also to students without disabilities? How can students with moderate to severe disabilities benefit from the strategies used in the general classroom?

WORKING **TOGETHER**

Collaborating to Support Students with Significant Disabilities

Collaboration is essential in order for students with low-incidence disabilities to have opportunities to participate in general education settings. One approach that has been useful for students, parents, and school professionals is called the McGill Action Planning System (MAPS). Developed in Canada by experts in inclusive practices for students with significant disabilities, MAPS is based on a set of questions focusing on strengths that parents, other family members, professionals, students, and peers answer in one or more meetings intended to ensure that a student has positive learning experiences. Here are the questions that guide this process:

1. *What is this student's history?* This question is answered by family members so that others have a better understanding of the student.

2. *What is your dream for the child?* As participants answer this question, they are encouraged to think about what they want for the student and what they think the student wants. This is a question of vision, not present-day realities. The team members should dream some here and verbalize those dreams.

3. *What is your nightmare?* Parents sometimes find this question particularly hard to answer because it requires thinking of their child facing difficulties. But if participants can verbalize their nightmares and fears, they will have taken an important step in becoming committed to making sure this nightmare never occurs.

4. *Who is the student?* Taking turns, everyone expresses in a few words what comes to their minds when they think of the student. Participants continue taking turns until no one has anything else to add. When the list is com-

pleted, particular people in the group, such as family members, are asked to identify what they believe are three especially important descriptors.

5. *What are the student's gifts?* The individuals collaborating to plan for the student might look back on the ways they have described the student in answering the previous question. They focus on what they believe the student can do, instead of what the student cannot do.

6. *What are the student's needs?* The parents' answers to this question might vary considerably from those of the student's peers or teachers. When the list has been completed, the group decides which needs are top priority, demanding immediate attention.

7. *What would an ideal day at school be like for the student?* Some MAPS groups answer this question by outlining a typical school day for students without disabilities who are the student's age. The team might think about how the needs outlined in answering the previous question could be met at school. After that, the team could think about the kinds of help a student needs to truly achieve inclusion at school.

REFLECTION

Why is it critical to include general education teachers in the MAPS process? What might be the unique contribution that a student's peers make? How does MAPS represent a model for collaboration that could also be useful in thinking about working together on behalf of other students?

SOURCE: From *The MAPS Process: Seven Questions*, by the Circle of Inclusion Project, University of Kansas, 2002. Retrieved November 22, 2004, from http://www.circleofinclusion.org/english/guidelines/modulesix/a.html.

factors, including their culture. For example, in some Puerto Rican, Mexican, and Colombian families, mothers or both parents are blamed for having children with significant disabilities, and these children are seen as penance for past sins (Rogers-Adkinson, Ochoa, & Delgado, 2003). These parents' degree of acceptance of a child at a low functioning level may frustrate teachers trying to help the student to learn skills and relying on parents to practice the skills at home. For students who are bilingual, issues may arise as educators try to teach English survival words (for example, *stop, danger*) at school while only the native language is spoken in the home.

TAKE ADVANTAGE OF ASSISTIVE TECHNOLOGY ● Both high- and low-technology options help students learn. For example, some students experience success when you provide them with pictures that remind them of key concepts, and with the widespread availability of digital cameras, infinite opportunities are created to take photos of signs, locations, people, and other items that can be used as tools for contextual learning. In another example, many students who cannot use language to communicate use various forms of **augmentative and alternative communication (AAC),** that is, various communication forms—unaided (for example, gestures) or aided (for example, computer software)—that enable students to convey their messages. These are addressed in the Technology Notes on page 199. Other students use technology to aid movement.

Students with Multiple Disabilities

Because students with multiple disabilities often have extraordinary needs, they are considered a distinct group in IDEA. Most students with multiple disabilities have an intellectual disability and a physical or sensory impairment. The needs of these students and the accommodations that help them succeed can be similar to those for students with moderate and severe intellectual disabilities, the differences being mostly a matter of degree and complexity.

However, a few issues may arise more often that particularly concern these students. You may find that the number of special service providers who come to the classroom to work with students with multiple special needs (for example, a special educator, a paraprofessional, a speech/language pathologist, or an occupational therapist) can become distracting for other students. Also, care must be taken that a wheelchair, computer equipment, other therapeutic equipment, and specialized materials (for example, large books in three-ring binders made with many pictures) for a student with multiple disabilities do not become problems for classroom traffic patterns, safety, and storage.

Because many students with multiple disabilities have limited speech and do not easily convey their preferences and needs, communicating with them can be a challenge. One strategy for communication is using augmentative communication systems, the same systems that are sometimes used by students with moderate or severe intellectual disabilities, described earlier in this chapter.

As a teacher, you can expect some but probably not all students with multiple disabilities to participate in general education activities in your school. They are likely to receive considerable support from a special education teacher or a paraprofessional. Thus, co-teaching and other classwide integration activities are likely (Giangreco & Doyle, 2002). These professionals and other members of the multidisciplinary team can assist you in setting expectations for students, planning appropriate educational experiences, monitoring their performance, and problem solving when concerns arise (Downing, 2002). In an elementary school, a student with multiple disabilities might attend your class for morning activities, remain in the room for language arts, and participate in art and music with other students. That student might also receive some services in other building locations (for example, the library, gym, learning center, or special education classroom). In a secondary school, a student with multiple disabilities

RESEARCH NOTE

In a study by Taber, Alberto, Hughes, and Seltzer (2002), students with severe disabilities were successfully taught to use the speed-dial function on a cell phone to call for assistance when lost in the community. Students unable to recognize when they were lost were taught to answer a ringing cell phone and provide descriptive information to the caller. How might you assist such students to learn comparable skills?

RESEARCH NOTE

In a study conducted by Poston and Turnbull (2004), families of children with developmental disabilities reported that they used their faith as a way to make sense of having children with disabilities. Many parents spoke about how their children were accepted into all facets of their religious communities.

> TECHNOLOGY
NOTES

Augmentative and Alternative Communication

Augmentative and alternative communication (AAC) is the term for an individual's use of ways other than speech to send a message to another individual. AAC includes non-aided communication, such as sign language or gestures and facial expressions, and it also includes aided communication, using computers or other simple or complex devices as tools. You might be familiar with a children's story that is about AAC, E. B. White's *The Trumpet of the Swan*, in which Louis, a swan who cannot make the same sounds as other swans, learns to use a trumpet as his voice.

Many students with low-incidence disabilities use AAC devices either as their primary means of communication or as supplements to traditional speech. In order to facilitate a student's use of such devices, a team that includes the student and family members, the speech/language pathologist, teachers, and others evaluates the communication needs and abilities of the student; explores options, sometimes by having the student try out different devices for a specific period of time; teaches the student to use the selected device; and monitors its effectiveness. These are some examples of AAC devices that your students might use:

- *Communication boards.* As introduced in Chapter 1, many students with significant disabilities use communication boards. These boards may be as simple as a set of pictures that depict common tasks or needs. The student points to the appropriate picture using a finger, fist, elbow, eyes, or alternative means such as a head pointer. More complex communication boards are electronic. Pointing at pictures may activate prerecorded messages, such as "I need to be excused to the restroom" or "Hello. My name is Jorge. What is your name?"

- *Switches and scanning devices.* Some students cannot push a button or point at a picture. However, they might be able to indicate a choice using a switch. Thus, when a scanning device is used, a series of options is presented (for example, "I am hungry," "I am thirsty," or "I am tired"), and the student chooses the one that communicates the intended message. The switch is the means for making the choice; students may have the motor control to slap a large button switch to stop items being shown on a computer screen or may make a slight head movement that activates a switch with an electronic voice that "responds."

Big Area Switches (BASs) are examples of simple switches for students with limited motor control.

The Discover Switch is designed for students who write using computers but operate them with a switch. This device includes picture and word banks, as well as other helpful tools.

Information about augmentative and alternative communication is available on many websites and from many organizations, including Augmentative and Alternative Communication Connecting Young Kids (YAACK), a website with basic information and links to many other resources (http://aac.unl.edu/), and the website of the International Society for Augmentative and Alternative Communication (ISAAC) (http://www.isaac-online.org).

SOURCE: Adapted from *Introduction to Augmentative and Alternative Communication*, by American Speech-Language-Hearing Association, 2004, Rockville, MD: Author. Retrieved November 22, 2004, from http://www.asha.org/public/speech/disorders/Augmentative-and-Alternative.htm.

might attend some core classes with peers, some classes with a vocational emphasis (for example, consumer and food sciences), and some special classes for learning community-based and other functional and job-specific skills.

Deaf-Blindness

Helen Keller (1880–1968) was an American author and lecturer. Born in Alabama, she became deaf and blind at 19 months of age from an illness. She learned to read and write from her special education teacher, Anne Sullivan, and eventually graduated with honors from Radcliffe College. She wrote seven books about her life and her disabilities.

Although students with dual sensory impairments, or *deaf-blindness*, typically are not totally blind or deaf, they do have extraordinary needs related to staying in touch with the environment, making sense of events that most teachers and students take for granted, and learning with a limited ability to see and hear (Sall & Mar, 1999). These students sometimes have average or above-average intelligence (as did Helen Keller), but they often have intellectual or other disabilities.

How a student with *deaf-blindness* is educated in any particular school varies considerably. In some schools, professionals, paraprofessionals, and parents judge that students who are deaf and blind can be successful in inclusive environments with extensive supports (Giangreco, Edelman, MacFarland, & Luiselli, 1997), but they disagree somewhat on the types of and approaches to service delivery. In addition to instructional support in general education settings, these students often need extensive training to learn to communicate through sign language, signals and gestures, touch cues, or other means (Engleman, Griffin, Griffin, & Maddox, 1999; Engleman, Griffin, & Wheeler, 1998). In addition, students who are deaf-blind need assistance in social interactions with their peers. Teachers can facilitate interactions by doing the following (Goetz & O'Farrell, 1999):

- Arrange the classroom to promote the active participation of students who are deaf-blind.

- Prompt the students with special needs and the typical learners to interact with each other.

- Interpret for typical students the behaviors of students who are deaf-blind (for example, pushing and shoving may be an indication that a student is excited about playing with the other students).

In other schools, a student who is deaf-blind may be a member of your class, accompanied by a special education teacher or personal assistant, only on some field trips, at assemblies, in selected class activities, or for particular school programs. The specialists working with the student can prepare both you and the other students in the class, letting you know how to approach and greet the student, telling you what to expect in terms of behavior, and explaining why inclusive activities are important for the student and what learning or social objectives are being addressed.

What Accommodations Can You Make for Students with Sensory Impairments?

Students with *sensory impairments* have either vision loss or hearing loss so significant that their education is affected. Their specialized needs can range from slight to complex. Because school learning relies heavily on seeing and hearing, students with these disabilities often experience academic problems and need both teacher accommodations and adaptive equipment. Some of the vocabulary used to describe sensory disabilities are included in the Professional Edge on page 201.

In some cases, a vision or hearing problem is identified by professionals in the school setting. If you notice any of the symptoms noted in the Professional Edge on

PROFESSIONAL EDGE

The Vocabulary of Sensory Impairments

To be effective in making adaptations for your students with sensory impairments, you should understand the terminology used to describe these disabilities. The following terms are some you may encounter in your dealings with students who have sensory impairments and the special educators who work with them. Remember that when you work with students with low-incidence disabilities, you should stay in close contact with special educators and related services personnel so that questions you have and concerns that arise can be promptly addressed.

Visual Impairment

- *Refractive disorders.* The way the eye focuses light is impaired, as in myopia (nearsightedness), hyperopia (farsightedness), and astigmatism (blurred vision).

- *Muscle disorders.* The ability to control eye movements is impaired, as in strabismus (crossed eyes).

- *Receptive disorders.* The ability to receive and process signals from light is impaired, as in retinal detachment caused by glaucoma or a blow to the eye.

Hearing Loss

- *Conductive disorders.* The way the ear transmits sound is impaired; these disorders are generally correctable through surgery or medication.

- *Sensorineural disorders.* The auditory nerve, by which we receive and process signals from sound, is impaired; these disorders are generally not correctable through amplification or hearing aids.

- *Mixed losses.* A combination of conductive and sensorineural impairments.

---

page 202, you should alert your school nurse or health technician as well as a student's parents.

Students with Visual Impairments

Students with **visual impairments** cannot see well enough to use vision as a primary channel for learning without significant assistance. Some students are considered *legally blind*, which means that the vision in the best eye, with correction, is 20/200 or lower, or the visual field is 20 degrees or less. In other words, what a person with normal vision can see at 200 feet, some of these students can see at a maximum of only 20 feet. Those students legally blind because of a limited visual field can see just a 20 percent or smaller "slice" of what a person with normal vision can see within his or her range of vision.

Although the concept of legal blindness is an important one that helps students access special services throughout their lives, a different set of terms is used in schools. For educators, the term *blind* generally is reserved to describe the few students who have little useful vision. They use touch and hearing for most learning. Most students with visual impairments are *partially sighted*, meaning that they have some useful vision; their vision is between 20/70 and 20/200, or they have another vision problem that has a serious negative effect on their learning.

Students with Hearing Loss

Students who are deaf or hard of hearing, sometimes referred to as having **hearing impairments,** cannot hear well enough to use hearing as a primary channel for learning without significant assistance. Because a huge proportion of both formal and incidental learning occurs through casual conversations, presentations by teachers and others,

FYI

Although IDEA uses the term *hearing impairment*, professionals and individuals with hearing loss prefer the expression *deaf or hard of hearing* (DHH), the term used throughout this chapter.

PROFESSIONAL EDGE

Warning Signs That Students May Have Vision or Hearing Loss

As a school professional, you sometimes will be in a unique position to judge whether a student may be experiencing a vision or hearing loss. If you observe any of these warning signs, you should alert your school nurse and follow district guidelines for seeking other assistance for the student.

Signs of Possible Vision Loss

- Frequent rubbing or blinking of the eyes
- Short attention span or daydreaming
- Poor reading
- Avoiding close work
- Frequent headaches
- A drop in scholastic or sports performance
- Covering one eye
- Tilting the head when reading
- Squinting one or both eyes
- Placing head close to book or desk when reading or writing
- Difficulty remembering, identifying, and reproducing basic geometric forms
- Poor eye–hand coordination skills

Signs of Possible Hearing Loss

- Failure to pay attention to casual conversation
- Giving wrong or inappropriately strange responses to simple questions

- Apparently functioning below cognitive potential
- Frequent, recurring ear infections
- Complaints of ringing in the ears, "head noises," and/or dizziness
- Complaints of pain in the ears or discharge
- Withdrawing from interactions with peers
- Frustration or other unexplained behavior problems
- Limited speech or vocabulary
- Frequent mispronunciation of words
- Placing head close to book or desk when reading or writing
- Watching a speaker intently to hear
- Failure to hear someone who is speaking from behind
- Turning up the volume on the television or when using the computer
- Difficulty hearing when using the phone

SOURCES: Adapted from *Warning Signs of Vision Problems,* by Eye Care Council, 1998. Retrieved November 22, 2004, from http://www.seetolearn.com/warning.html; *An Educator's Guide to Hearing Impairment,* by N. Crowe, November 2002. Retrieved November 22, 2004, from http://www.nsac.ns.ca/envsci/staff/ncr/hearing.pdf; and *Teaching Students Who Are Hard of Hearing,* by Northeast Technical Assistance Center, n.d., Rochester, NY: Author. Retrieved November 22, 2004, from http://www.netac.rit.edu/publication/tipsheet/teaching.html.

and overheard information and relies on understanding language, many professionals consider deafness and other hearing loss to be primarily language or communication impairments (for example, Luckner & Muir, 2001). A small number of students with hearing impairments are *deaf;* they cannot process linguistic information through hearing, either with or without hearing aids. Most students, however, are *hard of hearing,* meaning that they have some residual hearing that lets them process linguistic information through hearing, usually by using hearing aids or other assistive devices.

To determine the severity of a hearing loss, professionals check the loudness of sounds as measured in decibels (dB) and the pitch or tone of sounds as measured in hertz (Hz). Normal speech is usually in the 55–60 dB range at 500–2,000 Hz. In contrast, a whisper is about 15–25 dB, and a rock band plays at about 110 dB. Students with a hearing loss of 25–40 dB are considered to have a mild loss; they might not hear every word in a conversation or might not distinguish between words with similar sounds (*such as breathing and breeding*). Those with a loss of 40–60 dB have a moderate loss; they typically cannot hear enough of a conversation to follow it auditorily. Those with a loss of 60–80 dB have a severe loss, and those with a loss of more than 80 dB have a profound loss. Alyssa, whose story you read at the beginning of the chapter, has a profound hearing loss. Students with severe and profound hearing losses typically cannot process speech, even when amplification is used. They rely on sight as an alternative means of learning.

Another factor professionals consider in judging the seriousness of a student's hearing loss is the age when the loss occurred. Students who have been deaf or hard of hearing since birth are often at a disadvantage for language learning because they did not go through the natural process of acquiring language. These students can speak, but because they learned to talk without hearing how they sounded, their speech may be difficult to understand. They might prefer sign language and an interpreter for communicating with you and others. Students who lose their hearing after they learn language, that is, after about age 5, sometimes experience fewer language and speech difficulties.

Accommodations for Students with Visual Impairments

Although students with visual impairments have the same range of intellectual ability as other students, they typically have had fewer opportunities to acquire information usually learned visually (Pogrund & Fazzi, 2002). For example, students generally learn about maps by looking at them. Although students who are blind can learn by feeling a raised map, this method is not as efficient as seeing it. The same problem can occur with academics. Students with visual impairments often experience learning difficulties simply because they cannot easily use vision to process information. Think about how you read this text: You probably scan the pages, focus on words and phrases in boldface print, and visually jump between reading the type and looking at a figure, feature, or photo. If you could read this book only by magnifying it 15 times, or by listening to it on audiotape, or by reading it in braille, you would find it much more tedious to scan, to select important words and phrases, and to go back and forth between components. If you multiply this dilemma across all the visual learning tasks students face, you can begin to understand the challenges of learning with a visual impairment.

As is true for all individuals, students with visual impairments vary in their social and emotional development. Some students encounter little difficulty making friends, interacting appropriately with peers and adults, and developing a positive self-concept. Other students need support in these areas (Sacks & Silberman, 2000). For example, it is important to teach some students who cannot see to adhere to social norms such as facing a person when talking, taking turns, and keeping an appropriate social distance. Conversely, teachers should keep in mind that some students might miss another student's or a teacher's puzzled expression about something they had said and continue to interact as if they were understood. Teachers also should help other students to understand that a student with a visual impairment cannot help a wiggling eye, or that such a student stands a little too close during interactions because she has difficulty judging distance.

> Accommodations needed by students with visual impairments depend on many factors, and the INCLUDE strategy can guide your planning.

RESEARCH NOTE

As is true for other students with disabilities, self-determination is a concern for students with visual impairments. In one study, 54 students with visual impairments ages 8 to 23 reported that they had few opportunities to make choices at home, at school, with friends, for health care, and in physical education classes (Robinson & Lieberman, 2004).

PLANNING INSTRUCTION FOR STUDENTS WITH VISUAL IMPAIRMENTS ●
Accommodations needed by students with visual impairments depend on many factors, and the INCLUDE strategy can guide your planning. First, take into account students' overall ability level, use of learning strategies and other learning skills, and attentional and motivational levels, just as you would for any other student. Then, working with a special educator, make accommodations depending on the amount of students' residual vision and the nature of their vision problems, keeping in mind that

these students have many essential life skills to master that other students take for granted (for example, proper eating manners, appropriate social distance during interactions, keyboarding, signature writing, and proficiency in using adaptive technology) and that time must be made in their school careers to teach these skills (Sacks & Silberman, 2000). Some specific adaptations you can make and unique needs you must consider for students with visual impairments are covered in the following sections.

ORIENTATION AND MOBILITY ● One important area of need for students with visual impairments is orientation and mobility, that is, the sense of where they are in relation to other objects and people in the environment and the ability to move about within a space. For example, students with visual impairments need to understand where furniture, doorways, bookshelves, and the teacher's desk are in the classroom, in relation to their own location. In addition, they need to be able to move from the classroom to the auditorium to the cafeteria and out to the bus in a timely manner. Your first task in preparing for a student with a visual impairment might be to arrange your classroom carefully, leaving adequate space for all students to move about. Depending on the amount of sight the student has, you might need to keep furniture and supplies in consistent places and make sure the student has an opportunity to learn where everything is. If you decide to rearrange the room or move your supplies, alert your student with a visual impairment to the changes and allow opportunities to adapt to them. Another orientation and mobility issue is safety. Half-open doors or trash cans inadvertently left in aisles can be serious hazards for students with visual impairments. For fire drills or emergencies, pair all students with buddies to assist each other so as to avoid singling out any individual student with a visual impairment.

ANALYZE AND REFLECT

What type of accommodations might be necessary in order for students with visual impairments to be safe in the classroom? What implications might these accommodations have for students in the classroom without disabilities?

TEACHING STUDENTS WITH VISUAL IMPAIRMENTS ● You also might be asked to modify your teaching slightly to accommodate a student with a visual impairment. For example, you might need to identify the novels you plan to use in class prior to the start of the school year so they can be ordered in braille, large-print, or audiotape format. For visual clarity, you might need to use a whiteboard with a black felt-tipped marker instead of a traditional chalkboard, or to provide the student with paper that has heavy black lines instead of the traditional light blue ones. In addition, you should be sure to recite what is written on the board; call students by name so the student with a visual impairment can learn the sounds of everyone's voices and where they are seated; allow the student to move close to demonstrations and displays; give specific directions instead of using general words such as *here* and *there*; and seat the student so as to optimize visual learning (for example, away from bright light or near the front of the room). Usually, an itinerant vision specialist or another special educator will alert you to these types of accommodations and arrange for any classroom modification.

Some general modifications in your classroom also can help a student with a visual impairment. Meet with the itinerant vision specialist or other special educators to discuss the student's needs and the extent of assistance required, including the important matter of problems related to storing the student's specialized equipment. Based on this information, some or many accommodations might be appropriate. Assign a buddy to assist a new student at the beginning of the school year, especially in dealing with the cafeteria, moving from room to room, and locating supplies. This assistance might be discontinued later in the school year to avoid creating unneeded dependence.

Some students with visual impairments need additional time to complete assignments, whether during class or as homework. Monitor closely to ensure that a student is not spending too much time on a single task; this might be a signal that the task needs to be shortened or otherwise modified. Be alert for a student's need for a change-of-pace activity. A student who is fidgeting or refusing to work might be fatigued, a common problem for students who have to make extraordinary efforts to learn using vision. Letting the student take a break or substituting an alternative activity both helps the student and prevents discipline problems. Also keep in mind how to plan alternative learning opportunities for students. If you are talking about history and using a timeline, for example, use white glue or some other means of marking points on the timeline so that a student with a visual impairment can participate meaningfully in the discussion by touching the points in time and feeling the distance between them. A vision specialist can help you develop such alternative learning opportunities. Finally, teachers sometimes worry about the impact that words and phrases such as *Do you see my point?* and *That's quite a sight!* have on a student with a visual impairment. Generally, you should just use the vocabulary you normally would; avoiding words related to seeing is not necessary.

LEARNING TOOLS FOR STUDENTS WITH VISUAL IMPAIRMENTS ● Students with visual impairments use a wide variety of equipment or devices to facilitate their learning. If they have some residual vision, they can use devices to help them acquire information visually. Some use simple devices such as magnifying lenses or bright light to read or do other schoolwork. Others hold their books close to their eyes or at a specific angle to see the print. Many students with visual impairments use computers. For example, if students use a speech synthesizer or text enlarger with a standard word-processing program, they may be able to type their assignments exactly as their peers do. For students who read braille, assignments can be printed on a braille printer as well as a standard printer so that both teacher and student can read them. A further sample of the learning tools available for students with visual impairments, as well as tools used by students with hearing loss, is included in the Technology Notes on pages 206–209.

Accommodations for Students Who Are Deaf or Hard of Hearing

Students with hearing losses have the same range of intellectual ability as other students. However, if intelligence is assessed using a test based on language, students with hearing loss might have depressed scores. Academically, many students struggle because their hearing loss affects their ability to understand language, which in turn affects their learning. Alyssa, the student with a profound hearing loss introduced at the beginning of the chapter, finds this problem especially frustrating. Although evidence suggests that some students who are deaf or heard of hearing and are educated in general education settings usually read better than their peers who are educated in special education classrooms (Easterbrooks, 1999), students might have difficulty learning vocabulary and, as a result, understanding the materials they read and the lessons you present. For example, students with hearing losses often miss subtle meanings of words, which can affect both their learning and their social interactions. One simple example can illustrate the complexity of learning language. Think of all the meanings you know for the word *can*. As a noun, it refers to a container made of metal for storing food, for example, a can of peas. But it also means a container with a lid, as in the type of can that tennis balls are packaged in. *Can* also has slang meanings, as a synonym for both bathroom and prison. As a verb, it means "to be physically able," as in "I can lift that box." It also refers to preserving produce from the garden, as in "I plan to can green beans this year"; to losing a job, as in "I just got canned"; and to the state of being likely, as in "Can that be true?" If you think about all the words in the English language that have multiple and sometimes contradictory meanings, it becomes easier to understand the difficulties faced by students who are deaf or hard of hearing.

Socially and emotionally, students who are deaf or hard of hearing are sometimes immature (Marschark, 1997). This lack of maturity occurs for two reasons. First, much of the etiquette children acquire comes from listening to others and modeling what they say and do. This learning is not available to many students who are deaf or hard of hearing. Second, these students can become confused in interactions that involve many people and multiple conversations. Because these types of situations often are

text continues on p. 210

FYI

Although a few students have guide dogs, adults are more likely to use them because of the care they need, the training involved in obtaining them, and the expense of maintaining them.

WWW
R E S O U R C E S

You can learn more about visual impairments by accessing the American Foundation for the Blind website, at http://afb.org.

> TECHNOLOGY NOTES

Assistive Technology for Students with Sensory Impairments

For Students with Visual Impairments

Larger format books (such as the one shown here) and large-print books are low-tech options for students with visual impairments.

The electronic braillewriter is a device with six keys that the student simultaneously presses down in various combinations to produce the special system of raised dots that can be "read" through touch.

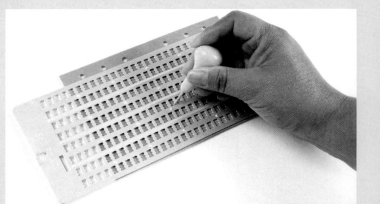

The slate and stylus is a simplified device for producing braille.

A portable notetaker is equipped with six keys and a spacebar, as well as a speech synthesizer.

Students with visual impairments can use specially designed magnifying glasses to help them to better see educational materials.

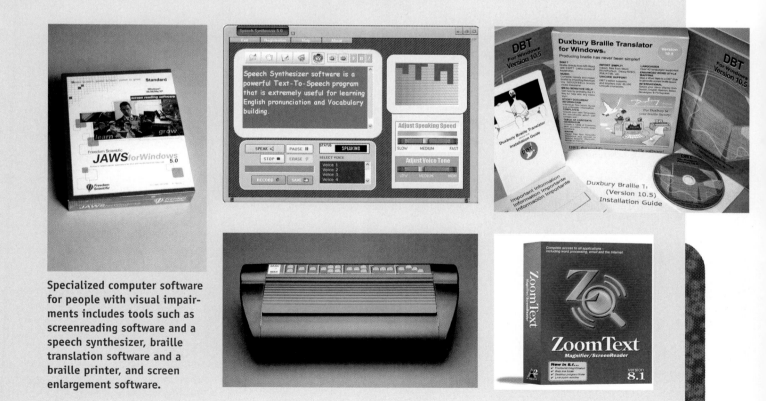

Specialized computer software for people with visual impairments includes tools such as screenreading software and a speech synthesizer, braille translation software and a braille printer, and screen enlargement software.

> TECHNOLOGY NOTES (continued)

Assistive Technology for Students with Sensory Impairments

For Students Who Are Deaf or Hard of Hearing

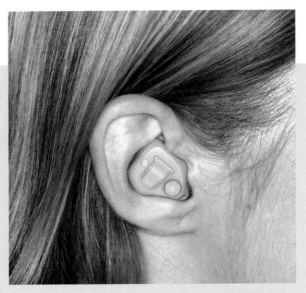

Hearing aids are common assistive technology for people with hearing impairments.

This is an FM system in which the teacher wears a microphone and the student wears a receiver.

A sound field system is similar to an FM system but uses speakers so that the teacher's voice is amplified for the entire class.

C-print is a system in which a typist enters a teacher lecture and student comments into a laptop computer for simultaneous display on a second computer used by the student.

HIMSELF WITH YES-MEN.
HE BASKS IN THEIR FAWNING
ADMIRATION WHICH HE SEEMS TO

Closed captioning, words printed at the bottom of the screen, enables students with hearing loss to watch videos and television.

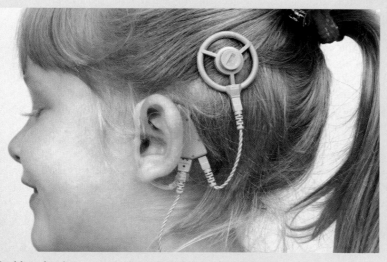

Cochlear implants are devices that electronically transmit sound to the brain, bypassing the ear itself.

uncomfortable for them, students with hearing impairments sometimes avoid them and fail to develop social skills needed in group interactions. For example, Jim is a seventh-grade student with a moderate hearing loss. When students work in lab groups in Mr. George's science class, Jim tends to tune out because he cannot follow what everyone is saying. Sometimes he tries to participate in the activity, but he often does so by making an exaggerated face or drawing a cartoon to show others. He does this even when the other students are working intently, and they become annoyed with his antics. When Jim realizes his attempts to participate are not being successful, he withdraws from the group and becomes passive. Mr. George and the special education teacher are working to address this problem. Mr. George makes sure that he monitors the groups' work, and he sometimes intervenes by asking Jim a question that helps him participate in his group. Mr. George reminds his students that unless every group member understands a science experiment, the group is not finished. Jim also receives help on his social interactions in a support group that he attends with several other students, led by a social worker twice each week.

TEACHING STUDENTS WHO ARE DEAF OR HARD OF HEARING ●

Accommodations for students with hearing impairments emphasize helping them use whatever residual hearing they may have and accessing language to promote formal and informal learning. Although the specific types of accommodations needed by a student you teach are determined by the multidisciplinary team that writes the student's IEP, the following are some common ones.

Because many students who are deaf or hard of hearing get some information through *speech reading*, or watching others' lips, mouth, and expressions, teachers should always face the class when presenting information and stand where no glare or shadow makes it difficult for a student to see, perhaps also using an overhead projector instead of writing on the chalkboard. A teacher also should stand in one location instead of moving around the room, and the student should sit near the teacher. These adjustments facilitate speech reading but also are necessary if an interpreter is present. Teachers should avoid exaggerating sounds or words; doing this makes it more difficult for the student, not easier. Because some students with hearing losses do not use speech reading and because even those who do get only part of the message that way, teachers should use as many visual aids as possible. Important directions can be written on the chalkboard, with either words or, for younger students, pictures. Major points in a lecture for older students can be written on an overhead projector or on the chalkboard. With an overhead projector, the teacher can face students while writing, thus enabling students with hearing impairments to speech-read.

If a student who is deaf or hard of hearing speaks to you and you do not understand what has been said, ask the student to repeat the information. If you still do not understand or the student becomes frustrated, switching to paper and pencil is sometimes appropriate. When a student appears confused following directions or answering a question you ask, the difficulty might be vocabulary. Try substituting a simpler word or offering a word you think the student might be trying to convey. Above all else, be patient when communicating with students who are deaf or hard of hearing.

As with students who have visual impairments, safety also needs to be kept in mind for students with hearing impairments. Assigning a buddy to assist such a student during a fire, tornado, or earthquake drill is a simple strategy for addressing this issue. For other specific adaptations regarding safety, a special educator with expertise in working with these students can assist you.

If a student who is deaf or hard of hearing uses sign language, you might consider enrolling in a sign class yourself and inviting a deaf education teacher to your class to teach some signs to the entire group. Students generally enjoy this experience, and both you and they will be better able to communicate with the student who cannot hear. For example, you might use the sign for "line up" instead of asking stu-

FYI

Even the best speech readers get only about 25 percent of a spoken communication. Most individuals receive only 5–10 percent of spoken communication using this strategy.

dents to do this; by using the sign, everyone, including the student with hearing loss, understands.

Finally, you should be aware that the field of deaf education is facing complex issues. Some professionals, parents, and community members believe that students should maximize their use of oral language; others argue that sign language should be the primary mode of communication. Yet others favor a combination of approaches (Easterbrooks, 1999; Gallimore & Woodruff, 1996). Controversy exists, too, about Deaf culture, that is, some individuals' view of deafness as a cultural phenomenon rather than a disability (Pagliaro, 2001). Some individuals believe students who are deaf should be educated in separate schools with specially designed curricula and experiences. Others believe that this approach leads to isolation for students. If your school includes students with hearing losses, you may hear discussion concerning these topics, and knowing about them may help you better understand the range of perspectives among professionals, parents, and students. An example of ways to include students who are deaf or hard of hearing in the general education classroom is described in the Case in Practice below.

WWW
RESOURCES

The National Association of the Deaf, at http://www.nad.org, has the goal of advocating for people who are deaf or hard of hearing, providing information on topics related to hearing loss, and serving individuals with these special needs.

LEARNING TOOLS FOR STUDENTS WHO ARE DEAF OR HARD OF HEARING ● Students with some residual hearing often use amplification devices such as hearing aids. If you have a student who wears hearing aids, you should be alert for

CASE IN PRACTICE

Including Students Who Are Deaf or Hard of Hearing

Ms. Skinner is a fifth-grade teacher at Lunar Elementary School. This year in her class of 31 she has 2 students with hearing loss. The girls, who are twins, have profound hearing losses present since birth. Because they use sign language as their primary means of communication, they are accompanied by Ms. Mohammed, their interpreter. Ms. Skinner discusses what it is like to teach in this class:

When I first heard I was going to get Jenna and Janice this year, I was worried. I knew they'd been in fourth grade and done well, but there's so much more curriculum at this level. I didn't know how I was going to teach everything and also do all the work necessary for Jenna and Janice and at the same time deal with end-of-grade testing and all that pressure.

As it turns out, it hasn't been much of an adjustment at all. Ms. Mohammed interprets for the girls, and she adds explanations if they need it. The hardest part for me was learning to stay in one place when I talk—for a teacher like me, who is constantly moving around the room, that has been very difficult. Ms. Mohammed has taught all of us some basic signs—that puts us all in touch. Jenna and Janice have some serious academic problems mostly related to vocabulary, but the other kids just think of them as classmates. I've learned a lot this year. I'm a lot more confident that I really can teach any student who comes through my door!

REFLECTIONS

Why might teachers be worried about having students like Jenna and Janice

in their classrooms? What is the best way to get over this worry? How would having these students in a middle school social studies class or high school civics class differ in terms of expectations and accommodations compared to those in an elementary class? What aspects of teaching might be particularly challenging for you if you had students like Jenna and Janice in your classroom? How would you help them compensate for their difficulty in vocabulary? What do you imagine is the impact of having an interpreter in a classroom most of the time? What type of assistance might you ask from the twins' parents to help them master the subjects you will be teaching?

signs of inattention that signal the hearing aid is not turned on or the battery needs to be replaced. Certain students might use an FM system consisting of a microphone worn by the teacher and a receiver worn by the student. When the teacher talks, the sound is converted into electrical energy carried on a specific radio frequency through the air. The receiver converts the electrical energy back to sound, amplifies it, and sends it to the student's ear. Alternatively with this system the classroom may be equipped with speakers so that all students can more clearly hear the teacher's voice. A third type of device also is becoming more common. Cochlear implants and related technology are creating options for some students to "hear" electronically.

Keep in mind that hearing aids and FM systems both amplify sounds, but they do not discriminate the teacher's voice from other sounds. Thus, a student wearing hearing aids can be distracted by the amplified noise of someone typing on the computer keyboard, a door slamming, or chairs scraping on the floor. A student using an FM device also hears the amplified sound of a teacher's jewelry hitting the microphone or the static from a teacher's fingering the microphone. Any of these extraneous noises can interfere with a student's understanding of spoken information and can distract from learning. Amplification clearly assists some students who have hearing impairments, but it also has limits.

Students who have a severe or profound hearing loss often use sign language. Sometimes they use *American Sign Language (ASL)*, a distinct language not based on standard English grammar and structures. Learning ASL is like learning any other second language. Other students use a manually coded English (MCE) system such as *signed exact English (SEE)*, that is, spoken English converted to a set of signs. With either method, students sometimes also use *finger spelling*, in which every letter of a word is spelled out. For example, finger spelling is needed for names or technical terms for which no signs exist.

> "Students who have a severe or profound hearing impairment often use sign language."

Especially in secondary schools, students who use sign language sometimes are accompanied by interpreters who translate your words and those of classmates into sign language (Yarger, 2001). An interpreter needs to sit facing the student and near you so that the student can both watch you and follow the interpreter. Some older students also use a note taker (who could be a classmate) because they cannot both watch an interpreter and a teacher and take notes. However, even if a student uses an interpreter, you should speak directly to the student when asking questions, giving directions, or otherwise conversing. Do not speak to the interpreter instead of the student. The interpreter will make sure the student understands what you say. For example, you should say to Paige, a student with a profound hearing loss, "Do the first five examples on the page." You should *not* direct your remarks to the interpreter by saying, "Tell Paige to do the first five examples on the page." Also keep in mind that interpreters need breaks; you might be asked to make small changes in your instructional pattern to ensure that the interpreter can take a break without negatively affecting student learning.

What Accommodations Can You Make for Students with Physical, Medical, or Health Disabilities?

Some students receive special education and related services because they have physical disorders, chronic or acute medical problems, or health impairments that interfere with their learning. In IDEA, three categories of disabilities can be loosely grouped in this area: orthopedic impairments, other health impairments, and traumatic brain injury. **Orthopedic impairments (OI)** are diseases or disorders related to the bones, joints, or muscles. **Other health impairments (OHI)** include medical or health conditions such as AIDS, seizure disorders, cancer, juvenile diabetes, and asthma. **Traumatic brain injury (TBI)** is any insult to the brain caused by an external force, including injuries sustained in auto accidents and during play. Students with these kinds of disabilities, caused by a wide variety of physical or health problems, differ greatly in their levels of ability and academic achievement and in their needs, which can range from modest to extensive. The following sections provide examples of the specific conditions that fall into these disability categories.

Orthopedic Impairments

Students with orthopedic impairments, often referred to as *physical disabilities*, are those with significant physical needs. The types of special needs these students may have include the following.

STUDENTS WITH CEREBRAL PALSY ● In public schools, the largest group of students with orthopedic impairments comprises those who have *cerebral palsy (CP)*. Some 9,750 infants and preschoolers are diagnosed each year as having this condition (United Cerebral Palsy, 2004), a 25 percent increase over the past decade. Cerebral palsy occurs because of injury to the brain before, during, or after birth and results in poor motor coordination and abnormal motor patterns. These problems can occur in just the arms or legs, in both the arms and legs, or in a combination of limbs, and with varying degrees of severity. For some students, CP also affects other muscle groups, such as those controlling the head and neck. Thus, some students with cerebral palsy walk on their toes with their knees close together. Their arms may be positioned with their elbows bent and their hands positioned near shoulder height. Other students with CP need braces or a walker to move about. Yet others use wheelchairs. For some students, head supports prevent their heads from lolling side to side. Intellectually and academically, students with CP can be gifted, average, or below average, or they might have mental retardation.

Don is a student with cerebral palsy. His arms and hands are drawn up close to his body and he does not control their movement. He moves around school in a motorized wheelchair, and Mike, his personal assistant, helps with personal care (for example, going to the bathroom, eating) and tasks such as writing. Don has low-average ability, but his physical disabilities sometimes cause others to think he has an intellectual disability as well, especially because his speech is difficult to understand. Don's teachers have learned to engage him in class activities by asking yes-or-no questions to which he can respond fairly easily. If they ask a question requiring a longer answer, they give Don time to form the words needed and do not let other students speak for him.

STUDENTS WITH MUSCULAR DYSTROPHY ● Another orthopedic impairment is *muscular dystrophy (MD)*, a disease that weakens muscles. Students with this disorder have increasing difficulty walking and otherwise actively moving about. Gradually, they lose their ability to stand and they require a wheelchair. They also tire more and more easily. Students with muscular dystrophy usually die during their late teens (National Institute of Neurological Disorders and Stroke, 2001). Frank was a student with MD. When he began elementary school, he seemed no different from any other student. However, he began middle school using a wheelchair when he became tired. By the end of that year, he was using the wheelchair all the time. By late in his sophomore

WWW
RESOURCES
Information about the causes, classification, prognosis, treatment, and psychological aspects of cerebral palsy can be found at the website for United Cerebral Palsy, at http://www.ucp.org.

FYI

Spina bifida is a physical disability that results when the spinal cord protrudes from an opening in the spine, and it may lead to paralysis and mental retardation. However, the incidence of this disability has been dropping rapidly since the U.S. Food and Drug Administration (FDA) in 1997 strongly recommended that some foods such as bread be fortified with folic acid, a nutrient known to prevent spina bifida.

year, Frank was too weak to attend school and received instruction from an itinerant teacher at his home. He died in late September of his junior year of high school.

STUDENTS WITH SPINAL CORD INJURIES ● A third orthopedic impairment is *spinal cord injury*. As the term implies, this injury occurs when the spinal cord is severely damaged or severed, usually resulting in partial or extensive paralysis (National Spinal Cord Injury Association, 2004). Spinal cord injuries are most often the result of automobile or other vehicle accidents. The characteristics and needs of students with this type of injury are often similar to those of students with cerebral palsy. Judy suffered a spinal cord injury in a car accident. She was hospitalized for nearly half the school year, and at the time she returned to school she could not walk and had the use of only one arm. She is as bright and articulate as ever and still gets in trouble when she challenges teachers' authority. What has changed is how she moves from place to place.

Cerebral palsy, muscular dystrophy, and spinal cord injuries are just a sample of the range of orthopedic impairments students can have. You may teach students who have physical disabilities caused by amputations or birth defects that result in the absence of all or part of a limb. Likewise, you might have a student with juvenile rheumatoid arthritis, a chronic swelling of the joints usually accompanied by soreness and limited mobility. Whatever the orthopedic impairment a student has, your responsibility is to learn about the student's needs and work with special education professionals to ensure those needs are met through various adaptations.

TEACHING STUDENTS WITH ORTHOPEDIC IMPAIRMENTS ● The adaptations you make for students with physical disabilities will depend on the nature and severity of the disabilities and on the students' physical status. For example, you need to be alert to changes you might need to make in the physical environment so that students can comfortably move into, out of, and around the classroom. Such changes include rearranging classroom furniture and adding supports such as handrails. Other physical adaptations, such as creating adapted work spaces with large tables and lowering chalkboards, can facilitate student learning. Of course, students with orthopedic impairments also may use assistive technology, a topic you have learned about earlier in this chapter and in other chapters. Ideas to help you think about the best uses of such technology are presented in the Technology Notes on page 215.

A second area of adaptation to consider for students with orthopedic impairments involves their personal needs (Friend, 2005). Many students become fatigued and might have difficulty attending to learning activities late in the school day. A few take naps or otherwise rest. Other students need to stop during the school day to take medication. Some students need assistance with personal care, such as using the bathroom and eating. Students who use wheelchairs might need to reposition themselves or be repositioned by an adult because of circulation problems. This repositioning can be done readily for young children, who can be moved to sit or lie on the classroom floor during stories or other activities. Paraprofessionals typically assume personal-care responsibilities and those related to moving students. If you have questions about these areas, a special educator can assist, or the student's parent can explain what is needed.

It is not possible to generalize about students' academic and social needs. Some students with orthopedic impairments enjoy school and excel in traditional academic areas. Some students with cerebral palsy are gifted. Other students with these disabilities experience problems in learning. Some are charming and gregarious students who are class leaders; others have a low self-concept and are likely to have problems interacting with peers. If you think about a student like Judy, the student introduced previously who has a spinal cord injury, you can imagine that her reaction to her accident and her need to use a wheelchair is influenced by many factors, including her family support system, her self-concept, and her peers' reactions. The suggestions through-

> TECHNOLOGY NOTES

Making Sense of Assistive Technology

Teachers in inclusive classrooms can be overwhelmed by the number and variety of technological options their students may have. As you consider the use of assistive technology for your students with disabilities, as well as for other students, these are points to keep in mind:

- When you are providing input related to the technology use, opt for open-ended devices whenever possible, ones that permit customizing for both student and tasks. For example, software that may be used by several students is preferable to programs designed for just one student.

- Try the lowest technology solution before assuming that high technology is needed. A larger mouse may adequately accommodate a student; an entirely different keyboard or computer may not be needed.

- Collaborate with others. Keeping abreast of all new developments is an impossible task for one person to accomplish. If you learn how to use a program or device, share your knowledge with others, and they can do the same for you. Also work closely with other professionals, such as assistive-technology specialists who might be employed in your school district.

- Collaborate with parents to be sure that technology devices that go home are used for the purpose intended and returned to school for use there.

- Ensure that devices used by students are age- and gender-appropriate. For example, a high school student using a talking word processor should use the adult voice option, not the child voice. Software, even if presenting very basic skills, should appear appropriate for a student's age.

- Avoid the belief that you have to understand completely a piece of assistive technology before you can use it and help your students use it. In many cases, "jumping in," even when you are uncertain, is the strategy of choice.

- Check on your school district policy concerning equipment use (home versus school), maintenance, and repairs. Although you are not responsible for these areas, being knowledgeable can help you and parents avoid problems.

- Ask for training on equipment or devices that your students will use. Given that you are teaching the student, you should not rely on the special educator to provide all expertise.

- Experiment with assistive technology. You may discover an option that will help some of your students or identify problems that should be addressed.

SOURCE: Adapted from "Using Assistive Technology in the Inclusive Classroom," by J. B. Merbler, A. Hadadian, and J. Ulman, 1999, *Preventing School Failure, 43,* pp. 113–117. Reprinted with permission of the Helen Dwight Reid Educational Foundation. Published by Heldref Publications, 1319 Eighteenth St., N.W., Washington, DC 20036-1806. Copyright © 1999.

out this text for working with students to help them learn and succeed socially are as applicable to this group of students as to any other.

Other Health Impairments

Students with health impairments often are not immediately apparent to a casual observer. However, their disabilities may be significant.

STUDENTS WITH SEIZURE DISORDERS ● One group of health impairments is seizure disorders, or *epilepsy*, a physical condition in which the brain experiences sudden but brief changes in functioning. The result is often a lapse of attention or consciousness and uncontrolled motor movements. A single seizure is not considered a symptom of epilepsy, but if several seizures occur, the disorder is diagnosed. About 125,000 new cases of epilepsy are counted each year, with half of them occurring among children and adolescents. Most cases have no specific cause determined (National Dissemination Center for Children with Disabilities, 2004a).

DIMENSIONS OF DIVERSITY

In choosing assistive technology, professionals should base decisions on a family's priorities, resources, and concerns, including stressors and cultural values, in order to avoid the possibility of assistive technology abandonment (Parett, Hourcade, & Huer, 2003).

FYI

Approximately 6.5 million Americans have epilepsy, and 315,000 of these individuals are children through the age of 14. Epilepsy can occur at any age, sometimes as a result of illness or injury but often for no apparent reason.

Epilepsy can produce different types of seizures. *Generalized tonic-clonic* seizures (previously called *grand mal* seizures) involve the entire body. A student experiencing a generalized tonic-clonic seizure falls to the ground unconscious; the body stiffens and then begins jerking. Breathing may become shallow, and the student might lose bladder or bowel control. After a minute or two, the movements stop and the student regains consciousness. Steps you should take when a student has a generalized tonic-clonic seizure are summarized in the Professional Edge below.

Other seizures do not involve the entire body. *Absence seizures* (previously called *petit mal* seizures) occur when students appear to "blank out" for just a few seconds. If they are walking or running, they might stumble because of their momentary lapse of awareness. When you observe a student with these symptoms, alert the school nurse or another professional who can further assess the student. It is not unheard of for students to attend school for several years before someone realizes that their inability to pay attention is actually the result of a seizure disorder.

Most students who have seizures take medication to control their disorder, and if necessary you should monitor the consistency with which the medication is taken, because that greatly affects its effectiveness. If the medication is carefully monitored and a student's size and status are not changing, you might not even be aware of the student's disability. However, when children are growing rapidly and gaining weight,

PROFESSIONAL EDGE

What to Do When a Student Has a Seizure

As an educator in an inclusive school and as a responsible citizen, you should know how to respond when someone has a seizure. The Epilepsy Foundation recommends these steps for responding to generalized tonic-clonic seizures:

1. Keep calm and reassure other people who may be nearby.

2. Clear the area around the person of anything hard or sharp.

3. Loosen ties, scarves, jewelry, or anything else around the neck that may make breathing difficult.

4. Put something flat and soft, like a folded jacket, under the head.

5. Turn the individual gently onto his or her side. This will help keep the airway clear. Do not try to force his or her mouth open with any hard implement or with your fingers. It is not true that a person having a seizure can swallow his or her tongue, and efforts to hold the tongue down can injure the teeth or jaw.

6. Do not hold the person down or try to stop his or her movements.

7. Do not attempt artificial respiration except in the unlikely event that an individual does not start breathing again after the seizure has stopped.

8. Stay with the person until the seizure ends naturally.

9. Be friendly and reassuring as consciousness returns.

10. Follow whatever procedures have been established for notifying parents that a seizure has occurred.

11. Call for medical assistance if
    - the seizure lasts more than 5 minutes
    - the person is not wearing an "epilepsy/seizure disorder" I.D.
    - the person is pregnant or is carrying other medical I.D.
    - there is a slow recovery, a second seizure, or difficult breathing afterward
    - any signs of injury are apparent

Further information about what to do in the case of seizures and more information about this disorder are available from the Epilepsy Foundation, at http://www.epilepsyfoundation.org/answerplace.

SOURCES: From *First Aid for Generalized Tonic Clonic (Grand Mal) Seizures* and *First Aid Steps for Convulsions,* by the Epilepsy Foundation, (2003). Retrieved November 22, 2004, from, respectively http://www.epilepsyfoundation.org/answerplace/Medical/firstaid/firstaidkeys.cfm and http://www.epilepsyfoundation.org/answerplace/Medical/firstaid/seizurefachart.cfm.

and when they approach puberty and undergo many physical and hormonal changes, seizures may occur as their bodies change.

Although no relationship exists between seizure disorders and academic performance, you may find that a student with this disability is reluctant to engage in interactions with peers out of fear of peers' reactions to the seizures (Speigel, Cutler, & Yetter, 1996). Students also may experience low self-esteem. If a student is likely to have recurring seizures, you may want (with student and parent support) to explain epilepsy to your class, or ask a specialist to do that. What is important is that typical learners understand that, although somewhat frightening, epilepsy is not dangerous, not controlled by the student who has the disorder, and not contagious.

STUDENTS WITH SICKLE-CELL DISEASE ● Another health impairment is *sickle-cell disease*. This disorder is inherited and occurs most often in African American individuals, with an incidence of 1 in 650. Out of every 12 African Americans, 1 carries the gene for the disorder. The disease also is occasionally found in other groups, including Greeks and Italians (Operation Sickle Cell, 2001). Sickle-cell disease occurs when normally round blood cells are abnormally shaped liked sickles. This makes the blood thicker and prevents it from efficiently carrying oxygen to tissues. The result for individuals who have this disorder is fatigue and reduced stamina, along with mild to severe chronic pain in the chest, joints, back, or abdomen; swollen hands and feet; jaundice; repeated infections, particularly pneumonia; and sometimes kidney failure (Operation Sickle Cell, 2001). No reliable treatments are currently available for individuals who have this disease. In children, sickle-cell disease can affect growth. Students with this disorder experience crises in which their symptoms are acute and include high fevers, joint swelling, and extreme fatigue; they are likely to miss school during these times. A student with this health impairment often needs assistance in making up for missed instruction and encouragement for dealing with the pain and discomfort.

STUDENTS WITH AIDS ● A third health impairment is **acquired immune deficiency syndrome (AIDS).** AIDS results when students are infected with the *human immunodeficiency virus (HIV)* and their bodies lose the ability to fight off infection (DePaepe, Garrison-Kane, & Doelling, 2002). In 2000, 4,061 cases of AIDS were reported for adolescents between the ages of 13 and 19 (Centers for Disease Control and Prevention, 2002). This figure is considered a significant underestimate of the incidence of this disease because several states, including some with a high incidence of reported AIDS infections, do not release HIV statistics to the Centers for Disease Control. Students with AIDS often can attend school with little assistance until their illness progresses to the point that they lack the stamina to complete schoolwork or that the risk of catching an infection or illness from a classmate becomes too great. As you probably know, no medical cure currently exists for AIDS. Studies of the impact of AIDS on children are just beginning.

STUDENTS WITH ASTHMA ● A fourth example of a health impairment is *asthma*. Children with asthma comprise the largest group of chronically ill children in the United States: Approximately 5 million youngsters have this illness, and at any single time, most educators have two students in their classrooms who have asthma (Getch & Neuharth-Pritchett, 1999). This disease of the lungs is characterized by episodes of extreme breathing difficulty (Gabe, Bury, & Ramsay, 2002). It can be triggered by allergens such as pollen, dust, and animal dander, but often it can be controlled with medication.

ANALYZE
AND**REFLECT**

Review the steps for treating a student or another individual having a seizure in the Professional Edge on page 216. Can you name each one? In what circumstances should you seek medical help?

Why is it important for teachers to understand health impairments, especially common ones such as asthma? What instructional adaptations can teachers make for different types of disabilities?

WWW
RESOURCES
•••••••••••••••••••••
At the website for the Sickle Cell Disease Association of America (http://www.sicklecelldisease.org), you can find news, research updates, discussion boards, and resources related to this genetic disorder.

Although only students with moderate or severe asthma are likely to be receiving special education services, any student with asthma may need special consideration in your classroom. For example, these students probably miss more school than other students and need assistance in mastering missed concepts. When in school, they sometimes feel tired or generally unwell, and they may need to be excused from some activities (Madden, 2000). For students who use inhalers to treat their condition, you should monitor that the student carries this medication as needed.

STUDENTS WITH CANCER ● Yet another health impairment is *cancer*, an uncontrolled division of abnormal cells. In 2001, 8,600 children were diagnosed with this disease (National Cancer Institute, 2002). The most common forms of cancer among children are leukemia (that is, blood-cell cancer) and brain tumors. Students with cancer may miss significant amounts of school because of hospitalization and other treatments; in some cases their cognitive functioning may be affected by radiation therapy or chemotherapy. Sometimes students first identified as having a health impairment because of cancer are identified after treatment as having one or more learning disabilities. At the beginning of the chapter, you were introduced to Julian, a fifth-grade student who has this disease.

ADDITIONAL DISORDERS AND CONDITIONS THAT MAY AFFECT STUDENTS ● Students may have many other health impairments. For example, you may have a student who has been badly burned and is undergoing medical treatment and physical or occupational therapy to restore range of movement in affected limbs. Other health impairments your students might have include hemophilia, a genetically transmitted disease in which blood does not coagulate properly; juvenile diabetes, a condition in which the body does not produce enough insulin to process the carbohydrates eaten; and cystic fibrosis, a genetically transmitted disease in which the body produces excessive mucus that eventually damages the lungs and causes heart failure. Keep in mind that some students with health impairments are not eligible for special education because their conditions do not negatively affect their educational performance. These students are likely to receive support through Section 504 plans, a topic introduced in Chapter 2 and discussed further in Chapter 8.

TEACHING STUDENTS WITH HEALTH IMPAIRMENTS ● As noted throughout this discussion, the adaptations you make for students with health impairments often relate to helping them make up for work missed because of an absence or hospitalization, and to recognizing and responding to their social and emotional needs (Closs, 2000). In one study of parents' and educators' perceptions of problems faced by children with chronic illness, parents reported that their children's most frequent problems were "feeling different," undergoing constant medical procedures, experiencing pain, and facing death. Educators listed absences, falling behind in school, lack of interaction with peers, the school's inability to meet the student's needs, and social adjustment as the most serious problems (Shepard & Mahon, 2002).

General strategies for working with students with health impairments include these:

1. Find out the students' most difficult problems and help them work through them. Strategies include having students write or draw about their concerns and referring students to the school counselor or social worker as you see a need.

2. Provide materials for the students about others who have a similar disease or disorder. Books, videotapes, websites, movies, and other informational materials can help students with health impairments understand how others have successfully

FYI ▰▰▰▰▰▰

Tourette syndrome (TS), a tic disorder that includes involuntary body movements (mild or severe), occurs in about 10 out of every 10,000 school-age children. The symptom most commonly associated with TS is uncontrolled shouted obscenities, but this actually occurs in only about 15 percent of cases (Centers for Disease Control and Prevention, 2004).

coped with their illnesses, and they can be useful for explaining the needs of these students to peers without disabilities.

3. Consider including death education in your curriculum if you have a student with a life-threatening condition such as cancer. A special educator, counselor, or social worker probably can prepare a unit and help you present it.

4. Work closely with families. Parents can often be the most valuable source of information concerning their children's status and needs. They can also alert you to upcoming changes in medications and emotional problems occurring at home, and they can help their children work on missed school assignments (Shepard & Mahon, 2002).

In terms of academic and curricular adaptations, you should respond to students who have health impairments as you would to other students with disabilities. Using the INCLUDE strategy, you can identify their needs. If modifications in the environment, curriculum, or instruction are needed, you can carry them out using the suggestions made throughout the remainder of this text.

Traumatic Brain Injury

Traumatic brain injury (TBI), sometimes called *acquired brain injury*, occurs when a student experiences a trauma to the head from an external physical force that results in an injury to the brain, often including a temporary loss of consciousness. TBI is the leading cause of disability and death among children, and it has many causes, including falls, bicycle and motor vehicle accidents, sporting accidents, accidents on playground equipment, child abuse, and gunshot wounds (Brain Injury Association of America, 2004; Youse, Le, Cannizzaro, & Coelho, 2002). More than 1 million children and adolescents sustain a TBI each year. Although most of these injuries are mild, some 30,000 youngsters have a lifelong disability as a result of TBI (Keyser-Marcus, Briel, Sherron-Targett, Yasuda, Johnson, & Wehman, 2002; Dissemination Center for Children with Disabilities, 2004b). Whether TBI is the result of a severe injury or a mild one, it can have a pervasive and significant impact on a student's educational performance.

Recovery from a TBI can take months or even years, and some students with severe TBI spend time in rehabilitation after their hospitalization and before returning to school. Other students with mild or moderate injuries are likely to go directly from the hospital back to their homes and schools (Clark, Russman, & Orme, 1999). Students with TBI often return to school at some point during the recovery process, but predicting their abilities and the point at which they will reach their best outcomes is impossible given various lengths of recovery time and alternative patterns for treatment.

One of the most perplexing aspects of teaching students with TBI is that they can appear just as they did prior to their injuries and yet have significant learning and social problems. They can also seem to be "back to normal" one day, only to seem lethargic and incapable of learning the next day. Because of the extreme variability in needs of students with TBI, the information presented in this section should be considered illustrative; if you teach a student with TBI, seeking input from a specialist is essential.

CHARACTERISTICS OF STUDENTS WITH TRAUMATIC BRAIN INJURY ● Intellectually, students with TBI might have the same abilities they had before, or they might experience a loss of capacity. For example, after an automobile accident, Michael, a high school honor student who used to be a class leader, was left struggling to remaster basic math facts. His injury affected his school learning. Students might experience difficulty initiating and organizing their learning tasks, remembering what

they have learned, and reasoning or problem solving. They might also have difficulty processing verbal information and producing spoken and written language.

Students with TBI also have physical needs. Depending on the severity of the injury and the extent of recovery, some students have limited use of their arms and legs. Others have problems in fine motor movements such as those needed to grasp a pencil or turn the pages of a book. Yet others have limited strength and stamina. Students with these needs sometimes attend school only part of the day.

Socially and emotionally, students with TBI experience many difficulties. Sometimes they have changes in their personalities; they are not who they used to be. For example, they often remember what they were able to do prior to their injuries and sometimes become depressed as they recognize their current limitations (National Dissemination Center for Children with Disabilities). Because they often need a high degree of structure and do not respond well to change, they can display behavior problems when a sudden change in schedule occurs, as when an assembly interrupts an accustomed routine. Some students lose their ability to interpret and respond appropriately to social cues. As a result, they might laugh at inappropriate times, speak loudly when everyone else has realized a whisper is needed, or wander off when distracted by something. Their behaviors can be puzzling or frustrating unless you understand how to respond to them. Some of the most common challenges for students with TBI, along with potential responses teachers can make, are included in Table 6.3.

FAMILIES AND TRAUMATIC BRAIN INJURY ● It is especially important to mention families as part of considerations about TBI. Often, parents or siblings have witnessed a student in a totally unresponsive state, and they have psychologically prepared for the possibility of death. They might be tremendously relieved that the student survived but at the same time traumatized by the amount of physical care the student needs and by the drain on financial and psychological family resources. Depending on the amount of uncertainty about the extent to which the student can eventually recover, the impact of the TBI on the student's intellect and personality, and the family's ability to provide for the student's needs, families can experience a range of emotions, including shock, denial, sorrow, and anger (Mason, O'Sullivan, O'Sullivan, & Cullen, 2000). Eventually, many families adapt. You need to be sensitive to the family's stress and their changing capacity to follow up on homework as well as schoolwork to support your efforts.

TEACHING STUDENTS WITH TRAUMATIC BRAIN INJURY ● If you teach a student with TBI, you might attend at least one planning meeting to discuss the details of the student's abilities and needs and to prepare you for helping the student in the classroom. This transition planning, which typically occurs when a student is moving from the hospital or rehabilitation center back to school, is essential to ensure that appropriate expectations are set for the student, procedures are established for responding to changes in the student's condition, and all services are coordinated (Lemanek, 2004).

> If you teach a student with TBI, you might attend at least one planning meeting to discuss the details of the student's abilities and needs and to prepare you for helping the student in the classroom.

In your classroom, adaptations relate to physical needs, instructional and organizational routines, academic content, and the social environment. Because students with TBI need structure and routine, you should follow a consistent pattern in classroom activities, expect the consistent types of student responses, and keep supplies and materials in a consistent place in the classroom. If a break in routine is necessary, you can prepare the student by alerting him, assigning a buddy, and staying in close proximity.

TABLE 6.3 Classroom Accommodations for Students with Traumatic Brain Injury

Post-TBI Cognitive Challenges	Macroenvironment	Microenvironment	Structure and Pacing	Teaching Style
Attention/ Concentration	• Seat student near teacher. • Minimize distractions. • Use FM unit and earplugs to minimize external noise. • Provide out-of-classroom activities in low-stimulation environments.	• Use peer note takers. • Use tape recorders. • Provide assignments and activities in writing. • Use large-print books with low density on the page.	• Use small groups for teaching. • Alternate instruction, activity, and rest. • Schedule classes to capitalize on periods of highest attention.	• Refocus student with verbal and/or nonverbal cues. • Plan frequent breaks.
Information-Processing Speed		• Use peer note takers and tape recorders. • Review taped materials/peer notes to identify missed critical information.	• Slow the pace of classroom instruction. • Allow extra time for completion of in-class tests/assignments/homework. • Reduce homework load. • Allow more time for student to respond.	• Do not rush or challenge the student. • Provide anticipatory cuing to prepare responses in advance. • Frequently repeat information, to enhance processing abilities.
Memory	• Provide written materials to back up classroom instruction.	• Use tape recorder to review critical information. • Use an organizer as an external memory aid. • Test using multiple-choice format. • Use fact cards and cue sheets to aid recall. • Use highlighters to focus attention to information.	• Utilize the student's best learning modality (e.g., visual, auditory). • Encourage tape-recording new class content. • Encourage writing down class assignments in daily organizer.	• Provide adequate repetition for mastery. • Encourage student to repeat information to ensure comprehension.
Executing Functioning	• Designate a specific location to return homework. • Display classroom schedule.	• Develop a system to indicate that homework has been handed in. • Use a binder with subject sections and pockets for homework. • Color-code sections of binder and book covers by subject. • Create maps to aid between-class travel; do in-school travel training.	• Review daily routines to reorient student. • Cue student to record homework assignments. • Encourage outlining oral and written assignments.	• Encourage student to use organizer daily. • Break large projects or tasks into component parts or steps. • Prepare student before the topic shifts.

SOURCE: Adapted from *Students with Traumatic Brain Injury: Identification, Assessment, and Classroom Accommodations,* by M. Hibbard, W. A. Gordon, T. Martin, B. Raskin, and M. Brown, 2001, New York: Research and Training Center on Community Integration of Individuals with Traumatic Brain Injury, Mount Sinai School of Medicine. Retrieved November 22, 2004, from http://mssm.edu/tbinet/alt/pubs/tbikids.pdf.

ANALYZE
AND**REFLECT**

What characteristics of students with TBI create challenges for teachers working with them? How do the suggestions in Table 6.3 apply to your own anticipated teaching situation?

WWW
RESOURCES

The Brain Injury Association of America, Inc. website, at http://www.biausa.org, includes information about causes, cost, prevention, and treatment of TBI. It even has a kid's corner.

You may need to make changes in the academic expectations for a student with TBI. Because students might know information one day but forget it the next, or learn with ease sometimes but struggle to learn at other times, the need for flexibility is ongoing. Students are also likely to become frustrated with their inability to learn the way they did in the past, so your patience in reteaching information, providing additional examples and exercises, and using strategies to help them focus attention is essential.

Socially, emotionally, and behaviorally, students with TBI rely on you to set clear expectations but also to be supportive of and responsive to their changing needs. One student, Gary, had been in a coma but gradually regained enough ability to function that he returned to his middle school, at first for only an hour or two each day and eventually for the entire day. However, he continued to forget common words and grew increasingly frustrated when he could not convey messages. His teachers began providing the words he needed. Because many students with TBI seem unable to form a realistic picture of how they are functioning, you might need to confront them gently about socially inappropriate behavior. Frustrated with his language skills, Gary yelled at friends, yet his sentences remained unclear. Teachers intervened to help him learn to control his anger and to assist friends to understand him. Students with TBI also might overestimate their abilities. Informally, you can assist in this area by discussing realistic options for the near future and, with older students, for career choices.

In general, many adaptations needed by students with TBI are much the same as those needed by students with physical or health disabilities, learning disabilities, and emotional disabilities. The uniqueness of students with TBI and the reason they are grouped as a separate category in IDEA is that their needs are difficult to predict, change either slowly or rapidly, and vary in intensity. With patience and a willingness by teachers to meet students wherever they are and work forward from there, students with TBI can achieve school success.

What Accommodations Can You Make for Students with Autism Spectrum Disorders?

Autism was first identified as a disorder in 1943 by Dr. Leo Kanner. Since then, it has been the source of much research and ongoing professional debate. At various times, autism was viewed as either a type of emotional disability or as a special form of mental retardation. However, professionals now recognize that autism is a unique disorder that occurs in many forms, and they usually refer to this disability as **autism spectrum disorder (ASD)** to convey its diverse nature. The prevalence of autism spectrum disorders has been rising steadily over the past decade, partly due to better diagnosis (for example, Gillberg, 1999; Fombonne, 2003). This disability affects boys more than girls, in a ratio of approximately 4:1 to 5:1, and it often occurs with other disorders. In particular, it is estimated that 70 percent or more of individuals with autism also have mental retardation (Ghaziuddin, 2000), but that number could be an overestimation because of the communication difficulties that accompany the disability and the resulting problems in obtaining accurate estimates of ability. What is important to remember is that some individuals with autism spectrum disorders do not have intellectual disabilities and may be gifted or talented (Nash & Bonsteel, 2002). If you teach a student with autism spectrum disorder, you will find that it is both rewarding and challenging, that sometimes the student is a frustrating enigma and others times the student's progress in learning and contributions to the school community are exciting.

Characteristics of Students with Autism Spectrum Disorders

Although autism is like most of the other low-incidence disabilities in that it can exist in many forms, from mild to severe, and cannot be treated as a single disorder with a single set of adaptations, it does have specific characteristics.

SOCIAL RELATIONSHIPS ● Students with autism have seriously impaired social relationships. Many students with autism resist human contact and social interactions from a very early age, and they have difficulty learning the subtleties of social interactions (Myles & Southwick, 1999). They often do not make eye contact with others, and they can seem uninterested in developing social relationships. For example, typical young children often ask teachers to watch them do something ("Look at me!"), and they bring interesting items to share with the teacher and their classmates. A young child with autism, however, may not seek out such opportunities for social interactions. Albert, a 13-year-old with autism, discussed his problems in the social domain. He maintained that others viewed him as extremely ugly, but he did not understand why he did not have friends. When an interviewer asked him what he talked about with others, the two topics he mentioned were wind and smells in the environment (Cesaroni & Garber, 1991). He did not take on the perspective of others, and he did not understand that others' interests, so different from his own, also were part of social interaction.

COMMUNICATION ● Many students with autism spectrum disorder also experience problems in both verbal and nonverbal communication (Scheuermann & Webber, 2002). They often have significantly delayed language development, and, if they have language skills, they struggle to maintain a conversation with another person. In writing about her experiences of being autistic, Temple Grandin, one of the most famous individuals with autism spectrum disorder and a university professor who has designed livestock facilities, provides clear examples of her communication problems (Grandin, 2002). She explains that when she was little she simply did not have the words to communicate, and so she frequently resorted to screaming. She also comments that as she grew up, she observed others, but she did not understand how to fit in. Unlike Grandin, many students with autism spectrum disorders cannot write or otherwise clearly communicate about their experiences, and they may use inappropriate behaviors instead of words to convey many needs. Unless taught alternative behaviors, they might hit a peer as a way of saying hello, or run from a classroom instead of saying they do not like the assignment just given. Some students with autism have *echolalic speech*; they repeat what others have said instead of producing original communication.

STUDENT INTERESTS ● Another characteristic of students with autism is a very limited range of interest. For example, a student may be fascinated with radios to the exclusion of nearly everything else. When students with autism have such an interest, they can spend literally hours and hours absorbed in a private world of exploration. They might act bored with every topic and every activity unless it relates to their special interest. Such a narrow range of interest often has a negative impact on social relationships with peers and adults because the student does not discern that others are not as interested in their preferred topic.

RESEARCH NOTE

Facilitated communication (FC) is a controversial communication approach sometimes implemented with individuals with autism. Based on the belief that these individuals have extreme difficulty with expressive communication, it requires that a coach support an individual's hand, wrist, or elbow, thus allowing that individual to type on a computer keyboard. Although some professionals claim extraordinary results from this method, a review of controlled studies finds no support for FC (Mostert, 2001).

RESEARCH
N O T E

Although some individuals contend that autism can be linked to MMR (measles-mumps-rubella) vaccine, the Centers for Disease Control and Prevention (2002) reports that no published scientific evidence supports this claim.

STUDENT STRESS ● Students with autism have a low threshold for and difficulty in dealing with stress (Myles & Adreon, 2001). A change in classroom seating assignments could be difficult for a student with autism, as could the introduction of a new route from the classroom to a bus or an alternative order for the day's activities. Particular noises or odors or a noisy environment also can be stressful. Many students with autism respond to stress with stereotypic behaviors. They complete the same action or motion again and again. For example, they may rock rapidly in their chairs, spin an object repeatedly, or twirl themselves or their arms. In other situations, students might develop a ritual to complete a task. They might need 10 minutes to prepare to complete an assignment because they need to arrange paper and pencil on the desk in a precise pattern, check that all books in the desk are also stored in a specific order, and make sure the desk is aligned precisely at the intersection of tiles on the classroom floor. In your classroom, you should be aware of potentially stressful situations for a student with autism. You can allow time for the student to prepare for the situation, talk about the situation well in advance, assign a peer partner to assist the student, and enlist the assistance of a special educator or paraprofessional. If a student's response to stress is demonstrated with aggressive or extremely disruptive behavior, you should work closely with a special educator, behavior consultant, or other specialist to address the problem. In some instances, the student might need to spend part of the school day in a more structured, less stressful environment, such as the school library or learning center.

STUDENTS WITH ASPERGER SYNDROME ● One group of students with autism spectrum disorder that should be highlighted is those with Asperger syndrome. A diversity of students may be identified with this disability (Barnhill, Hagiwara, Myles, & Simpson, 2000). Students with **Asperger syndrome** are characterized by extraordinary difficulty in social interactions such as making eye contact, using facial expressions appropriately and understanding those of others, and seeking out peers and other people, even though language and cognitive development are typical. They also may have difficulty in using language correctly, confusing whether to use first-person ("I"), second-person ("you"), or third-person ("she" or "he") pronouns. These students also may insist on specific routines in the classroom and at home, and as noted earlier, they may have extraordinary interest in a topic (for example, models of aircraft, countries in Asia) to the extent that they do not realize that others may not share their interest. Many students with Asperger syndrome have very high intellectual ability, and they appropriately spend the school day with peers in general education classrooms. However, because of their difficulty with social interaction, they may struggle to make friends. Carter, the student you met at the beginning of this chapter, has Asperger syndrome.

> " In your classroom, you should be aware of potentially stressful situations for a student with autism. "

Accommodations for Students with Autism Spectrum Disorders

Although it is impossible to provide a comprehensive list of strategies for helping students with autism spectrum disorders to succeed in your classroom, the following suggestions illustrate how your efforts can make a significant difference in these students' lives.

RESPONDING TO BEHAVIOR ● Students with autism spectrum disorders often have behaviors that are unusual and can be disturbing to teachers and students who do not understand them, and these behaviors can interfere with learning. However, many of the behaviors can be corrected with highly structured behavior support programs, some have relatively simple solutions, and some can be ignored. For example, if a student with autism withdraws from classroom activities and begins rocking every day at about 11:00 a.m., it could be a signal that the student is too hungry to work until an 11:45 a.m. lunchtime. Providing a snack in a quiet corner of the classroom could reduce the problem. Many students with autism spectrum disorders can receive some or all of their education in a general education classroom, provided that needed supports are in place for them (Simpson & Myles, 1998).

Generally, the accommodations that help to reduce behavior problems involve creating a structured and predictable environment and encouraging appropriate social interactions (Grandin, 2002; Moreno, 2000; Edelson, n.d.). To create a positive learning environment, establish clear procedures and routines for classroom tasks and follow them consistently. For example, in an elementary classroom, you can create procedures for students to retrieve their coats at lunchtime, or begin each day with the same activities in the same order. For secondary students, you can set a clear pattern in your instruction by beginning each class with a 3-minute review followed by a 20-minute lecture followed by a 15-minute individual or small-group work session. Instead of relying on words to prompt students about these procedures, work with a special educator to create picture cards that depict the procedures. Students with autism spectrum disorder often respond better to pictures than words. In the Professional Edge on page 226, several specific strategies for working with students with autism spectrum disorder are summarized.

In addition to structure, students with autism spectrum disorder may need opportunities during the day to work alone and be alone (Myles & Adreon, 2001). This time serves as a break from the stresses of the classroom and the social and communication demands of that setting. A special education teacher probably can advise you about whether this is necessary for a particular student and can assist in making arrangements for a quiet place, sometimes referred to as *home base*, for the student to work.

FOSTERING SOCIAL INTERACTIONS ●
To help students with social interactions with peers and adults, you can observe a student's behavior to understand its purpose from the student's perspective (Gagnon, 2001; Gray & Garand, 1993). If a student has been working in a small group but suddenly leaves the group and runs out the door, it could be a signal that the student has misunderstood a comment made by another student. Other social areas in which general education teachers can work with special educators to accommodate students with autism spectrum disorders include teaching them to wait, to take turns, to stop an activity before it is complete, to negotiate, to change topics, to finish an activity, to be more flexible, to be quiet, and to monitor their own behavior.

COMMUNICATING WITH STUDENTS ●
Communication with students with autism is accomplished through a wide variety of strategies (Durand & Merges, 2001; Bondy & Frost, 2002). Some students with autism can communicate adequately with speech, especially when they do not feel pressured. With young children, this sort of communication sometimes can be prompted by interrupting a child during a favorite activity (for example, playing with a toy), then permitting the child to resume the activity after communicating with you (Sigafoos & Littlewood, 1999). Other students learn to communicate through sign language, just as many students who are deaf or hard of hearing do. For some students, the motor activity of signing seems to help them successfully convey their needs and preferences. For yet other students, communication boards are useful tools: By simply touching pictures, students can communicate with others even when they cannot speak the appropriate words. Other communication devices that help students who have limited speech, including those with autism, were described previously in this chapter.

PROFESSIONAL EDGE

Teaching Students with Autism Spectrum Disorder

Specialized techniques can be used to teach students with autism spectrum disorder (ASD). These approaches are designed to draw on students' strengths, focus their attention, and address their unique needs. Three examples of approaches effective for these students are social stories, the Picture Exchange Communication System (PECS), and visual schedules.

Social Stories

Students with ASD often experience difficulty understanding social expectations, especially when those expectations vary across situations. An example situation concerns when it is OK to run at school. This social story might assist a student with autism:

Running

I like to run. It is fun to go fast.
It's OK to run when I am playing outside.
I can run when I am on the playground.
I can run during P.E.
It is not OK to run when I am inside, especially at school.
Running in the hallways is not safe.
Teachers worry that someone may get hurt if I run into them.
When people are inside, they walk.
I will try to walk in the hallways and run only when I am outside on the playground.

After preparing this type of story, the teacher reads it several times with the student, preferably just before the situation in which running is an issue. As the student learns to

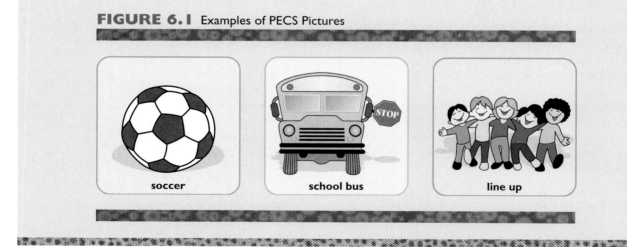

FIGURE 6.1 Examples of PECS Pictures

soccer   school bus   line up

SUMMARY

Students with low-incidence disabilities comprise only about 10 percent of all students with disabilities, but they account for eight of the federal categories of dis-

ability (that is, orthopedic impairments, other health impairments, traumatic brain injury, hearing impairments, visual impairments, deaf-blind, multiple disabil-

FIGURE 6.2 Examples of Visual Schedules

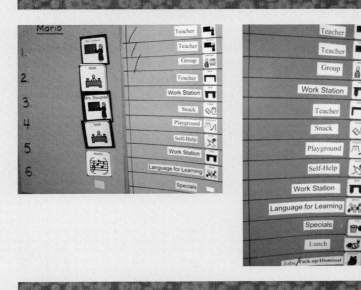

teacher or other person working with the student exchanges a picture of a desired item (for example, a crayon, a basketball) that the student points to or picks up for the actual item (see Figure 6.1). No words are used. As students learn the system, they begin to initiate communication by bringing a picture to another individual in order to obtain the pictured item or make a need known. Eventually students use this system to form sentences and answer questions. Research has demonstrated the effectiveness of this system (Magiati & Howland, 2003). If you teach students with autism, you might interact with them using PECS.

Visual Schedules

Most students with ASD benefit when they have a clear and consistent schedule that is explained ahead of time. Working with a special educator, you can develop visual schedules that use pictures only, pictures and words, or words only (see Figure 6.2). Visual schedules can be displayed in the classroom, placed on the student's desk, or kept in an assignment notebook.

follow the advice in the story, the teacher gradually reduces the repetition of the story until it is no longer needed.

Social stories can be used in many situations. Try writing a social story for these situations:

- a high school student who is using profanity when speaking with adults at school
- a middle school student who talks only about one topic
- an elementary student who takes her shoes off when in the cafeteria

Picture Exchange Communication System

The Picture Exchange Communication System (PECS) is a strategy for teaching individuals with ASD to initiate communication with peers and others. PECS is taught to students in a highly structured series of steps. Initially, the

SOURCES: From *Social Stories,* by the Center for Autism and Related Disabilities, University of Florida, n.d. Retrieved November 23, 2004, from http://card.ufl.edu/handouts/socialstories.html; *Visual Schedule Systems,* by L. Kamp and T. McElean, 2000, Vancouver, BC: Special Education Technology–British Columbia. Retrieved November 23, 2004, from http://www.setbc.org/projects/vss/default.html; *Beyond Autism Pecs Pictures/Icon Pages* (p. 15), n.d. Retrieved November 23, 2004, from the Beyond Autism website, http://trainland.tripod.com/pecs15.htm; and "A Pilot Evaluation Study of the Picture Exchange Communication System" (electronic version), by I. Magiati and P. Howland, 2003, *Autism: The International Journal of Research and Practice, 7,* pp. 297–320.

ities and autism) and part of the mental retardation category. Together, these students have tremendously diverse abilities, challenges, and needs. Many of them can succeed in your classroom if you take into account that you will teach only one or two students with these disabilities at any single time and that they are students first and have disabilities second. Many teaching strategies you have already learned are effective in teaching these students, and other professionals and parents are

available to assist you in creating successful learning experiences for them.

One group of students with low-incidence disabilities is composed of those with moderate or severe intellectual disabilities, multiple disabilities, and deaf-blindness. These students learn slowly, and they usually need assistance to maintain and generalize their skills and to combine skills to complete complex activities. They need a functional, community-based, and age-appropriate education that can be accomplished in general education settings that have appropriate supports and a commitment to effective teaching and learning practices, such as multiple levels of instruction in one classroom, heterogeneous student groupings, natural support systems, and development of partnerships with families.

Students with sensory impairments are those with significant limitations for processing information using visual or auditory channels. The impact of these students' disabilities on their education can be slight or significant. They often have needs related to academic learning, social and emotional skills, and skills for living in their environments. They also use adaptive equipment or materials to help them learn.

Some students have orthopedic impairments (that is, physical disabilities), other health impairments (that is, serious medical or health conditions), or traumatic brain injury (that is, trauma to the head from accident or other injury). Their special supports and services are determined by their needs. Students in these groups often have medical problems that directly or indirectly affect their learning. Their intellectual levels include an entire range. Most students in this group have social and emotional difficulties because of their illnesses, and accommodations in these areas are likely to be necessary.

Autism spectrum disorder (ASB), referred to as *autism* in federal special education law, is another low-incidence disability. Students with autism spectrum disorder have a wide range of intellectual and other abilities, and they have impairments in their social relationships, communication, range of interests, and capacity to respond to stressful events. They need highly structured learning environments with clear procedures and routines. Recently, more attention is being paid to students with one type of ASD, Asperger syndrome.

Applications in **Teaching Practice**

Planning Adaptations for Students with Low-Incidence Disabilities

Mr. Walker teaches English to ninth graders. This year he will have several students with learning disabilities and emotional disabilities in his class, but his primary concern is Terrell, a young man who has cerebral palsy and limited vision. Mr. Walker has been told that Terrell has average intelligence and is quite capable of following the standard course of study for English, but that he needs several accommodations. Mr. Walker is meeting with Ms. Bickel from the special education department to ask questions about Terrell.

Mr. Walker: I need more information about Terrell. Can he really do the work? How much can he see? How is he going to take tests? What is his assistant supposed to be doing? Am I accountable if Terrell has a medical problem during class? Is it likely that will happen? I hear that Terrell has all sorts of computer equipment and a motorized wheelchair—I have 32 other students in that class period, and I'm concerned about just fitting everyone in the door!

Ms. Bickel: It sounds like you haven't gotten the information I thought you had. Let me try to clarify. Terrell is quite a good student. He usually gets As and Bs in his core academic classes, and he is highly motivated to learn. He has every intention of going to college, and right now he hopes to be an editor. Because he can't use his voice, he "talks" using his communication board. I'll be working with you to be sure the board includes all the key words you want it to contain. All Terrell has to do is point his head toward the answer he wants and the laser pointer activates the board, which "says" the answer out loud. Probably one adaptation Terrell will need is extra time to answer; he really wants to participate but might need a moment to get the laser beam focused on the answer he wants to give. His equipment is all adapted to take into account his limited vision.

Mr. Walker: I'll have to see how that works. What does his assistant do?

Ms. Bickel: Mr. Owen is responsible for Terrell's personal care and for making sure he gets from class to class. He also takes notes for Terrell and records answers Terrell gives on his communication board. He can help you out in class if there's a chance, but Terrell needs his attention much of the time.

Mr. Walker: Oh, I wasn't trying to get more help. I just need a picture of what this will be like. I need an extra place for Mr. Owen in class, don't I?

Ms. Bickel: Yes, he'll need to sit right next to Terrell.

The teachers continue talking for another 45 minutes, problem solving about the space issue and trying to ensure that Terrell will experience success and that Mr. Walker understands Terrell's needs. In the first week of school, Ms. Bickel asks Mr. Walker how it is going with Terrell. Mr. Walker comments that he is surprised how smoothly and easily things are going. Terrell "spoke" in class on the first day, and the other students asked a few questions about the equipment, but that was all. Mr. Walker asks whether Ms. Bickel can help him deal with two other students who already seem to have behavior problems.

QUESTIONS

1. What type of disability does Terrell have? Why is he included in Mr. Walker's English class?
2. What accommodations should Mr. Walker make in his classroom and his instruction to address Terrell's special needs?
3. If you were meeting with Ms. Bickel, what additional questions would you ask about Terrell? About needed accommodations?
4. What assistance would you need from Ms. Bickel to feel comfortable teaching Terrell?
5. What would your expectation be for working with Terrell's parents? What might you learn from them that would help you be more effective in teaching Terrell? What expectations might you have of them in working with you?
6. Review the entire chapter and all the information about students with low-incidence disabilities presented in it. What are the benefits of inclusive practices related to students in this group? What are the concerns and questions you still have for working with students with low-incidence disabilities? What do you think will be your greatest personal and professional beliefs that will be challenged when you work with students with low-incidence disabilities?

WORKING THE **STANDARDS**

INTASC **INTASC PRINCIPLES REFLECTED IN THIS CHAPTER:**

Principle #2 states that all teachers have realistically high expectations for what students with disabilities can accomplish, and use this knowledge to create challenging and supportive learning opportunities for students with disabilities (Principle 2.02).

Principle #4 states that all teachers

- Understand that it is particularly important to provide multiple ways for students with disabilities to participate in learning activities (Principle 4.04).

- Modify tasks and/or accommodate the individual needs of students with disabilities in a variety of ways to facil-

itate their engagement in learning activities with other students (Principle 4.04).

- Use strategies that promote the independence, self-control, and self-advocacy of students with disabilities (Principle 4.07).

- Expect and support the use of assistive and instructional technologies to promote learning and independence of students with disabilities (Principle 4.08).

Principle #9 states that all teachers continually challenge their beliefs about how students with disabilities learn and how to teach them effectively (Principle 9.02).

WORKING THE **STANDARDS** (continued)

CEC STANDARDS REFLECTED IN THIS CHAPTER:

CEC Content Standard #2 states that special educators

- Know and demonstrate respect for their students first as unique human beings.

- Understand the similarities and differences in human development and the characteristics between and among individuals with and without exceptional learning needs.

- Understand how exceptional conditions can interact with the domains of human development.

- Understand how the experiences of individuals with exceptional learning needs can impact the individuals' ability to learn, interact socially, and live as fulfilled, contributing members of the community.

CEC Content Standard #3 states that special educators understand the effects that an exceptional condition can have on an individual's learning in school and throughout life.

CEC Content Standard #4 states that special educators select, adapt, and use these instructional strategies to promote challenging learning results in general and special curricula and to appropriately modify learning environments for individuals with exceptional learning needs.

CEC Content Standard #9 states that special educators are aware of how their own and others' attitudes, behaviors, and ways of communicating can influence their practice.

CEC Content Standard #10 states that special educators promote and advocate the learning and well-being of individuals with exceptional learning needs across a wide range of settings and a range of different learning experiences.

BACK TO THE CASES

The standards and principles just listed relate to the cases described at the beginning of this chapter: Kylie, Julian, Carter, and Alyssa. The questions and activities that follow demonstrate how these standards and principles, along with other concepts that you have learned about in this chapter, connect to the everyday activities of all teachers.

Kylie

Kylie appears to be having successful learning experiences in her first-grade year. Her teachers have made the necessary accommodations and modifications to support her learning needs. However, Kylie's mother is beginning to question whether Kylie should continue to be fully integrated into the general education classroom as she progresses into upper-elementary grades. She has requested a meeting with several of the upper-grade teachers. You have been invited to this meeting, which will be held tomorrow afternoon. (See INTASC Principles 2.02, 4.04, and 9.02; and CEC Standards 3, 9, and 10.) In preparation for the meeting, the principal has given each of you a list of questions to answer:

- Why is it important for Kylie to continue her education with same-age peers in the general education classroom?
- What can you do to support Kylie's learning needs?
- What life skills are essential for Kylie to learn that can best be taught in the general education classroom?

Julian

Julian's cancer has disrupted his education and personal life. While he has support from peers at this time, his frequent absences from school and special medical needs make him less available for active involvement with friends and classmates, which may cause him to feel isolated. In addition, some peers may not fully understand his changed physical appearance or may have misinformation about his condition that may cause them to avoid contact with him in school. As Julian's teacher, you are unsure how to discuss these concerns with Julian or his classmates. (See INTASC Principles 2.02, 4.04, and 4.07; and CEC Standards 2 and 3.) Turning to the Internet for information, you begin your search with the American Cancer Society (http://www.cancer.org/docroot/CRI/content/CRI_2_6x_When_Your_Child_Goes_Back_to_School.asp), Children's Cancer Web (http://www.cancerindex.org/ccw), and Brave Kids (http://www.bravekids.org). Based on information from these three websites and others you may find, what will you do to support Julian's special social and psychological needs?

Carter

In Chapter 5, you learned about using the INCLUDE strategy to guide your teaching of students with exceptional learning needs. Step 1 of the strategy requires teachers to consider their classroom demands. Given what you know about Carter and about autism spectrum disorder, explain how you would establish and maintain your classroom to provide a supportive environment for a student like Carter. (See INTASC Principles 2.02, 4.04, and 4.07; and CEC Standards 2 and 3.) Your answer should include topics such as physical classroom organization, routines, and learning groups, as well as any other areas that you consider important for Carter's welfare.

WORKING THE **STANDARDS** *(continued)*

Alyssa

English is the most difficult subject for Alyssa, particularly developing ideas logically and elaborating on them. Recall what you may have learned elsewhere about typical language development in children, and compare it to what you have learned in this text about problems that children with hearing loss encounter with language development. Now consider how general educators might have supported Alyssa's language development. (See INTASC Principles 4.04, 4.07, and 4.08; and CEC Standards 2 and 3.) What would you do to help Alyssa learn to develop ideas and the vocabulary needed for elaboration so that she might not face this problem as she prepares to enter college?

 Visit the companion website (http://www.ablongman.com/friend4e) for a complete correlation of this chapter to the INTASC Principles and CEC Standards.

Further **Readings**

Downing, J. E. (2002). *Including students with severe and multiple disabilities in typical classrooms: Practical strategies for teachers* (2nd ed.). Baltimore: Brookes.

This book addresses information for including students who have sensory disabilities as well as intellectual disabilities. An emphasis is placed on teaching strategies that are effective with both students with disabilities and their typical classmates.

Nash, J. M., & Bonesteel, A. (2002, May 6). The geek syndrome. *Time 159*(18), 50–51.

This article from a popular-press magazine captures some of the day-to-day characteristics and issues related to individuals with Asperger syndrome.

Lewis, S. (2002). Some thoughts on inclusion, alienation, and meeting the needs of children with visual impairments. *RE:view, 34*, 99–101.

This article offers a perspective on inclusive practices related to students with visual impairments.

Goldin-Meadow, S., & Mayberry, R. I. (2001). How do profoundly deaf children learn to read? *Learning Disabilities Research and Practice, 16*(4), 222–229.

If you are a general education teacher, you may find this article on reading for students who are deaf to be helpful in understanding the dilemma these students face.

Keyser-Marcus, L., Briel, L., Sherron-Targett, P., Yasuda, S., Johnson, S., & Wehman, P. (2002). Enhancing the schooling of students with traumatic brain injury. *Teaching Exceptional Children, 34*(4), 62–67.

This article offers practical suggestions for teachers who are working with students who have experienced a traumatic brain injury.

CHAPTER **7**

Students with High-Incidence Disabilities

SETH IS AN eighth-grade student at King Middle School. Most people who know Seth outside of school would never guess that he has a learning disability. He converses easily with children and adults, has a great sense of humor, and is renowned among his peers for his "street smarts." Things don't go as well for Seth in school; basic academic skills are particularly problematic. He reads slowly, struggling with each word, and as a result he often cannot tell his teacher what he has read. Seth's written language is also a problem. His handwriting is illegible, his spelling is inconsistent, and his written essays lack organization. In math, Seth still doesn't know basic math facts, and when faced with answering word problems, he simply gives up. ● *What disability does Seth have? What factors do you think may have contributed to Seth's academic problems? What kinds of adaptations should Seth's teacher make to help him progress in the general education curriculum? What other kinds of support do Seth and his teacher need?*

RICK IS HEADING toward his 15th birthday and major trouble both in and out of school. Rick's behavior in school has never been easy to manage. In the primary grades, he was disruptive in class but responded well when his parents gave him rewards at home for good behavior in school. When Rick was in fifth grade, his parents divorced and behavior problems in school began to worsen. Rick began to talk abusively to peers in class and to refuse loudly to do any work. He also began to bully other students, particularly those least likely to be able to defend themselves. In seventh and eighth grades, Rick attended an alternative school. Although his school behavior improved somewhat, he became involved in gang activities in eighth grade. This year, Rick is a ninth grader in high school and is attending all general education classes in addition to seeing a special education teacher once a day in the resource room. His school and class attendance has been spotty, and he occasionally engages in disruptive behavior in his classes. ● *What is Rick's disability? How do you think his general education teacher can accommodate his behavior? What kinds of support do Rick and his teacher need?*

ANALYZE
AND **REFLECT**

Compare Table 7.1 with Table 6.1 on page 189. How do these tables support the concept of high-incidence and low-incidence disabilities? How do the concepts of mild, moderate, and severe disabilities also contribute to a cross-categorical view of students with special needs?

FYI

The wide-spread practice of identifying students with learning disabilities solely on the basis of a discrepancy between ability (as measured by an intelligence test) and achievement has been criticized widely because this practice has resulted in over- and misidentification of learning disabilities and does not account for other possible reasons for academic failure such as poor instruction or the lack of appropriate interventions factors. That is why IDEA now gives states the option of identifying learning disabilities based on their response to scientifically based instruction in the general education classroom.

FYI

Students with mild intellectual disabilities make up two-thirds of the federal category of mental retardation. The federal definition of mental retardation is in Table 6.1 on page 189.

FYI

Stuttering is the most common kind of speech problem involving fluency. Stuttering is a speech impairment in which an individual involuntarily repeats a sound or word, resulting in a loss of speech fluency.

Students like Seth and Rick have high-incidence disabilities. These students' disabilities affect their language, learning, and behavior. You probably will teach students with high-incidence disabilities in your classroom. The expectation in IDEA is that students with high-incidence disabilities will spend most of their time in general education, while meeting the same curricular standards as their classmates without disabilities. In order to meet the goals set forth in IDEA, students with high-incidence disabilities require support from general and special education professionals. Usually this support is in the form of instructional accommodations rather than modifications. For instance, Seth is learning word-processing skills to help him overcome his problems with spelling and handwriting. He is also using texts on CD-ROM in his science and social studies classes, which are sometimes co-taught. Rick and his teachers have developed an individualized behavior contract in which Rick is allowed extra access to the auto mechanics shop for attending class and complying with teachers' requests. This chapter covers characteristics and needs of students with high-incidence disabilities and classroom adaptations that enable these students to gain better access to the general education curriculum.

What Are High-Incidence Disabilities?

Students with **high-incidence disabilities** have speech or language disabilities, learning disabilities, emotional disturbance, or mild intellectual disabilities. These students make up over 80 percent of all students who have disabilities (U.S. Department of Education). The federal terms for high-incidence disabilities and the proportion of students with these disabilities served through IDEA are summarized in Table 7.1. Students with high-incidence disabilities share three important characteristics:

1. They are often hard to distinguish from peers without disabilities, particularly in nonschool settings.
2. They often exhibit a combination of behavioral, social, and academic problems.
3. They benefit from systematic, highly structured instructional interventions such as those discussed in this chapter and throughout the remainder of this book. Having these interventions in place helps them meet the same standards as their classmates without disabilities.

What Accommodations Can You Make for Students with Communication Disorders?

Malcolm and Clarissa are part of a large group of students who have communication disorders. Communication is the exchange of ideas, opinions, or facts between people. Effective communication requires a sender to send a message that a receiver can decipher and understand. Students with communication disorders have problems with speech and/or language that interfere with communication. They need accommodations that help them better understand and express oral language.

Understanding Speech Problems

Speech is the behavior of forming and sequencing the sounds of oral language (Hallahan & Kauffman, 2003). One common speech problem is with **speech articulation,** resulting in the inability to pronounce sounds correctly at and after the developmentally

TABLE 7.1 Proportion of Students with High-Incidence Disabilities Receiving
Special Education Services in 2000–2001[a]

Federal Disability Category	Defining Characteristics	Total Number of Students	Percentage of All Students Receiving IDEA Services
Learning disabilities	General intellectual functioning within the normal range	2,887,217	50.0
	Significant difference between ability and school achievement and/or failure to respond to research-based interventions in the general education setting		
	Difference in ability/achievement *not* due to (a) a visual, hearing, or motor handicap; (b) mental retardation; (c) emotional disturbance; or (d) environmental, cultural, or economic disadvantage		
Emotional disturbance	Inability to learn that cannot be explained by intellectual, sensory, or health factors	473,663	8.2
	Inability to build or maintain satisfactory interpersonal relationships with peers and teachers		
	Inappropriate types of behavior or feelings under normal circumstances		
	General pervasive mood of unhappiness or depression; or tendency to develop physical symptoms or fears associated with personal or school problems		
Speech[b] or language[c] impairments	Speech is disordered when it deviates so far from the speech of other people that it calls attention to itself, interferes with communication, or causes the speaker or listeners distress.	1,093,808	18.9
	Three kinds of speech disorders are articulation (abnormal production of speech sounds), voice (absence of or abnormal production of voice quality, pitch, loudness, resonance, and/or duration), and fluency (impaired rate and rhythm of speech, for example, stuttering).		
	Language is disordered when comprehension and/or use of a spoken, written, and/or other symbol system is impaired or does not develop normally.		
	Language disorders may involve form (word order, word parts, word usage), content (word meaning), or function (words that communicate meaningfully).		

[a]Students ages 6–21 receiving services through IDEA, Part B (U.S. Department of Education, 2002). Additional students receive services under Part H of the same law, and under Chapter 1.

[b]From definitions developed by Van Riper and Emerick (1996).

[c]From definitions developed by the American Speech-Language-Hearing Association (1993).

SOURCE: From *Twenty-Fourth Annual Report to Congress on the Implementation of the Education of the Handicapped Act,* 2002, Washington, DC: U.S. Department of Education.

appropriate age. For example, Stacey is in second grade but cannot pronounce the *s* sound, a sound most students master by age 5. Other speech difficulties involve voice and fluency. Examples of these speech problems are shown in Figure 7.1.

Because communication is social, students with speech disorders, such as **stuttering,** often experience social problems. Students who can clearly communicate draw positive attention from peer relationships, but students who cannot are often avoided by their peers and sometimes ridiculed. The experience of peer rejection can be devastating, leading to a lack of confidence, a poor self-image, social withdrawal, and emotional

WWW
RESOURCES
For more information about stuttering, visit the website of the National Center for Stuttering, at http://www.stuttering.com.

FIGURE 7.1 Speech Problems

Articulation

1. Has difficulty pronouncing sounds correctly (at and after the developmentally appropriate age). Frequent articulation errors include *f, v, k, g, r, l, s, z, sh, ch,* and *j*. Sounds may be distorted or omitted, or one sound may be inappropriately substituted for another.

2. Speech may be slurred.

Voice

1. Speech is excessively hoarse.

2. May use excessive volume or too little volume

3. Speech has too much nasality.

4. Speech lacks inflection.

Fluency

1. Stutters when speaking

2. May have excessively slow rate of speech

3. May exhibit uneven, jerky rate of speech

SOURCE: *Adapting Instruction in General Education for Students with Communication Disorders,* by D. Barad, 1985, unpublished manuscript, De Kalb: Northern Illinois University.

DIMENSIONS OF DIVERSITY

Learning English is particularly challenging for students with learning disabilities whose native language is not English (Lerner, 2003). For these students, teachers need to draw on instructional methods from both bilingual education and special education.

FYI

In remembering the distinction between receptive and expressive communication disorders, think of the root words *receive* and *express*.

problems later in life (Cowen, Pederson, Babijian, Izzo, & Trost, 1973). For example, after years of being ridiculed by peers, Jeffrey, a high school ninth grader who stutters, speaks infrequently and has no friends. He would like to ask a girl in his math class to a dance but is petrified that he will not be able to do so without stuttering.

Understanding Language Problems

Language is a system of symbols that we use to communicate feelings, thoughts, desires, and actions. Language is the message contained in speech. Language can exist without speech, such as sign language for people who are deaf; and speech without language, such as birds that are trained to talk (Hardman, Drew, Egan, & Winston, 2002). Students who have language problems have trouble with either or both of two key parts of language: receptive language and expressive language. **Receptive language** involves understanding what people mean when they speak to you. **Expressive language** concerns speaking in such a way that others understand you. Receptive language problems occur when students are unable to understand what their teachers and peers are saying. For example, students with receptive language difficulties may not understand questions, may have trouble following directions, and may not be able to retain information presented verbally. Students with expressive language problems are unable to communicate clearly; their spoken language may include incorrect grammar, a limited use of vocabulary, and frequent hesitations. Some common receptive and expressive language problems are listed in Figure 7.2.

Students with language problems may also have difficulty using language in social situations. For example, they may be unable to vary their conversation to match the person with whom they are talking or the context in which it is occurring. Students with language problems may also have difficulty taking turns while speaking during a conversation, recognizing when a listener is not understanding the message and taking action to clarify, and, in general, being a considerate speaker and listener (Bos & Vaughn, 2001). As with problems in communicating clearly, problems in using lan-

FIGURE 7.2 Language Problems

Receptive Language Problems

1. Does not respond to questions appropriately

2. Cannot think abstractly or comprehend abstractions as idioms ("mind sharp as a tack"; "eyes dancing in the dark")

3. Cannot retain information presented verbally

4. Has difficulty following oral directions

5. Cannot detect breakdowns in communication

6. Misses parts of material presented verbally, particularly less concrete words such as articles (*the* book; *a* book) and auxiliary verbs and tense markers ("He *was* going"; "She *is* going")

7. Cannot recall sequences of ideas presented orally

8. May confuse the sounds of letters that are similar (*b, d; m, n*) or reverse the order of sounds and syllables in words (*was, saw*)

9. Has difficulty understanding humor or figurative language

10. Has difficulty comprehending concepts showing quantity, function, comparative size, and temporal and spatial relationships

11. Has difficulty comprehending compound and complex sentences

Expressive Language Problems

1. Uses incorrect grammar or syntax ("They walk down together the hill"; "I go not to school")

2. Lacks specificity ("It's over there by the place over there")

3. Frequently hesitates ("You now, um, I would, um, well, er, like a, er, soda")

4. Jumps from topic to topic ("What are feathers? Well, I like to go hunting with my uncle")

5. Has limited use of vocabulary

6. Has trouble finding the right word to communicate meaning (word finding)

7. Uses social language poorly (inability to change communication style to fit specific situations, to repair communication breakdowns, and to maintain the topic during a conversation)

8. Is afraid to ask questions, does not know what questions to ask, or does not know how to ask a question

9. Repeats same information again and again in a conversation

10. Has difficulty discussing abstract, temporal, or spatial concepts

11. Often does not provide enough information to the listener (saying, "*We* had a big fight with *them*," when *we* and *them* are not explained)

SOURCES: *Adapting Instruction in General Education for Students with Communication Disorders,* by D. Barad, 1985, unpublished manuscript, De Kalb: Northern Illinois University; and *Strategies for Teaching Students with Learning and Behavior Problems* (3rd ed.), by C. S. Bos and S. Vaughn, 1994. Copyright © 1994 by Allyn and Bacon. Reprinted by permission.

guage appropriately can seriously impede students' social development and peer relationships. General education teachers can intervene in the classroom to help such students socially.

Early language development forms the underpinning for much of the academic learning that comes when students go to school. It is not surprising, then, that students with speech and language disorders are likely to have trouble with academics as well. Problems with sounds can result in students' having difficulties acquiring word analysis and spelling skills. Receptive language problems can make comprehension very difficult and can result in trouble understanding mathematical terms such as *minus*, *regroup*, and *addend* and confusion in sorting out words with multiple meanings, such as *carry* and *times* (Mercer & Pullen, 2005). Furthermore, language disabilities can

DIMENSIONS
OF **DIVERSITY**

It is incorrect to view students as having communication disorders when they use ethnic or regional dialects, speak a form of nonstandard English learned at home, or are native speakers of languages other than English and have limited English proficiency.

seriously impede the content-area learning stressed in middle, junior high, and high school. In these settings, much information is provided orally using lecture formats, the vocabulary and concepts covered are much more abstract, and students are expected to learn with less support from the teacher. These demands are difficult for students with language disorders.

Another part of learning independently is solving problems. Students with language disorders may have difficulty verbalizing the steps to solve a problem. For example, when Veronica, a language-proficient student solves story problems, she talks to herself as follows: "First I need to read the whole problem. Then I need to decide what the problem is asking for and whether I need to add, subtract, multiply, or divide. Okay, the problem is asking how much Alex weighs. It says that Alex is 3 pounds heavier than Dominique and that Dominique weighs 125 pounds. So, if Alex weighs 3 pounds more, his weight will be a bigger number than Dominique's so I need to add." A student with language problems cannot talk herself through such problems.

Accommodations for Students with Communication Disorders

As discussed in Chapter 5, the INCLUDE strategy suggests that before you make adaptations, you carefully consider potential student problems in view of your instructional demands. For students with speech and language problems, note especially any areas in which students are required to understand oral language (for example, listening to a lecture or a set of verbal directions) or to communicate orally (for example, responding to teacher questions or interacting with classmates when working in cooperative groups). The following discussion highlights specific suggestions for working with students with speech and language disorders.

CREATE AN ATMOSPHERE OF ACCEPTANCE ● You need to help students who have difficulty expressing themselves believe they can communicate without worrying about making mistakes. You can foster this nonjudgmental atmosphere in several ways. First, when a student makes an error, model the correct form instead of correcting the student's mistakes directly:

> *Teacher:* Kareem, what did Jules do with the frog?
>
> *Kareem:* Put pocket.
>
> *Teacher:* Oh. He put it in his pocket?
>
> *Kareem:* Yes.

Second, try to allow students who stutter or have other fluency problems more time to speak, and do not interrupt them or supply words that are difficult for them to pronounce. Offering praise or other reinforcement for successful efforts to communicate, as you would for your other students, is also helpful. Sometimes, you should praise even an attempt:

> *Teacher:* Anthony, what did you do when you went home yesterday?
>
> *Anthony:* Television.
>
> *Teacher:* Great, you told me one thing you did. You watched television.

Finally, try to minimize peer pressure. One effective way to do this is to model and reinforce tolerance of individual differences in your classroom.

ENCOURAGE LISTENING AND TEACH LISTENING SKILLS ● Even though students spend more time listening than doing any other school activity, very little time is devoted to teaching listening skills (Lerner, 2006). Stressing listening is particularly important for students with receptive language disorders. You can take the following four steps to stress listening:

1. Listen carefully yourself and praise listening among your students. For example, when Ms. Hernandez listens to a student speak, she leans forward and nods. Many of her students copy these listening actions.

2. Be sure to engage your students' attention before you begin speaking by increasing your proximity to the listeners, by giving direct instruction (such as, "Listen to what I'm going to say"), and by reducing competing stimuli (have only one activity going on at one time, or have only one person speak at a time). You can also use verbal, pictorial, or written advance organizers to cue students when to listen (for example, "When we get to number 3 on this list, I want you to listen extra carefully for an error I am going to make") (Sabornie & deBettencourt, 2004).

3. Make oral material easier to understand and to remember by simplifying vocabulary, simplifying sentence structure using high-frequency words, repeating important information, giving information in short segments using visual aids for emphasis, having students rehearse and summarize information, and using cues that signal when you are going to say something important (Mandlebaum & Wilson, 1989).

4. Teach listening skills directly. Provide practice on skills such as predicting what might be heard, following directions, appreciating language, identifying main ideas and supporting details, drawing inferences, differentiating fact from fiction, and analyzing information critically.

When you speak, you can also enhance your students' listening skills by stressing words that are important to meaning. For example, say "He *hit* the *ball*" or "*He* hit the ball," depending on what you want to emphasize. Stressing inflectional patterns, such as using an upward inflection when asking a question, also helps students better understand what you are saying.

USE MODELING TO EXPAND STUDENTS' LANGUAGE ● You can expand the language of students with expressive language problems by adding relevant information to student statements:

Student: John is nice.

Teacher: Yes, he is very nice, and polite, too.

You can also expand language by broadening a minimal statement:

Student: My shoe.

Teacher: Your shoe is pretty.

Modeling to expand students' language is most effective when it is done as an ongoing part of your everyday communications with students. Students can also learn to model behavior for themselves. The Technology Notes feature on page 240 explains a high-tech method of self-modeling using video.

PROVIDE MANY MEANINGFUL CONTEXTS FOR PRACTICING SPEECH AND LANGUAGE SKILLS ● The goal of successful language programs is to teach students to use appropriate language in a variety of social and academic situations both in and out of school. You can help students with all types of speech and language problems meet that goal by providing as many opportunities as possible to practice language skills within meaningful contexts (Hardman et al., 2002). Practice helps students refine language skills and make them more natural and automatic. When students

> ❝ Even though students spend more time listening than doing any other school activity, very little time is devoted to teaching listening skills. ❞

CONNECTIONS

Using modeling, providing meaningful learning contexts, and developing other instructional methods are discussed in greater detail in Chapters 9–11.

RESEARCH NOTE

Carlo and colleagues (2004) improved the reading vocabulary of mixed groups of Anglo and Latino fifth graders using two strategies. They allowed native Spanish speakers access to the text's meaning in Spanish. They also presented vocabulary words in meaningful contexts and reinforced word meaning through activities that stressed spelling, pronunciation, meaningful word parts, syntax, and depth of meaning.

> TECHNOLOGY NOTES

Changing Behavior Using Video Self-Modeling

One of the time-tested truths of education is that students learn by example. According to social learning theory, one important way students learn new behaviors is by watching other students perform or model them. Given that modeling is most effective when the person doing the modeling is similar to the observer, what would happen if the modeling were done by the person herself? There is a method of instruction that does just that. It is called *video self-modeling*. The idea is that seeing themselves perform successfully provides clear information on how to best execute skills while at the same time strengthening the students' beliefs in their own capabilities (Bandura, 1969).

Video self-modeling can be used to help students of all ages perform a variety of behaviors successfully in school settings.

Video self-modeling has been used to help students of all ages perform a variety of behaviors successfully in school settings, including on-task behavior, fluent speech, following teacher directions, talking with adults, reading fluently, raising hands, and answering teacher questions (Hitchcock, Dowrick, & Prater, 2003). Furthermore, this technique can provide a motivational boost for students with learning, behavior, and communication problems, who often see themselves as incapable of doing the right thing. Video self-modeling is most helpful when students engage in a behavior at some times but not others. For example, Cedric stutters in class but not when he is with the speech teacher. Ronald is able to resolve conflict with other students while in the classroom but not on the playground. Delaney can read fluently in her small reading group but not when she reads a play in front of the entire class.

To implement video self-modeling, you first need to produce a video of the student engaging in the target behavior. Select a setting for modeling that is the same as or similar to the setting where you eventually want the student to engage in the behavior. For example, modeling hand-raising would take place during a real class; a demonstration of self-control when there is a conflict during play could take place on the playground. Next, make sure that the student is able to engage in the behavior required. For example, for reading fluency, students should be modeling using books at their reading level. For question answering, students must have answered questions in class before, and the questions must be ones to which they know the answers. Finally, create a situation in which students re-

ceive positive consequences for engaging in the behavior. For example, Floyd could earn points every time he raised his hand in the modeling session and then was able to cash the points in for minutes on the computer. Carmella was told she would earn a special sticker for solving a conflict with a classmate during free play. For situations when you will be doing the teaching, enlist the help of school support staff to shoot the video. Be sure to obtain parent permission prior to taping.

Once you have shot your video, edit it so that it shows only a sample of exemplary behavior. The tape needs to be long enough to completely show the behavior in question, but it should be only as long as it needs to be; often that is 5 minutes or less. Don't worry if your school doesn't have sophisticated editing equipment. The rudimentary equipment available in most schools should work fine. When your video is edited, you are ready to show it to the student. For maximum effect, show the video once per day, over a period of days, on an every-other-day basis. Be sure to specify the settings where you want the student to perform the behavior as well as the general expectation that you want her to do the behavior more often.

Research Note

Hitchcock and colleagues (2003) reviewed the research literature for studies looking at the effectiveness of video self-modeling in school-based settings. They found 18 studies consistently showing that video self-modeling was effective for strengthening academic skills and classroom behavior. The review also showed that video self-modeling helps students maintain appropriate behaviors and apply them in new settings.

How do you think teachers can help to create an atmosphere of acceptance for students with communication disorders? What are the benefits of group work?

FYI

Students with emotional disturbance often are referred to as *behavior disordered (BD)*. Another term for students with mild intellectual disabilities is *educable mentally handicapped (EMH)*.

RESEARCH NOTE

Glassberg, Hooper, and Mattison (1999) studied a sample of 233 students ages 6–16 years who were newly identified with behavior disorders to see how many of them also had learning disabilities. Overall, they found that 53 percent of the students had a learning disability based on criteria for at least one of four accepted definitions for learning disabilities.

practice in many different contexts, they can apply what they learn more readily. For example, Ms. Crum just taught her class the meaning of the word *ironic*. During health class, the students discussed the irony of the government's warning people against fat consumption and then funding school lunches that are high in fat. During a trip to the museum, Ms. Crum pointed out the irony of the guard's telling them to be quiet when he was wearing shoes that squeaked loudly when he walked.

It is also helpful to encourage students with communication disorders to talk about events and experiences in their environment, describing them in as much detail as possible (Hardman et al., 2002). For example, Ms. Cusak, a first-grade teacher, starts every Monday by having two students tell about something they did over the weekend. Mr. Drake, a sixth-grade teacher, uses a *Saturday Night Live* format whereby students in his class act out something funny that happened to them over the weekend.

Finally, whenever possible, instruction should be embedded in the context of functional areas. For example, in Ms. Taylor's consumer math class, she has students go out to appliance stores, talk to salespeople about service contracts, and then describe and compare the various service contracts that are available. In Ms. Ellen's second-grade class, students invite and converse with classroom visitors.

What Are the Academic Needs of Students with Learning and Behavioral Disabilities?

INCLUDE

Students with learning and behavioral disabilities have learning disabilities, mild intellectual disabilities, and emotional disturbance. These are the students who are most likely to be included in your classroom. Students with **learning disabilities** are students who achieve less than typical students academically because they have trouble with processing, organizing, and applying academic information. Students with learning disabilities are of normal intelligence, have presumably received adequate instruction, and have not been shown to be sensory impaired, emotionally disturbed, or environmentally disadvantaged. Students with **mild intellectual disabilities** are students who have some difficulty meeting the academic and social demands of general education classrooms, in large part because of below-average intellectual functioning (that is, scoring 55–70 on an IQ test). Students with mild intellectual disabilities can meet at least some of the academic and social demands of general education classrooms. Students with **emotional disturbance** are of average intelligence but have

FYI

Some advocacy groups prefer the term *specific learning disability* to *learning disability,* because it emphasizes that only certain learning processes are affected.

DIMENSIONS OF DIVERSITY

African American students, especially those in urban middle schools, are at risk of being overidentified for behavior disorders; children from Latino or Asian American families are at risk of underidentification (Peterson & Ishii-Jordan, 1994). Why do you think this is so?

WWW RESOURCES

The Learning Disabilities Association of America is a helpful support group for parents of students with learning disabilities. Valuable information on parental rights and tips for parenting are available on its website at http://www.ldanatl.org.

problems learning primarily because of external (acting out, poor interpersonal skills) and/or internal (anxiety, depression) behavioral adjustment problems.

Students with learning disabilities, mild intellectual disabilities, and emotional disturbance differ in a number of ways (Hallahan & Kauffman, 2003). The behavior problems of students with emotional disturbance are more severe, and students with mild intellectual disabilities have lower levels of measured intelligence. Students with learning disabilities may have more pronounced learning strengths and weaknesses than students with mild intellectual disabilities, who are likely to show lower performance in all areas. Still, the academic and social characteristics of students with these disabilities overlap considerably. All three groups may experience significant problems in academic achievement, classroom behavior, and peer relations.

Although scientists have developed sophisticated computerized imaging techniques to detect neurological differences in children who experience learning and behavioral disabilities, the precise causes of these disabilities in individual children are largely unknown because learning and behavior result from a complex interaction between students' individual characteristics, the various settings in which they learn, and the tasks or other demands they face in those settings (Hallahan et al., 2005; Smith, 2004; Ysseldyke, Algozzine, & Thurlow, 2000). It is often difficult to identify the primary cause of a learning or behavior problem. For example, Thomas is lagging behind his classmates in acquiring a sight-word vocabulary in reading. Learning disabilities tend to run in his family, but Thomas's school district also changed reading series last year. In addition, Thomas's parents separated in the middle of the school year and divorced several months later. Why is Thomas behind in reading? Is it heredity? Is it the new reading program? Is it his parents' marital problems? All these factors may have contributed to Thomas's problem.

The most important reason students with high-incidence disabilities are grouped together for discussion is that whatever behaviors they exhibit and whatever the possible causes of these behaviors, these students benefit from the same instructional practices (Algozzine, Ysseldyke, & Campbell, 1994; Kameenui et al., 2002). These practices are introduced in this chapter and covered in considerable depth throughout the rest of this book. For example, Raeanna has a mild intellectual disability. She has difficulty reading her classmates' social cues. As a result, she does not recognize when she is acting too aggressively with her classmates and often is rejected by many of them. Del is a student with learning disabilities. He also has trouble reading the social cues of his peers. Although Raeanna and Del may learn new social skills at different rates, both can benefit from social skills training that provides considerable guided practice and feedback on how to read social cues. The point to remember is that categorical labels are not particularly useful in describing specific students or developing instructional programs for them (Hardman et al., 2002). For example, both Damon and Aretha have learning disabilities, yet their areas of difficulty differ. Damon has a severe reading problem but excels in mathematics and various computer applications. Aretha, on the other hand, is reading at grade level but has significant problems with math. Though both students are categorized as having learning disabilities, they have very different needs. You must analyze each individual student's needs and then make adaptations as necessary. This individualization is at the heart of the INCLUDE strategy, introduced in Chapter 5.

> " Whatever behaviors they exhibit and whatever the possible causes of these behaviors, students with high-incidence disabilities benefit from the same instructional practices. "

INCLUDE

Students with learning and behavioral disabilities have many academic needs. They have difficulty acquiring basic skills in the areas of reading, written language, and math. They also may lack skills necessary for efficient learning, such as attending to task, memory, organizing and interpreting information, reasoning, motor coordination, independent learning skills, and academic survival skills.

Reading Skills

Students with learning and behavioral disabilities have two major types of reading problems: decoding and comprehension. Decoding problems involve the skills of identifying words accurately and fluently. Accuracy problems are most readily observed when students read orally, mispronouncing words, substituting one word for another, or omitting words (Lerner, 2006). Students with reading fluency problems can read words accurately but do not recognize them quickly enough. They read slowly, in a word-by-word fashion, without grouping words together meaningfully (Hallahan et al., 2005; Lerner, 2006). Many of these reading decoding problems are exemplified in the following oral reading sample by a student with a learning disability.

> Then Ford had, uh, other i . . . a better idea. Take the worrrk to the men. He deee. . . . A long rope was hooked onto the car . . . wheels. . . . There's no rope on there. The rope pulled the car . . . auto . . . the white wheels along . . . pulled the car all along the way. Men stood still. Putting on car parts. Everybody man . . . put on, on, a few parts. Down the assembly line went the car. The assembly line saved . . . time. Cars costed still less to buh . . . bull . . . d . . . build. Ford cuts their prices on the Model T again. (Hallahan et al., 2005, p. 370)

Here is the passage the student tried to read:

> Then Ford had another idea. Take the work to the men, he decided. A long rope was hooked onto a car axle and wheels. The rope pulled the axle and wheels along. All along the way, men stood still putting on car parts. Down the assembly line went the car. The assembly line saved more time. Cars cost still less to build. Ford cut the price on the Model T again. (Hallahan et al., 2005, p. 370)

Students who have serious difficulties decoding written words are sometimes referred to as having *dyslexia*. The Professional Edge on page 244 discusses the meaning of this term and suggests instructional approaches.

Students with learning and behavioral disabilities often have problems comprehending stories in the elementary grades and content-area textbooks and advanced literature in the upper grades. Although these difficulties result in part from poor decoding skills, they may also occur because these students lack strategies for identifying the key elements of stories and content-area texts. For example, Todd's teacher asked him questions about a book he had just read as part of his classroom literature program. Todd was unable to tell her where the story took place (setting) or the lesson of the story (moral) because the answers to these questions were not directly stated in the story and Todd lacked the necessary inference strategies to figure them out. In another instance, Patsy was unable to answer a study question comparing the causes of World Wars I and II because she could not locate key words, such as *differences* and *similarities*. In addition, students with these disabilities may not be able to adjust their reading rate to allow for skimming a section of text for key information or for reading more slowly and intensively to answer specific questions. For example, Dennis takes a lot of time to locate key dates in his history book because he thinks he needs to read every word in the chapter while he is looking for the dates.

Written Language Skills

The written language difficulties of students with learning and behavioral disabilities include handwriting, spelling, and written expression. Handwriting problems can be caused by a lack of fine motor coordination, failure to attend to task, inability to perceive and/or remember visual images accurately, and inadequate handwriting instruction in the classroom (Mercer & Pullen, 2005). Students may have problems in the

DIMENSIONS OF **DIVERSITY**

Research from the National Institute of Child Health and Human Development has shown that reading disabilities affect boys and girls at roughly the same rate. Boys, however, are more likely to be referred for treatment, as they are more likely to get the teacher's attention by misbehaving. Girls may escape the teacher's attention, as they may withdraw into quiet daydreaming (Bock, 1999).

RESEARCH N O T E

Research shows that fewer than one child in eight who is failing to read by the end of first grade ever catches up to grade level (Juel, 1988). Many at-risk readers benefit from early intervention that includes the explicit, systematic teaching of our letter–sound system, often referred to as *phonics* (Ehri, 2004).

CONNECTIONS

Assessment strategies to identify at-risk readers in kindergarten and first grade are described in the Professional Edge in Chapter 4 on page 119.

FYI

Graham (1999) suggests that you can make spelling engaging by including student choice as part of the selection and study of words, allowing peers to study and work together, helping students discover patterns in the spelling of words, and using games to learn and practice spelling skill approaches.

PROFESSIONAL EDGE

Understanding Dyslexia

The term *dyslexia* is used a lot these days. You hear that a friend's child has dyslexia, or you see a person who is dyslexic on television, or you read that Albert Einstein and Thomas Edison had dyslexia. The word *dyslexia*, which means "developmental word blindness," has a medical sound to it, but until recently there was little convincing evidence to show that it was medically based. Thanks to the development of computerized imaging techniques, such as functional magnetic resonance imaging (fMRI) and positron-emission tomography (PET scan), evidence of an organic basis for dyslexia is beginning to accumulate.

Recent studies using computerized imaging show that the brain activity of students with dyslexia differs from that of students who are good readers (Shaywitz, 2003). For example, from an early age, and often into adulthood, dyslexics show a pattern of underactivation in a region in the back of the brain that enables first accurate and then automatic reading. This pattern of underactivity appears to be present in dyslexics regardless of their age, sex, or culture (Shaywitz, 2003). That is why dyslexics have problems initially "cracking the code," and then problems later on developing reading fluency. Still, knowing the cause of severe reading problems is one thing; knowing what to do to help students who have these problems is another altogether.

Put very simply, students with dyslexia have serious problems learning to read despite normal intelligence, normal opportunities to learn to read, and an adequate home environment. Although the precise organic cause of dyslexia continues to be researched, considerable evidence suggests that reading problems associated with dyslexia are phonologically based (Blachman, 1997; Foorman, 2003; Stanovich & Siegel, 1994). Students with dyslexia have difficulty developing phonemic awareness, the understanding that spoken words are made up of sounds. Phonemic awareness problems make it hard for them to link speech sounds to letters, ultimately leading to slow, labored reading characterized by frequent starts and stops and multiple mispronunciations. Students with dyslexia also have comprehension problems largely because their struggle to identify words leaves little energy for understanding what they read.

Students with dyslexia also have trouble with the basic elements of written language, such as spelling and sentence and paragraph construction. Finally, students with dyslexia may have difficulty understanding representational systems, such as telling time, directions, and seasons (Bryan & Bryan, 1986). Dyslexia commonly is considered a type of learning disability, and students with dyslexia are served under the learning disability classification of IDEA.

It is important to identify students with dyslexia or other severe reading disabilities early, before they fall far behind their peers in word-recognition reading skills. Early identification is particularly urgent given recent studies showing that effective language instruction appears to generate repair in underactivated sections of the brain (Shaywitz, 2003). Students who appear to be learning letter names, sounds, and sight words at a significantly slower rate than their classmates are at risk for developing later reading problems. See the Professional Edge in Chapter 4 on page 126 for specific assessment strategies to identify children at risk for reading failure early.

From the Research

A large body of research (Blachman, 2000; National Reading Panel, 2000; Foorman, 2003; McCardle & Chhabra, 2004; Oakland, Black, Stanford, Nussbaum, & Balise, 1998; Snow, Burns, & Griffin, 1998; Swanson, 2000) shows that many students with severe reading disabilities benefit from a beginning reading program that includes the following five elements:

1. *Direct instruction in language analysis.* For example, students need to be taught skills in sound segmentation by orally breaking down words into their component sounds.

2. *A highly structured phonics program.* This program should teach the alphabetic code directly and systematically by using a simple-to-complex sequence of skills, teaching regularity before irregularity, and discouraging guessing.

3. *Writing and reading instruction in combination.* Students need to be writing the words they are reading.

4. *Intensive instruction.* Reading instruction for at-risk students should include large amounts of practice in materials that contain words they are able to decode.

5. *Teaching for automaticity.* Students must be given enough practice that they are able to read both accurately and fluently.

For students who are dyslexic, visit the website Dyslexia: The Gift, at http://www.dyslexia.com, for curriculum aids, a bookstore, discussion board, and links to further information.

areas of letter formation (is the letter recognizable?), size, alignment, slant, line quality (heaviness or lightness of lines), straightness, and spacing (too little or too much between letters, words, and lines).

Students with learning and behavioral disabilities also have trouble with spelling. The English language consists largely of three types of words: those that can be spelled phonetically, those that can be spelled by following certain linguistic rules, and those that are irregular. For example, the words *cats*, *construction*, and *retell* can be spelled correctly by applying phonics generalizations related to consonants, consonant blends (*str*), vowels, root words (*tell*), prefixes (*re*), and suffixes (*ion*, *s*). The word *babies* can be spelled by applying the linguistic rule of changing *y* to *i* and adding *es*. Words such as *said*, *where*, and *through* are irregular and can be spelled only by remembering what they look like. Students with learning and behavioral disabilities may have trouble with all three types of words.

Students with learning and behavioral disabilities have two major types of written expression problems: product problems and process problems (Isaacson, 2001; Mercer & Pullen, 2005). Their written products are often verb-object sentences, characterized by few words, incomplete sentences, overuse of simple subject-verb constructions, repetitious use of high-frequency words, a disregard for audience, poor organization and structure, and many mechanical errors, such as misspellings, incorrect use of punctuation and capital letters, and faulty subject-verb agreements and choice of pronouns (Mercer & Pullen, 2005).

These students also have trouble with the overall process of written communication. Their approach to writing shows little systematic planning, great difficulty putting ideas on paper because of a preoccupation with mechanics, failure to monitor writing, and little useful revision (Mercer & Pullen, 2005). A writing sample from a student who has a disability is shown in Figure 7.3. What types of product problems do you see in this sample? What process problems do you think might have led to these problems?

FIGURE 7.3 Written Expression Sample of a 14-Year-Old Student with a Learning Disability

W W W
RESOURCES
IEPs for most students with
learning and behavioral
disabilities include goals
and supports in the academic areas of reading, math,
and writing. The IEP page
of the website LDOnLine at
http://www.ldonline.org/ld
_indepth/iep/iep.html,
provides many links to help
parents and teachers de-
velop IEPs in academic
areas.

FYI

Adaptations of materials
and formats for math in-
struction include keeping
models on the board; pro-
viding graph paper to align
problems; and using visual
cues, such as color-coded
or boldfaced signs and arrows, as reminders of direction, and frames to set off
problems and answers.

Math Skills

Math also can be problematic for students with learning and behavioral disabilities. Their problems tend to occur in eight key areas (Cawley, Parmar, Foley, Salmon, & Roy, 2001; Smith, 2004; Strang & Rourke, 1985).

1. *Problems with spatial organization.* Students may be unable to align numbers in columns, may reverse numbers (write a 9 backward, read 52 as 25), or may subtract the top number from the bottom number in a subtraction problem such as

$$\begin{array}{r} 75 \\ -39 \\ \hline 44 \end{array}$$

2. *Lack of alertness to visual detail.* Students misread mathematical signs or forget to use dollar signs and decimals when necessary.

3. *Procedural errors.* Students miss a step in solving a problem. For example, they may forget to add a carried number in an addition problem or to subtract from the re-grouped number in a subtraction problem:

$$\begin{array}{r} 29 \\ +53 \\ \hline 72 \end{array} \qquad \begin{array}{r} 41 \\ -28 \\ \hline 23 \end{array}$$

4. *Failure to shift mind-set from one problem type to another.* Students solve problems of one type but, when required to solve problems of another type, solve them in the way they did those of the first type. For example, Kristy just completed several word prob-lems that required addition. The next problem requires subtraction, but she continues to use addition.

5. *Difficulty forming numbers correctly.* Students' numbers are too large or are poorly formed, which makes solving computational problems awkward, particularly when the students are unable to read their own numbers.

6. *Difficulty with memory.* Students are frequently unable to recall basic math facts.

7. *Problems with mathematical judgment and reasoning.* Students are unaware when their responses are unreasonable. For example, they do not see the obvious errors in 9 − 6 = 15 or 4 + 3 = 43. They may also have trouble solving word problems. For example, they may be unable to decide whether to add or subtract in a word problem, focusing on cue words such as *less, more,* or *times* rather than comprehending accurately the situation described in the problem. This difficulty is shown in the following problem: "A boy has 3 times as many apples as a girl. The boy has 6. How many does the girl have?" Stu-dents with disabilities are likely to answer 18 instead of 2 because they think the pres-ence of the word *times* in the problem means they need to multiply (Cawley et al., 2001, p. 325).

8. *Problems with mathematical language.* Students may have difficulty with the mean-ings of key mathematical terms, such as *regroup, place value,* and *minus* (Lerner, 2003; Mercer & Pullen, 2005). They may also have trouble participating in oral drills (Lerner, 2006) or verbalizing the steps in solving word or computational problems (Cawley, Miller, & School, 1987).

Students from culturally and linguistically diverse backgrounds may have addi-tional problems learning math skills. Some potential trouble spots and strategies for dealing with these trouble spots are shown in the Special Emphasis On . . . feature on page 247.

CONNECTIONS

Approaches to adapting instruction for students with
ADHD, which are covered
in Chapter 8, are also applicable here.

Special EMPHASIS On …

Adapting Math Instruction for Students Who Are Linguistically and Culturally Diverse

Math can be a challenging subject for all students, including students with learning and behavioral difficulties. Students from linguistically and culturally diverse backgrounds may face additional challenges when learning math. In the following table, Scott and Raborn (1996) present some potential trouble spots and suggested strategies for teaching math to students from linguistically and culturally diverse backgrounds.

Trouble Spot	Recommendation
Learning a new language	• Determine the student's level of proficiency in both English and the native language. • Assess math abilities in both languages. • If a student is stronger in math than in English, provide math instruction in the primary language. • Listen to the words you most frequently use in teaching math. Work together with the ESL teacher to help the student learn these words or to help you learn them in the student's language. • Use a variety of ways to communicate such as gesturing, drawing sketches, writing basic vocabulary and procedures, rewording, and providing more details. • Provide time and activities that will allow students to practice the English language and the language of math.
Cultural differences	• Use story problem situations that are relevant to the student's personal cultural indentity (e.g., ethnicity, gender, geographical region, age). • Share examples of the mathematical heritage of the student's culture (e.g., folk art, African and Native American probability games, measurement systems). • Involve family and community members in multicultural math.
Tricky vocabulary	• Use concrete activities to teach new vocabulary and the language of math. • Use only as many technical words as are necessary to ensure understanding. • Give more information in a variety of ways to help students understand new vocabulary. • Develop a picture file; purchase or have students make a picture dictionary of math terms and frequently used vocabulary.
Symbolic language	• Allow students to draw pictures, diagrams, or graphic organizers to represent story problems. • Make clear the meanings and function of symbols. • Point out the interchangeable nature of operations. • In algebra, teach students to translate phrases to mathematical expressions.
Level of abstraction and memory	• Allow students to develop mathematical relationships using concrete representations accompanied by verbal descriptions. • Develop mathematical understanding from concrete to abstract form. • Use visual and kinesthetic cues to strengthen memory. • Keep distractions to a minimum.

Research Note

Grossen (2002) implemented a math curriculum with middle school English-language learners that stressed the use of scaffolding to teach students explicit problem-solving strategies. After a year, the percentage of students at grade level significantly increased; the number of children significantly below grade level dropped considerably.

SOURCE: From "Realizing the Gifts of Diversity among Students with Learning Disabilities," by P. Scott and D. Raborn, 1996, *LD Forum, 21*(2), pp. 10–18. Reprinted by permission of the Council of Learning Disabilities.

CONNECTIONS

Specific strategies for helping students remember information are described in Chapter 11.

RESEARCH NOTE

Many educators claim that students have certain learning preferences or styles and that teaching to accommodate these styles enhances instruction, particularly in reading. In a review of more than 40 research studies on learning styles, Kavale and Forness (1987) found no evidence for teaching based on learning styles. Yates (1999), in a more recent review of the literature, concluded that learning-style questionnaires cannot reliably differentiate instructional groups, have not generated a consistent body of research verifying their effectiveness, and may distract teachers from approaches that do have a sound research base. Our advice is to meet individual needs by always teaching to as many senses as possible.

ANALYZE AND REFLECT

What learning needs might students with learning and behavioral disabilities share? How might their needs be different? How might you modify instruction for basic academic skills for these students?

Learning Skills

Students with learning and behavioral disabilities have difficulty performing skills that could help them learn more readily. One such skill is attention. Students may have difficulty coming to attention or understanding task requirements (Hallahan et al., 2005). For example, Janice frequently fails essay tests; she is unable to focus on key words in the questions to help her organize a response. As a result, she loses valuable writing time just staring at the question and not knowing how to begin. Benito misses important information at the beginning of science lectures because he takes 5 minutes to attend to the teacher's presentation. Students may also have trouble focusing on the important aspects of tasks. For example, Anita can tell you the color of her teacher's tie or the kind of belt he is wearing, but nothing about the information he is presenting. When Arman tries to solve word problems in math, he is unable to tell the difference between information that is needed and not needed to solve the problem. Finally, students with learning and behavioral disabilities may have trouble sticking to a task once they have started it. This lack of task persistence is largely due to a lack of confidence resulting from a history of school failure. The emotional repercussions of school failure are covered later in this chapter in the discussion of the personal and psychological adjustment of students with learning and behavioral disabilities.

Memory problems may also make learning difficult for students (Lerner, 2006; Hallahan et al., 2005). Some problems occur when information is first learned. For example, Carla cannot remember information when it is presented just once. Sal has practiced math facts many times but still cannot remember some of them. Students may also fail to retain what they learn. For example, Abby had learned addition facts in the fall but remembered only about 50 percent of them when tested in the spring. Finally, students sometimes learn something but do not remember to use the information to solve problems or to learn other information. For example, John learned a note-taking strategy in a resource room but failed to use the strategy in his content-area classes.

Students with learning and behavioral disabilities may have trouble organizing and interpreting oral and visual information despite adequate hearing and visual skills (Lerner, 2006). For example, Rodney is a student with a learning disability who has trouble with visual tasks. He frequently loses his place while reading and copying; has trouble reading and copying from the chalkboard; does not notice details on pictures, maps, and photographs; is confused by worksheets containing a great deal of visual information; and often cannot remember what he has seen. LaTonya has trouble with auditory tasks. She has difficulty following oral directions, differentiating between fine differences in sounds (*e/i, bean/been*), taking notes during lectures, and remembering what she has heard.

Students also may lack reasoning skills necessary for success in school. Important reasoning skills include reading comprehension, generalization (the ability to recognize similarities across objects, events, or vocabulary), adequate background and vocabulary knowledge, induction (figuring out a rule or principle based on a series of situations), and sequencing (detecting relationships among stimuli) (Salvia & Ysseldyke, 2003). For example, Stu has difficulty understanding a lecture on the civil rights movement because he lacks necessary background information; he is unsure what a civil right is. Tamara has trouble recognizing a relationship on her own, even after repeated examples; her teacher presented five examples of how to add *s* to words that end in *y*, but Tamara still could not figure out the rule.

Some students with learning and behavioral disabilities may have motor coordination and fine motor impairments (Lerner, 2003). For example, Denise is a first-grade student who has some fine motor and coordination problems. She has trouble using scissors, coloring within the lines, tying her shoes, and printing letters and numbers. Cal is in third grade. His handwriting is often illegible and messy. He is also uncoordinated at sports, which has limited his opportunities for social interaction on the playground, because he is never selected to play on a team.

Independent learning also can be a challenge for students with learning and behavioral disabilities. They have been referred to as *passive learners*, meaning that they do not believe in their own abilities; have limited knowledge of problem-solving strategies; and even when they know a strategy, cannot tell when it is supposed to be used (Hallahan et al., 2005; Lerner, 2006). Being a passive learner is particularly problematic in the upper grades, where more student independence is expected. For example, when Laverne reads her science textbook, she does not realize when she comes across information that she does not understand. So instead of employing a strategy to solve this problem, such as rereading, checking the chapter summary, or asking for help, she never learns the information. As a result she is doing poorly in the class. When Darrell studies for tests, he reads quickly through his text and notes but does not use strategies for remembering information, such as asking himself questions, saying the information to himself, or grouping into meaningful pieces the information he needs to learn.

Students with learning and behavioral disabilities may also have problems in the area of **academic survival skills** such as attending school regularly, being organized, completing tasks in and out of school, being independent, taking an interest in school, and displaying positive interpersonal skills with peers and adults (Brown et al., 1984; Kerr & Nelson, 1998). For example, Duane is failing in school because he rarely shows up for class; when he does attend class, he sits in the back of the room and displays an obvious lack of interest. Nicole is always late for class and never completes her homework; her teachers think she does not care about school at all.

As you can see, students with learning and behavioral disabilities have problems in a number of academic and learning areas. Some parents and teachers have tried unproven interventions in search of quick fixes for students with learning and behavioral disabilities. The issue of using unproven, controversial therapies is discussed in the Professional Edge on pages 250–251.

> Being a passive learner is particularly problematic in the upper grades, where more student independence is expected.

FYI

Estimates of the percentage of students with learning disabilities who are at risk for social problems range from 34 to 59 percent (Bryan, 1997).

What Are the Social and Emotional Needs of Students with Learning and Behavioral Disabilities?

Considering students' social needs is crucial because students who have social adjustment problems in school are at risk for academic problems (Epstein, Kinder, & Bursuck, 1989; Anderson, Kutash, & Duchnowski, 2001; Coleman & Webber, 2002) as well as serious adjustment problems when they leave school (Carter & Wehby, 2003; Kauffman, 2005). Students with learning and behavioral disabilities may have needs in several social areas, including classroom conduct, interpersonal skills, and personal and psychological adjustment.

Students with learning and behavioral disabilities may engage in a number of aggressive or disruptive behaviors in class, including hitting, fighting, teasing, hyperactivity, yelling, refusing to comply with requests, crying, destructiveness, vandalism, and extortion (Deitz & Ormsby, 1992; Friend, 2005; Hallahan & Kauffman, 2003). Although many of these behaviors may be exhibited by all children at one time or

CONNECTIONS

The use of strategies for responding to student behavior, including punishment, is the topic of Chapter 12.

PROFESSIONAL EDGE

Controversial Therapies in Learning and Behavioral Disabilities: What Does the Research Say?

Being the parent or teacher of a student with learning disabilities is not easy. Students with learning disabilities often do not respond favorably to the first approach tried—or, for that matter, to the first several. Failure and frustration can lead to the search for miracle cures. This problem is compounded by the fact that journals that publish research about the effectiveness of various treatments are not normally read by parents and teachers. Unfortunately, this void is readily filled by a steady stream of information, much of it not substantiated by research, from popular books, lay magazines, television talk shows (Silver, 1998; Vaughn, Klingner, & Hughes, 2004), and now the Internet.

As a teacher, you need to be well informed about these therapies so you can give parents reliable, up-to-date information when they come to you for advice. The best way to get this information is to read professional journals. Any treatment may work for a few students, but this is not the same as demonstrating effectiveness in a controlled research study. If you or a student's parents decide to use a controversial therapy, you must monitor its effectiveness carefully and discontinue it if necessary. Several controversial therapies are summarized here, including the latest research findings for their effectiveness.

Neurophysiological Retraining

In this group of approaches, learning difficulties are seen as the result of dysfunctions in the central nervous system that can be remediated by having students engage in specific sensory or motor activities. One common example of this approach is patterning (Doman & Delacato, 1968), in which students are taken back through earlier stages of development (creeping and crawling). Another approach is optometric visual training, in which students do eye exercises designed to improve their visual perception and hence their reading skills. A third approach, vestibular training, takes children through tasks involving spatial orientation, eye movements, and balance, with the goal of improving their academic performance, especially in reading. No research evidence suggests that patterning, optometric visual training, or vestibular training improves students' cognitive functioning or reading ability (Hallahan et al., 2005; Silver, 1998).

Diet Control Therapies

A number of therapies involve using diet to control hyperactivity and other learning disorders. One of these (Feingold, 1975) claimed to decrease student hyperactivity by eliminating various artificial flavors, colors, and preservatives from the student's diet. Most research studies have shown that the Feingold Diet is not effective in controlling hyperactivity (Smith, 2004). Others have suggested that refined sugars in the diet lead to hyperactivity. Again, these claims have not been proven by research (Barkley, 1995; Connors & Blouin, 1982/1983). Another diet therapy for learning disorders involves using megavitamins to treat emotional or cognitive disorders (Cott, 1977, 1985). This therapy has not been verified by research (Smith, 2004). Another theory purports that deficiencies in trace elements such as copper, zinc, magnesium, manganese, and chromium along with the more common elements of calcium, sodium, and iron cause learning disorders; but these claims remain unsubstantiated (Silver, 1998). Finally, one theory claims hypoglycemia (low blood-sugar levels) causes learning disabilities. Clinical studies on this theory have been inconclusive (Rappaport, 1982/1983; Smith, 2004).

Scotopic Sensitivity Syndrome

This syndrome has been defined as a difficulty in efficiently processing light, which causes a reading disorder (Irlen, 1991; Lerner, 2006). Symptoms include abnormal sensitivity to light, blinking and squinting, red and watery eyes, frequent headaches, word blurriness, print instability, slow

another, the classroom conduct of students with behavioral disorders is viewed by teachers as abnormal, and their behavior has a negative impact on the other students in class (Cullinan, Epstein, & Lloyd, 1983; Hallahan & Kauffman, 2003). For example, Kenneth is an adolescent with learning and behavior problems. His father died last year, and his mother has been working two jobs just to make ends meet. Kenneth has begun to hang out with a rough crowd and has been getting into fights in school. He

reading, skipping and rereading lines, and difficulty reading at length because of general eye strain and fatigue (Irlen, 1991). Following a screening test, students identified as having scotopic sensitivity are treated with plastic overlays or colored lenses, which can be expensive. Although many people treated with tinted lenses claim that the lenses eliminate their symptoms and help them read better, research shows that tests for scotopic sensitivity are flawed (Silver, 1998; Woerz & Maples, 1997), and the effects of the lenses have not been verified (American Academy of Pediatrics, 1998; Fletcher & Martinez, 1994). Caution is advised.

Allergies

Although there seems to be a relationship between allergies and brain functioning, a clear cause-and-effect relationship has yet to be established (Silver, 1998). Two persons who have written a lot about the relationship between allergies and learning disabilities and ADHD are Dr. Doris Rapp and Dr. William Crook. Dr. Rapp suggests the elimination of certain foods from the diet, such as milk, chocolate, eggs, wheat, corn, peanuts, pork, and sugar. She performs an "under-the-tongue" test (not validated) that she claims determines whether a child is allergic to any or all of these foods. Dr. Crook's recent work has focused on child reactions to a specific yeast and the development of specific behaviors following a yeast infection. According to Silver (1998) and Smith (2004), neither Crook nor Rapp supports these findings with research. In addition, the established profession of pediatric allergies does not accept either of these treatments (Silver, 1998).

Controversial Therapies and the Internet

As the number of Internet sites created for specific disabilities and related health issues increases, so too does information about controversial therapies. Because information on the Internet is not reviewed for quality, Ira (2000) suggests that you do the following to determine the credibility of the various websites you visit.

1. Click on the About Us or Contact Us links or buttons at a website. These links may inform you of who is on the team of people running a particular website. Many sites, particularly those that want to prove their credibility, feature a page describing their background, history, and affiliations (the About Us section) and mailing and e-mail addresses and phone number (the Contact Us section).

2. Try to establish links with other sites. Sites with reliably usable information may have endorsements from prominent special needs organizations or may have links to other websites with more information on the subject. Look for links to other associations or educational or even government-supported institutions related to the subject. The more independent sites that validate a recommendation, the more credible it is. The following are specific sites that may address doubts about the credibility of a particular controversial therapy.

   http://www.interdys.org International Dyslexia Society

   http://www.ldanatl.org Learning Disabilities Association of America

   http://www.ncld.org National Center for Learning Disabilities

   http://www.cldinternational.org Council for Learning Disabilities

3. Ask friends and special needs associations to recommend websites that are informative. You can also e-mail people you think can clue you in on the credibility of a particular site.

4. Examine the content of the site for typographical or grammatical errors. As with books, magazines, and journals, credibility is often reflected in editorial excellence.

5. Check to see how often the site is updated. A site that is updated regularly with new research findings is most likely to be run by people interested in learning the truth rather than perpetuating their own point of view.

6. Check to be sure that a given finding has been validated by a credible, refereed research publication. Many of these publications are available on the web.

has also been talking back to his teachers frequently and refusing to comply with their demands. Kenneth's behavior has gotten so bad that other students and their parents are complaining about it to the teacher. Some cautions involved in disciplining students like Kenneth are presented in the Professional Edge on pages 252–253. Ways to get support from colleagues in solving academic and behavior problems in your classroom are described in Working Together on page 254.

PROFESSIONAL EDGE

Disciplining Students with Emotional Disturbance

Students with emotional disturbance sometimes behave in ways that disrupt the education of other students in the class or threaten their safety. When this happens, you may need to punish such a student both to defuse the situation and to deter the student from acting out again. Punishment involves decreasing inappropriate behavior by either presenting something negative or taking away something positive. Although the courts have held that it is permissible to punish students with emotional disturbance, they have also held that the punishment must be delivered according to the following eight principles (Hartwig & Ruesch, 2000; Yell, 1990; Yell, Clyde, & Puyallup, 1995; Yell, Drasgow, Bradley, & Justesen, 2004):

1. Teachers must be careful not to violate the due process rights of their students. This means that you need to communicate clearly to parents and students the behaviors you expect and the specific consequences for inappropriate behaviors. As needed, these items should be written in students' IEPs as part of the behavioral intervention plan.

2. When using punishment, do not violate the educational rights of students with emotional disturbance. Punishments such as expulsion, serial suspensions (successive, consecutive suspensions), prolonged in-school suspensions, and prolonged periods of time-out (removing students from classroom activities; see Chapter

12) constitute a change of placement and therefore cannot be done without due process. Temporary suspensions of 10 days or fewer are permissible; possession of a weapon or illegal drug, or infractions involving the infliction of serious bodily injury will automatically result in a student's being pulled from the classroom for up to 45 school days. To expel a student for more than 10 days, a committee, including the student's parents, must determine whether the misconduct had anything to do with the disability, or the school's failure to implement the IEP by engaging in a process called the *manifestation determination*. Finally, in the cases of suspension, students must be presented with the evidence against them and given the opportunity to present their side of the story. However, schools may remove a student who has seriously injured another person while at school, on school premises, or at a school function without a hearing officer ruling.

3. The punishment of students with emotional disturbance must serve an educational purpose, and clearly written guidelines for its use must exist. For example, Calvin was told that his verbal outbursts in class were preventing him and his classmates from learning. He was handed a written contract indicating that if he engaged in more than one verbal outburst in class, he would be required to sit in the back of the room and not participate in any classroom activities for 3 minutes.

DIMENSIONS OF DIVERSITY

Social skills are learned in cultural contexts. Teach your students about the variance in social behavior within all cultures and emphasize the notion that families and individuals experience their cultures in personal ways.

Interpersonal Skills

Students with learning and behavioral disabilities are likely to have difficulty in social relations with their peers. Evidence for these problems comes from more than 20 years of research showing that these students have fewer friends, are more likely to be rejected or neglected by their peers (Bryan, 1997), and are frequently rated as socially troubled by their teachers and parents (Smith, 2004). Many of these problems can be traced to the failure of students to engage in socially appropriate behaviors or social skills in areas such as making friends, carrying on conversations, and dealing with conflict.

There are a number of explanations for why students have social skills problems. Some students may simply not know what to do in social situations. They may lack knowledge because they do not learn from naturally occurring models of social behavior at home or in school. Students also may have trouble reading social cues and may misinterpret the feelings of others (Lerner, 2006; Silver, 1998; Bryan & Bryan, 1986). For example, a story was told recently about five boys sitting on the floor of the principal's office, waiting to be disciplined. Four of the boys were discussing failing or near-failing grades and the trouble they were going to be in when the fifth boy, a student

4. The punishment procedure used must be reasonable according to these guidelines:
   a. Is the rule being enforced reasonable?
   b. Does the punishment match the offense?
   c. Is the punishment reasonable in light of the student's age and physical condition?
   d. Is the teacher dealing out the punishment without malice or personal ill will toward the student?

5. More intrusive punishments should be used only after more positive procedures based on a careful assessment of the student's behavior in the classroom, called a *functional assessment* (see Chapter 12), have been tried. For example, Mr. Shu was concerned about Calvin's verbal outbursts in class. He noticed that the outbursts came when it was time to complete seatwork independently. After making sure Calvin was able to complete the work, Mr. Shu first tried giving him 5 extra minutes of computer time for not having a verbal outburst. When this approach did not work, he tried a different reward. When this positive procedure failed, Mr. Shu resorted to seating Calvin by himself for a period of time as described in Mr. Shu's written contract with Calvin.

6. When you use punishment, keep records of all the procedures you try. Write down the behavior that precipitates the punishment, the procedures used, the length of time they were used, and the results. This information can help you make informed decisions about a student's behavior management program. It can also help clarify for parents why you used a particular procedure.

Students who are experiencing emotional problems might be withdrawn, anxious, or depressed. What can you do to help these students in your classroom?

7. Punishment procedures for students with emotional disturbance should be carried out in conjunction with the special education teacher as agreed on in the student's IEP. Any major changes in punishment should be decided on only in collaboration with these same people. For example, Mr. Shu consulted with Calvin's special education teacher and parents each time he tried a different punishment procedure.

8. Remember that punishment should always be used in conjunction with positive consequences for appropriate behavior. The use of positive consequences can greatly reduce the need for using punishment in the future and can help build positive behaviors that will benefit students throughout their lives.

with a learning disability, chimed in to say that his grandparents were coming to visit the next week.

Other students may know what to do—but not do it. For example, some students with learning and behavioral disabilities are impulsive; they act before they think. In Del's sessions with the school social worker, he is able to explain how he would act in various social situations, but in an actual social setting he gets nervous and acts without thinking. Some students may choose not to act on their previous knowledge because their attempts at socially appropriate behavior may have gone unrecognized and they would rather have negative recognition than no recognition at all. For example, James was rebuffed by one group of students so often that he began to say nasty things to them just to provoke them. He also began to hang out with other students who chronically misbehaved because, according to James, "At least they appreciate me!" Finally, some students may know what to do socially but lack the confidence to act on their knowledge in social situations, particularly if they have a history of social rejection or lack opportunities for social interactions. Consider Holly, a student who is socially withdrawn. Holly worked for a year with her school counselor to learn how to initiate a social activity with a friend but is afraid to try it out for fear of being rejected.

FYI

Social cues are verbal or nonverbal signals people give that communicate a social message.

WWW
RESOURCES

The website of Internet Mental Health, http://www.mentalhealth.com, is a virtual encyclopedia of mental health information.

WORKING TOGETHER

Learning from Others

Marcia Lamb is beginning her first year of teaching third grade at a large urban elementary school. She has 25 students in her class. Three students have IEPs: 1 student has behavior disorders, and 2 have learning disabilities. After the first full week of school, Marcia is clearly struggling to get control of her class. During large-group instruction many children are off task. Even when students are paying attention, they call out answers without raising their hands. Transitioning from one subject to the next seems to take forever because few students do as they are told. There is constant complaining that the work is too hard. Although some of the problems involve her students with disabilities, Marcia is having problems with most of the students at one time or another.

Marcia doesn't know what to do. She was assigned a faculty mentor, but every time she sees her in the hall she seems so busy that Marcia is reluctant to ask her anything. The special education teacher also seems busy and is still in the process of setting up her schedule. Marcia is afraid to tell the principal she is having problems. What should Marcia do?

- An important part of working together is recognizing that problem solving works best when it is done in teams. Seeking help from an individual or team is not a sign of weakness but an effective strategy that also sends the message that you recognize you have a problem and want to do something about it. Marcia needs to set up an appointment with her mentor right away to discuss the problems she is having with her class. The mentor can share her experiences with Marcia and give her ideas for structuring her class to prevent many of her current problems from recurring.

- Another key part of working together is recognizing the strengths of your colleagues and accessing their particular areas of expertise as needed. Marcia needs to make an appointment with the special education teacher to discuss her efforts with the 3 students with disabilities included in her class. These students may require a more individualized effort, and special education teachers specialize in making such accommodations for students with disabilities. Marcia may also be able to set up a co-teaching arrangement whereby she and another teacher teach together sometime during the day. Co-teaching is a powerful way for new teachers to acquire expertise from their more experienced colleagues.

- As for contacting her principal, although there is no need to directly involve the principal at this time, Marcia should not feel reluctant to let her know she has been working with her colleagues to help her be a more effective teacher. No doubt they value the act of self-improvement as an important quality in a new teacher.

DIMENSIONS OF DIVERSITY

Gans, Kenny, and Ghany (2003) studied the self-concept of a primarily Latino group of middle school children with and without learning disabilities. They found that the children with LD rated themselves significantly lower in intellectual ability (in answers to, for example, "How smart am I?") and in school status (for example, in responses to "I am an important member of my class") than the children without LD.

Personal and Psychological Adjustment

Students with little success at academics and/or social relationships may have personal and psychological problems as well (Kerschner, 1990; Torgesen, 1991; Vaughn & Haager, 1994). One common personal problem is self-image. Students with learning and behavioral disabilities often have a poor self-concept; they have little confidence in their own abilities (Lerner, 2006; Licht, Kistner, Ozkaragoz, Shapiro, & Clausen, 1985; Silver, 1998). Poor self-image, in turn, can lead to **learned helplessness.** Students with learned helplessness see little relationship between their efforts and school or social success. When these students succeed, they attribute their success to luck; when they fail, they blame their failure on a lack of ability. When confronted with difficult situations, students who have learned helplessness are likely to say or think, "What's the use? I never do anything right anyway." For example, Denny is a 15-year-old sophomore in high school. He has been in special education since the second grade. He has never received a grade better than a C and has received quite a few D's and F's. Last quarter, Denny started to skip classes because he felt that even when he went to class he did not do well. Denny is looking forward to dropping out of school on his 16th birthday and going to work for a fast-food chain, where, he reasons, at least he will be able to do the work.

Students with learning and behavior problems may also have severe anxiety or depression (Cullinan, Evans, Epstein, & Ryser, 2003; Friend, 2005). Depressed or anxious students may refuse to speak up when in class, may be pessimistic or uninterested

FIGURE 7.4 Diagnostic Criteria for Major Depression

Depression is a dysphoric mood (unhappy; depressed affect), a loss of interest or pleasure in all or almost all usual activities. At least five of the following symptoms also must have been present consistently *for at least 2 weeks*.

1. change in appetite or weight
2. sleep disturbance
3. psychomotor agitation or retardation
4. loss of energy
5. feelings of worthlessness
6. complaints of difficulty concentrating
7. thoughts of death or suicide
8. depressed mood most of the day
9. diminished interest or pleasure

SOURCE: *Diagnostic and Statistical Manual Disorders* (4th ed., text rev.), by the American Psychiatric Association, 2000, Washington, DC: Author. Reprinted by permission.

in key aspects of their lives, may be visibly nervous when given an assignment, may become ill when it is time to go to school, or may show a lack of self-confidence when performing common school and social tasks. For example, Barrett is a 9-year-old boy with a consistent history of school failure. Barrett is sick just about every morning before he goes to school. At first his mother let him stay home, but now she makes him go anyway. When at school, Barrett is very withdrawn. He has few friends and rarely speaks in class. Barrett's teachers tend not to notice him because he is quiet and does not cause problems. If you have a student in your class who exhibits the signs of depression shown in Figure 7.4, get help for him or her by contacting your school counselor, psychologist, or social worker.

What Accommodations Can You Make for Students with Learning and Behavioral Disabilities?

As you have just read, students with learning and behavioral disabilities have a range of learning and social-emotional needs. Although these needs may make learning and socializing difficult for them, students with learning and behavioral disabilities can succeed in your classroom if given support. Some initial ideas about how you can accommodate students with learning and behavioral disabilities in your classroom are discussed next. A more in-depth treatment of such accommodations can be found in Chapters 8–13.

Addressing Academic Needs

As we have already discussed, you can discern whether students with learning and behavioral disabilities need adaptations by using the INCLUDE strategy to analyze their academic needs and the particular demands of your classroom. In most cases students with learning and behavioral disabilities are expected to meet the same curricular expectations as their classmates without disabilities. Therefore, provide them with in-

**RESEARCH
N O T E**

Heath and Ross (2000) studied the prevalence of depression and its symptoms among 100 fourth- through sixth-grade children with learning disabilities and 100 children who were not disabled. They found that girls with LD reported higher levels of depressive symptoms and a higher prevalence of depression than girls without LD. There were no differences in prevalence or depressive symptoms for boys with and without LD.

WWW
R E S O U R C E S

LDOnLine is an interactive guide to learning disabilities for parents, students, and teachers. This website offers newsletters, teaching tips, and more, at http://www.ldonline.org.

C O N N E C T I O N S

Review all the steps of the INCLUDE strategy (see Chapter 5). What are they? How can you use them for students with high-incidence disabilities?

In what ways might students with cognitive, emotional, and behavioral disorders have difficulty learning? How can teachers address each of these areas of difficulty?

RESEARCH
N O T E

Sutherland, Wehby, and Copeland (2000) found that the rate of on-task behavior of nine fifth-grade students with emotional and behavior disorders was significantly increased by simply increasing the number of times their teacher praised them for appropriate behavior.

ANALYZE
AND REFLECT

What social-emotional needs might students with learning and behavioral disabilities share? To what extent are students' social-emotional problems related to their academic problems? Why is it important to address students' social and emotional needs?

WWW
R E S O U R C E S

The Center for Effective Collaboration and Practice promotes collaboration among federal agencies serving children who have or are at risk of developing emotional disabilities. Its website provides many links to resources on issues of emotional and behavioral problems in children and youth. Visit http://cecp.air.org.

structional accommodations rather than modifications. Try the three types of accommodations described in Chapter 5: bypassing a student's need by allowing the student to employ compensatory learning strategies; making an adaptation in classroom organization, grouping, materials, and methods; and providing the student with direct instruction on basic or independent learning skills. For example, Jessica, who has learning disabilities, has enrolled in Mr. Gresh's high school general science class. Mr. Gresh uses a teaching format in which the students first read the text, then hear a lecture, and finally conduct and write up a lab activity (demands). Jessica has severe reading and writing problems. She is reading at about a sixth-grade level and has difficulty writing a legible, coherent paragraph (student learning needs). However, she does have good listening skills and is an adequate note taker (student strength). In Mr. Gresh's class, Jessica will have difficulty reading the textbook and meeting the lab-writing requirements independently (problem). She will be able to get the lecture information she needs because of her good listening skills (success). Mr. Gresh, with help from Jessica's special education teacher, brainstorms a number of possible accommodations for Jessica and then agrees to implement three of them. He develops a study guide to help Jessica identify key points in the text (adaptation). He also sets up small groups in class to review the study guides (adaptation) and assigns Jessica a buddy to help her with the writing demands of the lab activity (bypass). Finally, Mr. Gresh and the special education teacher set up a schedule to monitor Jessica's progress in writing lab reports and reading the textbook. Several more examples of how the INCLUDE strategy can be applied are provided in Table 7.2.

Addressing Social and Emotional Needs

One of the most important reasons given to explain the trend toward inclusive education is the social benefit for students with and without disabilities (Dorn & Fuchs, 2004; Freeman & Alkin, 2000; Stainback & Stainback, 1988). Unfortunately, experience shows that many students with learning and behavior problems do not acquire important social skills just from their physical presence in general education classes (Hallahan et al., 2005; Sale & Carey, 1995). Although much of the emphasis in your training as a teacher concerns academics, your responsibilities as a teacher also include helping all students develop socially, whether or not they have special needs. As with academics, the support students need depends largely on the specific social problems each student has.

TABLE 7.2 Making Adaptations for Students with Learning and Behavioral Disabilities Using Steps in the INCLUDE Strategy

INCLUDE

Identify Classroom Demands	Note Student Strengths and Needs	Check for Potential Successes, Look for Potential Problems	Decide on Adaptations
Student desks in clusters of four	*Strengths* Good vocabulary skills *Needs* Difficulty attending to task	*Success* Student understands instruction if on task *Problem* Student off task—does not face instructor as she teaches	Change seating so student faces instructor
Small-group work with peers	*Strengths* Good handwriting *Needs* Oral expressive language—problem with word finding	*Success* Student acts as secretary for cooperative group *Problem* Student has difficulty expressing self in peer learning groups	Assign as secretary of group Place into compatible small group Develop social skills instruction for all students
Expectation for students to attend class and be on time	*Strengths* Good drawing skills *Needs* Poor time management	*Success* Student uses artistic talent in class *Problem* Student is late for class and frequently does not attend at all	Use individualized student contract for attendance and punctuality—if goals are met, give student artistic responsibility in class
Textbook difficult to read	*Strengths* Good oral communication skills *Needs* Poor reading accuracy Lacks systematic strategy for reading text	*Success* Student participates well in class Good candidate for class dramatizations *Problem* Student is unable to read text for information	Provide taped textbook Highlight student text
Lecture on women's suffrage movement to whole class	*Strengths* Very motivated and interested in class *Needs* Lack of background knowledge	*Success* Student earns points for class attendance and effort *Problem* Student lacks background knowledge to understand important information in lecture	Give student video to view before lecture Build points for attendance and working hard into grading system
Whole-class instruction on telling time to the quarter hour	*Strengths* Good coloring skills *Needs* Cannot identify numbers 7–12 Cannot count by 5s	*Success* Student is able to color clock faces used in instruction *Problem* Student is unable to acquire telling-time skills	Provide extra instruction on number identification and counting by 5s
Math test involving solving word problems using addition	*Strengths* Good reasoning skills *Needs* Problems mastering math facts, sums of 10–18	*Success* Student is good at solving problems *Problem* Student misses problems due to math fact errors	Allow use of calculator
Multiple-choice and fill-in-the-blanks test	*Strengths* Good memory for details *Needs* Cannot identify key words in test questions Weak comprehension skills	*Success* Student does well on fill-in-the-blank questions that require memorization *Problem* Student is doing poorly on multiple-choice parts of history tests	Use bold type for key words in multiple-choice questions Teach strategy for taking multiple-choice tests

DIMENSIONS
OF DIVERSITY

Altwerger and Ivener (1996) suggest that teachers can build up the self-esteem of English-language learners by embracing the common and diverse strengths brought from their home culture, by considering all learners capable of constructing and reconstructing meaning over time, and by providing opportunities for students to share their knowledge and questions and to view themselves as important contributors to their own language.

CONNECTIONS

Ways of teaching students self-control are covered in Chapters 10 and 12.

FYI

Having a good sense of humor is important when working with youth with emotional and behavioral disorders. Richardson and Shupe (2003, p. 11) suggest that you check your sense of humor in class by asking yourself these questions: How often do I laugh as I teach? Do I use humor to defuse difficult situations or avoid potential power struggles? Does humor used in my classroom (by me or my students) tend to bring people closer together or push them further apart?

Students who have significant conduct problems benefit from a classroom with a clear, consistent behavior management system. In classrooms that are effectively managed, the rules are communicated clearly and the consequences for following or not following those rules are clearly stated and consistently applied. Conduct problems can also be minimized if students are engaged in meaningful academic tasks that can be completed successfully. Still, conduct problems may be so significant that they require a more intensive, individualized approach. For example, Rick, whom you read about at the beginning of this chapter, repeatedly talked out and loudly refused to carry out any requests his teachers made of him. His school attendance was also spotty. Rick's general education teachers got together with Rick's special education teacher to develop a **behavior contract.** According to the contract, each teacher was to keep track of Rick's attendance, talk-outs, and refusals to comply in class. The contract specified that when Rick talked out or refused to comply once, he would be given a warning. If he engaged in either of these behaviors again, he would be required to serve 5 minutes of detention for each violation. The contract also specified that for each class Rick attended without incident, he would receive points that his parents would allow him to trade for coupons to buy gasoline for his car.

Adaptations depend on the types of interpersonal problems your students have. You can use **social skills training** for students who do not know how to interact with peers and adults (Goldstein, Sprafkin, Gershaw, & Klein, 1980; Sabornie & deBettencourt, 2004). For example, Tammy is very withdrawn and has few friends. One day her teacher took her aside and suggested that she ask one of the other girls in class home some day after school. Tammy told her that she would never do that because she just would not know what to say. Tammy's teacher decided to spend several social studies classes working with the class on that skill and other skills such as carrying on a conversation and using the correct words and demeanor when asking another student whether he or she would like to play a game. She felt that many of the students in class besides Tammy would benefit from these lessons. First, Tammy's teacher posted the steps involved in performing these skills on a chart in front of the classroom. Then, she and several students in the class demonstrated the social skills for the class. She next divided the class into small groups, and each group role-played the various skills and was given feedback by classmates and peers. To make sure that Tammy felt comfortable, the teacher put her in a group of students who had a positive attitude and liked Tammy. An example of how to carry out social skills training is presented in the Case in Practice on page 259.

For students who know what to do in social situations but lack the self-control to behave appropriately, **self-control training** can be used (Kauffman, 2005). Self-control training teaches students to redirect their actions by talking to themselves. For example, Dominic did not handle conflict very well. When his friends teased him, he was quick to lose his temper and to verbally lash out at them. His outbursts only encouraged the students, and they continued teasing and taunting him any chance they got. Dominic's teacher taught him a self-control strategy to help him ignore his friends' teasing. Whenever he was teased, Dominic first counted to 5 to himself, to get beyond his initial anger. He then told himself that what they were saying wasn't true and that the best way to get them to stop was to ignore them and walk away. Whenever he walked away, Dominic told himself he did a good job and later reported his efforts to his teacher.

Some students may know what to do socially but lack opportunities for using their social skills. For example, students who are newly included in your classroom and/or new to the school need opportunities to interact with classmates to get to know them better. One way to create opportunities for social interaction is to allow students to work in small groups with a shared learning goal. For example, Thomas is a student with a mild intellectual disability who is included in Mr. Jeffreys's sixth-grade class. This is Thomas's first year in general education; until this year, he was in a self-contained special education classroom. Mr. Jeffreys has decided to use peer learning groups in science because he thinks they will be a good way for Thomas to get to know

CASE IN PRACTICE

A Social Skills Training Session

Ms. Perez and her fourth-grade class are working on a unit on social skills in social studies. They are learning the skill of listening to someone who is talking by doing the following:

1. Look at the person who is talking.
2. Remember to sit quietly.
3. Think about what is being said.
4. Say yes or nod your head.
5. Ask a question about the topic to find out more.

Jeanine, a student in the class, has just practiced these listening skills in front of the class by role-playing the part of a student who is talking to her teacher about an assignment. In the role-play, Ms. Perez played herself. The class is now giving Jeanine feedback on her performance.

Ms. Perez: Let's start with the first step. Did Jeanine look at me when I was talking? Before you answer, can someone tell me why it's important to look at the person who is talking?

Lorna: You don't want the other person to think you're not listening even though you are. So you really have to *show* them you are listening.

Ms. Perez: That's right, Lorna. Well, how did Jeanine do on this one?

Charles: Well, she looked at you at first but while you were explaining the assignment she looked down at her feet. It kind of looked like she wasn't listening.

Jeanine: I was listening, but I guess I should have kept good eye contact all the way through.

Ms. Perez: Yes, Jeanine. To be honest, if I didn't know you better, I would have thought that you didn't care about what I was saying. You need to work harder on that step. The next step is to remember to sit quietly. How did Jeanine do with this one?

Milton: I think she did well. She remembered not to laugh, fidget, or play with anything while you were talking.

Ms. Perez: I agree, Milton. Nice work, Jeanine. Now, can someone tell me what the next listening step is?

Kyrie: It's to think about what the person is saying.

Ms. Perez: Right, Kyrie. Let's let Jeanine evaluate herself on this one.

Jeanine: Well, I tried to think about what you were saying. Once I felt my mind start to wander, but I followed your suggestion and started thinking about a question that I could ask you.

Ms. Perez: Good, Jeanine. Trying to think of a question to ask can be very helpful. How did you think you did on the next step? Did you nod your head or say yes to show you were following me?

Jeanine: I think I did.

Ms. Perez: What do the rest of you think? Did Jeanine nod her head or say yes?

Tara: Well, I saw her nod a little, but it was hard to tell. Maybe she needs to nod more clearly.

Ms. Perez: Jeanine, you need to nod more strongly or the teacher won't realize you are doing it.

REFLECTIONS

What teaching procedures is Ms. Perez using to teach her students listening skills? Do you think they are effective? What could she do to make sure that her students use this skill in their classes? For what settings outside of school would these and other social skills be important?

---

his classmates and make some friends. Every 2 weeks, Thomas has the opportunity to complete various lab activities with a different group.

Students who exhibit learned helplessness can benefit from **attribution retraining** (Ellis, Lenz, & Sabornie, 1987b; Fulk, 1996; Mercer & Pullen, 2005). The idea behind attribution retraining is that if you can convince students that their failures are due to lack of effort rather than ability, they will be more persistent and will improve their performance in the face of difficulty (Hallahan et al., 2005; Schunk, 1989). You can enhance student self-image by using the following strategies (Mercer & Pullen, 2005):

1. *Set reasonable goals.* When setting goals for students, make sure that they are not too easy or too hard. Self-worth is improved when students reach their goals through considerable effort. Goals that are too ambitious perpetuate failure. Goals that are too easy can give students the idea that you think they are not capable of doing anything difficult.

2. *Provide specific feedback contingent on student behavior.* Feedback should be largely positive, but it should also be contingent on completion of tasks. Otherwise, students are likely to perceive your feedback as patronizing and just another indication that you think they are unable to do real academic work. Do not be afraid to correct students when they are wrong. Providing corrective feedback communicates to students that you think they can succeed if they keep trying and that you care about them.

3. *Give students responsibility.* Assigning a responsibility demonstrates to students that you trust them and believe they can act maturely. Some examples include taking the class pet home on weekends, taking the lunch count, being a line leader, taking messages to the office, and taking attendance.

4. *Teach students to reinforce themselves.* Students with poor self-images say negative things about themselves. You can help students by reminding them of their strengths, encouraging them to make more positive statements about themselves, and then reinforcing them for making these statements.

5. *Give students a chance to show their strengths.* Part of the INCLUDE strategy is to identify student strengths and then help students achieve success by finding or creating classroom situations in which they can employ their strengths. For example, Cara cannot read very well but has an excellent speaking voice. After her group wrote a report on the 1960 presidential election, Cara was given the task of presenting the report to the whole class.

S U M M A R Y

Students with high-incidence disabilities are students who have speech and language disabilities, learning disabilities, emotional disturbance, or mild intellectual disabilities. These students make up over 80 percent of all students who have disabilities. They are often hard to distinguish from their peers; exhibit a combination of behavior, social, and academic problems; and benefit from systematic, highly structured interventions.

Students with communication disorders have a number of learning, social, and emotional needs. Their language problems can affect their performance in academic and social areas. The academic and social performance of students with speech and language problems can be enhanced through a number of adaptations, including creating an atmosphere of acceptance, actively encouraging and teaching listening skills, using modeling to expand students' language, and teaching within contexts that are meaningful for students.

Students with learning and behavioral disabilities receive special education services within the categories of learning disabilities, mild intellectual disabilities, and emotional disturbance. Students with learning and behavioral disabilities have many academic needs. They may also lack skills necessary for efficient learning, such as attending to task, memory, organizing and interpreting information, reasoning, motor coordination, independent learning skills, and academic survival skills. You can make adaptations for these students in academic areas using the INCLUDE strategy.

Students with learning and behavioral disabilities have social and emotional difficulties in classroom conduct, interpersonal skills, and personal and psychological adjustment. Adaptations for students with learning and behavioral disabilities in social areas include individualized behavior management, social skills training, self-control training, and attribution retraining.

Applications in **Teaching Practice**

Using the INCLUDE Strategy with Students with High-Incidence Disabilities

INCLUDE

Answer the following questions to show how you would apply the INCLUDE strategy to accommodate the students described in the vignettes at the beginning of this chapter. To help you with this application, refer to Table 7.2 on page 257 and to the section on the INCLUDE strategy in Chapter 5.

QUESTIONS

1. What communication, academic, behavioral, and social and emotional needs does each student have?
2. Keeping in mind the major aspects of the classroom environment, including classroom organization, classroom grouping, instructional materials, and instructional methods, what kinds of problems are these students likely to have?
3. What types of adaptations would you make for each of these problems?
4. Are these accommodations reasonable in terms of teacher time and ease of implementation? What support (if any) would you need to carry them out?
5. How can you monitor the effectiveness of your adaptations? What can you do next if your first adaptation is ineffective?

WORKING THE **STANDARDS**

INTASC

INTASC PRINCIPLES REFLECTED IN THIS CHAPTER:

Principle #2 states that all teachers have realistically high expectations for what students with disabilities can accomplish, and use this knowledge to create challenging and supportive learning opportunities for students with disabilities (Principle 2.02).

Principle #4 states that all teachers

- Understand that it is particularly important to provide multiple ways for students with disabilities to participate in learning activities (Principle 4.04).

- Modify tasks and/or accommodate the individual needs of students with disabilities in a variety of ways to facilitate their engagement in learning activities with other students (Principle 4.04).

- Use strategies that promote the independence, self-control, and self-advocacy of students with disabilities (Principle 4.07).

- Expect and support the use of assistive and instructional technologies to promote learning and independence of students with disabilities (Principle 4.08).

Principle #9 states that all teachers continually challenge their beliefs about how students with disabilities learn and how to teach them effectively (Principle 9.02).

CEC CONTENT STANDARDS REFLECTED IN THIS CHAPTER:

CEC Content Standard #2 states that special educators

- Know and demonstrate respect for their students first as unique human beings.

- Understand the similarities and differences in human development and the characteristics between and among individuals with and without exceptional learning needs.

- Understand how exceptional conditions can interact with the domains of human development.

WORKING THE **STANDARDS** (continued)

- Understand how the experiences of individuals with exceptional learning needs can impact the individuals' ability to learn, interact socially, and live as fulfilled, contributing members of the community.

CEC Content Standard #3 states that special educators understand the effects that an exceptional condition can have on an individual's learning in school and throughout life.

CEC Content Standard #4 states that special educators select, adapt, and use these instructional strategies to promote challenging learning results in general and special curricula and to appropriately modify learning environments for individuals with exceptional learning needs.

CEC Content Standard #7 states that special educators

- Use individualized strategies to enhance language development and teach communication skills to individuals with exceptional learning needs.

- Are familiar with augmentative, alternative, and assistive technologies to support and enhance communication of individuals with exceptional needs.

CEC Content Standard #9 states that special educators are aware of how their own and others' attitudes, behaviors, and ways of communicating can influence their practice.

CEC Content Standard #10 states that special educators promote and advocate the learning and well-being of individuals with exceptional learning needs across a wide range of settings and a range of different learning experiences.

BACK TO THE CASES

The standards and principles just listed relate to the cases described at the beginning of this chapter: Seth and Rick. The questions and activities that follow demonstrate how these standards and principles, along with other concepts that you have learned about in this chapter, connect to the everyday activities of all teachers.

Seth

For a number of reasons, Seth lacks basic math skills. In the next eighth-grade team meeting, one team member suggests that you (the math teacher) just give him a calculator and be done with it. However, you think you can teach Seth these skills. (See INTASC Principles 2.02, 4.07, and 9.02; and CEC Standards 4, 9, and 10.) Based on what you learned about instructional methods in Chapter 5 and characteristics of students like Seth in this chapter, what instructional methods will you tell the team member you will use with Seth? Explain why you think these will work for him.

Rick

Rick has been punished for his behavior many, many times, with little resulting change in his behavior patterns. After reading about disciplining students with emotional disturbance (see the Professional Edge on page 252), you determine that you should be proactive rather than reactive. Outline a plan that you might use with Rick based on those principles. (See INTASC Principles 2.02, 4.04, and 4.07; and CEC Standards 4 and 7.) You may not be able to include specific strategies, reinforcers, or punishments at this point, but you should be able to explain how you can meet each of the principles found in the Professional Edge by referring to previous chapters as well as this one.

Visit the companion website (http://www.ablongman. com/friend4e) for a complete correlation of this chapter to the INTASC Principles and CEC Standards.

Further **Readings**

Forness, S. R., Walker, H. M., & Kavale, K. A. (2003). Psychiatric disorders and treatments: A primer for teachers. *Teaching Exceptional Children, 36*(2), 42–49.

This article provides essential information for teachers on the diagnosis and treatment of child psychiatric disorders including oppositional defiant and conduct disorders, attention deficit–hyperactivity disorders, depression, anxiety, schizophrenia, and autism spectrum disorder.

Rhode, G., Jensen, W. R., & Morgan, D. P. (2003). *The tough kid new teacher kit: Practical classroom management survival strategies for the new teacher.* Longmont, CO: Sopris West.

This book offers a variety of practical strategies and ideas that can be readily carried out by classroom teachers. The book also suggests a number of resources to help teachers in the area of behavioral, social, and academic assessments for challenging students.

Shaywitz, S. (2003). *Overcoming dyslexia: A new and complete science-based program for reading problems at any level.* New York: Knopf.

This is an excellent introductory book for parents and teachers on the causes of and treatments for severe reading problems. The author takes the latest scientific research on reading disabilities and translates it into a very readable, practical book.

Silver, L. B. (1998). *The misunderstood child: Understanding and coping with your child's learning disabilities* (3rd ed.). New York: Times Books.

This is another very readable book on the topic of learning disabilities: What they are and how to treat them.

CHAPTER 8

Other Students with Special Needs

LEARNER OBJECTIVES

After you read this chapter, you will be able to

1. Describe students protected through Section 504 and the accommodations general education teachers can make for them.

2. Explain accommodations general education teachers can make to address the special needs of students with attention deficit–hyperactivity disorder.

3. Outline the adaptations that students who are gifted and talented may need in general education classrooms.

4. Explain how cultural diversity influences education, critically analyzing your own response to students from cultures other than your own and your skills for addressing their needs.

5. Describe how general education teachers can accommodate students at risk for school failure, including students affected by poverty, abuse or neglect, substance abuse, and other factors.

KEY TERMS AND CONCEPTS

Attention deficit–hyperactivity disorder (ADHD) (p. 271)

Bilingual education programs (p. 291)

Child abuse (p. 293)

Child neglect (p. 293)

English-language learners (ELLs) (p. 291)

Fetal alcohol effects (FAE) (p. 294)

Fetal alcohol syndrome (FAS) (p. 294)

Gifted and talented (p. 278)

Multicultural education (p. 291)

Section 504 (p. 267)

JOSÉ IS A STUDENT in Mr. Lee's seventh-grade math class. Mr. Lee comments that José is never completely still in class—he drums his pencil, plays with his calculator, or tears paper into thin strips. He also has noticed that José's attention is drawn to nearly anything that goes on in class—or outside. He watches as another student looks for something in her backpack, stares at a student sharpening a pencil, and stops working when the fan comes on in a computer at the side of the classroom. José seems distracted even when a cloud blocks the sun, momentarily dimming the light in the classroom. Instead of raising his hand during class discussions, José just blurts out what is on his mind, and he is as likely to make a comment about his older brother or his latest adventure in his neighborhood as he is to contribute a comment relevant to the topic being presented. José frequently is written up for behavior problems; the principal keeps reminding him that if he would *think* before he *acts* he would avoid most of the problems. José's grandmother reports that he is "all boy," much like his father was. She readily admits, however, that keeping up with him can be exhausting. ●

Does José have a disability? What are José's special needs? What is the responsibility of school personnel for meeting those needs?

LYDIA IS A FOURTH-GRADE student who is gifted and talented. She has been reading since age 3, and she frequently borrows her sister's high school literature anthology as a source of reading material. She knew most of the math concepts introduced in fourth grade before the school year began. She has a strong interest in learning Spanish and playing flute and piano, and she volunteers to read to residents of a local nursing home. Lydia's idea of a perfect afternoon is to have a quiet place to hide, a couple of wonderful books, and no one to bother her. Lydia's teacher, Mr. Judd, enjoys having her in class because she is so enthusiastic about learning, but he admits that Lydia's abilities are a little intimidating. He also has noticed that Lydia doesn't seem to have much in common with other students in class. She is a class leader but does not appear to have any close friends as other students do. ● *Is Lydia entitled to receive special services because of her giftedness? Is Lydia typical of students who are gifted or talented? What can Mr. Judd do to help Lydia reach her full potential? What social problems do students like Lydia encounter?*

TAM IS A JUNIOR in high school, but he doubts that he'll finish the school year. He describes school as pointless, and he sees that he has more important things to do than sit in classrooms learning about topics he believes have no relevance in his life. He is still coming to school only because he hates to hurt his mother's feelings by dropping out. He is absent often, especially from his first-block U.S. history class, and he usually does not bother to do homework or read assignments. Tam does not belong to any clubs at school nor does he participate in any athletics, and his counselor is concerned about his circle of friends outside of school. Last month, he was questioned by the police about a convenience-store robbery and then released, but rumors around school suggest he was part of a gang that committed the crime. After school, Tam hangs out with his friends, often congregating in the alley behind an electronics store and not returning home until well after midnight. Tam is considering an offer to run drugs that was recently made by Michael, a 21-year-old dropout whom Tam looks up to. Tam has a juvenile record; he is on probation for stealing a car with yet another of his friends. Michael told him, though, that the risks are minimal until he turns 18 and that his records will be expunged at that time even if he gets arrested. Tam's teachers describe him as unmotivated, a student who has vastly more potential than they see him using. ● *How common are students like Tam? What other characteristics and behaviors might Tam display in school? If Tam were your student, how would you try to reach him? What are your responsibilities to students like Tam?*

Most educators agree that many students who are not eligible to receive special education have needs as great as or greater than those of students protected by IDEA. For example, even though José has a significant attention problem, he does not qualify for special education. Lydia's teacher is concerned that he cannot possibly make time to provide the advanced instruction that would benefit her, but his school district does not offer any programs for students who are gifted or talented until middle school. Tam's teachers worry about his future and are frustrated that they cannot make his life better and help him reach his potential. They feel powerless to influence students like Tam who have so many difficulties in their young lives, and they question how traditional academic standards and activities can be made relevant for those students.

This chapter is about students who are not necessarily eligible for special education but whose learning is at risk and whose success often depends on the quality of the instruction they receive and the care taken by general education teachers. Did you attend school with students with special needs such as these? Were you one of those students? If either is the case, you bring to your teacher-preparation program an understanding and empathy that other teacher candidates may not have, and you may have a perspective on student diversity that you can draw on in addressing student needs. The students examined in this chapter include those who have functional disabilities protected by Section 504, the civil rights law introduced in Chapter 1, but not protected by IDEA, including those with attention deficit–hyperactivity disorder; as well as those who are gifted and talented; those whose native languages are not English and whose cultures differ significantly from that of most of their classmates; and those who are at risk because of life circumstances, including poverty, child abuse, drug abuse, and others factors.

CONNECTIONS

Review the information about IDEA and the procedures for serving students through special education in Chapters 1 and 2.

The rationale for discussing José, Lydia, Tam, and other students like them in this text has four parts:

1. Students with these types of special needs often benefit greatly from the same strategies that are successful for students with disabilities. Thus, one purpose is to remind you that the techniques explained throughout this text are applicable to many of your students, not just those who have IEPs.

2. You should recognize that you will teach many students with a tremendous diversity of needs resulting from many different causes, disability being just one potential factor. Creating appropriate educational opportunities for all your students is your responsibility.

3. Students with special needs often are referred for special education services because caring teachers recognize that they need help. It is essential that you realize that special education is much more than "help" and is reserved for just the specific groups of students already described in Chapters 5 and 6.

4. Although many special educators are committed to helping you meet the needs of all your students, including those at risk, they cannot take primary responsibility for teaching students like José, Lydia, and Tam. These are not students who "should be" in special education. They represent instead the increasingly diverse range of students that all teachers now instruct, and they highlight the importance of creating classrooms that respect this diversity and foster student learning regardless of students' special needs.

> These are not students who "should be" in special education. They represent instead the increasingly diverse range of students that all teachers now instruct.

This chapter also highlights how complex student needs have become (Bennett, 2003; Boethel, 2003). For example, you probably realize that students with disabilities also can have the special needs described here. For example, a student with a physical disability also might be academically gifted. A student with an intellectual disability also might live in poverty. A student with a learning disability might speak a language other than English at home. You probably recognize, too, that the student groups emphasized in this chapter are not necessarily distinct, even though it is convenient to discuss them as if they were. Students who live in poverty can also be gifted and members of a cultural minority. An abused student can be at risk because of drug abuse. Keep in mind as you read this chapter that your responsibility as a teacher for all students, regardless of their disabilities or other special needs, is to use the INCLUDE strategy to identify strengths and needs, arrange a supportive instructional environment, provide high-quality instruction, and foster student independence. When students have multiple special needs, these tasks can be especially challenging, and you should seek assistance from colleagues, parents, and other professional resources.

Which Students Are Protected by Section 504?

In Chapter 1, you learned that some students with special needs who do not meet the eligibility criteria for receiving services through IDEA are considered functionally disabled as defined by **Section 504** of the Vocational Rehabilitation Act of 1973. Students in this group are entitled to receive reasonable accommodations that help them benefit from school. These accommodations can include some of the same types of services and supports that students eligible through IDEA receive, but there are crucial differences between the two statutes as well (Miller, Bieker, & Copenhaver, 2002).

Understanding Section 504

First, the definition of a disability in Section 504 is considerably broader than it is in IDEA. In Section 504, any condition that substantially limits a major life activity, such as the ability to learn in school, is defined as a disability. This definition means that students with a wide range of needs that do not fall within the 13 federal disability categories for education are eligible for assistance through Section 504. For example, a student who is photophobic (that is, highly sensitive to bright light) might receive services through Section 504, and so also might students with significant attention problems, drug addiction, chronic health problems, communicable diseases, temporary disabilities resulting from accidents or injury, environmental illnesses, or alcoholism (Smith, 2001).

Second, unlike IDEA, no funds are provided to school districts to carry out the requirements of Section 504 (deBettencourt, 2002; Henderson, 2001). The expectation is that schools should take whatever steps are necessary, even if additional funds are required, to eliminate discrimination as defined through this statute. Third, the responsibility for making accommodations for students who qualify as disabled through Section 504 belongs to general education personnel, not special education personnel. Special educators might provide some informal assistance, but their aid is not mandated as it is in IDEA. The types of accommodations required vary based on student needs but could include alterations in the physical environment, such as providing a quiet workspace or a room with specialized lighting; modifications in instruction, such as decreasing the number of items in an assignment or allotting additional time to complete it; organizational assistance, such as checking a student's backpack to ensure that all materials for homework are there; and changes in a student's schedule, such as allowing a rest period. Individual school districts establish policies for meeting the requirements of Section 504 (Henderson, 2001). Table 8.1 summarizes the differences between these important laws.

For students to receive assistance through Section 504, their needs must be assessed and a decision made concerning their eligibility (deBettencourt, 2002). The regulations for Section 504 advise that a team be convened to manage this process, but this is not required. The assessment procedures can be similar to those used for IDEA, but school districts probably should assess some students for Section 504 assistance who would not be assessed at all for special education services. Students determined eligible have Section 504 plans that cover their instructional programs as well as after-school programs, field trips, summer programs, and other extracurricular activities (Smith, 2002). The plans outline the accommodations needed, who is to implement them, and how they will be monitored. A sample of the types of accommodations that may be incorporated into a Section 504 plan is presented in the Professional Edge on page 270.

Section 504 and Students with Medical or Health Needs

Although many students can qualify for assistance through Section 504, two common groups are addressed in this chapter: students with medical or health needs and students with attention deficit–hyperactivity disorder (ADHD). The first group is discussed here; students with ADHD are covered in the subsequent section.

Students with chronic health or medical problems, for example, those with communicable diseases, who are not eligible for IDEA services according to established criteria and as determined by a multidisciplinary team, comprise one of the major

W W W
R E S O U R C E S

You can find a wide variety of presentation materials and papers related to Section 504 at the website of the Council of Educators for Students with Disabilities, at http://www.504idea.org/504resources.html.

TABLE 8.1 Examples of Differences between IDEA and Section 504

Component	IDEA	Section 504
Purpose	To provide federal financial assistance to state and local education agencies to assist them in educating children with disabilities.	To eliminate discrimination on the basis of disability in all programs and activities receiving federal financial assistance.
Individuals protected	All school-age children who fall within 1 or more of 13 specific categories of disability and who, because of such disability, need special education and related services.	All school-age children who have a physical or mental impairment that substantially limits a major life activity, have a record of such an impairment, or are regarded as having such an impairment. Major life activities include walking, seeing, hearing, speaking, breathing, learning, working, caring for oneself, and performing manual tasks.
Free and appropriate public education (FAPE)	Requires that FAPE be provided to only those protected students who, because of disability, need special education or related services.	Requires that FAPE be provided to only those protected students who, because of disability, need regular education accommodations, special education, or related services.
	Defines FAPE as special education and related services. A student can receive related services under IDEA if and only if the student is provided special education and needs related services to benefit from special education.	Defines FAPE as regular or special education and related aids and services. A student can receive related services under Section 504 even if the student is in regular education full-time and is not provided any special education.
	Requires a written IEP and a required number of specific participants at the IEP meeting.	Does not require a written IEP document, but does require a plan prepared by a group of persons knowledgeable about the student.
Funding	Provides additional funding for protected students.	Does not provide additional funds. IDEA funds may not be used to serve students protected only under Section 504.
Evaluations	Requires reevaluations to be conducted at least every 3 years.	Requires periodic reevaluations. The IDEA schedule for reevaluation can suffice.
	Does not require a reevaluation before a change of placement, but evaluation data, including progress toward goals and objectives, should be considered.	Requires reevaluation before a significant change in placement.
Placement procedures	An IEP meeting is required before any change in placement.	A reevaluation meeting is required before any "significant change" in placement.
Grievance procedures	Does not require a grievance procedure, nor a compliance officer.	Requires districts with more than 15 employees to (a) designate an employee to be responsible for assuring district compliance with Section 504, and (b) provide a grievance procedure for parents, students, and employees.
Due process	Contains detailed hearing rights and requirements.	Requires notice, the right to inspect records, the right to participate in a hearing and to be represented by counsel, and a review procedure.
Exhaustion	Requires the parent or guardian to pursue an administrative hearing before seeking redress in the courts.	Does not require an administrative hearing prior to Office for Civil Rights involvement or court action; compensatory damages possible.
Enforcement	Enforced by the U.S. Office of Special Education Programs (OSEP). Compliance is monitored by State department of education and OSEP.	Enforced by the U.S. Office for Civil Rights.

SOURCE: *Meeting the Needs of All Students,* by the Parent Advocacy Coalition for Educational Rights, 2004, Minneapolis, MN: Author. Retrieved December 5, 2004, from http://www.pacer.org/parent/504.html#IDEA504.

PROFESSIONAL EDGE

Section 504 Accommodations

Many types of accommodations can be written into Section 504 plans. The only guidelines are that the adjustments should be (a) individualized to meet students' needs and (b) reasonable, that is, designed to "level the playing field" for them. These accommodations should go beyond those typically offered to all students (for example, allowing students to choose from among several projects). Here are some examples of accommodations that are commonly found in Section 504 plans.

- Seat the student nearest to where the teacher does most of his or her instruction.

- Provide clues such as clock faces indicating beginning and ending times for instruction or assignments.

- Establish a home–school communication system for monitoring behavior.

- Fold assignments in half so that the student is not overwhelmed by the quantity of work.

- Make directions telegraphic, that is, concise and clear.

- Tape-record lessons so the student can listen to them again.

- Use multisensory presentation techniques, including peer tutors, experiments, games, and cooperative groups.

- Provide practice tests that are very similar in structure and appearance to actual tests.

- Mark right answers instead of wrong answers.

- Send a set of textbooks to be left at home so that the student does not have to remember to bring books from school.

- Provide books on tape so that the student can listen to assignments instead of reading them.

Remember that Section 504 accommodations may vary greatly depending on a student's special needs such as a medical condition or physical problem, drug or alcohol abuse, ADHD, or others.

SOURCES: Adapted from *Ideas for an IEP or Section 504 Plan*, by D. Simms, 2000. Retrieved on September 13, 2000, from http://www.angelfire.com/ny/Debsimms/education.html; and *Sevier County (TN) School System Section 504 Examples of Program Accommodations and Adjustments*. Retrieved December 3, 2004, from http://ww.slc.sevier.org/504ana.htm.

groups that can qualify for assistance through Section 504. For example, a student who has asthma not serious enough to be considered a disability under IDEA might have a Section 504 plan. The plan could address accommodations related to the student's need for occasional rest periods, opportunities to take medication, exemption from certain physical activities, and provisions to make up assignments and tests after absences. A student with severe allergies might have a plan that specifies materials in school that cannot be used (for example, paints, chalk, peanut products), guidelines for participation in physical education, and requirements for providing assignments that can be completed at home if necessary. A student who is diabetic might have a plan that addresses permission to use the restroom whenever requested; permission to keep a bottle of water present even during class; permission to test blood glucose whenever necessary, including in the classroom; and postponement of high-stakes testing without penalty if blood glucose is too high or too low.

> You may find that some students with Section 504 plans have learning and behavioral problems that at times seem very similar to those of students with disabilities.

As you can tell, some of the responsibility for implementing Section 504 plans belongs to administrators, who authorize physical modifications to classrooms and make arrangements for students to have rest periods or take medications. Your responsibility is to implement instructional adaptations outlined in the plan, such as providing assignments in advance and allowing extra time for work completion. Your interactions with students protected by Section 504 differ from your interactions with other students only in your responsibility to make the accommodations that are required. However, you may find that some students with Section 504 plans have learning and behavior problems that at times seem very similar to those of students with disabilities. These students benefit from the many strategies presented in this text.

How Can You Accommodate Students with Attention Deficit–Hyperactivity Disorder?

Students with attention problems have been a concern of teachers for many years. In fact, labels such as *hyperkinesis* and *minimal brain dysfunction* have been applied to these students since the 1940s (Barkley, 1998a), and the first medication to help them was developed in the 1950s (Eli Lilly, 2003). The challenges that these students present for teachers, parents, and peers have raised awareness that they have a disorder, have prompted research about their characteristics and needs, and have fostered the development of new interventions for assisting them in school and everyday life. Some students with significant attention problems as described in this section are eligible for services through IDEA, but many receive assistance through Section 504 (National Institute of Mental Health [NIMH], 2002).

The term for significant attention problems is **attention deficit–hyperactivity disorder (ADHD),** a condition defined in the *Diagnostic and Statistical Manual of Mental Disorders (DSM–IV–TR)* (American Psychiatric Association, 2000). ADHD is diagnosed when individuals have chronic and serious inattentiveness, hyperactivity, and/or impulsivity that is more severe and occurs more frequently than in peers. You also might hear the term *attention deficit disorder (ADD)* being used to label the condition. *ADD* is an earlier term for describing attention problems, and some professionals use the terms *ADHD* and *ADD* interchangeably.

Students with ADHD generally have symptoms that fall into one of these three categories:

1. *ADHD—predominantly inattentive type.* Students in this group often appear to daydream. They may not hear teacher directions, sometimes skip parts of an assignment that they do not notice, and frequently lose things. However, they do not move around more than their peers.

2. *ADHD—predominantly hyperactive-impulsive type.* Students in this group are hyperactive, that is, they move around far more than their peers, and they tend to be impulsive, acting before thinking. They squirm in their seats, tap pencils or fingers, and blurt out answers during instruction.

3. *ADHD—combined type.* Students in this group display the characteristics of both of the other types of ADHD. They experience extraordinary difficulty both in focusing their attention and in restricting their movement.

Think about José, the student you met at the beginning of the chapter. Which type of ADHD seems to best characterize him?

Estimates of the prevalence of ADHD range from less than 1 percent to more than 20 percent of school-age children (National Center on Birth Defects and Developmental Disabilities, 2003), but experts seem to agree that it affects approximately 3 to 7 percent of students (Salend & Rohena, 2003), making it the most commonly diagnosed childhood psychiatric disorder. Estimating prevalence is difficult because no single "official" census of these students is gathered and research results vary depending on the sample of students studied (American Academy of Pediatrics [AAP], 2000). Boys are diagnosed with ADHD approximately three times more frequently than girls, but that may be because boys' symptoms are more noticeable than girls' (Newcorn et

WWW
RESOURCES

You can access the website for Children and Adults with Attention-Deficit/ Hyperactivity Disorder (CHADD) at http://www. chadd.org. CHADD is a nonprofit organization dedicated to bettering the lives of those with ADHD and their families.

FYI

Although most professionals in the United States agree that ADHD is a serious and potentially lifelong disorder, a few authors and some professionals from other countries speculate that ADHD is mostly a phenomenon of American culture.

al., 2001). ADHD also occurs frequently with other disabilities. Specifically, approximately 26 percent of students with learning disabilities and 43 percent of students with behavioral or emotional disabilities also have ADHD (Forness & Kavale, 2001).

The causes of ADHD are not clear. Researchers find that one important factor is heredity (Joseph, 2000). Students who have ADHD are likely to have a family pattern of this disorder. In fact, if two parents have ADHD, their child is 3 times more likely than other children to have it as well (NIMH, 2000). Researchers also have found that the brains of individuals with ADHD are different from those of others: The amount of electrical activity is unusually low in the parts of the brain regulating attention, and the chemicals in the brain that transmit information may not function properly (Barkley et al., 2002; Swanson, 2000). The environment also may play a role in causing ADHD. Children prone to have this disorder who live in very unstructured homes are more likely to actually develop it. A few authors have suggested that ADHD is the result of food additives or food allergies, inner ear problems, vitamin deficiencies, or bacterial infections, but none of these causes has been demonstrated to be valid (NIMH, 2003).

Usually, a diagnosis of ADHD is the result of individualized testing for cognitive ability and achievement, a medical screening completed by a doctor, and behavior ratings completed by family members and school professionals (AAP, 2000). Based on that information, a school team decides whether the student's disorder meets the criteria of other health impairment under IDEA, whether a Section 504 plan is needed, or whether no specific intervention is warranted.

Characteristics and Needs of Students with Attention Deficit–Hyperactivity Disorder

The characteristics and needs of students with attention deficit–hyperactivity disorder can vary considerably. However, although all students might occasionally demonstrate some symptoms of ADHD, students diagnosed with this disorder display many of them prior to 7 years of age. Further, their symptoms are chronic and extraordinary. For example, Mr. Mitchell, a high school social studies teacher, talked about Benjamin, one of his students:

> I keep Ben seated right in the front of the room, next to where I'm most likely to stand while I'm teaching the large group. When I ask the class a question, Ben is likely to jump out of his seat and wave his hand in my face or jump up and down to get me to call on him. Sometimes I try to make eye contact with him to get him to sit down, but it usually works better if I just put my hand on his shoulder and push a little. When my students are working on their own, I may turn around to notice that Ben is "sitting" by balancing on the top of the back of his seat. If I make a general comment to the class about settling down, everyone does—except Ben. I try very hard not to correct him publicly since he really doesn't seem to know what he is doing. Having Ben certainly has taught me a new kind of patience.

Cognitively, students with ADHD can function at any level, although the disorder is usually diagnosed in students who do not have intellectual disabilities. Students who are below average in ability and achievement, students who are average learners, and students who are gifted and talented all can have ADHD. Their shared characteristics relate to how their brains function. That is, ADHD is not really about inattention; rather, it is the inability to *regulate* attention. The disorder develops when students fail to develop *executive functions*, that is, the ability to carry out the mental activities that help most people regulate their behavior. Executive functions include these four activities:

1. *Working memory.* The ability to remember what tasks are supposed to be done and how much time there is to do them

2. *Self-directed speech.* The silent self-talk that most people use to manage complex tasks

FYI

Behavior rating scales frequently are used to determine whether a student has ADHD. Commonly used rating scales include the Achenbach Behavior Checklist for Parents, the Connors Rating Scale, and the Behavior Problems Checklist.

ANALYZE
AND REFLECT

What characteristics of ADHD does Ben display? What are some examples of environmental, instructional, and behavior strategies that might help Ben in Mr. Mitchell's class and throughout the school day?

3. *Control of emotions and motivation.* The ability to talk oneself into calming down when faced with a difficult or frustrating task

4. *Reconstitution.* The ability to combine skills learned across a variety of settings in order to carry out a new task, such as a student's knowledge that the rule for speaking in a low voice applies not only in their classrooms but also in the hallways, lunchroom, and office

Think about friends from high school who were diagnosed with ADHD or students with whom you now work. How do they display these problems in executive functions in school? At home? In other settings?

Academically, students with ADHD may have difficulty in reading, especially long passages for which comprehension demands are high; in spelling, which requires careful attention to detail; in listening, especially when a large amount of highly detailed information is presented; and in math, which often requires faster computational skills than students with ADHD can handle. All these learning problems can be related to students' problems in executive functions.

Socially and emotionally, students with ADHD are at risk for a variety of problems (Bagwell, Molina, Pelham, & Hoza, 2001; Lesesne, Abramowitz, Perou, & Brann, 2000). For example, they are more likely to be depressed or to have extremely low confidence or self-esteem. Likewise, they are likely to have conflicts with parents, teachers, or other authority figures. They are often unpopular with peers, frequently are rejected by them, and have difficulty making friends. Students with ADHD may feel demoralized, but they may also be bossy and obstinate.

The frequency of behavior problems of students with ADHD varies. Students whose disorder is inattention might not act out in class, but they can be disruptive when they try to find lost items or constantly ask classmates for assistance in finding their place in a book or carrying out directions. Students with hyperactive-impulsive disorder often come to teachers' attention immediately because they have so many behavior problems. Their constant motion, refusal to work, and other behaviors can be problematic even in the most tolerant environments. Examples of the behaviors displayed by students with ADHD are included in Figure 8.1.

FYI

Determining whether a student has ADHD is a decision that can be made only by a pediatrician or a family physician. Educators should never offer a diagnosis to parents, but they may encourage the parents to contact their child's doctor to discuss their concerns.

FIGURE 8.1 Behavior Characteristics of Students with Attention Deficit–Hyperactivity Disorder

Inattention

- Making careless mistakes
- Having difficulty sustaining attention
- Seeming not to listen
- Failing to finish tasks
- Having difficulty organizing
- Avoiding tasks requiring sustained attention
- Losing things
- Becoming easily distracted
- Being forgetful

Hyperactivity

- Fidgeting
- Being unable to stay seated
- Moving excessively (restless)
- Having difficulty making and keeping friends
- Being "on the go"
- Talking excessively
- Being prone to temper tantrums
- Acting in a bossy way
- Being defiant

Impulsivity

- Blurting answers before questions are completed
- Having difficulty awaiting turn
- Interrupting/intruding upon others
- Acting before thinking
- Being viewed by teenage peers as immature
- Failing to read directions

SOURCES: Adapted from "The Practical Aspects of Diagnosing and Managing Children with Attention Deficit Hyperactivity Disorder," by M. L. Wolraich and A. Baumgaertel, 1997, *Clinical Pediatrics, 36,* pp. 497–504; and "Arranging the Classroom with an Eye (and Ear) to Students with ADHD," 2001, *Teaching Exceptional Children, 34*(2), pp. 72–81.

How can you arrange your classroom to improve learning for students with ADHD? What are other interventions you can try for these students?

Interventions for Students with Attention Deficit–Hyperactivity Disorder

As a result of recent studies (MTA Cooperative Group, 2004), professionals now are recommending that five types of interventions be used for students with ADHD: environmental supports, academic interventions, behavior interventions, parent education, and use of medication.

ENVIRONMENTAL SUPPORTS ● The way you arrange your classroom can either foster learning for students with ADHD or impede it. To help students, your classroom should be free from distracting items such as mobiles hung from the ceiling that twirl in the air currents and piles of extra books or art supplies. Some students might benefit if you let them work using a desk carrel, a three-sided cardboard divider that blocks visual distractions. You also can provide a classroom environment conducive to learning for these students by having very clear classroom rules and routines. Further, if a change in the normal pattern of classroom activities is necessary, you can alert all students and make sure to support students with ADHD by assigning peer partners to assist them or by quietly letting them know what activity is next. Finally, you can consciously pace your instruction to mix tedious or repetitive classroom activities with those that permit students more variety and activity.

ACADEMIC INTERVENTIONS ● Students with ADHD typically struggle with academic achievement, although the extent of their learning problems varies considerably (Reid, 1999). To assist students with ADHD academically, try to emphasize only essential information. For example, keep oral instructions as brief as possible. Rather than giving directions, providing multiple examples, and then recapping what you have said, instead list directions by number using very clear language (for example, "First, put your name on the paper; second, write a one sentence response for each question; third, put your paper in the basket on the counter by the door"). When reading for comprehension, students with ADHD tend to perform better on short passages than on long ones. Thus, it is better to ask a student with ADHD to read just a small part of a long story or expository passage and check comprehension at that point, then have him or her read another part and so on, than to read an entire story or chapter. Similarly, when older students have lengthy assignments, it is better to break them into smaller parts, assigning each component individually and checking progress. In math, students should be given extended periods of time to complete computational work because their attentional problems interfere with their efficiency in this type of task. In all large-group instruction, keep the pace rapid and provide many opportunities for students to participate, such as trading answers to questions with a partner, working with manipulatives, or repeating answers as a class after one student has responded. Additional suggestions for helping students with ADHD attend during instruction are presented in Figure 8.2.

In addition to the types of interventions just outlined, most recommendations for helping students with ADHD academically are similar to those used for students with learning and emotional disabilities, and for other students who need highly structured and especially clear instruction. The chapters that follow this one feature many instructional approaches that meet the needs of students with ADHD.

BEHAVIOR INTERVENTIONS ● For responding to behavior, professionals generally recommend interventions that emphasize structure and rewards, such as specific verbal praise ("Martin, you began your work as soon as I gave the assignment"), stickers or other symbols of appropriate behavior ("Tamatha, you will earn a sticker for each five math problems you complete"), and games that emphasize rewards for positive classroom behaviors (Wells et al., 2000). Reprimands or consequences may be

FIGURE 8.2 Strategies for Teaching Students with ADHD

- Give clear and complete directions for all in-class assignments and homework, including the amount of time allotted and evaluation criteria.
- Provide a rationale to students for the assignments they are asked to complete.
- Check students' understanding of assignments by having them repeat the directions back.
- Break long assignments into several shorter assignments.
- Schedule time while students work in class for them to obtain teacher feedback about their progress.
- Use the Internet to remind students about homework assignments.
- Motivate students by commenting on their strengths and accomplishments.
- Ensure that instruction is fast-paced.
- Use high levels of student participation and movement during instruction.
- Tailor questions to students' knowledge and skill levels.
- Use visual organizers (for example, graphic organizers, semantic webs).
- Help students remember important instructional tasks by using learning strategies (see Chapter 11).
- Draw on student interests during instruction (for example, their culture and experiences).
- Have students work with a peer partner.

SOURCE: Adapted from "Educational Interventions for Students with ADD," by S. J. Salend, H. Elhoweris, and D. vanGarderen, 2003, *Intervention in School and Clinic, 38,* 280–288.

needed at times, but these should be mild and used less often than rewards. As the IN-CLUDE strategy outlines, you should first consider environmental demands and address these as a means of preventing behavior problems. For example, students with ADHD exhibit less acting-out behavior when they sit near the front of the room, and as noted earlier, they often benefit from working in an area with few visual or auditory distractions (for example, away from posters or bulletin board displays and computers signaling with tones and music). Likewise, allowing a student to move from one desk to another in the classroom and permitting the student to stand while working are examples of simple environmental support strategies that may help prevent serious behavior problems.

If a student needs to be corrected, provide a clear and direct but calm reprimand. If you say, "Tamatha, I know you are trying hard, but please try to remember to raise your hand before speaking," Tamatha might not even realize that you are correcting her. A preferred response would be to say quietly to her, "Tamatha, do not call out answers. Raise your hand." This message is much clearer.

PARENT EDUCATION ● Yet another dimension of working successfully with students with ADHD involves parent education (Wells et al., 2000). Although offering parent education generally is not the sole responsibility of a new teacher, you can contribute in this area by suggesting that parents of students with this disorder be invited to sessions to learn strategies for responding to their children's behavior, ways to create a discipline system that includes both rewards and consequences, tips for helping these children to make friends, and skills for working with school professionals to ensure academic success. Parents of students in middle school and high school also benefit from learning about their children's rights and responsibilities as they graduate from school and enter college or a work setting. Parent education by itself is not sufficient to address the needs of your students with ADHD, but it can help to maximize the benefits of the other interventions.

INCLUDE

RESEARCH
N O T E

Research indicates that students with ADHD are likely to have other disabilities or disorders as well. For example, approximately 26 percent of students identified as having learning disabilities are also diagnosed with ADHD, and approximately 43 percent of students identified with emotional and behavior disorders also are diagnosed with ADHD (Forness & Kavale, 2001).

USE OF MEDICATION ● The most common intervention for students with ADHD, and the intervention that has been demonstrated by researchers to have the most benefit (MTA, 2004), is the prescription of medication. Prescribing medication is a decision that is made by parents with their physicians; educators may not tell parents that a child needs this intervention. Approximately 2.5 million students take medication for ADHD (Head, Robison, Sclar, Skaer, & Galin, 1999), and medication is effective for 70 to 80 percent of the students for whom it is prescribed, especially if combined with other interventions (that is, environmental supports, academic and behavior interventions, and parent education) (Forness & Kavale, 2001).

> The most common intervention for students with ADHD is the prescription of medication.

The most common type of medication prescribed for students with ADHD is stimulant medication, including Ritalin, Cylert, Adderall, and Focalin. However, students may take other medications, including antidepressants such as Norpramin, Tofranil, and Zoloft; antihypertensives such as Clonidine and Tenex; and Strattera, a relatively new medication developed specifically for this disorder. More information about medications prescribed for ADHD is described in Table 8.2.

Despite the apparent effectiveness of medications in treating ADHD, their use remains somewhat controversial (Kollins, Barkley, & DuPaul, 2001). For example, teachers encounter the problem of students not consistently taking their medication, or of them sharing their medication. This situation can result in a loss of learning or even endanger other students. Another issue concerns the proper dosage. Some researchers contend that dosages high enough to cause an improvement in behavior can negatively affect students' academic learning and performance (Forness & Kavale, 2001). A third area of concern pertains to side effects. Some parents and professionals believe that medication may suppress weight and height gain, even though recent research indicates that this side effect is temporary (Kollins et al., 2001). Yet other parents are concerned that taking medication may predispose their children to future drug use and problems in adulthood, another perception that has not been supported by research (Barkley, 2004; Biederman, 2003). As a teacher, your responsibilities related to medication are indirect. You should know about the medications commonly prescribed, alert your school nurse and parents if you suspect that a change in student learning or behavior might be related to medication, and be prepared to respond to parental and medical inquiries regarding the effect of medication on particular students.

FYI

Although parents who chose to address their children's ADHD with medication used to have few choices—mostly whether to give standard or sustained-release Ritalin—the number of medications now makes such decisions far more complex. You may be asked to monitor students who are being tried on new medication to determine whether any adverse effects (for example, drowsiness) are occurring.

Families of Children with Attention Deficit–Hyperactivity Disorder

Just like families of other students with disabilities or special needs, families of students with ADHD cannot be described using a single set of characteristics. However, it is fair to say that for many families, having a child with ADHD affects every area of family functioning and adds significant stress for parents and siblings both at home and in interactions with school personnel (Colson & Brandt, 2000). For example, Tate is a student with ADHD. Nearly every day at school, he has some sort of negative experience, because of either inattention during instruction or a behavior disruption during lunch or passing periods. Because of this, Tate's parents receive quite a few late-afternoon phone calls from school personnel, and they, trying to respond to the teachers and keep clear their expectations for his school performance, often punish Tate by taking away computer time or some other privilege. Tate dislikes school, dreads the phone ringing when he gets home, and feels like all his parents ever do is criticize him. His parents are very concerned that they are having a more and more difficult time "getting through" to Tate about his behavior. What seems to be developing

TABLE 8.2 Overview of Medications Commonly Used for ADHD

Brand Name [Generic Name]	Type of Medication	Advantages	Disadvantages	Comments
Concerta [Methylphenidate]	Psychostimulant	Works quickly. Lasts up to 12 hours.	Not recommended for children in families with a history of tic disorders.	First true once-a-day ADHD medication approved by the FDA.
Ritalin [Methylphenidate]	Psychostimulant	Excellent safety record. Easy to use and evaluate. Works in 15–20 minutes.	Lasts only 4 hours. Must be administered frequently.	The most frequently prescribed medication. Watch for tics or Tourette's syndrome.
Ritalin SR (sustained release) [Methylphenidate]	Psychostimulant	Excellent safety record. Easy to use and evaluate. Longer-lasting (6–8 hours).	Does not work as well as regular Ritalin.	Can be used along with regular Ritalin.
Focalin [Dextromethylphenidate]	Psychostimulant	Works quickly. Only half the dose of Ritalin is needed.	Lasts only 4–5 hours.	A refined form of Ritalin.
Dexedrine [Dextroamphetamine]	Psychostimulant	Excellent safety record. Rapid onset (20–30 minutes).	Lasts only 4 hours. Must be administered frequently.	Some students have fewer side effects than when on Ritalin.
Dexedrine (sustained release) [Dextroamphetamine]	Psychostimulant	Excellent safety record. Longer-lasting (6–8 hours).	Slower onset (1–2 hours).	Can be used along with standard Dexedrine. This permits once-daily dosing.
Adderall [Single-entity amphetamine product]	Psychostimulant	Works quickly. May last somewhat longer than other standard stimulants (3–6 hours).	High potential for abuse.	May help students for whom Ritalin has not been effective.
Adderall XR [Single-entity amphetamine product]	Psychostimulant	Works quickly and lasts about 12 hours.	High potential for abuse.	Not recommended for long-term use.
Tofranil and Norpramin [Imipramine and desipramine]	Antidepressant	Long-lasting (12–24 hours). Can be administered at night. Often works when stimulants do not.	Has possible side effects. May take 1–3 weeks for full effects. Should not be started and stopped abruptly.	High doses may improve depression symptoms and mood swings.
Catapress [Clonidine]	Antihypertensive	Can be used with students with Tourette's syndrome.	Tablets are shorter-lasting (4 hours). Patches are expensive.	Often has positive effect on defiant behavior.
Strattera [Atomoxetine hydrochloride]	Norepinephrine reuptake inhibitor	Lasts about 8–10 hours. A noncontrolled prescription medication.	Relatively new medication. Long-term effects on children are not known.	First nonstimulant ADHD medication approved by the FDA.

SOURCE: Medication chart to treat attention deficit disorders, by H. C. Parker, 2003. Retrieved December 2, 2004, from http://www.ldonline.org/ld_indepth/add_adhd/add_medication_chart.html; and *Special Education: Contemporary Perspectives for School Professionals* (p. 231), by M. Friend, 2005, Boston: Allyn and Bacon.

is a negative cycle of teacher–parent–child interactions that is likely to lead to frustration and ineffective intervention (LeFever, Villers, Morrow, & Vaughn, 2002).

When working with families like Tate's, your job as a teacher is to try to build positive relationships by encouraging parents to reward their children for their successes and by helping parents see their children's strengths. Some parents struggle with their own role in their children's disorder, particularly when they believe that a child is "just like his father." Teachers have to be careful not to blame parents for their children's

ADHD, but, at the same time, not to condone inappropriate student behavior that a parent might excuse by saying that the child can't help it.

Families face additional concerns as their children with ADHD reach adolescence and adulthood. Although professionals used to think that children outgrew ADHD as they approached adolescence, it is now clear that for most individuals it is a lifetime disorder (Barkley, 2004; Casey, 2003). Adolescents with ADHD may experience more negative moods than other teens, and they may spend more time with friends, and less time with family, and be prone to tobacco and alcohol abuse (Whalen, Jamner, Henker, Delfino, & Lozano, 2002). Parents and family members are faced with responding to these children's emotions and potentially harmful behaviors (McCleary, 2002).

> Although professionals used to think that children outgrew ADHD as they approached adolescence, it is now clear that for most individuals it is a lifetime disorder.

Finally, mention should be made of varied family responses to ADHD diagnosis and treatment based on cultural differences. For example, in one study researchers investigated the perceptions of Mexican, Mexican American, and Puerto Rican mothers toward the behavior of their children with ADHD (Schmitz & Velez, 2003). They found that, across these three Latino subgroups, mothers who were the least acculturated were the least tolerant of their children's hyperactive behavior. In another study, parents from Caucasian, African American, and Hispanic groups in one community were queried about ADHD. Although children from the three groups were identified as having ADHD in approximately the same proportion, African American parents were less likely than Caucasian parents to agree to medication as an intervention, and Hispanic parents were the least likely to agree (Rowland, Umback, Stallone, Nafetl, Bohlig, & Sandler, 2002).

How Can You Accommodate Students Who Are Gifted and Talented?

WWW
RESOURCES

At the website for the University of Connecticut's Neag Center for Gifted Education and Talent Development (http://www.gifted.uconn.edu), you can read about current trends in the field, programs for students who are gifted and talented, and resources to help teachers to address these students' needs.

In addition to students who are not able to meet typical curricular expectations, you also will have in your classroom students who have extraordinary abilities and skills. The term used to describe these students is **gifted and talented.** *Giftedness* traditionally has referred to students with extraordinary abilities across many academic areas and *talent* to students with extraordinary abilities in a specific area. Now, however, the terms often are used interchangeably. The federal definition for this group of students is stated in the 1988 Gifted and Talented Students Education Act (P.L. 100-297), which identifies children and youth who possess demonstrated or potential high-performance capability in intellectual, creative, specific academic and leadership areas, or the performing and visual arts. The federal definition further clarifies that these students need services in school that other students do not. However, unlike services offered through IDEA, federal legislation does not require specific services for gifted and talented students, and so the extent to which programs exist is largely determined by state and local policies.

An ongoing discussion in defining giftedness and serving these students concerns prevalence. Just like several other groups of students with special needs that you have learned about, the reported prevalence of giftedness varies considerably from location to location, depending largely on the definitions adopted by states and school districts, funding, and identification procedures. Currently, between 2 and 22 percent of the students in any school district may receive services as gifted and talented, but the average is 12 percent (Council of State Directors of Programs for the Gifted, 2001). This is approximately the same percentage of students as the overall percentage receiving services as students with disabilities.

Prevalence of giftedness and talent also is greatly affected by two other factors. First, over the past several years, researchers and writers have offered alternative definitions of giftedness and have questioned traditional criteria for identification that rely on intelligence measures (that is, IQ tests). For example, Tomlinson (2001) notes that intelligence is not static and that schools should create opportunities in supportive environments to maximize the potential of all instead of limiting services to just a few selected students.

Another conceptualization of giftedness is one that you may already have studied. Gardner (1993) conceptualizes intelligence as being multifaceted. He argues that measured IQ is far too narrow a concept of intelligence and that a person's ability to problem solve, especially when in a new situation, is a more useful way of thinking about intelligence. Gardner (1983) has proposed that there are *multiple intelligences* that describe the broad array of talents that students possess, and he describes eight of these:

1. verbal/linguistic
2. visual/spatial
3. logical/mathematical
4. bodily/kinesthetic
5. musical
6. intrapersonal (that is self-understanding)
7. interpersonal
8. naturalist

Notice how wide a range of abilities is captured in this notion of intelligence. What is the impact of this and the other alternative views of intelligence on services for students who are gifted and talented? What does this information imply for you as a school professional?

The second factor that affects the number of students identified as gifted and talented is the notion of potential. Although some students who are talented can be easily identified because they use their special abilities and are willing to be recognized for them, some gifted students go unnoticed. These students mask their skills from peers and teachers because low expectations are set for them or their unique needs are not nurtured. Groups at risk for being underidentified include young boys, adolescent girls, students who are so highly gifted and talented as to be considered geniuses, students from racially or culturally diverse groups, and students with disabilities (for example, Donovan & Cross, 2002; Gavin & Reis, 2003). In many school districts, focused attention has been placed on these groups to ensure that they are identified.

CONNECTIONS

The use of performance-based assessments, often helpful in identifying students who are gifted and talented, was discussed in more depth in Chapter 4.

> " Although some students who are talented can be easily identified because they use their special abilities and are willing to be recognized for them, some gifted students go unnoticed. "

Characteristics and Needs of Students Who Are Gifted and Talented

Students who are gifted and talented have a wide range of characteristics, and any one student considered gifted and talented can have just a few or many of these characteristics. Although early studies presented a limited number of descriptors, the studies frequently were conducted with high achievers from privileged backgrounds and did not take into account the diverse nature of today's society (Terman, 1925). More recently, especially with the increasingly recognized need to address giftedness and talent

FYI

Students who have disabilities but who also are gifted and talented are referred to as *twice exceptional*. These students are entitled to special education services because of their disabilities, and they also access programs designed to nurture their talents.

among the entire population, including students from diverse groups (for example, Bonner, 2003), deciding whom to identify as gifted and talented and how to describe them has become complex. For example, professionals now recommend that identification procedures include both traditional and nontraditional measures. Traditional measures include intelligence and achievement tests, grades, and teacher recommendations. Nontraditional measures include nonverbal ability tests, creativity tests, student portfolios, performance-based measures (for example, giving a presentation or performing a dance), and parent and peer recommendations. The following information about student characteristics is intended to provide an overview of students who are gifted and talented and should be viewed as a sample of what is known, not as a comprehensive summary.

Cognitive Abilities and Academic Skills

The area of cognitive functioning and academic skills is the most delineated aspect of gifted education. Students who are gifted and talented generally have an extraordinary amount of knowledge because of insatiable curiosity; a keen memory; an unusual ability to concentrate; a wide variety of interests; high levels of language development and verbal ability; and the ability to generate original ideas. They also have an advanced ability to comprehend information using accelerated and flexible thought processes, a heightened ability to recognize relationships between diverse ideas, and a strong capacity to form and use conceptual frameworks. These students tend to be skilled problem solvers because they are better able than other students to pick out important information that helps them solve a problem and are more likely to monitor their problem-solving efforts (Donovan & Cross, 2002; Gallagher, 2002).

Students who are gifted and talented often are difficult to identify and challenging to teach. What kinds of intelligence might you recognize in your students? Within your inclusive classroom, how might you address the academic, social, and emotional needs of students who are gifted and talented?

The cognitive abilities of students who are gifted and talented sometimes lead them to high academic achievement, but not always. Consider these three students who are gifted and talented: Belinda was identified as gifted and talented in second grade. She has been reading since the age of 3, seems as comfortable interacting with adults as with her peers, and invariably becomes the leader of the groups of children with whom she plays, even if they are older. She enjoys school immensely and wants to be a university professor when she grows up. She is similar to Lydia, whom you read about at the beginning of this chapter. Tomas also is identified as gifted and talented. He has been taking violin and piano lessons since the age of 5, and now in the seventh grade he is a veteran pianist. He already plans to major in music theory when he goes to college, and he offers his own interpretations of both classical and contemporary music. In his academic studies, however, Tomas is slightly below average in achievement. He is also somewhat shy; he appears more comfortable with his musical instruments than with his peers. A third student to think about is Charles, a sophomore in high school. Charles lives in a neighborhood where education is not valued and getting high grades is viewed as showing off. As a result, the nearly straight A's that used to define Charles's report cards have dropped over the past year, and now he is earning mostly C's and D's. How might the needs of each of these students differ? How could you encourage them to reach their potential?

SOCIAL AND EMOTIONAL NEEDS ● Socially and emotionally, gifted and talented students can be well liked and emotionally healthy, or they can be unpopular and at risk for serious emotional problems. Affectively, they tend to have unusual sensitivity to others' feelings as well as highly developed emotional depth and intensity, a keen sense of humor that can be either supportive or hostile, and a sense of justice (Schuler, 2002). They often have a sense of obligation to help others and may become involved in community service activities. Teachers sometimes assign these students to help other students, an acceptable practice unless done so often that it interferes with advanced learning opportunities. These students often set high expectations for themselves and others, which can lead to frustration when those expectations are not met.

Because some gifted students have a superior ability to recognize and respond to others' feelings, they can be extremely popular with classmates and often sought after as helpmates. However, if they tend to "show off" their talents or repeatedly challenge adult authority, they may be perceived negatively by peers and teachers and may have problems developing appropriate social relationships (Colangelo & Davis, 2003). For example, Ms. Ogden is concerned about eighth grader Esteban. On some days, Esteban seems to have just a four-word vocabulary: "I already know that." He says this to teachers, to peers, and to his parents about nearly any topic under discussion. Although it is often true that Esteban does know about the subjects that are being discussed, Ms. Ogden finds herself becoming annoyed at Esteban's style of interacting, and she knows the other students do not want to be grouped with Esteban because of it.

Students' emotional status is one factor that contributes to their social skills. Some gifted and talented students are self-confident, have a strongly positive self-concept, and are generally happy (Colangelo, 2002). Others, however, feel isolated or alienated and can experience depression, low self-concept, and other emotional problems, especially as they move from childhood to adolescence. If they find school boring and have difficulty forming friendships, students who are gifted and talented also can have poor attitudes toward learning and school activities in general. These students are at risk for dropping out of school (Renzulli & Park, 2002).

BEHAVIOR PATTERNS ● Students who are gifted and talented display the entire range of behaviors that other students do. They can be model students who participate and seldom cause problems, often serving as class leaders. In this capacity, students are sensitive to others' feelings and moderate their behavior based on others' needs (Colangelo, 2002). However, because students who are gifted and talented often have an above-average capacity to understand people and situations, their negative behavior can sometimes be magnified compared with that of other students. This behavior can be displayed through an intense interest in a topic and refusal to change topics when requested by a teacher. Other behavior problems some students who are gifted and talented display include being bossy in group situations, purposefully failing, and valuing and participating in counterculture activities (Colangelo, 2002).

Interventions for Students Who Are Gifted and Talented

Although some school districts operate separate classes and programs for students who are gifted and talented, you likely will be responsible for teaching these students in your classroom. The concept used to think about meeting the needs of students who are gifted and talented is *differentiation* (Tomlinson, 2001), the same concept that is suggested for thinking about the instruction of students with academic and behavior problems. Four strategies often used to challenge gifted and talented students are curriculum compacting, acceleration and enrichment, differentiation, and individualized interventions (VanTassel-Baska, 2003). As you read the following descriptions of these strategies and the example of their implementation in the Case in Practice on page 282, think about how the INCLUDE strategy could guide you in implementing them.

CURRICULUM COMPACTING ● Some gifted and talented students already have mastered much of the traditional curriculum content of the public schools, and they may be bored when asked to listen to a lecture or complete an assignment that does not challenge them (Reis & Renzulli, 2004). In curriculum compacting, teachers assess students' achievement of instructional goals and then eliminate instruction on goals already met. The time gained is used to pursue special interests, to work with a mentor, or to study the same topic at a more advanced level. How could you use curriculum compacting in your planned teaching?

FYI

Adolescents who are gifted and talented may face unique challenges, including reconciling competing expectations from family, teachers, and peers and recognizing that they may not always be able to reach the extraordinarily high standards they set for themselves.

DIMENSIONS OF DIVERSITY

Donovan and Cross (2002) reported that in many states Caucasian students were 3 to 4 times more likely than African American students to be identified as gifted.

CASE IN PRACTICE

Meeting the Needs of a Gifted Student

INCLUDE

It is Wednesday morning and Ms. Ollendorf is preparing for the school day. She is thinking about what to do with Mary Jo, a student in her class who is clearly gifted in a number of areas. Mary Jo writes with surprisingly sophisticated vocabulary, and she seldom makes any type of error. Her true talents, however, lie in math, science, and music. She either knows or masters within minutes any math concept introduced, and she has a grasp of science that is just a little intimidating to Ms. Ollendorf. Mary Jo most likes searching for information on the Internet related to topics addressed in school.

Yesterday, Mary Jo's mother came in for a conference. She said that Mary Jo's love of science was waning and was concerned. She offered this explanation:

> Mary Jo has said probably 20 times during the past month that science is boring. She thinks the book is too simple and doesn't explain "interesting" things. She says she could finish her reports on the experiments before doing them because they are not complex enough to challenge her. She also

said that she doesn't do the extra-credit work that you give students as an option because she can get perfect scores on everything anyway. Why would she want to do extra work?

In thinking about Mary Jo, Ms. Ollendorf has to admit that the child made a few good points. What concerns Ms. Ollendorf most, though, is the possibility of Mary Jo's becoming uninterested in science when she so clearly has the potential to pursue a science-related career if she chooses.

A week later, Ms. Ollendorf introduces a different sort of science to Mary Jo. She has gathered advanced supplemental science textbooks and has contacted several friends who work in local businesses to be mentors for Mary Jo. She has also spoken with a friend who is a science education professor about how to challenge Mary Jo. She offers Mary Jo these options:

- She will take unit tests prior to instruction.

- If she scores at least 80 percent on a unit test, she can work 4 days per week in the alternative science ma-

terials. If she does not achieve 80 percent, she will participate in the lessons on the parts of the unit she has not mastered.

- For each unit of instruction completed in this manner, Mary Jo is to select and create a product that demonstrates the science concepts she has explored.

- Mary Jo will have a once-per-month visit with a mentor. Mentors might include a high school student, one of the local businesspeople, or another teacher.

REFLECTIONS

What type of gifted student is Mary Jo? If you had to make a prediction, how do you think she behaves in other subject areas? What did Ms. Ollendorf do to make science a more challenging subject for Mary Jo? Which of the four approaches to providing appropriate instruction to gifted and talented students did Ms. Ollendorf use? What other strategies could Ms. Ollendorf implement to expand Mary Jo's science instruction further?

ANALYZE AND REFLECT

What are your beliefs about professionals' responsibility for providing special instruction and programs for students who are gifted and talented? How should you balance this responsibility with those for teaching average students? Those at risk for school failure? Those who have disabilities?

ACCELERATION AND ENRICHMENT ● In some school districts, you may learn that acceleration is part of the programming available for students who are gifted and talented. That is, these students may skip a grade or complete the standards for two grades in a single year. In high school, acceleration may relate to a specific subject. For example, a student with extraordinary math skills might enroll in advanced coursework in that area while following the traditional curriculum for English and social studies. Acceleration also is seen in high schools that offer the College Board Advanced Placement (AP) program. Students have the option of completing college credit for one or more advanced courses taken in high school. Are you aware of other acceleration options offered to high school students?

Enrichment is an instructional approach that provides students with information, materials, and assignments that enable them to elaborate on concepts being presented as part of the regular curriculum and that usually require high levels of thinking (Freeman, 2000). This common classroom option requires you to find related information, prepare it for the students who need it, and create curriculum-relevant alternative activities for them. For enrichment to be effective, you need to ensure that students have opportunities to complete assignments designed to encourage advanced thinking and product development, that they do such assignments in lieu of other work instead of as additional work, and that many learning resources are available to them both in and out of the classroom (Smith & Weitz, 2003).

DIFFERENTIATION ● Perhaps one of the most practical approaches you can use for working with students in your class who are gifted and talented is to systematically plan lessons based on differentiation, the same approach introduced for your work with students who have disabilities. Recall that differentiation is based on the understanding that students should have multiple ways to reach their potential. As a teacher, you can use the INCLUDE strategy to think about the specific strengths and needs of these students; identify problem areas in critical thinking, analysis, and other advanced skills; and decide how to address those problem areas through activities integrated into instruction.

INDIVIDUALIZED INTERVENTIONS ● All of the previously described approaches may be effective for students who are gifted and talented, but students who have special circumstances—those who live in poverty, those from nondominant cultures, or those who also have disabilities—may need even further special attention. For example, some students may downplay their abilities because academic achievement is not valued in their immediate communities and they fear being rejected. For these students, you may want to find mentors from similar backgrounds so that students see that drawing on their talents can lead to positive outcomes. For some students, interacting with peers from a similar background can be helpful, especially if they are given tasks that foster critical-thinking skills. In addition, students in this group may benefit when technology is integral to instruction, either as a resource for learning or as a tool for accessing learning, as might be the case for students with disabilities. The Professional Edge on page 284 provides a checklist that can be useful for recognizing students who might be gifted underachievers.

Many professionals contend that strategies for instructing students who are gifted and talented are appropriate for most students (Gubbins, 2002; Tomlinson, 2001). They suggest that your job as a general education teacher is to design effective instruction for all students, and that this instruction also meets the needs of students who are gifted and talented. To reach all your students, you need to offer activities that address several ability levels at one time, that accommodate a variety of interest areas, and that enable students to integrate their learning and maximize their potential. In the Professional Edge on page 285 you can review some strategies for accomplishing this goal.

What Are the Needs of Students from Culturally Diverse Backgrounds?

The racial, cultural, and linguistic diversity of U.S. classrooms has been increasing for decades, and all indications are that it will continue to do so. For example, in 1972 just 22 percent of students enrolled in grades 1 through 12 were members of minority groups; in 2000, the number had risen to 38.7 percent (National Center for Education Statistics, 2002). Researchers predict that by 2025 half of all students in U.S. schools will be non-Anglo-American (Hodgkinson, 2000/2001). However, trying to accurately capture the diversity of today's students is a complex matter. Consider the following facts: If you live in an area near a large city, the diversity of your student population is likely to increase dramatically over the next decade. If you teach in an inner-city area

RESEARCH NOTE

The Schoolwide Enrichment Model (SEM) is a research-based approach to gifted education that stresses integrating services for students with extraordinary ability with the entire array of programs and services found in a school (Renzulli & Reis, 2002).

INCLUDE

RESEARCH NOTE

Serving students who both are gifted and have learning disabilities can be particularly challenging. General educators may not have the training to work with students who have multiple exceptionalities and special educators typically are not trained to address the unique needs of students with gifts and talents. Collaboration is imperative to effectively teach these students (Kennedy, Higgins, & Pierce, 2002).

PROFESSIONAL EDGE

Gifted Underachievers

One of the challenges you will face as an educator is maximizing the potential of all your students. One group that can be difficult to identify is students who are gifted and talented but who are underachievers. The following checklist is designed to help you to decide whether any of your students might be in this group. If some students have many of the following characteristics, their potential may be unrealized and you should collaborate with colleagues to better reach them either through differentiation in your class or through referral for special programs.

❑ Poor test performance

❑ Achieving at or below grade-level expectations in one or all of the basic skill areas: reading, language arts, mathematics

❑ Daily work frequently incomplete or poorly done

❑ Superior comprehension and retention of concepts when interested

❑ Vast gap between qualitative level of oral and written work

❑ Exceptionally large repertoire of factual knowledge

❑ Vitality of imagination; creative

❑ Persistent dissatisfaction with work accomplished, even in art

❑ Seems to avoid trying new activities to prevent imperfect performance: evidences perfectionism, self-criticism

❑ Shows initiative in pursuing self-selected projects at home

❑ Has a wide range of interests and possible special expertise in an area of investigation and research

❑ Evidences low self-esteem in tendencies to withdraw or to be aggressive in classroom

❑ Does not function comfortably or constructively in a group of any size

❑ Shows acute sensitivity and perceptions related to self, others, and life in general

❑ Tends to set unrealistic self-expectations: goals too high or too low

❑ Dislikes practice work or drill for memorization and mastery

❑ Easily distracted: unable to focus attention and concentrate efforts on tasks

❑ Has an indifferent or negative attitude toward school

❑ Resists teacher efforts to motivate or discipline behavior in class

❑ Has difficulty in peer relationships; maintains few friendships

SOURCE: *Giftedness, Conflict and Underachievement,* by J. Whitmore, 1980, Boston: Allyn and Bacon, as cited in *A Checklist to Identify Gifted Underachievers,* retrieved December 3, 2004, from http://theheights.webzone.net.au/programs_gifted_underachievers.shtml.

ANALYZE AND REFLECT

Why are students with culturally and linguistically diverse backgrounds given special attention in a textbook about students with special needs? How could classroom practices inadvertently cause African American students or others to be referred inappropriately for special education services?

or a rural district, you may find little change in diversity but decreasing student enrollment. The Harvard Civil Rights Project has published data suggesting that, despite the now 50-year-old *Brown v. Board of Education* court decision ending segregated schooling, U.S. public schools are gradually resegregating (Orfield & Lee, 2004). In particular, students who are African American or Latino are more likely than they were in the 1980s to be educated in schools with few Caucasian students. But diversity itself is being redefined. In the 2000 U.S. Census, individuals could indicate that they were members of more than one race. The result is that traditional approaches to calculating racial diversity in schools are losing meaning.

Evidence suggests that students from cultures other than Anglo-European ones sometimes experience an extraordinarily high failure rate in school. For example, in 2002, approximately 11 percent of all young adults in the United States ages 16 through 24 did not have a high school diploma and were not enrolled in school. However, this number included 26 percent of Hispanic young adults and 12 percent of African American young adults, but only 7 percent of non-Hispanic white individuals (National Center for Education Statistics [NCES], 2002). Although some of these students may later return to complete school in a GED program, many will not (NCES, 2004).

The reasons for these students' failure to complete school are complex and interrelated but involve several identifiable factors. First, students from racial and ethnic mi-

PROFESSIONAL EDGE

Differentiating for Students Who Are Gifted and Talented

You have learned that differentiation is a way to meet a wide variety of learning needs in your classroom, including the needs of students who are gifted and talented. Tomlin-son (2001) suggests that you think about your learners as being on a continuum that can be applied to several dimensions of learning.

Dimension	Ideas for Advanced Learners
Concrete to abstract	Provide more abstract materials and ideas and more applications than for other learners.
Simple to complex	Ask students to solve more complex problems, to complete more complex research, or to accomplish more complex learning goals.
Basic to transformational	Expect students to manipulate information and to integrate concepts from several areas into an integrated whole.
Fewer facets to multiple facets	Give students activities that have multiple parts and that require more planning.
Smaller leaps to greater leaps	Offer student learning activities in which they can make mental leaps related to insight and application.
More structured to more open	Arrange learning activities that do not have single correct solutions and that may be tackled using any of several approaches.
Less independence to more independence	Allow students to work independently in planning, implementing, and self-monitoring learning activities.
Quicker to slower	Sometimes, permitting students to complete tasks very rapidly is preferred. At other times, more time is needed for in-depth study.

SOURCE: Adapted from *How to Differentiate Instruction in Mixed-Ability Classrooms* (2nd ed.), by C. A. Tomlinson, 2001, Alexandria, VA: Association for Supervision and Curriculum Development.

nority groups often lack role models because most teachers are from the majority Anglo-European culture (Gordon, Piana, & Keleher, 2000). In addition, instructional practices can negatively affect students. In particular, textbooks with cultural biases can promote stereotypes and omit culturally important information. Teaching practices that do not allow opportunities for student-centered learning also can put students from different cultures at a disadvantage because students' background and experiences may lead them to learn more effectively from small-group peer interactions (Bennett, 2003; Nieto, 2002/2003). A mix of teaching approaches is needed. Finally, school policies and organization can penalize students. For example, few schools operate mentor programs specifically designed to connect students from diverse cultures with leaders in business, industry, and education. These contacts can be essential for helping students succeed.

Diversity and Special Education

The relationship among school failure, special education, and diverse student needs is not a comfortable one (Ladner & Hammons, 2001). Historically, students from racial or cultural minorities were sometimes inappropriately placed in special education programs based on discriminatory assessment practices. Evidence suggests that this unfortunate bias is still an issue today (U.S. Department of Education, 2002), particularly for African

WWW RESOURCES

The National Center for Education Statistics' Common Core of Data (http://nces.ed.gov/ccd) can inform you about diversity in schools nationwide, about schools in your state, or about specific schools in a district. This website also has information designed to help students understand their schools.

American students, and that the bias extends to the types of placements for students. For example, African American students identified as having disabilities are more likely than other students (including white, Hispanic, Asian, and Native American) to be placed in separate settings for more than 20 percent of the day. Conversely, this group of students is less likely than students in other groups to be identified as being gifted and talented (Donovan & Cross, 2002). The reasons for this bias continue to be studied. Some researchers maintain that the issue concerns poverty more than race, a topic addressed later in this chapter, but it also includes bias in curriculum and instruction, teacher attitude, and the special education referral process (Artiles, Harry, Reschly, & Chinn, 2002).

Cultural Awareness

Understanding the characteristics of students who are members of racially and culturally diverse groups involves recognizing that the contradictions between some of these students' home and community experiences and the expectations placed on them at school can lead to learning and behavior problems (Banks, 2001). It also includes acknowledging that teachers sometimes misunderstand students and their parents, which can lead to miscommunication, distrust, and negative school experiences.

The makeup of today's general education classrooms reflects the racial, linguistic, and cultural diversity of the communities they serve. The Technology Notes feature on page 287 describes how computers can be used to foster students' cultural awareness. However, as the preceding discussion of cultural bias suggests, such awareness and sensitivity also must be cultivated among general and special education teachers.

If you live in an area in which many different cultures are represented in a single classroom, the thought of learning about all of them can be intimidating. It is probably not possible, nor is it necessary, to learn many details about all the cultures of your students (Benner, 1998). However, it is your responsibility to learn fundamental characteristics students might have because of their backgrounds. For example, some students might keep their questions to themselves instead of asking you because of concern about interacting with the teacher, who is perceived as an authority figure. If you understand this reticence, you can make a special effort to initiate interactions with those students. Further, when a student displays behavior that you find troublesome, you should determine whether a cultural reason prompted the behavior before responding to it or before assuming that it represents misbehavior. Of course, you should also keep in mind that not all students from diverse backgrounds encounter these problems, nor do all families from racial or ethnic minority groups use discipline practices different from those schools use.

DIMENSIONS
OF DIVERSITY

Since 1990, the gap in graduation rates between Caucasian and African American students has remained nearly constant. Hispanic students are the most likely to drop out of high school.

How are students from culturally diverse backgrounds at risk for school failure? How can you promote student acceptance of cultural differences in your classroom?

> TECHNOLOGY NOTES

Using Computer Technology to Foster Cultural Awareness

Technology can be used effectively to build a greater understanding of world politics and cultural differences. In the following lesson plan, the teacher assists students in using a variety of technologies as they develop a multicultural resource center for the employees of an international business.

Computers with access to the Internet offer a wealth of multicultural learning opportunities.

Activity:

Training for Cultural Awareness

Level:

Grades 9–12

Purpose of Activity:

To familiarize students with the intricacies of other cultures through the development of a project

Instructional Activity:

Setting the Stage: The Training Department Dilemma. Over the past 2 years your company, NUTECH, has experienced a surge in overseas business. This has resulted in a tremendous increase in the amount of foreign travel for NUTECH employees, who have conducted business in locales where they knew very little about the local cultures. The employees report that they believe this has put them at a distinct disadvantage, and they would like to get training on how to relate more effectively to indigenous populations when traveling abroad.

Your training team has been assigned the task of putting together a multicultural center to provide employees with an easy-to-access compilation of resources. At a team meeting, a brainstorming session identified several ideas for potentially valuable resources.

Ideas for Multicultural Resource Center:

1. *Brochure.* The brochure should include a brief description of the history of the country along with relevant geographic and cultural data. It would be helpful to stress any cultural differences that visitors should recognize; for example, in Thailand it is considered very rude to sit with one leg crossed over the other with a foot pointing at another person. You should use a desktop-publishing or word-processing program to develop the brochure. Graphics should enhance the layout.
2. *Videotape.* Create a videotape that provides useful information to a traveler in a specific country. The information should enable that person to function more effectively in the local culture by stressing customs, values, and historical perspectives.
3. *Bar-coded videodisc presentation.* Develop a bar-code-driven program that accesses relevant segments of a DVD that pertain to a specific culture. You should use a bar-code generator and a word processor for the project materials, which you should mount on tagboard and laminate.
4. *Multimedia display.* Create a multimedia display that provides suggestions for travelers in a particular country. Video segments would enhance the program, either by being imported into the program or through interaction with a videodisc player.
5. *Database.* Develop a database of resources for each country to which employees might travel. This should include magazine and newspaper articles, videos, books, and so forth. You can access much of this information via the Internet.

Suggestions for Teacher:

For this activity, students choose a country on which to focus. They must understand the purpose of the product—to provide a resource for someone who needs help functioning in another country's culture. To develop a quality product, students will need to strive to truly understand the culture of the chosen country. Encourage students to use telecommunication resources to locate information. The Internet may offer them an opportunity to actually converse with citizens of the chosen country. They may also have access to foreign nationals living nearby.

SOURCE: *Integrating Educational Technology into Teaching*, by M. D. Roblyer, J. Edwards, and M. A. Havriluk, 1997, Columbus, OH: Merrill.

The INCLUDE strategy can be a valuable tool for making decisions about instruction for students from culturally and linguistically diverse groups. First, you should consider the demands of the classroom setting, and then identify strengths and interests that students bring to the learning environment. Next, you should look for potential problem areas throughout your entire instructional program and use that information to brainstorm ideas for ameliorating the problems and select those with the most potential for success. As you go through this process, it is essential to monitor student progress and make adjustments as needed.

The impact of cultural and linguistic diversity in educational settings can be examined from three perspectives: how cultural factors affect student behavior, how teaching approaches can be tailored to culturally diverse groups, and how communication with non-native English speakers can be enhanced. We examine each perspective briefly.

CULTURAL FACTORS AND STUDENT BEHAVIOR ●
Various cultural values have an impact on students' behaviors and the way educators interpret these behaviors. For example, for some Native American and immigrant students, time is a fluid concept not necessarily bound by clocks (Hodgkinson, 2000/2001). A student might come to school "late" by Anglo-European cultural standards that measure time precisely, but "on time" according to events happening at the student's home. Another example of the differences between Anglo-European standards and some students' cultures concerns school participation. Hispanic students sometimes are more likely to participate when they have established a close relationship with their teachers and peers (Banks, 2001). Contrast this fact with the common high school structure in which one teacher sees as many as 180 students each day and often uses an instructional format that minimizes interactions. In such settings, some Hispanic students—especially those who have only recently come to the United States—can be at a great disadvantage. Similarly, recent research suggests that some African American students learn better when they can socialize during learning (Townsend, 2000). If these opportunities are not offered in the classroom, some students are being denied an essential learning tool.

INFORMED INSTRUCTIONAL DECISION MAKING ●
Decisions about teaching approaches occur by matching the needs of students from culturally diverse backgrounds to instructional approaches (Banks, 2001). For example, many African American students as well as many Hispanic American and Asian American students respond well to cooperative rather than competitive teaching and learning environments (Bennett, 2003). Likewise, because traditional Native American students sometimes dislike responding individually and out loud in a large-group situation, you may need to create opportunities for individual contacts and quiet participation. Such instructional thinking and approaches, referred to as *equity pedagogy*, should become integral to your teaching (Cushner, McClelland, & Safford, 2000).

CROSS-CULTURAL COMMUNICATION ●
For students who do not speak English as their native language, school can be a frustrating experience, resulting in some common problems. First, students who do not use English proficiently can easily be discriminated against when they are assessed. For example, NCLB requires that students be assessed in the standard way after a limited period of exemption because of language differences. However, some students may not be ready to participate in high-stakes assessments, so their scores may underestimate their actual achievement. Second, students with limited English skills sometimes are perceived by teachers and classmates as deficient; teachers might have difficulty understanding students and might assume they have limited ability, and peers may exclude students from social activities because of language differences (Oakes & Lipton, 2003). Third, language-related issues sometimes lead to a belief that, when English is not students' primary language, they must be segregated from other students to learn. If you understand your students' levels of language proficiency as summarized in the Professional Edge on page 289, you can ensure

---

INCLUDE

DIMENSIONS
OF DIVERSITY

Equity pedagogy is the term to describe the use of instructional strategies that addresses the learning characteristics and cognitive styles of diverse populations. If you complete an Internet search using this term, you can find research and teaching resources for effectively working with all your students.

PROFESSIONAL EDGE

Levels of Language Proficiency

When you teach students who are English-language learners, you will find that you must understand their level of language proficiency in order to design effective instruction. Further, you will need to keep in mind that language proficiency for any single student could vary significantly de- pending on whether the task at hand involves speaking, lis- tening, reading, writing, or a combination of those. The fol- lowing are the five levels of language proficiency, including the performance definition and some of the ways students function for each.

At the given level of English-language proficiency, English-language learners will process, understand, produce, or use:

5 Bridging	• the technical language of the content areas • a variety of sentence lengths of varying linguistic complexity in extended oral or written discourse, including stories, essays, and reports ➢ oral or written language approaching comparability to that of English-proficient peers when pre- sented with grade-level material
4 Expanding	• specific and some technical language of the content areas • a variety of sentence lengths of varying linguistic complexity in oral discourse or multiple, related paragraphs ➢ oral or written language with minimal phonological, syntactic, or semantic errors that do not impede the overall meaning of the communication when presented with oral or written connected discourse with occasional visual and graphic support
3 Developing	• general and some specific language of the content areas • expanded sentences in oral interaction or written paragraphs ➢ oral or written language with phonological, syntactic, or semantic errors that may impede the com- munication but retain much of its meaning when presented with oral or written narrative or expository descriptions with occasional visual and graphic support
2 Beginning	• general language related to the content area • phrases or short sentences ➢ oral or written language with phonological, syntactic, or semantic errors that often impede the meaning of the communication when presented with one- to multiple-step commands, directions, questions, or a series of statements with visual and graphic support
1 Entering	• pictorial or graphic representation of the language of the content areas • words, phrases, or chunks of language when presented with one-step commands, directions • WH-questions (that is questions beginning with the words who, what, where, when, or why) or statements with visual and graphic support

SOURCE: *English Language Proficiency Standards for English Language Learners in Kindergarten through Grade 12: Frameworks for Large-Scale State and Classroom Assessment,* by M. Gottlieb, 2004, Madison, WI: WIDA Consortium. Retrieved December 1, 2004, from http://www.doe.state.de.us/DPIServices/Desk_Ref/ELP_StandardsOV.pdf.

ANALYZE
AND**REFLECT**

What types of communication problems may occur between school professionals and parents of students from racially and ethnically diverse groups? How can professionals bridge the gap between themselves and families different from their own?

that your instruction takes language into account and can avoid or reduce some of the challenges non-native English speakers face.

For students from culturally and linguistically diverse backgrounds, home–school communication is critical. You might have difficulty even in basic communication, though, because of language differences and the lack of availability of an interpreter. A second problem you may face concerns cultural values and parent responses to school personnel (Obiakor, Utley, Smith, & Harris-Obiakor, 2002). For example, in traditional Asian American families, pride and shame are often emphasized, and indirectness is valued. Imagine a parent conference in which an insensitive teacher describes in detail the academic and learning problems an Asian American child is having and directly asks the parents whether they can assist in carrying out a home–school behavior change program. If they follow traditional Asian values, the parents might be humiliated by the public accounting of their child's failures and embarrassed at the teacher's direct and unnecessary request for their assistance.

A third example of the importance of communication relates to the parents' perceptions of school and the ways they should interact with school personnel contrasted to school staff expectations for parent involvement. For example, the parents of some students may find school foreign and intimidating, and they may believe that their role is to listen passively to what school personnel say. For students from diverse cultural backgrounds who have disabilities, it is particularly important to be sure that adequate information is communicated to parents about a student's instructional program and the procedures used in special education (Zhang & Bennett, 2003). You share this responsibility with special education professionals.

Families and Diversity

Not only may you find that it takes a focused effort to understand students and family members because of language barriers and global cultural differences, but you also may learn that you simply do not grasp the day-to-day realities of your students' and their families' lives. Probably the single most recommended strategy for gaining a better understanding is to set aside books and lesson plans, release your conceptual ideas about diversity and multiculturalism, and simply to listen to families (Ladson-Billings, 1999). In addition to being willing to make the time to learn about families, Sánchez (1999, pp. 354–357) recommends the following:

CONNECTIONS

The role of cultural awareness in teacher–parent communication and in professional collaboration was introduced in Chapters 2 and 3.

1. Be willing to step outside your comfort zone, by going into the community to learn about your students' and similar families.

2. Adopt the unequivocal view that all families are involved in and significant to their children's education and that schooling is only one source of education.

3. Be willing to examine your own story more deeply.

4. Be willing to challenge stereotypes and reduce prejudice.

5. Be willing to explore the sociocultural context in the lives of families and teachers.

6. Be willing to examine your own teaching practices from a family perspective.

7. Be willing to distribute power.

By carefully listening to families and by recognizing that the most important factor about working with others is that, unless you have been in the same situation, you cannot completely understand, you can respond with respect and sensitivity to your students as well as their families. Working Together on page 291 provides some suggestions for fostering collaboration with families by focusing on making them feel welcomed and valuable in their children's education.

WORKING **TOGETHER**

Creating a School Environment for Collaborating with Parents

Collaboration between parents or families and school professionals is an attitude, not an activity, and it occurs when motivation is prompted by a "want to" way of thinking rather than an "ought to" approach. This is especially important when working with families from diverse racial and cultural groups. To foster this attitude, here are a few ideas:

- Survey the parents of your students to find out what information they need. Arrange to have your survey translated into the languages spoken in the homes of your students.

- Call to invite uninvolved parents to come to a school event or activity.

- Let parents know that there is a specific time and/or day of the week that they can reach you by telephone at school.

- Ask parents to volunteer in your classroom, either tutoring students or teaching mini lessons about their hobbies, interests, or jobs.

- Call parents to praise their child—and do this more than once.

- Develop home learning activity packets that are related to your learning objectives, but be sure they are family-friendly, that is, that only basic supplies are needed to complete them.

- With parent permission, connect an uninvolved parent in your class with a parent who is involved.

- Keep a list of community resources at your fingertips. Although your school social worker or other professionals also might have this information, you may be able to offer informal assistance in a way that is respectful and low-key.

- Have your students create a newsletter to send home. In it, describe important activities. Have secondary students journal to their parents, outlining what is being studied.

- Ask for parents' input regarding what works best with their child, especially regarding discipline and rewards.

SOURCE: *Home-school collaboration: Building effective parent-school partnerships,* by S. L. Christenson, 2002, Minneapolis: Children, Youth, and Family Consortium, University of Minnesota. Retrieved December 5, 2004, from http://www.cyfc.umn.edu/schoolage/resources/home.html.

Multicultural and Bilingual Education

Creating a classroom in which students' cultures are acknowledged and valued is a fundamental characteristic of **multicultural education,** that is, curriculum and instruction that reflect the diversity of our society. Multicultural education begins with examining how you decorate your classroom and how you select learning materials (Banks, 2001). Do your bulletin boards display the work of students from ethnic and cultural minority groups? When you portray historical events, do you include information about members of several cultural groups? Does your classroom contain stories or literature about successful individuals from a variety of cultures? Is respect for diversity infused throughout your curriculum? Two points are especially noteworthy regarding multicultural education. First, professionals agree that multicultural education should not be an event that occurs for one week out of each school year. It is better addressed through integration of multicultural information in students' educational activities. Second, multicultural education is not a topic that is confined to social studies, as some educators believe. It should pervade all subject areas, being reflected in the stories or literature addressed in language arts or English, in assignments given in science and math classes, and in the community contacts students make in vocational classes.

If the school in which you teach has a very diverse student population, programs for supporting **English-language learners (ELLs)** also will be important. For example, **bilingual education programs** are based on the assumption that students need to learn English by being immersed in the language environment, but until a level of proficiency in English is achieved, many students do not learn concepts and skills from English-language instruction (Bennett, 2003). In bilingual programs, students spend part of the school day receiving instruction in core academic areas in their native language and the remainder of the day with English-speaking students. For students

WWW RESOURCES

The National Association for Bilingual Education is an organization concerned with the quality of education received by students whose native language is not English. You can learn more about this organization by visiting its website, at http://www.nabe.org.

WWW
R E S O U R C E S

You may wish to locate more resources related to multicultural education. One good website that has many listed resources, including information about African American and Native American children, fact sheets, tips for teachers, and materials to challenge your thinking is EdChange's Multicultural Pavilion Teachers Corner, at http:// curry.edschool.virginia.edu/ go/multicultural/teachers. html.

C O N N E C T I O N S

Many students discussed in this chapter benefit from systematic approaches to addressing behavior. This topic is covered in depth in Chapter 12.

INCLUDE

receiving special education services, a bilingual special education program staffed by a bilingual special education teacher may be provided in which students receive individualized services designed to strengthen their learning and drawing on their language and culture. Yet other students learn through English as a second language (ESL) programs in which instruction occurs primarily in English although separate from general education, and no specific attempt is made to preserve students' native language. In a few elementary schools, students who are English-language learners are participating in the typical classroom, with a bilingual teacher joining the class for all or part of the day (Bahamonde & Friend, 1999).

If you develop curiosity about your students' cultures and languages, you can be sensitive to their learning needs and responsive to them. If you consider yourself as much a learner in interacting with these students as a teacher, you will truly become culturally competent and help them effectively access the curriculum and succeed in school.

How Can You Meet the Needs of Students Who Are at Risk?

In addition to all the other special needs you find among students, you are likely to encounter one that is found in virtually every public school classroom in the country. That special need is being at risk for school failure. Students who are *at risk* are those who have been exposed to some condition or situation that negatively affects their learning. Most teachers include in this description students who were prenatally exposed to drugs, including alcohol; students who are homeless; and students who have been neglected. Others include students who are bullies and those who are victims, as well as those who have recently experienced the death of someone close to them. Students who are school-phobic are at risk, as are those considering suicide, those who are considered physically unattractive or obese, those who are socially underdeveloped, and those considered slow or marginal learners. It is difficult to understand the range of problems students face and the tremendous impact these problems have on their lives. One school district committee, formed to identify the district's at-risk learners and to create options for helping them succeed, became overwhelmed at the enormity of their task. One teacher finally suggested that at-risk students were all students who were not achieving in the way teachers thought they could.

You might be wondering why students who are at risk are discussed in a text about students with disabilities. Three reasons are central: First, with a well-designed education, many students who are at risk for school failure succeed in school. The strategies for accommodating the needs of students with disabilities are usually effective for students at risk; these strategies are discussed throughout this text. By using the INCLUDE strategy, you can identify ways to help these students reach their potential. Second, effective early-school experiences for students who are at risk can establish a pattern of success in school learning that carries through high school (Neace, Munoz, Weber, & Johnson, 2002). Without such experiences, students at risk are more likely to be identified as having learning or emotional disabilities. Third, many students with disabilities also are students at risk. Many students with disabilities have been abused, some live in poverty, and others use illegal drugs. Increasing your understanding of risk factors and approaches for working with students at risk benefits all students at risk for school failure.

Characteristics and Needs of Students at Risk

Cognitively, socially and emotionally, behaviorally, and physically, students considered at risk are as diverse as students in the general school population. What distinguishes them from other students is the high likelihood that they will drop out of school prior to earning a high school diploma and that they will experience difficulty throughout their lives. Some also share other characteristics and needs, including a tendency to be noncompliant, problems in monitoring their own learning and behavior, language delays, difficulties with social relationships, and problems understanding the consequences of their behaviors (Wenz-Gross & Siperstein, 1998). To illustrate further the needs these students have, three representative groups of at-risk students are briefly discussed: children living in poverty, including those who are homeless; children who have been abused or neglected; and children who live in homes in which substance abuse occurs or who themselves are substance abusers. Keep in mind that even though this discussion treats each group as distinct for the sake of clarity, any single student could be in all three groups.

> " Cognitively, socially and emotionally, behaviorally, and physically, students considered at risk are as diverse as students in the general school population. "

STUDENTS WHO LIVE IN POVERTY ●

More than one-third of American children under 18 years of age live in low-income families, that is, in families whose income is up to double the level considered poverty, or $18,500 for a family of four (National Center for Children in Poverty, 2004). A total of 16 percent of children live in poverty. These children live in all parts of the country, but most are in the South and West. Keep in mind, too, that 56 percent of these children (that is, 14.6 million) have parents who work full-time year-round; just 16 percent do not have an employed parent. Overall, the United States has the highest rate of childhood poverty among all wealthy countries (Children's Defense Fund, 2003).

Students who live in poverty have many problems that affect their learning. For example, these children score significantly lower on academic assessments than students who do not live in poverty, and they are more likely to have been retained at least once (Children's Defense Fund, 2003). They also might not have nutritious meals, a safe and warm place to play and sleep, or needed supplies to complete homework. They are sometimes worried about their families' circumstances, and older students might be expected to work evenings and weekends to help support the family or to miss school to babysit for younger siblings. Students living in poverty also are more likely than advantaged students to experience parental neglect, to witness violence, and to change schools and residences frequently.

Some poor families are homeless; it is now estimated that 1.35 million children are homeless each year, with an average age of 6 years (Homes for the Homeless, 2004). In addition to those who are homeless, many families are in temporary living arrangements with relatives or friends. Homelessness results in many educational problems. Students sometimes leave their neighborhood school or transfer from school to school when they move to a shelter or stay with family or friends. This can leave gaps in their learning. Some students are placed in foster care when the family is homeless, and this arrangement affects their social and emotional adjustment. In addition to learning problems, students who live in poverty or who are homeless sometimes (although not always) display acting-out, restless, or aggressive behaviors; depression; regressive behaviors; and anxiety (Popp, Stronge, & Hindman, 2003).

STUDENTS WHO ARE ABUSED OR NEGLECTED ●

A second group of students at risk are the approximately 4 million who are physically abused, sexually abused, psychologically abused, or neglected each year (Lonergan, 2000). Some 1,400 children die each year as a result of abuse. Although the precise meaning of the term **child abuse** varies from state to state, it generally refers to situations in which a parent or other caregiver inflicts or allows others to inflict injury on a child, or permits a substantial risk of injury to exist. **Child neglect** is used to describe situations in which a parent or other caregiver fails to provide the necessary supports for a child's well-being,

FYI

Because poverty affects life chances in so many ways, students often face multiple risk factors simultaneously. Some children experience both poverty and abuse, for example. Family problems, crime, youth violence, teen pregnancy, and sexually transmitted diseases also place students at risk.

FYI

Homeless children have to make many educational and personal adjustments as a result of four conditions in their lives: constant moving, frequent change of schools, overcrowded living quarters, and lack of basic resources such as clothing and transportation.

WWW
R E S O U R C E S

The National Clearinghouse on Child Abuse and Neglect Information website, at http://nccanch.acf.hhs.gov, provides updated information on prevention, identification, and treatment of child abuse and neglect.

RESEARCH
N O T E

According to data gathered in 1998 by the National Child Abuse and Neglect Reporting System (NCANRS), two-thirds of the 2.8 million referrals to child protective services were determined to be valid enough to merit investigation. One-third of those investigations resulted in evidence of abuse or neglect.

whether these are basic food and shelter, education, medical care, or other items. Figure 8.3 summarizes demographic characteristics of students who are abused and of the individuals who abuse them.

Some students who have been abused or neglected show visible signs such as bruises, burns, or other untreated physical problems. They might also complain of hunger. The following student characteristics might signal to school professionals the presence of abuse or neglect (*Child Abuse Characteristics*, 2000):

- wears clothes inappropriate for weather
- cries excessively or shows little or no response to pain
- seems wary of physical contact
- appears apprehensive when approached by other students
- engages in vandalism
- arrives early to or departs late from school, or is frequently absent
- attempts to explain away unusual injuries
- is fatigued, falls asleep
- shows precocious or bizarre sexual behavior

You should be aware that you have a legal and ethical obligation to report any suspected child abuse among your students (Hinson & Fossey, 2000). Although the specific reporting requirements for teachers vary from state to state, federal law requires that every state maintain a hotline and other systems for reporting abuse, and every state has statutes that define abuse and neglect and that establish reporting procedures. If you suspect that one of your students is being abused, you should follow your school district's procedures for reporting it. If you are unsure about those procedures, you should notify your principal, school social worker, or school nurse.

STUDENTS WHO LIVE WITH SUBSTANCE ABUSE OR ARE SUBSTANCE ABUSERS ● A third group of students at risk for school failure are those involved in substance abuse. Some students' parents have abused drugs and alcohol. The impact on students can begin before they are born and often affects them throughout their lives. Babies born to mothers who drink heavily during pregnancy may have a medical condition called **fetal alcohol syndrome (FAS)**, or a milder form known as **fetal alcohol effects (FAE)**. Babies with FAS or FAE are smaller than expected, may have facial and other slight physical abnormalities, and often experience learning and behavior problems when they go to school. The prevalence estimate for these disorders is 1 in every 100 live births or some 40,000 infants each year. Some researchers estimate that as many as 1 in 8 children in the United States has some type of permanent brain damage related to the mother's alcohol use during pregnancy (National Organization on Fetal Alcohol Syndrome, 2004). Students with FAS or FAE tend to use poor judgment, leaving a situation when things do not go as planned or failing to predict the consequences of their behavior.

Babies born to mothers who have been abusing drugs often are low in weight. They also are likely to become overstimulated, which leads to an array of behaviors associated with irritability. When these children reach school age, they are likely to experience a wide variety of learning and behavior problems. Some are low achievers, and others may become eligible for special education services. They may be inattentive, hyperactive, and impulsive.

Researchers estimate that nearly one in four children grows up in a home in which alcohol or drugs are abused. These children are at risk because of a number of factors. For example, they are at risk for being neglected or abused. In homes in which drugs are abused, these students may be passive recipients of drugs that can be inhaled, or they may accidentally ingest other drugs. Students who live in homes in which alcohol

FIGURE 8.3 Child Abuse: A National Profile

In 2002, more than 2.6 million children were reported to child protective services because of suspected abuse or neglect. Some 896,000 of these cases were substantiated. This was a slight decrease (12.3 cases per 1,000 children versus 12.4 cases per 1,000 children) from 2001.

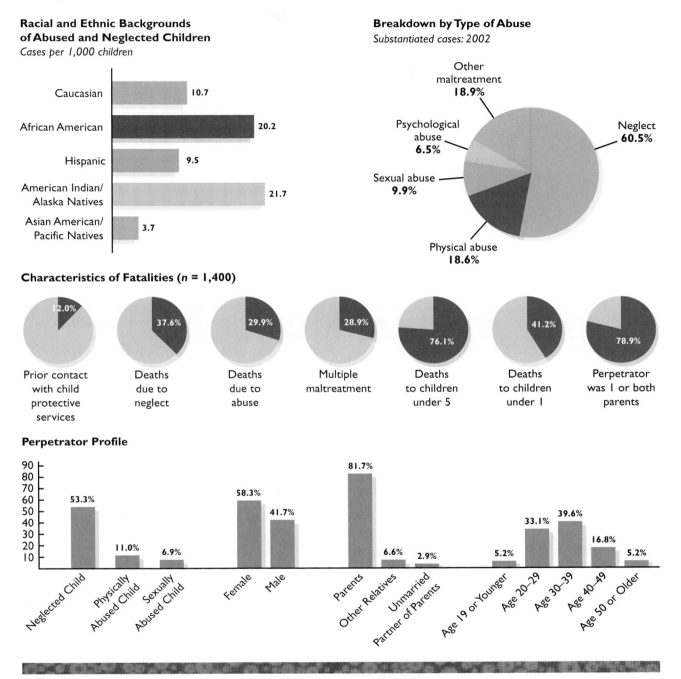

Racial and Ethnic Backgrounds of Abused and Neglected Children
Cases per 1,000 children

- Caucasian: 10.7
- African American: 20.2
- Hispanic: 9.5
- American Indian/Alaska Natives: 21.7
- Asian American/Pacific Natives: 3.7

Breakdown by Type of Abuse
Substantiated cases: 2002

- Other maltreatment 18.9%
- Psychological abuse 6.5%
- Sexual abuse 9.9%
- Neglect 60.5%
- Physical abuse 18.6%

Characteristics of Fatalities (*n* = 1,400)

- Prior contact with child protective services: 12.0%
- Deaths due to neglect: 37.6%
- Deaths due to abuse: 29.9%
- Multiple maltreatment: 28.9%
- Deaths to children under 5: 76.1%
- Deaths to children under 1: 41.2%
- Perpetrator was 1 or both parents: 78.9%

Perpetrator Profile

- Neglected Child: 53.3%
- Physically Abused Child: 11.0%
- Sexually Abused Child: 6.9%
- Female: 58.3%
- Male: 41.7%
- Parents: 81.7%
- Other Relatives: 6.6%
- Unmarried Partner of Parents: 2.9%
- Age 19 or Younger: 5.2%
- Age 20–29: 33.1%
- Age 30–39: 39.6%
- Age 40–49: 16.8%
- Age 50 or Older: 5.2%

SOURCE: Adapted from *Child Maltreatment 2002,* 2002, Washington, DC: Department of Health and Human Services. Retrieved November 29, 2004, from http://www.acf.hhs.gov/programs.cb/publications/cm02/cm02.pdf.

RESEARCH
N O T E

Fujiura and Yamaki (2000) used large data sets to analyze the relationship between poverty and disability. They found that the two clearly are linked and that when poverty was controlled as a factor, links between ethnicity or culture and disability did not exist. This contradicts some other researchers' findings.

or drugs are abused often display at least several of the following characteristics at school (Germinario, Cervalli, & Ogden, 1992, p. 106):

- poor or erratic attendance
- frequent physical complaints and visits to the nurse
- morning tardiness, especially on Mondays
- inappropriate fear about the possibility of parents being contacted
- equating any drinking with being drunk or being alcoholic
- perfectionistic and/or compulsive behavior
- difficulty concentrating, hyperactivity
- sudden emotional outbursts, crying, temper tantrums
- regression (for example, thumb sucking)
- friendlessness, isolation, withdrawn behavior
- passivity during routine activities but active or focused during drug and alcohol awareness lessons
- lingering after drug and alcohol awareness lessons to ask unrelated questions
- signs of abuse or neglect

A third group of students affected by substance abuse includes students who themselves abuse drugs or alcohol. It is estimated that 10.8 percent of youth ages 12 through 17 reported currently using illicit drugs in 2001, an increase from the 2000 figure of 9.7 percent (Substance Abuse and Mental Health Services Administration [SAMHSA], 2002). This survey of youth beliefs and behaviors also indicated a significant decrease in marijuana use, an increase in disapproval of the use of Ecstasy, but a decline in the perceived risk of inhalant abuse (National Institute on Drug Abuse, 2004). Also in 2001, 10.1 million youth ages 12 through 20 indicated they were current drinkers, with 19 percent of those classified as binge drinkers. Among youth ages 12 through 17, 13 percent were current cigarette smokers. The number of new daily smokers was 747,000, down from 1.1 million in 1997. Youth who smoke are 11.4 times more likely to use illicit drugs and 16 times more likely to drink heavily than nonsmokers (SAMHSA, 1999). It should be noted that students with emotional disabilities are at particularly high risk for alcohol and drug abuse. Students who are substance abusers often have poor diets and sleep disturbances, feel a great deal of stress, and are at risk for depression and suicide. In school, they typically recall only information taught while they are sober, interact poorly with peers and teachers, and display excessive risk-taking behavior.

As you can see, students who live in poverty, who are abused or neglected, or who live with substance abuse, as well as other at-risk students, collectively have many characteristics and needs that affect their learning. Although some of them are resilient and do not suffer long-term consequences because of their stressful lives (Henderson & Milstein, 1996), the majority do not thrive without the support of an understanding school system and knowledgeable and committed teachers.

FYI

By age 18, 66 percent of young women and 68 percent of young men have had sexual intercourse. Among those adolescents, one in four develops a sexually transmitted disease.

Interventions for Students at Risk

As a classroom teacher, you will be faced with the sometimes frustrating situation of not being able to take away from your students the stresses that often prevent them from learning to their potential—although your school counselor may be able to help address some needs as explained in the Special Emphasis On . . . feature on page 297. However, you can offer them a safe environment, with clear expectations and instructional support, that might become an important place in their lives.

Generally, recommendations for intervening to teach students at risk include four goals, none of which is completely unique to these students: set high but realistic expectations, establish peers as teaching partners, collaborate with other professionals, and work closely with parents or other caregivers. Each recommendation is discussed briefly here.

Special **EMPHASIS** On ...

Counselors and Students at Risk

If you plan to become a school counselor, you have an essential role to play in helping all the staff members of a school work effectively with students at risk and their families. For example, many students at risk are socially isolated. This increases the likelihood that students will be the victims or perpetrators of bullying; that they will experience physical, sexual, or psychological abuse by adults; and that they will become depressed and at risk for suicide. These are some of the strategies counselors can use to help students who are socially isolated:

- Develop a personal relationship with the students. This helps to break the notion some students have that "there is no one to help me."
- Assist students to increase their social contacts and relationships with peers. Options for implementing this intervention include teaching social skills through role-playing, arranging small-group interactions that are based on the needs of a targeted student, and encouraging the student to participate in clubs, organizations, and activities that are primarily social.
- Arrange activities that bring together several families. When the social contacts of the adults in a student's life

are expanded, the student is likely to benefit. One example is school-based "Family Nights" at which computers are available, the media center is open, and informal parent education is offered.

Not surprisingly, many of the strategies for helping students also involve helping families. If family members feel marginalized, that is, they do not feel comfortable and welcomed at school, counselors also face the task of overcoming this barrier. They may do this by arranging for family members to meet with school staff members at a site other than school, by involving church or other trusted community leaders in developing family advocacy programs, and working with teachers to find friendly ways to invite family members to participate in their children's education.

Reflections

If you are a teacher, which of the above ideas could you take responsibility for implementing? What questions do you have about the role of counselors in fostering success for students who are at risk? What other ideas do you have for working effectively with at-risk students and their families?

SET HIGH BUT REALISTIC EXPECTATIONS ● When you are teaching students who are at risk, it is tempting to make assumptions about how much they are capable of learning. For example, you might think that because a student does not have books at home and the parent is either unable or unwilling to read with the student, the student cannot be a successful learner. The result of such thinking is often inappropriately low expectations that students might "live down" to (Janisch & Johnson, 2003). Low expectations can also lead to overusing teaching strategies that emphasize drilling students on lower level academic skills. Although drill activities have a place in educating at-risk students, they must be balanced with other approaches. For example, students need to learn thinking processes along with basic skills, and they need to learn to construct their own knowledge along with receiving it from you. This approach is illustrated in the description of Wesley Elementary School (Pollard-Durodola, 2003), an inner-city school with a surprising record of academic success for students that is attributed to a safe and structured school environment, high expectations for students and teachers, a curriculum designed to directly address student needs, plans to prevent problems, and strong instructional leadership. This project demonstrates that when school professionals collaborate, they can reach the wide range of needs their students may have.

One other strategy for setting high expectations should be mentioned. Many professionals now believe that the still-common practice of tracking, that is, grouping students for instruction by perceived ability, can discriminate against students at risk. Tracking leads to a sense of failure among some students, and it tends to lead to lowered expectations for at-risk students (Richardson & Hines, 2002). Grouping students heterogeneously generally does not place high-achieving students at a disadvantage, and it may help raise the achievement of at-risk learners. Although teachers appropriately group students by their needs for instruction in specific skills as part of their overall instructional plan, and some secondary schools offer advanced classes that result in a limited amount of tracking, you should be aware of the potential negative effects of tracking. As a teacher, you can ensure that you do not overuse this type of grouping in your classroom, and you can work with your colleagues to create a school in which students of many different abilities learn together.

One word of caution about setting standards is necessary. Some students who are at risk live in such high stress situations outside school that they might not have much support from their parents and other family members for school assignments and work. Two examples from teachers help to illustrate this point. One talked about a student who was not returning homework. The teacher was penalizing the student by giving her lower grades and making her complete the work during recess. She later found out that the family was penniless and had a single light bulb in their tiny apartment. When the bulb burned out, there was no light after sunset, and homework was not the priority. Another teacher described a high school student who always slept in class. In-school suspension did not help, nor did attempts to contact the parents. The teacher later learned that this student left school each day, cooked dinner for her younger siblings, and then worked at a fast-food restaurant until midnight. High expectations are important, but they need to be tempered with understanding of the circumstances in a student's life outside school.

Effective instruction for students at risk includes the same strategies you would use for other students, with particular attention to the physical and social-emotional challenges these students often face. Students at risk need a structured learning environment, systematic instruction in basic skill areas, and strategies for learning independence. The Technology Notes feature on page 299 provides specific strategies on how to use computers to maximize at-risk students' learning.

ESTABLISH PEERS AS TEACHING PARTNERS ●

Peers learning from one another is a strategy recommended earlier for students from diverse cultural and linguistic backgrounds; it is also useful for at-risk students. For example, in the Success for All (SFA) Program (Munoz, Dossett, & Judy-Gullans, 2003), an intensive early reading program designed to help at-risk learners acquire foundational learning that helps them throughout their school careers, a key component is a cooperative learning approach. Students work with each other in structured groups to learn vocabulary, writing, comprehension, and other reading skills. This program appears to have great potential for helping students achieve school success.

COLLABORATE WITH OTHER PROFESSIONALS ●

A third strategy for teaching at-risk students involves increasing your problem-solving capability by adding the skills and resources of your colleagues. The purpose of problem solving with your colleagues about at-risk students is that you can check your own perspectives against theirs, gain access to their expertise, and coordinate your efforts. For example, if you are teaching Shaneal, a student who you suspect has been abused, you can first ask the counselor or social worker whether there is any past documentation of abuse, and you can request that one of these professionals speak with the student. If you are teaching Jack, a student who is missing quite a few school days and increasingly refuses to complete assignments, you might want to consult with colleagues about the causes of Jack's behavior and how to address them.

SUPPORT FAMILY AND COMMUNITY INVOLVEMENT ●

As with all students, it is essential that you maintain positive contact with parents or other caregivers of your at-risk students. However, the level of participation you can expect will vary considerably. Some parents are anxious to ensure that their children have all the advantages a positive education can give them, and they will do all they can to assist you in teaching. Other parents are not functioning well themselves, and they probably cannot be

CONNECTIONS

Peer tutoring and other forms of peer-mediated instruction are discussed in Chapter 13.

High expectations and family involvement contribute to the greater academic success of some students at risk. In your classroom, how can you identify students who are at risk? What other interventions and instructional strategies can you use to help them succeed in school?

> TECHNOLOGY NOTES

Technology and Students at Risk

Have you ever considered how access to technology could make a positive difference to at-risk students and how those students may have less access to technology than other students? Brown (2000) included students of color, those who live in poverty, and those with limited English proficiency in her review of scholarly literature on access and barriers to technology. She found that whereas nearly 33 percent of Caucasian students used computers at home, only 11 percent of African American students and 10 percent of Hispanic students used home computers. She also found that computers in schools typically are placed in locations more readily used by high achievers than by struggling learners (for example, in library and media centers instead of in classrooms). She provided evidence that the instructional uses of computers for students at risk tended to be for remedial and routine tasks instead of complex and challenging ones. She also raised issues related to the role models for technology use available to students of color and females.

The following table lists suggestions for fostering equitable access to technology for all students.

Problem	Suggestions
Location of labs	• Create minilabs throughout the building (McKenzie, 1998). • Have roving computer stations that stay in classrooms for extended periods (McKenzie, 1998). • Create computer labs for each department (e.g., math, science, English).
Promotion of technology use by different groups	• Offer and allow the typically underserved students opportunities to take technology courses and earn credits toward graduation. • Invite guest speakers who will serve as role models for students of color and female students. • Encourage all students to join technology clubs (for example, meet during lunch). • Encourage students to use technology during their own time and for their own purposes. Technology does not always have to be used for academics. • Actively encourage students of color and female students to use technology to help overcome some of the negativisms they may hold about technology (for example, have a female students' technology day, use female students and students of color as technology monitors, and have more technology sign-up slots for female students during free time). • Seek software that meets the needs and special interests of all students (for example, instructionally sound simulations). • Encourage students of color and female students to attend summer technology camps (Wolfe, 1986).
Quality access for the entire student body	• Assure equal technology use regardless of gender, ethnicity, or achievement level by removing some of the biases and stereotypes associated with technology use (Martin, 1990; Wolfe, 1986). • Target all students for higher-level cognitive skills by having them use more problem-solving tools and learn programming (Emihovich, 1992). • Consider summer school courses that meet at atypical times to accommodate students who work after school.
Computer scheduling	• Blend technologies into daily routines to promote learner-centered environments. • Schedule individual and group time for students. • Offer evening classes to involve parents and other community members. • Provide appropriate activities for each special population in the school and classroom.

SOURCE: From "Access, Instruction, and Barriers: Technology Issues Facing Students at Risk," by M. Brown, 2000, *Remedial and Special Education, 21*, p. 188. Copyright © 2000 by PRO-ED, Inc. Reprinted with permission.

expected to participate actively in their children's education. To involve families and communities in their children's education, you might try these ideas. Sometimes it might be more appropriate to require a student to bring to school something personally important from home and to base an assignment on that, rather than to assign more traditional homework. It also can be helpful to assist parents in connecting with community resources such as health clinics and social service agencies. One school district, struggling because of the rapidly increasing number of at-risk students, worked with local church leaders to connect families with resources and improve the communication between school personnel and families.

When you think about the diversity of students you may teach, it is easy to become overwhelmed by the challenge of meeting all students' instructional needs. Keep in mind that classrooms structured to celebrate diversity rather than treat it as a deficiency or an exception are classrooms with many options for learning and a blend of structure and flexibility.

SUMMARY

In addition to students with disabilities, you will teach many other students who have extraordinary learning needs. Some students receive specialized services through Section 504, federal legislation requiring that accommodations be provided by general educators to students who have functional disabilities that might limit their access to an education.

One group of students who receive Section 504 assistance is students with attention deficit–hyperactivity disorder (ADHD), a medically diagnosed problem characterized by chronic and severe inattention and/or hyperactivity-impulsivity. Students with ADHD are served through a variety of environmental, academic, and behavior interventions, and they often are helped by medication. Most other students protected through Section 504 have physical conditions or medical problems, and their plans outline needed academic, behavioral, and physical or medical accommodations.

Students who are gifted and talented comprise a second group with special needs. Students who are gifted and talented include those with generally high intellectual ability as well as those with specific talents in areas such as music. The interventions most often used to help them achieve school success are curriculum compacting, enrichment and acceleration, differentiation, and individualized interventions.

A third group with special needs includes students from culturally and linguistically diverse backgrounds. These students and their families sometimes have values that differ from those of schools. Teachers need to learn about students' cultures, teach in a manner that is responsive to those cultures, and acknowledge and value diverse cultures in the classroom to teach students from diverse cultural backgrounds effectively.

Finally, students at risk for school failure because of environmental influences such as poverty, child abuse, and drug addiction also have special needs. Because students at risk often live in unpredictable and stressful environments, strategies for teaching them include setting appropriate expectations, establishing peers as teaching partners, collaborating with other professionals, and working closely with families and community members.

Applications in **Teaching Practice**

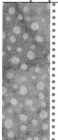

Diversity in a High School Class

Ivan Robinson is a first-year high school teacher in an urban school district. Although it is only the fourth week of school, he is concerned. He is confident of his knowledge of history and civics as well as his teaching skills, and he has a strong commitment to teaching all the students assigned to him, but he is worried that he won't be able to meet the vast array of needs represented in his second-block class this year.

Mr. Robinson is well aware that student needs in school are becoming increasingly diverse, and this current class group clearly demonstrates that fact. For example, Thuan, who just im-

migrated to the United States from Vietnam, speaks very little English and seems overwhelmed by nearly everything at school. Mr. Robinson can't recall ever seeing Thuan smile. As he discusses U.S. history, he knows that much of the information is beyond Thuan's understanding, and he knows that Thuan does not have the context for grasping the themes in history.

Then there is Sonny. Sonny is supposed to be taking medication for ADHD, but it doesn't seem to be having the right effect on him. At an after-school meeting, Mr. Robinson, the school psychologist, the counselor, and the assistant principal discussed the matter with Sonny, and it was noted that Sonny recently had decided he had outgrown the need for medication and was sometimes not taking it. He did say, though, that a few times he decided to "catch up" by taking a double dose. The counselor is supposed to follow up on this unhealthy and potentially dangerous thinking about medication and keep Mr. Robinson informed. In the meantime, Sonny is in his class and, as Mr. Robinson puts it, is either "bouncing off the walls or drugged out."

Jenny is a concern as well. She and her twin sister, Jenna, are struggling academically despite lots of individual attention and supportive parents. Neither girl is reading well enough to complete the chapters in the history text. Both girls have been referred in the past for special education services, but neither is eligible to receive them. Mr. Robinson knows that the twins' father has been out of work for nearly a year, that the girls both work after school and have little time for homework or any type of tutoring assistance, and that the family is barely getting by on donations from friends and their church. He wonders how much of the twins' learning problems are related to their home situation.

Mr. Robinson also teaches Kimberly, who just moved into the district and who is so far ahead of other students that Mr. Robinson wishes she were taking his course through the local community college. Two other students, Lisa and Paul, are from families that have very little; they come to school without supplies and seem reluctant to interact with the other children.

In thinking about his class, Mr. Robinson realizes that at least half the students have special needs of one sort or another. He wants to reach them all to share his love of history, but he is not sure he can accomplish his goal.

QUESTIONS

1. How typical is the type of class group Mr. Robinson has? What other types of diverse needs might you expect to be represented in a class you are responsible for teaching?
2. What general strategies might Mr. Robinson use in his class that would benefit many students with special needs and would harm none?
3. For each student with special needs Mr. Robinson has identified, consider how the INCLUDE strategy could be used. Fill in this chart, perhaps working with a classmate to generate ideas for information not specifically outlined in the preceding student descriptions. Be sure to address academic, social-emotional, behavioral, and medical-physical needs.

INCLUDE

	Thuan	Sonny	Jenny and Jenna	Kimberly	Lisa	Paul
Identify						
Note						
Check						
Look						
Use						
Decide						
Evaluate						

4. There are eight special education teachers in Mr. Robinson's school, and he works extensively with Mr. Settle. What is Mr. Settle's role in assisting Mr. Robinson and other teachers in the school to meet the diverse needs of students, including those who do not have IEPs?

5. How might Mr. Robinson work with the parents of his students to help ensure their needs are addressed? What barriers might he encounter? How should he address these barriers? What inadvertent biases could he have toward his students' families? How could these biases relate to your own views as a novice educator?
6. What realistic expectations can Mr. Robinson set for himself as a teacher for this school year? How can he reach his goal of meeting the needs of all his students?

WORKING THE **STANDARDS**

INTASC **INTASC PRINCIPLES REFLECTED IN THIS CHAPTER:**

Principle #2 states that all teachers

- Continually examine their assumptions about the learning and development of individual students with disabilities (Principle 2.02).

- Have realistically high expectations for what students with disabilities can accomplish, and use this knowledge to create challenging and supportive learning opportunities for students with disabilities (Principle 2.02).

Principle #4 states that all teachers

- Understand that it is particularly important to provide multiple ways for students with disabilities to participate in learning activities (Principle 4.04).

- Modify tasks and/or accommodate the individual needs of students with disabilities in a variety of ways to facilitate their engagement in learning activities with other students (Principle 4.04).

- Use strategies that promote the independence, self-control, and self-advocacy of students with disabilities (Principle 4.07).

- Expect and support the use of assistive and instructional technologies to promote learning and independence of students with disabilities (Principle 4.08).

Principle #9 states that all teachers continually challenge their beliefs about how students with disabilities learn and how to teach them effectively (Principle 9.02).

CEC CONTENT STANDARDS REFLECTED IN THIS CHAPTER:

CEC Content Standard #2 states that special educators

- Know and demonstrate respect for their students first as unique human beings.

- Understand the similarities and differences in human development and the characteristics between and among individuals with and without exceptional learning needs.

- Understand how exceptional conditions can interact with the domains of human development.

- Understand how the experiences of individuals with exceptional learning needs can impact the individuals' ability to learn, interact socially, and live as fulfilled, contributing members of the community.

CEC Content Standard #3 states that special educators understand the effects that an exceptional condition can have on an individual's learning in school and throughout life.

CEC Content Standard #4 states that special educators select, adapt, and use these instructional strategies to promote challenging learning results in general and special curricula and to appropriately modify learning environments for individuals with exceptional learning needs.

CEC Content Standard #9 states that special educators are aware of how their own and others' attitudes, behaviors, and ways of communicating can influence their practice.

CEC Content Standard #10 states that special educators promote and advocate the learning and well-being of individuals with exceptional learning needs across a wide range of settings and a range of different learning experiences.

BACK TO THE CASES

The standards and principles just listed relate to the cases described at the beginning of this chapter: José, Lydia, and Tam. The questions and activities that follow demonstrate how these standards and principles, along with other concepts that you have learned about in this chapter, connect to the everyday activities of all teachers.

José

Mr. Lee has come to the student assistant teacher for help with José, because nothing he has tried has worked. After

WORKING THE **STANDARDS** (continued)

hearing his concerns, the team decides to write a Section 504 plan; as a member of the team, you will help select appropriate accommodations for José. After reviewing this chapter, the Professional Edge on page 270, and Figure 8.2, share the accommodations you would recommend. (See IN-TASC Principles 2.02, 4.04, and 4.07; and CEC Standards 4 and 7.) List each accommodation, and explain why you believe each is most appropriate for José.

Lydia

Lydia's family is very concerned that she is not getting appropriate opportunities to use her talents and academic ability. You have invited family members to a conference tomorrow afternoon where you will address their concerns with a proposal for future accommodations. (See INTASC Principles 2.02, 4.04, and 4.07; and CEC Standards 4, 7, and 10.) In preparation, you ask a peer to work with you to

- Develop a matrix of pros and cons for the instructional strategies commonly used with students who are gifted and talented.

- Write a rationale for using or not using each strategy for Lydia.
- Create a proposal to present to the family that includes a combination of strategies you believe would be most appropriate.

Tam

Tam's first-block history teacher sat at your table during lunch today. During a general conversation about working with at-risk students, the teacher shared Tam's story. Based on the three types of interventions you read about in this chapter for students who are at risk, what strategies might you suggest your colleague employ to help Tam? (See INTASC Principles 2.02, 4.04, 4.07, and 4.08; and CEC Standards 4, 7, and 10.)

 Visit the companion website (http://www.ablongman.com/friend4e) for a complete correlation of this chapter to the INTASC Principles and CEC Standards.

Further **Readings**

Payne, R. K. (2001). *A framework for understanding poverty.* Highlands, TX: Aha! Press.

This book helps educators and others to understand deeply the challenges faced by children in poverty and the strategies school professionals should take in working with them. In particular, the book addresses the resilience of children who grow up in poverty.

Popp, P. A., Stronge, J. H., & Hindman, J. L. (2003). *Students on the move: Reaching and teaching highly mobile children and youth* (Urban Diversity Series). Washington, DC: National Center for Homeless Education and ERIC Clearinghouse on Urban Education (ERIC Document Reproduction Service No. ED482661).

This handbook, available without charge through the ERIC system, is designed to help teachers and other professionals learn about students who move frequently (for example, children of migrant workers, children living in deep poverty, children of military families). The handbook blends research summaries with case studies and includes a checklist of interventions to support these students as well as a list of related children's literature and activities.

Salend, S. J. (Ed.). (2003). ADHD [Special issue]. *Intervention in School and Clinic, 38(5),* 257–315.

This special issue on students with ADHD summarizes their rights under Section 504; overviews academic, behavioral, and medical interventions; and includes a mother–son interview describing the experience of living with ADHD.

Tomlinson, C. A., Kaplan, S. N., Renzulli, J. S., Purcell, J., Leppien, J., & Burns, D. (2002). *The parallel curriculum: A design to develop high potential and challenge high-ability learners.* Thousand Oaks, CA: Corwin.

This book provides a wealth of information on working with students who are gifted and talented. It is based on the notion of looking at four dimensions of curriculum—the core curriculum, the curriculum of connections (for example, connect across disciplines), the curriculum of practice (for example, use information to produce a product), and the curriculum of identity (for example, examine the impact of knowledge on people throughout the world). The book has many ideas that teachers can use across grade levels to challenge their high-ability students.

CHAPTER 9

Instructional Adaptations

LEARNER OBJECTIVES

After you read this chapter, you will be able to

1. Describe accommodations you can make for students who do not have the preskills necessary to learn new skills.

2. Select and sequence instructional examples to help students access basic skills instruction.

3. Accommodate individual learners by providing the direct instruction, practice, and review needed to help them acquire basic skills.

4. Describe accommodations you can make when activating background knowledge, organizing content, and teaching terms and concepts to help students acquire academic content.

5. Make lessons accessible for students with special needs by improving the clarity of your written and oral communication.

6. Describe strategies for involving parents in teaching their children.

7. Adapt independent practice activities for students.

8. Describe how you can make modifications in your classroom materials and activities for students with moderate to severe disabilities.

KEY TERMS AND CONCEPTS

MS. DIAZ WAS TEACHING

her fourth-grade class how to write percentages for fractions using this example from her math book:

Write a percent for $\frac{7}{8}$.

$\frac{7}{8}$ means $7 \div 8$.

$$0.87\frac{4}{8} = 0.87\frac{1}{2} = 87\frac{1}{2}\%$$

$$8)\overline{7.00}$$

$$\underline{64}$$

$$60$$

$$\underline{56}$$

$$4$$

Divide until the answer is in hundredths. Give the remainder as a fraction.

$\frac{7}{8} = 87\frac{1}{2}\%$, or 87.5%

To show her students how to do this problem, Ms. Diaz wrote the example on the board, pointing out that the fraction $\frac{7}{8}$ means 7 divided by 8. She then explained that they would have to divide until the answer was in hundredths and would have to give the remainder as a fraction. Following this instruction, Ms. Diaz assigned the students 15 similar problems to do independently. Abdul, who is a student in this class, has a learning disability. He has difficulty learning new skills unless he is given many opportunities for instruction and practice. Abdul answered none of the 15 problems correctly. He missed converting the fractions to percentages, because he forgot that means 7 divided by 8; Abdul divided 8 by 7 instead. ●

How could this lesson have been taught to Abdul to prevent this misunderstanding?

CECILY IS A STUDENT

with a hearing impairment who is in Ms. Boyd's U.S. history class. Cecily is failing history because the tests are based mainly on the textbook and she has trouble picking out main ideas in the text and understanding important vocabulary words. Cecily can read most of the words in the text but she reads very slowly, word by word. Last week, she was assigned a chapter to read for homework; she spent almost 2 hours reading 15 pages, and when she was done, she couldn't remember what she had read. The key words are highlighted, but Cecily can't figure them out from the context and doesn't know how to use the glossary. ●

What can Ms. Boyd do to help Cecily read and remember key

ideas in her textbook? What can she do to help Cecily understand new vocabulary words?

ALBERT HAS ADHD and is included in Ms. Olivieri's second-grade class. Albert has trouble following written directions and doing independent practice assignments that have more than one part. He also complains that his seatwork as-

signments are too hard for him. During seatwork, Albert is frequently out of his chair, either getting help from or bothering other students in the class. Ms. Olivieri feels that she is already spending too much time helping Albert. ● *What should she do to make seatwork a more successful experience for Albert and give herself more time to work with other students?*

As you have already learned, the curriculum methods and materials teachers use have a strong influence on how readily students learn in the classroom. In fact, the better the materials and the teaching, the fewer individual accommodations are required for students with special needs. However, for a variety of reasons, you may not have control over the materials used in your school. Furthermore, despite your best teaching efforts, some students will still need individual accommodations or modifications to gain access to important skills and content. For example, in the chapter-opening cases just described, merely showing Abdul how to do one problem is not enough. He needs guidance through a number of examples before he is ready to do problems independently. In addition, you can help Cecily focus on important information in her textbook by giving her a study guide that has questions pertaining to the most important content in each chapter. You can also have Cecily identify words she does not know and ask a classmate to help her with the meanings before she reads. For Albert, you can make sure all directions are clearly written using words he can identify; you can also give the directions orally and guide students through several practice examples before they are required to work independently. Of course, you also want to be sure that Albert has the necessary academic skills to complete assignments independently.

The purpose of this chapter is to provide you with strategies for adapting curriculum materials, teacher instruction, and student practice activities that are reasonable to carry out and that increase the likelihood of success for students with special needs. Remember, most students with disabilities included in your classroom are expected to meet the same curricular goals as their classmates without disabilities. Therefore, most of the adaptations covered in this chapter fall under the category of accommodations, which we learned in Chapter 5 are supports that allow students to more readily access the general education curriculum.

It is also important to note that the instructional accommodations described in this chapter can at times be carried out with your entire class. At other times, they might be presented with individual students or as a part of small groups. The way you choose to accommodate your students with special needs depends on classroom demands, the characteristics of individual students, and the overall level of functioning of your class. For example, in the case above, if Abdul has many other classmates who are struggling to write percentages for fractions, and if Abdul can attend to a task in a large group, then Ms. Diaz can accommodate him by building more guided practice into her large-group instruction. If only Abdul and a few of his classmates are having trouble learning percents, and/or if Abdul has trouble paying attention in a large group, then Ms. Diaz would be better off accommodating Abdul either one-to-one or in a small group. You can use the INCLUDE strategy to help you make decisions about the best way to make accommodations for your students with special needs.

INCLUDE

" The instructional accommodations described in this chapter can at times be carried out with your entire class. At other times, they might be presented with individual students or as a part of small groups. "

Instructional modifications, as we learned in Chapter 5, are used for students who have more severe disabilities and who have an alternative curriculum specified on their IEPs. Strategies for making appropriate instructional modifications are covered at the end of this chapter, as well as in Chapter 6.

How Can You Make Accommodations for Students with Special Needs in Basic Skills Instruction?

Basic skills instruction primarily means instruction in the academic skills of reading, writing, and math. However, you may also apply effective principles for adapting basic skills instruction to content areas such as science. Four aspects of basic skills instruction for which you may need to make accommodations for students with special needs are preskills; the selection and sequencing of examples; the rate of introduction of new skills; and direct instruction, practice, and review.

Teaching Preskills

Darrell is in Ms. Rayburn's second-grade class. In language arts, he is experiencing a problem common to many students with special needs. On Tuesday, Darrell was at his desk reading a book on his favorite topic: magic. However, when Ms. Rayburn asked Darrell specific questions about the book, he was unable to answer them. It turned out that Darrell was unable to identify most of the words in the book and was just pretending to read. Another student, Tamika, is in Mr. Thomas's Algebra 1 class. She is having difficulty solving basic equations with one unknown because she has yet to master basic math computational skills.

Preskills are basic skills necessary for performing more complex skills. Prior to teaching a skill, you should assess students on the relevant preskills and, if necessary, teach these skills. Darrell was unable to comprehend the book about magic because he lacked the word-identification skills needed to read the words. He may need instruction in word-attack skills; he may also need to be encouraged to read trade books at his reading level. Tamika will need additional instruction and practice on her computational skills if she is going to be successful in Algebra 1. Because textbooks do not generally list preskills, you need to ask yourself continually what preskills are required, and you need to be on the lookout for students who lack them. Looking at the instructional demands in this way is a key part of applying the INCLUDE strategy. Determining the potential impact of student preskills on instruction may mean informally assessing such skills. For example, before Ms. Tompkins taught her kindergartners to tell time, she checked to see whether they could identify the numbers 1–12 and count by 5s to 60. Before teaching students to look up words in a dictionary, Mr. Thurman checked to see whether his students could say the letters in the alphabet, could alphabetize words to the third letter, and knew whether to turn to the front, middle, or end of the dictionary when looking up a certain word. Mr. Thomas began his Algebra 1 class by assessing his class on basic computational skills.

If you are teaching a skill and find that most of your students lack the necessary preskills, teach these preskills directly before teaching the more complex skill. If only one or two stu-

WWW
RESOURCES

The Education 4 Kids website, at http://www.edu4kids.com, was set up to help students learn basic math skills on the Internet. Users can decide what type of math they want to be quizzed on and can also control the complexity of the equations and the size of the numbers. The site even keeps score so students can see how they are doing.

DIMENSIONS OF DIVERSITY

Children learn many basic preskills both directly and vicariously before they reach school age. Children's cultural backgrounds and life conditions greatly affect what they know and can do.

FYI

Assessing student preskills does not always have to be done using paper-and-pencil tasks. Simply questioning your students orally takes less time and can give you relevant information immediately.

INCLUDE

66 If you are teaching a skill and find that most of your students lack the necessary preskills, teach these preskills directly before teaching the more complex skill. 99

dents lack preskills, you can accommodate these students with extra practice and instruction through a peer or parent volunteer, or with the help of a special service provider. For example, Ms. Cooper was preparing a lesson on how to find the area of a rectangle. Before beginning the lesson, she gave her students a multiplication probe and found that almost half the class was still having problems with their multiplication facts. Ms. Cooper set up a peer tutoring program in which students who knew their facts were paired with students who did not; the pairs practiced facts for 10 minutes each day for a week. Ms. Cooper still introduced finding the area of rectangles as scheduled but she allowed students to use calculators until they had mastered their facts in the peer tutoring sessions.

Selecting and Sequencing Examples

The way you select and sequence instructional examples can affect how easily your students learn. For example, Alex's practice activities for a week in Mr. Huang's third-grade math class are shown in Figure 9.1. Mr. Huang has been covering two-digit subtraction with regrouping. On Monday through Thursday, Alex was given five of these problems and got them all right. On Friday, he was asked to do a mixture of problems,

FIGURE 9.1 Alex's Math Work

Monday's Seatwork

$\overset{2}{\cancel{3}}5$	$\overset{3}{\cancel{4}}2$	$\overset{2}{\cancel{3}}8$	$\overset{3}{\cancel{4}}1$	$\overset{6}{\cancel{7}}4$
-17	-15	-19	-22	-49
18	27	19	19	25

Tuesday's Seatwork

$\overset{5}{\cancel{6}}4$	$\overset{6}{\cancel{7}}0$	$\overset{8}{\cancel{9}}1$	$\overset{5}{\cancel{6}}8$	$\overset{7}{\cancel{8}}2$
-38	-32	-58	-39	-28
26	38	33	29	54

Wednesday's Seatwork

$\overset{8}{\cancel{9}}4$	$\overset{5}{\cancel{6}}1$	$\overset{2}{\cancel{3}}3$	$\overset{6}{\cancel{7}}6$	$\overset{7}{\cancel{8}}1$
-57	-45	-19	-38	-47
37	16	14	38	34

Thursday's Seatwork

$\overset{4}{\cancel{5}}5$	$\overset{2}{\cancel{3}}0$	$\overset{6}{\cancel{7}}2$	$\overset{8}{\cancel{9}}6$	$\overset{7}{\cancel{8}}3$
-29	-18	-28	-59	-38
26	12	44	37	45

Friday's Seatwork

$\overset{8}{\cancel{9}}6$	$\overset{3}{\cancel{4}}3$	$\overset{7}{\cancel{8}}9$	$\overset{5}{\cancel{6}}7$	$\overset{6}{\cancel{7}}5$
-53	-18	-33	-28	-57
313	25	416	39	18

some requiring regrouping and some not. Alex got only three of the problems correct because he was unable to discriminate between subtraction problems that required regrouping and those that did not. He was unable to differentiate these two types of problems in part because his daily practice pages had included only one problem type. Carefully preparing the **example selection** you use for instruction and student practice can help students learn to differentiate among problem types.

You can help students make key discriminations between current and previous problem types by using examples that at first require the application of only one particular skill (Carnine, Silbert, Kame'enui, & Tarver, 2004). When students can perform these problems without error, add examples of skills previously taught, to help students discriminate between the different problem types. Doing this also provides students with needed review. An easy accommodation for Alex would have been to add several problems that did not require regrouping to each daily teaching and practice session once he had shown that he could compute the regrouping problems accurately when they were presented alone.

Ms. Owens ran into a different example-related problem when teaching her students word problems in math. In her examples, when a word problem included the word *more*, getting the correct answer always involved subtracting, such as in the following problem:

> Alicia had 22 pennies. Juanita had 13. How many more pennies does Alicia have than Juanita?

However, on her test, Ms. Owens included the following problem:

> Mark read 3 books in March. He read 4 more books in April. How many books did Mark read?

Several students with special needs in Ms. Owens's class subtracted 3 from 4 because they thought the presence of the word *more* signaled subtraction. Ms. Owens needed to include problems of this latter type in her teaching to prevent such misconceptions.

Consider this example: When Mr. Yoshida taught his students how to add *ed* to a word ending in *y*, he demonstrated on the board as follows:

> carry + ed = carried   hurry + ed = hurried

Next, Mr. Yoshida had his students add *ed* to five words ending in *y*. Finally, he assigned students 10 practice problems in their English books that looked like this:

> Write the past tense of *marry*.

A number of students were unable to answer the questions in the book, even though they knew how to add *ed* to words ending in *y*, because the practice examples in the book required students to know what the meaning of past tense and how to form the *past tense* was by adding *ed*. The book's practice activity was very different from the instructional examples Mr. Yoshida used, which only required students to add *ed* to words ending in *y*.

Both Ms. Owens's and Mr. Yoshida's examples demonstrate an important aspect of selecting instructional examples: The range of your instructional examples should match the range of the problem types used when you assess student learning. Ms. Owens could have prevented problems in her class by expanding her range of examples to include word problems that contained the word *more* but that were not solved by subtracting. Mr. Yoshida could have better prepared his students for the practice activities in the English book by using examples that referred directly to forming the past tense by adding *ed*. Note that some students with special needs may still struggle even when the instructional examples used are appropriate. These students may require an individual accommodation that could be as simple as a reminder that the word *more* can have more than one meaning or that the past tense is formed when adding *ed* to a verb; or that could be as involved as additional instruction.

The following example shows a different example selection problem. Tawana's class was covering several high-frequency sight words that appeared in their classroom reading program. On Wednesday Tawana learned the word *man*, but on Thursday, after the word *men* was presented, she was unable to read *man* correctly. Tawana's word-identification problem illustrates another example selection problem, namely, **example sequencing.** The visual and auditory similarities of *man* and *men* make learning these words difficult for many at-risk students and students with learning disabilities, who may have trouble differentiating words that look and/or sound the same. One way to prevent this problem is to separate the introduction of *man* and *men* with the introduction of other, dissimilar high-frequency words, such as *dog*, *house*, and *cat*. Students with special needs may also need an individual accommodation such as more practice learning the words.

This same sequencing idea can be applied to teaching letter sounds. For example, when deciding on the order in which to teach the sounds, consider separating letters that look and sound the same, such as *b* and *d*, *m* and *n*, and *p* and *b*. The careful sequencing of instruction can also be applied to teaching higher level content. For example, when Mr. Roosevelt, a high school chemistry teacher, taught the chemical elements, he separated those symbols that look and/or sound similar, such as bromine (Br) and rubidium (Rb), and silicon (Si) and strontium (Sr).

Deciding the Rate of Introduction of New Skills

Students sometimes have difficulty learning skills when they are introduced at too fast a rate. For example, Mr. Henry was teaching his ninth-grade English students how to proofread rough drafts of their writing for errors in using capital letters and punctuation marks. He reviewed the rules for using capital letters, periods, commas, question marks, and exclamation points. Next, he had students take out their most recent writing sample from their portfolios to look for capitalization and punctuation errors. Carmine found that he had left out capital letters at the beginning of two sentences, but he did not find any of the punctuation errors he had made. He missed them because Mr. Henry taught his students to proofread their papers for capital letters and punctuation marks simultaneously. A better pace would have been first to work on proofreading for capitalization errors and then to add one punctuation mark at a time (first periods, then commas, followed by question marks, and then exclamation points).

In another example of the **rate of skill introduction,** Ms. Stevens was working on reading comprehension with her students. She introduced three new comprehension strategies at once: detecting the sequence, determining cause and effect, and making predictions. However, when applying the INCLUDE strategy, she recognized that Carlos, a student with a mild intellectual disability, learned best when he was taught one strategy at a time. Ms. Stevens accommodated Carlos by forming a group with three other students who, like Carlos, would benefit from learning these comprehension strategies one by one. As an additional adaptation, she temporarily removed cause-and-effect and prediction questions from these students' written comprehension exercises until they had been taught these strategies directly in their small group. When Mr. Wallace, the special education teacher, came to co-teach, he worked with these students on detecting the story sequence. Learn more about working with special education teachers in the Working Together feature on page 311.

These examples demonstrate an important principle about introducing new skills to students with special needs: New skills should be introduced in small steps and at a rate slow enough to ensure mastery prior to the introduction of more new skills. Furthermore, you may want to prioritize skills and even postpone some, as Ms. Stevens did. Many commercially produced materials introduce skills at a rate that is too fast for students with special needs. As just illustrated, a common accommodation is to slow down the rate of skill introduction and provide more practice. Other students in the

DIMENSIONS OF**DIVERSITY**

Listening is the weakest academic language skill for English-language learners. Khisty (2002, p. 34) suggests the following strategies when teaching math to Latino students:
(a) write words on an overhead projector or on the board as they are spoken, or point to words in a prepared written text as they are delivered; (b) always contextualize instruction through the use of models, real objects, drawings, and other visual aids; and
(c) have students act out problems or concepts.

INCLUDE

www
RESOURCES

The ProQuest K–12 website, at http://www.proquestk12.com, provides lesson plans that include modifications for students with special needs.

WORKING **TOGETHER**

Asking for Help

Ms. Gabriel is starting her first year as a high school history teacher. She just found out that she will have four students with learning disabilities included in her fifth-period American History class. The special education teacher, Mr. Colbert, left the students' IEPs in her mailbox with a brief note asking her to look them over to see what kind of accommodations she is required to make in her teaching. The IEPs state that she is supposed to give them their tests orally, modify their homework assignments, and adapt the textbook.

Ms. Gabriel is confused. In the first place, she is unsure exactly what an accommodation is. Second, how is she supposed to give tests orally to these students and still give the rest of the students written tests? Also, she doesn't know what the IEP means by modifying homework and adapting the text. She's particularly worried about homework because she knows students won't like it if they know that other students are doing less homework. Ms. Gabriel feels that Mr. Colbert should have met with her to explain more clearly what she needed to do. Still, she is new to the school and is afraid to admit she doesn't know what to do. Mr. Colbert is also the wrestling coach, and Ms. Gabriel doesn't feel very comfortable communicating with "jocks."

If you were Ms. Gabriel, what would you do?

- Including students with special needs is a team effort. In order for the team to be effective, all of the team members need to be clear about student goals and faculty responsibility for helping meet those goals. Ms. Gabriel is correct that a meeting needs to be called to clarify what she needs to do with the students.

- In calling the meeting, Ms. Gabriel should set a positive tone for problem solving. Rather than complaining that a meeting should have been called, Ms. Gabriel should write a note to Mr. Colbert explaining that she is excited about the challenge of working with these students in her class, has some questions as to how she can best meet their needs, and would like to meet briefly with him about it.

- At the meeting, Ms. Gabriel must be careful to not put Mr. Colbert on the defensive. One way to put him at ease right away would be to establish empathy. Ms. Gabriel can do that by recognizing how busy he is and thanking him for taking the time to meet with her.

- Even though Ms. Gabriel may not feel comfortable interacting with a coach, she needs to be careful to react to his ideas, not his personality. She needs to realize that good ideas can come from persons whose personalities don't match hers.

- Ms. Gabriel can further establish good communication with Mr. Colbert by explaining her questions using nonevaluative language. For example, rather than addressing the subject by saying that she doesn't see how she can give tests two different ways or modify homework without being unfair to the other students, she should ask Mr. Colbert for his ideas about how to carry out these accommodations. For example, for the problem with homework, she could say, "What specific homework adaptations do these students need? Do the other students ever complain when you make homework adaptations for students with disabilities? What do you say to them?"

- The need to keep her interaction with Mr. Colbert positive and productive should not compromise the equally important need for Ms. Gabriel to attain the appropriate supports for her included students with special needs. An effective team player is assertive yet at the same time treats colleagues with respect.

class, including those with no formally identified special needs, often benefit from such accommodations as well. If a student happens to be the only one having a problem, you can seek additional support from special needs staff, paraprofessionals, peers, and/or parent volunteers.

Slowing down the rate of skills introduced is an adaptation in the way curriculum is presented, but it is not the same thing as reducing the amount of curriculum to be learned. You need to be careful not to reduce the expectations for your students with special needs who are expected to meet the goals of the general education curriculum. Otherwise, they will have difficulty meeting state standards. However, for your students with moderate to severe intellectual disabilities it may be appropriate to make an instructional modification by decreasing the amount of curriculum. For example, Ms. Evers modified Robin's curriculum by shortening her spelling lists from 15 to 3 words and selecting only high-frequency words specified on her IEP.

CONNECTIONS

Direct instruction may help Abdul, whom you read about at the beginning of the chapter. His teacher, Ms. Diaz, could teach the skill of writing percentages for fractions directly by listing the steps in solving such problems on the board; having students say all the steps; solving several sample problems for students by following the listed steps; leading students through solving similar problems using the steps until they are able to do them independently; and assigning problems for students to do independently, reminding them to follow the steps listed on the board.

RESEARCH
NOTE

Research shows that many students with learning disabilities need direct instruction in letter sounds in order to eventually learn to identify words systematically (Ehri, 2004).

Some students need additional instruction and practice when they are learning new skills. What prerequisite concepts and skills might you teach for this assignment on vocabulary? What kinds of additional practice might you provide?

Providing Direct Instruction and Opportunities for Practice and Review

Students with special needs may require more direct instruction and review if they are to acquire basic academic skills. Consider the following example. Youn is in Ms. Howard's spelling class. On Monday, Ms. Howard gave students a pretest on the 15 new words for the week. On Tuesday, the students were required to use each word in a sentence. On Wednesday, the teacher scrambled up the letters in all the words and had the students put them in the correct order. On Thursday, students answered 15 fill-in-the-blank questions, each of which required one of the new spelling words. On Friday, Youn failed her spelling test even though she had successfully completed all the spelling activities for that week. She did poorly on her spelling test because the daily spelling activities did not provide her with enough direct instruction and practice on the spelling words. Although activities such as using spelling words in sentences are valuable in the right context, they do not provide practice on the primary objective of this particular lesson, which is spelling all 15 words correctly from dictation. One way to accommodate Youn individually would be to have a peer tutor give her a daily dictation test on all 15 words, have Youn write each missed word three times, and then retest her on all 15 words again.

These examples demonstrate another problem that students with special needs have when learning basic skills: retention. Melissa had mastered addition facts to 10 as measured by a probe test in October, but when she was given the same test in January, she got only half of the facts correct. Similarly, Thomas, in his world history class, could state the major causes of World War I in November, but he could not remember them when asked to compare them to the causes of World War II in February. A common adaptation you can use for such students is to schedule more review for them. This review should be more frequent following your initial presentation of the material, and then can become less frequent as learning is established. For example, instead of waiting until January to review addition facts, Melissa's teacher could first provide review weekly, then every other week, and then every month. Thomas's history teacher could periodically review key concepts and information that Thomas may need to apply later, either through homework, an instructional game or contest, or an activity in a co-taught class. If Thomas and Melissa were the only ones in their classes in need of review, their teachers could accommodate them individually by giving them extra help before school or while the rest of the class was working independently.

A related concern is that indirect instructional approaches may be appropriate for some students but may need to be supplemented for others. For example, Felix and Bill

were learning to read in Ms. Farrell's class. Neither boy had mastered the *ch* sound (as in *chin*). On Monday, Felix came across the word *chair* in a trade book he was reading. His teacher pronounced the word and stated, "When *c* and *h* are together in a word, they usually say *ch*." The next day, Felix came to the word *chip* in his book, and he figured it out, remembering what Ms. Farrell had told him the day before. For Felix, one example in his book and a brief teacher explanation were enough for learning to occur. On Monday, Bill also came across a *ch* word, and he, too, was told what the word was and what sound *c* and *h* make when they come together in a word. Unlike Felix, however, when Bill came across another *ch* word the next day, he could not remember the sound of these letters. Having the teacher tell him just once the sound *ch* made was not enough. Bill required more direct instruction and practice than Felix, such as that provided in the activity shown in Table 9.1.

This discussion of Felix and Bill raises an important issue: General education teachers need to know more than one approach to meet the needs of individual students. Felix can learn sounds with minimal instruction while reading books; Bill cannot. Bill's teacher may need to accommodate Bill and maybe other students in the class, by providing them with some direct instruction on letter–sound correspondence. Learn more about how to provide differentiated instruction in reading in the Professional Edge on pages 314–315.

Another example reinforces the idea that some of your students with special needs may need more direct instruction and practice. Mr. Diaz was teaching his high school English students how to write a persuasive essay, including how to develop a topic sentence, add supporting details, reject counterarguments, and end with a conclusion. He described the steps in writing a persuasive essay while showing students an example of

DIMENSIONS OF DIVERSITY

In Native American cultures, children learn new skills by first observing them and then doing them. Native American students can benefit from direct teaching approaches that first stress modeling or demonstrating skills. You can make demonstrations particularly effective for your Native American students by showing them what the final product looks like before the demonstration (Sparks, 2000).

ANALYZE AND REFLECT

Under what circumstances would you accommodate individual students by changing how you teach the entire class? When would accommodating students be more appropriately carried out individually or in small groups?

TABLE 9.1 Direct Instruction of *ch* Sound

Teacher	Students
1. Teach directly the *ch* sound in isolation.	
Teacher writes on the board: *ch, or, ee, ch, th, sh, ch,* and *ing.*	
1. Teacher models by saying the sound of the new letter combination and tests by having the students pronounce it. Teacher points to *ch*. "These letters usually say *ch*. What sound?"	*"ch"*
2. Teacher alternates between the new combination and other combinations. Teacher points to a letter combination, pauses 2 seconds, and asks, "What sound?"	Say the combination sound
3. Teacher calls on several individual students to identify one or more letter combinations.	
2. Teach directly the *ch* sound in words.	
Teacher writes on the board: *chin, chair, chip, boot, beam, chomp, stain, chum, moon,* and *chat.*	
1. a. Students identify the sound of the letter combination in *chin,* then read the word. Teacher points under the combination letters and asks, "What sound?"	*"ch"*
b. Teacher points to left of word. "What word?"	*"chin"*
c. Teacher repeats step 1(a–b) with remaining words.	*"chin"*
2. a. Students reread the list without first identifying the sound of the letter combination. Teacher points to *chin,* pauses 2 seconds, and asks, "What word?"	
b. Teacher repeats step 2(a) with remaining words.	
3. Teacher calls on individual students to read one or more words.	

SOURCE: From *Direct Instruction Reading* (4th ed.), by D. Carnine, J. Silbert, and E. J. Kame'enui, and S. G. Tarver, 2004, Upper Saddle River, NJ: Merrill/Prentice Hall. Copyright © 2004. Reprinted with the permission of Prentice-Hall, Inc.

PROFESSIONAL EDGE

Providing Differentiated Instruction in Reading

The idea behind differentiated instruction is that a variety of teaching and learning strategies are necessary to meet the range of needs evident in any given classroom. According to Tomlinson (2000, p. 9), students' diverse needs can be met by "providing materials and tasks at varied levels of difficulty, with varying degrees of scaffolding, through multiple instructional groups, and with time variations." Nowhere is the need for differentiated instruction more evident than in beginning reading. Research tells us that while about 20–30 percent of students acquire reading skills readily without the need for extra support, another 20–30 percent require some additional support, and about 30 percent require intensive support if they are to learn to read (Lyon, 1998). Bursuck and colleagues (2004) implemented a multitiered model of differentiated beginning reading instruction in grades K–3 in three urban schools. The model had originally been implemented successfully in two rural schools (Dickson & Bursuck, 1999, 2003). Failure rates for the three urban schools on the state third-grade reading test ranged from 50 to 78 percent. Clearly, many students were in need of a different approach to beginning reading. The purpose of the multitiered model was to provide varying levels of student support depending on student need. The model is shown in Figure 9.2.

Tier 1 was the standard general education reading program but with some teaching strategies added because of the high percentage of students in the three schools who were struggling to learn to read. These enhancements included many of the teaching methods described in this chapter such as careful example selection, a gradual rate of introducing new skills, direct teacher instruction, and the provision of many opportunities for practice and review. The general education reading program was also adapted to make the teaching of phonics more explicit and systematic, a key recommendation by the National Reading Panel (2000). The performance of students in Tier 1 was continually monitored using curriculum-based measures of key literacy skills such as phonemic awareness, letter sounds, word identification, passage-reading fluency, and reading comprehension. Students who were not acquiring key literacy skills according to the assessments continued to receive instruction in Tier 1 but were provided with Tier 2 instruction as well which consisted of extra daily practice on skills covered in the classroom reading series using small, same-skill groups of 2–8 students.

The booster sessions represented in Tier 2 of the model were delivered by the classroom teacher or a trained paraprofessional using either one-to-one or small-group instruction. The progress of Tier 2 students continued to be regularly monitored. If these students continued to show problems acquiring beginning reading skills, they moved to more intensive instruction in Tier 3.

Tier 3 was an intensive alternative reading program designed for at-risk readers called *Reading Mastery* (Engelmann & Bruner, 2003). The phonetically based *Reading Mastery* curriculum is characterized by a carefully designed instructional sequence as well as the extensive use of scaffolding to support student learning. Tier 3 instruction was carried out in small groups by either a Chapter I or special education teacher. Children in Tier 3 were pulled out of their general

INCLUDE

a well-written persuasive essay. He then asked the students to write a one-page persuasive essay for homework. Brenda handed in her essay the next day; although her paper showed some potential, her topic sentence lacked clarity, her details were sketchy, and she forgot to reject possible counterarguments. Brenda needed more instruction and guided practice on how to write a persuasive essay than Mr. Diaz had provided. He could have applied the INCLUDE strategy, anticipated Brenda's problems, and provided guided practice by writing essays with the class until even the lower performers such as Brenda seemed comfortable performing the task. He could also have had the students write a persuasive essay independently in class so that he could monitor their performance and accommodate individual students using corrective feedback and more instruction if necessary.

Finally, it is important to remember that practice is most effective when it follows direct instruction; practice is never an adequate substitute for direct instruction. For example, Mr. Hanesworth designs a board game in which students get to move ahead

education classes when the rest of the students were involved in word-reading activities that were too difficult for them. Tier 3 students still participated in many of the general education reading activities, but care was taken to coordinate those activities with the students' Tier 3 reading program. Preliminary results showed that about half of the students were making adequate progress in Tier 1. Another 20 percent required Tier 2 boosters, and about 30 percent required an alternative, more intensive reading program in Tier 3 (Bursuck et al., 2004). Similar to other research (O'Connor, 2000; Torgesen, 2000), this study found that approximately 5 percent of the students continued to struggle to acquire beginning reading skills, even with Tier 3 instruction. These students moved to Tier 4.

Tier 4 instruction was provided by a special education teacher and was characterized by smaller instructional groups (no more than three students per group), a slower rate of skill introduction, and more extensive scaffolds or supports, such as in-depth auditory discrimination training (Lindamood & Lindamood, 1998). The results also showed that the overall performance of the three schools on the state reading test in grade 3 exceeded levels of performance in the same schools before the model was implemented (Bursuck, Damer, & Dickson, 2005). Also of interest was that children receiving help in Tiers 2 and 3 had attitudes toward reading that were as positive as their Tier 1 classmates, minorities were not overrepresented in Tiers 2 and 3, and referrals to special education decreased in all three schools (Bursuck & Damer, in press).

FIGURE 9.2 Multitiered Model of Differentiated Reading Instruction

Tier 1
Grade-Level Instruction with Added Strategies

Tier 2
Boosters for Poor Responders to Tier 1

Tier 3
Intensive Alternative Program for Poor Responders to Tiers 1 and 2

Tier 4
Special Education Instruction

if they can answer a division fact problem. The problem is that five students in his class still do not understand the concept of division. For them, the board game practice activity is likely to result in failure. Mr. Hanesworth can accommodate these learners in a small group by providing additional instruction on division for them while allowing the rest of the class to play the board game independently. Of course, later on, Mr. Hanesworth can reward the hard work of the small group by allowing them to practice a skill they know using a game-like format.

Clearly, you may need to adapt instruction to enable students with special needs to acquire basic skills. An example of how to adapt basic skills instruction using INCLUDE is presented in the Case in Practice on pages 316–317. In addition, the Technology Notes feature on pages 318–319 introduces ways to use technology to assist students with special needs with their writing. Students may also need accommodations when subject-area content is presented, the primary teaching focus as students move into the upper grades.

CASE IN PRACTICE

Applying INCLUDE to a Basic Skills Lesson

Ms. Dettman loves to look on the Internet for what she calls "teacher-tested" lesson plans. She found a lesson yesterday on the topic of math story problems (Bowen, n.d.), an area in which her students often struggle and in which she is always looking for something different to do. The teacher who used this technique claimed that it had had a positive impact on her class's performance last year on the state's high-stakes test in math. Ms. Dettman decided to try it.

In this lesson, the teacher posts a daily story problem on tagboard. The skill targeted (for example, division, fractions) varies from day to day. The problem is read aloud first thing in the morning and students have until lunchtime to solve it. The children keep a special file folder containing an answer sheet for the week's problems. Children are required to show their work. After lunch, three or four students go to the board to solve the problem. They talk aloud about how

they solved the problem. Each child has an incentive chart posted in class. Every day, two students collect and score papers and a sticker is awarded for correct answers. Students receive a prize when they reach five stickers, and then a new chart is posted.

Ms. Dettman has a group of four students in class who have trouble in math; three of these students have learning disabilities in both reading and math. Because the curricular goals for these students are the same as those of everyone else in the class, instructional modifications are not required. Ms. Dettman reviewed the demands of this activity to see whether any accommodations were needed. She identified the following seven demands:

1. Read the problem.
2. Identify the operation needed to solve the problem (for example, add, subtract).
3. Write a number sentence.

4. Convert the number sentence to a computation problem.
5. Solve the computation problem.
6. Label the answer.
7. Check work.

Next, Ms. Dettman thought about areas where she might need to make accommodations. She considered the students' preskills. Three of the students have reading problems, but the fact that the story problems would be read out loud eliminated the need for an accommodation such as a bypass strategy. However, Ms. Dettman thought the students would have trouble translating the story problems into a sentence; they all have reading comprehension problems and had previously struggled to pick the correct operation when they solved story problems in class. The four students also don't know their math facts, and their computational accuracy is inconsistent, even though they understand the concepts behind the

CONNECTIONS

Teaching preskills, selecting and sequencing examples, deciding the rate of introduction of new skills, and providing opportunities for direct instruction, practice, and review are all elements of *universal design,* a concept discussed in Chapter 5. Adaptations in these areas can help you provide *differentiated instruction,* another idea discussed in Chapter 5.

How Can You Make Accommodations for Students with Special Needs When Teaching Subject-Area Content?

The instruction of academic content includes areas such as history and science. This instruction mainly involves the use of textbooks and lecture-discussion formats, but it also can include other activities, such as videos, films, and cooperative learning. Although content-area instruction generally is associated with instruction in secondary schools, the information presented here is relevant for elementary teachers as well. In this section, you learn how you can adapt your teaching and materials to help students with special needs learn subject-area content. Strategies for making accommodations are stressed for activating background knowledge, organizing content, and teaching terms and concepts. As with basic skills, you can provide accommodations for your students with special needs

four basic operations. Computation could be a definite problem as well. None of the students struggle with handwriting, so the writing demands of solving the word problem would not be problematic. In addition, one student is artistically inclined, a strength that Ms. Dettman planned to build on. Ms. Dettman was concerned about the fact that different types of story problems were selected for the activity each day in the lesson plan. She thought that this variety might confuse the four students who seem to work best when new problem types are added gradually as others are learned. Ms. Dettman was also concerned that student modeling of problem solving at the board by thinking out loud was a great idea, but she felt the students with problems in math might not benefit from it without more careful structuring.

Ms. Dettman decided to make the following accommodations for the four students. Although she would

continue to work with them on improving the accuracy of their math computation skills, for this activity she would allow them to bypass their current difficulties in this area by letting them use calculators. Ms. Dettman also decided to provide the students with a visual diagram to guide them through the problem-solving steps, along with small-group guided practice to ensure they used the strategy appropriately. Part of that small-group guided practice would include teacher and student think alouds to make the problem-solving steps more conspicuous for the students. Also, when students came to the board to solve problems out loud in the large group, bonus points would be awarded to those students paying careful attention, particularly to the think-aloud part. Ms. Dettman would use only story problems that the students were capable of solving independently. That way they would get needed indepen-

dent practice as well as a realistic opportunity to earn stickers and cash them in for a prize at the end of the week. Finally, Ms. Dettman would appoint the student with artistic talent to be the class artist; she would come to the board and draw a picture representing the problem.

REFLECTIONS

Why do you think Ms. Dettman made instructional accommodations for the four struggling students rather than instructional modifications? How did Ms. Dettman use the INCLUDE strategy to come up with instructional accommodations for those students? How effective and feasible do you think these accommodations are? What would you do differently if you were the teacher?

by changing how you teach the entire class or by making more individualized adaptations either one-to-one or in small groups. Strategies for teaching science to English-language learners are described in the Special Emphasis On. . . on page 320.

Activating Background Knowledge

The amount of background knowledge students have can greatly influence whether they can read subject matter with understanding. To illustrate, read this list of words:

are	making	between
only	consists	often
continuously	vary	corresponding
one	curve	points
draws	relation	variation
set	graph	table
if	values	isolated
variables	known	

DIMENSIONS OF DIVERSITY

Relating subject-area content to students' background knowledge makes material more relevant for students. It also motivates students to draw on their own background knowledge when they encounter new information, thereby helping them assume responsibility for their own learning (Gersten et al., 1998).

> TECHNOLOGY NOTES

Supporting Student Journal Writing Using Word-Recognition and Speech-Synthesis Software

A dialogue journal is a written conversation between the teacher and each individual student (Staton, Shuy, Kreeft-Peyton, & Reed, 1988). Dialogue journals can benefit students with special needs in a number of ways. Journals can provide students with an opportunity to practice writing without the fear of being continuously corrected. Teacher responses to students' journal entries can also model good writing for students. Dialogue journals also motivate students' writing by giving them a specific reason to write.

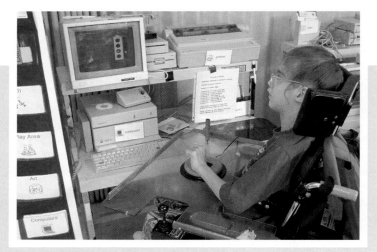

How might speech-synthesis and word-prediction programs help this student with her journal entries? What other types of assistive technology might help her with her writing?

Although journals can benefit students with special needs, problems with basic skills can disrupt the journaling process. Illegible handwriting and severe spelling problems can render student work unreadable, making it impossible for the teacher to respond to entries. Dictation can help, but that takes a lot of individual attention—more than you may be able to provide. A word processor with a spell-checker can also be used, but the spelling errors of some students may be too severe for a spell-checker to help.

MacArthur (1998) researched the use of assistive technology as a support for students engaging in dialogue journals with their teachers. He equipped the computers of third-grade students with special needs with speech-synthesis and word-prediction capabilities. Speech synthesis translates words typed by students into speech. Speech synthesis helps students read their teachers' messages without having to ask for help. It also helps students read their own writing, allowing them to detect more spelling and grammatical errors than they would spot by reading

alone. Word-prediction programs help students "predict" words they intend to write. Students type the first letter, or first few letters, and then choose from a list of predictions instead of having to type the whole word. Word prediction can help students with severe spelling problems. For example, the prediction program called Penfriend predicts words that students are most likely to type using a variety of knowledge including English grammar, frequently used words, and a learned knowledge of the students' personal writing styles. Predictions are made from an alphabetical word list that is visible on the screen. A sample screen display is shown in Figure 9.3. As students type the first letter or letters of a word, the word list automatically scrolls to the first word beginning with those letters. Students can then click on the word they want from the list to insert it in their story. They can also hear the word pronounced by the speech synthesizer before selecting it.

MacArthur (1998) found that the use of speech-synthesizer and word-prediction programs greatly improved

Were you able to read all of them? Do you know the meanings of all these words? Now read the following passage:

> If the known relation between the variables consists of a table of corresponding values, the graph consists only of the corresponding set of isolated points. If the variables are known to vary continuously, one often draws a curve to show the variation. (From Michaelson, 1945, as cited in Lavoie, 1991)

Chances are, if you were asked to summarize what you just read, you would be unable to do so despite the fact that you probably answered yes when asked whether you could read and understand all the words individually. You may lack the background knowledge necessary to understand this very technical paragraph. The knowledge students

FIGURE 9.3 Penfriend Software

Thomas has typed the first letter of *poisonous;* the word list has scrolled to the first word beginning with those letters; and Thomas is about to double-click on the word to insert it in his text.

From Penfriend software published by Crick Software Ltd. Copyright. Used by permission.

the spelling accuracy and legibility of the journal entries of four of the five students with severe writing problems who participated in the study. However, student spelling performance reverted to previous problematic levels when the synthesizer and word-prediction programs were taken away. This shows that programs such as the ones described here are useful as bypass or compensatory strategies but do not by themselves result in improved independent spelling skills. Such skills need to be directly and systematically taught.

bring to a content-area lesson is often as important for understanding as the quality of the textbook or instructional presentation (Langer, 1984; Pressley, 2000). For students to understand content material, they need to relate it to information they already know. Unfortunately, teachers often fail to consider background information. Students with disabilities and students who are at risk may have two problems with background knowledge: They may simply lack the necessary knowledge, or they may know the information but be unable to recall it or relate it to the new information being presented.

USING THE PREP STRATEGY ● One teaching strategy for determining how much knowledge students already have about a topic so that you can decide how much

RESEARCH NOTE

Studies of English-language learners show that making connections with students' culture, background, and experiences can lead to high levels of student engagement in instruction (Foorman et al., 2004).

Special EMPHASIS On ...

Strategies for Teaching Science to English-Language Learners

You learned in Chapter 8 that the racial, cultural, and linguistic diversity of U.S. classrooms has been increasing and will continue to do so. English-language learners (ELLs), or students for whom English is not their primary language, are an increasingly large proportion of this group. For example, in the 2003–2004 school year, 5.5 million ELLs attended American public schools (Leos, 2004, as cited in Short & Echevarria, 2005). Unfortunately, ELLs struggle in school (Snow & Biancarosa, 2003), and nowhere is this fact more evident than in science, where information about teaching ELLs can be hard to find (Watson, 2004).

While ELLs share the characteristic of having limited English proficiency, it is important to realize that they are a diverse group; ELLs come to your science classroom with different levels of background knowledge, literacy in their native language, family involvement in their education, intellectual ability, and motivation to do well in school, to name a few areas. All of these factors, in addition to English proficiency, should be considered when adapting ELLs' science instruction using these strategies (Short & Echevarria, 2005; Watson, 2004):

- For students in your class who speak little or no English but are fluent in Spanish, label parts of your classroom and lab equipment with both English and Spanish names (for example, *science book/ciencia libro*). Besides helping to initiate communication with your ELLs, labeling in English and Spanish also demonstrates to English-speaking students the difficulties students face when learning a new language. Requiring all of your students to learn both names effectively reinforces this idea.

- Place less emphasis on the traditional approach of having students read the textbook prior to engaging in a laboratory activity. Instead, start with the laboratory experience. The concreteness of laboratory experiences makes the text more comprehensible.

- Whenever possible, show objects, draw pictures, or act out the meaning of key terms. For example, when teaching the concept of scientific classification, one teacher demonstrated the concept by having students take off their left shoes and put them in a pile in the front of the room. The students classified the shoes in different ways such as shoes that lace, slip on, or buckle.

- Repeat instructions, actions, and demonstrations as needed, speaking slowly and using simple sentence structure whenever possible.

- Demonstrate procedures and provide clarifying diagrams and illustrations before students begin lab work. For example, before students begin a lab exercise, provide them with a written procedural guide, go over key terms by placing them on the board, demonstrate the procedures, and actively monitor students' performance by circulating among them as they are completing the lab.

- Assign lab partners to ELLs. The lab partners should be strong in science and willing to work with students who are ELLs. Placing two ELLs together in a group along with one English speaker is also effective, particularly if one of the ELLs is more advanced than the other in English skills. Encouraging ELLs to express their thoughts to a partner before reporting to the whole class promotes language learning and the confidence to speak out in class.

- If appropriate, enlist the support of parents in building students' background knowledge about topics before they are introduced in class. Background knowledge provided in students' native language allows them to better follow what is discussed, even if they don't know every word.

- Schedule time for review at the end of each lesson, pointing out key concepts and vocabulary while making connections to lesson objectives and state standards. This is essential, because ELLs may concentrate so intently on processing language during instruction that they are unable to identify the most important information expressed.

- Give feedback to your students on their language use in class. For example, model for your students how scientists talk about their experimental findings. Have students try to use the language of scientists when orally presenting their lab reports, and give them feedback on their performance.

background information to present in class prior to a reading assignment is called the **PReP (PreReading Plan) strategy** (Langer, 1984). The PReP strategy has three major steps:

1. Preview the text or lesson, and choose two to three important concepts. For example, for a science lesson, Mr. Amin chose the concept of photosynthesis and the key words cycle and oxygen.

2. Conduct a brainstorming session with students. This process involves three phases. In Phase 1, students tell you what comes to mind when they hear the concept. This gives you a first glance at how much they already know about the topic. In Phase 2, students tell you what made them think of their responses in Phase 1. This information can help you judge the depth of and/or basis for their responses, and it also provides a springboard for students to refine their responses in Phase 3. In Mr. Amin's class, he discovered in Phases 1 and 2 that two of the students mistakenly thought that photosynthesis had to do with photography because of the presence of photo in the word. This error provided an opportunity to build on students' knowledge. Mr. Amin explained that *photo* means light and that in photography, a camera takes in light and combines it with certain chemicals on film to make pictures. He then said that plants take in light, too, and when the light combines with chemicals in the plant, carbohydrates and oxygen are made. This process is called photosynthesis. In this way, Mr. Amin used what the students already knew to teach them a concept they did not know. In Phase 3, students can add to their responses based on the discussion in Phase 2.

3. Evaluate student responses to determine the depth of their prior knowledge of the topic. During this step, you can decide whether students are ready to read the text and/or listen to a lecture on photosynthesis or whether they first need more information. Determining the needs of your students with respect to the demands of your instruction is an important part of INCLUDE. In Mr. Amin's class two students continued to have trouble understanding that photosynthesis was something plants did with light to make carbohydrates and oxygen. They needed more information before they were ready to read the chapter. Mr. Amin accommodated these students by showing them a video illustration of photosynthesis including concrete examples that weren't necessary to use with the rest of the class.

PREPARING ANTICIPATION GUIDES ● Anticipation guides can help you activate student knowledge about a particular topic and construct bridges to new information by encouraging students to make predictions (Readence, Moore, & Rickelman, 2000; Vacca & Vacca, 2004). **Anticipation guides** consist of a series of statements, some of which may not be true, related to the material that the student is about to read (Burns, Roe, & Ross, 2001). Before teaching, students read these statements that either challenge or support ideas they may already have about the subject. This process catches their interest and gives them a reason for listening and reading. Providing questions or statements prior to reading also aids comprehension for all students, including those with special needs.

For example, Ms. Henry constructed an anticipation guide prior to teaching a unit on the nervous system. Her anticipation guide included the following statements:

- A person cannot function without the nervous system.
- The nervous system helps us study and learn about new things.
- There are gaps between the nerve cells in our bodies.
- Nerve cells do different jobs in the body.
- The central nervous system is only one part of the nervous system.

WWW
RESOURCES

Education World, at http://www.education-world.com, provides a searchable database of more than 50,000 sites related to curriculum ideas. Many of the resources are geared especially to students with exceptionalities.

DIMENSIONS OF DIVERSITY

Use concrete examples and experiences to make instruction more comprehensible for English-language learners with learning difficulties (Gersten et al., 1998). These include visuals, computer software, CD-ROM, films, field trips, and science experiments. Also, use materials and subject matter that relate to the students' experiences and interests, allow students to share information and experiences in their native language, and intersperse lectures with hands-on activities.

- Our brains do not control our reflexes.
- Persons cannot hold their breath until they die.
- Some people can swim without thinking about it.

When using the anticipation guide, Ms. Henry needed to make an accommodation for several of her students with reading problems. After distributing the guide, she met with these students in a small group and read each item out loud, clarifying terms such as *central nervous system*, *reflexes*, and *nerve cells*.

PROVIDING PLANNING THINK SHEETS ● Activating background information and building bridges to current knowledge is also of concern to teachers when asking students to write. Some researchers recommend **planning think sheets** to help writers focus on background information as well as on the audience and purpose of a paper (Englert et al., 1988). For audience, students are asked to consider who will read the paper. For purpose, students clarify why they are writing the paper (for example, to tell a story, to convey information, or to persuade someone). Finally, students activate background knowledge and organize that knowledge by asking themselves questions such as, "What do I know about the topic? How can I group or label my facts?" (Englert et al., 1988). A planning think sheet for a paper assignment might contain write-on lines for students to answer the following questions (Raphael, Kirschner, & Englert, 1986):

- What is my topic?
- Why do I want to write on this topic?
- What are two things I already know that will make it easy to write this paper?
- Who will read my paper?
- Why will the reader be interested in this topic?

Students with special needs may need more teacher modeling and guided practice before being able to complete the think sheets independently. You can deliver these accommodations using a small, teacher-led group.

Organizing Content

Research shows that many students, including students with special needs, have difficulty understanding important ideas and their interrelationships in content areas such as social studies and science (Kame'enui, Carnine, Dixon, Simmons, & Coyne, 2002; Lawton, 1995). These students can benefit from the use of supports or scaffolds that help them identify and understand important information. As we discussed in Chapter 5, one form of support is to organize the curriculum according to big ideas rather than facts in isolation. Another form of support is to make these big ideas more evident to students through the use of advance organizers, cue words for organizational patterns, study guides, and graphic organizers.

USING ADVANCE ORGANIZERS ● **Advance organizers** include information presented verbally and/or visually that makes content more understandable by putting it within a more general framework. They are particularly effective for students with special needs who may have limited background knowledge and reading and listening comprehension skills (Swanson & Deshler, 2003). Examples of advance organizers include the following (Lenz, 1983):

- identifying major topics and activities
- presenting an outline of content
- providing background information

WWW
RESOURCES

The TESOL (Teachers of English to Speakers of Other Languages) website, at http://www.tesol.org, provides news and links regarding the fastest-growing sector of school-age children: those who come from non-English-speaking backgrounds.

FYI

Advance organizers help activate prior learning, keep students on task, and provide reference points for remembering tasks that need to be completed.

- stating concepts and ideas to be learned in the lesson
- motivating students to learn by showing the relevance of the activity
- stating the objectives or outcomes of the lesson

EMPLOYING CUE WORDS FOR ORGANIZATIONAL PATTERNS ● Big ideas are often the central focus of an **organizational pattern** of information. The most common patterns of information include the descriptive list and the sequence of events in time, comparison/contrast, cause/effect, and problem/solution (Baxendell, 2003; Ellis, 1996). Each of these patterns of information can be made more conspicuous for students through the use of cue words. For example, cue words for a list, description, or sequence might include *first, second,* and *third;* cue words for comparison/contrast would be *similar, different, on the one hand,* and *on the other hand;* cue words for cause/effect might be *causes, effects, because,* and *so that;* and cue words for problem/solution would be *problem, solution,* and *resolve.* Cue words are important for students with special needs, many of whom have difficulty telling the difference between important and unimportant information (Hallahan et al., 2005; Kame'enui et al., 2002).

Consider the following two passages, about the formation of the two-party system, which are taken from two different social studies textbooks.

DIMENSIONS OF DIVERSITY

Direct teaching of organizational patterns can greatly assist English-language learners in comprehending content-area textbooks (Schifini, 1994).

Text 1

Ordinary People Formed a Political Party

The problem.   You have learned how the policies of the Federalist party of the wealthy business people did not directly help the ordinary people. Small farmers had to pay the Whiskey Tax, but wealthy farmers who grew other crops did not. Ordinary people had lost a great deal of money when they sold their bonds to speculators. Government money was being paid primarily to wealthy people. The Alien and Sedition Acts were passed to keep ordinary people from gaining political power. A serious problem for the first few years in our country's history was that the party of the wealthy business people ignored the *viewpoint* of ordinary people.

What was a serious problem during the first few years of our country's history?

The solution.   Although Thomas Jefferson didn't like the idea of political parties, Jefferson felt that ordinary people needed to be brought together and organized to get the political power that would result in the government doing things to help the ordinary person. Thomas Jefferson was a popular leader who gathered up the support of a great number of skilled workers, such as carpenters, blacksmiths, and other craftsmen, as well as shopkeepers and small farmers.

Jefferson began to organize a political party before the Presidential election of 1800. He felt confident that a political party of ordinary people could win elections because there were many more common people than wealthy business people. The political party of the ordinary people wanted to elect enough representatives to control Congress and to elect Thomas Jefferson to be President in the next Presidential election in 1800. That new political party was called by several names: the Democratic-Republicans, the Republicans, and also the Jeffersonian party. During the election campaign, the political party of the ordinary people made an issue of the unpopular Whiskey Tax and also the unpopular Alien and Sedition Acts. In the election of 1800, the party of the ordinary people won, and *Thomas Jefferson,* who also wrote the Declaration of Independence, became the third President of the United States. Also, enough legislators from the party of the ordinary people were elected to make those legislators the new majority in charge of Congress.

Why was Thomas Jefferson important to the development of political parties in the United States? (Carnine, Crawford, Harniss, & Hollenbeck, 1995, p. 207)

Text 2

The Constitution said nothing about the political parties that Washington had warned against. As early as the presidential election of 1792, however, something resembling two major parties appeared in American politics. These parties centered around Alexander Hamilton and Thomas Jefferson.

Rise of the two-party system. In the election of 1792, Washington was re-elected by unanimous vote. Vice-President John Adams was also re-elected but against strong opposition. He was opposed by George Clinton of New York, a candidate backed by Thomas Jefferson and his followers.

Hamilton's followers came to be called Federalists. The Federalist Party was strongest in New England and along the Atlantic seaboard. It included many wealthy merchants, manufacturers, lawyers, and church leaders. John Adams, himself a Federalist, said that Federalists represented "the rich, the well-born, and the able."

The opposition party was led by Thomas Jefferson. Its members called themselves Republicans. Although some wealthy people were Republicans, most of Jefferson's supporters were the owners of small farms or wage earners in the growing towns. (Todd & Curti, 1982, p. 212)

Which passage is easier to understand? Most teachers would say the first one. The major heading is specific. The relationship between Federalist legislation and the formation of the Republican Party is clear. This relationship is cast in the form of a problem/solution framework; the formation of the Republican Party was the solution to a problem involving the Federalists' trying to grab power from the ordinary people. This problem/solution structure is clearly signaled by boldface headings. Notice, too, that each section in the first passage is followed by a question that helps students sort out the main idea. Clearly, students will have an easier time accessing the content in this text. Still, some students may require more individualized accommodations, such as highlighting cue words, teacher modeling, and guided practice on how to use cue words to comprehend different text structures.

> You can accommodate students by helping to make the key concepts more explicit using teaching strategies described in this text such as study guides and graphic organizers.

The second passage contains no explicit signals of the relationship between Federalist policies and the formation of the Republican Party. It is also unclear why ordinary people so hated these policies. Students reading this passage are required to make a number of inferences, which may be difficult for students with special needs to make. Rewriting the book is obviously not a reasonable adaptation here, so instead you can accommodate students by helping to make the key concepts more explicit using teaching strategies described in this text, such as study guides and graphic organizers.

CONSTRUCTING STUDY GUIDES ● The general term **study guide** refers to outlines, abstracts, or questions that emphasize important information in texts (Mercer & Mercer, 2001). Study guides are helpful in improving comprehension for students with special needs in content-area classrooms (Lovitt, Rudsit, Jenkins, Pious, & Benedetti, 1985). For example, at the beginning of this chapter, Cecily was having trouble picking out key ideas in her American history text, a common problem for students at all educational levels. She might benefit from a study guide that cues students to important information by asking them questions about it. Procedures for constructing study guides are shown in the Professional Edge on page 325. A sample study guide for a section of a social studies text on Truman's Fair Deal is shown in Figure 9.4.

PROFESSIONAL EDGE

How to Develop Study Guides

Study guides help improve the comprehension of all students, especially those with special needs who are included in content-area classrooms. The following steps show you how to develop a study guide from a content-area textbook.

1. Go through the entire book and mark the chapters you want to cover for the term and those you do not.

2. Indicate the sequence in which you will assign the chapters; that is, note the one that comes first, second, and so forth.

3. Read the material in the first chapter carefully. Mark the important vocabulary, facts, and concepts that you expect students to learn. Cross out any material you do not intend to cover.

4. Divide the chapter into logical sections of 1,000 to 1,500 word passages. (The length will depend, of course, on how detailed the material is and how much of it you deem important.)

5. Write brief sentences that explain the main ideas or emphasize the vocabulary, facts, or concepts in the passage. Write 15 sentences per passage.

6. Place those sentences in order so that the material in one leads to the next, and so forth.

7. To create questions, either leave out a few words in each sentence or change each sentence into a question. For example, the following statement was identified as important in a chapter on natural disasters:

   A 2 percent sales tax was passed to pay for relief efforts after the massive floods of 1993.

   This statement could be turned into a question by leaving out several words:

   _____ was passed to pay for relief efforts after the massive floods of 1993.

   You could also change the statement into a question:

   How did the people pay for the relief efforts after the massive floods of 1993?

8. Make a transparency of sentences and/or questions using large type.

9. Prepare sheets for the students, using regular type.

10. Prepare an answer sheet for the teacher.

11. Develop a multiple-choice test to cover the material in the study guide. The test should have 10–15 items, with four possible choices for each question.

SOURCE: From *Study Guides: A Paper on Curriculum Modification,* by S. V. Horton, 1987, Seattle: University of Washington.

FIGURE 9.4 Sample Study Guide for Truman's Fair Deal

VOCABULARY

Consumables are products that _____.

Some positive examples of consumables are _____, _____,

and _____. A negative example of a consumable is _____.

BIG IDEAS

The **problem** was that after World War II, price controls were lifted and the cost of

_____, _____, and other consumer goods

went _____.

The **solution** was for workers to _____.

The **effect** was that _____ and _____.

Study guides can be used with the entire class or as an accommodation for individuals or small groups of students. Horton (1987) suggested the following additional modifications you might want to try:

1. Allow 2 or 3 inches of margin space in the study guide in which students can take notes. Draw a vertical line to indicate the margin clearly. For example, in the study guide in Figure 9.4, the answer to the first vocabulary question is "Consumables are products that cannot be used over again." You may want to have students write this vocabulary word along with its complete definition in the margin. Some students with special needs find new words easier to understand if you first use the overhead to discuss the definition along with a series of positive and negative examples. Specific strategies for presenting new vocabulary are presented later in the chapter.

2. Print page numbers next to the sentences in the study guide to show where to find the missing word in the textbook.

3. Print the missing words at the bottom of the page to serve as cues.

4. Leave out several words for more advanced students and fewer for students with special needs. For example, in Figure 9.4, the *effect* part of the big idea could be simplified as "The *effect* of strikes such as the railroad strike was that the stability of the American economy was threatened, and _____."

4. Arrange for peer teaching situations; pair students and have them take turns being the teacher and the student.

5. Use the study guide for homework assignments. Assign students a passage in the text and give them accompanying study guides (either with or without the pages marked for easy reference). Have them complete the guides and study the material for homework.

6. Ask students to keep and organize their study guides from a number of passages and to study them as they review for unit or end-of-semester tests.

7. Place reading passages, study guides, and tests on a computer.

8. Whenever possible, write the study guide at a reading level that fits most of your students. Students with reading and writing problems may need to have the study guide read to them or may need to respond to the questions orally.

9. Use INCLUDE to decide whether to put related but more basic information in the guide. For students with more significant challenges, make an instructional modification by changing the content load so that it remains related to the topic at hand but is more basic. For example, Ms. Hall required that Al, a student with a mild intellectual disability in her fourth-grade class, identify fruits and vegetables that were high in fiber, while the rest of the class responded to questions about the biochemical processes involved when the body digests fiber. When the students were tested on the content covered in the guide, Al was held responsible for answering his more basic questions, which covered content that had been previously specified on his IEP.

Of course, study guides are not a substitute for direct instruction. The amount of direct instruction necessary varies with the difficulty of the material. In general, students need more help completing study guides for texts that assume high levels of student background knowledge and in which key information needs to be inferred as opposed to being explicitly presented. The INCLUDE strategy can help you determine whether more direct instruction is needed and whether it needs to be delivered as part of large- or small-group instruction.

CREATING GRAPHIC ORGANIZERS ● Another way teachers can help students organize content is to use **graphic organizers.** This strategy gives students a visual format to organize their thoughts while looking for main ideas (Baxendell, 2003). Archer and Gleason (2004) suggest the following five guidelines for constructing graphic organizers:

1. Determine the critical content (for example, vocabulary, concepts, ideas, generalizations, events, details, facts) that you wish to teach your students. Helping students focus on the most critical information is important for several reasons. First, students with special needs may have trouble identifying the most important information in an oral lesson or textbook chapter. In most cases this will be content stressed in your state's standards. Second, it is easier for students to remember several main ideas than to remember many isolated details. Third, putting too much information on a graphic organizer can make it so visually complex that students may have trouble interpreting it.

2. Organize the concepts into a **concept map,** a type of graphic organizer or visual representation that reflects the structure of the content, such as stories, hierarchies (top-down and bottom-up), feature analysis, diagrams, compare/contrast, and timelines. Because the purpose of a graphic organizer is to clarify interrelationships among ideas and information, you should keep it as simple as possible. Figure 9.5 shows a completed comparison/contrast concept map.

3. Design a completed concept map. Completing the map before you teach with it ensures that the information is clear and accurate and can be presented to your students in a timely manner.

4. Create a partially completed concept map to be completed by students during instruction. Having students fill out the map as you present your lesson is an excellent way to keep them on task. Also, many students with special needs benefit from a multisensory approach; seeing the information on the graphic, hearing it from the teacher, and writing it on the map helps them better retain the information presented.

5. Create a blank concept map for students to use as a postreading or review exercise. This structure for review is easy for students to use.

Once you have constructed graphic organizers, you can use them as follows (Carnine et al., 2004):

1. Distribute partially completed concept maps to your students.

2. Project the map on a screen using PowerPoint or an overhead projector, displaying only those portions you wish students to attend to. Limiting the amount of information you present at one time helps students with attention problems who have trouble focusing on more than one piece of information at a time.

FIGURE 9.5 Comparison/Contrast Concept Map

Attribute	Native Americans	Colonists
Land	Shared	Owned
	Lived close to it without changing it	Cleared it
	Respected it	Used it

Summary

Native Americans and colonists had different ideas about land. Native Americans shared the land whereas the colonists owned individual pieces of it. Native Americans lived close to the land; they respected it and did not change it. Colonists used the land for their own gain.

3. Introduce the information on the concept map, proceeding in a logical order; stress the relationships between the vocabulary, concepts, events, details, facts, and so on.

4. At natural junctures, review concepts you have introduced. You can do this by placing the blank map on the overhead and asking students questions about the content. This review is essential for students who have difficulty learning large amounts of information at one time.

5. At the end of the lesson, review the critical content again using the blank concept map. You can also have students complete the blank maps for homework. These maps help students organize their studying and also help you find out what they have learned.

In most cases, graphic organizers are helpful for your entire class. Students with attention or listening problems may benefit from the additional accommodations of having a completed graphic explained to them prior to instruction for use as an advance organizer, and then completing a blank organizer after instruction with the teacher for extra practice and review. The Case in Practice on pages 330–331 illustrates how one teacher uses a graphic organizer called a *story map* to help her students better comprehend a particular story. Also, the Professional Edge on pages 332–333 shows how graphic organizers can be used to enhance the teaching of higher level problem-solving skills in algebra.

Teaching Terms and Concepts

Content-area instruction is often characterized by a large number of new and/or technical vocabulary words and concepts. Students who have special needs or who are at risk are likely to have difficulty with the vocabulary and concept demands of many content-area texts and presentations. For example, consider the following passage from a general science text:

> Thousands of years ago, Scandinavia was covered by a thick ice sheet. The mass of the ice forced the crust deeper into the denser mantle. Then the ice melted. The mantle has been slowly pushing the land upward since then. This motion will continue until a state of balance between the crust and mantle is reached again. This state of balance is called *isostasy* (ie-soss-tuh-see) (Ramsey, Gabriel, McGuirk, Phillips, & Watenpaugh, 1983).

Although the term *isostasy* is italicized for emphasis, other technical terms and concepts, such as *crust* and *mass*, also may pose a problem for students and require special attention. These words may be particularly difficult because students are likely to be familiar with their nonscientific meanings, which are quite different from their technical meanings (for example, *mass* as in church; *crust* as in bread). You need to check student understanding and teach vocabulary directly, if necessary, using one of the strategies covered in this section.

MODELING EXAMPLES AND USING SYNONYMS AND DEFINITIONS ●
Carnine and colleagues (2004) propose an approach to teaching terms and concepts that entails three related ways of teaching new vocabulary to students: modeling examples, synonyms, and definitions. Although there is some variation from method to method, all three use the following five steps:

1. Pick a range of both positive and negative examples to teach your new word. Example selection is most important. A range of positive examples is used to make sure students can apply the word to a variety of contexts or forms. For example, if you are teaching your students the word *rectangle*, you want them to identify a rectangle whether it is big, small, empty, or shaded. Therefore, when showing students examples of rectangles, show them big rectangles, small rectangles, empty rectangles, and shaded rectangles. If you are teaching your students the word *vehicle*, you

This teacher is modeling positive and negative examples to clarify the meaning of a new concept. How can using both examples and nonexamples help make the meaning of new terms and concepts clear?

want them to recognize a vehicle whether it is a car, boat, or bicycle. Whereas positive examples help students learn the range of a word, negative examples help them discriminate the new word from other words that may be similar. For example, for teaching *rectangle*, use figures such as triangles, circles, and trapezoids as negative examples. For teaching *vehicle*, use a chair, a house, and even an exercise bike as a negative example. Generally, you should use at least six examples to teach a new word and include among them at least two negative examples.

2. If you are teaching a word using a synonym, students must already know the synonym. For example, when teaching the word *gigantic* using the synonym *huge*, first make sure students know what *huge* means. If you are teaching a word using a definition, the definition should be stated simply and clearly and should contain only words for which students know the meaning. Consider the following definition of *vehicle* for third grade:

> *Vehicle:* A method of transportation that takes a person from one location to another

This definition uses a number of words that third graders might not know. Instead, consider a simpler definition that younger students can understand:

> *Vehicle:* An object that takes you from place to place

3. Tell students the meaning of the words either through modeling positive and negative examples or by presenting positive and negative examples using a synonym or a definition. For example, if you were teaching *rectangle* by modeling positive and negative examples, you might say the following as you pointed to your examples:

> This is a rectangle. . . . This is a rectangle. . . . This is *not* a rectangle. . . .
> This is a rectangle.

If you were teaching *vehicle* using a definition, you might say:

> A vehicle is an object that takes you from place to place. What is a vehicle? [Point to a picture of a car.] This is a car. It is an object that takes you from place to place. It is a vehicle. . . . This is a boat. It is an object that takes you from place to place. A boat is a vehicle. . . . This is a chair. A chair is an object, but it doesn't take you from place to place. It is *not* a vehicle.

CASE IN PRACTICE

Teaching with Story Maps

Story maps are graphic organizers that provide students with a visual guide to understanding and retelling stories. They have been shown to help students with special needs read with better comprehension (Carnine et al., 2004; Pearson & Fielding, 1991). In the account that follows, Ms. Barrows, a second-grade teacher, is using the story map in Figure 9.6 to teach her students the story *The*

Funny Farola (Miranda & Guerrero, 1986). She has demonstrated using the maps for a week now, so her students are familiar with the format. Today, she is providing guided practice for her students on how to use the maps.

Ms. Barrows: Boys and girls, today we're going to read a story entitled *The Funny Farola*. A farola is a lantern

used to give light. What do you think the story is going to be about?

Juliane: Maybe it's going to be about a lantern that looks funny.

Lee: Maybe it's about something funny happening to someone who has a farola.

Ms. Barrows: Well, before we read and find out, who can tell me what a story map is?

FIGURE 9.6 Story Map

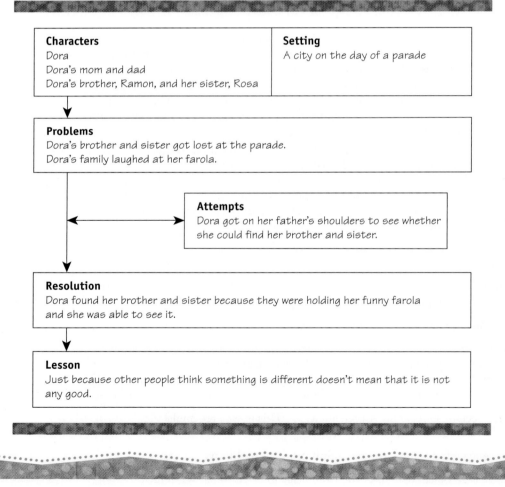

Characters
Dora
Dora's mom and dad
Dora's brother, Ramon, and her sister, Rosa

Setting
A city on the day of a parade

Problems
Dora's brother and sister got lost at the parade.
Dora's family laughed at her farola.

Attempts
Dora got on her father's shoulders to see whether she could find her brother and sister.

Resolution
Dora found her brother and sister because they were holding her funny farola and she was able to see it.

Lesson
Just because other people think something is different doesn't mean that it is not any good.

Darwain: Well, it's a map that guides us through a story kind of like a regular map tells us where we're going when we're driving a car.

Ms. Barrows: That's right, Darwain. Now let's read the first page and find out who the main characters in this story are and where the story takes place. When you find out, we'll fill them in on our story maps. [She distributes a blank story map to each student.]

Harley: I know, the story is about Dora Rivers, her sister Rosa, her brother Ramon, and her mom and dad. I think Dora is the main character.

Ms. Barrows: That's right, Harley. Let's all fill in the main characters on our maps.

Ms. Barrows: Where do you think the story takes place? It's hard to tell, because the writers don't come right out and say it.

Lovell: I think it takes place in a city.

Ms. Barrows: Why do you think so, Lovell?

Lovell: Because it sounds like it's a big parade, and cities have big parades.

Ms. Barrows: Good thinking, Lovell. When stories don't come out and say things, we have to figure it out by thinking hard, and that's what you did. Let's all fill in the setting on our maps. [They do.] Remember, we said last week that all stories have a problem that needs to be solved. Read the next four pages and find out what the problem is here. [The students read the passage.] What's the problem?

Harley: Well, Dora's little brother and sister got lost at the parade.

Ms. Barrows: Right. That's one problem. Write it on your maps. Now, does anyone see another problem?

Eliseo: I know. Dora made a farola that looked like a frog and everybody laughed at her.

Ms. Barrows: Eliseo, what's wrong with a farola that looks like a frog? I thought it looked cute.

Eliseo: Well, I think it was because Dora's was different from everyone else's. In the pictures in the story, there were no farolas that looked like animals.

Ms. Barrows: That's right, Eliseo. Let's all put this problem on our maps. [They do.] Let's read the next page and find out what Dora and her mom and dad attempted to do to try to find her brother and sister.

Lovell: Dora got up on her father's shoulders to see whether she could see her brother and sister.

Ms. Barrows: Do you think this will help Dora find her brother and sister?

Lesa: I don't think so. There are so many people there.

Ms. Barrows: Well, let's all finish the story and find out. [They finish reading the story.] So, did Dora find her brother and sister?

Juliane: Yes. She found them because they were carrying her funny farola and it really made them stand out in the crowd.

Ms. Barrows: That's right. Let's fill in how Dora solved the problem on our story maps. [They do.] What about Dora's other problem? Was it solved, too?

Juliane: Yes. They didn't think Dora's farola was so funny anymore, because it helped them find Dora's brother and sister.

Ms. Barrows: That's right. How do you think Dora felt at the end?

Lovell: I think she felt happy.

Ms. Barrows: Why do you think that, Lovell?

Lovell: Well, because she found her brother and sister and no one thought her farola was stupid anymore.

Ms. Barrows: Good thinking, Lovell. I'd like the rest of you to put how *you* think Dora felt, and why, on your maps. Remember, we said a part of stories is a lesson that they teach us. What lesson do you think this story teaches?

Harley: Well, just because something is different doesn't mean it's no good.

Ms. Barrows: Good thinking, Harley. Let's all put down the lesson of this story on our maps.

REFLECTIONS

How did Ms. Barrows use the story map to help her students comprehend the story? Which students do you think would benefit most from this approach? What should Ms. Barrows do to get her students ready for completing story maps on their own? How could you incorporate the use of story maps into a literature-based classroom reading program?

PROFESSIONAL EDGE

Using Graphic Organizers to Teach Algebra

Graphic organizers are very well suited for helping students visualize the steps needed to solve higher level problems. Ives and Hoy (2003) describe a successful strategy that uses graphic organizers to teach solving three linear equations with three variables. Note that to benefit from this strategy students need the preskills of (a) combining linear equations; (b) substituting values in place of variables in equations; (c) solving linear equations in one variable; and (d) recognizing that linear equations in one variable typically have unique solutions (that is, they can be solved) whereas linear equations with more than one variable do not (Ives & Hoy, 2003, p. 44). The strategy uses the frame shown in Figure 9.7.

In Figure 9.7a, the blank graphic organizer, the lines that make up the borders of the rectangles divide the symbolic content into cells representing the problem-solving steps. When solving the equations, students are taught to use the graphic organizer by working from cell to cell in a clockwise fashion starting from the top left cell (see Figure 9.7b). The clockwise movement helps students anticipate where they will be working next. The position on either the top or bottom row also communicates important information. The top row is used to combine equations in order to eliminate variables until an equation of one variable is made (see Figures 9.7c and 9.7d). When this equation is found, the bottom row guides the successive steps used to solve for the remaining variables until the entire problem is solved (see Figures 9.7d and 9.7e).

The roman numerals indicate the number of variables below them in the top boxes: Equations with three variables are placed in the top left cell, those with two in the top middle cell, and those with one in the top right cell. The roman numerals reinforce the idea that when solving systems of linear equations, the goal is to come up with equations having fewer and fewer variables. The bottom boxes, where specific variables are solved for, are also clarified by the roman numerals: The first value solved for is carried down to the bottom right box; the second value is solved for in the bottom middle box; and the third in the bottom left box.

FIGURE 9.7

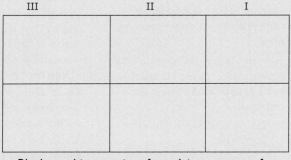

a. Blank graphic organizer for solving systems of linear equations in three variables

---

Finally, if you were teaching the word *gigantic* using the synonym *huge*, you might say:

> Today we're going to learn the meaning of the word *gigantic*. What's the word? *Gigantic* means huge. [Point to picture of an elephant.] An elephant is a gigantic animal. It is huge. [Point to a picture of a redwood tree.] This is a redwood tree. It is gigantic. It is huge. [Point to a smallish dog.] This is a dog. The dog is not gigantic. The dog is not huge.

4. Ask students a series of yes-or-no questions to ascertain whether they can discriminate positive examples from negative examples. For example, ask, "Is this a rectangle?" If students have been taught a word using a definition or synonym, follow your question with, "How do you know?" Their reasons for answering yes or no will reveal whether the students are correctly using the definition or just guessing. For example, to test whether students know what a vehicle is, you might say:

> What is this? (A car.) Is a car a vehicle? (Yes.) Why do you say that? (Because it is an object that takes you from place to place.) What is this? (A chair.) Is a

III	II	I
$2x + 4y + 2z = 16$ $-2x - 3y + z = -5$ $2x + 2y - 3z = -3$		

b. Graphic organizer for solving systems of linear equations in three variables as it may appear after the original equations have been entered

III	II	I
$2x + 4y + 2z = 16$ $-2x - 3y + z = -5$ $2x + 2y - 3z = -3$	$y + 3z = 11$ $-y - 2z = -8$	$z = 3$
		$\boxed{z = 3}$

d. Graphic organizer for solving systems of linear equations in three variables as it may appear after the first variable has been solved

III	II	I
$2x + 4y + 2z = 16$ $-2x - 3y + z = -5$ $2x + 2y - 3z = -3$	$y + 3z = 11$ $-y - 2z = -8$	

c. Graphic organizer for solving systems of linear equations in three variables as it may appear after two linear equations in two variables have been found

III	II	I
$2x + 4y + 2z = 16$ $-2x - 3y + z = -5$ $2x + 2y - 3z = -3$	$y + 3z = 11$ $-y - 2z = -8$	$z = 3$
$2x + 4(2) + 2(3) = 16$ $2x + 14 = 16$ $2x = 2$ $\boxed{x = 1}$	$y + 3(3) = 11$ $y + 9 = 11$ $\boxed{y = 2}$	$\boxed{z = 3}$

e. A completed graphic organizer for solving systems of linear equations in three variables

SOURCE: From "Graphic Organizers Applied to Higher-Level Secondary Mathematics," by B. Ives and C. Hoy, 2003, *Learning Disabilities: Research and Practice, 18*(1), pp. 36–51.

chair a vehicle? (No.) Why do you say that? (Because it doesn't take you from place to place.)

5. The purpose of this step is to discover whether students can discriminate the new word from words they have learned previously. This step is carried out through a series of open-ended questions. For example, in teaching *rectangle*, the teacher points to a rectangle along with other figures already taught and asks, "What is this?"

Teaching vocabulary by modeling examples or by using synonyms and definitions can benefit all your students. Use modeling examples when students may not understand words that explain the meaning of the new word (for example, teaching students what a herringbone design is). Use synonyms when students already know another word with a meaning similar to the new word; for example, you could teach the word *bow* (of a ship) using the synonym *front*. Use definitions

> Teaching vocabulary by modeling examples or by using synonyms and definitions can benefit all your students.

FIGURE 9.8 Concept Diagram

Concept Name:	Nonviolent resistance
Definition:	Protesting in a peaceful way

Always	Sometimes	Never
Peaceful	Done in a group	Violent
	Done individually	

Positive Examples	Negative Examples
Picketing	Shouting match
Boycott	Physical attack
Sit-in	Revolutionary war
Hunger strike	Riot

when a longer explanation is needed to define a word and students already understand the words that make up the explanation. Regardless of which procedure you use, be sure to monitor the performance of your students with special needs carefully using periodic questioning as you teach.

MAKING CONCEPT DIAGRAMS ● Constructing **concept diagrams** is a method that combines graphic organizers with the methods just described using definitions, synonyms, and positive and negative examples (Bulgren, Schumaker, & Deshler, 1988). A sample concept diagram for the concept of nonviolent resistance is shown in Figure 9.8. First, the teacher selects a key word from a story or lecture. Next, he or she constructs a diagram that features the definition of the word; the characteristics that are always present, sometimes present, or never present; and positive and negative examples that can be used to model the word. Finally, the concept diagram is presented to students as follows (Carnine et al., 2004):

1. Present the word and its definition.
2. Discuss which characteristics are always, sometimes, or never present.
3. Discuss one of the positive examples and one of the negative examples in relation to the characteristics.
4. Check other positive and negative examples to discover whether they match the characteristics.

ANALYZE
AND**REFLECT**

Stahl and Shiel estimate that teachers can realistically teach 300 words per year, which translates to about 8–10 per week (as cited in Armbruster et al., 2001). This means that there will never be enough time to teach all of the words students are unlikely to know. If you were teaching a new unit in a subject area, what criteria would you use for word selection? What would you do with words that you were unable to select?

How Can You Improve Clarity in Written and Oral Communication?

In effective instruction, ideas are clearly tied together, which enables students to understand them more easily. The need for instructional clarity applies to both written communication and oral communication. Written communication, in many school situations, involves the use of textbooks and other printed materials, such as handouts, homework, and written tests. Oral communication can include instructional behaviors such as giving directions, asking questions, and delivering lectures. When a textbook is not written clearly or a lecture is not presented clearly, students have to make critical connections between ideas on their own, a skill that many at-risk students may not have. Students with special needs may not be able to recognize that they do not understand the material, or they may not be aware of strategies to try when instruction is difficult to understand. For example, when reading a text, they may not know how to use key words and headings or how to look at the end-of-chapter questions to get main ideas. During oral presentations students may not feel comfortable asking questions to clarify the information presented because often they are not sure what to ask and are afraid of looking stupid. Finally, students with special needs may lack the background knowledge necessary to construct meaning on their own. If you communicate clearly and use materials that do so as well, students with special needs can be more successful.

Clarity in Written Communication

The importance of clearly written communication is illustrated by these two textbook passages about western migration in the United States:

> Many of the farmers who moved in from New England were independent farmers. Land cost about a dollar an acre. Most men could afford to set up their own farms. Livestock farming was quite common on the frontier. Hogs could be fed in the forests. The cost of raising hogs was low. (Senesh, 1973, as cited in Armbruster, 1984)

> Most of the farmers who moved in from New England were independent farmers. Being an independent farmer means that the farmer can afford to own his own farm. Around 1815, most men could afford their own farms because lands were cheap—it cost only about a dollar an acre. Many of these independent farms were livestock farms. For example, many frontier farmers raised hogs. Hog farming was common because hogs were inexpensive to keep. The cost of raising hogs was low because the farmer did not have to buy special feed for the hogs. The hogs did not need special feed because they could eat plants that grew in the surrounding forests. (Armbruster, 1984)

The second passage is much easier to understand; it requires fewer inferences by the reader and less adaptation by the teacher. It also defines *independent farmer* for the reader. If students were reading the first passage, you might have to provide this definition—which you could do orally or in a study guide. The reason farmers turned to raising livestock can be inferred from the first paragraph, but it is stated directly in the second. For students reading the first paragraph, teachers may need to make the accommodation of posing questions prior to reading to establish an understanding of this relationship: For example, "Why did the farmers turn to raising livestock?" Obviously, adapting every paragraph like this is not feasible. But this example underscores the need for adopting structurally and organizationally coherent textbooks. Adaptations may still be needed to accommodate individual learners, but they should be made only for sections containing the most important information.

Problems with textbook organization and clarity can also occur in explanations, especially when a sequence of events is being described. The ease with which students can understand the sequence depends on a number of factors, including the number of steps, the format used (list or paragraph), and the presence of distracting information or material not related to the sequence. For example, students with special needs may struggle to understand the following passage about how baby alligators are hatched.

> Adult female alligators make large cone-shaped nests from mud and compost. The female lays from 15 to 100 eggs with leathery shells in the nest and then

WWW
RESOURCES

Get practical ideas about specific teaching problems from actual teachers in the field from Teachers Helping Teachers, at http://www.pacificnet.net/ ~mandel.

INCLUDE

covers it. The heat from both the sun and the decaying compost keeps the eggs warm. The eggs hatch in about 9 weeks. Unlike other reptiles that hatch from eggs, baby alligators make sounds while they are still in the shell. The mother then bites off the nest so the baby alligators can get out. When first hatched, baby alligators are about 15 to 25 cm long. (Berger, Berkheimer, Lewis, & Neuberger, 1979, p. 55, as cited in Armbruster, 1984)

As you can see, the passage states a sequence of events leading up to the hatching of a baby alligator. It is written in paragraph format, which is harder to decipher than a list. Although the events are described in chronological order, the presence of a distractor, the sentence "Unlike other reptiles that hatch from eggs, baby alligators make sounds while they are still in the shell," breaks up the sequence and makes it harder for students to comprehend. Use the INCLUDE strategy to identify written work that is hard to comprehend and students who are likely to struggle with it most. A relatively easy accommodation for these students would be to highlight the sentences in the sequence or have them put numbers next to each key sentence in the sequence. Of course, if a number of students in your class are having trouble with distracting information, you can accommodate them by providing direct instruction on how to identify and/or ignore distracting or irrelevant information.

Another aspect of written language that can make comprehension more difficult is the use of pronouns. A general rule of thumb is, the closer a pronoun is to its referent, the easier it is to translate. Consider the following section of text:

> Another aspect of written language that can make comprehension more difficult is the use of pronouns. A general rule of thumb is, the closer a pronoun is to its referent, the easier it is to translate.

Now life began to change. The Eskimo hunters could see that these tools were useful. So they became traders, too. They trapped more furs than their families needed.

Then they brought the furs to the trading posts. There they could trade the furs for supplies they had never had before. Because the new tools helped Eskimo hunters get along better, they became part of the Eskimo environment. (Brandwein & Bauer, 1980)

Many readers may have trouble figuring out whom *they* refers to in this passage. Although the placement of most pronouns is not this problematic, understanding pronouns can be difficult for students with special needs. However, students can be taught to make sense of pronouns (Carnine et al., 2004). Before students read, identify unclear pronouns. Have students underline the pronouns in a passage. Then show them how to find the pronouns' referents by asking questions. Study the following example:

WWW
RESOURCES

The CAST (Center for Applied Special Technology) website, at http://www. cast.org, has many helpful suggestions for the universal design of learning materials and teaching practices to reduce the need for developing special accommodations and modifications for individual students in general education classes. This site also provides a link to the National Center on Accessing the General Curriculum web page, which also offers research, solutions, and resources for universal design.

Passage

Curtis and Dorva skipped school. They were grounded for a week. He was sorry. She got mad.

Student Questioning

Teacher: "Curtis and Dorva skipped school." Who skipped school?

Students: Curtis and Dorva.

Teacher: "They were grounded for a week." Was Curtis grounded?

Students: Yes.

Teacher: Was Dorva grounded?

Students: Yes.

Teacher: "He was sorry." Was Curtis sorry?

Students: Yes.

Teacher: Was Dorva sorry?

Students: No.

Teacher: "She got mad." Did Dorva get mad?

Students: Yes.

Depending on the level of sophistication of your class, this instruction could be done with the entire class or performed as an accommodation for individual students who struggle to understand sentences containing pronouns.

Clarity in Oral Communication

Just as the quality of textbook writing affects student learning, so, too, does the quality of teachers' oral language. Three particularly important areas of oral language are giving directions, asking questions, and presenting subject matter (such as in a lecture).

GIVING ORAL DIRECTIONS ● Giving oral directions is the most common way that teachers tell their students what they want them to do. When directions are not clear and have to be repeated, valuable instructional time is wasted. Consider this set of directions given by a middle school teacher at the beginning of a social studies lesson:

Unclear Instruction

All right, everyone, let's settle down and get quiet. I want you all to get ready for social studies. Shh. . . . Let's get ready. Alice and Tim, I want you to put those worksheets away. We need our books and notebooks. (Evertson et al., 1983, p. 143)

How clear is the teacher about what she wants her students to do? Now read this alternative set of directions:

Clearer Instruction

All right, everyone, I want all of you in your seats facing me for social studies. [Teacher pauses.] Now, I want you to get out three things: your social studies book, your spiral notebook, and a pencil. Put everything else away so that you have just those three things—the social studies book, the spiral notebook, and the pencil—out on your desk. [As students get out their materials, the teacher writes "Social Studies, page 55, Chapter 7 on Italy" on the chalkboard. She waits until students have their supplies ready and are listening before she begins talking.] (Evertson et al., 1983, p. 143)

In the first example, the teacher does not get the students' attention before giving them directions. She is also unclear in communicating what she wants her students to do. For example, the words *settle down* and *get ready* are not defined for the students. In the second example, the teacher first gets her students' attention and then very specifically states all the things they need to do. Lavoie (1989) has suggested four guidelines for giving directions that are helpful either for your entire class or as accommodations for individual students with special needs:

1. State commands specifically, using concrete terms. In the Clearer Instruction example, the teacher was very specific about what the students needed to do to get ready for social studies. They had to get out three things: their books, notebooks, and pencils. The first teacher told them only to "get ready."

FYI

Another use of cuing is to let a student know that he or she can expect to be called on to respond orally when you present a particular cue that only the student knows. This way the student can attend to a lesson with less anxiety about speaking in class.

CONNECTIONS

Strategies for questioning students with limited English proficiency are covered in Chapter 8.

CONNECTIONS

Students with special needs benefit from being taught to think because efficient thinking may not come naturally to them or they may not have been exposed to good models of thinking. Strategies for teaching students thinking skills are described further in Chapter 10.

2. Give "bite-size" directions; avoid a long series of directions. The second teacher first had her students sit down and face her; then she had them take out their materials; finally, she had them turn to the chapter they were going to read that day.

3. Whenever possible, accompany explanations with a demonstration. For example, Mr. Gaswami asked his students to take out their science books, turn to the beginning of the chapter, identify five key words, and define them using the glossary. Mr. Gaswami showed his students what he wanted them to do by opening his book to the chapter, pointing out that the key words were italicized, and then defining several key words to demonstrate how to find and paraphrase the meanings using the glossary in the back of the book. He also wrote these directions on the board to help students remember all the steps.

4. Use cuing words such as "Look up here" and "Listen, please" before giving directions. Gestures such as a raised hand are also effective in getting students' attention.

ASKING QUESTIONS ● Asking students questions is a vital part of instructional clarity. The way you question your students is important for several reasons. Questioning is a quick way of assessing what your students have learned. In addition, questioning through the use of follow-up probes can help you analyze your students' errors. For example, Ms. Dilworth's third-grade class was given the following math problem:

> Three-fourths of the crayons in Bob's box of a dozen crayons are broken. How many unbroken crayons are there?

Ms. Dilworth asked Kareem what the answer was, and Kareem answered that there were 4 unbroken crayons left. Ms. Dilworth asked Kareem to explain how he got that answer. Kareem said, "Because three-fourths means 3 groups of 4, and because there is only one group left, that group has 4 in it." By asking a question, Ms. Dilworth found out that Kareem did not know the concept of three-fourths. Questions can also be used to redirect students to the correct answer when they make mistakes. For example, Ms. Dilworth might have asked Kareem a number of follow-up questions: "How many crayons did you start with? How many is a dozen? What fraction of the crayons were broken? What does three-fourths mean? What would one-fourth of 12 be?"

Last, and perhaps most important, it is through effective questioning that your students can learn thinking skills. Well-constructed questions provide students with a model for effective thinking; in time, students learn to ask themselves these same questions as they solve problems. For example, Ms. Collins wanted her students to ask themselves key questions while they read stories to help improve their comprehension. At first she asked them questions while they read, such as, "What is the story about? What is the problem? What is the solution? What's going to happen next? Is your prediction still good? Do you need to change your prediction? What makes you think so?" In time, she taught the students to ask themselves these questions as they read independently.

Although asking questions can be a very potent teaching strategy, in order to achieve maximum benefit, questioning needs to be carried out correctly. Wilen, Ishler, Hutchinson, and Kindsvatter (1999) have suggested the following guidelines for using questions in your classroom:

1. *Phrase questions clearly to ensure that students know how to respond.* For example, a vague question, such as, "What about the Great Depression?" forces students to guess rather than to consider carefully a direct response to the question. Better wording would be, "What were the two primary causes of the Great Depression?"

2. *Provide a balance between higher and lower level questions.* The important point to keep in mind is that both kinds of questions are important. Lower level, or convergent, questions help you find out whether students have the basic understanding necessary for higher level thought. Further, critical and creative thinking can be developed by using convergent and evaluative questions. Although incorporating more higher level skills into the curriculum is positive, it is important to realize that lower level knowledge is still important, particularly for students with special needs. Students with special needs may not readily acquire lower level knowledge. Failing to help them acquire this understanding can prevent them from ever developing higher level understanding. Also, lower level questions can give students an opportunity to succeed in class. Finally, research suggests that lower level questions may be most appropriate in teaching basic skills to students who are at risk (Emmer, Evertson, Sanford, Clements, & Worsham, 1983; Berliner, 1984).

3. *Adapt questions to the language and skill level of the class, including individual students in the class.* Your questions should accommodate a range of needs, from lower-performing students to gifted students. For example, a question for a lower-performing student might be, "From what you have just read, how does the demand for a product affect its supply?" For students with more skills, the question might become, "Going beyond the article a little, how does price affect supply and demand and at what point is market equilibrium reached?"

4. *Vary the "wait time" you give students to answer questions.* Wait time is the amount of time you give students to respond to questions in class.

5. *Involve all students in classroom questioning by calling on nonvolunteers as well as volunteers.* Calling on all students also allows you to monitor student learning efficiently. In addition, calling on nonvolunteers (who frequently are students with special needs) demonstrates that you hold them accountable for listening and leads to higher levels of on-task behavior. However, as mentioned before, you should match questions with student ability to maximize the likelihood of student success. Finally, for lower level questions, consider using unison responding, or having all students respond at once, together. Unison responding allows more student opportunities for practice and recitation and can lead to higher levels of correct responses and on-task behavior (Carnine, 1981). Use the INCLUDE strategy to ensure that the questions you ask in class match the instructional levels of your students.

PRESENTING CONTENT ORALLY ● Communicating clearly to your students when you are presenting subject-area content orally, such as in a lecture, also is important. The following section of a lecture was delivered during a geography lesson on Italy:

Teacher 1

Italy is in southern Europe, down by France and the Mediterranean Sea. It's a peninsula in the Mediterranean. There are a lot of beautiful islands in the Mediterranean off of Italy and Greece as well. Sardinia and Sicily are islands that are part of Italy. Corsica, Capri, and some other islands like Crete and Cyprus are in the same part of the world, but they don't belong to, although they may be close to, Italy. You could turn to the map of Europe that's in your text to see where Italy is. (Evertson et al., 1983, pp. 143–144)

The language used by this teacher lacks clarity. For example, he presents information about a number of islands but is unclear in explaining how these islands relate to the main topic, which seems to be the location of Italy. The teacher is also vague when he says, "[The islands] don't belong to, although they may be close to, Italy." In addition, the teacher uses the word *peninsula* but does not define it. Finally, this explanation needs the visual display of a map to bring clarity to it, but the teacher refers to a map only at the end of the explanation, almost as an afterthought; and rather than requiring students to refer to it, he leaves students with the impression that its use is voluntary. The only students who will know where Italy is after this lecture is over are those

who already knew in the first place. Many students with special needs may be left behind. An example of another lecture on the same topic is much clearer:

Teacher 2

Now, I want all eyes on me. [The teacher then gestures to the world map next to her.] Raise your hand if you can show the class where Italy is. [Several students raise their hands. The teacher then has Maria read the names and show the class where France, Switzerland, Austria, Slovenia, and the Mediterranean Sea border on Italy.] Italy is in Europe. It is a large peninsula shaped like a boot that extends into the Mediterranean Sea. [She writes *peninsula* on the board, sounding the syllables as she writes. Because students have studied the word once before, she calls on a student to define it.] Agnes, what is a *peninsula?*

How Can You Involve Parents in Teaching Their Children?

Teachers are always looking for ways to find extra help for students who take more time to learn new content or skills. That is why we often hear teachers say, "If only his parents would work with him more at home." Although we know parents can promote learning by showing affection for their children, by displaying interest in their children's schoolwork, and by expecting academic success, the effectiveness of parents' tutoring their children at home is less clear. The results of research on the effectiveness of parent teaching is mixed; some experts say it is effective whereas others question it (Mercer & Pullen, 2005). When determining whether to involve parents in tutoring their children, Mercer and Pullen (2005, p. 125) suggest that the following factors be taken into account.

1. Are there reasons for deciding against tutoring (for example, mother–father disagreement over the necessity of tutoring, health problems, financial problems, marital problems, or a large family with extensive demands on parental authority)?

2. Do parents have the resources of a professional (for example, a teacher) to assist them? The success of home tutoring may depend on cooperative efforts.

3. Can the sessions be arranged at a time when there is no interruption from siblings, callers, or other demands? These children need sustained attention in order to learn.

4. Will the child become overwhelmed with academic instruction and resent the home sessions or feel overly pressured?

5. Do the parents become frustrated, tense, disappointed, or impatient during the tutorial sessions? These parents may spend their time better with the child in activities that are mutually enjoyable.

6. Do the tutorial sessions create tensions among family members? For instance, do the siblings view the sessions as preferential treatment?

7. Does the parent resent tutoring the child or feel guilty every time a session is shortened or missed? Are the sessions usually enjoyable and rewarding?

Of course, if you decide to have parents tutor their child, the same strategies for teaching skills and content to students with special needs covered earlier in this chapter still apply. For example, only skills or content at a student's level should be presented, and the progression of skills or content should be gradual and based on student mastery. In addition, parents should be carefully trained to present new information or skills clearly and enthusiastically and to provide appropriate corrections and encouragement as needed. Parents should also limit the length of the tutoring sessions to 15 minutes for children up to grade 6 and 30 minutes for older students, and should begin and end each session with an activity that is fun and that the child is successful at (Cummings & Maddux, 1985, as cited in Mercer & Pullen, 2005). Too, care must be taken to select the most appropriate time to tutor and to select a place that does not restrict the activities of other family members and is not too distracting. Finally, tutoring should be held at the same time and place to establish a clear routine (Mercer & Pullen, 2005).

What Adaptations Can You Make to Help Students Succeed in Independent Practice?

As discussed in Chapter 5, the main purpose of practice activities is to provide students with opportunities to refine skills or solidify content that they have already learned and to allow you to monitor their performance. To achieve these purposes, students should be able to complete practice activities such as seatwork and homework independently.

Even under ideal circumstances and with the best intentions, it is difficult to design practice activities that meet the needs of all students in your class. Problems arise because of individual characteristics, and individual accommodations need to be made using INCLUDE. For example, students with severe reading problems may have difficulty reading directions that are quite clear to everyone else. Students with attention problems may have trouble answering questions that have multiple steps. Students with physical disabilities may be unable to perform the writing requirements of their assignments. In the case of students with severe cognitive disabilities, practice activities may need to be modified totally so that they are consistent with the students' skill levels and the goals and objectives on their IEPs.

INCLUDE

> Even under ideal circumstances and with the best intentions, it is difficult to design practice activities that meet the needs of all students in your class.

Adapting Seatwork Assignments

One problem with seatwork is that the practice activities may not contain enough items for the student to achieve mastery. This limitation is important, because students with disabilities often require more practice to master skills or content. For example, Ms. Jennings has just taught her students to solve two-step story problems in math that require first adding and then subtracting. She demonstrated three problems in front of the class and then guided her students through three more. Ms. Jennings then had students independently complete five problems in the math book. She found that only half the students answered all the problems correctly and that the rest of the class needed more practice. Many math books have extra problems for students who need more practice, but some do not. You may need either to make up your own items or to find similar items from other books.

Another common problem with seatwork is that the directions are too difficult. Complicated or confusing directions can prevent students from completing their seatwork successfully. For example, some directions are excessively wordy: "Use the words letters stand for and the sense of the other words to find out what the new word in heavy black print is" (Center for the Study of Reading, 1988, p. 14). This is just a convoluted way of saying, "read." Other directions have too many steps: "Read the first sentence, and fill in the missing word. Read the second sentence. Find the word from the first sentence that makes sense in the second sentence and print it where it belongs. Then, do what the last sentence says. Repeat for all the other sentences" (Center for the Study of Reading, 1988, p. 14).

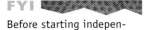

Affleck, Lowenbraun, and Archer (1980) have suggested five adaptations you can make to directions to ensure that students with special needs know what to do prior to working independently. Use INCLUDE to figure out whether these adaptations need to be done with your entire class or only with one or a small group of students.

1. Verbally present the tasks. This adaptation can be applied to the whole class, particularly when many students are having problems with the directions. You can accommodate the needs of individual students by pairing a worksheet with an auditory tape that explains the directions.

2. Add practice examples that you can do with the whole class or a small group of students who are having particular difficulty.

3. Write alternative sets of directions. You can project these onto a screen using an overhead projector or distribute individual copies to students.

4. Highlight the important words in the directions.

5. Have students help each other when the directions are difficult.

Students may also have trouble when single pages of seatwork contain a number of different tasks. This combination of tasks can cause problems for students with special needs, who often have difficulty making the transition from one task to another. Consider the example shown in Figure 9.9. This worksheet has three different tasks. Students need to make a number of transitions within one worksheet to complete the activity successfully. Also, students are required to use words circled in Part A as answers to Part C. Using answers from one part of a worksheet as answers to questions on another part is confusing and assumes that students will answer the first part correctly. You could adapt this worksheet by visually cuing the change of task on the page (for example, draw a line between tasks) and by correcting Part A before the students do Part C.

Finally, seatwork should provide opportunities for students to practice skills that they have already learned, not teach them new skills. In Part A of the seatwork activity shown in Figure 9.9, students are required to circle the words that contain the same vowel sound as in the word *hit*. This task is appropriate for practice, because students must already be able to read the words to tell whether they have the short *i* sound. The exercise is not appropriate for teaching students to read the words for the first time. A more effective way to teach that concept would be to have the students read to you words in passages and lists and then provide them with corrective feedback on missed words. Before you give a seatwork assignment to your students, ask yourself whether students can already perform the skill. If the answer is no, you need to spend more time teaching it first.

Providing Feedback on Independent Practice Activities

You can also adapt student practice by providing feedback on students' performance. It makes good sense to correct and return students' work as soon as possible. Timely feedback allows you to find out right away where students are making mistakes so you can reteach material if necessary. Providing feedback as quickly as possible is particularly important for students with special needs, who are less likely to learn material the first time it is presented. Returning papers soon after they are handed in also helps students know what they are doing correctly or incorrectly, and gives them the opportunity to make corrections while the material is still fresh in their minds and before they have forgotten why they responded as they did. In addition, regular feedback makes students feel more accountable for their work.

FIGURE 9.9 Seatwork Activity

Name _____

The Sound of Short *i*

A. Say each word. Circle the words that have the vowel sound you hear in *hit*.

lick	milk	cane	time
might	away	drink	gone
rabbit	house	sing	girl
this	come	five	fish

B. Make new words by changing the first letter or letters.

pick _____ _____ _____

wing _____ _____ _____

slip _____ _____ _____

C. Fill in each blank with one of the words that you circled above to complete the sentences.

1. The boys and girls will _____ a song in school.

2. My father and I went to the river and caught a big _____.

3. _____ is not the book I want to read.

4. The fluffy little _____ ran across the road.

5. My mother gave me a glass of _____.

Although providing timely feedback to students is a good practice, as a professional teacher and an individual with a personal life as well, you may have limited time during and after school. Therefore, in grading your students' papers, efficiency is imperative. The following list of suggestions is designed to help you save time.

1. *Correct papers as you circulate.* You can correct some papers as you circulate throughout the room during the seatwork period. Carry a pen with a different color of ink than students use when they correct their own papers. Begin correcting the papers of students with special needs first. This ensures that those who are most likely to need your help receive it. Each time you stop at a student's desk, correct at least two items. Correct answers can be marked with a C, a star, a happy face, or whatever you prefer. Mark errors with a dot. When you find an error, try to determine whether the student simply made a careless mistake or did not know how to do the item correctly. If the student does not know how to do the item, show him or her how to do it, assign several similar problems, and say that you will be back to check the work in several minutes (Paine et al., 1983).

2. *Use spot-checking.* Reading 3 of the 10 comprehension answers assigned should give you a fairly good idea of whether students understand the material (Lavoie, 1989).

3. *Use shared checking.* Allow the first two students finished with an assignment to go to a corner together and compare their answers. When they reach agreement on the answers, they can design a "key." They can then check the other students' answers. If you have students exchange papers, have the corrector sign the paper at the bottom. This strategy helps ensure that students correct fairly and accurately (Lavoie, 1989).

4. *Use easy checking.* Design assignments in a way that makes them easy to correct. For example, put problems or questions in neat, orderly rows. When checking assignments from consumable workbooks, cut off the corners of the pages you have checked or corrected. This helps you (and the student) find the next page quickly (Lavoie, 1989).

5. *Use self-checking.* Dictate or display answers using an overhead projector while students correct their own papers. Require that pencil assignments be corrected in pen and vice versa. Making corrections in a different shade or color enables you to monitor the number of mistakes students make before completion of their final corrected copy. Having students color over each answer with a yellow crayon before the correction activity serves the same purpose because their original answers are impossible to erase. After collecting papers, spot-check them for accuracy, and provide corrective feedback for errors and positive feedback for correct answers (Lavoie, 1989).

Adapting Homework Assignments

As they do with in-class practice activities, students with special needs may have difficulty completing traditional homework assignments. A major reason for student failure to complete homework assignments independently, successfully, and without undue stress is that the assignments are too difficult to begin with. Before you give your students an assignment, ask yourself the following questions:

1. What skill (for example, reading, written expression, or math) demands does the assignment make on the students? Are the students capable of meeting these skill demands?

2. What background knowledge (for example, vocabulary or concepts) does the assignment demand of the students? Are the students capable of meeting the demand for background knowledge?

3. Is the purpose of the assignment made clear to the students?

4. If the assignment involves skill practice, does it include much practice on a few skills rather than little practice on many skills?

5. Are clear, written directions provided for how to complete the assignment?

6. Is enough time allotted for completion of the assignment?

WWW
R E S O U R C E S

For homework help, students can go to these two sites—http://www.infoplease.com/homework and http://www.highschoolhub.org/hub/hub.cfm—and be linked instantly to information on the academic subject of their choice, including math, English, literature, social studies, and science. Students can also be linked to tutorials in a wide range of subject areas.

All students can benefit from homework and other independent practice activities. What are some strategies you can use to adapt homework and other assignments for students with special needs?

Homework problems may also be related to how the homework process is managed and how competent students are to work independently. A list of effective homework practices for each of these factors is shown in Figure 9.10.

Even if you answered yes to all the questions listed above, students with special needs may require additional accommodations. For example, students with reading problems may need extra assistance with homework directions. Students with physical disabilities may need assignments shortened, or they may need to respond orally rather than in writing. Remember to use the INCLUDE strategy to make adaptations that fit your assignments and the individual characteristics of your students with special needs. A survey of general education teachers (Polloway, Epstein, Bursuck, Jayanthi, & Cumblad, 1994) showed that teachers favored the following homework adaptations: adjusting the length of assignments; providing extra teacher help; providing a peer tutor for assistance; setting up student study groups; providing auxiliary learning aids (for example, computers and calculators); checking more frequently with students about assignments (for example, clarifying when they are due and what is required); and allowing alternative response formats (for example, oral or written).

Successful homework also depends on individual student skills. Not only do students need to be proficient in basic academic skills, but also they need to be able to learn independently. For example, they need to recognize their homework problems and seek help when necessary. They also need to manage their time effectively. Strate-

INCLUDE

ANALYZE AND **REFLECT**

Select a commercially prepared student practice activity in the subject area and grade level you plan to teach. Critique the activity in light of the guidelines for assigning homework. How might you adapt this worksheet for a student with special needs?

FIGURE 9.10 Recommended School-Based Homework Practices

Management Considerations

- Communicate clear expectations for homework from the beginning of the year.
- Establish a routine for assigning, collecting, and evaluating homework.
- Write assignments on the board so students can easily record them.
- Remind students of assignment due dates.
- Communicate consequences for completing and for not completing homework.
- Present homework instructions clearly, and verify student understanding.
- Allow students to start homework in class.
- Use assignment organizers or homework planners.
- Implement classroom-based incentive programs.
- Coordinate homework assignments with other teachers.

Student Competencies

- Teach interdependent learning skills (how to do homework with others).
- Teach independent learning or study skills.
- Teach time management skills.
- Teach self-advocacy skills, including the ability to ask for help if needed.

SOURCES: Adapted from "Practical Recommendations for Using Homework with Students with Disabilities," by J. R. Patton, 1994, *Journal of Learning Disabilities, 27*(9), pp. 570–578; "Home-School Collaboration about Homework: What Do We Know and What Should We Do?" by J. R. Patton, M. Jayanthi, and E. Polloway, 2001, *Reading and Writing Quarterly, 17*(3), pp. 227–242; and "Homework Practices of General Education Teachers," by E. A. Polloway, M. H. Epstein, W. D. Bursuck, M. Jayanthi, and C. Cumblad, 1994, *Journal of Learning Disabilities, 27*(8), pp. 100–109.

gies for teaching these and other independent learning skills are covered in more depth in Chapter 10.

Involving Parents in the Homework Process

The success of homework depends in large part on the successful involvement of parents. Parents play two key roles: overseeing the homework process while their children are at home and communicating with the school regularly and clearly regarding homework exceptions.

FYI

Sometimes, homework is not a viable option, as in the case of students who work so hard during the day that they need a break, or students whose life circumstances make homework irrelevant.

WWW
R E S O U R C E S

Webmath, at http://www.webmath.com, is a website designed to help students with specific math problems they encounter in class or in homework. Answers to problems are generated and produced in real time, at the moment web users type in their math problems and click on Solve.

RESEARCH
N O T E

Nelson and colleagues (1998) surveyed middle school students of varying achievement levels about their preferences for homework adaptations. The most preferred adaptations were completing assignments entirely at school, working on assignments in small groups, beginning homework in class with the teacher checking understanding, and allowing extra-credit assignments. The least preferred adaptations were making changes to assignments for individual students and using assignment notebooks.

OVERSIGHT OF HOMEWORK COMPLETION ● One way parents oversee the homework process is by having daily discussions about homework with their children (Bursuck et al., 1999). For example, every night after dinner, Mr. Rojas asks his son Juan what assignments he has for that day, when they are due, and whether he thinks he is going to need some help with any of them. Mr. Rojas also asks Juan whether he has any tests coming up or long-term assignments due and asks him what his plan is for getting things done. Parents can also create an environment at home that is conducive to getting homework done. For example, at the beginning of the school year Ms. Lange and her son Damon determined how much time Damon needed to set aside each night for homework, identified a set time each night and materials needed, and then selected a setting in which Damon could complete his homework relatively free of distractions. Parents also need to supervise homework activities periodically during the time scheduled for homework and to provide support and encouragement for their children's homework completion. For example, Mr. and Ms. Brown frequently praise their child's efforts to complete his homework, and they take him out from time to time for ice cream when he completes a particularly difficult assignment.

HOME–SCHOOL COMMUNICATION ● The quality of home–school communication about homework is very important to a successful homework process (Polloway, Bursuck, & Epstein, 2001). Yet, despite its importance, home–school communication about homework is likely to be a problem (Harniss, Epstein, Bursuck, Nelson, & Jayanthi, 2001; Munk et al., 2001). Parents feel the need for much more communication with teachers about homework and feel that teachers need to make more of an effort to initiate such communication (Munk et al., 2001). Likewise, teachers feel that parents do not (a) initiate communication about homework often enough, (b) take homework seriously enough, and (c) follow through with commitments they make about helping their children with homework. Teachers also feel they lack the time to communicate often enough with parents because of large class sizes and increased paperwork demands. In addition, teachers feel they lack knowledge and training about adapting homework for students with special needs (Epstein et al., 1997).

Contacts with parents about homework can be increased by conducting parent–teacher meetings in the evening for working parents and by taking advantage of the ever-increasing use of e-mail, a great potential time-saver (Harniss et al., 2001). Another strategy for increasing communication is to establish homework hotlines that can be accessed by phone, or websites that provide certain types of homework assistance. You can also involve parents in the homework process at the beginning of the school year and on an ongoing basis thereafter. For example, at the open house at the beginning of the school year, Ms. Ordonez gives parents information about course assignments for the semester, homework adaptations available in the classroom, and policies on missed homework and extra-credit assignments. She then sends home school progress updates every 4 weeks; the progress reports include a section on homework completion. It is also important to understand that homework may be a lower priority for families when compared to other home issues. For example, Mr. Gentry knew that Dominique's family had recently been evicted from their apartment and were living in their car. Until Dominique's family was able to find another place, Mr. Gentry arranged for him to complete his homework before or after school.

Making Instructional Modifications for Students with Moderate to Severe Disabilities

Students with moderate to severe disabilities often cannot perform some or all of the steps in tasks carried out every day by students without disabilities. In the past, this inability to perform tasks in the same way as other students was interpreted to mean that these students could not benefit from these activities. Today, the emphasis is on making modifications for students with moderate to severe disabilities so that they can meet curricular standards in a more functional way as guided by their IEPs (Lowell-York, Doyle, & Kronberg, 1995; Nolet & McLaughlin, 2000).

One way to adapt materials and activities for students with moderate to severe disabilities is to conduct an **environmental inventory.** The purpose of an environmental inventory is to find out what modifications are needed to increase the participation of these students in the classroom as well as in community environments (Vandercook, York, & Forest, 1989) and to help them meet more functional curricular objectives specified on their IEPs. The environmental inventory process involves asking yourself four questions:

1. What does a person who does not have a disability do in this environment?
2. What does a person who has a disability do in this environment? What is the discrepancy?
3. What types of supports and/or adaptations can be put in place to increase the participation level or independence of the person who has a disability label?
4. What functional outcomes can the student meet as a result of this participation?

An example of how this process is used in a classroom environment is shown in Figure 9.11. This example involves Roberto, the student with moderate to severe disabilities whom you read about at the beginning of Chapter 4. Roberto is in Ms. Benis's sixth-grade social studies class. The class is working in small groups on depicting the steps in the recycling process for paper, metal, and plastic. Each group is studying a different recycled material. Roberto lacks the motor and cognitive skills necessary to participate like everyone else. Ms. Benis decides to implement instructional modifications with Roberto. She assigns him to the group that his friend Seth is in. She also decides to use different materials with Roberto. Ms. Benis has a paraprofessional help Roberto find pictures of recycled products; Seth helps Roberto paste these pictures onto the group's diagram. Mr. Howard, Roberto's special education teacher, helps Roberto identify recycled products in grocery stores and restaurants. Roberto's parents help him sort the recycling at home. All of these activities help Roberto meet his IEP goal of participating in community recycling efforts. Examples of making instructional modifications using INCLUDE are described in the Case in Practice on page 349.

WWW
RESOURCES

Do you want to post your own homework assignments on the Internet without a website of your own? Go to Ed Gate's SchoolNotes web page, at http://www.schoolnotes.com.

ANALYZE AND**REFLECT**

Students with special needs often require more practice when learning a new skill or content. Logistically, how can you provide more practice for some students while at the same time meeting the needs of your students who are ready to move to new material?

CONNECTIONS

Other information on including students with moderate to severe disabilities is included in Chapters 4 and 6.

CONNECTIONS

Observe a student with moderate to severe disabilities in a general education classroom. Observe how the teacher has used INCLUDE or the environmental inventory process of modifying instruction.

INCLUDE

FIGURE 9.11 Environmental Inventory Process

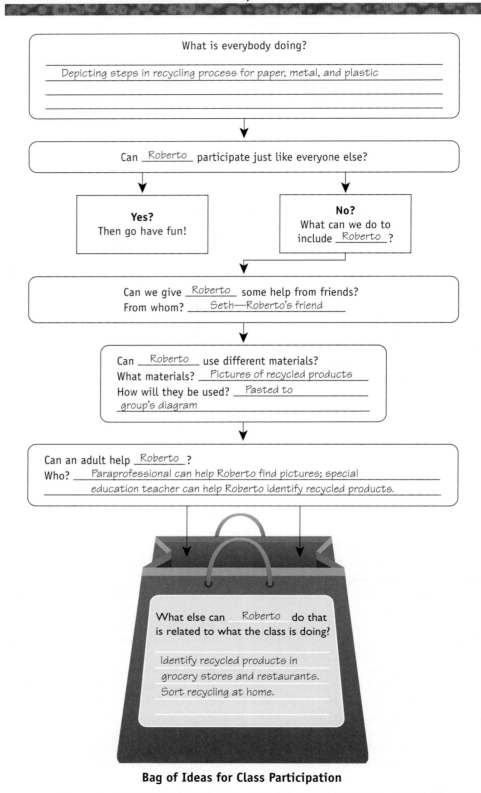

Bag of Ideas for Class Participation

SOURCE: From "The McGill Action Planning System (MAPS): A Strategy for Building the Vision," by T. Vandercook, J. York, and M. Forest, 1989, *Journal of the Association for Persons with Severe Handicaps, 14*(3), pp. 205–218.

CASE IN PRACTICE

Making Instructional Modifications in a Middle School Consumer and Food Science Class

INCLUDE

Mr. Gagliano teaches a middle school Consumer and Food Science class. He recently taught a unit on the topic of cooking and nutrition, including how to shop for food. The targeted state standards for the unit were as follows:

1. Students demonstrate the knowledge and skills needed to remain physically healthy.
2. Students evaluate consumer products and services and make effective consumer decisions.

One part of the unit covered vegetarianism. The goal was for the students to plan, shop for, and cook a vegetarian meal. After defining *vegetarianism* and providing a brief history of vegetarianism in the United States, Mr. Gagliano planned to show a video on the FDA nutritional guidelines, including how to decipher nutritional information on a food product label. Mr. Gagliano then planned to break the class into four groups and assign each group the task of designing a vegetarian meal meeting FDA nutritional guidelines.

Ramone is a student with moderate intellectual disabilities who is included in Mr. Gagliano's class. Ramone can do basic math at about the second-grade level and reads below the first-grade level. Although his oral language skills are adequate to carry on a conversation, his ability to interact with others in a small group is limited. Ramone's IEP objectives include the following:

1. Prepare three basic meals independently.
2. Use a calculator to budget money while shopping.
3. Make purchases with the "next dollar" strategy (for example, paying $6.00 and "one more dollar for cents" for an item that costs $6.62).
4. Increase functional sight-word vocabulary to 200 words.
5. Work appropriately in small groups for up to 50 minutes.

Mr. Gagliano and Ms. Henning, Ramone's special education teacher, met to decide how Ramone's instruction during this unit could be adapted. They agreed that the curricular demands for the rest of the class were not appropriate for Ramone, and they planned the following instructional modifications based on Ramone's IEP:

1. Ramone will record the possible choices for the menu (for example, main dishes, dessert, drink). He will actively participate in the making of the final choices. A classmate will help him with spelling as needed.
2. Ramone will record the choices for the grocery list. He will also be assigned the job of checking the kitchen to make sure that items on the list are not already there.
3. Ramone will practice reading the words from the grocery list with the help of his group.
4. Ramone will assist with the shopping, using his calculator to budget the group's money, making purchases using the "next dollar" strategy, and reading his grocery words to find his items. Ramone will be assisted by his group as needed.
5. Ramone will assist the group in cooking the meal.

Following the activity, Ramone, with assistance from Mr. Gagliano and Ms. Henning, evaluated his performance using checklists based on his related IEP objectives. The evaluations were placed in Ramone's alternative assessment portfolio.

REFLECTIONS

Do you think it was appropriate for the teachers to plan instructional modifications for Ramone rather than instructional accommodations? How were the expectations for Ramone different from those of his classmates? How were they similar? Do you think that students such as Ramone should get credit for meeting state standards when their instruction is modified? How useful is the INCLUDE strategy in planning instructional modifications for students with moderate to severe disabilities?

SOURCE: Adapted from "Creating and Using Meaningful Alternate Assessments," by H. Kleinert, P. Green, M. Hurte, J. Clayton, and C. Oetinger, 2002, *Teaching Exceptional Children*, 34(4), pp. 40–47.

SUMMARY

Teachers who communicate clearly through the curriculum materials they use and the information they present orally in class can meet the needs of a broad range of students without having to make adaptations. Nonetheless, despite your best efforts, you will still need to make some accommodations or modifications for students who are at risk or have other special needs. Sometimes accommodations are delivered while teaching the entire class, while other times they are made with individual students or as part of small groups.

In teaching basic skills, you may need to make adaptations in the areas of preskills; selecting and sequencing examples; the rate of introduction of new skills; and the amount of direct instruction, practice, and review.

In teaching subject-area content to students with special needs, adaptations may need to be made in acti-

vating background knowledge, organizing content, and teaching terms and concepts. Your written and oral communication with students must be clear.

Including parents in teaching their children can be helpful. You may also need to make accommodations for students in independent practice activities such as seatwork and homework.

Students with moderate to severe disabilities often cannot perform some or all of the steps in everyday tasks. These students require instructional modifications based on an alternative curriculum set forth on their IEPs. You can use an environmental inventory as well as the INCLUDE strategy to modify your classroom activities for these students.

Applications in **Teaching Practice**

Developing a Repertoire of Instructional Adaptations

You want to teach a group of at-risk students to spell the following contractions: *can't, aren't, couldn't, shouldn't, wouldn't, don't, won't,* and *isn't.*

QUESTIONS

1. How can you evaluate whether your students have learned the contractions?
2. What preskills should you be concerned with, how can you assess them, and what can you do with students who do not know them?
3. How can you sequence your instruction? Why did you choose this particular sequence?
4. How can you provide direct instruction, practice, and review for your students?
5. At what rate should you introduce the contractions?

Design a study guide for a section of Chapter 2 of this text.

QUESTIONS

1. What steps did you go through in constructing your study guide?
2. How did you select the vocabulary and concepts that you included?
3. How would you use the study guide to teach at-risk students or other students with special needs?

Develop a graphic organizer for a major concept in Chapter 1 of this text.

QUESTIONS

1. How did you select the concept? Is it a big idea?
2. How would you use the graphic organizer to teach at-risk students or other students with special needs?

Design a lesson to teach the concept of reasonable accommodations using a definition.

QUESTIONS

1. Is your definition stated clearly, simply, and concisely?
2. What positive and negative examples did you use?
3. How can you find out whether your students know the meaning of the concept?
4. How can you find out whether your students can differentiate this concept from other concepts presented in the text?
5. How would you teach the concept using a concept diagram format?

You are teaching a lesson on the respiratory system. First you describe the respiratory process (for example, diaphragm contracts; air rushes into nose and/or mouth; air travels down trachea; air enters lungs through bronchial tubes; and so forth) using a chart showing the key parts of the respiratory system (for example, nose, throat and trachea, bronchial tubes, lungs). Next you plan to have students work in small, heterogeneous groups on labeling a model of the respiratory system and describing all the key steps in the respiratory process.

QUESTIONS

1. Based on this lesson, complete an environmental inventory for Timothy, the student with a moderate cognitive disability described at the beginning of Chapter 5 in your text.
2. Using INCLUDE, what other adaptations might you make for Timothy?

WORKING THE **STANDARDS**

INTASC INTASC PRINCIPLES REFLECTED IN THIS CHAPTER:

Principle #1 states that all teachers understand that students with disabilities may need accommodations, modifications, and/or adaptations to the general curriculum depending on their learning strengths and needs (Principle 1.03).

Principle #4 states that all teachers

- Understand that it is particularly important to provide multiple ways for students with disabilities to participate in learning activities (Principle 4.04).

- Use research-based practices, including explicit instruction and planned maintenance and generalization, to support initial learning and generalization of concepts and skills for students with disabilities (Principle 4.03).

Principle #7 states that all teachers

- Plan ways to modify instruction, as needed, to facilitate positive learning results within the general curriculum for students with disabilities (Principle 7.02).

- Collaborate to plan instruction related to an expanded curriculum in general education classrooms for students with disabilities who require such a curriculum (Principle 7.03).

- Design the learning environment so that the individual needs of students with disabilities are accommodated (Principle 7.04).

CEC CONTENT STANDARDS REFLECTED IN THIS CHAPTER:

Council for Exceptional Children

CEC Content Standard #3 states that special educators understand the effects that an exceptional condition can have on an individual's learning in school and throughout life.

CEC Content Standard #4 states that special educators

- Possess a repertoire of evidence-based instructional strategies to individualize instruction for individuals with exceptional learning needs.

- Select, adapt, and use these instructional strategies to promote challenging learning results in general and

WORKING THE **STANDARDS** (continued)

special curricula and to appropriately modify learning environments for individuals with exceptional learning needs.

CEC Content Standard #6 states that special educators

- Match their communication methods to an individual's language proficiency and cultural and linguistic differences.

- Provide effective language models.

- Use communication strategies and resources to facilitate understanding of subject matter for individuals with exceptional learning needs whose primary language is not English.

BACK TO THE CASES

The standards and principles just listed relate to the cases described at the beginning of this chapter: Ms. Diaz, Cecily, and Albert. The questions and activities that follow demonstrate how these standards and principles, along with other concepts that you have learned about in this chapter, connect to the everyday activities of all teachers.

Ms. Diaz

Abdul has experienced some difficulties with math skills since he entered second grade. Ms. Diaz notes that lately he has been showing signs of losing his motivation to try new math skills. She has increased the number of examples and practice opportunities each time she introduces a new skill and provides oral and written directions for all seatwork activities. Another teacher has suggested that she use an advance organizer whenever she introduces a new skill. Ms. Diaz has asked you (her student teacher) to help her develop an advance organizer for the lesson in the case study for teaching conversion of fractions into percentages. (See INTASC Principles 1.03, 4.03, and 7.02; and CEC Standard 4.) After you have completed that task, she asks you why using advance organizers might help increase Abdul's motivation to learn new skills, especially math skills. What do you tell her?

Cecily

At the end of this case, we ask how Ms. Boyd might help Cecily read and remember content in her history text. Later in the chapter, we suggest that a study guide might be a useful tool for Cecily. Developing effective study guides that move beyond the knowledge (recall) level of Bloom's taxonomy is a skill that requires practice. (See INTASC Prin-

ciples 1.03, 7.02, and 7.04; and CEC Standard 3.) Construct a study guide that would effectively support and extend Cecily's learning as she reads the history text, using the following instructions.

Ask one to three classmates to form a work group. Select a portion of a chapter from this text and individually develop a study guide for that portion (see the Professional Edge on page 325, "How to Develop Study Guides"). Once everyone in the group has completed a study guide, compare your guides using these questions:

- Do you and your peers agree on the important or key topics? Do you agree on the important vocabulary words to be included? Note and discuss differences.
- Do the study guides match the objectives listed at the beginning of the chapter?
- Are your questions written to help Cecily understand the material at the higher levels of Bloom's taxonomy (application, analysis, and synthesis), and are they also written to help her with knowledge and comprehension of specific facts?
- Collaborate with your peers to incorporate everyone's ideas into a single study guide that will meet Cecily's needs.

Albert

Ms. Olivieri has taken several steps to improve Albert's ability to complete seatwork independently. First, she starts lessons in which she will introduce a new skill by reviewing the skills previously learned that apply to the new skill. Next, as she teaches the new skill, she regularly offers numerous examples of work she expects students to complete during independent practice. Finally, she provides clear, step-by-step directions in both oral and written formats. She has noted that Albert's ability to do correct work has improved. However, he still has difficulty completing the same quantity of work that his peers are able to complete. Once he has completed some portion of the work, he is out of his seat to sharpen a pencil, throw away scrap paper, or chat with a friend. Since Ms. Olivieri has experienced some success with Albert, she is encouraged to continue working to help him become independent in completing his seatwork. What might she try next? (See INTASC Principles 1.03, 4.04, and 7.02; and CEC Standards 3 and 4.) Explain why you selected these strategies or interventions.

Visit the companion website (http://www.ablongman. com/friend4e) for a complete correlation of this chapter to the INTASC Principles and CEC Standards.

Further **Readings**

Beck, I. L., McKeown, M. G., & Kucan, L. (2002). *Bringing words to life: Robust vocabulary instruction*. New York: Guilford.

Rarely do the terms *practical* and *research-based* merge as they do in this indispensable little book on teaching vocabulary to all learners.

Cooper, H., & Valentine, J. C. (2001). Using research to answer practical questions about homework. *Educational Psychologist, 36*(3), 143–153.

This article answers the complex and controversial question, How much time should students spend on homework each night?

Kame'enui, E. J., Carnine, D. W., Dixon, R. C., Simmons, D. C., & Coyne, M. D. (2002). *Effective teaching strategies that accommodate diverse learners* (2nd ed.). Upper Saddle River, NJ: Merrill/Prentice Hall.

This book discusses how the principles of universal design can be practically applied to day-to-day instruction in both basic skill and subject areas.

Thorndike, E. L., & Barnhart, C. L. (1998). *Thorndike Barnhart children's dictionary: Medallion edition*. Chicago: Scott Foresman–Addison Wesley.

Clear definitions are essential for student understanding of new vocabulary. The definitions in this dictionary, though not perfect, are the best we have seen as compared to similar children's dictionaries.

Strategies for Independent Learning

LEARNER OBJECTIVES

After you read this chapter, you will be able to

1. State ways that teachers can encourage student self-awareness and self-advocacy.

2. Describe ways that independent learning strategies can be developed and taught.

3. List and describe successful learning strategies in the areas of reading and reading comprehension, listening and note taking, written expression, math problem solving, and time and resource management.

4. Describe ways that students can learn to use learning strategies independently.

KEY TERMS AND CONCEPTS

Controlled materials (p. 364)

Learning strategies (p. 358)

Pattern guide (p. 379)

Peer editing (p. 380)

Reciprocal teaching (p. 371)

Self-advocacy (p. 357)

Self-instruction (p. 390)

Self-monitoring (p. 390)

Self-questioning (p. 391)

Self-reinforcement (p. 391)

Task analysis (p. 388)

GERALD IS A STUDENT

with learning disabilities in Mr. Mc-Crae's ninth-grade English class. Gerald has had problems in the area of written expression throughout his school years, consistently failing to meet standards on the state high-stakes assessment. It is not that he does not have good ideas. When Gerald talks about what he is going to write, it sounds great. However, when he tries to get his ideas on paper, writing becomes a very frustrating experience for him. First of all, Gerald's papers lack organization. They rarely have a good introduction and conclusion, and the body is usually out of sequence. Gerald also makes a lot of mechanical errors; his papers are full of misspellings, and he frequently leaves out punctuation marks and capital letters. When asked by Mr. McCrae why he does not proofread his papers, Gerald responded that he does. ● *What can Mr. McCrae do to help Gerald learn to organize his papers better? What can be done to help Gerald proofread his papers better for mechanical errors?*

TRACI IS A STUDENT in Ms. Cord's third-

grade class. Traci has yet to meet standards on the state high-stakes assessment in math, but her scores have never been low enough to make her eligible for special education services. Traci has trouble solving story problems in math because she does not have a systematic way of working on them. When she starts a problem, she looks for the numbers right away rather than first reading the problem carefully. For example, one day she saw the numbers 23 and 46 in a problem and automatically added them to get a sum of 69. The problem called for subtraction, but Traci did not know that, because she had not read the problem. ● *What can Ms. Cord do to help Traci solve math word problems more successfully? How can Ms. Cord help Traci become a more independent problem solver?*

RON IS A TWELFTH-GRADE student with

a moderate intellectual disability who has problems with organization. He is often late for school, because, according to his parents, he rarely plans ahead and is always getting his materials ready for school at the last minute. Ron is usually late for class as well. He says that he cannot keep track of what he needs to bring to each class, so he is constantly going back to his locker, which makes him late. His locker is a complete mess. In the afternoons, Ron has a part-time job helping to clean copying and fax machines as part of a work-study program. His supervisor has expressed concern that Ron has been late for work several times and frequently misses his bus, causing his coworkers to have to drive him home. ● *What can Ron's teachers do to help him become better organized?*

DIMENSIONS OF **DIVERSITY**

The value placed on student independence may differ depending on a student's culture. For example, compared to European American students, many Hispanic, Native American, Filipino, and Southeast Asian students are more interested in obtaining teacher direction and feedback than in working on their own (Grossman, 1995). Because being independent and taking direction are both important behaviors, you should teach your students to function in both manners.

" Being able to work independently is a skill that has become increasingly important as more and more students are expected to meet state and federal standards. "

CONNECTIONS

Strategies for achieving independence that are relevant for students with moderate to severe intellectual disabilities are discussed in Chapters 6 and 9.

All these students share a common problem: They are unable to meet the academic and organizational demands of school independently. Being able to work independently is a skill that has become increasingly important as more and more students are expected to meet state and federal standards. Gerald needs to be able to organize his papers better, not just in English but in all areas, because teachers often judge quality on the basis of organization, neatness, or the number of spelling or punctuation errors. Traci needs to solve problems more systematically, not just in math but in other classes and outside of school as well. Ron needs a strategy for managing his time: Being punctual and having the necessary supplies or materials are essential for success on his alternative assessments as well as eventually in the world of work. The fact is, as students move through the grades and on to careers or postsecondary education, more and more independence is expected and is necessary for success.

Students need to perform independently in five key areas: gaining information, storing and retrieving information, expressing information, self-advocating, and managing time (Ellis & Lenz, 1996). Gaining information involves skills in listening to directions during lessons and on the job, and in reading and interpreting textbooks, source books, and other media. Storing information consists of strategies for taking notes and preparing for tests or other evaluations. Students also need to retrieve information when needed. For example, they need to remember how to carry out a task such as cleaning and clearing a table, or how to follow safety procedures during science lab. Expressing information includes the tasks of taking tests and writing papers. It also involves employment tasks such as developing a printed menu for a fast-food restaurant. Self-advocacy skills help students set realistic school or life goals and develop and carry out a plan to meet those goals. Finally, students need to have the time management skills to organize their time and efforts toward meeting their goals.

Although all these skills become more important as students progress through school, independence should be stressed at all levels of instruction. Unfortunately, many students, including those who are at risk or have other special needs, lack basic independent learning skills. Traditionally, when students needed learning-strategy instruction, they were referred to special education classes, remedial reading or math programs, or special study-skills courses. But in inclusive classrooms, learning strategies can be taught to students with special needs in several ways. Moreover, often learning strategies can be covered in class so that all students can benefit. For example, when Mr. Cooper discovered that many of his students in U.S. history were having trouble taking notes, he presented a note-taking strategy to his whole class. Similarly, Ms. Carpenter taught her biology class a strategy for taking multiple-choice tests because her students were scoring low as a group on these kinds of questions.

Sometimes, when students have more intensive skill needs, more individualized strategy instruction might take place outside the classroom. For example, some students with special needs may need to have a strategy broken down into small steps, view multiple demonstrations of a strategy, and practice the strategy many times before they learn it. If the collaborative support of other education professionals is lacking, this level of instruction may be difficult to deliver within the time and curricular constraints of the general education classroom. Ron, from the chapter-opening cases, has just such extraordinary needs. He needs a strategy designed specifically for his organizational problems; a plan for getting to his afternoon job on time would not be relevant for the rest of his classmates. In cases such as these—in which a special educator teaches a strategy to individual students—your job is to encourage and monitor student use of the strategy in your class and to provide students with feedback on their performance. However, in most cases, you can teach many of these skills in your class while still covering the required academic content. In fact, teaching learning strategies to students allows you to cover more material because your students become able to learn on their own.

You should do all you can to encourage and teach independent learning strategies to your students. This chapter focuses on three major ways you can build student independence in learning:

1. encouraging student self-awareness and self-advocacy skills
2. developing and teaching independent learning strategies directly in class
3. teaching students to use specific strategies on their own

Keep in mind that the strategies discussed apply most directly to students with high-incidence or sensory disabilities and to students who are at risk for learning problems.

How Can You Encourage Student Self-Awareness and Self-Advocacy?

As we have said, as students move through elementary, middle, and high school and on to postsecondary education or the world of work, the level of independence expected by those around them increases. Teachers expect students to come to class on time, master content through reading and lectures, keep track of assignments, organize study and homework time, set realistic career goals, and participate in curricular and extracurricular activities to meet these career goals. Students also are expected to recognize when they have a problem and to know where to go for help. Clearly, students need to look out for themselves, to become self-advocates.

Adjusting to these changing expectations can be difficult for all students, but especially for students with disabilities. Many students with special needs are not aware of their strengths and weaknesses (Brinckerhoff, 1994; Scanlon & Mellard, 2002) and lack self-advocacy skills (Durlak, Rose, & Bursuck, 1994; Janiga & Costenbader, 2002). They need to learn these skills while still in school.

In effective student **self-advocacy** training, students learn their strengths and weaknesses, the potential impact of these strengths and weaknesses on their performance, the support they need to succeed, and the skills required to communicate their needs positively and assertively. Generally speaking, special educators have much of the responsibility for teaching self-advocacy directly. However, general education teachers are in a good position to teach all students about the opportunities and expectations of the adult world related to self-awareness and self-advocacy. For example, in applying the steps in INCLUDE, when Ms. Gay observed that Meredith was getting F's on her independent work in class, Ms. Gay surmised that Meredith's problem was at least in part due to her being afraid to ask for help. Ms. Gay decided to spend 5 minutes with the whole class to talk about knowing when and how to ask for help. She felt this discussion would help Meredith and other students in the class be more assertive when they had a problem. In

DIMENSIONS OF DIVERSITY

Self-advocacy relates to social and cultural factors that affect a student's self-concept and self-esteem. Strategies for achieving independence can help students at risk or with special needs overcome learned helplessness and develop a stronger sense of self-efficacy.

RESEARCH NOTE

Three research studies have established the effectiveness of teaching the IPARS self-advocacy strategy to students with disabilities for their use in IEP meetings (Hammer, 2004). The steps in this strategy are as follows: **Inventory** your learning strengths, weaknesses to be improved, goals and interests, and choices for classroom learning. **Provide** your inventory information during the IEP conference. **Ask** questions. **Respond** to questions. **Summarize** your IEP goals.

ANALYZE AND REFLECT

Why might guiding students in establishing or choosing their own learning goals be an effective approach for introducing self-advocacy skills? What problems might occur when teaching students to advocate for themselves? What can general education teachers do to make the process of teaching self-advocacy skills to students with disabilities more effective?

another situation, Cecil, a student with a vision impairment who was in Mr. Jordan's algebra class, sat in the front row but was still unable to see the problems on the board, because Mr. Jordan formed his numbers too small. However, Cecil did not feel comfortable asking Mr. Jordan to write larger. With his special education teacher, Cecil practiced asking Mr. Jordan for help. Cecil then asked Mr. Jordan directly, who responded that it would be no problem to write bigger. Mr. Jordan also gave Cecil some additional pointers on how to describe his disability and how to ask his teachers for accommodations. The Working Together feature below stresses the importance of teachers working together as a team when helping students acquire self-advocacy skills.

WWW
RESOURCES

The following websites can be valuable resources for students as they develop self-advocacy skills:
Wrightslaw: http://www.wrightslaw.com
Disability Rights Education and Defense Fund (DREDF): http://www.dredf.org

How Can You Effectively Teach Independent Learning Strategies in Class?

In addition to teaching students to advocate for their own educational needs, another way you can help your students become more independent is to teach them strategies for learning how to learn (Dickson, Collins, Simmons, & Kameenui, 1998). These methods are collectively referred to as learning strategies. **Learning strategies** are techniques, principles, or rules that enable a student to learn to solve problems and

WORKING TOGETHER

Fostering Team Communication and Self-Advocacy

Avery was a student in Mr. Katz's sophomore biology class. In about the third week of school, Avery approached Mr. Katz after class. Avery said he had a learning disability and that his special education teacher said he had a legal right to receive more time to take his classroom tests. Mr. Katz was concerned. He felt that it wasn't fair to let Avery have extra time when he couldn't do that for the rest of the class. Mr. Katz also knew that new state tests in science were going into effect soon and that getting more time to take classroom tests was not a good way to prepare Avery for these tests. In Mr. Katz's eyes, if Avery failed to meet standards in science, he, Avery's teacher, would be accountable. Furthermore, Mr. Katz was furious that no one had told him about this issue. He knew Avery had learning disabilities and that he might need extra help, but no one had said anything about changing how he took tests. Mr. Katz remembered that he had been unable to attend Avery's IEP meeting due to a scheduling conflict, but shouldn't someone have told him about something as important as this?

What has gone wrong here? What should Mr. Katz do?

- Even though Avery has a legal right to testing accommodations, Mr. Katz seems to have little knowledge of what this right involves and how eligibility for testing accommodations is determined by the IEP team. The proper time to address Mr. Katz's concerns about testing accommoda-

tions was before the plan was put in place, not afterward. At the high school level, it is common for some teachers not to attend IEP meetings. However, even if a teacher is not at the IEP meeting, it is the responsibility of the team to inform all relevant staff members about what has been decided.

- The more basic problem here is that Avery's IEP team has not been operating as such. In effective teaming, the group's goals, as well the means toward attaining those goals, need to be clear to all team members. While Avery's special education teacher might be doing the right thing in teaching Avery to advocate for himself, the success of this effort depends on all of the team members' understanding the goal and working together to help the student attain it.

- Unfortunately, communication problems such as this one can happen in this era of teacher shortages and school regulation. What should Mr. Katz do? An understandable response would be to play the victim and complain bitterly to whomever would listen. However, this response would undermine Mr. Katz's obligations as a member of Avery's IEP team, the purpose of which is to work together for the betterment of Avery's education. A more proactive approach would be to view the situation as a team communication problem in need of a solution. Mr. Katz should request a meeting, express his concerns about Avery's accommodations, and work to reach a team consensus consistent with Avery's unique needs.

complete tasks independently (Lenz, Ellis, & Scanlon, 1996; Schumaker, Deshler, & Denton, 1984). Learning strategies, which are similar to study skills, not only emphasize the steps needed to perform a strategy (for example, steps to follow in reading a textbook) but also stress why and when to use that strategy as well as how to monitor its usage. For example, when Ms. Blankenship taught her students a strategy for reading their textbook, she pointed out that the strategy would save them time yet improve their test scores. She also taught them to judge how well they are using the strategy by filling out a simple checklist as they read. The Case in Practice below shows how the INCLUDE strategy can be used to select the appropriate learning strategies for your students.

CASE IN PRACTICE

Using INCLUDE to Guide Instruction in Learning Strategies

Mr. Devereau taught social studies at Martin Luther King Jr. Middle School. He had a reputation for expecting a lot from his students; throughout the year, he expected them to be able to learn an increasing amount of subject matter independently. Prior to the first day of school, Mr. Devereau was informed that his first-period class included eight students with learning disabilities and two with behavior disorders. He was also told that a special education teacher, Ms. Finch, was assigned to the class as a co-teacher. Mr. Devereau had never had this many students with disabilities at one time before; he also had never worked with a co-teacher. Still, he was hopeful that Ms. Finch would be able to help him, so he set up an appointment to meet with her.

Ms. Finch: What demands do students have to meet to be successful in your class?

Mr. Devereau: I expect students to begin to learn on their own. That is what is expected when they get to high school. I assign most of the reading of the text to be done outside of class, and I require students to take notes from class lectures or DVDs that I show. With my lectures, I use mainly PowerPoint slides. I distribute copies of the slides to students before class.

Ms. Finch: How does your grading system work?

Mr. Devereau: Grades are based on student performance on two multiple-choice tests and a five-page report on a famous person in pre–Civil War America.

Ms. Finch: Based on how your class is structured, my concern is that the students' IEPs show that they all are likely to have problems finding main ideas in both the textbook and the class lectures. But I know of some learning strategies that would help them be more successful in these areas.

Mr. Devereau: That sounds good. It's likely that other students in the class would benefit from these strategies as well.

Mr. Devereau and Ms. Finch decided to each take a strategy. Mr. Devereau would teach the note-taking strategy while he was lecturing in class. Ms. Finch would assist by modeling note taking at the board and/or monitoring student note-taking performance and providing corrective feedback as necessary. Ms. Finch was to teach the students two textbook-reading strategies, one for scanning a text and another for summarizing the big ideas in the text. She was to work on these strategies daily, during the last 15 minutes of class, until the students were able to perform them independently. While Ms. Finch and Mr. Devereau thought that the students with special needs would also have trouble with the multiple-choice tests and the five-page report, they decided that covering these strategies at the same time would be too much. However, they agreed to show the students how the strategies they were learning for note taking and textbook reading could also help them with their tests and research paper.

REFLECTIONS

How did Mr. Devereau and Ms. Finch use INCLUDE to help their students? Do you think it was appropriate for them to teach the strategies to the entire class? Why? Under what circumstances might it have been more appropriate to teach the learning strategies to smaller groups? Which strategies described in this chapter might be appropriate for Mr. Devereau and Ms. Finch to use? What might they do to tie the strategies the students are learning to their needs in test taking and report writing?

An important component of teaching learning strategies effectively is to present well-designed strategies. As you recall from the discussions of effective materials in Chapters 5 and 9, the better your materials are designed, the greater the chance that they will work for your students with special needs without requiring you to make major accommodations. Some effective guidelines for designing learning strategies are presented in the Professional Edge below.

For students to use learning strategies independently, they must first learn to perform them accurately and fluently. The following steps have proven effective for teaching learning strategies (Deshler et al., 1996). These steps include many of the effective teaching practices described in Chapters 5 and 9.

Assessing Current Strategy Use

INCLUDE

Students often are receptive to instruction when they can clearly see what problems they are having and how the strategy you are teaching can help them overcome these problems. Therefore, learning-strategy instruction begins with an assessment of how well your students can currently perform a skill, a part of the N and C steps of INCLUDE. As you learned in Chapter 4, specific learning strategies can be assessed using direct observation checklists, analyses of student products, and student self-evaluations.

You also need to assess whether your students have the preskills necessary to perform the strategy. For example, on the one hand, students who can discriminate be-

PROFESSIONAL EDGE

Developing Your Own Learning Strategies

You can use the guidelines here either to create your own learning strategies or to evaluate ones that are commercially produced. By following these suggestions, you will not always need to depend on commercial publishers for your learning materials. Rather, you can develop learning strategies to fit the students in your class.

1. Identify skill areas that are problematic for most of your students, such as taking multiple-choice tests or writing lecture notes.

2. For each skill area, specify student outcomes, such as scoring at least 10 percent higher on multiple-choice tests or writing down key main ideas and details from a lecture.

3. List a set of specific steps students need to follow to reach the identified outcomes. You may want to ask other students who have good test-taking and note-taking skills what they do. Presented here is a sample reading comprehension strategy called *RAP* (Ellis & Lenz, 1987):

   R **Read** a paragraph.

   A **Ask** yourself what were the main idea and two details.

   P **Put** the main idea and details in your own words.

4. Your strategy should contain no more than eight steps. Having more steps makes the strategy difficult to remember.

5. Your steps should be brief; each should begin with a verb that directly relates to the strategy.

6. To help students remember the steps, encase the strategy in a mnemonic device (for example, the acronym RAP for the reading strategy just presented).

7. The strategy should cue students to perform behaviors for thinking (remembering), for doing (reading), and for self-evaluation (surveying or checking their work).

8. A textbook-reading strategy that was developed by teachers (Bartelt, Marchio, & Reynolds, 1994) and that meets the guidelines for developing an effective learning strategy follows:

   R **Review** headings and subheadings.

   E **Examine** boldface words.

   A **Ask**, "What do I expect to learn?"

   D **Do** it—Read!

   S **Summarize** in your own words.

SOURCE: Adapted from "Generalization and Adaptation of Learning Strategies to Natural Environments: Part 2. Research into Practice," by E. Ellis, K. Lenz, and E. Sabornie, 1987, *Remedial and Special Education, 8*(2), pp. 6–23. Copyright © 1987 by PRO-ED, Inc. Reprinted with permission.

tween main ideas and details in a lecture are ideal candidates for learning a note-taking strategy; students who can read all the words on a test and understand the class content will benefit most from a test-taking strategy. On the other hand, students who cannot identify most of the words in their texts are not logical candidates for learning a textbook-reading strategy; students whose seatwork activities are too hard for them will not benefit from a strategy to help them organize their independent practice activities. As you have learned, students with special needs often lack critical preskills. Before you decide to teach a particular strategy, you should identify its preskills and assess them separately. If most students lack the preskills, they can be taught as part of your everyday instruction. If only a few have problems with preskills, these students need to receive additional instruction in class, with a peer or adult tutor, through co-taught lessons, or in a learning center or special education setting.

Clarifying Expectations

Learning strategies have the potential of empowering your students because they enable students to learn and succeed in and out of school on their own, without undue help from others. When you introduce learning strategies to students, you need to point out their potential benefits clearly and specifically. Carefully explained expected outcomes can be motivating, particularly as students get older and teacher encouragement alone may no longer be enough to keep them interested. The first step in getting and keeping students motivated to learn is to provide a strong rationale for why learning the strategy is important. This rationale should be directly tied to current student performance as well as to the demands of your class, two essential pieces of information derived from the INCLUDE process. For example, when introducing a new note-taking strategy, Mr. Washington pointed out that the class was able to identify on average only half of the main ideas presented on a note-taking pretest. He also told his class that half of the material on his tests would come from information presented during his lectures. Finally, Mr. Washington explained that taking good notes can help students outside of school as well; in many job situations, employers give directions that need to be written down.

The next step in clarifying expectations is to explain specifically what students should be able to accomplish when they have learned the skill. For example, Ms. Thompson told her class that after learning a textbook-reading strategy, they would be able to do their homework faster. Also, give students an idea of how long it will take them to learn the strategy. For example, you could make a chart showing the instructional activities to be covered each day and the approximate number of days it will take to learn the strategy. The advantage of presenting the information on a chart is that steps can be crossed out or checked off as completed. The act of checking off completed activities can be very motivating for students. It is also a way of demonstrating self-monitoring, an effective independent learning skill that we discuss later in this chapter.

Demonstrating Strategy Use

In demonstrating strategies, keep in mind three important points. First, remember that the process one goes through in performing a task or solving a problem should be carefully explained. For example, demonstrate both thinking and doing behaviors. Talking aloud to yourself while performing the skill is particularly important for many students with special needs, who often do not develop spontaneously organized thinking patterns. Second, present both positive and negative examples of appropriate strategy use, carefully explaining why they are positive or negative. This explanation can help students tell the difference between doing a strategy the right way and doing it incorrectly, a distinction that can be difficult for students with special needs to make without direct instruction. For example, Mr. Washington demonstrated effective and ineffective note-taking strategies using the overhead projector. As a student listened to a short video-taped lecture, he took notes systematically, writing down key ideas and details. Next,

CONNECTIONS

The assessment strategies described in Chapter 4 apply to this discussion. Also recall the information in Chapter 9 on teaching preskills and providing direct instruction.

CONNECTIONS

Applying the INCLUDE strategy is an effective way to identify strategies that students need to succeed in your class.

WWW RESOURCES

The following websites can provide information about helping students make the transition from school to work:

LD OnLine: http://www.ldonline.org/ld_indepth/transition/transition.html

All Means All School-to-Work Project: http://ici.umn.edu/all

Vocational and Educational Services for Individuals with Disabilities: http://www.vesid.nysed.gov/do/transition.htm

Reed Martin, Special Education Law and Advocacy Strategies—Transition Planning and the Child with a Disability: http://www.reedmartin.com/transitionresources.htm

Demonstrating the use of a learning strategy involves explaining both the thinking and the doing parts of a process, showing examples and nonexamples of effective strategy use, and checking learners' understanding. How do these steps help students with special needs acquire learning strategies?

using the same lecture, he demonstrated ineffective note taking by trying to write down every word. Third, after you demonstrate, ask frequent questions to test student understanding. Frequent questioning can help you monitor student understanding and determine whether more demonstration is needed. Keep in mind that for many students, including those with disabilities, one demonstration may not be enough. See the Case in Practice on page 363 for a sample script for demonstrating the KWL Plus (K = what you already know; W = what you want to know; L = what you learned) textbook-reading strategy (Ogle, 1986).

DIMENSIONS
OF DIVERSITY

Schifini (1994) reports that the KWL strategy is particularly helpful for second-language learners, because it gives them the immediate opportunity to relate class discussions and their own thinking to the text and to extend ideas beyond the text. The activities also give students the opportunity to contribute, regardless of their language proficiency, because everyone knows something and has something he or she wants to learn.

CONNECTIONS

Strategies for memorizing information are covered in Chapter 11 as part of study strategies.

Encouraging Students to Memorize Strategy Steps

The purpose of having students memorize the steps in the strategy is to make it easier for them to recall the strategy when they need to use it. To help students learn the steps, you can post them prominently in your classroom at first so that you and your students can refer to them throughout the class or day. Students may also need to be drilled on saying the strategy steps. To practice, students could pair off and quiz each other; or you could ask students the strategy steps before and after class. For example, each day during the last several minutes of class, Ms. Henry quizzed four of her social studies students on the steps of the KWL reading strategy.

Even though memorizing a strategy can help students recall it, you may not want to spend too much time on this step, particularly for some of your students with special needs, who may have memory problems. For these students, you might include the steps to all the strategies they are learning in a special section of their assignment notebooks. For strategies used most often, cue cards listing strategy steps can be taped to the inside cover of textbooks or notebooks.

Providing Guided and Independent Practice

As we have already stated, students must learn how to perform strategies accurately and fluently before they can attempt them independently. Such proficiency requires considerable practice. Five ways of providing practice on learning strategies are suggested. One way is to have students practice with controlled materials when they are first

CASE IN PRACTICE

Teaching Script for Demonstrating KWL Plus

An important component of teaching a learning strategy effectively is to demonstrate its appropriate use. The following script shows how one teacher uses modeling to present a textbook-reading strategy to her eighth-grade class.

Teacher: Let's review the textbook-reading strategy we talked about yesterday. Please take out the cue cards you made in class yesterday.

The teacher has students read each step individually and asks them what each step involves. Questions such as, "What are the steps? What might you do with the information you think of when brainstorming? What do you do after you read the passage?" are used.

Teacher: Now that we've reviewed each step, we need to learn how to use the whole strategy effectively. Before we move on, though, let's read aloud all of the steps together as a group. When I point to the letter, say the letter, and when I point to the meaning, you read its meaning.

The students read the steps aloud: "*K* means 'what you already know,' *W* means 'what you want to know,' and *L* is 'what you learned.'"

Teacher: Good. Now I'm going to demonstrate how to use the strategy with a story I found about crayons. I'll put the passage on the overhead, as well as give each of you a copy so you can follow along at your desk. I'll work through each step of the strategy orally and write the information obtained at each step on the board. Use your cue cards to help you see what step of the strategy I'm on.

The teacher then goes through the story, demonstrating correct usage of the steps and asking for feedback. The teacher also goes back over each step, asking the students to verify that all of the steps to the strategy were followed and to explain how they were followed.

Teacher: What do I do now that I have a passage assigned to read? First, I brainstorm, which means I try to think of anything I already know about the topic and write it down.

The teacher writes on the board or overhead known qualities of crayons, such as "made of wax," "come in many colors," "can be sharpened," and "several different brands."

Teacher: I then take this information I already know and put it into categories, like "what crayons are made of" and "crayon colors." Next, I write down any questions I would like to have answered during my reading, such as "Who invented crayons? When were they invented? How are crayons made? Where are they made?" At this point, I'm ready to read, so I read the passage on crayons. Now I must write down what I learned from the passage. I must include any information that answers the questions I wrote down before I read any additional information. For example, I learned that colored crayons were first made in the United States in 1903 by Edwin Binney and E. Harold Smith. I also learned that the Crayola Company owns the company that made the original Magic Markers. Last, I must organize this information into a map so I can see the different main points and any supporting points.

At this point, the teacher draws a map on the chalkboard or overhead.

Teacher: Let's talk about the steps I used and what I did before and after I read the passage.

A class discussion follows.

Teacher: Now I'm going to read the passage again, and I want you to evaluate my textbook-reading skills based on the KWL Plus strategy we've learned.

The teacher then proceeds to demonstrate the strategy incorrectly:

Teacher: The passage is about crayons. Well, how much can there really be to know about crayons besides that there are hundreds of colors and they always seem to break in the middle? Crayons are for little kids, and I'm in junior high so I don't need to know that much about them. I'll just skim the passage and go ahead and answer the question. Okay, how well did I use the strategy steps?

The class discusses the teacher's inappropriate use of the strategy.

Teacher: We've looked at the correct use of the strategy and we've seen how mistakes can be made. Are there any questions about what we did today? Tomorrow we will begin to memorize the strategy steps so that you won't have to rely on your cue cards.

SOURCE: From *A Script for How to Teach the KWL Strategy*, by S. Butson, K. Shea, K. Pankratz, and M. Lamb, 1992, unpublished manuscript, DeKalb: Northern Illinois University. Used with permission.

CONNECTIONS

Providing support for students when they first learn a skill is discussed in Chapter 5 as part of scaffolding.

learning a strategy. **Controlled materials** are generally materials at the student's reading level, of high interest, and relatively free of complex vocabulary and concepts. Because controlled materials remove many content demands on the learner, they allow students to focus all their energy on learning the strategy. Controlled materials also allow for initial success, which is important for motivation. For example, Mr. Bernard was teaching his students a strategy for taking essay tests in current events. At first, he had his students practice this strategy on simply worded, one-part essay questions about material familiar to the students, such as people and events in the areas of rock music, movies, television, and sports. As students became better at using the strategy, Mr. Bernard gradually introduced more complex questions on less familiar topics, such as the AIDS epidemic in Africa and the economic conditions in Mexico. Finally, he used sample test questions.

A second way to provide students with practice is first to guide them and then to allow them to perform independently. By *guided practice*, we mean giving students verbal cues when they are first attempting a skill. For example, before and while her students were practicing a strategy, Ms. Waters asked them questions such as, "What will you do first?" "Why did you do that?" "What should you do after you are done with the strategy steps?" "Which key words are you going to look for in the questions?" "How will you know which are the main ideas?" and "Was the sentence I just read a main idea? Why?" Once most students seem able to answer your reminder questions, you can gradually stop asking them so that students are eventually performing independently. Some students may need little guided practice or none at all. These students can be allowed to work independently right away.

A third practice technique is to give feedback that is specific and encourages students to evaluate themselves (Lenz et al., 1996). For example, Dominique has just performed the steps of a proofreading strategy in front of the class. Her teacher says, "Good job, Dominique! I knew you could do it." Denise performed the same strategy in front of her class and her teacher asked, "How do you think you did? What do you need to focus on most the next time?" The feedback Dominique received does not clearly tell her what she did right, nor does it encourage self-evaluation. The feedback given to Denise encourages self-evaluation, a critical part of independent learning. Of course, if Denise cannot evaluate her own performance at first, the key parts of good performance have to be pointed out to her and practice on self-evaluation provided.

A fourth aspect of practicing learning strategies is to praise students only when they have produced work that is praiseworthy. Praise that is not tied to student performance or is exaggerated, often for the purpose of enhancing student self-image, may only reinforce student inadequacy. For example, because of a history of failure in learning situations, students with special needs often see little relationship between their efforts and classroom success. When you give nonspecific praise to these students, it is easier for them to attribute your praise to something other than competence, such as sympathy ("I'm so bad at this, she has to pretend I did well").

> " Encourage students to reinforce themselves and to take responsibility for both their successes and their failures. "

Fifth, encourage students to reinforce themselves and to take responsibility for both their successes and their failures. For example, after doing well on a note-taking strategy, Alicia was encouraged by her teacher to say, "I did a good job. This time I paid attention and wrote down all the main ideas. I need to do the same the next time." Alicia's teacher was showing her how to attribute her success to factors under her control. This approach can help her become a more active, independent learner.

FYI

Knowing which strategies to teach your students is an important outcome of using the INCLUDE strategy.

Administering Posttests

When it appears from your practice sessions that most students have acquired the strategy, give them the pretest again, this time as a posttest, to test their mastery. If according to your posttest students have not acquired the strategy, identify where the breakdown occurred and then provide additional instruction and/or practice. If more than 20 percent of the students need extra practice or instruction, they can receive additional help in a large or small group. If fewer than 20 percent of the students require more assistance, those needing more individualized practice can be provided with peer tutors or support staff.

What Are Some Examples of Successful Learning Strategies?

There is a growing research base of learning strategies that work for students who are at risk or who have special needs. These strategies cover many areas, including reading and reading comprehension, listening and note taking, written expression, math-problem solving, and time and resource management. An array of strategies that incorporate many of these effective practices are summarized in the following sections.

Word-Identification and Reading Fluency Strategies

Students cannot always depend on the teacher to help them figure out difficult words. They also need to read fluently enough so that they can understand what they are reading and finish assignments in a timely manner. The next two strategies are designed to help students help themselves in the important areas of word identification and reading fluency.

IDENTIFYING WORDS IN TEXTBOOK READING ● Middle and high school students are likely to encounter technical words in their content-area textbooks that have multiple syllables, making them difficult for students to identify. A strategy designed to help students with special needs identify difficult words in their textbook reading is described here (Archer, Gleason, & Vachon, 2003, p. 95). The strategy helps students break apart words and then put them back together again. First, teach your students to break words apart on paper by having them do the following:

1. Circle the word parts at the beginning of the word (prefixes).
2. Circle the word parts at the end of the word (suffixes).
3. Underline the letters representing vowel sounds in the rest of the word.
4. Say the parts of the word.
5. Say the parts fast.
6. Make it a real word.

Here is an example of this strategy:

r e c o n s t r u c t i o n

Once your students can perform all of these steps on paper, they are gradually encouraged to perform the steps in their heads, as follows (Archer et al., 2003, p. 95):

1. Look for word parts at the beginning and end of the word, and vowel sounds in the rest of the word.
2. Say the parts of the word.
3. Say the parts fast.
4. Make it a real word.

To be successful with this strategy, students need to be able to perform two critical preskills. They need to know sounds the vowels make, and they need to be able to pronounce prefixes and suffixes. Students lacking in these preskills need to be taught them prior to strategy instruction. For words that have parts that are hard to decode, encourage students to say the parts they know and then use the strategy described next for using the context to figure out the word. Of course, it is fair to get help from a classmate or the teacher if all of these strategies have been tried and students are still unable to figure out the word.

WARF ● To be successful understanding content-area textbooks, students need to read quickly enough so that they can think about word meaning rather than squander their energy on word identification. Students may also have to adjust their rate of reading, depending on their purpose for reading (Mercer and Pullen, 2005). Minskoff and Allsopp (2003) suggest a strategy to help students who can read accurately at least at the third-grade level but need to increase and/or adjust their reading speed. It is called *WARF*.

W   *Widen* your eye span.
A   *Avoid* skip-backs.
R   *Read* silently.
F   *Flex* your reading rate.

Students are first taught to widen their eye span and not read word by word. They are taught to group words, not reading the articles (for example, *the* or *a*) or auxiliary words (for example, *is* or *are*), so they can focus on words that give meaning. As part of this **W** step, they are also taught to try to group words meaningfully (for example, for the words *a sunny day*, focus on *sunny* and *day*). In the **A** step, avoiding skip-backs, students are taught to keep reading if they don't understand something, using context clues to gain understanding. They are told to go back only if this is unsuccessful. In the **R** step, students are taught to read silently, avoiding reading aloud in a whisper by pressing their lips together. In the final step, **F,** students learn to change their reading rate depending on the difficulty and/or familiarity of the material. For example, when students are looking for information, they need to know to read quickly as they search for key words on the page. When students read important information they need to understand or memorize, they need to be aware to read more slowly. Conversely, if students are reading information they know well, they can adjust their rate and read faster.

Vocabulary Strategies

In addition to being able to identify technical vocabulary, students must also know what words mean if they are to understand what they read. Strategies for using direct instruction to teach new vocabulary were covered in Chapter 9. Realistically, however, teachers have the time to teach only about two vocabulary words per day at the most (Armbruster et al., 2001). Therefore, students need strategies to help them figure out the meaning of words independently.

> ❝ Teachers have the time to teach only about two vocabulary words per day at the most. Therefore, students need strategies to help them figure out the meaning of words independently. ❞

USING CONTEXT CLUES ● Using context clues to figure out the meaning of new words is an important independent vocabulary strategy students need to know. Ruddell (2006) has identified five types of context clues that can help students learn the meaning of new vocabulary in context. These are shown in Table 10.1.

Learning to identify all of the types of context clues is likely to be overwhelming for younger students. For them, a more general strategy for using the words around an unknown

TABLE 10.1 Types of Context Clues

Context Clue	Example
Definition	The author gives you a definition for the word *zenith* in the sentence: When the sun hits its **zenith,** which means *right overhead,* I could tell it was noon by the tremendous heat.
Synonym	The author uses another word that means about the same thing as the word you are trying to understand: Captain Jackson's uniform was **impeccable.** In fact, it was so *perfect* that she always had the highest score during inspection.
Antonym	The author uses another word that means the opposite or nearly the opposite of the word you are trying to understand: The soldier was **intrepid** in battle, in contrast to the person next to him, who was quite *cowardly.*
Example	The author gives you several words or ideas that are examples of the word you are trying to understand: *Tigers, lions, panthers, and leopards* are some of the most beautiful members of the **feline** family.
General	The author gives you some general clues to the meaning of a word, often spread over several sentences: **Patriotism** was a *very strong force* in the South. People *loved their part of the country* and were *very proud to be Southerners.*

Note: In the Example column, italicized words provide context clues for boldfaced words.

SOURCE: *Teaching Children to Read and Write: Becoming an Influential Teacher* (2nd ed.), by R. B. Ruddell, 1999, Boston, MA: Allyn & Bacon. Copyright © 1999 by Pearson Education. Reprinted/adapted by permission of the publisher.

word may be more appropriate. Whatever the situation, however, students need to be taught directly to find and interpret words in context. It is also important to remember that using the context to figure out the meaning of a new word is not always helpful. Sometimes the words needed to infer the meaning of the new word are separated from the word and are hard to find. At other times the words around a word may not offer usable clues to deciphering its meaning and may even be misleading (Beck et al., 2002).

DECODING MORPHEMES ● There are times when looking at *morphemes*, or the smallest parts of word meaning, can help students figure out the meaning of a new word. A list of the most common morphemes compiled by Ruddell (2006) is shown in Table 10.2.

Once you have taught students to decode each of these morphemes and identify its meaning, a strategy that combines using morphemes with using the context can be applied. That strategy is shown in Figures 10.1 and 10.2.

Reading Comprehension Strategies

Reading comprehension strategies are intended to help students meet the independent reading demands of content-area classes successfully, particularly in the middle and upper grades. Although reading primarily involves textbooks, students must be able to read and understand a variety of source books as well. The following are examples of proven reading comprehension strategies for students of all grade levels.

SCROL ● One example of a reading comprehension strategy is *SCROL* (Grant, 1993). The SCROL strategy enables students to take notes when they are reading, an important study strategy, and use text headings to aid their comprehension and help

TABLE 10.2 Useful Morphemes in Vocabulary Development

Prefix and Suffix Family or Type	Meaning	Instructional Vocabulary Example Words
"Not" prefix family	*un, dis, in, im* = not	*disloyal, unaware, invisible, imperfect*
"Before," "during," and "after" prefix family	*pre* = before *mid* = during or middle *post* = after	*prejudge, midtown, postgame*
"Excess" prefix family	*out* = better or more than *over* = too much or too many *super* = more, better, or higher	*outlive, overflow, superhuman*
Number prefix family	*uni, mono* = one *bi* = two *semi* = part, half, or occurring twice	*uniform, monofilament, bicolor, semiarid*
Prefix *re*	*re* = again or back	*recharge, rehire*
"State or quality of" suffix family	*ship, ness, ment* = state or quality of	*friendship, loneliness, excitement*
Suffix *ward*	*ward* = in the direction of	*skyward, northward*
Suffix *ful*	*ful* = full of or characterized by	*merciful, helpful*

SOURCE: *Teaching Children to Read and Write: Becoming an Influential Teacher* (2nd ed.), by R. B. Ruddell, 1999, Boston, MA: Allyn & Bacon. Copyright © 1999 by Pearson Education. Reprinted/adapted by permission of the publisher.

FIGURE 10.1 Word-Part Clues

1. Look for the *root word,* which is a single word that cannot be broken into smaller words or word parts. See if you know what the root word means.

2. Look for a *prefix,* which is a word part added to the beginning of a word that changes its meaning. See if you know what the prefix means.

3. Look for a *suffix,* which is a word part added to the end of a word that changes its meaning. See if you know what the suffix means.

4. Put the meaning of the *root word* and any prefix or suffix together and see if you can build the meaning of the word.

SOURCE: *Teaching Children to Read and Write: Becoming an Influential Teacher* (2nd ed.), by R. B. Ruddell, 1999, Boston, MA: Allyn & Bacon. Copyright © 1999 by Pearson Education. Reprinted/adapted by permission of the publisher.

FIGURE 10.2 Vocabulary Clues

When you come to a word and you don't know what it means, use these clues:

1. *Context clues:* Read the sentences around the word to see if there are clues to its meaning.

2. *Word-part clues:* See if you can break the word into a root word, prefix, or suffix to help figure out its meaning.

3. *Context clues:* Read the sentences around the word again to see if you have figured out its meaning.

SOURCE: *Teaching Children to Read and Write: Becoming an Influential Teacher* (2nd ed.), by R. B. Ruddell, 1999, Boston, MA: Allyn & Bacon. Copyright © 1999 by Pearson Education. Reprinted/adapted by permission of the publisher.

them find and remember important information. The SCROL strategy has five steps. Advise students to follow steps 3–5 (**R–L**) every time they encounter a section with headings in the text they are reading.

S *Survey* the headings. In the assigned text selection, read each heading and subheading. For each heading and subheading, try to answer the following questions: What do I already know about this topic? What information might the writer present?

C *Connect.* Ask yourself, How do the headings relate to one another? Write down key words from the headings that might provide connections between them.

R *Read* the text. As you read, look for words and phrases that express important information about the headings. Mark the text to point out important ideas and details. Stop to make sure that you understand the major ideas and supporting details. If you do not understand, reread.

O *Outline.* Using indentations to reflect structure, outline the major ideas and supporting details in the heading segment. Write the heading and then try to outline each heading segment without looking back at the text.

L *Look* back. Now, look back at the text and check the accuracy of the major ideas and details you wrote. Correct any inaccurate information in your outline. If you marked the text as you read, use this information to help you verify the accuracy of your outline.

Taking notes using SCROL improves student comprehension while also providing students with a product that can help them study more effectively for tests.

PARS ● *PARS* is a simplified textbook-reading strategy that is good for younger students or students without much experience using textbook-reading strategies (Cheek & Cheek, 1983). The four steps of PARS follow:

P *Preview* the material by scanning the chapter and surveying the introductory statement, headings, graphic aids, and chapter summary to identify main ideas.

A *Ask* questions that relate to the main ideas discovered when surveying the chapter.

R *Read* the chapter to answer the questions developed.

S *Summarize* the main ideas in the chapter.

Remember that just telling students the steps of a learning strategy is not enough. Letting students watch you perform the strategy and then carefully guiding students as they learn to perform it are essential if students are to learn to use PARS to access the content of their textbooks more independently.

CAPS ● You have learned that students who can comprehend stories are able to identify key parts of stories called story grammars (see the Case in Practice in Chapter 4). *CAPS* is a self-questioning strategy that guides students as they look for these important story elements (Leinhardt & Zigmond, 1988). The strategy is composed of the following steps:

C Who are the *characters?*
A What is the *aim* of the story?
P What *problem* happens?
S How is the problem *solved?*

CAPS is particularly effective in elementary school, where key reading demands involve understanding stories.

SLiCK ● A common accommodation for students with reading disabilities is the bypass strategy of providing them with an oral text. However, some students still struggle to understand a text, even when they no longer have to read it. *SLiCK* (Boyle et al.,

CONNECTIONS

Strategies for developing and using graphic organizers were covered in more depth in Chapter 9.

2002) is a strategy designed to help students comprehend textbooks prerecorded on CD-ROM. It involves the following steps:

S   *Set* it up.
L   *Look* ahead through the chapter.
C   *Comprehend.*
K   *Keep* it together.

In the **S** step, the student sets it up by opening the textbook to the start of the assigned section; readying a worksheet containing the SLiCK strategy steps at the top, with spaces to record key information such as headings, subheadings, and key vocabulary words; and putting the CD in the CD player. In the **L** step, the student looks ahead through the chapter using the CD book, player, and print textbook. The student notes key words, headings, and subheadings and records them on the worksheet. In the comprehend, or **C**, step, the student reads along with the CD, pausing to record important details under the headings and subheadings previously identified. The student is encouraged to think of big ideas by writing minisummaries as he or she reads. In the final step, **K,** the student combines all of the minisummaries to get the big picture about what the section of text means.

Boyle and colleagues (2002) report that students acquire the **S** and **L** steps quickly, while the **C** and **K** steps require considerable teacher modeling and practice before they are learned.

RUDPC ● You have learned that successful comprehension requires an understanding of how information in stories and expository text is organized and that students with learning disabilities and ADHD often have trouble identifying organizational patterns. While we typically think of organizational patterns as applying to written text, information presented on computer screens has an organizational scheme as well (Minskoff & Allsopp, 2003). Research assignments in school routinely require students to access information on the Internet. Students need to learn how to navigate the different parts of a website to acquire efficiently the information they need. Often this involves ignoring the many distractions that can appear on the computer screen. Minskoff and Allsopp (2003) developed the *RUDPC* strategy for helping students derive important information from a web page. The steps are as follows:

R   *Read* the title and headings.
U   *Use* the cursor to skim the page.
D   *Decide* whether you need the page.
P   *Print* the page.
C   *Copy* the bibliographic information.

When reading a website, students need to make quick decisions about whether a given section of a web page provides information they are looking for. Reading everything on the screen is inefficient. Students with special needs may need explicit instruction on the **D** step in order to learn to make these judgments. Minskoff and Allsopp (2003) also suggest that for some students, printing pages prevents them from being distracted by graphics or frustrated by small fonts.

POSSE ● Another reading comprehension strategy is *POSSE* (Englert & Mariage, 1991). This strategy includes many reading practices that have been shown to aid reading comprehension, such as graphic organizers, text structures, stimulation of student background knowledge, and self-monitoring. The steps in this strategy are as follows:

P   *Predict* ideas.
O   *Organize* the ideas.
S   *Search* for the structure.
S   *Summarize* the main ideas.
E   *Evaluate* your understanding.

These students are engaged in a structured dialogue about the newspaper they are reading, a peer-modeled comprehension strategy called reciprocal teaching. What strategies must students be taught before they can practice reciprocal teaching?

When students are predicting, they can be given a sentence starter such as *I predict that. . . .* For this step, students are taught to use signals from a variety of sources, including title, headings in bold, pictures, key words, and so on. Brainstorming is very important in this step.

A technique used for teaching the POSSE strategy steps is a process called reciprocal teaching. **Reciprocal teaching** is a way to teach students to comprehend reading material by providing them with teacher and peer models of thinking behavior and then allowing them to practice these thinking behaviors with their peers (Palincsar & Brown, 1988). At first, the teacher leads the dialogue, demonstrating how the strategies can be used during reading. As instruction goes on, the teacher gives the students more and more responsibility for maintaining the dialogue. Eventually, students are largely responsible for the dialogue, though the teacher still provides help as necessary. Research shows that the most important part of the technique is the teacher's releasing control and turning the dialogue over to the students (Englert & Mariage, 1991).

A sample dialogue for reciprocal teaching is presented in the Case in Practice on page 372. After reading the Case in Practice, think of the reasons why reciprocal teaching is such a powerful technique for teaching reading comprehension to students who are at risk or who have special needs. In what other areas could reciprocal teaching be used?

The Technology Notes feature on pages 374–375 describes computer software that teaches students key reading comprehension strategies geared to their individual reading levels.

Listening and Note-Taking Strategies

Students in all grades need to be able to understand information presented orally by their teachers. In elementary school, students are required to follow many oral directions and to listen when the teacher is reading aloud or presenting information orally. In middle school, junior high, and high school, where lecturing is a common way for teachers to present subject-area content, students are required to discern and record key information in lectures so they can study it later. As you have already learned, students with special needs may have problems understanding information presented orally. These problems can make access to the general education curriculum more difficult for them. The listening and note-taking strategies described in the next section were designed to help all students learn more successfully from their teachers' presentations.

SLANT ● Students who are actively participating in class are much more likely to stay on task, understand what the teacher is saying, and take good notes. One strategy

ANALYZE
AND **REFLECT**

What makes reciprocal teaching a powerful technique for teaching reading comprehension to students who are at risk or who have special needs? In what other areas could reciprocal teaching be used?

CASE IN PRACTICE

Teaching Script for Demonstrating POSSE

The students in this class have just read a section of text that focuses on Loch Ness. They are now applying the search, summarize, and evaluate steps of POSSE.

Teacher: What is the main topic the text is talking about?

Peg: The Loch Ness monster.

Teacher: What was this section about? What was the main idea?

Peg: Oh, the lake. I have two questions: "What is a lake?" and "What lives in it?"

Teacher: Do you mean this particular lake or any lake?

Peg: This lake. Joe?

Joe: It's foggy, it's deep, and it's long and narrow.

Peg: Don?

Don: The land beside the lake, you don't know if it is real soft and you could fall through it.

Teacher: So it could be soft and swampy.

Ann: I think the Loch Ness monster lives there.

Teacher: Is Ann answering your question, Peg?

Peg: No.

Teacher: What was your question?

Peg: I had two: "What is a lake?" and "What lives in the lake?"

Joe: But the book never answered that. I have a question about the main idea. Aren't we supposed to do a question about the main idea?

Teacher: Just about what we read.

Joe: Yes, but Peg asked us, "What lives in the lake?" but it doesn't really mention that in the book.

Teacher: That's true. The major idea has to do with Loch Ness and what it looks like. A minor idea that we really inferred rather than directly read in

the article was that the Loch Ness monster lives in the lake.

Peg: Are there any clarifications?

Students: [No response.]

Teacher: I have a clarification. You had trouble reading some of these words and I wondered if you know what some of them mean. What does *ancestors* mean?

[The teacher continues discussing vocabulary.]

SOURCE: From "Making Students Partners in the Comprehension Process: Organizing the Reading 'POSSE,' " by C. S. Englert and T. V. Mariage, 1991, *Learning Disability Quarterly, 14,* pp. 133–134. Used by permission of Council for Learning Disabilities.

that can help students stay engaged while the teacher is talking is called *SLANT* (Mercer & Mercer, 2001). The steps are these:

S   *Sit* up straight.
L   *Lean* forward.
A   *Ask* questions.
N   *Nod* your head.
T   *Track* the teacher with your eyes.

This strategy can be used effectively with students at all grade levels. When teaching SLANT, model both positive and negative examples of strategy usage for your students. Showing examples of inappropriate strategy usage is instructive, and students love to see the teacher doing the wrong thing. Next, have students role-play both appropriate and inappropriate strategy usage. Even after learning the strategy, many students will still not know when to apply it. To assure consistent strategy application, post the steps of the strategy in your classroom and use the posting to remind students to use the strategy.

GIVE ME FIVE ● The *Give Me Five* strategy focuses students' attention on five body parts in order to improve their listening skills: *eyes* on the speaker, *mouth* quiet, *body* still, *ears* listening, and *hands* free (Prouty & Fagan, 1997, as cited in Swain, Friehe, & Harrington, 2004). See Figure 10.3 for a helpful illustration of this strategy. The con-

FIGURE 10.3 The Give Me Five Listening Strategy

SOURCE: From *Language Strategies for Children,* by V. Prouty and M. Fagan, 1997, Eau Claire, WI: Thinking Publications.

crete nature of this strategy makes it ideal for use with younger students. Its multisensory emphasis may be especially helpful for your students with disabilities.

TALS ● Once students marshal their body parts to help them pay careful attention to what the teacher is saying, Swain and colleagues (2004) suggest introducing another strategy, *TALS*, to help them prepare for the material to come and sift through all they hear for the most important information. Identifying important ideas in a lecture is expected of all students as early as middle school. This means that students need to learn this important skill early, and TALS is designed specifically for younger children. The steps in TALS are as follows:

T   *Think.*
A   *Ask* why.
L   *Listen* for what?
S   *Say* to self.

Mr. Lewis's students used the TALS strategy when learning the key parts of stories using story maps. When reading stories out loud, he instructed the students, "Think about the story parts, ask why a story map is important, listen for the different parts of a story map, and say to yourself the parts of the story."

RESEARCH NOTE

Boyle and Weishaar (2001) examined the effects of a strategic note-taking strategy on the recall and comprehension of students with learning and behavior disabilities. Students were taught to prompt themselves to tap into their background knowledge before the lecture and to identify and summarize main ideas and details during and after the lecture. The study found that students who were taught this strategy scored significantly higher on measures of immediate recall, long-term free recall, comprehension, and the volume of notes recorded than students in a control group who used conventional note taking.

> TECHNOLOGY NOTES

Thinking Reader: The Textbook of the Future

Textbooks are the most common method of delivering subject-area information to students of all grades, but particularly to those who are in middle school or high school. Yet many students with and without special needs experience problems comprehending their textbooks. Whereas some of these problems are due to reading slowly and/or inaccurately, students also lack strategies for locating and retaining important information in their texts. Unfortunately, standard textbooks provide teachers and students with little support in teaching and learning important comprehension strategies. Enter the Thinking Reader.

The Thinking Reader incorporates a variety of supports into electronic text in order to teach research-based reading comprehension strategies such as summarizing, questioning, clarifying, predicting, and visualizing. The supports can be customized to accommodate individual student reading abilities by systematically reducing the level of structure as students become more proficient in the reading comprehension strategies. The goal is for students to select independently the strategy that best fits their comprehension needs.

The specific supports in the program include a human voice feature that reads the text while highlighting it and natural intonation to support the finding of main ideas and the development of fluency. Comprehension is supported through a series of strategy prompts that guide students as they practice the comprehension strategies. For example, at the end of each passage, students might be asked to predict what will happen in the story, clarify something that they find confusing, summarize the passage, or visualize what is happening. Students respond to the prompts in three formats: open-ended, fill-in-the-blank, and oral response. There are also supports for vocabulary development including a contextual glossary with Spanish translations for ELL students.

Perhaps the most helpful aspect of the Thinking Reader is the availability of supports to help students think about the passage. The program employs an "agent" who provides hints for each strategy (for example, "Try predicting what will happen to one of the characters") or think alouds (for example, "I remembered that both Winnie's grandmother and the stranger are very interested in music. She is excited to hear the music again, and he seems to find it meaningful that she has heard it before. So I predict that the music will be important in some way"). A sample screen display is shown in Figure 10.4.

From the Research

While more carefully controlled studies remain to be done, a recent federally funded experiment (Dalton & Pisha, 2001) evaluated the effectiveness of the Thinking Reader with 102 readers in the bottom quartile in reading based on performance on a standardized test. Students using the Thinking Reader made greater gains in comprehension than a control group receiving more traditional strategy instruction. The results also revealed that students reading with the Thinking Reader spent significantly more time on task and had significantly more opportunities to respond and to practice strategies than did their classmates receiving the traditional strategy instruction (Coyne et al., 2004).

TASSELL ● As students move into the upper grades, they are required to take notes for longer periods of time. Longer lectures require sustained attention, a skill that is often problematic for students with special needs (Smith, 2004). The *TASSELL* strategy is recommended for students who have trouble maintaining their level of attention (Minskoff & Allsopp, 2003). It includes the following steps:

T   *Try* not to doodle.
A   *Arrive* at class prepared.
S   *Sit* near the front.
S   *Sit* away from friends.
E   *End* daydreaming.
L   *Look* at the teacher.

For the **E** step, encourage students to monitor their attention. When they find they are daydreaming, they should immediately change their position, sit forward, and make eye contact with the teacher. Then they should write down whatever the teacher is saying, regardless of its importance (Minskoff & Allsopp, 2003). For the **L** step, encourage students to keep their eyes on the teacher when they are not taking notes or

FIGURE 10.4

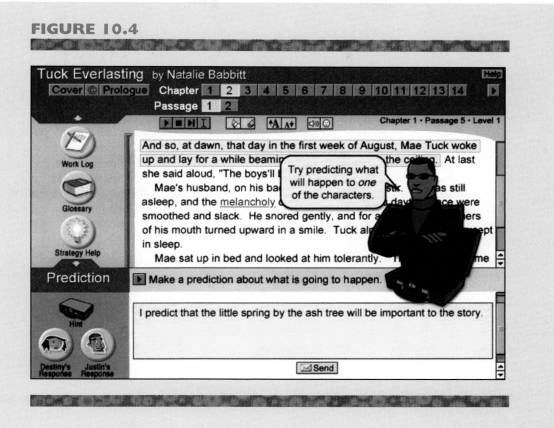

Note: The Thinking Reader was developed by Dr. David Rose and Dr. Bridget Dalton at the Center for Applied Special Technology (CAST). The program is based on research cited in this text, including a report of the National Reading Panel (2000), principles of universal design (Dalton & Pisha, 2001), and reciprocal teaching (Palincsar & Brown, 1988). The Thinking Reader has been used successfully to teach comprehension strategies to students with learning disabilities (Dalton & Pisha, 2001).

looking at the chalkboard, overhead, PowerPoint presentation, or computer screen (Minskoff & Alsopp, 2003).

Another self-monitoring strategy for helping students sustain attention is addressed in the Special Emphasis On . . . feature on page 376.

The next section describes two research-based note-taking strategies. Before you read about them, consider the note-taking tips listed in Figure 10.7 on page 377. These tips help no matter which note-taking strategy is used.

CALL UP ● *CALL UP* is a strategy for taking lecture notes that has the following steps (Czarnecki, Rosko, & Fine, 1998):

C   *Copy* from the board or transparency.
A   *Add* details.
L   *Listen* and write the question.
L   *Listen* and write the answer.
U   *Utilize* the text.
P   *Put* in your own words.

Special EMPHASIS On …

Getting Students to Study in Study Hall

The idea behind study hall seems simple enough: Give students extra time during the day to study or do homework and they will get better grades in their classes. Unfortunately, the idea of study hall and its everyday reality can be very different. While the effectiveness of study hall depends on a number of factors, a key element is the ability of the students to study.

Studying requires that students remain on task for continuous periods of time, an ability that can be a problem for students with special needs. A program of self-monitoring, a skill for fostering student independence, can be used to increase the time on task in study hall for adolescents with learning disabilities (Dalton, Martella, & Marchand-Martella, 1999). This self-monitoring program consists of two parts: a self-monitoring form and a behavior checklist and rating form (see Figures 10.5 and 10.6).

On the self-monitoring form, every 5 minutes the students circle yes if they are working or on task at the designated time, or no if they are not working or are off task. On the behavior checklist, students check yes or no in answer to whether they engaged in certain behaviors before class, during class, and after class. Students also rate their overall behavior in class on a scale of 1 to 5, with 1 being *poor* and 5 being *great*.

If you are using this strategy with students in study hall, you need to be sure that they know what to do. First, they need to understand what on- and off-task behavior is. This can be easily covered by providing them with several examples and having them tell you whether they are on task or off task. Students also need to practice using the self-monitoring form with someone supervising to be sure they are completing it correctly. The hard part is getting them to look up at the clock at the appropriate time. Students who struggle with this step can benefit from a tape or CD that signals at regular intervals when to look at the clock. Begin the strategy when the students show you that they know what to do.

In the research by Dalton and colleagues (1999) using this strategy, the rate of student off-task behavior in study hall was decreased. The students' study hall teacher also noted improved behavior when the self-monitoring program was being used.

FIGURE 10.5 Study Hall Self-Monitoring Form

Name _____

Date _____

Are you working?

9:05	☐ Yes	☐ No
9:10	☐ Yes	☐ No
9:15	☐ Yes	☐ No
9:20	☐ Yes	☐ No
9:25	☐ Yes	☐ No
9:30	☐ Yes	☐ No
9:35	☐ Yes	☐ No
9:40	☐ Yes	☐ No
9:45	☐ Yes	☐ No
9:50	☐ Yes	☐ No

SOURCE: Adapted from "The Effects of a Self-Management Program in Reducing Off-Task Behavior," by T. Dalton, R. C. Martella, and N. E. Marchand-Martella, 1999, *Journal of Behavioral Education, 9*(3–4), pp. 157–176.

FIGURE 10.6 Study Hall Behavior Checklist and Rating Form

Before Class

Did you get your homework done?	☐ Yes	☐ No
Did you find out what you'll be doing in class?	☐ Yes	☐ No
Did you get started on time?	☐ Yes	☐ No

During Class

Did you self-monitor to stay on task?	☐ Yes	☐ No

After Class

Did you follow the teacher's directions?	☐ Yes	☐ No
Did you work on the assignment for the entire time you were given?	☐ Yes	☐ No
Do you have homework tonight?	☐ Yes	☐ No

How Was Your Behavior?

Poor	Needs Improvement	Okay	Good	Great
(1)	(2)	(3)	(4)	(5)

SOURCE: Adapted from "The Effects of a Self-Management Program in Reducing Off-Task Behavior," T. Dalton, R. C. Martella, and N. E. Marchand-Martella, 1999, *Journal of Behavioral Education, 9*(3–4), pp. 157–176.

FIGURE 10.7 Tips for Note Taking

1. Take notes using either a two- or three-column system.

2. Take notes on only one side of the paper.

3. Date and label the topic of the notes.

4. Generally use a modified outline format, indenting subordinate ideas, and numbering ideas when possible.

5. Skip lines to note changes in ideas.

6. Write ideas or key phrases, not complete sentences.

7. Use pictures and diagrams to relate ideas.

8. Use consistent abbreviations (for example, w/ = with, & = and).

9. Underline or asterisk information the lecturer stresses as important.

10. Write down information the lecturer writes on the board or transparency.

11. If you miss an idea you want to include, draw a blank line so that you can go back and fill it in.

12. If you cannot automatically remember how to spell a word, spell it the way it sounds or the way you think it looks.

13. If possible, review the previous session's notes right before the lecture.

14. If the lecture is about an assigned reading topic, read the information before listening to the lecture.

15. As soon as possible after the lecture, go over your notes, filling in key concepts in one column and listing any questions you still have.

16. After going over your notes, try to summarize the major points presented during the lecture.

17. Listen actively! In other words, think about what you already know about the topic being presented and how new information is related to old information.

18. Review your notes before a test.

SOURCE: From *Strategies for Teaching Students with Learning and Behavior Problems* (6th ed.), by C. S. Bos and S. Vaughn, Boston: Allyn & Bacon. Copyright © 2006 by Allyn & Bacon. Reprinted by permission.

When copying from the board or transparency, students listen and look for cue words or phrases that identify main ideas, copy them down in the margin, and underline them. Students also listen for details, writing them 1 inch from the margin with a dash (—) in front of each detail. Students listen for teacher or student questions that they think can inform their understanding and write them, indented, under the appropriate main ideas. Students also record answers under the main ideas. The last two steps can be carried out at home or in study hall. Students first read about the main ideas in their textbooks and then paraphrase the information under each main idea in a space previously left blank. Students record relevant text pages in the margins so they can refer to the text at a later time if needed. Try posting the CALL UP steps prominently in your classroom. As you lecture, model the various steps while explicitly telling your students which steps you are performing and why. For example, Mr. Sauter was lecturing his class on the topic of the respiratory system. He wrote *respiratory system* on the board and directed his students to write down this main idea of the lecture. He then told them to add the details of the parts of the respiratory system (for example, *nose, lungs, mouth,* and *windpipe*) to their notes. Mr. Sauter posed important questions as he lectured such as "What is the purpose of the bronchial tubes?" He directed students to copy down these questions as he raised them. Finally, Mr. Sauter asked students to answer all questions raised for homework.

ANOTES ● Staying organized is a challenge for all students, but particularly for students with special needs. Part of the trick of being a successful note taker is being able to retrieve the notes at a later time and use them to study for tests. *ANOTES* is another research-based strategy that is useful for revising notes to organize them for test preparation. It includes the following steps:

A   *Ask* yourself whether you have a date and topic.
N   *Name* the main ideas and details.
O   *Observe* ideas also in text.
T   *Try* margin noting and use the SAND strategy.
E   *Examine* for omissions or unclear ideas.
S   *Summarize* key points.

In the first step, students skim their notes for a main idea mentioned several times or recall what the teacher said the lesson was about. Students then highlight or underline all the main ideas and supporting details in their notes. Students note main ideas that are also in the text. Next students use the *SAND* strategy to organize their notes visually: They *star* important ideas, especially those that are also in the text, *arrange* arrows to connect ideas, *number* key points in order, and *devise* abbreviations and write them next to the items. Students then reread the notes to find any missing information and unclear ideas. Finally, students write the overall idea of the lecture in a sentence or two immediately following the notes. Most students will need considerable modeling and guided practice in order to learn this strategy. Also helpful are regularly scheduled note checks, whereby the teacher randomly selects the notes of several students and provides feedback on how well they performed the ANOTES strategy. Adding bonus points toward student grades for effective strategy usage is a good way to encourage your students to use the strategy correctly. Of course, receiving higher grades because of having better notes to study can be the most powerful motivation for strategy usage.

As we have said, to learn these or other note-taking strategies, students need the preskill of being able to tell the difference between main ideas and details. Some students choose key words that represent main ideas, but others attempt to write down everything and need to be taught directly how to differentiate main ideas and details.

> **To learn note-taking strategies, students need the preskill of being able to tell the difference between main ideas and details.**

For example, Mr. Abeles discovered that many students in his history class were unable to identify main ideas in his lectures. First, he explained the difference between main ideas and details: Main ideas are what a whole section or passage is about; details are what just one part of a section or passage is about. For several weeks he stopped after presenting a section of material and put three pieces of information on the board—one main idea and two details. He asked the students which was the main idea and why. When his students were doing well at these tasks, Mr. Abeles had them write their own main ideas for a section of a lecture, which were shared with the class, and then he provided corrective feedback as necessary.

To take effective notes, students also must be able to summarize material in their own words. Here is an effective strategy for writing summaries (Sheinker & Sheinker, 1989, p. 135):

1. Skim the passage (or listen to a section of lecture).

2. List the key points.

3. Combine related points into single statements.

4. Cross out the least important points.

5. Reread the list.

6. Combine and cross out to condense points.

7. Number the remaining points in logical order.

8. Write out points in paragraph format in numbered order.

Students should also learn strategies for studying their notes, such as covering up one column and trying to say what is in the column, and then uncovering the column and comparing their responses to the actual information. Although some students can master this study strategy with only a verbal explanation, others may need more support, perhaps in the form of a demonstration and guided practice. More strategies for studying for tests are described in Chapter 11.

Writing Strategies

Another area that requires student independence is writing and proofreading papers. Several research-based strategies are useful to help students in this area.

POWER ● One strategy that helps students organize all the steps in the writing process is called *POWER* (Englert et al., 1988). The process involves the use of self-questioning, graphic organizers, and peer editing using the following steps:

P Planning
O Organizing
W Writing
E Editing
R Revising

The POWER strategy teaches students four different organizational structures for writing papers: stories, comparison/contrast, explanations, and problem/solution (Englert et al., 1988). When writing stories, students use key story elements—Who? When? Where? What happened? How did it end?—to organize their papers. A comparison/contrast structure includes information on what subjects are being compared (for example, Native Americans and settlers), on what characteristic of those subjects is being compared (views about land), and on how the subjects are alike and/or different in relation to that characteristic (Native Americans shared land; settlers owned land). Explanations involve telling how to do something, such as explaining the steps in changing a tire. In a problem/solution structure, a problem is identified (for example, it took too long to travel from the East to the West in the early 1800s in the United States), the cause of the problem is explained (the only way to go from the East to the West was by stagecoach), and the solution is stated (the transcontinental railroad was built).

For the *planning* stage, students focus on the audience for the paper, the purpose, and the background knowledge that is necessary to write the paper. In the *organizing* step, students decide which organizational pattern fits their paper (for example, story, comparison/contrast) and then complete a pattern guide to help them organize their ideas. A **pattern guide** is a graphic organizer designed to help students organize their papers. A sample pattern guide for a comparison/contrast paper is shown in Figure 10.8. Notice that the words that are not in boxes—Both same, In contrast to, Similarly, and However—are key words that are used frequently when making comparisons. These words help students make the transition to writing sentences. For example, in Figure 10.8, two kinds of pizza are being compared and contrasted. The student might write, "The crusts of deep dish and regular pizza are the same in that they both are made of white flour. This is in contrast to their thickness; deep dish pizza crust is much thicker."

In the *writing* stage, the teacher demonstrates and thinks aloud to show students how to take the information gathered in the planning and organizing steps and produce a first draft. For example, you can compose an essay comparing two kinds of pizza using an overhead projector, thinking out loud as you write. You can involve students by asking questions such as, "What would a good topic sentence be? Is this a good example? How do you think I should end this? Why?" You could also have students write the paper along with you.

The *editing* step teaches students to critique their own writing and to identify areas in which they need clarification or assistance, an important self-evaluation skill. Editing is a two-step process involving student self-evaluation and peer editing. For self-evaluation, students reread and evaluate their drafts, starring sections of the paper they

FIGURE 10.8 Pattern Guide for Comparison/Contrast Paper

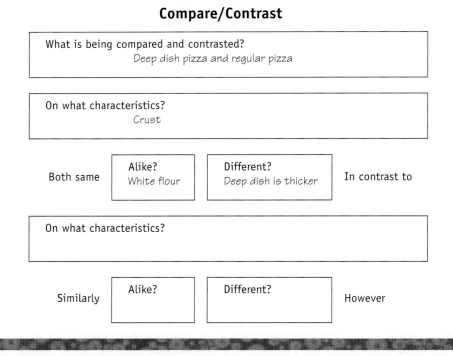

SOURCE: From "A Case for Writing Intervention: Strategies for Writing Informational Text," by C. S. Englert, T. E. Raphael, L. M. Anderson, H. M. Anthony, K. L. Fear, and S. L. Gregg, 1988, *Learning Disability Quarterly, 3*(2), p. 108.

like best and putting question marks in the margins by passages they think may be unclear. Finally, students think of two questions to ask their peer editors. For example, Jorge asked his peer editor whether he had used capital letters and punctuation correctly. He was also concerned about whether his paper was long enough and asked for suggestions on how to add information.

For **peer editing,** several steps are followed. First, the writer reads the paper to a peer editor while the editor listens. The peer editor then summarizes the paper. Next, the editor evaluates the paper, sharing with the writer an analysis of salient features of the writing that might guide a revision or lead to improvement. For example, the peer editor might suggest that the writer add key words or reorganize the paper for clarity. Then the peer editor and the writer brainstorm ways to improve the paper.

A research-based strategy called *TAG* can also help students with the peer editing process (Carlson & Henning, 1993; MacArthur & Stoddard, 1990). The TAG strategy involves three simple steps:

T *Tell* what you like.
A *Ask* questions.
G *Give* suggestions.

As discussed previously, students need to be provided with models and guided practice for doing these steps prior to doing them independently.

In the *revising* step, students decide on changes to be made using their self-evaluation marks and peer feedback. Englert and colleagues (1988) suggest that the teacher model how to insert or change the order of information, all the while providing a rationale for any changes. All modifications are made directly on the first draft. Last, the teacher and student have a conference, and changes in writing mechanics are suggested. Following this conference, a final draft is composed on clean sheets of paper.

COPS ● When students have to proofread their papers independently, they might use a strategy called *COPS* (Alley, 1988). In the COPS strategy, students question themselves as follows:

C   Have I *capitalized* the first word and proper nouns?
O   How is the *overall appearance* of my paper? Have I made any handwriting, margin, or messy errors?
P   Have I used end *punctuation*, commas, and semicolons carefully?
S   Do words look like they are *spelled* right; can I sound them out or use the dictionary?

Although COPS has been shown to be effective, students need preskills to perform this strategy adequately. Before teaching COPS, consider the following questions: Can the students recognize misspelled words? Do the students know rules for using capital letters and punctuation? Can they apply these rules? Can the students use a dictionary? If the answer to any of these questions is no, teach these skills directly before teaching students the COPS strategy.

STOP & LIST, SPACE, AND DARE ● Several additional strategies can be used to help students with the various aspects of written expression. Troia, Graham, and Harris (1999) used the STOP & LIST, SPACE, and DARE strategies to teach story writing and the writing of persuasive essays to students with learning disabilities.

STOP & LIST is introduced to help students plan their writing. In the STOP step, students *stop* to think of their purpose for writing. For the LIST step, students *list* their ideas and put them in a sequence.

The *SPACE* strategy emphasizes five key elements when writing stories:

S   Setting
P   Problem
A   Actions
C   Consequence
E   Emotions

When teaching SPACE, use these steps, which were employed successfully by Troia and Graham (2002). Present an example of each story element (for example, problems; actions taken to solve problems; consequences, or what happens when someone acts to solve the problem) from sample stories. Then, read new stories together with your students and identify the same elements in these stories. Next, ask students to identify the elements in one or more stories until they can perform this task without error. Finally, ask students to tell a story based only on pictures, and note each element as it is included. Once students are able to do this, they are ready to begin to write original stories under the direction of the teacher.

DARE is a strategy designed to teach a different form of writing: persuasive essays. DARE stresses four key steps:

D   *Develop* a topic sentence.
A   *Add* supporting details.
R   *Reject* counter-arguments.
E   *End* with a conclusion.

DEFENDS ● *DEFENDS* (Ellis & Lenz, 1987) is another strategy designed to help students write persuasive papers:

D   *Decide* on an exact position.
E   *Examine* the reasons for the position.
F   *Form* a list of points that explain each reason.
E   *Expose* the position in the first sentence.
N   *Note* each reason and supporting points.
D   *Drive* home the position in the last sentence.
S   *Search* for errors and correct.

ANALYZE AND REFLECT

How would you use INCLUDE to find out whether students needed to learn the COPS strategy? What assessment information would you collect to monitor student progress in learning COPS?

DIMENSIONS OF DIVERSITY

Cohen and Riel (1989) conducted a study to explore the effects of writing using the Internet for authentic audiences of peers from different cultural backgrounds. They found that essays written for distant peers were superior to essays written to be graded by their teachers; essays for authentic peers were more explicit and detailed.

When first teaching this strategy, motivate students to learn DEFENDS by having them write about topics they are familiar with and feel strongly about. Whenever possible, try for authentic writing contexts such as having students write letters to the editor of a newspaper or to a company, lodging a complaint.

LEARNING SPELLING WORDS ● A study strategy can help students learn unknown spelling words (Graham & Freeman, 1986). Students are required to carry out the following five steps:

1. Say the word.
2. Write and say the word.
3. Check the word.
4. Trace and say the word.
5. Write the word from memory and check your spelling.

If students misspell the word in step 5, they need to repeat all five steps.

> Using the Internet for writing can lead to many positive outcomes in addition to better written products.

Strategies for Using Technology to Improve Student Writing

USING THE INTERNET ● The Internet can enhance the writing process for all your students, including those with special needs. Smith, Boone, and Higgins (1998) have described the different ways the Internet can expand the writing process (see Figure 10.9). They believe that using the Internet for writing can lead to many positive outcomes in addition to better written products, including the following outcomes:

1. Students are no longer limited to community or school libraries for information and ideas.
2. Students can develop a better sense of research as they comb the Internet for information.
3. Students can learn how to locate information more efficiently using web search engines such as Yahooligans!
4. Students can learn to gather information from many sources and make judgments about its accuracy.
5. Students can learn about important aspects of writing not often covered extensively or clearly in school, such as copyright laws, plagiarism, and publishing restrictions.
6. Students can learn to solve problems and cope with frustration as they experience problems, such as long delays, when using the Internet.

REVISING ESSAYS ● This strategy uses a word processor for revising essays (Graham & Harris, 1987). Students instruct themselves using the following six steps:

1. Read your essay.
2. Find the sentence that tells you what you believe—is it clear?
3. Add two reasons why you believe it.
4. SCAN each sentence:

    S Does it make *sense?*
    C Is it *connected* to your belief?
    A Can you *add* more?
    N *Note* errors.

www RESOURCES

The Write Site, at http://www.writesite.org, is designed for language arts students in middle school. The site allows students to take on the roles of journalists and editors to research, write, and publish their own newspaper. The site provides unit outlines, handouts, exercises, downloadable teaching material, information about how to write, and more.

FIGURE 10.9 The Internet-Expanded Writing Process

Writing Process Phases	Typical Activities	Internet Activities
Prewriting	Brainstorming	Keyword searching
	Outlining	Browsing
	Clustering	Downloading information
	Collecting information	
Writing	Writing series of drafts	
Revision	Peer responding	E-mailing drafts to other kids for response
	Teacher responding	
	Editing	E-mailing drafts to experts for response
	Revising	
Publishing	Final drafting	
	Binding into a book	
	Reading by others in class	
	Reading by parents	
WWW Revision		Final draft is reviewed for possible hypertext links to other WWW sites.
		Additional searches are made for possible links.
		Story is pasted into a WWW creation program.
		Hypertext links are added.
WWW Publishing		Story file is transferred to a classroom WWW site on a networked computer.
		URL address is established.
		The story WWW page is registered with search page Yahooligans! for international access.
		Uncle in Kathmandu can read it.

SOURCE: From "Expanding the Writing Process to the Web," by S. Smith, R. Boone, and K. Higgins, 1998, *Teaching Exceptional Children, 30*(5), pp. 22–26.

5. Make changes on the computer.
6. Reread your essay and make final changes.

USING SPELL-CHECKERS EFFECTIVELY ● Spelling checkers can help students identify misspelled words and spell them correctly. However, one problem with spell-checkers is that the correctly spelled version of a word that the student is attempting to write is not always presented as an alternative. This happens when the combination of letters that the student has typed does not approximate closely enough the intended word for the software to offer the needed choices. Because the correct word does not appear on the first attempt, students often click on Go to Next Word or Skip Word without making a change. The result is a paper with many misspelled words. Ashton (1999) describes the *CHECK* strategy, a sequence of steps designed to help students use any spell-checker more effectively. The sequence of steps in the strategy follows.

RESEARCH
N O T E

Hetzroni and Shrieber (2004) studied the use of a word processor for enhancing the written expression of junior high school students with learning disabilities. They found a clear difference in quality between handwritten and computer-produced writing. Using paper and pencil, students wrote papers that had more spelling mistakes and lower overall quality of organization and structure.

C   *Check the beginning sounds.* Most spell-checkers search for similar words beginning with the same letter as the word typed. Therefore, the correctly spelled version of the word is more likely to appear when at least the first letter is correct. For this step, students check the beginning sound of the word and ask themselves what other letter could make that beginning sound. For example, if the student is attempting to spell the word *elephant* but has begun the word with *ul*, teach him or her to ask what other letter(s) make that beginning sound.

H   *Hunt for the correct consonants.* If trying a new beginning sound does not help, have students change other consonants in the word. Ashton (1999, p. 26) tells of a boy who was writing about Egypt and wanted to use the word *pyramid*. His first spelling attempt was *perament*, but the only suggested word was *per*. The boy continued to sound out the word and changed the spelling to *peramed*. This still did not produce the word he was looking for, so he changed his spelling again to *peramid*. *Pyramid* then appeared in the suggested word list, and the student recognized it as being the correct spelling.

E   *Examine the vowels.* Selecting the correct vowel when spelling is especially difficult, because vowels make so many sounds. Spell-checkers can help students figure out which sound to use for a particular vowel or vowel combination. For example, a student spelled the place where she ate lunch as *cafitirea*. After substituting other possible vowels in the word, she came close enough to the actual spelling to elicit the word *cafeteria* on the suggested list.

C   *Changes in word lists give hints.* Sometimes students can use words in the suggested word list to find the correct spelling. For example, a student trying to spell the word *favorite* first tried *fovoriute*. When this spelling did not produce the correct alternative, she changed her original spelling to *foariute*, then *fovaritue*, then *favaritue*. After the last try, the word *favor* was given as a suggested spelling. Using that word, she typed *favoritue*, which brought *favorite* to the list—the correct spelling, which she recognized.

K   *Keep repeating steps 1 through 4.* The most important aspect of using this strategy effectively is to give it repeated chances, trying as many different letter combinations as you can. However, at some point students may want to use another source, such as a dictionary, personalized word list (a continually updated list of words students have looked up before), classmate, teacher, or parent.

Strategies for Problem Solving in Math

Increasingly, teachers are focusing on problem solving as a major component of the math curriculum. This concentration is consistent with the math standards developed by the National Council of Teachers of Mathematics (2000), which also stress the importance of teaching problem solving. However, research indicates that if students with special needs are to become good problem solvers, they must be taught how to problem-solve directly. A common (but by no means the only) way to introduce problem solving to students in a classroom context is through story or word problems. An effective technique for teaching word problems for students with special needs is presented in the Professional Edge on page 388.

DRAW ● *DRAW* is a strategy for teaching students with special needs to solve multiplication facts that are not yet committed to memory (Harris, Miller, & Mercer, 1995). The DRAW strategy has the following steps:

D   *Discover* the sign. (The student looks at the sign to figure out what operation to perform.)

R   *Read* the problem. (The student says the problem aloud or to himself or herself.)

A   *Answer* or draw, and check. (The student thinks of the answer or draws lines to figure out the answer. The student checks his or her drawing and counting.)

W   *Write* the answer. (The student writes the answer in the answer space.)

RESEARCH
NOTE

DeLaPaz (1999) reviewed the research on dictation and speech-recognition systems and concluded that these systems can allow students with disabilities to circumvent handwriting, spelling, and punctuation problems, freeing them to focus on higher level concerns, such as planning and generating content. DeLaPaz warns, though, that students need to be taught carefully how to use this technology and that students with disabilities still need to be taught skills for critical planning and content generation that many of them lack.

CONNECTIONS

The NCTM standards also stress the use of manipulatives, covered in Chapter 5, and performance-based tests, examined in Chapter 11.

FASTDRAW ● You can help students make the transition from pictures to abstract numbers in multiplication by teaching them the *FASTDRAW* strategy. In addition to the preceding DRAW strategy, the FAST part of the strategy has the following steps (Harris et al., 1995, p. 6):

F	*Find* what you're solving for. (Students look for the question in the problem.)
A	*Ask* yourself, "What are the parts of the problem?" (Students identify the number of groups and the number of objects in each group.)
S	*Set up* the numbers. (Students write the two numbers in the problem in a vertical format.)
T	*Tie down* the sign. (Students add the multiplication sign to the problem.)

STAR ● The *STAR* strategy has been used successfully to teach older students with disabilities to solve math problems, including algebra (Gagnon & Maccini, 2001, p. 10). It consists of the following steps:

S	*Search* the word problem, reading the problem carefully and writing down knowns or facts.
T	*Translate* the word problem into an equation in picture form by choosing a variable, identifying the operation, and representing the problem through manipulatives or picture form.
A	*Answer* the problem.
R	*Review* the solution by rereading the problem and checking the reasonableness of the answer.

Examples of how STAR can be used to solve division problems with integers are shown in Figure 10.10.

LAMPS ● The *LAMPS* strategy (Reetz & Rasmussen, 1988) can be used as an aid to help remember the steps in regrouping or carrying in addition:

L	*Line up* the numbers according to their decimal points.
A	*Add* the right column of numbers and ask . . .
M	"*More* than 9?" If so, continue to the next step.
P	*Put* the 1s below the column.
S	*Send* the 10s to the top of the next column.

SLOBS ● To help with borrowing in subtraction, teach students to follow the steps in the *SLOBS* strategy (Reetz & Rasmussen, 1988):

S	*Smaller:* Follow steps.
L	*Larger:* Leap to subtract.
O	Cross *off* the number in the next column.
B	*Borrow* by taking one 10 and adding to the next column.
S	*Subtract.*

For the problem

$$\begin{array}{r} 72 \\ -\,46 \\ \hline \end{array}$$

students look at the top number on the right to see whether it is smaller or larger than the bottom right number. If it is smaller, the students follow the rest of the steps. They cross off the number in the next column to the left to borrow one unit from that column (reducing that number by one) and add it to the other column. In the problem shown, they borrow 10 from the left column, then subtract. If the number is larger, students proceed directly to the subtract step. They repeat the steps if more digits are to be subtracted.

RESEARCH NOTE

Tournaki (2003) compared the effectiveness of two kinds of instruction to teach students two-digit addition facts (2 + 3 = 5): strategy instruction and drill and practice. Strategy instruction consisted of teaching the students to start with the larger number and then count upward using the smaller number. For drill and practice, students memorized the answers to the facts. The results showed that the students with learning disabilities improved their performance only when they used the strategy. General education students performed equally well with both kinds of instruction, but on a transfer task requiring the addition of three digits (for example, 2 + 4 + 4 = 10), the strategy groups performed better.

FIGURE 10.10 Using the STAR Strategy to Solve Division Problems with Integers

Sample problem: Suppose the temperature changed by an average of –2°F per hour. The total temperature change was –16°F. How many hours did it take for the temperature to change?

Phase of Instruction   ⭐ **Star Strategy**

1. Concrete Application

Students use blocks to represent the problem. General guidelines: inverse operation of multiplication.

Algebra tiles: ▨ = 1 unit

Prompts students to:

Search problem (read carefully, ask questions, write down facts); translate the problem using blocks; answer the problem using the tiles; and review the solution (reread the problem, check reasonableness and calculations).

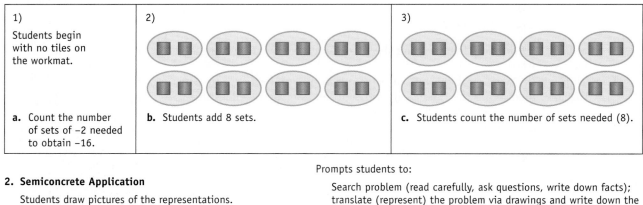

1)

Students begin with no tiles on the workmat.

a. Count the number of sets of –2 needed to obtain –16.

b. Students add 8 sets.

c. Students count the number of sets needed (8).

2. Semiconcrete Application

Students draw pictures of the representations.

Prompts students to:

Search problem (read carefully, ask questions, write down facts); translate (represent) the problem via drawings and write down the equation; answer the problem using drawings and write the answer; and review the solution (reread the problem, check reasonableness and calculations).

3. Abstract Application

Students first write numerical representations:

–16÷2 = x, apply the rule for dividing integers to obtain x = +8, and reread and check the answer.

Prompts students to:

Search problem (read carefully, ask questions, write down facts); translate the problem into an equation; answer the problem (apply the rule for division integers); and review the solution (reread the problem, check reasonableness and calculations).

SOURCE: "Preparing Students with Disabilities for Algebra," by J. C. Gagnon and P. Maccini, 2001, *Teaching Exceptional Children, 34*(1), 8–15. Reprinted with permission.

FOIL ● The *FOIL* strategy (Crawford, 1980) helps prevent algebra students from missing one of the four products needed to calculate multiplication of a binomial by another binomial. Four steps are followed:

F   Multiply *first* terms.
O   Multiply *outermost* terms.
I   Multiply *innermost* terms.
L   Multiply *last* terms.

For example, the FOIL strategy can be applied to the following problem:

$(x + 4)(x + 3)$
A   B C   D

In the **F** step, the student multiplies the first two factors in each binomial, $x \times x = x^2$, or, using the letters, *AC*. Next, in the **O** step, the student multiplies the first factor in the first binomial and the second factor in the second binomial, $x \times 3 = 3x$, or *AD*. Then, in the **I** step, the student multiplies the second factor of the first binomial and the first factor of the second binomial, $4 \times x = 4x$, or *BC*. Finally, in the **L** step, the second factors of both binomials are multiplied: $4 \times 3 = 12$, or *BD*. This strategy applies only to the special case of multiplying two binomials.

Strategies for Managing Time and Resources

A lack of organization is a common characteristic of students with disabilities (Lerner, 2006; Silver, 1998). For example, Ron, one of the students introduced at the beginning of the chapter, has trouble organizing.

Organizing study materials involves having the appropriate school supplies, making sure these supplies are brought to class when they are needed, and having an organized notebook to ensure easy access to information. First, you can make sure that your students obtain the appropriate school supplies by requiring that they tell their parents what materials they need, because you will not be able to call each of their parents individually each day to remind them what to bring. In many cases, teachers tell their students what to bring and assume that the students will do the rest on their own. However, this method may not be structured enough for some students who, like Ron, are likely to forget what you said; are not organized enough to write it down; or even when they write it down, cannot find it when they get home.

Second, you can encourage students to write the information down rather than try to remember it. Having the information on the board or overhead helps ensure that their lists are accurate. You may also want to duplicate the list and distribute it to your students.

Finally, encourage your students to ask themselves the following, or similar, questions, which can help them remember school supplies as well as assignments throughout the school year:

- What is due tomorrow in school?
- What do I need to do to get it done tonight?
- What materials or other things do I need to get the job done?
- Whom can I ask for help in doing this?

These questions can at first be posted on the board to help students remember them and to prompt their use. You can help motivate students to bring needed materials by providing positive recognition for those who do bring their supplies to school. For example, Mr. Gutierrez gave school pencils to students who had all their supplies in school. Ms. Habner put the names of her students on a "responsible students" list, from which she chose people for classroom jobs. You may need to make adaptations for students with special needs. For example, students with physical disabilities may need a classmate or parent to bring their supplies into school. Students who live in poverty might be unable to afford supplies other than materials the school or teacher provides.

Besides having to organize their materials, students also need to organize their time, particularly as they get older and the demands made on their time increase. More schools are now teaching their students to use schedule books to help them arrange their time (Bryan, Burstein, & Bryan, 2001; Jenson, Sheridan, Olympia, & Andrews, 1994; Patton, 1994). You can teach your students to use a weekly schedule book in the following three ways:

1. *Teach students to differentiate between short- and long-term assignments.* Short-term assignments are those that can be completed in 1 or 2 days and that take one or two steps to complete, such as reading a chapter in the history textbook and answering the questions at the end of the chapter. Long-term assignments take more than 2 days to complete and take more than two steps to get done. Writing a five-page report on a current event is an example of a long-term assignment. The difference between short- and long-term assignments can be taught readily to the whole class at once by giving them the definitions and teaching them to apply these definitions to a series of examples.

Strategies for managing time and organizing materials help provide the structured routines that many students need to succeed in school. What are the three steps in teaching students how to use weekly assignment calendars?

DIMENSIONS OF DIVERSITY

Teachers with a multicultural perspective take into account that students from different cultural backgrounds might have different routines as well as different resources for addressing, structuring, and completing projects.

WWW RESOURCES

TimeLiner is a software program designed to help students organize information for research projects using a timeline. For more information, go to http://www.teachtsp.com.

PROFESSIONAL EDGE

The Key Word Strategy for Solving Math Story Problems: Is There a Better Way?

The key word strategy is an example of an ineffective strategy that many students with special needs use or are taught to use in solving math story problems (Kelly & Carnine, 1996). In this approach, students associate key words such as *more, in all, gave away,* and *left over* with certain mathematical operations. The key word strategy is attractive to teachers and students because sometimes it works. For example, the word *more* is commonly associated with subtraction, as in the following problem:

> Jose has 15 cents. Carmen has 10 cents. How much *more* money does Jose have?

Unfortunately, many times the word *more* appears in word problems that call for addition, as in the following problem:

> Charmaine had 15 cents. Her mother gave her 10 *more* cents. How many cents does she have now?

Kelly and Carnine (1996) suggest teaching students with special needs a more effective strategy for solving math word problems using problem maps and math fact families. Their strategy for teaching single-operation addition and subtraction problems follows:

> For any addition/subtraction situation, there are two "small" numbers and a "big" number (the sum).
>
> An addition/subtraction number family is mapped this way:
>
> $$\xrightarrow{\quad 7 \qquad 9 \quad} 16$$

The preceding family represents the following addition/subtraction facts:

$$7 + 9 = 16 \qquad 16 - 9 = 7$$
$$9 + 7 = 16 \qquad 16 - 7 = 9$$

A missing *big* number implies addition:

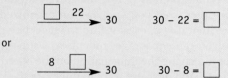

$$8 + 22 = \square$$

A missing *small* number implies subtraction:

$$\xrightarrow{\quad \square \qquad 22 \quad} 30 \qquad 30 - 22 = \square$$

or

$$\xrightarrow{\quad 8 \qquad \square \quad} 30 \qquad 30 - 8 = \square$$

These maps can then be applied to a variety of addition and subtraction word problems. Kelly and Carnine (1996, p. 6) give the following example involving comparison problems:

> In comparison problems, the difference between two values being compared may be information given in a problem (for example, Marco sold 57 fewer subscriptions than Lui) or the unknown in a problem (for example, How much heavier was Mary?). Because of the words *sold fewer* in the following problem, many students with LD will subtract.
>
> Marco sold 57 fewer magazine subscriptions than Lui. Marco sold 112 subscriptions. How many subscriptions did Lui sell?

2. *Teach students to task analyze long-term tasks.* Start by modeling the task-analysis process of breaking long-term tasks into component subtasks, estimating the amount of time it will take to perform each subtask, and then scheduling time to complete the subtasks in a schedule book. You can model this by distributing an already completed **task analysis** and timeline for your first several long-term assignments. Then, have students begin to develop their own task analyses, first under your guidance and, eventually, independently.

3. *Show students how to record information in their schedule books.* Have students enter fixed activities or activities you do every week, occasional activities or activities that are different from week to week, and due dates for assignments. Students can also prioritize assignments; schedule time to work on assignments; and monitor assignment completion, including rescheduling or adding time to work on assignments.

Many schools have had success using schoolwide programs with a single system of keeping track of assignments in schedule books that students use in every class. The consistency and repetition that are naturally a part of such a system seem to benefit students, including those with disabilities, many of whom are more successful when teach-

Students can use number families to avoid this confusion. The first step is to represent the problem using a number family; students must determine whether each of the two numbers given in the problem is a small number or the big number. The students are shown a simple way to do this:

They find the sentence that tells about the comparison and read it without the difference number. For example, students are taught to read the first sentence without the 57: "Marco sold fewer subscriptions than Lui." Because Marco sold fewer subscriptions, Marco is represented by a small number. By default, Lui is the big number. The students write M for Marco and L for Lui:

The word problem also gives a number for the difference between Marco and Lui. That number always has to be a small number. Marco sold 57 fewer, so 57 is the other small number:

Next the students read the rest of the problem. The problem asks about Lui and gives a number for Marco, so the students draw a box around L and replace the M with 112:

112
57   M̶ ──────▶ L

Because the problem gives both small numbers, the students write an addition problem.

```
   57
+112
```

The answer tells how many magazine subscriptions Lui sold.

See Stein, Silbert, and Carnine (1997) for similar word problem strategies as applied to multiplication, division, and multistep story problems.

FROM THE RESEARCH

Darch, Carnine, and Gersten (1984) compared the effectiveness of the problem-solving strategy described here with a traditional basal approach that emphasized key words. The subjects were 73 fourth-grade students who were unable to successfully solve math story problems. The results showed that the group receiving the problem-solving strategy outperformed the basal group on a posttest that included 26 math story problems. A student satisfaction survey given at the end of the study showed that more students in the strategy group liked the way the unit was taught and said they were using the strategy to solve problems in their general education classrooms.

SOURCE: Excerpt from "The 'Key Word' Strategy for Solving Math Story Problems," by B. Kelly and D. Carnine, 1996, reprinted by permission of Council for Learning Disabilities.

ers stick to a daily routine. Students with special needs may require additional adaptations, however, such as the classroom teacher's checking and/or initialing their schedule books before they leave class. This step is particularly important when students are first learning to use a schedule book.

How Can Students Learn to Use Strategies Independently?

Some students may have trouble using a learning strategy independently, even after they have learned how to do it. Their problem could be that they do not know when to use a strategy, or how to keep track of how well they are using it and how to change their behavior if necessary.

CONNECTIONS

The "self" strategies covered in this chapter apply to academic learning. These same strategies are sometimes referred to as *cognitive behavior management,* which is discussed in Chapter 12.

> Some students may have trouble using a learning strategy independently, even after they have learned how to do it.

Four strategies that can help students perform tasks more independently are self-instruction, self-monitoring, self-questioning, and self-reinforcement. Like all learning strategies, these "self" strategies may need to be carefully taught using the teaching practices described in this chapter.

Self-Instruction

In **self-instruction,** learners are taught to use language to guide their performance. In essence, students are taught to talk themselves through a task. The idea is, if they can talk themselves through a task, they will not need help from anyone else. Self-instruction has been successfully used to teach students with disabilities strategies for math, test taking, reading comprehension, and writing (Uberti, Mastropieri, & Scruggs, 2004). The first step needed to teach students self-instruction techniques is to explain that self-instruction involves giving oneself instructions on how to do a task. For example, self-instruction can be used to help get seatwork done or to remember to use a strategy for a multiple-choice test. Next, ask students to identify a situation that requires the use of a specific skill, such as getting their seatwork done in reading or taking a 10-minute science quiz on Friday. Demonstrate how to write down the steps needed to perform that task. For example, to get seatwork done, the student first decides how much effort to put into this task. Next, he or she decides what is supposed to be done. Finally, the student decides what the first step in completing the task should be, what the next step should be, and so forth, until the seatwork is done. When students are finished, they praise themselves for a job well done. Ask students to rehearse the steps through self-talk or peer review, going over all the steps involved in completing a seatwork task from beginning to end.

After you have demonstrated how to apply self-instruction, have the students practice in a role-play situation, and give them feedback. In the seatwork task, for example, you could put a sample reading task on the classroom screen using PowerPoint or the overhead projector and demonstrate the steps by thinking out loud. The students could then practice in pairs and give each other feedback, with you monitoring and also giving feedback. Students could keep a chart or index card listing the task steps, which they should be encouraged to glance at periodically while performing the task.

Self-Monitoring

In **self-monitoring,** students watch and check themselves to make sure they have performed targeted behaviors. Self-monitoring has been shown to be effective in making positive changes in the academic and social behavior of students with disabilities (Daly & Ranalli, 2003). Self-monitoring is a critical aspect of independent learning because being independent often requires students to check their performance to see whether it is effective and make a change when a particular strategy is not working (Hallahan et al., 2005; Reid, 1996). Self-monitoring can also be a strong motivator for students by providing them concrete evidence of their progress. In teaching self-monitoring to your students, first explain to them that self-monitoring is a way that they can check their own behavior to make sure they are doing the right thing. Ask the students to identify a behavior or a learning strategy that they need to do in class. For example, students may select a behavior such as being on task or on time for classes, or they may choose a strategy such as the COPS proofreading strategy described earlier in the chapter.

The next step is to select a practical and expedient way for students to measure the behavior. One possibility is to have them count on a card or pocket counter the number of times the behavior occurs. For example, Yashika recorded on an index card the number of her talk-outs in reading class. Another possibility is to use a checklist to keep track of behaviors as they occur.

RESEARCH NOTE

McDougall and Brady (1998) taught fourth-grade students with and without disabilities self-monitoring skills in math. Students monitored their attention by asking themselves at regular points during the lecture whether they were paying attention. Students were reminded to check their attention by a prerecorded audio cue. Students monitored their math performance by graphing their scores on daily math fact quizzes. Results showed that students' time on task and math fact performance were greatly improved and that the improvements in math fact performance generalized to a math word problem task.

Teach students to use the measurement system through demonstration, practice, and feedback, and continue to encourage and reinforce the use of self-monitoring in your class. Self-monitoring can be applied to any learning strategy.

Self-Questioning

Self-questioning is a form of self-instruction in which students guide their performance by asking themselves questions. The idea behind self-questioning is that if students can guide their own behavior by asking themselves questions, then they will not always need a teacher or other adult present to perform. In teaching students self-questioning, have them first identify the behaviors, duties, or tasks that are required in class. For example, students can identify steps needed to proofread a written paper, such as checking the correct use of capital letters, punctuation, spelling, and appearance. Have students write these tasks in question form, asking, for example, "Have I capitalized all words correctly? Have I used the right punctuation marks in the right places? Have I spelled all the words correctly? Is my paper neat?"

As in self-monitoring, the next step is to select a practical and expedient way for students to measure the behavior, such as recording behaviors as they occur using a checklist. Students might practice self-questioning in pairs for feedback. Other practical measures include keeping task questions on index cards and putting them in a convenient place. For example, students might put the proofreading questions on an index card and tape it to the inside cover of their notebooks.

Montague, Warger, and Morgan (2000) taught students with disabilities to solve math word problems using a strategy that included elements of self-instruction, self-monitoring, and self-questioning. The strategy is shown in Figure 10.11. Also, applications of self-strategies to student behavior in study hall are shown in the Special Emphasis On . . . feature on page 376.

Self-Reinforcement

As the term implies, **self-reinforcement** occurs when students reward themselves for behaving appropriately or achieving success in learning tasks. An important part of being an independent learner is recognizing when one has done a good job. As discussed before, students with special needs often attribute their success to factors other than their own efforts, such as luck. Teaching self-reinforcement is an effective way of helping students replace negative attributions with more positive ones. Students need to be coached to use self-reinforcement by praising or rewarding themselves explicitly for doing something right or being successful academically. The first step is to have students set a particular goal for themselves, such as getting all their homework in on time, getting all their seatwork done, being on time for class, taking accurate and complete notes during a lecture, studying for a test, or reading a book. Allow students to decide when and how they can reinforce themselves. For example, younger students might give themselves a star or sticker each time they beat their highest score on a math facts timed test. Older students might give themselves a point for each day they complete their homework. If they have four points by the end of the week, they could go out to lunch with a friend. Self-praise is also a good way of rewarding progress toward personal goals.

Practice setting goals, acknowledging when a goal has been attained, and using different kinds of self-reinforcement. You will want to model for students how self-reinforcement works by demonstrating how you set goals for yourself, knowing when

> " If students can guide their own behavior by asking themselves questions, then they will not always need a teacher or other adult present to perform. "

CONNECTIONS

Reinforcement and related behavioral principles are explored further in Chapter 12.

RESEARCH N O T E

Wehmeyer and colleagues (2003) studied the use of self-monitoring and self-reinforcement with students with developmental and intellectual disabilities. They found that the use of these strategies improved the students' class participation and decreased their rate of problem behaviors.

FIGURE 10.11 Using Self-Instruction, Self-Monitoring, and Self-Questioning in a Math-Problem-Solving Strategy

Math-Problem Solving

Read (for understanding)
Say:	Read the problem. If I don't understand, read it again.
Ask:	Have I read and understood the problem?
Check:	For understanding as I solve the problem.

Paraphrase (in your own words)
Say:	Underline the important information.
	Put the problem in my own words.
Ask:	Have I underlined the important information?
	What is the question? What am I looking for?
Check:	That the information goes with the question.

Visualize (a picture or a diagram)
Say:	Make a drawing or a diagram.
Ask:	Does the picture fit the problem?
Check:	The picture against the problem information.

Hypothesize (a plan to solve the problem)
Say:	Decide how many steps and operations are needed.
	Write the operations symbols $(+, -, \times, \div)$
Ask:	If I do . . . , what will I get?
	If I do . . . , then what do I need to do next?
	How many steps are needed?
Check:	That the plan makes sense.

Estimate (predict the answer)
Say:	Round the numbers, do the problem in my head, and write the estimate.
Ask:	Did I round up and down?
	Did I write the estimate?
Check:	That I use the important information.

Compute (do the arithmetic)
Say:	Do the operations in the right order.
Ask:	How does my answer compare with my estimate?
	Does my answer make sense?
	Are the decimals or money signs in the right places?
Check:	That all the operations are done in the right order.

Check (make sure everything is right)
Say:	Check the computation.
Ask:	Have I checked every step?
	Have I checked the computation?
	Is my answer right?
Check:	That everything is right. If not, go back.
	Then ask for help if I need it.

SOURCE: From "Solve It! Strategy Instruction to Improve Mathematical Problem Solving, "by M. Montague, C. Warger, and T. H. Morgan, 2000, *Learning Disabilities: Research and Practice, 15,* pp. 110–116.

ANALYZE AND REFLECT

Research suggests that once students learn a self-strategy, they have trouble recognizing when it is appropriate to use it. Why do you think this is so? What can you do as a teacher to ensure that your students apply the strategies they are learning?

you have reached a goal, and reinforcing yourself for reaching the goal. For example, Mr. Hughes explained to his class that he needs to work on getting his lawn cut on time. Each time he cuts the lawn and has to rake up only one bag of grass clippings or less (his measure of lawn length is the longer the lawn, the more grass to rake), he treats himself to a milk shake at the local ice cream shop. Mr. Hughes also praises himself for saving time and effort each time he cuts the lawn and has little grass to rake up.

As students get older, they are expected to learn at home, at school, and in the workplace with less support. They are also expected to set goals for themselves and take independent actions to meet those goals. For some students, being an independent learner does not come naturally. These students need to be taught directly independent learning and self-advocacy skills. They also need to be taught how to apply those skills in school and in real-world settings with minimal support.

SUMMARY

General education teachers can help all their students, including students with special needs, become independent learners. One way teachers can build student independence is to encourage student self-awareness and self-advocacy.

Another way to help your students become more independent is to design and teach effective learning strategies in class. Effective learning strategies can be developed by identifying skills that are problematic for most of your students, specifying relevant student outcomes, and listing a set of specific steps students need to follow to reach the identified outcomes; these steps should be brief, should number no more than eight, and should be encased in a mnemonic device. They should also cue students to perform thinking, doing, and self-

evaluating behaviors. Methods of teaching learning strategies to students include assessing current strategy use, clarifying expectations, demonstrating strategy use, encouraging students to memorize strategy steps, providing guided and independent practice, and administering posttests.

Many strategies that can help students become independent learners are available in the areas of reading and reading comprehension, listening and note taking, writing, problem solving in math, and managing time and resources. Four strategies that can help students learn to use these strategies independently are self-instruction, self-monitoring, self-questioning, and self-reinforcement.

Applications in **Teaching Practice**

Designing Strategies for Independence

Latasha is a student who has a moderate hearing loss. Although her hearing aid helps, she still has to depend a lot on speech reading to communicate. She also speaks slowly and has trouble saying high-frequency sounds such as *sh* and *t*. Latasha has a poor self-image and is reluctant to interact with her peers and teachers. Design a self-advocacy program for Latasha.

QUESTIONS

1. What skills would you teach Latasha to use for self-advocacy?
2. How would you get Latasha to use these skills in your class and in other in-school and out-of-school situations?

Cal is a student with organizational problems; he is chronically late for class and rarely finishes his homework. Design an organizational strategy for Cal using the guidelines for developing strategies covered in this chapter.

QUESTIONS

1. How would you teach the organizational strategy you have designed using the guidelines covered in this chapter for effectively teaching a learning strategy?
2. How would you teach Cal to apply the strategy independently using self-instruction? Self-monitoring? Self-questioning? Self-reinforcement?

Evaluate the design of any one of the learning strategies in the chapter using the guidelines in the Professional Edge on page 360.

QUESTIONS

1. Is there anything you would change about the strategy? How would you teach the strategy using the six steps described in this chapter?
2. How would you help students apply the strategy independently using the four "self" strategies discussed in this chapter?

WORKING THE **STANDARDS**

INTASC PRINCIPLES REFLECTED IN THIS CHAPTER:

Principle #2 states that all teachers are knowledgeable about multiple theories of learning and research-based teaching practices that support learning (Principle 2.04).

Principle #4 states that all teachers

- Work collaboratively and individually to provide effective instruction that results in positive learning outcomes for students with disabilities (Principle 4.01).

- Use strategies that promote the independence, self-control, and self-advocacy of students with disabilities (Principle 4.07).

Principle #5 states that all teachers help students with disabilities recognize the relationship between their own efforts and positive outcomes (Principle 5.04).

CEC CONTENT STANDARDS REFLECTED IN THIS CHAPTER:

CEC Content Standard #4 states that special educators emphasize the development, maintenance, and generalization of knowledge and skills across environments, settings, and the life span.

CEC Content Standard #5 states that special educators shape environments to encourage the independence, self-motivation, self-direction, personal empowerment, and self-advocacy of individuals with exceptional learning needs.

CEC Content Standard #7 states that special educators individualize instructional plans to emphasize explicit modeling and efficient guided practice for acquisition and fluency through maintenance and generalization.

BACK TO THE CASES

The standards and principles just listed relate to the cases described at the beginning of this chapter: Gerald, Traci, and Ron. The questions and activities that follow demonstrate how these standards and principles, along with other concepts that you have learned about in this chapter, connect to the everyday activities of all teachers.

Gerald

Gerald's problems in written expression include organization and mechanical errors. Mr. McCrae has determined that organization is most important, because the mechanical errors can be corrected after Gerald has produced an organized written product. Mr. McCrae has selected the POWER strategy to teach Gerald to use. You are interested in applying this strategy in your teaching, so you work with Mr. McCrae to develop a script for teaching it (see the Case in Practice on page 372 for a sample script). In the planning portion of POWER, you may want to consider an editing strategy such as COPS and a graphic organizer from Chapter 9. After you have written your script, compare scripts with a peer partner from your class. (See INTASC Principles 4.01, 4.07, and 5.04; and CEC Standards 5 and 7.)

Traci

After helping Traci with a strategy for solving word problems, Ms. McCord reflects on Traci's skills in other academic areas. Traci often cannot answer comprehension questions regarding details in short passages of text or storybooks. Ms. McCord wonders whether Traci's difficulties in reading might be similar to the ones she experienced in word problems. (See INTASC Principle 4.01; and CEC Standard #5.) What do you think? Explain your thinking. Suppose that she does discover that the difficulties are similar. What

WORKING THE STANDARDS *(continued)*

strategies might she teach Traci that would be useful in reading in the content areas? Provide a reason for each of your choices.

Ron

After several weeks of his teachers working with Ron, he is now coming to class with all of the books and materials he needs. In fact, he completed his homework assignments every day this week. He is proud that he has been remembering to check his schedule book and the checklist in his locker. However, he still experiences difficulty getting to school and work on time, and on four days last week he missed the bus that takes him home. After deciding that the next step is to teach Ron to use self-instruction and self-monitoring strategies for the home and work situations, you develop a strategy that will help him manage time when he is away from the school environment. (See INTASC Principles 4.07 and 5.04, and CEC Standards 4 and 5.) After you have written the strategy, share it with two or three peers for feedback.

 Visit the companion website (http://www.ablongman.com/friend4e) for a complete correlation of this chapter to the INTASC Principles and CEC Standards.

Further **Readings**

Daly, P. M., & Ranalli, P. (2003). Using countoons to teach self-monitoring skills. *Teaching Exceptional Children, 35*(5), 30–35.

Countoons are cartoon versions of self-recording devices that students can use to keep track of their behaviors, even when they cannot read. This practical article describes how to use countoons to teach your students with special needs important self-management skills.

Lancaster, P. E., Schumaker, J. B., & Deshler, D. D. (2002). The development and validation of an interactive hypermedia program for teaching a self-advocacy strategy to students with disabilities. *Learning Disability Quarterly, 25*(4), 277–302.

This article reports research showing the effectiveness of using an interactive hypermedia program (IHP) to teach high school students with high-incidence disabilities to advocate for themselves.

Minskoff, E., & Allsopp, D. (2003). *Academic success strategies for adolescents with learning disabilities and ADHD.* Baltimore: Brookes.

This text is full of practical learning strategies for organization, test taking, studying, note taking, reading, writing, mathematics, and advanced thinking.

Strichart, S. S., & Mangrum, C. T. (2001). *Teaching study skills and strategies to students with learning disabilities, attention deficit disorders, or special needs* (3rd ed.). Boston: Allyn and Bacon.

This book includes 169 reproducible activities that provide opportunities for learning and student practice in study skills and learning strategies, selected because of their relevance for students with special needs.

Evaluating Student Learning

MR. STEVENS IS a high school earth science teacher. One of his students, Stan, has a learning disability that causes him to have trouble reading textbooks. Stan also has difficulty figuring out multiple-choice test questions, the kind that Mr. Stevens uses on his exams and quizzes. Stan says that he knows the material but just needs more time to take the tests, because he reads slowly. During the past marking period, Mr. Stevens gave four multiple-choice tests, each worth 20 percent of the final grade. Scores on homework assignments counted for the remaining 20 percent. Stan earned a grade of B on his homework, but he had two D's, one C, and one F on the tests. Mr. Stevens assigned him a grade of D for the marking period. Mr. Stevens felt this was a fair grade because most of Stan's peers scored much higher on the tests. Mr. Stevens is also committed to keeping his reputation as a teacher with high standards. When Stan received his grade for the marking period, he asked his parents why he should work so hard when he couldn't seem to get good grades anyway. Stan's parents felt that he had improved during the last marking period but that his grade did not show it. They were afraid that Stan would stop trying and eventually drop out of school. ● *What are the issues here? What could Mr. Stevens do to help Stan?*

JENNIFER IS IN Ms. Robinson's third-grade class. She has a hearing impairment and has some trouble in reading but is doing well in Ms. Robinson's classroom reading program. Ms. Robinson is pleased with her progress and has given her an A in reading for the first two grading periods. Recently, Jennifer's parents became very upset when they learned that Jennifer was reading only at the first-grade level according to district standardized tests. They wondered how she could have done so poorly on the standardized tests when she has been bringing home A's on her report card. ● *What would you tell Jennifer's parents if she were in your class? How could you change your grading procedures to prevent communication problems like this from occurring?*

LUCILLE IS A STUDENT with a mild intellectual disability who is in Ms. Henry's fourth-grade math class. On the basis of her current performance in math, which is at the first-grade level, Lucille's IEP team set math goals for her in the areas of basic addition and subtraction. The rest of the class is working on more difficult material based on the fourth-grade math curriculum. Lucille's IEP objective for the second marking period was to compute in writing, within 20 minutes, 20 two-digit–by–two-digit addition problems with regrouping with 80 percent accuracy. She received direct instruction on these problems from Mr. Brook, her special education teacher, who was co-teaching with Ms. Henry. As a result, she met her goal for the marking period. ● *How should Ms. Henry grade Lucille? School policy mandates letter grades.*

One of a teacher's major jobs is to evaluate the educational progress of students. The information collected during evaluation activities can indicate whether teaching has been effective and can help teachers alter instruction as needed. Classroom evaluations also are helpful in giving students (and their parents) an idea of how well they are performing in school, and they can be used by principals and school boards to evaluate the effectiveness of their schools.

Even though evaluation activities are very important, the ways in which students are evaluated most frequently—testing and grading—can be problematic for students with disabilities, their teachers, and their parents. For example, Stan and his earth science teacher have a problem because Stan's test scores more often reflect his learning disability than his knowledge of earth science. Jennifer's teacher has a problem in communicating the meaning of Jennifer's grades to her parents. She graded Jennifer based on Jennifer's progress and effort in class. Jennifer's parents, however, thought she was being graded in comparison with her peers and therefore expected their daughter to be performing at or above grade level, not below. Lucille's teacher needs to give Lucille a grade even though she has different curricular goals than the other students in the class. Further complicating these problems are the current climate of accountability and the expectation that most students with disabilities will meet standards. This expectation makes it imperative that accommodations in evaluation be done without compromising students' ability to meet standards on high-stakes tests. As you work with students with disabilities or special needs, you will experience these and other challenges in evaluating their learning. In this chapter, you learn a number of ways to solve these problems.

> " The ways in which students are evaluated most frequently—testing and grading—can be problematic for students with disabilities, their teachers, and their parents. "

How Can Classroom Tests Be Adapted for Students with Special Needs?

CONNECTIONS

How do the topics in this chapter fit into the INCLUDE framework presented in Chapter 5?

Although testing has always been a major part of U.S. education, the recent emphasis on school reform, with its dominant theme of raising educational standards, promises to make educators rely even more on tests in the future (Albrecht & Joles, 2003; Nolet & McLaughlin, 2000; Roebber, 2002). This increasing emphasis on test performance accompanies concerns about the test performance of students with disabilities. As described in the vignette about Stan at the beginning of this chapter, testing can be a very trying experience for many of these students and their families.

Most important in testing students with disabilities is ensuring that test results reflect their knowledge and skills, not their disabilities. Fortunately, classroom tests can be adapted in ways that help you test students with disabilities fairly and with a reasonable

TABLE 11.1 Examples of Testing Adaptations

Before the Test	During the Test	After the Test
Study guide	Alternative forms of questions	Changed letter or number grades
Practice test	Alternative ways of administering tests	Changed grading criteria
Individual tutoring		Alternatives to letter and number grades
Teaching test-taking skills		
Modified test construction		

amount of accuracy. As shown in Table 11.1, adaptations can be made in three contexts: before the test, during test administration, and after the test during grading procedures. Many of these adaptations can also benefit students who do not have disabilities.

Adaptations before the Test

You can do a number of things before a test to help students with disabilities. First, you can prepare a *study guide* that tells students what to study for the test. A study guide can help students avoid wasting valuable time studying everything indiscriminately and instead help them concentrate on the most important information. Study guides can also assist students with memory problems by focusing their efforts on only the most critical material. Second, you can give a *practice test*. This test can clarify your test expectations and also benefits the class by familiarizing students with the test format. Practice tests are also helpful to students who have trouble following directions and to those who are anxious about taking tests and often fail to cope immediately with an unfamiliar test format. Finally, many students with disabilities also benefit from *tutoring* before tests. Tutoring can be offered before or after school and may be carried out by peer tutors or paraprofessionals. Tutors can provide guidelines for what to study or help directly with particularly difficult content.

FYI

Planning your tests and test adaptations at the beginning of instruction helps you clarify what is essential to teach and achieve a good match between your tests and instruction.

CONNECTIONS

Strategies for developing and using study guides appear in Chapter 9.

Students can help each other prepare effectively for tests using directly taught study strategies. What strategies might these students be using to prepare for an upcoming test?

Another option is to teach students *test-taking skills.* This option can help students take your classroom tests and state high-stakes tests as well. Students may need a number of test-taking skills, including ones for studying for tests, for taking objective tests, and for writing essay tests.

When studying for tests, students often are required to remember a lot of material. This can be difficult for students with learning or intellectual disabilities, who may have memory problems. Students can benefit from strategies that help them remember important content for tests. For example, Georgia uses a memorization technique called **chunking.** After she studies a chapter in her text, she tries to recall five to seven key ideas. These key thoughts help trigger her recall of more significant details. After reading a chapter about the life of Harriet Tubman, for example, she remembers information in chunks—Tubman's early years, her experiences with the underground railroad, and so on. These general ideas help her remember details such as when Harriet Tubman was born and how many slaves she helped to free.

Mnemonic devices also can help students remember information for tests. **Mnemonics** impose an order on information to be remembered using words, poems, rhymes, jingles, or images to aid memory. For example, Mr. Charles wants his class to remember the six methods of scientific investigation. He tells the students to think of the word *chrome* (Cermak, 1976). The following six steps make up the *CHROME* strategy:

C   Categorization
H   Hypothesis
R   Reasoning
O   Observation
M   Measurement
E   Experimentation

FIGURE 11.1   Keyword for de Soto

SOURCE: From "Mnemonic Strategies: Instructional Techniques Worth Remembering," by R. N. Carney, M. E. Levin, and J. R. Levin, 1993, *Teaching Exceptional Children, 25*(4), p. 27. Reprinted by permission of the Council for Exceptional Children.

Another mnemonic device that can help students remember definitions and factual information is called the keyword method (Mastropieri, 1988; Uberti, Scruggs, & Mastropieri, 2003). The **keyword method** uses visual imagery to make material more meaningful to students and hence easier to remember. First, a vocabulary word or fact is changed into a word that sounds similar and is easy to picture. For example, to help remember that the explorer Hernando de Soto came from Spain, students might be shown the picture in Figure 11.1, a bull (to symbolize Spain) at a counter sipping a soda (the keyword for *de Soto*) (Carney, Levin, & Levin, 1993). When students are asked to name an explorer who came from Spain, they are told to think of the keyword for de Soto. Next, they are told to think back to the picture the keyword was in and remember what was happening in the picture. Finally, they are told to answer the question. (So who was an explorer from Spain?)

Many students do poorly on tests because they do not study for tests systematically. Teach students to organize their materials so that they avoid wasting time searching for such items as notes for a particular class or the answers to textbook exercises. Making random checks of students' notebooks is one way to find out how well organized they are. For example, Ms. Barber stresses note taking in her fifth-grade social studies class. Every Friday afternoon, she checks the notebooks of five students in her class. She gives students bonus points if they have notes for each day and if their notes are legible and include key information. Also, teach students strategies for how to process material when they are studying. For example,

Ms. Treacher shows her third graders a verbal **rehearsal strategy** for learning spelling words. She says the word, spells it out loud three times, covers the word, writes the word, and then compares her spelling to the correct spelling. Mr. Jacobs shows his class how they can summarize text and class material on the topic of nonviolent resistance using a concept map such as the one shown in Figure 11.2. Another effective rehearsal strategy is for students to ask themselves questions about the most important information to be learned.

Many students, including those with special needs, do not test well because they lack strategies for actually taking the tests. For example, Sal rarely finishes tests in science because he spends too much time on questions that he finds difficult. Laura has trouble with true–false questions because she does not pay attention to key words such as *always, never, usually,* and *sometimes.* Lewis's answers to essay questions contain much irrelevant information and do not focus on what the questions are asking. The Professional Edge on page 402 offers suggestions for teaching students strategies for taking objective tests. These strategies work for taking high-stakes tests too.

Students also need strategies for taking essay tests. Performing well on essay tests requires that students know the content covered; can follow directions, including identifying and understanding key words; and can organize their ideas. All these areas can be problematic for students with disabilities. The following six suggestions might prove helpful to students taking essay tests:

1. Read over the entire exam before you begin. If you have memorized information related to specific questions, jot it down before you write your answer.

2. Look for key instructional words in the questions to help you determine how to structure your answer and determine what information to include. For example,

FIGURE 11.2 Concept Map: Summarizing Material

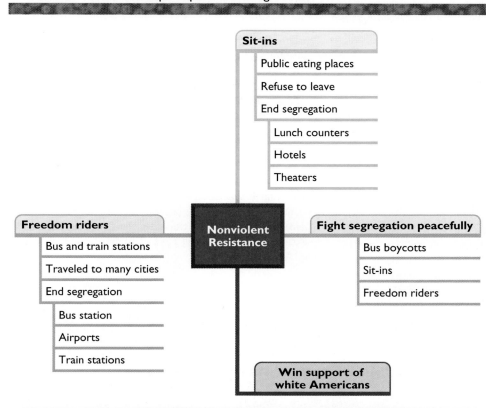

W W W RESOURCES

The Study Guides and Strategies website (http://www.studygs.net) provides study guides as well as strategies for preparing for and taking tests. The site provides study-skills resources including several links to study-skills guides and interactive tutorials.

FYI

The keyword method recommended here for learning vocabulary is not to be confused with the keyword strategy for teaching students to solve math story problems referred to in the Professional Edge on pages 388–389 in Chapter 10.

RESEARCH NOTE

Terrill, Scruggs, and Mastropieri (2004) compared two methods of learning SAT vocabulary words by high school students with learning disabilities. They compared the keyword mnemonic strategy with a more traditional approach consisting of oral drill and written practice. They found that the students learned 92 percent of the targeted words using key words, but only 42 percent using the more traditional approach.

RESEARCH NOTE

Robinson and colleagues (1998) found that students who studied for tests using graphic organizers and who delayed reviewing their notes by 2 days performed better on tests than students using traditional outlines who studied their notes immediately after recording them.

PROFESSIONAL EDGE

Teaching Strategies for Taking Objective Tests

Many students flounder when taking tests because they do not approach tests in any organized way. You can help your students approach their objective tests more systematically by teaching them the strategies described here. The following six rules for responding to multiple-choice and true–false items are based on a comprehensive review of the research literature.

1. Respond to the test maker's intention. Answers to test questions should take into account the way material is treated in class. For example, Rob had this item on his social studies test:

> During the occupation of Boston, the British received their most severe losses at Bunker Hill.
> True
> False

Even though Rob had learned at a recent trip to the museum that the Battle of Bunker Hill was actually fought on Breed's Hill, his teacher had not brought up this point in class. Therefore, Rob responded by circling *true*.

2. Anticipate the answer. Before students attempt to answer the question, they should fully understand its meaning. Therefore, they should try to figure out the answer before they read the possible answers. For example, Armand was answering the following multiple-choice item:

> What does an astronomer study?
> a. plants
> b. music
> c. history
> d. stars

After he read the question, Armand thought about the word *astronomy* and what his teacher had talked about in class, such as the fact that astronomers use telescopes and that they look at stars and planets. He then read all the possible choices and circled *d, stars,* as the correct answer.

3. Consider all alternatives. Many students with special needs, such as students with learning disabilities, tend to answer too quickly, choosing the first available choice. Students should be encouraged to read all the choices before responding. Students can monitor their behavior by putting a check mark next to each choice after they have read it.

4. Use logical reasoning strategies to eliminate unlikely answers. Even if students do not know the answer to a question, they can improve their chances of getting it right by using what knowledge they do have to eliminate unlikely choices. For example, Dolores read the following item:

> In which country would it be impossible to use a sled in the winter?
> a. Guatemala
> b. Canada
> c. Zimbabwe
> d. Norway

Dolores did not know the geographical locations of Guatemala or Zimbabwe, but she did know that Canada and Norway were countries where it snowed often. She then took a guess between *a* and *c,* and chose *a,* the correct answer. By eliminating two of the items, she improved her chance of getting the question right by 25 percent.

5. Use time wisely. As already mentioned, a frequent test-taking problem is failing to budget time. Some students spend so much time on some items that they have little time left for others. While taking tests, students should check the time periodically to make sure they have enough time left to answer the remaining questions. You can assist students by writing the time remaining on the chalkboard several times during the testing period. Students also can be taught to estimate the amount of time they should spend on each question. For example, if students are taking a 100-item test in a 50-minute period, they should figure on spending no more than one-half minute per question. After 25 minutes, they can then check to see that they have completed at least 50 items. Finally, teach students to spend more time on items on which they have at least partial knowledge and less time on questions for which they have no knowledge.

6. Guess, if all else fails. Most tests do not have a penalty for guessing. On standardized tests especially, tell your students that if they do not answer a question, they have no chance of getting it right, but if they guess, they have a 50 percent chance of getting true–false questions right and a 25 percent chance of getting most multiple-choice questions right.

SOURCE: From "Are Learning Disabled Students 'Test-Wise'? A Review of Recent Research," by T. Scruggs and M. Mastropieri, 1988, *Learning Disabilities Focus, 3*(2), pp. 87–97.

you would include different information and use a different structure if you were asked to list the reasons for the American Revolution versus discuss them.

3. Organize your answers. A rule of thumb in answering essay questions is that you should spend at least one-fourth of your time planning what you are going to write.

4. Leave time to proofread your answers for clarity, legibility, spelling, and grammar.

5. When writing an answer, leave margins and do not write on the back of the paper. If your writing is large, write on every other line. Leaving some extra space makes the exam easier for the teacher to grade.

6. If you do not have time to write an answer, write your outline for the answer. Often, teachers give you a substantial amount of credit if they can see that you knew the information and simply did not have time to write the answer.

All students benefit from tests that are written clearly and assess pertinent knowledge or skills. Thus, everything that you have learned about writing good tests in your teacher-education program applies here. Still, test items can be well written but constructed in a way that results in problems for students with special needs. When this situation occurs, *modified test construction* is necessary. For example, Carmen has difficulty reading tests that are visually cluttered. She might benefit from triple spacing between test items and extra space between lines. Juan scores poorly on tests because he is unable to read many of the words used in the items; the items contain complex sentences with many words that are above his reading level and that his teacher did not use while teaching. Consider, for example, the following item taken from a social studies test:

> Circle the answer that best fits in the blank.
>
> A country in southern Europe, that is on the Mediterranean Sea, _____ has a capital city by the name of Athens.
>
> a. Greece
> b. Italy
> c. Poland
> d. Croatia

This item could be written much more simply and still test the same information as follows:

> Circle the answer that best fits in the blank.
>
> The southern European country whose capital is Athens is _____.
> a. Greece
> b. Italy
> c. Poland
> d. Croatia

A student with a reading problem may answer the first question incorrectly because of its awkward wording, not because he or she does not know the answer.

In essay-test construction, several adaptations might benefit students with problems in reading and written expression. For students with reading problems, highlight key words such as *analyze, compare/contrast, describe,* and *list.* You can also give students a form to complete to help them organize their responses. For example, this question was used on a science test:

> Compare and contrast plant and animal cells by describing three ways they are alike and three ways they are different.

> " All students benefit from tests that are written clearly and assess pertinent knowledge or skills. "

WWW RESOURCES

Search for tips on writing tests on the Classroom website (http://www. gradebook.org).

FYI

Another consideration in constructing tests is to arrange test items in chronological order to match the sequence of instruction.

The following **response format** might aid students in writing an answer:

Ways that plant and animal cells are alike
 1.
 2.
 3.

Ways that plant and animal cells are different
 1.
 2.
 3.

Other practical ways of constructing objective tests that allow you to measure student knowledge more accurately are shown in the Professional Edge on page 405. Strategies for constructing test items for English-language learners are shown in the Special Emphasis On . . . feature on page 406.

Adaptations during the Test

If changes in test construction are intended for the whole class, they can be incorporated into the original master before duplicating. However, when changes are intended only for one or two students, you can make them as students take the test. For example, Ms. Minter's co-teacher, Ms. James, was working with Barry on his test-taking skills. She was helping Barry consider each choice in multiple-choice questions carefully, rather than always picking the first choice. Ms. James began by using an alternative form of question for Barry. When using **alternative forms of questions,** the teacher changes the type of question asked (for example, multiple-choice instead of essay questions) or the construction of the question (for example, adding a word bank for fill-in-the-blank questions). Ms. James used an alternative form of question by decreasing the number of choices on Barry's test items from four to two to make it easier to apply the strategy, on Barry's tests, she blackened two of the four choices. Eventually, however, she added choices to be sure that Barry was able to take the same tests as his classmates. Ms. James used this type of test adaptation for another student with reading comprehension difficulties by underlining key words in each question. She gradually eliminated the underlining as the student showed he was able to identify the key words in questions without them.

CONNECTIONS

Issues of fairness and other topics concerning student relations are taken up in more detail in Chapter 13.

The way that tests are given to students with disabilities can also affect the accuracy of the results. Students who, like Stan from the chapter-opening cases, have reading comprehension problems might do better on tests if given more time to finish them or if allowed to take them orally. Students with written expression problems might benefit from a dictionary or a handheld spell-checker or by dictating their answers. Seating students with attention problems near you when they take a test might help them stay on task longer. These are all examples of **alternative ways of administering tests.** The alternative ways of giving tests that are shown in the Professional Edge on page 407 are grouped according to students' areas of difficulty.

As the Professional Edge indicates, students might also benefit from the use of an **alternative test site,** such as a resource room. For example, testing in the resource room might help students with attention problems (by allowing them to take their tests in a setting with fewer distractions) and students with written language problems (by permitting them to answer test questions orally). Changing the test site also protects students who are taking the test in a different way from being embarrassed. However, before sending a student out of class to take a test, you should first try other options.

DIMENSIONS OF DIVERSITY

Some African American, Brazilian American, Filipino American, and Hawaiian students are accustomed to working at a slower pace. These students may benefit from extended time when taking tests (Grossman, 1995).

For example, Ms. Edwards allows her students to choose whether to have a test read to them. Those who do not want the test read aloud can work independently while she reads the test to the rest of the students. She also gives the students to whom she reads the test more help with directions and the meaning of key vocabulary or difficult questions. Mr. Collins and Ms. Klein are co-teaching. Mr. Collins supervises students

PROFESSIONAL EDGE

Modifications in Test Construction for Students with Disabilities

All of your students will do better on clearly written tests that ask questions pertaining specifically to the material covered in class and in the textbook. But your students with disabilities especially require well-phrased and visually accessible tests if they are to succeed at test taking. The following modifications, although beneficial to all your students, can be crucial for your students with special needs.

1. Tests should be typewritten and photocopied.

2. Make tests visually uncluttered by leaving sufficient space between items (3 spaces) and between lines within items (1½ spaces). Do not crowd pages with items; keep wide margins.

3. Use symmetrical spacing. For multiple-choice tests, align possible responses vertically rather than horizontally, and type the question and possible responses on the same page. Permit students to circle the letter of the correct answer rather than write it in front of the item.

4. Provide additional spacing between different types of test questions. Provide separate directions and a sample item for each type of test question.

5. For completion, short-answer, and essay questions, leave sufficient space to write the answer. Students do not do as well when they must continue their answers on the back of the page or on the next page.

6. Leave space for students to answer on the test rather than using machine scoring or answer sheets. Some students have difficulty transferring answers from one page to another.

7. For students who have difficulty with multiple-choice questions, reduce the number of possible answers. Students might choose the correct answer from three, for example, rather than from four or five possible responses.

8. For students who read slowly and students who have organizational problems, avoid the following constructions in matching items: long matching lists—keep lists to five or six items and group by concepts; lengthy items; and drawing lines to the correct answer, which can be confusing for students with visual–motor problems (Wood, Miederhoff, & Ulschmid, 1989). Lists with 10 to 15 entries in the first column can be simplified by preselecting three to four choices from the second column for each item in the first column. Record these choices beside the item in the first column and have the student select the correct answer from the smaller pool. Consider the following example:

Match the definition on the left with the word on the right by writing the letter for the word in the blank next to the definition.

1. in a sudden way ____	a. brightness
2. not able ____	b. visitor
3. to make bright ____	c. suddenly
4. one who visits ____	d. happiness
5. in a happy way ____	e. rearrange
6. to tell again ____	f. brighten
7. to arrange beforehand ____	g. retell
8. state of being happy ____	h. prearrange
9. to arrange again ____	i. unable
10. state of being bright ____	j. happily

These questions will be less confusing for your students with disabilities if you modify them using the guidelines just described:

1. in a sudden way ____	a. brightness
	b. visitor
	c. suddenly
	d. retell
2. to make bright ____	a. happily
	b. unable
	c. brighten

9. Change fill-in-the-blank items to a multiple-choice format, providing three or four choices for the blank. Students select the correct answer only from the choices given. This modification changes the task from one of recall (memory) to one of recognition.

10. For essay questions, review the questions, key words, and tasks with students individually and help students develop answer outlines. Permit dictated or taped responses when appropriate.

11. Consider color-coding, underlining, enlarging, or highlighting key words and mathematical symbols.

SOURCE: Adapted from *Accommodations for Secondary Learning Disabled/Mainstreamed Students on Teacher-Made Tests,* by J. N. Williams, 1986, unpublished manuscript, Wheaton, MD: Wheaton High School.

Special EMPHASIS On …

Testing English-Language Learners in Math-Problem Solving

Recent research reveals two important findings about English-language learners and tests. The bad news is that the test scores of English-language learners in all subject areas, including math, are much lower than those of native English speakers (Abedi, Hofstetter, & Lord, 2004). The poorer test performance of ELLs in math occurs not because they know less about the math content but because they have a hard time understanding the language used in test items. In effect, the language demands of the test render the test invalid and unfair. However, the good news is that test scores for English-language learners can be improved by decreasing the complexity of the language (Abedi et al., 2004). In fact, simplifying the language of test items is more helpful to ELLs than translating the items into their native language (American Institutes for Research, 1999). Here are some examples of how you can simplify language when writing math problems for your students (Abedi et al., 2004):

- Change unfamiliar or infrequently used nonmath vocabulary. For example, the phrase "a certain business concern" is unfamiliar and difficult to understand; the substituted phrase "Acme Company" is more common and easier to understand.
- Change the voice of verbs from passive to active. For example, change "if a marble is taken from the bag" to "if you take a marble from the bag."
- Shorten the length of noun phrases. For example, the phrase "the pattern of the puppy's weight gain" can be changed to "the pattern above."
- Replace conditional clauses with separate sentences or change the order of the conditional and main clauses. For example, consider the sentence "If two batteries in the sample were found to be dead, then the workers had to inspect all of the batteries." This sentence can

be simplified by changing it into two sentences: "The workers found two dead batteries in the sample. Because of this, they had to inspect all of the batteries." You could also change the order of the clauses: "The workers had to inspect all of the batteries when they found that two batteries in the sample were dead."

- Remove or change relative clauses. For example, change "What is the total number of newspapers that Lee delivers in 5 days?" to "How many papers does Lee deliver in 5 days?"
- Change complex question phrases to simple question words. For example, change "which is the best approximation of the number . . . ?" to "approximately how many . . . ?"
- Make abstract wordings more concrete. For example, change "2,675 radios sold" to "2,675 radios that Mr. Jones sold."

Examine the following word problem from the Massachusetts Comprehensive Assessment System (at http://www.doe.mass.edu/mcas/2003/release):

Students in Mr. Jacob's English class were giving speeches. Each student's speech was 7–10 minutes long. Which of the following is the best estimate for the total number of student speeches that could be given in a 2-hour class?

a. 4 speeches
b. 8 speeches
c. 13 speeches
d. 19 speeches

What problems do you think an English-language learner might have with this question? How would you change the item to make it more understandable?

---

taking the test silently while Ms. Klein reads the test to another group of students. If you do find it necessary to send a student out to take a test, be sure to coordinate your plans in advance with the special education teacher to avoid scheduling problems.

Adaptations after the Test

You may also need to use alternative test-grading procedures for students. For example, because Matt has a learning disability, he has trouble remembering large amounts of information for tests. This memory problem has affected Matt's test scores, which so far include two F's and one D. Matt's teacher, in collaboration with the special

WWW
RESOURCES

You can create online quizzes on the Quiz Center page of the DiscoverySchool website, at http://school.discovery.com/quizcenter/quizcenter.html.

PROFESSIONAL EDGE

Adaptations in Administering Classroom Tests

Even a well-constructed test can fail to measure the knowledge of students with disabilities accurately if it is inappropriately administered. The adaptations you make in administering tests to students who have special needs depends on the students' area of difficulty. Use the following chart to help you decide which modifications to try with students with disabilities included in your class.

Adaptation	Area of Difficulty				
	Reading	Writing	Listening	Speaking	Organizing: Paying Attention
Oral explanation of directions	X				X
Repetition of directions; student repetition of directions	X		X		X
Oral, taped, or dictated test; oral clarification of written answers by student	X	X			X
Written test; written directions			X	X	
Extra time	X	X		X	
Time checks during the test					X
Segmented test with separate directions for each section	X		X		X
Peer or other assistance:					
to read directions	X				
to check comprehension	X				
to check spelling		X			
Technological aids:					
placemarks or markers	X				X
word processor		X			
tape recorder	X	X		X	
Visual aids and cues; verbal and visual prompts for word retrieval			X	X	
Use of outlines, diagrams, charts, tables, and webs to organize or answer	X	X			X
Permitted use of noncursive writing		X			
Use of previously prepared notes or rehearsed answers				X	
Alternative sites:					
to minimize noise/distraction			X		X
for alternative testing	X	X			
Seating proximity to teacher			X		X
Teacher paraphrase or summary of student answers in complete thoughts				X	
Checklist for materials needed and preparation					X
Allowing answering directly on test rather than answer sheet		X			

SOURCE: Adapted from *Accommodations for Secondary Learning Disabled/Mainstreamed Students on Teacher-Made Tests,* by J. N. Williams, 1986, unpublished manuscript, Wheaton, MD: Wheaton High School.

education teacher and Matt's parents, identifies the most important information in the chapter and tells Matt to study that for the test. When Matt takes the test, he answers only the 15 questions that his teacher marked with an asterisk, which test the key information he was told to study. The rest of the class answers 30 questions—the 15 that Matt answers plus 15 more covering other material in the chapter. Out of his 15 questions, Matt gets 13 correct. In deciding how to grade Matt, the teacher considers three grading options: changing letter or number grades, changing the grading criteria, and using alternatives to traditional letters and numbers.

Changing letter or number grades by adding written comments or symbols or by giving multiple grades can help clarify what a grade means. In Matt's case, his teacher could give him a B on the test but with an asterisk meaning that his test covered a different amount of content than that of the rest of the class. Giving multiple grades can be helpful on tests that require written responses. For example, on an English test, Jacinto is required to write an essay on the character Boo Radley in the novel *To Kill a Mockingbird.* When his teacher grades his essay, she assigns him one grade based on the quality of his analysis of the character and another grade for writing mechanics. Having *grading rubrics* or guidelines to follow when evaluating student performance helps students understand the criteria by which their work is judged. A strategy designed to help students use grading rubrics to improve their performance is described in the Professional Edge below.

CONNECTIONS

The IEP team (see Chapter 2) provides guidelines for making testing and grading adaptations for individual students.

PROFESSIONAL EDGE

Using Grading Rubrics with Students

The use of grading guidelines called *rubrics* benefits students in many ways. Rubrics help students:

- better understand their teachers' expectations
- monitor their progress
- judge the quality of their work (Jackson & Larkin, 2002)

Steps for creating and using rubrics, developed by Goodrich (1996/97, as cited in Jackson & Larkin, 2002), are described in Table 11.2.

Jackson and Larkin (2002) created the *RUBRIC strategy* to help students use rubrics to assess the quality of their work. The steps of the RUBRIC strategy are shown in Figure 11.3.

Jackson and Larkin (2002) make suggestions for teaching students to carry out the RUBRIC strategy. Teach students what rubrics are by showing them some examples. Internet resources for finding rubrics include RubiStar, at http://rubistar.4teachers.org; the rubrics page of Teach-nology, at http://www.bestteachersites.com/web_tools/rubrics; Kathy Schrock's guide to assessment and rubric information, at http://school.discovery.com/schrockguide/assess.html# rubrics; and Project Based Learning, at http://pblchecklist. 4teachers.org/.

Once students know what rubrics are, they are ready to learn to apply the RUBRIC strategy. In general, apply the same steps described in Chapter 10 for teaching learning strategies, including clarifying expectations, demonstrating strategy use, and providing guided and independent practice. When students are performing the **R** step, encourage them to familiarize themselves with the criteria to be applied to each component of the task. Getting the "big picture" prevents students from diving into the task without thinking, a common problem for students with disabilities. In the **U** step students work individually and apply the rubric to one of their products, giving it a score. During this step students are encouraged to ask questions about the clarity of the scoring guidelines as well as to verbalize their thought processes to someone else, receiving feedback as needed. For the **B** step, students select a buddy to help them rate the product again. The student and the buddy then review the material together in the **R** step, forming a team to compare scores and ideas. They then present their scores to the larger group of students, explaining how they used the rubric and why they agreed or disagreed. Next, the group gives the team feedback on how they applied the rubric, which the team then use to identify and award a new set of scores together in the **I** step. In the final step, **C**, students check their work.

A second option is to change the **grading criteria,** or the standard on which the grade is based. For example, Matt's teacher could give him a grade of B by basing his grade on a different standard: 15 questions rather than 30. You may instead want to base a student's grade on the percentage correct of the items tried instead of on the total number of questions. This alteration may help students who work accurately but slowly. Giving partial credit is another possible option. For example, when Ms. Jordan grades student answers to math story problems, she gives students points for underlining key words in the question and setting up the equation correctly. These extra points can motivate students who are improving but do not increase their test scores significantly. Students can also be allowed to retake tests. They can then be graded using their score on the retake or averaging their original score with their retake score.

A third grading option you may want to try is using **alternatives to letter and number grades,** such as pass/fail grades and checklists of skill competencies. For example, Matt could be given a grade of P (pass), because he mastered 7 of 10 key concepts in the chapter, or he could be rated on a **competency checklist** showing which key concepts in the chapter he learned. While all of these test-grading adaptations allow students to be more successful, care must be taken to assure that students are prepared to meet state standards. For example, Matt's teacher needs to be certain that the content for which Matt is held responsible reflects state standards and that reducing the content for which he is held responsible will not interfere with his attainment of state standards.

WWW
RESOURCES

EdWeb: Exploring Technology and School Reform (http://edwebproject.org) is a website that includes education-focused discussion groups in which you can discuss testing, grading, and many other educational issues.

TABLE 11.2 Steps for Creating and Using Rubrics

Step 1. Look at models	Show students good and poor examples of student work for a particular task. Help students identify characteristics of each.
Step 2. List criteria	Use the characteristics to generate a discussion about what is considered quality work.
Step 3. Articulate gradations of quality	Describe best and worst levels of quality on a continuum, and then fill in the middle levels of quality.
Step 4. Practice on models	Have students use the rubric created in Steps 2 and 3 to assess the examples of good and poor work in Step 1.
Step 5. Use self-assessment and peer assessment	Stop students occasionally as they are working on a task to have them assess the work.
Step 6. Revise	Encourage students to revise their work based on the feedback they receive in Step 5.
Step 7. Use teacher assessment	Assess students' work by using the same rubric they have used to assess their own and their peers' work.

SOURCE: Adapted from Goodrich, as cited in "Rubric: Teaching Students to Use Grading Rubrics," by C. W. Jackson and M. J. Larkin, 2002, *Teaching Exceptional Children, 35*(1), 40–45.

FIGURE 11.3 The Rubric Strategy

R	**Read** the rubric and the material to be graded
U	**Use** the rubric to give an initial score
B	**Bring** a buddy to help you rate again
R	**Review** the material together
I	**Identify** and award the scores together
C	**Check** the scores again

SOURCE: "RUBRIC: Teaching Students to Use Grading Rubrics," by C. W. Jackson and M. J. Larkin, 2002, *Teaching Exceptional Children, 35*(1), pp. 40–45.

How Can Report-Card Grades Be Adapted for Students with Special Needs?

Report-card grading is perhaps the most prevalent and controversial evaluation option used in schools. The practice of grading by letters and percentages began in the early 20th century, a time of great faith in the ability of educational measures to assess students' current levels of learning accurately and also predict future levels of learning. High grades were seen as a sign of accomplishment, intended to spur students on to greater achievements. Those who received low grades were either placed in basic-level or special classes or were encouraged to join the workforce (Cohen, 1983).

Times certainly have changed. Laws have been passed guaranteeing that our evaluations do not discriminate on the basis of disability, race, or ethnicity. These laws also guarantee an appropriate education for all students, not just those who can succeed with minimal intervention. Furthermore, our ability to compete in the emerging global economy depends on better educational outcomes for all our citizens, not just a privileged few. These changes have led to new demands that go beyond the relatively simple matter of identifying "good" and "poor" students. For example, how can evaluations be modified to ensure that they do not discriminate against students with disabilities? How can they be used to motivate students to stay in school, to communicate educational competence and progress to parents and students, and to guide our teaching as we strive to meet the needs of an increasingly diverse student body?

Although answers to these and other questions about grading are beginning to emerge, in large part we continue to use a grading system that was intended to fulfill a purpose much more narrow in scope. The use of traditional letter and number grades has caused problems for teachers, who must communicate with many audiences, including parents, students, administrators, and legislators. These audiences often are looking for information that is not readily communicated using a single number or letter (Munk & Bursuck, 2001a, 2003). For example, students may be interested in how much progress they have made, whereas their parents want to know how their children compare to their classmates as well as to children nationwide. Principals, on the other hand, may need to provide college admissions offices with indicators of student potential to do college work. Teachers also are increasingly left with many conflicting concerns about grading, including upholding the school's standards, maintaining integrity with other teachers, being honest with students, justifying grades with other students, motivating students for better future performance, communicating accurately to the students' next teachers, and avoiding the reputation of being an "easy" teacher (Munk & Bursuck, 2003).

DIMENSIONS OF DIVERSITY

What do grades mean in the United States? How are grades used and to what ends? How do values about grades in the national culture affect students with special needs? How do they affect students from other cultures?

DIMENSIONS OF DIVERSITY

In what ways might grading systems be unfair? Which student groups are affected the most? What provisions do school districts make for evaluating students who are culturally different or whose first language is not English?

Modifications of report-card grades for students with disabilities and other students with special needs must be carefully explained to prevent misunderstandings. What grading modifications might these people be discussing?

Increased inclusion in schools has put even more burdens on grading systems. As illustrated in the vignettes at the beginning of the chapter, grading can present serious challenges for students with disabilities and their teachers. Stan was not a good test taker, yet 80 percent of his report-card grade in earth science was based on his test performance. He was concerned that his grade did not accurately reflect his effort or progress in class. Jennifer's parents were surprised to find that their daughter had received A's in reading all year but was reading below grade level on a recent standardized achievement test. Lucille was working on math skills that were more basic than those the rest of the class covered, and her teacher was unsure how to grade her performance. Add to these problems the concern that grades need to relate to student performance on state high-stakes assessments used in conjunction with No Child Left Behind.

Despite these problems, a number of reasons support the continued use of grades. First, many parents want to see how their children compare to other students, and they demand grades. In addition, grades are efficient and can make decision making easier, particularly for schools making decisions about promotion to the next grade level and for colleges and universities making admissions decisions (Munk & Bursuck, 2001a). Despite their many limitations, therefore, grades are likely to be used by teachers and schools for many years to come. Teachers need to recognize the limitations of certain types of grades, however, and, when necessary, adapt grading systems to ensure they are fair to all students.

Changes to Letter and Number Grades

You can clarify the grades of all of your students by making changes to letter and number grades. Changes to letter and number grades clarify grades by supplementing them with other ways of evaluating and reporting student progress, such as written or verbal comments, logs of student activities, and portfolios. Written or verbal comments can be used to clarify areas such as student ability levels as compared with peers and the extent of student effort. For example, Roberto's teacher gave him an O (outstanding) in reading, because he increased the number of trade books he read but she also commented on his report card that the books he read were below grade level.

Comments about student ability levels can prevent misunderstandings, particularly when parents find their children are performing below standard on state tests. For instance, in the chapter-opening vignette, Jennifer's mother thought her daughter's high grade in reading meant that she was reading at grade level. An explanation on Jennifer's report card would have put her grade in context. Keep in mind, however, that students sometimes compare report cards with their classmates and might be embarrassed by comments that indicate they are working below grade level. To prevent this situation, you might use an alternative procedure, such as talking to parents or sending them a separate note of clarification. In addition, report-card comments should never state that the student is receiving special services; this would be a violation of student confidentiality.

Finally, the basis for arriving at number or letter grades on report cards is often not clear. For example, does the grade represent a student's performance in comparison with his or her classmates, or is it based on the student's progress toward meeting objectives on his or her IEP? Failure to clarify the bases for grades can lead to communication problems with parents, as shown in the Case in Practice and Working Together features on pages 412 and 413.

Because report-card grades are primarily summaries of student performance, they provide few specifics about student performance over a period of time. You can use **daily activity logs** of student activities and achievement to provide ongoing information for students and their parents. Daily observations

> Because report-card grades are primarily summaries of student performance, they provide few specifics about student performance over a period of time.

CASE IN PRACTICE

Explaining Grades

Jose is a student in Ms. Wittrup's fourth-grade class. When Ms. Diaz, Jose's grandmother, received Jose's most recent report card, she had some questions and made an appointment to see Ms. Wittrup and Ms. Talbot, Jose's special education teacher.

Ms. Wittrup: Ms. Diaz and Jose, I'm so glad you came in today. Ms. Diaz, I understand you have some questions about Jose's report card.

Ms. Diaz: Thank you for taking the time to see me. Yes, I do have some questions about Jose's report card. First of all, I noticed that Jose got a B in reading. This is an area where he's getting help in special education. Does this mean he doesn't need any more help?

Ms. Talbot: Jose's IEP objective for the first grading period was to read fluently and comprehend literature books that are at the second-grade reading level. His word-identification skills in that material are good, but he is still having some trouble with comprehension. Sometimes he has trouble summarizing what he has just read; other times he has a hard time answering questions that I ask him.

That is why he received a B rather than an A. I think Jose has a good chance of meeting this objective by the end of this marking period. Still, he is pretty far behind his fourth-grade classmates, so I think he needs to keep getting help from me.

Ms. Diaz: I think I understand better what his reading grade means, but I don't understand how Jose got only a C in math. He has always done better in math than in reading. Has he been fooling around in class and not paying attention?

Ms. Wittrup: No, Jose has been working hard in math. Jose doesn't have any special needs in math so he is in the regular program. As you can see from looking at my grade book, Jose scored an average of 75 percent on his math tests. His average for homework and in-class work was 80 percent. His overall average for the marking period was 78 percent, which is a C.

Ms. Diaz: Is there something I can do to help Jose with his math so that maybe he can get a B next time?

Ms. Wittrup: One thing that hurts Jose on his tests is that he is still

making careless mistakes on basic math facts, particularly the multiplication facts. If you could help him with these at home, I think Jose might be able to pull his grade up to a B.

Ms. Talbot: We're very proud of Jose for getting an A in social studies. Remember we had all agreed that because Jose had reading problems we would let him use a taped text and take his tests orally. Well, Ms. Wittrup told me that Jose had an average of 95 percent on the two tests, which is an A. Good for Jose!

REFLECTIONS

Ms. Diaz had a difficult time understanding what Jose's grades meant. What could Jose's teachers have done to prevent this confusion from occurring? Jose received a grade of A in social studies because he was allowed to use a taped textbook and to take the tests orally. How would you explain this adaptation to a concerned student who took the test without any of these supports and received only a C?

---

of students can be recorded in a notebook or journal, directly on a calendar, or on self-sticking notes.

Whatever type of daily activity log is used, entries should at least include the date, student's name, classroom activity, and a brief description of the observation. For example, Ms. Parks was concerned about the progress of one of her students, Carrie, in the area of word-identification skills. Each day during an hour-long literature class, Ms. Parks observed how Carrie approached the trade books she was reading. One day she recorded that Carrie spontaneously used the parts of a multisyllable word to figure out its pronunciation and meaning.

Information taken from the logs can be summarized periodically. These summaries can then be shared with parents as often as necessary to clarify student grades. For example, Leroy received a D in math for the marking period. His parents called his teacher to set up a conference to discuss the grade and find out how Leroy could improve. Leroy's teacher shared a log summary indicating that Leroy had not followed

WORKING TOGETHER

Communicating with Parents about Grades

Mr. and Mrs. Washington's son Delarnes is in Mr. Campbell's junior English class. Delarnes received an F in English for the last marking period, and Mr. and Mrs. Washington were upset. They knew Delarnes was working hard in the class because they were spending a lot of time helping him with his English homework at night. They scheduled a meeting with Mr. Campbell to learn more about the problem.

When Mr. and Mrs. Washington arrived at the meeting, Mr. Campbell was seated at a table with the chairwoman of the English department, Dr. West. The Washingtons hadn't expected someone else to be at the meeting and it made them fear that Delarnes had done something terrible. After asking the Washingtons to sit down, Mr. Campbell introduced Dr. West, who talked for what seemed like forever on the state English standards and on how the state "seemed to be setting the bar higher every year." The Washingtons weren't sure how the state standards affected Delarnes' English grade but were afraid to ask. Mr. Washington was beginning to grow impatient. He had expected the meeting to be about helping Delarnes. Next, Mr. Campbell said that while Delarnes seemed to be working hard, he had failed both of the grammar tests during the quarter, and his essay on Frederick Douglass had received a score of D–. Mrs. Washington had helped Delarnes outline that paper but hadn't heard anything about it since. Delarnes hadn't told his parents about the grammar tests. When Mr. Campbell asked the Washingtons if they would help Delarnes more at home, Mr. Washington exploded, saying that they *had* been helping him at home, asking why they hadn't been told about Delarnes's problem in English before, and demanding that the school do something to help him.

Why do you think Mr. and Mrs. Washington were upset? What do you think Mr. Campbell could have done to make the meeting more productive?

- Mr. Campbell needs help on how to conduct a more effective parent conference. Even though the Washingtons had initiated the meeting, Mr. Campbell could have set the stage for a more comfortable and productive meeting by telling Mr. and Mrs. Washington beforehand what Delarnes's problem was and explaining to them that the purpose of the meeting was to get their ideas about Delarnes's problem and to come up with a plan to help him improve. Parents are often unaware of the specifics of their child's performance in class. Telling the Washingtons in advance about Delarnes's performance in the class would have given them a chance to get over their shock and come to the meeting better able to help solve the problem. Also, by expressing his interest in the Washingtons' ideas, Mr. Campbell would have communicated to them that they had valuable information to offer—a critical precursor to a successful parent conference.

- Mr. Campbell should have also explained to Mr. and Mrs. Washington in advance that Dr. West was going to attend and why. For example, if Mr. Campbell had said that he was going to invite Dr. West because she could be of great help, her presence would not have been as intimidating. Also, Dr. West should have stuck to the topic at hand when addressing Mr. and Mrs. Washington, which was how to solve Delarnes's problem. Telling them about the difficulties of being an educator was irrelevant and served to further alienate them. Mr. Washington was correct in thinking that the focus of the meeting should be about his son.

- Finally, Mr. Campbell should have invited someone to the meeting with whom the Washingtons felt comfortable, such as a special education teacher, guidance counselor, or social worker. Lacking that, he could have encouraged them to bring someone along for help and/or moral support.

In the end, the meeting failed to accomplish what should have been its purpose, namely, helping Delarnes learn more and get a better grade in English class. Mr. Campbell and Dr. West should have involved Mr. and Mrs. Washington in developing an improvement plan for Delarnes that included both parental and school responsibilities, as well as a way to monitor the plan's effectiveness. Had a plan with a realistic chance for success been put in place, Mr. Washington would have left the meeting with a handshake, rather than shaking his head.

along while she was demonstrating solutions to math problems on the chalkboard. Leroy's teacher and parents set up a contract for Leroy that encouraged him to attend to such demonstrations.

Adding written comments to report-card grades also enables you to communicate clearly to your students exactly what they need to do to improve in your class. This is important for students with special needs, who are less likely than their peers to be able to evaluate their performance and set goals for themselves based on grades alone (Gersten, Vaughn, & Brengelman, 1996). One large school district in Canada uses computer-generated report-card templates and a large database of teacher comments to personalize teachers' report cards by providing more prescriptive information for

FIGURE 11.4 Personalized Grade Report

In English 10, the class has just completed a unit on poetry that focused on developing an appreciation and understanding of this literary form. Students continue to use exploratory writing to respond to literature read in class. Mander failed to complete two assignments worth 25% collectively this term. This has significantly affected his overall mark. Mander can improve his performance by ensuring assignments are completed and handed in on time.

Mark to Date	70%
Previous Mark	80%
Effort	
Excellent	
Satisfactory	✓
Needs Improvement	
Periods Absent since Beginning of Course	4
Periods Late since Beginning of Course	6

This term Mander has studied the basic skills of algebra. In particular, he has studied units on the operations of polynomials, equation solving, and factoring polynomials. Class time is used wisely. He organizes work effectively. He aims for excellence. Keep up the good work, Mander!

Mark to Date	90%
Previous Mark	75%
Effort	
Excellent	✓
Satisfactory	
Needs Improvement	
Periods Absent since Beginning of Course	None
Periods Late since Beginning of Course	None

SOURCE: Adapted from "Reporting Achievement at the Secondary Level: What and How," by J. Bailey and J. McTighe, in *ASCD Yearbook: 1996, Communicating Student Learning* (pp. 119–140), edited by T. Guskey, Alexandria, VA: Association for Supervision and Curriculum Development.

their students (Bailey & McTighe, 1996). An adaptation of a progress report from this district is shown in Figure 11.4.

In this sample progress report, note the presence of two key pieces of information: a clear statement of what the student needs to do to improve his English grade, and specification of the important content and/or requirements for each class. Note also that the student's level of effort is evaluated, an important aspect of student performance that we will address later.

Making Grading Adaptations for Students with Disabilities

Grading adaptations are procedures or strategies that can be used to individualize your grading system for students with disabilities (Munk, 2003). These adaptations are legal modifications for students with disabilities as long as they appear on students' IEPs. However, they should not be used with students without IEPs unless they are available to all students in the class (Salend & Duhaney, 2002). All school districts have some grading policy, and you should check to see whether grading adaptations are covered by your policy. See the Professional Edge below for a discussion of the legalities of making grading adaptations for students with disabilities.

Broadening the factors considered in grading is helpful for students with disabilities, who as a group tend to receive low or inaccurate grades (Munk & Bursuck, 2005).

PROFESSIONAL EDGE

The Legalities of Grading Students with Disabilities

Report-card grades are often used to make important educational decisions about students such as eligibility for honors awards, graduation, and admission to postsecondary education. Because of the importance of grades, teachers need to exert great care when modifying their grading systems for students with and without disabilities. While most schools have a written grading policy containing guidelines for giving and interpreting grades, many grading policies focus on the grading scale and the schedule for reporting grades to parents, not on judgments required for adapting grades for students with disabilities (Munk, 2003). The following are some answers to commonly asked questions about grading students with disabilities (LRP Publications, 1997; Salend & Duhaney, 2002). As legal guidelines for grading are constantly being refined, consult your school policies and your building administrator prior to modifying your grading system. It is also important to document all grading modifications for students with disabilities on their IEPs.

1. *Can I give modified grades to a student with a disability who is in my classroom and receiving accommodations?*

Using alternative grading systems for students with disabilities is appropriate, but only if you make the same ones available for your students without disabilities as well. However, you do not need to make grading modifications available to all students when grading adaptations are specified on a student's IEP.

2. *If a student who is enrolled in my class has alternative curricular objectives specified on her IEP, can I exclude her from my regular grading system and evaluate her based on her IEP objectives?*

In effect, students in an alternative, more basic curriculum are not considered to be officially enrolled in your class for credit. Therefore, you may grade them solely on the basis of their IEP objectives.

3. *Can I collaborate with an included student's special education teacher when assigning the student a grade?*

Collaborating with a student's special education teacher is entirely appropriate (and desirable) as long as collaboration is specified on the student's IEP.

4. *If I want to communicate to parents and employers that a student in my class has a modified curriculum, can my school indicate on the student's transcript that the class was a special education class?*

No. It is illegal to specify that a class is *special education*. However, there is general agreement that alternative terms can be used to communicate curricular differences, though as yet no terms have been officially sanctioned by the courts. Use a term such as *basic, level 1,* or *modified curriculum,* as long as those terms are also used in courses besides special education such as classes within gifted and talented programs. Asterisks or other symbols can also be used to communicate a modified curriculum as long as courses for all students are handled in a similar way.

5. *Can we include grades earned in special education classes or general education classes taken with support when we calculate districtwide GPAs and rank them for purposes of creating an honor role or assigning scholarships?*

Grades earned by students in special education classes or general education classes taken with support cannot be arbitrarily or categorically dismissed by the district. However, districts can implement systems of weighted grades that assign points to grades depending on the difficulty of the subject matter. Weighted systems are permissible as long as they are fair and simple to understand. Districts can also establish a list of "core courses" that must be completed to be eligible for honors, class rankings, or participation in certain activities. Again, the important consideration is that all students are similarly affected, not just students with disabilities.

While teachers are willing to make grading adaptations (Bursuck et al., 1996), these adaptations can be unsystematic (Polloway et al., 1996). Informal or unsystematic decisions, even when done in a student's best interest, can lead to confusion and threaten the meaningfulness of the resulting grade (Silva, Munk, & Bursuck, in press). The grading adaptations described here involve making judgments, but in a more systematic way. They are also done in conjunction with the student's IEP. Grading adaptations that are part of the IEP are legally binding and can prevent grading problems such as the ones described at the beginning of the chapter for Stan, Jennifer, and Lucille.

Researchers have identified five types of individualized grading adaptations that can be used to assign student report-card grades (Munk, 2003). They involve basing all or part of a student's grade on the following criteria:

1. progress on IEP objectives (Munk, 2003)
2. improvement over past performance (Bradley & Calvin, 1998; Munk, 2003)
3. performance on prioritized content and assignments (Guskey & Bailey, 2001; Munk, 2003)
4. use of balanced grading that takes into account student performance of learning strategies and effort (Guskey & Bailey, 2001; Munk, 2003)
5. use of modified grading weights and scales (Munk, 2003)

These five individualized grading adaptations are summarized in Table 11.3 and described in more detail in the following sections.

BASING ALL OR PART OF THE GRADE ON PROGRESS ON IEP OBJECTIVES

● For this type of grading adaptation, **progress on IEP objectives** is used as the basis for part or all of a student's report-card grade (Munk, 2003). Grading on the basis of progress on IEP objectives would have been an appropriate adaptation for Lucille, the student in the opening vignettes whose math curriculum was modified on her IEP. Whereas the rest of the class was working on decimals, she was working on two-digit–by–two-digit addition problems with regrouping. Because her IEP objective was to score 80 percent or better when given 20 of these problems, her fourth-grade teacher and special education teacher agreed to give her an A if she met her objective, a B if she scored between 70 and 80 percent, a C if she scored between 60 and 70 percent, and so forth. To ensure that Lucille's mother had an accurate picture of Lucille's standing in relation to her peers, Lucille's teacher included a written comment on Lucille's report card indicating that her grade was based on different curricular objectives as agreed to on her IEP.

Basing grades on progress on IEP objectives can also be helpful for students who are in special education but do not have modified curricular expectations. For example, Manny is a student with a learning disability who is included in Mr. Ottens's middle school science class. Manny receives pullout services in writing but is still expected to meet the same curriculum standards in science as his classmates. During Manny's IEP conference, it was decided that 10 percent of his science grade would be determined by progress on an IEP objective stating that "Manny will write complete sentences using correct spelling, grammar, and sentence structure." Mr. Ottens agreed to evaluate Manny's written work in science using these criteria. Mr. Ottens would give each assignment Manny submitted a writing grade along with a regular grade. Manny's average writing grade would count 10 percent toward his report-card grade in science.

Basing all or part of a student's daily work grade or report-card grade on his or her IEP objectives, as done for Lucille and Manny, is advantageous in that it

1. allows the team to consider how and when IEP objectives can be addressed in the general education classroom
2. informs students, parents, and teachers which objectives are important and how supports can be provided

ANALYZE
AND **REFLECT**

How might the strategy of grading on the basis of improvement help Stan and his parents, whom you read about at the beginning of the chapter? What other grading adaptations described in this chapter might be helpful?

TABLE 11.3 Types of Individualized Grading Adaptations

Adaptation	Example	Benefits	Cautions
Progress on IEP Objectives	A percentage of a student's report-card grade is determined by progress on IEP objectives.	• Addresses IEP objectives in the general education classroom • Informs IEP team which objectives are important and how supports can best be provided • Ensures that student's grade reflects progress on skills identified as most important • Eliminates redundancy of reporting grades separately from progress on IEP objectives • Improves communication between parents, students, and teachers about grading in the general education classroom	• To the maximum extent possible, IEP objectives should be based on the general education curriculum.
Improvement	A student's spelling grade is increased by a letter grade for making at least a 20% increase in test average as compared to the previous grading period.	• May motivate students to try harder • May motivate students to make better use of instructional supports	• Students should not become too dependent on special incentives to try their best on assignments. • Criteria on which a student's improvement is based should be gradually increased. • Students must possess skills needed to show improvement.
Prioritization of Educational Content and Assignments	A student is responsible for learning 6 essential ideas related to cell development. Grade is based on performance on short-answer tests and lab reports related to these ideas.	• Allows team to focus support on most important assignments • Reduces risk that performance on less important content will reduce grade • Informs teacher decisions regarding planning and grading for the entire class	• Prioritization should stress state learning standards.
Balanced Grading: Learning Strategies	Part of a student's grade is based on the effective use of an editing strategy.	• Considers learning strategies and effort in determining how work will be graded for whole class or individual student • Leads to greater collaboration and coordination between general education and special education teachers.	• Focusing too heavily on effort and learning processes can lead to low-quality products.
Balanced Grading: Effort	Part of a student's grade is based on attendance at after-school tutoring sessions.	• Gives students credit for learning and using supports that help them build new skills • Gives students credit for the extra steps or time they must spend improving learning skills or using assistive technology	• Effort is harder to assess than academic progress. • Students may work hard but master little content.
Modified Grading: Weights and Scales	The point value assigned to tests is reduced and the point value assigned to homework is increased.	• May motivate students to keep trying	• Grades can become inaccurate if weights are modified too much. • Weights should be shifted to alternative assessments that reflect student learning and not to requirements that are merely easier.

SOURCE: Adapted from Munk, D. D., & Bursuck, W. D. (2005). *Personalized grading plans for students with disabilities.* Manuscript in preparation.

3. ensures that a student's grade reflects progress on skills that have been identified as most important for him or her by the team

4. eliminates the redundancy of reporting grades separately from progress on IEP objectives

5. improves communication between parents, students, and teachers about grading in the general education classroom

BASING PART OF THE GRADE ON IMPROVEMENT OVER PAST PERFORMANCE ● A second type of grading adaptation involves basing part of a grade on improvement. **Improvement grades** can be incorporated into a traditional grading system by assigning extra points for improvement or by moving students up a grade on the scale if they improve, particularly if they are on the border between grades. Consider the case of Aretha, whose average on spelling tests in her general education classroom for the last marking period was 77 percent, an improvement of more than 40 percentage points over the preceding marking period. Although her true grade for spelling was technically a C, Aretha's IEP team had agreed in advance that her teacher would raise her grade a letter if she were to bring her test average up to at least 75 percent. The team also agreed, however, that once she reached 75 percent, she would be graded using the same scale as the rest of the class for the remaining grading periods. In another example, Roberto's IEP team agreed that if he read a minimum of five trade books during the grading period—an improvement of four over his performance for the previous grading period—he would receive a grade of O (outstanding) in reading, because he read so many more books than before. The team felt that even though other students in the class were reading more books at a more difficult level, Roberto deserved an O if he improved that much. His teacher did note on Roberto's report card, however, that the books he read were one to two years below grade level. The team also decided that Roberto would have to improve his performance by at least one book per marking period if he were to continue to receive a grade of O in reading.

Of course basing grades or progress on IEP objectives carries the risk that students with disabilities will be evaluated using criteria unrelated to expectations in general education. When curricular objectives in general and special education are out of synch, student access to the general education curriculum is compromised. That is why, to the maximum extent possible, IEP objectives should be based on the general education curriculum.

Perhaps the greatest benefit of adapting grades based on improvement is that it motivates students to try harder. In fact, basing part of students' report-card grades on improvement can motivate students to take better advantage of available supports or attempt more work than they would do ordinarily. In the preceding examples, Aretha worked more conscientiously during her instructional support time in the resource room because she thought it would improve her spelling grade in general education. Roberto read even more books than the minimum of five required in his IEP.

One potential drawback of grading on the basis of improvement is the risk that students will become dependent on special contingencies. For example, when Aretha finally reaches 75 percent on her spelling tests, will she balk when asked to perform better to receive a grade of B next time? Will Roberto expect that he will always be able to receive an O in reading by reading just five trade books? As was done for Aretha and Roberto, teachers need to continue to increase the criteria for successful performance until students are performing under the same conditions as their classmates without disabilities. Another problem can arise if students do not possess the skills needed to show improvement. For example, if Aretha's knowledge of sound–spelling relationships is well below that needed to spell her weekly spelling words correctly, no level of incentive will be enough to improve her performance. If there are no books in the classroom library that Roberto can read, he will be unable to reach his objective of

reading five books and answering comprehension questions, regardless of the grading incentive. Teachers should select improvement as a grading adaptation only when the student's performance clearly demonstrates the presence of the prerequisite skills needed to meet the goal.

BASING ALL OR PART OF THE GRADE ON PERFORMANCE ON PRIORITIZED CONTENT AND ASSIGNMENTS ● The third type of grading adaptation is basing all or part of a student's grade on his or her performance on prioritized curriculum content and assignments deemed most important by the teacher (Munk, 2003). **Prioritization of curriculum** benefits students for whom remembering, organizing, and accessing the content in the general education curriculum is a difficult and time-consuming process. Limiting the content load and assignments to the essentials for these students can make learning success more likely. Teachers can prioritize their content based on a number of sources including state learning standards, local curriculum guidelines, skills or content needed for future classes or postsecondary education, relevance to students' lives, or other criteria established by the IEP team (Munk, 2003). Basing priorities on standards is particularly important in the current climate of school accountability.

Claudia is included in Mr. Gonzales's middle school science class. She has learning disabilities; she has difficulty remembering factual material, reads quite slowly, and has problems organizing what she reads into main ideas. Claudia's IEP team decided that content prioritization would help her access the science curriculum more efficiently, particularly since the science textbook was hard to read and very content-dense. Mr. Gonzales agreed to prioritize the content for the next grading period when he was covering the topic of cells. He identified the following content as most important based on state learning standards (Munk, 2003, p. 74):

1. Identify nine major parts of all cells.
2. Use a microscope to view cells of different organisms.
3. Describe the stages in photosynthesis.
4. Describe the functions of cells.
5. Describe the similarities and differences between cells of animals and plants.
6. Identify parts of cells as viewed under a microscope.

Mr. Gonzales assured the team that this content reflected the major information in the state standards pertaining to cells. He explained that content ideas 1, 3, and 4 would be evaluated using short-answer tests, and ideas 2, 5, and 6 would be evaluated based on Claudia's performance on submitted lab reports. The team decided that her labs and tests would be graded based on the percentage correct on all items pertaining to her prioritized content. The resulting number grade would be converted to a letter grade using the same grading scale used schoolwide. Mr. Gonzales said that Claudia would be encouraged to participate in all of the other class activities for the grading period, including answering end-of-chapter questions in the textbook, but that the activities related to her prioritized content would be emphasized in arriving at her grade.

Using prioritization as a grading adaptation has a number of advantages. It directs the team to focus the need for supports on the most important content and assignments. For example, Claudia needed the most support on completing lab reports related to her curricular objectives and preparing for short-answer tests. Less support was needed for end-of-chapter questions in the text and producing lab reports on other topics. Prioritization may also reduce the risk that students' performance on

W W W
R E S O U R C E S
For a Listserv that carries messages on a range of topics relevant to inclusive education, go to the relevant page of JISCmail, at http://www.jiscmail.ac.uk/lists/inclusive-education.html.

ANALYZE
AND **REFLECT**

What are the advantages of making grading adaptations a part of students' IEPs? Under what circumstances might you want to make grading adaptations for your students without disabilities?

66 Prioritization directs the IEP team to focus the need for supports on the most important content and assignments. 99

less important content and activities will pull down their grade. For example, end-of-chapter questions are difficult for Claudia because they take her so long. In the past, she never completed them, and her low grades on these activities reduced her overall grade for the marking period. Finally, the process of prioritizing content can help teachers identify the most important elements of the curriculum. Knowing and communicating what is most important about the curriculum benefits all students, not just those with disabilities.

A problem that could arise when using prioritization involves the choice of which content to stress and which to de-emphasize. This decision is best made collaboratively by the student, parents, and teachers as part of the IEP process and, of course, while keeping state standards clearly in mind.

EMPHASIZING LEARNING STRATEGIES AND EFFORT IN A BALANCED GRADING SYSTEM ● Traditionally, grading systems have focused on the evaluation of student products without taking into account the learning strategies and effort required to come up with the products. For example, in Mr. Kellogg's sophomore English class, students write a five-page persuasive essay and are graded on various qualities of the essay submitted, such as length, organization, mechanics, and the integration of elements essential to a persuasive essay. When grading his students, Mr. Kellogg does not consider the amount of effort students put into the paper or the extent to which the students employ learning strategies. Brad is a student included in Mr. Kellogg's class. He is receiving help from his special education teacher, Ms. Laslow, in writing, but he feels discouraged. His grades in Mr. Kellogg's class have remained at D− despite all the hard work he has been doing with his special education teacher, Ms. Laslow, on learning strategies for writing such as outlining key essay elements, proofreading, self-monitoring, and using word processing. Mr. Kellogg has indicated that he has seen no changes in Brad's writing since the beginning of the year.

Brad's IEP team decided to use a **balanced grading adaptation** that took into account Brad's learning-strategy performance and effort. The team decided to give Brad credit for performing the writing strategies that he was learning from Ms. Laslow. When Brad submitted the final draft of his paper, he also gave Mr. Kellogg a copy of his paper outline and a completed self-monitoring checklist of all of the writing steps he followed. The team agreed that the quality of the outline and checklist would count 25 percent toward Brad's final grade on the paper. As a way of recognizing Brad's effort, the team also agreed to give him bonus points for submitting his paper to Mr. Kellogg once, early, for feedback, and for getting the final paper in on time.

Brad's individualized grading adaptation is an example of a grading system that attempts to balance an emphasis on the quality of the product with the effort and skill that went into producing it. A balanced grading system like this has a number of advantages. First, as you have already learned, students with disabilities may have difficulty performing learning strategies that typical students complete effortlessly (Munk, 2003). These strategies include the basic reading, writing, math, and computer skills covered in Chapters 5 and 9, and the independent learning strategies described in Chapter 10. Often these are the skills on which students receive help from special educators but have difficulty applying in their general education classes. Including student performance on these academic learning skills in the grading process helps focus students' attention on applying them in their general education classes. Balanced grading also leads to greater collaboration and coordination between general education and special

WWW
RESOURCES
Find out about testing and grading policies being used around the country by visiting the website of the Council of Chief State School Officers (CCSSO), at http://www.ccsso.org.

> " Balanced grading leads to greater collaboration and coordination between general education and special education teachers. "

education teachers. Once Brad's grading adaptation was agreed to, Mr. Kellogg took a greater interest in Brad in class. For example, he began to remind Brad to perform the skills present on his self-monitoring checklist. As a result, Brad was better able to apply what he had learned from Ms. Laslow to meeting the requirements in Mr. Kellogg's class.

While rewarding effort is a key part of a balanced grading adaptation and a potentially effective way to sustain student motivation, it is a grading adaptation that must be done with great care. First, effort is much more difficult to assess than academic progress (Gersten et al., 1996). Also, the relationship between effort and achievement is not always predictable; a student may work hard but master little of the content (Munk, 2003). Munk (2003, p. 90) advises IEP teams to ask the following questions when considering incorporating effort into a student's grading adaptation:

- Do you have evidence that when the student tries harder, he or she performs better on assignments?
- Can the team agree on how to measure effort?
- Will the student perceive the adaptation as an incentive to keep working hard?

In Brad's case, based on input from his mother, the committee felt that rewarding him for effort was necessary and would be effective. The team also agreed that they could measure his level of effort by noting whether he handed in an early draft of the paper to Mr. Kellogg for feedback and whether he submitted the final draft of the paper on time.

Finally, while learning processes and effort are important, ultimately, it is the product or outcome that is most important. Placing too much emphasis in grading on process use or effort can send the message that the quality of the final product is not important—a message inconsistent with most grading policies.

MODIFYING GRADING WEIGHTS AND SCALES ● The last type of individualized grading adaptation involves changing the grading scale used to assign a specified letter grade or changing the weights assigned to different requirements when determining a report-card grade. In the case of Stan from the chapter-opening vignettes, for example, his teacher, Mr. Stevens, counted tests as 80 percent of the grade and homework as 20 percent. Stan's IEP team decided that they could help Stan become less discouraged by using a **modified weights and scales** grading adaptation. The team decided to reduce the percentage Mr. Stevens counted for tests from 80 to 50 percent, while keeping homework at 20 percent. However, the team also added a new assignment: Stan would be required to make a taped summary of responses to a study guide at the end of each text chapter. This assignment would count for 20 percent of Stan's grade. The remaining 10 percent of Stan's grade would comprise other accomplishments such as being prepared, attempting all class activities, and participating in class. Mr. Stevens defined these other accomplishments as the percentage of school days for which Stan had his materials for class, completed in-class assignments, and asked at least one question in class. Because Stan's IEP team members were concerned that Stan would drop out of school, they also decided to make a temporary change in the grading scale for him. Stan's modified scale would be as follows: A = 90–100%; B = 80–89%; C = 70–79%; and so on. The regular school scale was this: A = 93–100%; B = 85–92%; C = 77–84%, and so on. Stan's IEP team planned to move him back to the school grading scale when his grades improved for two consecutive marking periods.

DIMENSIONS
OF DIVERSITY

Elliott (1998) reviewed the research on the use of performance assessments with students from different ethnic and cultural backgrounds and found mixed results; sometimes these students performed better on performance tests than on traditional standardized tests, and sometimes they did not. Elliott suggests that although of great potential value, performance tests should continue to be used along with, rather than as a substitute for, traditional standardized assessments.

RESEARCH
N O T E

Lane and colleagues (2002) surveyed principals and teachers about the utility of their states' performance-based assessments in math. Both principals and teachers tended to support performance-based assessments as a useful tool for making changes in instruction. They also thought that such assessments caused teachers to make positive changes in mathematics instruction in their classrooms.

DIMENSIONS
OF DIVERSITY

Because teachers' evaluations of lower income and non-European students can be prejudiced, performance-based assessments can be subject to bias. However, anecdotal evidence shows that when teachers follow specific scoring procedures, performance-based assessments provide much useful information about non-European students and students with limited English proficiency (Heath, 1993).

The benefit of using grading adaptations that change the grading scale or weights is that these adaptations may motivate students to keep trying because they can earn a higher grade that seemed "out of reach" before the adaptation. This was certainly the case for Stan, who was in need of a motivator because he had been trying hard but with little success to show for it. However, changing the grading scale and/or the weights for class requirements must be implemented cautiously because these adaptations do not require a change in the student's performance. This lack of increased performance expectations may send a message to students that they have no need to improve. Changing the weights and/or the grading scale may also be perceived by classmates and other teachers as unfair. Because of this we do not recommend changing the grading scale unless other adaptations are used as well. In the case of Stan, a number of adaptations were used in conjunction with changing weights and the grading scale. While Stan's tests counted less toward his grade, he was still expected to learn key content by submitting an orally completed study guide for each chapter in the text. He was also expected to be prepared for class, attempt all class activities, and ask questions in class. Often, changing weights is perceived to be fairer if weight is shifted to alternative ways to assess student learning, not simply away from a requirement that is particularly difficult for a student (Munk, 2003). Finally, the IEP team planned to reestablish the regular grading scale as soon as Stan showed signs of success in class.

How Can Performance-Based Assessment Benefit Students with Special Needs?

Ms. Johnson is just completing a unit on persuasive writing and has her students write letters to the editor of a local newspaper, trying to persuade readers to support the building of a new county facility for elderly people. Mr. Repp is teaching drawing to scale as part of a map-reading unit and has his students make a map of the neighborhood that could be used by visitors from Japan. Ms. Overton's class is working on basic bookkeeping skills and she has her students plan a budget for a fund-raiser to earn money to build a new jungle gym for the playground.

All these teachers are checking their students' progress with a method of evaluation called performance-based assessment. **Performance-based assessment** "provides students with opportunities to demonstrate their mastery of a skill or concept through performance of a task" (Haager & Klingner, 2005, p. 66). Performance-based assessments measure learning processes rather than focusing only on learning products. They frequently involve using **authentic learning tasks,** or tasks that are presented within real-world contexts and lead to real-world outcomes. Mr. Repp could have asked his students to compute the mileage between several cities using a mileage key, a more traditional map-reading assignment. Instead, he has them create their own maps within a real context, because he wants to see how well they can apply what they have learned to an actual problem. Not only does Mr. Repp evaluate students' maps, but he also evaluates parts of the learning process, such as how well his students select and implement learning strategies and collaborate with their classmates during problem solving.

Using performance-based assessments can be very helpful for students with disabilities or other special needs who may be included in your classroom. Performance-based assessments can offer students options for demonstrating their knowledge that do not rely exclusively on reading and writing, areas that often impede the successful testing performance of students with disabilities. For example, Calvin, a student with reading problems who is in Mr. Repp's class, completed the map activity successfully but would have had trouble with a traditional paper-and-pencil test of the same material.

Performance-based tests also are not subject to the same time constraints as traditional tests. Time flexibility can benefit students who need more time, such as students with reading fluency problems, or students who need to work for shorter time periods, such as students with attention deficit–hyperactivity disorder. Again using the example of Mr. Repp's map-drawing activity, students had some time limits (they had to finish in one week) but did not have to do the entire project in one sitting.

Students with disabilities may also have particular difficulty making the connection between school tasks and tasks in the real world. Performance-based assessments can help them understand this connection, particularly if an assessment is followed up with instruction directly geared to skill applications. For example, Ms. Johnson, whose students were required to write letters to the editor, discovered that many of her students were unable to support their arguments directly with specific examples. She therefore spent some class time demonstrating to students how they could support their arguments and guiding them through several practice activities.

As you can see, using performance-based assessments has many potential benefits for students with special needs. Nonetheless, you may still need to adapt performance-based tests for students with disabilities. For example, Gregory is a student with cerebral palsy in Mr. Repp's social studies class. Gregory has very little control over fine motor movements in his hands. As a result, he is unable to write or draw. Gregory obviously needs to have the drawing-to-scale map task adapted. One possible adaptation would be to have Gregory make an audiotape to accompany the map that would provide the Japanese visitors with a self-guided tour. Or consider Rhonda, a student with a learning disability who has difficulty expressing herself in writing. Rhonda is included in Ms. Johnson's class, which is writing letters to the editor as a way of practicing persuasive writing skills. As an adaptation, Ms. Johnson has Rhonda develop an oral editorial that is sent to the local public radio channel. In some cases, then, adaptations for performance-based tests can be made just as readily as adaptations for traditional tests.

Some students with special needs may have problems with performance-based tests that are more difficult to accommodate. For instance, students might have difficulty making the connection between school tasks and real-world tasks. You need to teach these students directly how to make those connections. For example, Ms. Riley's class is learning to compute subtraction problems. As a performance-based test, Ms. Riley has her class compare prices of various brands of the same products in the grocery store and compute price differences using subtraction. Cleo, a student in the class who has a mild intellectual disability, is unable to perform the task because he has never used subtraction as it applies to money or products in the grocery store. The next day in class, Ms. Riley includes examples of subtracting amounts of money in her daily instruction. She also includes story problems dealing with the subtraction of money, some of which involve grocery store products. This adaptation helps Cleo make the connection between money and the supermarket.

Students with special needs also lack important preskills that are necessary for problem solving. You need either to teach these preskills or to allow such students to bypass the preskills altogether to carry out performance-based tasks. For example, Sam has a learning disability in math; he does not know basic math facts and as a result cannot get Ms. Riley's product comparisons correct. Ms. Riley allows him to perform the task with a calculator. She also requires that he spend 5 minutes per day using a computer-based math fact program until he learns basic math facts. Anna has visual disabilities; another student reads to her the prices of the brands and she writes them down.

For students with more severe disabilities, you may need to modify or scale down performance-based tasks by using the guidelines for developing alternate assessments

As an alternative to pencil-and-paper tests, performance-based assessments allow students to demonstrate their knowledge and skills through application in real-world contexts. What are some ways to adapt performance-based assessments for students with special needs?

RESEARCH
N O T E

Johnson (2000) studied whether the accommodation of reading state performance tests in math to students with and without reading disabilities affected the validity of the test results. She found that reading the tests improved the scores of the students with reading disabilities, but not those of students without reading disabilities. Johnson concluded that reading math questions to students with reading disabilities is a valid recommendation for performance tests in math.

CONNECTIONS

Review Chapters 4 and 9 for information on testing and teaching preskills.

> Students with special needs may have trouble meeting the problem-solving demands of performance-based tests.

CONNECTIONS

Scaffolding (see Chapter 5) and learning strategies instruction (see Chapter 10) are good ways to support students as they learn to carry out performance-based tasks.

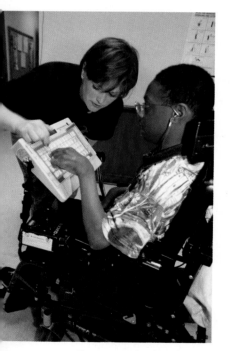

How can technology help teachers develop alternate assessments for students with moderate to severe disabilities?

described in Chapter 4 and the environmental inventory process described in Chapter 9. For example, Derek has severe intellectual disabilities and lacks basic math skills other than simple number identification. Ms. Riley has Derek participate in the same task as the other students but has him perform an easier step. She has Derek pick groups of products that students are to compare. This task is more consistent with Derek's IEP goal of being able to classify similar objects, such as three kinds of cola or two types of bread.

Finally, students with special needs may have trouble meeting the problem-solving demands of performance-based tests. For example, Peter has attention deficits and approaches problems impulsively; he rushes to find an answer and fails to consider all the options. For Peter, performance-based tests are important because they give him the opportunity to learn critical problem-solving skills. Nonetheless, for students like Peter to succeed, performance-based tasks need to be modified, and problem-solving skills need to be taught directly. For example, Mr. Kelsey's class is applying work they have done in computing areas and perimeters to the task of planning a garden. Before having students design their own gardens, Mr. Kelsey carefully demonstrates how he would design his. This demonstration is very helpful for students in the class, such as Peter, who are not natural problem solvers and need a model to guide them. Mr. Kelsey also scales down Peter's assignment, asking him to design only one section of a smaller garden.

As you can see, the use of performance-based tests with students with disabilities can be helpful, but it can also be problematic. For this reason, use performance-based tests in conjunction with other classroom-based and standardized tests.

How Can Portfolio Assessment Benefit Students with Special Needs?

Portfolio assessment is a method of evaluation in which a purposeful collection of student work is used to determine student effort, progress, and achievement in one or more areas (Montgomery, 2001). A portfolio collection typically contains the observable evidence or products of performance assessment, evidence that may or may not reflect authentic tasks (Poteet, Choate, & Stewart, 1993). This evidence includes many different sources of information, such as anecdotal records, interviews, work samples, and scored samples such as curriculum-based assessment probes. As an example, sources of information for language arts that can be placed into a portfolio are shown in Table 11.4.

Portfolios can be very helpful for teachers working with students with disabilities. Portfolios can assist teachers in evaluating student progress toward IEP objectives and in guiding instruction. For example, Ms. Pohl is interested in finding out whether the extra math practice sheets she is sending home with Robert are improving his scores on weekly math computation tests. She consults Robert's portfolio and finds that his performance has improved quite a bit over the last 2 months. Ms. Pohl tells Robert's parents of his progress. They agree to continue the extra practice for at least another month.

Portfolios also emphasize student products rather than tests and test scores. This emphasis benefits students with special needs, many of whom are poor test takers. It may also highlight student strengths better than traditional tests, which tend to have a

TABLE 11.4 Examples of Language Arts Portfolio Contents

Type of Portfolio Sample Contents

Reading	Audiotape of oral reading of selected passages
	Original story map
	Transcript of storytelling
	Log of books read with personal reactions, summaries, vocabulary
	Representative assignments: responses to pre- and postreading questions
	Favorite performance
	Journal entries, including self-evaluation
Writing	Scrapbook of representative writing samples
	Selected prewriting activities
	Illustrations/diagrams for one piece
	Log or journal of writing ideas, vocabulary, semantic maps, compositions, evaluations
	Conference notes, observation narratives
	Student-selected best performance
	Self-evaluation checklists

narrow academic focus. For example, Leshonn's teacher uses portfolios to evaluate her social studies students. Leshonn has problems in reading and writing but has good artistic ability and excellent oral language skills. During the last marking period, his class studied the growth of suburban areas after World War II, a content area included in the state standards. Leshonn designed a scale model of Levittown, one of the first planned communities. He also developed a tape-recorded explanation to go with the model that explained the key features of the community. His performance on these projects was excellent and enabled him to raise his overall grade for the class because his scores on the two tests given during the marking period were low.

Finally, a key component of portfolio assessments is student self-evaluation. Students with special needs, who are often described as not being involved in their own learning, can benefit greatly from self-evaluations. For example, students might complete a self-assessment after they have finished a unit of instruction. This evaluation can then become a part of the students' portfolios. The Technology Notes on page 426 features the use of assistive technology in helping students with severe intellectual disabilities construct their own portfolios.

You may have to make adaptations when using portfolios with students with special needs, particularly in selecting and evaluating portfolio pieces. For example, Jerome was asked to select an example of his best work in written expression for his portfolio. However, he was uncertain what "best work" meant: Was it a paper that he tried his hardest on? Was it a paper that was the hardest to write? Or was it one that he or his teacher liked best? Because he did not know, Jerome simply selected one paper at random. Similarly, when Thanh was asked to evaluate, for his portfolio, his efforts to solve a word problem in math, all he could come up with was whether he had the correct answer. You need to teach students such as Jerome and Thanh how to select and evaluate portfolio pieces.

DIMENSIONS OF **DIVERSITY**

Student-centered evaluation, a key component of portfolio assessment, is an important part of effective multicultural education because it takes into account unique student perceptions and experiences. Student-centered evaluation strategies include self-evaluation questionnaires, interviews, student entries in journals and learning logs, and think alouds (Dean, Salend, & Taylor, 1994).

DIMENSIONS OF **DIVERSITY**

Barootchi and Keshavarz (2002) found that portfolio assessments increased Iranian English-language learners' achievement and feelings of responsibility toward monitoring their own academic progress.

RESEARCH NOTE

Johnson and Arnold (2004) examined the validity of one state's alternate assessment portfolio system using commonly accepted professional standards and found serious shortcomings. While portfolios are potentially valuable evaluation tools, they should supplement, not supplant, standardized achievement, psychological, and curriculum-based measures.

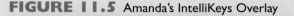

> TECHNOLOGY NOTES

Conducting Alternative Assessments Using Electronic Portfolios

In Chapter 4 you learned that students with moderate to severe intellectual disabilities working on a more functional curriculum are not required to take state high-stakes tests but must show that they have met state standards in more basic ways using alternative assessments. You also learned how the state of Kentucky implements its alternate assessments using student portfolios. Denham and Lahm (2001) reported the efforts of four students who used assistive technology to make their portfolios. All four students had moderate to severe disabilities and were unable to use the standard computer keyboard effectively. They used the IntelliKeys keyboard as an adaptation.

IntelliKeys is an enlarged keyboard that enables users with physical, visual, or intellectual disabilities to easily type, enter numbers, navigate on-screen displays, and execute menu commands. IntelliKeys helps students produce artifacts for their portfolios related to their IEP objectives and can be customized for specific students using individually designed overlays. The overlay for Amanda, a student with severe intellectual disabilities, is shown in Figure 11.5.

Amanda's teacher constructed this overlay using Overlay Maker 3, a software program. The response keys were grouped according to color and were used to facilitate the making of correct choices. The overlay provided response choices that Amanda was to use to complete an activ-

ity sheet shown on the computer. Amanda's activity sheet is shown in Figure 11.6.

For Amanda, questions on the activity sheet were tied to her performance on activities related to her IEP goals such as loading a soda machine, recycling cans, and shopping at the store. The activity sheet and overlay were designed to allow Amanda to read the text with text-reading software and construct a variety of sentences in response to the questions asked on the activity sheet using the overlay. By pressing a response choice on the overlay, Amanda caused the text programmed into that cell to be entered into the activity sheet. All answers were read back to

FIGURE 11.5 Amanda's IntelliKeys Overlay

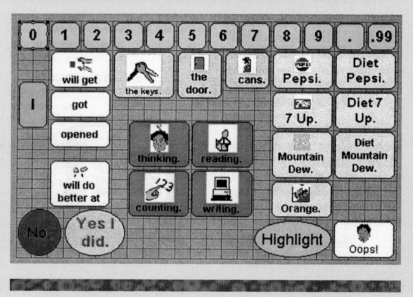

S U M M A R Y

As a teacher, you have a number of tools at your disposal for evaluating your students' progress, including tests, report-card grades, performance-based assessments, and portfolios. Although each of these evaluation methods can also help you measure the progress of students with special needs included in your class, any one of them may need to be adapted to ensure that the evaluation information measures the students' skill levels or content knowledge, not their disabilities or other special needs.

Testing adaptations can be made before testing, during testing, and after testing when tests are graded. Adaptations before the test include study guides, practice tests, tutoring, teaching test-taking skills and strategies, and modifying test construction. During the test, you can make alternative forms of questions and allow alternative ways of administering tests. Adaptations after the test involve grading tests and include changing letter or number grades, changing the criteria on which grades

FIGURE 11.6 Amanda's Soda Machine Activity Sheet

Prompt	Response			
Did I use my schedule?				
Did I use my sheet so I know what to do next?				
Did I write what sodas were needed?				
How many cans did we need?				
Did I put the can in the right place?				
Did I do a good job?				
Next time I will do better at . . .				

Amanda, allowing her to confirm the correctness of her answers. Note that some of the questions required a yes or no response while others required a more open-ended answer. The complexity of these questions was based on what Amanda was able to do. Amanda was assisted in her effort by a classroom peer without disabilities. The peer provided prompts and assistance when needed. When Amanda answered with assistance, her answer was shown in a different color, allowing her teacher to monitor her level of independent performance.

According to Denham and Lahm (2001, p. 13), "Before using the IntelliKeys, Amanda was limited to hand-writing her responses, which was painstakingly slow. The IntelliKeys system allowed her to write 56 words in 20 minutes, a feat she could not have accomplished without it. Amanda's reaction to the IntelliKeys system was, 'This is neat.'"

SOURCES: "Using Technology to Construct Alternate Portfolios of Students with Moderate and Severe Disabilities," by A. Denham and E. Lahm, 2001, *Teaching Exceptional Children, 33*(5), pp. 10–17; and Overlay Maker (Version 3) (computer software), 2004, Petaluma, CA: IntelliTools.

are based, and using alternatives to letter and number grades.

Adaptations in report-card grades involve making changes to letter and number grades, and grading on the basis of IEP objectives, improvement, prioritized curriculum and assignments, learning strategies and effort, and modified grading weights and scales. Grading adaptations for students with disabilities should be done as part of the IEP process.

Performance-based assessments measure learning processes rather than focusing exclusively on learning products and they frequently involve authentic, or real-world, tasks. They can be helpful in evaluating the performance of students with special needs because they do not rely exclusively on formats that create problems for students with disabilities. However, performance-based tests may need to be adapted for students with special needs by teaching directly the connection between school tasks and real-world tasks, allowing students to bypass preskills, scaling down the tasks, and teaching problem solving directly using performance-based tasks.

Portfolio assessment can also benefit students with special needs. Portfolios typically contain the observable evidence or products of performance assessment, such as anecdotal records, interviews, work samples, and scored samples. While portfolios can be helpful for teachers working with students with special needs, students with special needs may need to be taught how to select and evaluate their portfolio pieces.

Applications in **Teaching Practice**

Adapting Evaluations for Students with Special Needs

Eugene, Tara, and Jamie are students in your fourth-grade class. Eugene has been identified as having a specific learning disability. He has good study skills, but his problems in reading and written expression place him at a disadvantage when he takes tests. Failure on tests has increased his test anxiety; he often misses items he knows because when he is anxious during a test he tends to get careless.

Tara has a learning disability and receives intensive reading instruction in the resource room. Her short-term objectives for this marking period include reading a first-grade literature book at a rate of 20 words correct per minute with four or fewer errors per minute, and discerning who the main character of the story is, what the main problem in the story is, and how the problem is solved.

Jamie is a student with mild intellectual disabilities. You are about to start a unit on adding and subtracting fractions. The IEP objective for Jamie is to identify the fractions $\frac{1}{4}$, $\frac{1}{3}$, and $\frac{1}{2}$.

QUESTIONS

1. What tests will you be giving in this class?
2. For one of these tests, what adaptations might you need to make for Eugene before testing? In constructing the test? In administering the test? In grading the test?
3. At the end of the marking period, should you give Tara a grade in reading? Why or why not? Assuming that Tara has met her short-term objectives in reading, what do you think her grade for the marking period should be? Should her grade be adapted in any way?
4. Describe a performance-based test that you could use to measure Jamie's knowledge of her target fractions. How would you score this test? How could you use portfolio assessment to measure Jamie's progress on this unit?

WORKING THE **STANDARDS**

INTASC

INTASC PRINCIPLES REFLECTED IN THIS CHAPTER:

Principle #4 states that all teachers provide a variety of ways for students with disabilities to demonstrate their learning (Principle 4.05).

Principle #8 states that all teachers

- Use a variety of assessment procedures to document students' learning, behavior, and growth within multiple environments appropriate to the students' age, interests, and learning (Principle 8.02).

- Collaborate with others to incorporate accommodations and alternative assessments into the ongoing assessment process of students with disabilities when appropriate (Principle 8.03).

- Understand that students with disabilities are expected to participate in district and statewide assessments and that accommodations or alternative assessments may be required when appropriate (Principle 8.05).

Principle #10 states that all teachers communicate with families in ways that honor families' beliefs and practices, and seek to promote families' confidence and competence in furthering their children's development and learning (Principle 10.04).

CEC CONTENT STANDARDS REFLECTED IN THIS CHAPTER:

CEC Content Standard #8 states that special educators

- Use multiple types of assessment information for a variety of educational decisions.

- Understand the appropriate use and limitations of various types of assessments.

- Conduct formal and informal assessments of behavior, learning, achievement, and environments to design learning experiences that support the growth and development of individuals with exceptional learning needs.

Council for Exceptional Children

WORKING THE **STANDARDS** *(continued)*

CEC Content Standard #10 states that special educators

- Use collaboration to ensure that the needs of individuals with exceptional learning needs are addressed throughout schooling.

- Promote and advocate the learning and well-being of individuals with exceptional learning needs across a wide range of settings and a range of different learning experiences.

BACK TO THE CASES

The standards and principles just listed relate to the cases described at the beginning of this chapter: Stan, Jennifer, and Lucille. The questions and activities that follow demonstrate how these standards and principles, along with other concepts that you have learned about in this chapter, connect to the everyday activities of all teachers.

Stan

Stan's reading problem during tests is a common one for students with learning disabilities. Many teachers face the dilemma that Mr. Stevens must solve to give Stan an opportunity to demonstrate what he has learned rather than reflect his disability for reading quickly. One obvious and sometimes-used accommodation is to allow the student more time on the test. However, this may place students at a disadvantage during mandated state assessments, college-placement exams, and other standardized testing situations. Review the information in your text regarding adaptations that can be made before, during, and after a test. Develop plans for working with Stan to improve his test-taking situation and for grading procedures that might be used to assess his learning. (See INTASC Principles 4.05, 8.03, and 8.05; and CEC Content Standards 8 and 10.) Share your plan with a peer to discuss its pros and cons.

Jennifer

Jennifer's parents have questions about her grade in reading, but they are not the only ones who have noticed the difference. Jennifer shared her report card with a classmate, who then reported Jennifer's A to several other classmates. Three of those classmates are distressed, because they did not earn A's and feel that they are reading much harder books than Jennifer. You overhear two of the students taunting Jennifer by calling her the "teacher's pet" and laughing about the "baby books" she reads. When you stop the girls and ask them why they are being cruel to Jennifer, they complain about the unfairness of Ms. Robinson's grading system. What can teachers do to avoid situations such as this one? How might you respond to the girls? (See INTASC Principle 10.04; and CEC Content Standard 10.)

Lucille

Lucille's previous teachers used one of the five types of grading adaptations identified by researchers: progress based on IEP objectives. This year, Lucille will be in your classroom, and you have thought carefully about the issue of adapting your grading procedures to reflect Lucille's learning and progress in your class. You are planning a conference with her guardians and the special education teacher to discuss a change in the grading adaptation. You would like to use another of the five adaptations that you feel is more appropriate for your grade and content area. To prepare for the conference, outline your plan for using one of the other grading adaptations in your content area and list your reasons for selecting this alternative adaptation. (See INTASC Principles 4.05, 8.03, and 10.04; and CEC Content Standards 8 and 10.)

Visit the companion website (http://www.ablongman. com/friend4e) for a complete correlation of this chapter to the INTASC Principles and CEC Standards.

Further **Readings**

Guskey, T. R., & Bailey, J. M. (2001). *Developing grading and reporting systems for student learning.* Thousand Oaks, CA: Corwin.

This thoughtful book provides essential background knowledge on effective grading and reporting practices in education.

Munk, D. D. (2003). *Solving the grading puzzle for students with disabilities.* Whitefish Bay, WI: Knowledge by Design.

This very practical book includes a careful description of a research-based process that IEP teams can follow to grade students with disabilities. The book contains numerous case studies and many reproducible grading adaptation tools.

Popham, W. J. (2004). *Classroom assessment: What teachers need to know* (4th ed.). Boston: Allyn and Bacon.

This readable text covers practical ways teachers can use and interpret assessments within an educational context of accountability, including No Child Left Behind.

Thurlow, M. L., Elliott, J. L., & Ysseldyke, J. E. (2002). *Testing students with disabilities: Practical strategies for complying with district and state requirements* (2nd ed.). Thousand Oaks, CA: Corwin.

This practical book covers a range of topics, including maximizing the IEP; fostering collaboration among teachers, parents, and administrators; optimizing assessment accommodations; and using test scores to improve instruction. The book also features many reproducible tools.

Responding to Student Behavior

1. Outline strategies for promoting positive behavior and preventing misbehavior with groups of students, including students with special needs.

2. Explain simple techniques for responding to individual student misbehavior.

3. Describe the purpose of a functional behavior assessment and its steps for deciding how to respond to chronic, inappropriate individual student behavior.

4. Outline systematic approaches for increasing individual students' positive behaviors and decreasing their negative behaviors.

5. Identify how to help students manage their own behavior.

6. Articulate your own beliefs regarding your responsibilities for addressing student behavior in positive ways and describe how your beliefs may influence student actions.

KEY TERMS AND CONCEPTS

Behavior contracts (p. 462)

Behavior intervention plan (BIP) (p. 451)

Cognitive behavior management (CBM) (p. 464)

Differential reinforcement of incompatible behaviors (p. 459)

Discipline (p. 432)

Extinction (p. 459)

Functional behavior assessment (FBA) (p. 442)

Negative reinforcement (p. 456)

Positive behavioral interventions and supports (PBIS) (p. 434)

Positive reinforcement (p. 456)

Presentation punishment (p. 461)

Removal punishment (p. 460)

Response cost (p. 460)

Surface behaviors (p. 441)

Time-out (p. 460)

Token economy (p. 438)

JOSEPH, A JUNIOR with a learning disability and an emotional disability, comes late to his algebra class at least twice each week. He seldom participates in class discussions, and he does not ask questions. Unless Mrs. Akers repeatedly asks him not to, Joseph sits with his head down on his desk. When discussing Joseph with the special education teacher, Mrs. Akers describes his demeanor as sullen. Mrs. Akers has been teaching high school math for many years, and she believes that students have the responsibility to be interested in the subject, to attend class, and to participate. She knows that Joseph is heading toward a failing grade for this grading period, even though she thinks he could do the work with a little more effort. She believes that Joseph has given up on learning since he failed to pass the math section of the high school proficiency test. ● *What is Joseph's responsibility for his learning? What is Mrs. Akers's responsibility for making instruction appealing to students like Joseph? What strategies could help Joseph meet Mrs. Akers's class expectations for him?*

KATIE HAS A MODERATE intellectual disability. Every time she enters the classroom she says loudly, "I'm ba-ack," even if she has been gone for only a moment. Although she is in sixth grade, she frequently sucks her thumb and rocks in her chair. When she sees a student in the hallway, she waves—and continues waving long after the student has passed by. If she needs assistance, she leaves her seat and goes to the teacher, no matter what activity is occurring in the class. Katie's language arts teacher, Mr. Lowell, is losing patience with her "babyish" behaviors. He believes that Katie is learning many social skills through the small-group work the class does, and he knows Katie's paraprofessional is ensuring that she is learning basic prereading skills. Mr. Lowell is most concerned about the impact of Katie's behaviors on the class. Despite class discussions about how best to respond to Katie's outbursts, several students continue to snicker when Katie calls out, which often leads to other behavior problems. ● *How could Mr. Lowell address both*

Katie's inappropriate classroom behaviors and other students' responses to them?

MR. MORGAN HAD HEARD about David from his colleagues at Bessie Coleman Elementary School, but he was surprised nonetheless. David has ADHD and serious behavior problems. Although in the sixth grade, he reads at a second-grade level, and he often expresses frustration with schoolwork by acting out. He slams the book shut when he does not understand the words, and he recently overturned his desk at the end of a day filled with small behavior problems. During large-group instruction, he sometimes comments that the work is "boring" or creates a disturbance by taking another student's materials. Two parents recently have contacted Ms. Averitte, the school's principal, because of concerns that David is bullying their children at recess and on the bus. Mr. Morgan admits that he sometimes does not insist that David complete his assignments because "it's not worth the disruption it causes to my class." ● *What purpose might David's behavior be serving for him? How could Mr. Morgan constructively respond to David's behavior? What is a teacher's responsibility for making accommodations for a student like David?*

All teachers are responsible for the behavior of their students. Whether you teach 5-year-olds in a kindergarten class or 17-year-olds in junior English, the environment you create in your classroom affects whether students' inappropriate behaviors escalate or improve, and your response to such behaviors significantly influences students' learning. The public is concerned about student behavior, too. Despite the fact that incidents of school violence have decreased over the past 20 years (Austin, 2003), disruptive behavior is increasing each year (U.S. Department of Health and Human Services, 2000), and Americans still list lack of discipline and fighting, violence, and gangs among the top problems facing public schools (Rose & Gallup, 2004). The Professional Edge on page 433 takes a brief look at school violence and related student warning signs.

To begin a discussion of classroom discipline, we present some basic concepts to provide a context within which you should consider managing student behavior. First, it is essential to recognize that the root word of *discipline* is *disciple*, meaning a follower of a teacher. Even though discipline often is associated with obedience, **discipline** mostly is about learning. It is a means to ensure that students have the maximum opportunity to learn from their teachers. Discipline is never an end in and of itself. As you learn about approaches for ensuring classroom discipline in this chapter, you will be finding ways to enhance your students' learning.

Second, some professionals characterize discipline and classroom management strategies as negative, as being about teacher control and power (for example, Wilson & Corpus, 2001). That view fails to take into account the very real dilemma teachers face in attempting to keep a classroom full of students interested in learning in a way that is safe and respectful of all students. Rather than managing student behavior for your convenience or to command compliance, by using strategies that encourage appropriate behavior you will be creating conditions that enable your students to reach their potential (for example, Schoen & Nolen, 2004).

Third, teacher beliefs about discipline have a strong cultural basis, and some evidence suggests that a teacher is far more likely to refer students for discipline problems when they are from a culture other than the teacher's (Skiba, Michael, Nardo, & Peterson, 2002; Salend, Taylor, 2002; Townsend, 2000). In addition, teachers may unintentionally vary their use of discipline techniques (for example, talking to the student versus taking away a privilege) depending on the student's culture or ethnicity (Ishii-Jordan, 2000; Jensen, 2004). All teachers have an obligation to monitor their behavior to ensure that their responses are not based on racial bias or cultural ignorance.

FYI

While some students must have explicit instruction to function successfully socially, it is likely that all students can benefit from social instruction at some point in their lives (Skiba & Peterson, 2003).

PROFESSIONAL EDGE

Addressing School Violence

As a school professional, you have a responsibility to be alert for students who are at high risk for committing acts of violence against themselves or others. Most students display early warning signs that should signal to you a need for help. As you review the warning signs listed here, keep in mind that your concern for a student should not lead you to jump to conclusions. Instead, if you have serious concerns about a student, you should ask for assistance from your colleagues, including school counselors, social workers, and administrators, and with their support you should work with parents and the student to address the issues at hand.

Early Warning Signs of Potential for Violence

- *Social withdrawal.* Some students gradually withdraw from social contact because of depression, rejection, or a lack of confidence.

- *Excessive feelings of isolation.* Although most students feel this way occasionally, in some cases a sense of isolation is associated with aggression and violence.

- *Excessive feelings of rejection.* Some aggressive students who are rejected by peers seek out other aggressive students who, in turn, reinforce their violent tendencies.

- *Victimization by others.* Students who have been physically or sexually abused are at risk of becoming violent themselves.

- *Feelings of being picked on and persecuted.* Students who believe they are teased, bullied, or humiliated at home or at school may vent their feelings through aggression or violence.

- *Low school interest and poor academic performance.* A drastic change in school performance, or poor school achievement accompanied by frustration, can be a warning sign for acting out.

- *Expression of violence in writings and drawings.* When violent themes are directed at specific individuals (for example, teachers, peers) over time, a student should be referred to a counselor or another professional for assistance.

- *Uncontrolled anger.* Anger is natural, but if it is frequent and intense in response to minor incidents it may signal a potential for violence.

- *Patterns of impulsive and chronic hitting, intimidating, and bullying behavior.* If behaviors such as these are not addressed, they can escalate to violence.

- *History of discipline problems.* Chronic behavior problems sometimes signal underlying emotional needs that are unmet.

- *Past history of violent and aggressive behavior.* Unless students with a history of aggressive and violent acts receive counseling, the behaviors are likely to continue and escalate.

- *Intolerance for differences and prejudicial attitudes.* Intense prejudice (regarding, for example, race, religion, gender, or sexual orientation) may lead to violence against individuals perceived to belong to the targeted group.

- *Drug use and alcohol use.* Use of drugs and alcohol tends to reduce self-control, thus increasing the chance of being a perpetrator or victim of violence.

- *Affiliation with gangs.* Students who are members of gangs that support antisocial values may act on group beliefs.

- *Inappropriate access to, possession of, and use of firearms.* Students who have a history of aggression, impulsiveness, or other serious emotional problems should not have access to firearms or other weapons.

- *Serious threats of violence.* One of the most reliable indicators that a student is likely to commit a violent act is a specific and detailed threat.

SOURCE: Adapted from *Early Warning, Time Response: A Guide to Safe Schools,* by U.S. Department of Education, Special Education and Rehabilitative Services, 1998, Washington, D.C.: Author. Retrieved January 1, 2005, from http://cecp.air.org/guide/guide.pdf.

Teachers who actively, carefully, and creatively apply approaches for classroom management and who monitor the success of their strategies, adapting them as needed, can have a positive influence on student learning (Algozzine et al., 2000; Witzel & Mercer, 2003). Many issues are beyond a teacher's control—you do not have the power to increase the financial support available to schools, nor can you remove the public pressures that surround many curriculum, instruction, and school reform initiatives. However, you can affect and are ultimately accountable for the learning of your students, and your skills for addressing discipline can help you to maximize time available for instruction.

What Are Positive Behavioral Interventions and Supports?

RESEARCH
NOTE

Since 1968, lack of discipline often has topped the annual Gallup Poll of public attitudes toward public schools (Mitchell & Arnold, 2004).

Over the past several years, researchers from several universities have worked to identify strategies for preventing behavior challenges as well as techniques for addressing common and intensive behavior problems. This body of work has been integrated at the University of Oregon through the U.S. Office of Special Education Programs (OSEP) National Technical Assistance Center on Positive Behavioral Interventions and Supports (PBIS) (U.S. Department of Education, 2004). **Positive behavioral interventions and supports (PBIS)** are based on four elements:

1. clearly defined outcomes
2. behavioral and biomedical science
3. practices demonstrated to be effective through research
4. systemic approaches that enhance the learning environment and outcomes for all students

PBIS interventions are grouped by their intensity. The first level is called *primary prevention*, and it is designed to create schoolwide and classroom environments that address the needs of approximately 80 percent of students. The second level is called *secondary prevention*. It is designed to quickly and efficiently address student behavior problems in order to prevent them from becoming more serious, and it addresses an additional 15 percent of students. The final level, *tertiary prevention*, includes intensive interventions for the 5 percent or so of students whose behavior problems are chronic or exceptionally serious.

The sections that follow present a wide array of procedures grounded in PBIS principles. Some aim for primary prevention of problems and some for fostering positive behavior in groups of students. Also addressed for the secondary and tertiary levels of intervention is a specific and federally mandated way of problem solving about student behavior called functional behavior assessment. In addition, strategies are outlined for responding to these more serious individual student behaviors and creating positive behavior supports. Together, these techniques provide the foundation teachers need for effective classroom management.

WWW
RESOURCES

To learn more about PBIS, visit the Positive Behavior Support web page of the Council for Exceptional Children (http://ericec.org/faq/behavdis.html), and the Center for Effective Collaboration and Practice (http://cecp.air.org).

How Can You Prevent Discipline Problems?

Over the past several years, researchers have focused not just on the prevalence of behavior issues and violence in U.S. schools but also on the characteristics of students who are perpetrators and victims. For example, males are most involved in incidents of school violence; bullying behavior is most common among upper-elementary students; African American students are victims of school violence slightly more often than other students; little difference is found in the rate of violence in urban, suburban, and nonmetropolitan schools; and overall student attitude is directly related to participation in violence (Furlong & Morrison, 2000; National Center for Education Statistics, 2004). Information such as this is helpful in addressing discipline and violence, but what it most clearly points out is that the starting point for intervention is prevention.

Thus, we begin by outlining ideas for preventing behavior problems (Garnes & Menlove, 2003; Hyman & Snook, 2000); these are the primary prevention strategies addressed in PBIS. In many cases, you can make the difference between having a classroom in which the stress level is high and "keeping control" is a constant struggle, and having a classroom in which student learning is supported by the environment and behavior problems are rare. You can make this difference by creating a caring instructional environment conducive to learning and using effective communication to foster a positive classroom climate.

Instructional Environments Conducive to Learning

In Chapter 5 you learned that many factors contribute to creating an instructional environment that fosters student learning. Many of these same factors also promote appropriate classroom behavior. For example, teachers need to set clear expectations in their classroom through rules that students understand and follow (Algozzine et al., 2000; U.S. Department of Education, 2004). You need only a few rules, but they should have the following characteristics:

1. be specific and based on positive wording
2. be posted and discussed with students early in the school year
3. be rehearsed while students learn them
4. be enforced consistently

Rules also should be monitored and changed as needed. Figure 12.1 contains sample rules and related student and teacher responsibilities that can be adapted for various grade levels.

Another key factor related to the instructional environment and discipline is establishing clear classroom routines. Routines should be established for beginning the school day or class period, for transitioning from one activity to another, for moving about in the classroom, and for ending the school day or class period. Students who have routines are less likely to misbehave because they can meet classroom expectations for behavior. In classes such as art, music, drama, and physical education in which students may be very active participants, routines are especially important. The Special Emphasis On . . . feature on page 437 provides additional specific tips for addressing discipline in such classes.

Effective Classroom Communication

Teachers who treat their students with respect and trust are more successful than other teachers in creating positive classroom environments in which fewer behavior problems occur (Guetzloe, 2000; Wheeler & Richey, 2005). Communication between teacher and students is integral to fostering this trust and respect. However, teacher–student communication is a complex matter, and problems often arise. For example, sometimes teachers provide students with too much information or information that is not clear, and students become confused. And sometimes teachers give one message with words but convey another message with their tone of voice or nonverbal behaviors.

Another dimension of teacher–student communication concerns language differences. When students struggle to understand English, their behaviors may, at first, appear to be challenging. For example, a first grader who is asked to complete several directions at one time may have a tantrum as a result of the frustration of not understanding. Similarly, a high school student apparently ignores a teacher's direction to put away project supplies and spend any remaining time beginning the homework assignment; when the teacher addresses this behavior, the student pushes everything off his desk. Is this a behavior problem or an example of misunderstanding and frustration? Teachers working with students who are not proficient English speakers should

FYI

An unstructured classroom environment can prompt students from inconsistent homes to act out in order to explore and understand the limits of the classroom.

FIGURE 12.1 Recommended Rules and Responsibilities for Inclusive Classrooms

Recommended Rule	Student Expectations	Teacher Responsibilities
Enter the classroom quietly.	Walk in and speak softly. Put away belongings. Take assigned seat.	Stand at the door. Wait to share conversations with students. Establish areas for putting away coats, turning in assignments, and so on. Create a permanent seating arrangement. Recognize appropriate behaviors.
Begin work on time.	Listen to or read instructions carefully. Begin to work immediately.	Prepare practice assignments in advance. Expect students to begin work promptly. Monitor student behavior. Recognize appropriate behaviors.
Stay on task.	Ignore distractions from others. Continue to work without interruptions.	Assign developmentally appropriate tasks. Check for student understanding. Provide positive and corrective feedback. Monitor student behavior and assignment completion progress. Prevent or end distracting behaviors. Recognize appropriate behaviors.
Complete work on time.	Check assignment completion requirements. Ask questions to better understand. Set goals for assignment completion.	State complete assignment information, including grading criteria. Provide appropriate models and demonstrations. Teach goal setting. Allow sufficient class time to work. Recognize appropriate behaviors.
Follow directions at all times.	Listen carefully. Ask questions for understanding. Do as all teachers request.	Gain student attention. Give clear directions for particular situations. Check for student understanding. Provide examples and/or demonstrations. Monitor student behavior. Recognize appropriate behaviors.
Listen while others speak.	Maintain a positive body posture. Look at the person speaking. Note important information. Signal for more information.	Teach listening skills. Model good listening skills. Encourage verbal elaboration. Encourage "risk-free" active participation. Recognize appropriate behaviors.
Use appropriate language.	Avoid angry and foul words. Use kind words to tell how you feel.	Teach appropriate statements for avoiding conflicts. Teach techniques for self-control. Model respect toward students and peers. Recognize appropriate behaviors.
Keep hands, feet, and objects to self.	Avoid hitting, kicking, or throwing things.	Teach safety habits and procedures. Teach techniques for self-control. Recognize appropriate behaviors.

SOURCE: From "How Do Your Classroom Rules Measure Up? Guidelines for Developing an Effective Rule Management Routine," by J. A. Rademacher, K. Callahan, and V. A. Pederson-Seelye, 1998, *Intervention in School and Clinic, 33,* pp. 284–289. Copyright © 1998 by PRO-ED, Inc. Reprinted with permission.

take care to distinguish problems that result from language differences from misbehavior. The overall quality of your communication with your students is built in numerous small ways. For example, finding time each week to speak privately with students lets them know that you value them as individuals. Asking older students sincere questions about their friends, out-of-school activities, or part-time jobs also conveys that you care. Taking the time to write positive comments on papers shows students that you appreciate their strengths and are not focusing only on their needs. Teachers who fail to take these small steps toward positive communication with students, or who publicly embarrass a student or punish a group for the behavior of a few,

Special **EMPHASIS** On ...

Discipline in Related Arts Classes

Classes such as art, music, physical education, drama, and others that go beyond the core academic curriculum often provide students with disabilities opportunities to demonstrate their unique talents. However, these classes also have a high risk for discipline problems unless principles such as those presented throughout this chapter are put into place. In addition, keep the following ideas in mind to ensure that these learning environments are designed to foster student learning:

- Carefully explain expectations for classroom behavior on the first day of school. Review these rules in subsequent classes. Ask students to explain the expectations.
- Reward students for following classroom expectations, particularly at the very beginning of the school year. Remember to always pair a reward with verbal praise.
- Be organized. Have specific places where materials and supplies are kept and specific procedures that students are to follow in getting and returning these supplies. Remember that whenever students have to wait, the likelihood of misbehavior increases.

- Related arts classes sometimes can become a bit noisy as students engage in their tasks. Have a nonverbal way of gaining student attention (for example, a series of claps that students join in repeating, or a chime), teach students to respond to it, and reward them for doing so.
- Watch your timing. One problem that can occur in related arts classes is a rush at the end of the class period to wrap up the planned activity. When students rush, behavior problems are more likely.
- Ask your special education teacher if any students have behavior intervention plans. If so, find out what your role should be in ensuring their plans are implemented. For students without plans, ask whether there are any suggestions you could use to foster positive behavior.
- Use peers to improve behavior. You might find that assigning every student a peer buddy can address minor sources of misbehavior, such as being unsure of directions. Alternatively, have peer buddies only for students who are likely to struggle in your class.

soon create a negative instructional environment that thwarts appropriate behavior and effective learning.

Effective Teaching Methods

Another critical strategy for preventing behavior problems is to provide instruction that is relevant, interesting, individualized, and active (Kern et al., 2001). Recall from Chapters 9 and 10, for example, that learning is enhanced through the use of clear and systematic instructional approaches and strategies that actively engage students in their learning. We remind you of this information because effective instruction plays a critical role in classroom behavior management. Students who are given boring or outdated materials, who are asked to complete dozens of worksheets with little instructional value, or who have few opportunities to create their own learning through projects or activities are likely to resort to misbehavior (Kohn, 2004).

Schoolwide Strategies

One additional prevention strategy goes beyond your classroom. PBIS supports the use of schoolwide prevention strategies that are developed in a systematic way (for example, Leedy, Bates, & Safran, 2004). To begin, a school identifies a leadership team to guide the PBIS development process. This team analyzes all available information concerning student discipline, obtains a commitment from all staff members for addressing identified problems, and manages the process of establishing schoolwide expectations based on input from teachers and other staff members. Once general

RESEARCH NOTE

Elementary teachers viewed self-control and cooperation as essential social skills for students, while assertion was perceived as less important (Lane, Givner, & Pierson, 2004).

expectations are set and specific applications of these expectations are created for classrooms and specific school areas, the leadership team monitors implementation and proposes revisions as needed. For example, a common schoolwide expectation is that students will be respectful of themselves, of others, and of property. In the lunchroom, the specific expectations might include these:

- Use an indoor voice at all times.
- Ask for assistance if something spills or is dropped.
- Remove all trays and dispose of all trash when you are finished eating.

What might the specific applications be for a locker room? A classroom? On the bus?

FYI

Suggested alternatives to zero-tolerance policies regarding serious behavior infractions include (a) in-school suspension; (b) school or community service in addition to academic work and tutoring; and (c) structured problem solving to specifically state what students need to do to address their behavior problems (Casella, 2003).

How Can You Promote Positive Group Behavior?

In effective classrooms, teachers and students respect each other and students are busily engaged in learning (Maag, 2004). Students attend to their work, interact with each other politely and without verbal or physical fighting, and ignore the occasional misbehavior of classmates instead of encouraging it. In many classrooms, you can promote positive behaviors such as these by using behavior management strategies that are designed specifically for the whole class (Bloom, Perlmutter, & Burrell, 1999; Nelson, 1996). For example, all students might participate in discussing classroom discipline issues, in helping each other to monitor their behavior, and in earning privileges or rewards as individuals or as members of cooperative learning groups. The following sections describe effective whole-group strategies, such as token economies and other peer-mediated approaches to behavior management.

> " A long-respected group behavior management procedure that might be effective in your classroom is a token economy. "

Token Economy

A long-respected group behavior management procedure that might be effective in your classroom is a **token economy** (Kazdin, 1977). This primary prevention strategy creates a system in which students earn "money" that they exchange for rewards. As in any economy, certain tasks have more or less value than others, and rewards have more or less cost. In one form of token economy, students receive imaginary money that they record in checkbooks. When they purchase a privilege, the cost of it is subtracted from the balance. Use the following steps to create a classroom token economy:

1. *Identify the behaviors for which students can earn credit.* You might select completing and turning in work, keeping hands to oneself, talking in a classroom voice, bringing to class all needed (and specified) learning supplies, returning homework, or exhibiting other behavior that can be clearly observed. A number of behaviors can be specified and posted in the classroom. Students can be involved in deciding what behaviors to include.

2. *Decide on the classroom "currency."* You could use points, punches on a card, poker chips or other tokens, play money, or any other system. In choosing a currency, keep in mind that you will need to award it and monitor its use. In large classrooms, efficiency in issuing and exchanging the currency can become critical.

3. *Assign a value to each target behavior.* Simple behaviors should have a lower value than more difficult behaviors. In a very simple system, you would assign the same value (for example, one point) for each target behavior on a daily basis.

4. *Decide on the privileges or rewards students can earn.* Having variety in the possible "purchases" students can make helps maintain interest in the system. For older students, the list of options might include a make-your-own-homework-assignment privilege; for younger students, tokens might be redeemed for lunch with the teacher. It is important to include on the reward list at least one item that costs the minimum amount of currency a student might earn (for example, one point). This ensures that all students have the opportunity to participate in the economy.

5. *Assign purchase "prices" to the privileges or rewards.* In general, if a reward is readily available and not limited in quantity, its purchase price should be lower. Items that are tangible (and perhaps literally cost more), limited in supply, high in perceived value, or time-consuming should have a higher cost. One teacher had access to hundreds of sets of plastic beads; the beads became quite the rage in the classroom, but they were not very costly. However, lunch alone with the teacher was a high-priced privilege. For secondary students, a low-cost reward might be computer use; a high-cost reward might be a free pass on a homework assignment.

6. *Explain the economy to students.* As you probably have discerned, you can make an economy as simple or complex as you have the creativity to develop and your students have the ability to understand. It is often beneficial to demonstrate the economy with several examples to ensure that students understand it. With younger students, this might mean showing them chips that have been earned and then "cashing them in" for a prize. For older students, the system can be described briefly and, more importantly, the accounting system can be explained.

7. *Establish a systematic way for students to exchange their currency for privileges or rewards.* In most classrooms, it is effective to allow students to use their currency once a week or once every 2 weeks on a particular day. By having a consistent time and a system for the exchange, you avoid a constant stream of student requests for privileges or rewards and the aggravation of the constant monitoring this would require.

How you establish your token economy depends partly on the age of your students (Hail, 2000; Kehle, Bray, & Theodore, 2000). For younger students, you may need to use tangible currency (for example, tokens, beads, play money). Older students are more capable of using points or other symbolic currencies. Likewise, younger students need more opportunities to exchange their currency, whereas older students are more able to save their currency to earn more expensive privileges or rewards over a longer period of time.

Teachers are tremendously creative in adapting token economies to their students' needs and their own teaching styles. For example, one teacher held an auction in her classroom every 2 weeks, offering items donated by local businesses or obtained at garage sales. Students bid on items using the currency they had earned. Another teacher wanted to encourage students to learn about real economies. She permitted students to borrow tokens from one another and to purchase items from one another using their currency. One student "sold" his designer pencils to classmates, with tokens as the currency of exchange.

To work effectively, a token economy should be carefully planned with flexibility for adjustment as the need arises. For example, you might need to change the reward list or the amount of currency required to obtain particular rewards. You should also keep in mind that token economies are best used when most or all students in a class group need support for appropriate behaviors. Thus, you might use a token economy early in the school year, again right after the holiday break, and not again until the last month of school. During other periods, less comprehensive strategies may be adequate.

What is the responsibility of general education teachers for creating systems to address minor behavior problems in their classrooms? How do such systems benefit all students, both typical learners and those with special needs?

ANALYZE
AND**REFLECT**

How would the implementation of a token economy differ when used with elementary, middle, and high school students? What are the advantages and disadvantages of this behavior management technique?

Other Peer-Mediated Approaches

Many teachers create their own whole-class approaches for supporting positive behavior and reducing negative behavior. For example, in a school near a Cherokee

DIMENSIONS
OF **DIVERSITY**

An important type of diversity to monitor in your interactions with students is gender. You need to ensure that you interact with boys and girls equitably and that you respond to their behavior needs without bias.

RESEARCH
N O T E

When Farmer, Goforth, Clemmer, and Thompson (2004) examined school discipline problems among African American middle school students in a rural community, they found that boys were referred for discipline problems far more than girls, that girls with major offenses had many school difficulties, and that aggression was a key determinant of whether boys were referred.

reservation, students have a weekly council they call Peacekeepers (Bloom et al., 1999). This classroom meeting is based on written compliments and concerns that students have placed into a specified box; the class applauds those who have received compliments and problem solves about concerns. Approaches such as this one are highly recommended as a strategy for promoting positive behavior for students from racially and culturally diverse backgrounds.

How you group students for instruction also can serve as a group behavior management technique. For example, if you have students work with a learning buddy or peer tutor, you can probably reduce the amount of misbehavior because students become more actively engaged in their learning and have the added responsibility of serving as a "teacher." Similarly, if you have students work in small instructional groups so that no one can earn a reward unless the group completes the work, students have a natural incentive for focusing on their learning activities and are less likely to misbehave. For a student like David, introduced at the beginning of this chapter, peer-mediated instructional approaches can foster appropriate social interactions because they create the need to interact positively within a small-group, structured environment.

What Are Effective Strategies for Responding to Minor Individual Behaviors?

For some students, including students with special needs, the steps you take to create a positive and productive learning environment may not be sufficient to eliminate behavior problems, nor do group behavior management strategies always work. These students may need much more specialized approaches—secondary prevention strategies—and you will find it helpful to follow the steps of the INCLUDE model outlined in Chapter 4 when planning and implementing these strategies. However, before you decide to use that approach, try a number of simpler strategies. Teachers long have relied on the principle of least intervention in addressing student behavior needs. The strategies described in the following sections include minimal interventions, such as Catch 'Em Being Good, and techniques for managing students' surface behaviors.

Use Minimum Interventions

Teachers sometimes contribute unintentionally but significantly to student misbehavior. They do this by inadvertently bringing out negative student behaviors and by responding too strongly to minor misbehaviors, actions that sometimes cause a student to misbehave more. For example, when asked directly to begin work, a student might refuse. However, when given choices regarding which assignment to do first, the student might comply. Similarly, when reprimanded for using profanity in the classroom, some students will use the reprimand as a signal to continue the language to get further attention. Ignoring occasional inappropriate language might lessen the problem.

When working with students with special needs, it is essential to stay alert to how you might be contributing to a student's behaviors, either through your own responses to the behavior or through your classroom structure and lesson format (Daniels, 1998). Four examples of minimum interventions teachers use to address minor student misbehavior follow.

CATCH 'EM BEING GOOD ● A versatile and long-recognized strategy for reducing inappropriate student behavior and increasing appropriate behavior is called Catch 'Em Being Good. When a student is behaving according to expectations, you acknowledge and reward the behavior. For example, if third-grader Jeff enters the room and immediately begins his work, you might say to him, "I like the way you went right

What individual strategies can you use in responding to individual behavior? How can teacher feedback strengthen positive behavior? How can you find out what types of rewards your students respond to?

to your desk, Jeff. That's exactly what you're supposed to do!" This comment has the effect of rewarding Jeff's behavior. At the same time, it clearly lets other students know that going directly to one's seat is a behavior they should do, too. In a middle school social studies class, a teacher might privately say to a student who is chronically late, "I noticed you were at your seat with materials ready when the bell rang. Nice going." Although the privacy of the comment eliminates its potential positive impact on other students, it has the benefit of preventing student embarrassment.

MAKE LOW-DEMAND REQUESTS FIRST ● Sprague and Horner (1990) described a successful strategy for helping students with significant intellectual disabilities who have difficulty transitioning between activities, such as transitioning from one activity to another within the classroom. With this approach, make several low-demand and unrelated requests of the student prior to expecting the targeted request. For example, if it is time for first-grader Angel to put away his crayons and join a group reading a story, first get Angel's attention by saying something like, "Angel, give me five." Follow this with asking Angel to tell you his address (or another appropriate piece of personal information that he is learning). Next ask him to shake hands. Finally, request that Angel leave his coloring and join the reading group. Each of the requests is followed by verbal praise (for example, "Right" or "Good job"). How could this approach be used with an older student?

USE GROUPING STRATEGIES ● In many schools, students with disruptive behaviors tend to seek out others who misbehave as seatmates or groupmates. A very simple strategy may significantly reduce misbehavior in such situations. When a highly disruptive student is partnered with students who are not disruptive, inappropriate behavior is likely to decrease (Tournaki & Criscitiello, 2003). This strategy should be part of any plan for addressing disruptive behavior. It also has potential for a student like Joseph, one of the students described at the beginning of the chapter. Because Joseph is extremely quiet, a teacher might decide to place him with a group of students who model positive social skills and who are unlikely to make fun of him or encourage misbehavior.

Manage Students' Surface Behaviors

Another relatively simple strategy for responding to student behaviors is managing their **surface behaviors** (Maag, 2001). Long and Newman (1971) long ago proposed that a teacher's initial response to student behavior often determines whether a problem situation develops and how intense it is. If a teacher treats a minor misbehavior as a major infraction, the result might be a strong negative student response followed by

DIMENSIONS
OF DIVERSITY

For students from diverse backgrounds, especially those with limited English proficiency, a private "catch" of good behavior can be more effective than a public one because you can better gauge the student's understanding of your message.

CONNECTIONS

Grouping strategies were introduced in Chapter 5. How to use them to promote student social interactions is described in Chapter 13.

a stronger teacher response until a serious behavior problem comes to exist. For example, if a student mutters under her breath something negative about an assignment and the teacher responds by stating in a stern voice, "What did you say?" the incident is likely to escalate. The student might reply, "Nothing"; the teacher repeats the request, and the student eventually says something that requires a negative consequence. Such interactions can be avoided if teachers are prepared to shift the focus of the interaction. Suggestions for heading off such problems include purposefully ignoring minor incidents and using humor to defuse tense classroom situations. Examples of initial response techniques are outlined in the Professional Edge on page 443.

These initial response techniques are most suited to minor misbehaviors and are unlikely to resolve serious discipline issues. Also, responding to students' surface behaviors sometimes can have the effect of increasing those behaviors. For example, if you use humor with a student and the student responds by talking back, then your humor may be increasing rather than decreasing the inappropriate behavior. If this happens, switch to another approach or work with your colleagues to examine the behavior more carefully and to devise a more individualized response to it, as described in the remainder of this chapter.

How Can Functional Behavior Assessment Help You Respond to Serious Individual Behaviors?

When students with disabilities have chronic and significant behavior problems, you are not expected to design and use tertiary prevention strategies by yourself. You will find that IDEA contains many provisions that guide how teachers and other school personnel should respond to serious student behaviors (Drasgow & Yell, 2001; Etscheidt, 2002). These procedures, addressing everything from contacting parents to guidelines related to suspension and expulsion, are summarized in Figure 12.2.

In addition, you will work with a team of colleagues to complete a more detailed analysis of the behaviors of concern and to plan, carry out, and evaluate systematically the effectiveness of a range of interventions. This legislatively mandated approach, referred to as **functional behavior assessment (FBA),** is a problem-solving process implemented for any student with a disability with chronic, serious behavior problems. Its basis is the ongoing conflict between protecting the rights of students with disabilities and respecting teachers' and school administrators' concerns about preventing school violence, maintaining safe schools, and disciplining students with disabilities (Conroy, Clark, Gable, & Fox, 1999). An FBA is a detailed and documented set of procedures designed to improve educators' understanding of exactly what a problem behavior looks like, where it occurs, when it occurs, and what function it serves for the student. It leads to ideas about how to change the behavior and a specific plan for doing so (Asmus, Vollmer, & Borrero, 2002; Sugai, Lewis-Palmer, & Hagan, 1998). In this section of the chapter you will learn why FBA is important and how the process works. Later sections of this chapter outline examples of the strategies that might be included in an FBA.

Rationale for Functional Behavior Assessment

When a student displays behaviors that are especially aggravating or seem directed at purposely causing a classroom disruption, it is tempting to respond by trying to just stop the behavior to get back to the business of educating the student. However, if you do not understand why the behavior is occurring and how to address that underlying cause, the behavior is likely to be a recurring issue. In FBA, inappropriate behaviors are

PROFESSIONAL EDGE

Strategies for Managing Students' Surface Behaviors

As an educator, you sometimes will be faced with the dilemma of how to respond to students' surface behaviors, that is, inappropriate behaviors that students display—refusal to work, sitting with head down, calling out answers. In some cases, these and other behaviors may be symptoms of serious problems that need the careful attention of a functional behavior assessment (described later in this chapter). However, a first approach can be to use simple techniques with the intent of heading off a potentially tense classroom situation. The following strategies, most suited for responding to minor misbehaviors, can help you deal with problem behaviors as soon as they occur.

1. *Planned ignoring.* If a student's behavior is not likely to harm others or to spread to others, you might decide to ignore it. For example, a student who repeatedly sighs loudly could be signaling a loss of interest; instead of responding to the sighing, recognize that the student needs to change activities soon. If you ignore inappropriate behavior, you should be sure to also give the student attention for appropriate behavior.

2. *Signal interference.* Communicate with students about surface behaviors by using nonverbal signals such as eye contact or gestures (for example, finger to lips to request silence). Reward students for responding to more direct signals (for example, "Take out your books"), and they are more likely to carry out requests promptly.

3. *Proximity control.* Sometimes, simply moving closer to a misbehaving student resolves the problem. However, if the behavior continues it may mean that your nearness is actually rewarding the student and a different technique should be used.

4. *Interest boosting.* If a student appears to be losing interest in a task or activity, refocus attention immediately by asking a specific question about the student's progress or by otherwise paying specific attention to the student's work.

5. *Tension reduction through humor.* For some minor misbehavior, your best response might be humor. For example, a student frustrated with an assignment tossed a textbook into the trash can. Instead of scolding or lecturing, the teacher exclaimed, "Two points!" and then went to assist the student with the assignment. Care must be taken, though, that the humor is not perceived as a way to embarrass or put down the student.

6. *Hurdle help.* For some students, beginning an assignment can be overwhelming. As a result, they refuse to start working or they misbehave to avoid starting. You can help them begin and avoid a behavior issue by assisting with the first example, asking questions to facilitate their thinking, prompting them to follow steps, or literally cutting an assignment into parts and giving one small part at a time to these students.

7. *Support from routine.* Creating more structure in the classroom can avert discipline problems. For example, having Rhonda begin each day by hanging up her coat, going to her seat, and coloring the picture you have placed on her desk might help her avoid being disruptive. Displaying the schedule and using clear patterns for classroom activities also help.

8. *Direct appeal to valued areas.* Students sometimes see their schoolwork as irrelevant. If you can identify a meaningful context for assigned work, students may be more likely to complete it. For example, work with decimals could be related to sports statistics.

9. *Removing seductive objects.* When students bring toys or other distracting items to school (for example, pens that light up, souvenirs from a recent trip, itching powder), teachers should usually hold them for "safekeeping." Other objects in the classroom environment also can become a focus for misbehavior and should be hidden. For example, if you have costumes at school for the play, keep them in a closet; if you set up an intriguing science experiment, cover the materials until it is time to use them.

10. *Antiseptic bouncing.* When behavior is starting to become an issue or perhaps when you see signals that a behavior problem is likely to occur (for example, a student seems to be angry as she comes into the classroom), some students benefit from the opportunity to move to a quiet corner of the classroom or to step outside the room to reduce tension. Similarly, some students benefit by being sent on a simple errand that takes them out of the classroom and provides them with a purposeful activity.

SOURCE: Adapted from "Management of Surface Behavior: A New Look at an Old Approach" (Electronic version), by J. W. Maag (2001), *Counseling and Human Development, 33*(9), pp. 1–10.

FIGURE 12.2 IDEA Provisions Related to Discipline

IDEA includes a number of provisions intended to address issues that relate to students with disabilities and their behavior. The following list is a sampling of those provisions.

- Parents must be given an opportunity to participate in all meetings with respect to the identification and evaluation, educational placement of the student, and the provision of a free appropriate public education for the student. This provision applies to behavior problems as well as academic problems.

- School personnel may consider on a case-by-case basis unique circumstances that may affect decisions about a change in placement for students who violate a school's student conduct code.

- When a student's placement is changed because of behavior, the student's education must continue so that progress can continue toward the accomplishment of IEP goals and, for some students, objectives. Access to the general curriculum must be assured, and any behavior intervention plan must continue.

- Within 10 school days of a decision to change the placement of a student because of a behavior code infraction, school officials must hold a special meeting to complete manifestation determination, that is, a decision about whether the behavior is related to the student's disability or poor implementation of the IEP. If the behavior is related to the disability, a functional behavior assessment (FBA) must be completed and a behavior intervention plan (BIP) created and implemented (detail on these topics is included later in this chapter).

- School officials can remove a student to an appropriate interim alternative educational setting or suspend the student for not more than 10 days in the same year (to the extent that such alternatives are applied to students without disabilities) if the student violates the school's student conduct code.

- Parents have to be notified of all procedural rights under IDEA, including expanded disciplinary rights, not later than the day on which the decision to take disciplinary action is made.

- School personnel may remove a student with disabilities to an interim alternative educational setting for up to 45 school days if the student has brought a weapon to school or a school function, knowingly possesses or uses illegal drugs or sells or solicits the sale of a controlled substance while at a school or a school function, or causes serious bodily injury to another person. This action may be taken whether or not the behavior is found to be related to the student's disability, and it may extend beyond 45 days if that policy is in effect for other students and if the student's behavior is not related to the disability.

- In the case of a student whose behavior impedes his or her learning or that of others, the IEP team must consider, when appropriate, strategies to address that behavior. The FBA must look across contexts to include school, home, and community.

SOURCES: Adapted from *Highlights of New Legislation to Reauthorize the Individuals with Disabilities Education Act (IDEA), PL 108–466: The Individuals with Disabilities Education Improvement Act of 2004,* by J. West, L. Pinkus, and A. Singer, January 2005, Washington, DC: Washington Partners; and *What Every Teacher Should Know about IDEA 2004,* by M. Madlawitz, 2006, Boston: Allyn & Bacon.

viewed as serving a function or purpose for the student; understanding this function helps you identify the actual problem the student is experiencing and decide how to respond to that problem instead of the symptomatic behavior (Reid & Nelson, 2002; Scott et al., 2004). Functions of behavior include avoiding something (for example, work, people) or obtaining something (for example, attention, help). Put simply, this conceptualization of student behaviors suggests that before responding you should ask, "Why is the student doing this?" Table 12.1 describes in more detail some common functions of student behaviors.

The following example might help to clarify the idea of identifying the function of behaviors. Daniel is in the sixth grade. When the sixth-grade teaching team meets to discuss student problems, Mr. Adams expresses concern that Daniel often swears in class. Ms. Jefferson adds that he picks fights with other students several times each week. Dr. Hogue agrees that Daniel is having problems and recounts a recent incident in which Daniel was sent to the office. As the teachers talk, they begin to look past Daniel's specific behaviors and focus instead on the function the behavior is serving.

TABLE 12.1 Possible Functions of Student Behaviors

Function	Goal	Example of Behavior
Power/control	Control an event or a situation	Acts to stay in the situation and keep control: "You can't make me!"
Protection/escape	Avoid a task or activity; escape a consequence; stop or leave a situation	Has a tantrum at the start of every math lesson; skips social studies class
Attention	Become the center of attention; focus attention on self	Puts self in the forefront of a situation or distinguishes self from others, for example, burps loudly during class instruction
Acceptance/affiliation	Become wanted or chosen by others for mutual benefit	Hangs out with troublemakers; joins a clique or gang
Self-expression	Express feelings, needs, or preoccupations; demonstrate knowledge or skill	Produces drawings, for example, of aerial bombings, body parts, occult symbols
Gratification	Feel good; have a pleasurable experience; reward oneself	Acts to get or maintain a self-determined reward, for example, hoards an object; indulges in self-gratifying behavior at others' expense
Justice/revenge	Settle a score; get or give restitution, apology, or punishment	Destroys another's work; meets after school to fight; commits an act of vandalism

SOURCE: Adapted from "Behavioral Intent: Instructional Content for Students with Behavior Disorders," by R. S. Neel and K. K. Cessna, 1993, in Colorado Department of Education Special Education Services Unit, *Instructionally Differentiated Programming: A Needs-Based Approach for Students with Behavior Disorders,* Denver: Author. Used by permission.

They realize that in one class, Daniel was disruptive when a difficult assignment was being given; in another, the problem was occurring as quizzes were being returned; and in the third, the incident happened immediately prior to Daniel's turn to give an oral book report. The teachers agree that Daniel's intent has been to escape situations in which he fears he might fail.

Once you identify the function of a problem behavior, you can assist the student in changing the behavior. In Daniel's case, it would be easy for the teachers to decide on a reward system to get Daniel to swear less in Mr. Adams's class. However, this has more to do with the teachers' need to have well-mannered students than it does with Daniel's need to avoid the possibility of failing. An alternative approach would be to permit Daniel to receive his quizzes before the start of class, or perhaps to participate in the after-school homework club that includes a group that studies for quizzes. Another intervention strategy might be to permit Daniel to give oral reports to one peer or to audiotape them beforehand. The question of intervening to address Daniel's behavior has shifted from "How can we get Daniel to be less disruptive in the classroom?" to "How can we help Daniel use more appropriate strategies to avoid situations in which he fears he will fail?"

This approach to understanding student behavior is more complex than looking at the surface behavior the student displays and trying to stop it; it requires looking for patterns in a student's behavior and describing them clearly in concrete terms (Dieterich, Villani, & Bennett, 2003; Shippen, Simpson, & Crites, 2003). It takes more time and effort, but it greatly increases the likelihood that you and your colleagues will be able to design an effective intervention to assist the student. In addition, you should keep in mind that although most students involved in functional assessment and the development of a behavior plan are those with high-incidence disabilities, this method of addressing behavior was first used with individuals with significant intellectual disabilities, primarily for appropriate social and communication behavior. It certainly can also be appropriately used to help students with those disabilities succeed in your classroom. The Case in Practice on page 446 explores using functional assessment for such students.

ANALYZE AND REFLECT

How would understanding the function of a student's behavior influence your response to it? How does this approach differ from traditional responses to student behavior? How could you use the notion of behavior functions to understand how students can find and press teachers' "hot buttons"?

CASE IN PRACTICE

Supporting a Student with Autism Using Functional Behavior Assessment

Mary Elizabeth is a student with autism who just moved to the area. At her previous school, she spent most of her day in the general education classroom with the support of an instructional assistant and a special educator, and she was nearly at grade level in math and just a year or so behind in reading.

In her first week at John Glenn Elementary School, however, she repeatedly tried to bite and hit staff and students, had several noisy tantrums, and refused to attempt any academic tasks. On two different days, it took two adults to remove Mary Elizabeth from the general education classroom to the resource room. Ms. Lieberman, the third-grade teacher, was astonished at this disastrous beginning, especially because she had carefully prepared her other students for their new classmate and had done some quick read-

ing about what to expect of a student with autism.

Within the week, she was at her wits' end and even more distraught when the instructional assistant quit. Mr. Poulos, the school psychologist, quickly called together the team, including Ms. Lieberman and himself as well as special education teacher Ms. Daugherty, principal Dr. Cook, and Mary Elizabeth's parents, Mr. and Mrs. O'Toole. Mary Elizabeth refused to be part of the meetings, but Ms. Daugherty spoke with her individually about the problems and about ideas to address them.

The first meeting included a brief review of the problems being encountered and a discussion of simple factors that might help to address them, including temporarily shortening the school day. Then the group looked at the functions of Mary Elizabeth's behavior, and they began to discuss how

they could provide positive behavior supports to help her through the difficult transition to her new school.

REFLECTIONS

What function do you think the team decided was relevant for Mary Elizabeth? What was she trying to communicate? What type of data might the team decide to gather to make the best decisions about a behavior intervention plan? What ideas might a review of what you have read about students with autism produce for creating a behavior intervention plan based on student strengths and emphasizing positive supports? If you were Ms. Lieberman, what types of assistance would you request during the transition time as the behavior plan was implemented? What expectations would you have for all the other people at this meeting to participate in implementing an intervention?

The following sections present in more detail the process of completing FBAs. The procedure includes seven specific steps (Lee & Jamison, 2003; Ryan, Halsey, & Matthews, 2003; Shippen et al., 2003):

1. verifying the seriousness of the problem
2. defining the problem behavior in concrete terms
3. collecting data to better understand the behavior
4. analyzing the data and forming hypotheses about function
5. developing a behavior intervention plan (BIP)
6. implementing the plan and gathering data on its impact on the behavior
7. monitoring intervention effectiveness and proceeding to appropriate next actions

WWW RESOURCES
At the Wrightslaw website, on the Behavior Problems and Discipline page (http://www.wrightslaw.com/info/discipl.index.htm), you will find information related to the legal perspective on discipline, particularly for students with disabilities.

Verifying the Seriousness of the Problem

As we have noted in this chapter, many classroom behavior problems can be eliminated or significantly reduced through the use of supportive classroom practices, group behavior management techniques, and low-key individual interventions. A first step in functional assessment is to determine whether these standard strategies have already been implemented. For example, if you have a student who is bullying others, a topic addressed in the Professional Edge below, your team might ask you to complete a questionnaire about the tactics you have used to address the student's behavior, and a psychologist, special education teacher, or other educator may observe and interview the student. In cases of acting-out behavior, other students may be observed. The latter approach is used to determine whether the student's behavior is typical or significantly different from that of classmates.

Defining the Problem Behavior

The second step of functional behavior assessment is to ensure that the behaviors of concern are defined and described in a specific way. Teachers working with students with serious behavior problems often use a type of verbal shorthand to describe their concerns. They may refer to a student as "disruptive," or they may describe the student as being "always off task." They may comment that the student is "often up and wandering around the classroom" or express concern that the student is "sullen and unresponsive." Although these general statements may have specific meaning to the teachers making them, they are too vague and tend to be too subjective to be useful in addressing the student's behaviors. The alternative is to describe behaviors in specific and

PROFESSIONAL EDGE

Bullying: The Problems and Some Interventions

Bullying is a serious problem. Approximately 30 percent of students report being a bully, being bullied, or both (Nansel et al., 2001). As a professional educator, you should be aware of what types of bullying occur, who is likely to be bullied, and what you can do to help.

What Is Bullying?

Bullies generally consider themselves bigger, stronger, more popular, or in some other way more powerful than the victim. Bullying can take several forms:

- physical violence
- verbal taunts, name-calling, put-downs
- threats and intimidation
- extortion or stealing money or possessions

Students who are bullied are often perceived as "different" from most students. These are some of the reasons students may be bullied:

- appearance (for example, overweight, clothing, presence of a disability)
- intellect (too smart or not smart enough)
- racial or ethnic heritage
- socioeconomic background
- cultural or religious background
- sexual orientation

What Can Educators and Schools Do?

Teachers and other school professionals can help all students feel safe using strategies such as these:

- Ensure that students understand what bullying means, what behaviors it includes, and how it makes people feel.
- Develop and post class rules against bullying (for example, "Treat others as you would like to be treated").
- Use appropriate consequences for bullying (for example, student pays for damaged belongings, apologize).
- Encourage students to discuss bullying and positive ways to interact with others.
- Take immediate action when bullying is witnessed or reported.
- Administer a bullying survey to students.
- Praise prosocial behavior and helpful student behavior.
- Pay close attention for bullying during recess and other unstructured times.
- Take student reports of bullying seriously.
- Involve parents in terms of sharing information and enlisting their assistance.
- Interview bullies, victims, and witnesses separately.

SOURCE: Adapted from "Bullying: What's New and What to Do" (Electronic version), by J. Rosiak, (2004), *Be Safe & Sound, 1*(4), pp. 3–6.

concrete terms. It is sometimes helpful to jot down the vague descriptions of behavior and then review them, focusing on the specific incidents and details characterizing the behaviors: "Yesterday during the first 30 minutes of language arts, Michael left his desk six times"; "When I ask Chenille a direct question, she looks away and does not answer"; "Juan talks out 3–5 times each class period—he does not raise his hand." If several behaviors are identified, it often is most helpful to prioritize the one that should be addressed first instead of trying to design interventions for several behaviors at one time.

Collecting Data to Better Understand the Behavior

The third step in FBA requires systematically gathering information about a behavior's occurrence and the situation in which it occurs. By doing this, team members are able to judge more accurately whether the behavior follows a particular pattern, for example, occurring during certain types of activities or at certain times of the day. Patterns assist team members in understanding the function and the seriousness of the behavior in relation to teachers' classroom expectations. At the same time, by measuring the behavior when it becomes a concern and continuing to do so after a plan for addressing it is implemented, team members can decide whether their efforts to change the behavior have been successful. Sometimes you may be able to observe and record student behavior yourself. However, if this is not feasible, a school psychologist, a special education teacher, an administrator, a paraprofessional, or another professional may help to complete this task.

ANECDOTAL RECORDING ● One useful strategy for measuring student behavior is to record specific incidents, including what happened immediately before the behavior (antecedents) and what happened as a result of the behavior (consequences). This approach is called an *antecedents-behaviors-consequences (ABC) analysis*. For example, whenever Ms. Carlisle directs the class to form cooperative groups (antecedent), Carlos gets up from his seat and heads for the pencil sharpener (behavior). Ms. Carlisle then tells Carlos to join his group (consequence). By observing Carlos and keeping an ongoing ABC log of Carlos's behaviors in the classroom, Ms. Carlisle has found out that whenever the class is transitioning from one activity to another, Carlos is likely to be off task. A sample ABC analysis is shown in Figure 12.3. Note that an ABC analysis should be completed for behaviors that occur only occasionally (for example, throw-

How might a behavior chart help you collaborate with others to develop a plan for responding to a student's behavior? What other methods of recording behavior might you use to determine whether your behavior management plan is working?

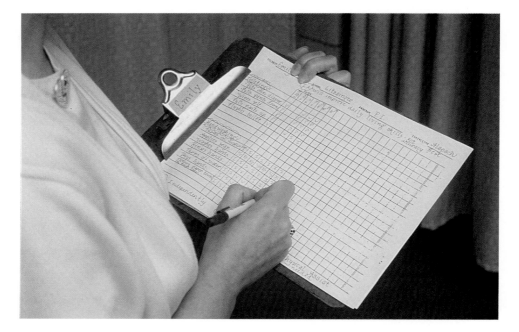

FIGURE 12.3 Sample ABC Analysis

Student Name ___Denton R.___ Date ___2/26___

Location ___Science—Mr. B___ Observer ___Mr. D___

Start Time ___1:02___ Stop Time ___1:15___

Antecedents	Behaviors	Consequences
1:03 Students get out books and open to begin class.	Denton pulls out his cap and puts it on.	Students around D. start laughing and saying, "Hey."
1:05 Teacher notices D. and tells him to remove cap.	D. stands, slowly removes cap, and bows.	Students applaud.
1:14 Teacher asks D. a question.	D. says, "Man, I don't know."	Another student says, "Yeah, you're stupid." Others laugh.

ing a chair, having a tantrum); if you have a student who engages in this type of behavior, a special education teacher, counselor, or psychologist might interview you to complete the ABC analysis.

EVENT RECORDING ● One straightforward way to measure a behavior is to count how many times the behavior occurs in a given period of time. This approach, called *event recording*, is appropriate when the behavior is discrete, that is, when it has a clear starting and stopping point. For example, it might be appropriate to use event recording to count the number of times John is late to class during a week or the number of times David blurts out an answer during a 30-minute large-group social studies lesson. Conversely, event recording probably would not be helpful in measuring Jane's tantrum or Jesse's delay in starting his assignment because these behaviors have more to do with how long they last than with the number of times they occur.

Event recording is relatively easy. You could keep a tally on an index card taped to your desk or plan book or kept as a bookmark in one of your textbooks. The key to event recording is to have an accurate total of the number of times a behavior occurred.

> One straightforward way to measure a behavior is to count how many times the behavior occurs in a given period of time.

PERMANENT PRODUCT RECORDING ● If your concern about student behavior relates to academics, it may be simplest to keep samples of work as a means of measuring behavior, a strategy called *permanent product recording*. For example, if students in a U.S. history class regularly have to respond to 10 discussion questions during a single class session, you might keep Sam's completed work to document the percentage of questions he is attempting or the percentage of his responses that are correct.

DURATION RECORDING ● For some behaviors, your concern is the length of time the behavior lasts. The strategy of *duration recording* might apply to a young student who cries each morning at the start of the school day, a middle school student who takes an extraordinary amount of time to locate all her learning materials, or a high school student who delays beginning assignments. Often, accurately recording duration requires that you have a stopwatch and are able to notice the moment the behavior begins and the moment it ends. However, duration recording also can measure how long students take to complete assignments if you ask students to write on their papers the times when they began and finished their work.

ANALYZE AND **REFLECT**

After recording the duration of a student's behavior, what is the next step you would take to decrease it? What factors should you consider when choosing a behavior intervention to implement in your classroom?

INTERVAL RECORDING ● Sometimes you have concerns about a student's behavior, but none of the systems just described offer a way to record the occurrence of the behavior. For example, you might be concerned about how well a student is staying on task during an independent assignment or the extent to which a student plays with others during free-choice time. In these cases, *interval recording* may be the preferred measuring strategy. To use this approach, you specify a length of time for the observation and then divide the time into smaller intervals. For example, you might observe a 10-minute work or play period divided into 30-second intervals. As you observe the student throughout each 30-second interval, you indicate whether the behavior has been present for that entire interval by marking + or – on the recording form.

TIME SAMPLING ● Time sampling uses a similar strategy but, whereas interval recording requires that you observe a student continually, time sampling, a similar strategy, involves only periodic observations of the student. For example, if you wanted to observe whether Patricia interacted with classmates during a 20-minute group assignment, you could divide the time period into ten 2-minute observations. At the end of each 2-minute interval, you would glance at that moment to see whether Patricia was interacting and record your observation accordingly. Time sampling is less demanding than interval recording because you observe only momentarily instead of continuously, but it does include the risk that the behaviors you observe at each sampling are not typical of what has occurred until that moment. This system also can be expedient when your goal is to observe several students at one time: By glancing at three different students and immediately recording the behavior of each one, you can look at the behavior patterns of each student during a single observational period. Teachers who use time sampling often need a signal to alert them to observe and record the behavior. For example, they might wear an earphone that enables them to hear a prerecorded tone after each interval.

OTHER DATA SOURCES ● A functional behavior assessment rarely consists of just classroom observations. Most likely, team members will ask questions about your perceptions of how the behavior has developed or changed and about your attempts to contact the parents and otherwise address the behavior. Family members may be interviewed, and an analysis of the structure, length, and characteristics of the student's entire school day may be considered, as may the physical classroom environment and classroom climate. The student also is likely to be interviewed; the student's perspective can add important information to other data gathered (Kinch, Lewis-Palmer, Hagan-Burke,

ANALYZE AND REFLECT

Which strategy—interval recording or time sampling—would be more appropriate for observing and recording the behavior of a seventh-grade student who is withdrawn and refuses to speak when he is asked to participate during instruction? Why?

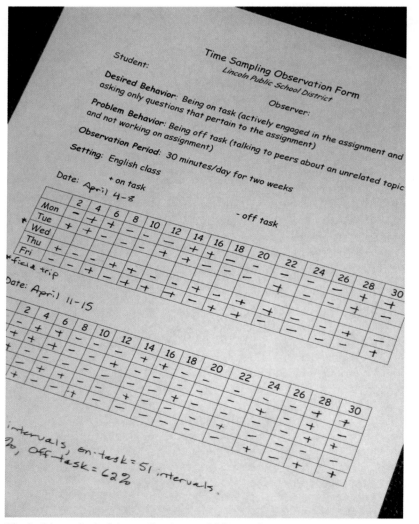

Why is this method of data collection useful for teachers?

& Sugai, 2001). Any factor that might contribute to the behavior may be explored.

Professionals sometimes say that such precise behavior measurement and exhaustive consideration of the causes of the behavior are not realistic. It is true that you would not routinely have the time to use these strategies. However, when you are faced with a student whose behavior is particularly persistent and puzzling, the time you and the team take to analyze it systematically can give you a clearer picture of how to address the problem and effectively alleviate it (Newcomer & Lewis, 2004). Further, by using generic, multipurpose recording forms and sharing the observation and interviewing tasks with other professionals and paraprofessionals, you may find that this step in a functional assessment is not as burdensome as you imagine.

> " When you are faced with a student whose behavior is particularly persistent and puzzling, the time you and the team take to analyze it systematically can give you a clearer picture of how to address the problem and effectively alleviate it. "

Analyzing the Data and Forming Hypotheses

At the fourth step in FBA, all the pieces come together. For example, Kyle's middle school teachers had expressed concern about his frequent loud and profane outbursts during class. Five 20-minute observation sessions revealed that Kyle spoke loudly using profanity an average of 2.2 times per session (event recording) during large-group instruction (classroom environment). An ABC analysis illustrated that the talking out occurred when the teacher asked the whole class group to read a paragraph in the books, review a chart or graph, or complete some other reading-related task (anecdotal recording). The other students looked at and laughed at Kyle after the talk-outs. The teacher nearly always corrected Kyle, and in just over half the instances he challenged the teacher's reprimand, saying for example, "I did not," or "You're picking on me." In an interview, Kyle said that he got called on in class only when he did not know an answer, and he said he knew more than teachers gave him credit for.

In analyzing these data, Kyle's teacher and other team members hypothesized that his talking out was serving two functions: First, it was a means of avoiding being called on when the question required a reading task, an area of significant academic difficulty for Kyle. Second, it was a means of getting attention from peers and the teacher.

This step in the process is something like detective work. With the data collected, team members try to identify patterns in the behavior, purposes it might serve for the student, and factors that might make the behavior better or worse. In Kyle's case, the teachers recognized that instead of responding to the profanity and outbursts, they needed to address his fear and his need for positive attention.

ANALYZE AND **REFLECT**

What information can a functional behavior assessment provide for teachers? How can this information be used to increase the likelihood of a student's success in school? Whose responsibility is it to complete a functional behavior assessment and behavior intervention plan?

Developing a Behavior Intervention Plan

Once hypotheses have been generated, team members can develop a **behavior intervention plan (BIP)** based on them. This fifth step in functional behavior assessment may include any number of interventions. For example, the BIP might include modifying the physical or instructional arrangement of the classroom (seating Kyle nearer to where the teacher usually stands, or using more cooperative groups); changing antecedents (teacher permitting students to ask each other for help while reading the material being discussed); altering consequences (teacher ignoring at least some occurrences of the talking out); teaching alternative behaviors to the student (having Kyle record his own behaviors and reward himself for raising his hand); or modifying curricular materials (using fewer questions for which reading is required) (Kauffman, Mostert, Trent, & Hallahan, 2002; Wheeler & Richey, 2005).

Different types of rewards and consequences that you might incorporate into a BIP are presented later in this chapter. Figure 12.4 contains an example of a behavior intervention plan.

DIMENSIONS OF **DIVERSITY**

Punishments vary from culture to culture. Your students may come from families that use punishments such as shame, ostracism, or physical punishment. Your knowledge of how students are punished at home should help you understand how they respond to punishment in school.

FIGURE 12.4 Sample Behavior Intervention Plan

Student: Tom Clark

Date Developed: 9/30/05

Grade: 7

School: Middle School

Date Implemented: 10/3/05

Baseline Data Results:
Tom destroyed assignments on 5 out of 5 observation days.

Hypothesis Statement:
Tom's behavior is related to frustration brought on by a discrepancy between his skill level and the skill level necessary to complete the assignments. Much of Tom's destructive behavior is related to his isolated seating from his peers in the classroom. Tom feels singled out because he sits at a table by himself.

Type of Intervention Plan: Educational __X__   Behavioral _____

Person(s) Responsible for Implementing Plan: Science teacher

DESCRIPTION OF THE BEHAVIOR

BEHAVIOR	BEHAVIOR DEFINED
Tom destroys his written assignments.	Tom wads up and tears up his assignment papers.

INTERVENTION GOAL:
To decrease the number of occurrences when Tom destroys his assignments to 0 per week

INTERVENTION PLAN:

1. Seat Tom with a peer who has good on-task behavior. The peer will review directions with Tom and assist him in getting started with assignments.

2. Provide Tom a daily monitoring assignment checklist to improve the following areas of difficulty:

Assignment Checklist

_____ I understood teacher directions.

_____ I answered all questions.

_____ I need more time.

_____ I asked for help when I needed it.

_____ I understood the assignment.

_____ I turned in my assignment.

3. Provide Tom with academic modifications, including these:
   a. Extend time to complete and turn in assignments if needed.
   b. Provide outlines, study guides, and graphic organizers with textbook assignments to assist Tom in identifying important information.
   c. Provide Tom with a word/definition list to use when completing worksheet assignments.
   d. Provide peer assistance with some assignments.
   e. Provide additional instructional modifications as needed.

4. Provide directions to Tom in a variety of ways (verbal, written, through direct instruction, and through peer assistance).

5. Reinforce Tom's academic productivity and assignment completion.

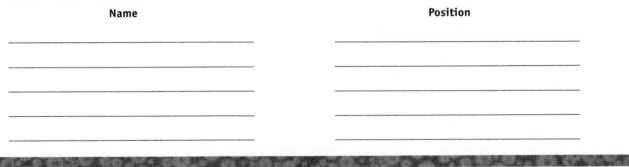

WHEN AND WHERE THE PLAN WILL BE IMPLEMENTED:

The plan will be implemented in Tom's science class for 3 consecutive weeks beginning 10/3/05.

INTERVENTION DATA COLLECTION SUMMARY:

Week 1.   Decrease in behavior to 3 occurrences.

Week 2.   Decrease in behavior to 2 occurrences.

Week 3.   Decrease in behavior to 1 occurrence.

FOLLOW-UP AND REVIEW DATE(S):

Follow-up and review meeting 10/24/05

COMMENTS:

The intervention plan is successful with Tom.

The team agreed to write the interventions outlined in this plan in Tom's IEP.

The team will meet in 3 weeks for review.

TEAM MEETING PARTICIPANTS:

Name	Position
_____	_____
_____	_____
_____	_____
_____	_____
_____	_____

SOURCE: From "Functional Assessment: A Systematic Process for Assessment and Intervention in General and Special Education Classrooms," by M. E. McConnell, P. B. Hilvitz, and C. J. Cox, 1998, *Intervention in School and Clinic, 34*(1), pp. 10–20. Copyright © 1998 by PRO-ED, Inc. Reprinted with permission.

Implementing the Plan

Once the BIP is developed, you and the team, often including the student, reach the sixth step in functional behavior assessment: the task of implementing your plan. Having a clear plan for implementation is important because the key to this approach is a systematic response to the behavior. This phase requires several actions: Teachers and other professionals implementing a BIP should monitor the consistency with which they implement the plan. In addition, if peers or family members have implementation responsibilities, every effort should be made to ensure that their roles are reasonable, that they understand and can carry out their parts of the plan, and that any concerns they may have are addressed (Peck-Peterson, Derby, Berg, & Horner, 2002). Throughout implementation, data on the BIP's impact should be gathered so that monitoring, described next, is facilitated.

Monitoring the Plan's Effectiveness

You began the process of functional behavior assessment gathering information about the student's behavior prior to thinking about how to respond to it. If you continue to keep behavior records as you implement the BIP, you can ascertain whether the plan is working (for example, Johnston & O'Neill, 2001). To proceed with the seventh step, monitoring the plan, you and the team use the same recording strategies presented in the third step of FBA, and you can provide data-recording forms to your peers or others who were not initially involved in the process. Remember that behavior does not change rapidly; the team should be committed to following the plan for a specified period of time—perhaps 2 or 3 weeks or even more—before deciding whether it is effective.

As you monitor the plan, you may observe any of a number of effects occurring. First, the inappropriate behavior may cease completely, or the desired behavior may be displayed consistently. If this happens, you may decide to gradually withdraw the plan. For example, if you are intervening to eliminate a student's profane language in class and no profane language is occurring, you can gradually increase the length of time without profanity required to earn a reward, and then move to using just verbal praise. This is called fading out a reward system.

Second, the plan you are implementing may have value but may need modification. Perhaps it requires too much time to implement, or the rewards need adjustment. Such alterations are not unusual; simply modify the plan and continue to monitor its effectiveness. For example, if you created a point system for your sophomore keyboarding student that includes earning points for being seated when the bell rings, points for turning homework in at the beginning of class, and points for having an assignment notebook and pen in class, you might discover that the system is too difficult to monitor. You might then eliminate the points for everything except homework for a student who chronically fails to come to class on time with assignments in hand.

Third, the plan may not be working. As you track the number and duration of tantrums for one of your students, you might learn that they are occurring more often and lasting longer. If a situation like this occurs, the team needs to analyze what is happening and create an alternative plan, following again the steps that have been outlined. If other options do not seem appropriate, a more significant change, such as a change in the student's placement, sometimes may need to be considered.

> **It is imperative that you work closely with parents to resolve student behavior problems.**

Finally, it is imperative that you work closely with parents to resolve student behavior problems. Parents sometimes can clarify reasons why a student suddenly is behaving in a particular way (for example, a death in the family, a divorce, a weekend trip, a cultural response to a school activity). In addition, they can reinforce school messages at home, and they can help provide rewards at home earned by appropriate behavior during the school day. Parents are likely to be members of the team completing the functional assessment and behavior intervention plan, and their contributions cannot be emphasized enough. You increase options for responding to student behavior by creating partnerships with parents, even when you may disagree with their perceptions, a topic addressed in the Working Together feature on page 455.

WORKING **TOGETHER**

When Differences of Opinion Occur

Few people would disagree that collaboration is essential for working with students with disabilities, and most professionals enjoy their interactions with colleagues and parents. However, collaboration can be challenging when differences of opinion occur. Think about dilemmas such as the one described here. Consider role-playing this interaction with your classmates to practice using the suggestions offered.

    Ms. Bonnet requests a meeting with you. She is quite upset, accusing you of treating her daughter Taylor unfairly. She says that Taylor has told her that other students are misbehaving more than she is but that you discipline only her. Ms. Bonnet wants you to stop.

- It is tempting in this type of interaction to become defensive, explaining that you are fair and that Taylor is not telling the whole story. Instead, first be sure that Ms. Bonnet has relayed her story. When she finishes speaking, paraphrase what she has said, succinctly summarizing the information without making any judgments. For example: "Taylor has told you that other students misbehave but that I discipline only her." Notice that you are not necessarily agreeing with this perspective.

- Try asking Ms. Bonnet for a specific example of what Taylor has described. That may help you to understand more about the situation.

- If Taylor is not present, it probably would be best to leave this matter unresolved and to arrange a meeting that includes her. That way, the situation can be more fully explored.

- As you discuss the situation with Taylor and her mother, ask Taylor what she thinks would make things fairer. You do not necessarily have to agree with her perspective, but it is important to know what she thinks should occur.

- Develop a strategy to address Taylor's concerns and try it for a week. This might include touching base momentarily with Taylor each day or keeping a record of your interactions with her. Even if you believe that Taylor's accusations are wildly inaccurate, trying to verbally reinforce her appropriate behavior can help to ease the tension.

- Consider the possibility that Taylor may be accurate in her perception. Are you inadvertently noticing because her voice tends to be louder than those of other students? Could you be responding to a cultural difference? Did Taylor do something earlier in the school year that has made you overly aware of her behavior? Are you especially watchful of her because you know that she has a behavior intervention plan?

Situations that involve conflict can be stressful, but with careful communication and a willingness to consider others' opinions, you can successfully address them.

What Are Effective Strategies for Responding to Serious Individual Behaviors?

The functional behavior assessment procedure provides educators with clear guidelines for assisting students whose behavior problems are significant. The strategies that are part of that process might include some of the simple approaches that you read about earlier in this chapter, but they also are likely to include interventions that are more long-term and systematic to increase preferred behaviors and decrease undesirable behaviors. The principles for interventions are the same whether you use simple strategies or more intensive interventions, but the latter are usually carried out across time in a consistent and well-documented manner. They also may involve the use of contracts in which the expectations for behavior are specified and rewards and consequences clearly spelled out. Such interventions covered in the following sections include increasing desirable behaviors, decreasing undesirable behaviors, and using behavior contracts.

Increasing Desirable Behaviors

All students, even the most challenging, have some appropriate behaviors you would like to increase. The primary strategy for increasing appropriate behavior is called *reinforcement.* Reinforcement is any response or consequence that increases a behavior (Jones & Jones, 2004; Safran & Oswald, 2003). It is important for you to keep in mind that reinforcement can increase negative as well as positive behaviors. For example, when a teacher puts a sticker on a student's chart because the student completed his assignment without calling out for unneeded help, the student is more likely in the future to continue to work independently. When a teacher says to a student who is wandering around the classroom, "Sit down!" the student is more likely in the future to be out of her seat again. In both instances, reinforcement was applied. In the first case, it rewarded a desirable behavior; in the second, it rewarded an undesirable behavior.

POSITIVE AND NEGATIVE REINFORCEMENT ● Anytime you respond to a behavior with a consequence that makes it more likely for the behavior to occur again, you are using **positive reinforcement** (Kauffman et al., 2002). When you reward a student for appropriate behavior and that behavior increases, positive reinforcement has occurred. For instance, if you tell a student that she may use the classroom computer after she completes five math problems and she completes all the problems, you are positively reinforcing math-problem completion through computer rewards.

> Although learning and behaving appropriately because of internal motivation rather than for external rewards certainly are preferable, some students who struggle to learn and behave as expected are simply not able or likely to do so.

Negative reinforcement operates somewhat differently. Suppose you set up a system with your ninth-grade English students whereby they must have their homework signed each night by their parents until they have brought it back to school on time at least 9 out of 10 times. Because students see having homework signed by parents as an undesirable consequence, they will increase their promptness in turning in homework to avoid the consequence. Any increase in behavior to avoid a consequence is the result of **negative reinforcement** (Wheeler & Richey, 2005). Although negative reinforcement can be effective, positive reinforcement should usually be tried first because having students work toward a positive outcome is preferable to having them work under the threat, or perception of a threat, of a negative consequence.

Some professionals object to using positive reinforcement with students because they fear it teaches students that they are entitled to a payoff for appropriate behavior. They contend that students should complete their schoolwork and behave appropriately simply because these are the right things to do. This discussion is often addressed as one of external versus internal motivation (for example, Kohn, 2003). Although learning and behaving appropriately because of internal motivation rather than for external rewards certainly are preferable, some students who struggle to learn and behave as expected are simply not able or likely to do so. These students may behave and respond appropriately in school because of internal motivation only when they are extremely interested in a subject or topic, or when they experience repeated success over an extended period of time. Additional strategies, including reinforcement, provide the support they need to succeed in their learning.

TYPES OF REINFORCERS ● For positive reinforcement to be successful for students with special needs, keep in mind that many different types of reinforcers can be used. Four types are described in the following list.

1. *Social reinforcers* are various types of positive interactions that a teacher, parent, or peer can give a student for appropriate behavior and to increase the behavior. These reinforcers might include a positive phone call home to parents, a pat on the back or a hug, verbal praise, or selection as citizen of the month. Social reinforcers, especially clear and specific verbal praise, always should be tried before other positive reinforcers because they are the most natural type of reward in a school environment. If you find

FYI

Your colleagues and the students you teach often can give you a wealth of ideas for rewards that will be effective. Keep in mind that simple, inexpensive systems of rewards are more likely to be feasible than ones requiring extensive record keeping or having a high cost.

it necessary to employ other types of rewards, you should use them only in conjunction with social reinforcers because your long-term goal should always be to have students respond to rewards that occur naturally in their classroom environment.

2. *Activity reinforcers* involve activities such as playing games, having extra recess, helping a teacher in another class, and participating in other coveted individual or group pastimes. Generally, activities that directly relate to a student's educational goals (for example, practicing math skills on the computer) are preferable to those that are solely recreational (for example, playing a noneducational computer game).

3. *Tangible reinforcers* are prizes or other objects that students can earn as symbols of achievement and that students want to obtain. A student who is earning baseball cards for completing assignments is receiving a tangible reinforcer. Stickers on papers is another example of this type of reinforcer. Tangible rewards can often be naturally integrated into classroom activities. For example, a student can earn the rocket pieces and household chemicals needed to create a highly interesting science experiment not offered to other students. However, make sure that the amount of the tangible reinforcer is appropriate for the amount of positive behavior required. Students earning the science materials just mentioned are expected to display appropriate behaviors over a lengthy period of time, not just for an afternoon. If the tangible reinforcer is a scented sticker, perhaps an afternoon of appropriate behavior is the right amount for the reward being given.

4. *Primary reinforcers* are food or other items related to human needs that a student finds rewarding. They are much more basic than secondary reinforcers, which comprise the three types just described—social reinforcers, activity reinforcers, and tangible reinforcers. Primary reinforcers used in schools often are edible and might include a piece of candy, a soft drink, or a piece of fruit.

Although you might occasionally employ primary reinforcers as a special treat, generally they should be used only if a student is incapable of understanding more natural rewards, or if other types of rewards are not effective. This is important for two reasons. First, the potential negative impact of food reinforcers on student health is a concern. Second, food reinforcers are not a natural part of the school learning process. In school, students are expected to work to learn; to prepare for adulthood; or, more immediately for some, to earn teacher praise or a grade. Candy is not a routine part of the learning environment. If you plan to use primary reinforcers such as food, check with a school administrator to find out about local policies governing their use. Also check with parents, both for permission and about possible student food allergies. You also should keep in mind nutritional issues.

EFFECTIVE USE OF POSITIVE REINFORCERS ●

In addition to understanding that there are different types of positive reinforcers, you need to know some principles for using them effectively (Walker, Shea, & Bauer, 2003). Three principles include the following:

1. *Make sure that the positive reinforcers are clear and specific and that students understand the relationship between their behavior and rewards.* The rewards students earn need to be specific. For example, rewarding with time on the computer is not precise enough. If it is a reward, the amount of computer time for the specific behavior displayed should be clarified. Clarity and specificity are especially important when you use verbal praise. Saying to a student, "Good job!" is far less effective than saying, "Good job! You asked three other students for help before you asked me." The former praise is vague; the latter praise explicitly states what behavior is being rewarded.

2. *Vary how much and how often you reward students.* If a student displays very little positive behavior, you may reward it heavily at first just to increase it. As the student learns to use the appropriate behavior more readily, you should decrease the amount and

ANALYZE
AND **REFLECT**

Which types of reinforcers might be most appropriate for each of the students described at the beginning of this chapter? How did you make these decisions?

intensity of the reward. For example, if at first you were rewarding a student with free-choice computer time for every two assignments completed, you might gradually change the reward so that the student must complete four assignments—and get at least 90 percent on each—to use the computer to review vocabulary. Another way to vary rewards is to enlist parent assistance. For example, Donna's mother might agree to provide a privilege when the teacher sends a note home indicating that Donna completed her independent work within a specified time. The only caution in asking parents for their help is the uncertainty of knowing for sure whether the parents are providing the reward agreed upon and whether they are withholding it when their child has not behaved according to expectations.

3. *Make sure a student desires the reward selected.* If you propose to make a positive phone call home when a student participates in group work but the student does not care what his or her parent thinks, your reward is unlikely to work. Instead, the student may be far more motivated to choose three homework problems *not* to do. You can determine your students' preferences for rewards by asking them what types of incentives they like or having them rank their preferences from a list of rewards you provide.

Related to the concept of reward desirability is that of *satiation*. Simply stated, a student who receives the same reward over a period of time may no longer find it rewarding (Schloss & Smith, 1994). If 5 minutes of free time is given repeatedly, after a while the student may come to expect the free time and not work to receive it. When this happens, it is important to change the reward. You can often avoid the problem of satiation by using a *reinforcement menu*. A reinforcement menu is a list of rewards from which students may choose. The menu can be posted in the classroom, or students can keep individual lists. Some rewards might be reserved for extraordinary performance. Many websites provide ideas for rewards and other ways to increase student behavior. Some of these are outlined in the Technology Notes on page 459.

Decreasing Undesirable Behaviors

Many teachers find that some students with special needs have inappropriate classroom behaviors that need to be decreased. These might include aggressive behaviors such as calling classmates names or poking, pinching, or hitting others; verbal outbursts such as calling out answers, swearing, or making nonsense statements during large-group instruction; and other behaviors such as fleeing the classroom when feeling stressed, copying others' work, or refusing to work. Just as some strategies increase desirable behaviors, other strategies are designed to decrease undesirable behaviors.

Decreasing behavior generally is accomplished through one of these four strategies (Jones & Jones, 2004; Kauffman et al., 2002):

1. differential reinforcement of behaviors that are incompatible with the undesirable behavior

2. extinction, or ignoring the behavior until the student stops it

3. removing something desirable from the student

4. presenting a negative or aversive consequence

The latter two strategies—removing something desirable and presenting a negative or aversive consequence—are considered *punishment*. Punishment occurs when a consequence applied has the effect of decreasing a behavior. These strategies violate the principles of PBIS, and they should be employed only when accompanied by strategies that increase desired behaviors. Each of the four strategies is explained in the following sections.

DIFFERENTIAL REINFORCEMENT OF INCOMPATIBLE OR OTHER BEHAVIORS ● Reinforcers can be used to decrease inappropriate behavior by increasing re-

FYI

If your school has students with extraordinarily challenging behaviors, you may learn that they sometimes need to be physically restrained. Physical restraint is used only by staff members who have specific training so that students and adults remain safe, and most school districts have strict policies concerning its use.

> TECHNOLOGY NOTES

Help on the Web for Responding to Student Behavior

The Internet is a valuable resource for information about responding to student behavior. You can find specific strategies for responding to common student behavior problems (for example, talking out, moving around the classroom without purpose, failing to start or complete an assignment in class). You also can find checklists for deciding whether a behavior problem is serious, forms for recording behaviors, and templates for interventions such as student contracts. Here is a sampling of particularly valuable websites.

- Dr. Mac's (McIntyre's) Amazing Behavior Management Advice Site,
  http://www.behavioradvisor.com

  This website lives up to its name. It offers basic information for new teachers related to setting up positive classroom behavior management systems, strategies for addressing common student behavior problems, examples and explanations of interventions such as contracts and token economies, and links to hundreds of additional websites. There is also a teacher bulletin for posting problems and receiving assistance. Recent examples ranged from a 4-year-old who chronically bullies classmates to a high school student with Down syndrome who does not want to leave the gym after his physical education class ends.

- Center for Effective Collaboration and Practice,
  http://cecp.air.org/fba/problembehavior/main.htm

  This organization is dedicated to improving the lives of students with emotional and behavior problems. Of par-

ticular interest is the detailed but easy-to-read information on this page of its website about completing a functional behavior assessment and creating and implementing a behavior intervention plan. Moreover, this site contains many other types of valuable information regarding school violence, prevention of behavior problems, and related topics.

- Kentucky Department of Education Behavior Home Page,
  http://www.state.ky.us/agencies/behave/interact/interaction.html

  This web page enables you to find strategies for addressing students' needs at the primary, secondary, and tertiary levels of the PBIS system described in this chapter. It also contains information about the provisions in federal special education law regarding disciplining students with disabilities and other helpful topics.

- North Carolina Department of Juvenile Justice and Delinquency Prevention, Center for the Prevention of School Violence,
  http://www.ncdjjdp.org/cpsv.html

  This web page provides information about making schools safe environments conducive to learning. It features specific sections for topics not frequently addressed, including ideas related to physical education and foreign language as well as specific locations in the school, such as restrooms.

---

lated appropriate behavior. Perhaps you have a student like Patrick in your classroom. Patrick has a severe learning disability. He tends to be very dependent on you for affirmation that he is doing his work correctly; he seems to be constantly at your elbow asking, "Is this right?" To change this behavior, you might want to try praising Patrick when you can catch him working independently at his desk. This technique is called **differential reinforcement of incompatible behaviors.** You are reinforcing a positive behavior—working independently at the student's own desk—that is incompatible with the negative behavior—being at your desk asking for affirmation (Conyers et al., 2003; Walker et al., 2003). Your goal in this case is to decrease Patrick's tendency to come to your desk (inappropriate behavior) by systematically rewarding him for staying at his desk (appropriate behavior), which prevents him from being at your desk. You also could decide to reward him for asking a classmate for assistance, that is, by reinforcing other behaviors.

EXTINCTION ● Another approach to decreasing negative behavior is **extinction.** To extinguish a behavior, you stop reinforcing it; eventually the behavior decreases (Walker et al., 2003). This strategy often is appropriate when a student has a minor but annoying undesirable behavior, such as tapping a pencil or rocking a chair, which inadvertently you have been reinforcing by calling attention to it or otherwise responding to it. However, extinction is appropriate only when the behavior is minor and does not threaten student well-being. Also, before an ignored behavior decreases, it is likely to increase; that is, at first the student might tap the pencil more loudly or rock more rapidly before stopping. If you respond to the behavior at this higher level (by telling the student to stop the noise or to keep still), you inadvertently reward the student for the exaggerated behavior through your response. If you think you cannot ignore a behavior while it increases, then extinction is not the strategy to use.

REMOVING REINFORCERS ● In some instances, you can decrease inappropriate behavior by taking away from the student something desired, a strategy called **removal punishment.** One example of removal punishment is **response cost,** which involves taking away a privilege, points, or some other reward (Schloss & Smith, 1994). An informal use of response cost occurs when teachers take away recess, a field trip, or attendance at an assembly because of misbehavior. More systematically, a student may lose a certain amount of free time each time he or she swears in class. Similarly, a student may lose the privilege of helping in the classroom because he or she refuses to begin assigned tasks.

If you are considering using response cost, keep in mind that it is effective only if the student currently has reinforcers that you can remove. For example, denying a student access to a special school program will decrease negative behavior only if the student wants to attend the program. Also, response cost sometimes fails because the negative behavior is being reinforced so strongly that the response cost is not effective. In the example just described, if the student receives a lot of peer attention from acting out in class, the response cost of not attending the school program might be too weak to counteract the strong appeal of peer attention. Finally, because response cost teaches a student only what not to do, it is essential that you simultaneously teach the student desired behaviors—what he or she should do.

Another removal punishment strategy is **time-out.** Time-out involves removing a student from opportunities for reward (Wolfgang, 2001). Many elementary school teachers use a simple form of time-out when they require students who are misbehaving on the playground to spend a few minutes in a "penalty box." The reward from which students are removed is playtime with classmates. Time-out can be used in a number of ways depending on the age of the student, the nature of the inappropriate behaviors, and the student's response to isolation. For example, it may be sufficient in a kindergarten or first-grade classroom to have a time-out chair in a quiet corner of the classroom. When Heather pushes another child, she is told to sit in time-out, where she can observe other students in the reading circle and yet cannot interact with them. If this is not effective, placing a carrel on the student's desk or using a screen (possibly made from a large box) around a chair might be the next step. For older students and for those with more challenging behaviors, time-out may need to be in a location totally removed from the student's class. For example, when Louis swears at his teacher, he is sent to the time-out room, a small, undecorated room with just a desk and chair that adjoins the counselor's office. However, for Cherri, time-out means going to Ms. Eich's room across the hall, where she doesn't know the students. The school district in which you work may have a policy concerning whether time-out is used and if it is, how to effectively implement it. The following are considerations to keep in mind:

1. The length of the time-out should vary depending on the student's age, the type of challenging behavior, and the amount of time it takes for the time-out to achieve the result of decreasing an undesirable behavior. Younger students and those with limited intellectual ability often require shorter time-out periods than older students with learning and behavior problems.

2. When using time-out, students should be given a warning, should know why they are given the time-out, and should not have access to attractive activities during

**ANALYZE
AND REFLECT**

How could extinction be implemented in your classroom to decrease a student's undesirable behavior? What implications does using extinction have on the other students in the classroom? How would you decide that extinction is not an appropriate technique to try?

time-out. The warning provides students an opportunity to correct the behavior; the explanation ensures that students understand the reason for time-out; and the absence of attractions guarantees that time-out does not become a reward for the student.

3. Giving a student attention as part of a time-out process sabotages its effectiveness. Sometimes, teachers who are using time-out accompany a student to the time-out area, explaining the student's behavior on the way, arguing with the student about the time-out procedure, or otherwise providing the student with a great deal of attention. This attention may reinforce the student's behavior and, in effect, negate the purpose of using time-out.

4. If a student refuses to go to a time-out location, you may need to ask for assistance in enforcing your decision. However, you should also keep in mind that if time-out becomes a power struggle between you and a student, it might not be the appropriate strategy to use.

5. Be aware that for some students, isolation is in itself rewarding. For time-out to be effective, the environment from which the student is removed must be rewarding. Some students are happy to be left completely alone for as long as possible. For students who prefer isolation, time-out is clearly not an appropriate strategy for reducing misbehavior.

6. Attend to the safety needs of students in time-out settings. It is highly unethical to send an upset student to an unsupervised time-out location. If time-out is employed, it must include adult supervision, a safe location for the student, and monitoring for student comfort and safety.

PRESENTING NEGATIVE CONSEQUENCES ● The final strategy for decreasing undesirable student behavior is the least preferable because it involves presenting negative consequences to students (Gardner et al., 1994). It is referred to as **presentation punishment.** For example, when a teacher verbally reprimands a student, the *reprimand* is a negative consequence intended to decrease student misbehavior. It is a mild punisher, one of the most common used in schools.

Another type of presentation punishment is *overcorrection*, in which a student is directed to restore a situation to its original condition or to a better condition than existed before the misbehavior. This strategy is useful when a student has damaged classroom property or has otherwise created a mess. For example, a student who scribbles on a chalkboard might be assigned to erase and wash all the boards in the room. A student who writes on a desktop might be required to stay after school to clean all the desktops in the class. A student who throws trash on the floor might be given the task of sweeping the classroom and adjoining hallway. This strategy can make clear the undesirable consequences of negative behaviors, but it is not without problems. First, the student must be willing to complete the overcorrection activity; it might be extremely difficult to compel this behavior. If a student refuses to complete the task, a confrontation might occur. In addition, the overcorrection requires close teacher supervision. A student should not be left alone to complete the assigned task, which could translate into a significant time commitment from the teacher.

Physical punishment is another traditional presentation punishment. Although corporal punishment, carried out within specific guidelines, is still permitted in schools in nearly half of the states, most educators strongly oppose its use (Hinchey, 2003). Physical and other types of punishment have many potential negative effects, including the following (Straus, 2001):

1. Punishment often suppresses a student's undesirable behavior but does not change it. Once a student realizes or observes that physical punishment no longer follows a behavior, that behavior is likely to recur. Thus, a student who is physically punished for stealing is likely to steal again if he or she is relatively sure that no one can discover the theft.

FYI

School districts that allow corporal punishment usually have clear guidelines, including obtaining advance parent permission, specifying how punishment is administered, and requiring the presence of a witness.

2. Although punishment might reduce or eliminate a particular behavior, other undesirable behaviors might be substituted. For example, a student strongly scolded for talking out might, at the first opportunity, deface a bulletin board as a way of "getting even."

3. Punishment sometimes has an opposite effect on behavior, increasing instead of decreasing it. This is especially true when the student craves adult attention. For example, if you verbally correct a student for not working, the student may enjoy your attention and attempt even less work to obtain your attention again. In this case, the intended punishment clearly has not served its purpose.

4. Through the teacher's modeling, students might learn that they, too, can control people by using punishment. For example, a student might imitate a teacher's scolding when tutoring a younger student. Likewise, the student might hit a classmate perceived as weaker if physical punishment is part of the school's disciplinary procedures. Similarly, students who are physically punished at home might use hitting at school with peers.

In general, then, the message for you as a teacher responding to student behaviors in class is this: Increasing positive behaviors through the use of reinforcers, especially when these desirable behaviors can substitute for undesirable behaviors, is the preferred approach to behavior management. If you find it necessary to decrease undesirable behaviors, the preferred strategies are reinforcing the positive incompatible behaviors and extinction. The use of removal or presentation punishment should be a last resort, should be only a part of an ongoing behavior intervention plan, and should involve a team decision. If you do use punishment, keep in mind all the potential problems with it and monitor its use closely.

> " Behavior contracts are one straightforward way to use the strategies for increasing or decreasing behavior. "

Using Behavior Contracts

Behavior contracts are one straightforward way to use the strategies for increasing or decreasing behavior. A behavior contract is an agreement between the teacher and student that clearly specifies the expectations for the student, the rewards for meeting expectations, the consequences of not meeting expectations, and the time frame for which the agreement is valid (Lassman, Jolivette, & Wehby, 1999). Contracts are best used with students like Joseph and perhaps David (from the chapter-opening vignettes) who are old enough to understand their content and whose disabilities either do not affect their cognitive functioning or affect it only marginally. However, simple contracts can be used with almost any student (Jones & Jones, 2004). As you review the sample contract in Figure 12.5, notice that it has more detail than some student contracts you may have seen. For students with special needs who have behavior challenges, contracts with less detail often are ineffective in changing behavior. The added components of the contract in Figure 12.5 significantly increase its impact on the student.

The original and still most comprehensive information on how to write student behavior contracts comes from Homme (1970). He stresses the following points:

1. The reward that goes with the contract should be immediate, that is, as close in time as possible to the performance of the desired behavior.

2. An initial contract should call for and reward small amounts of the desired behavior. For example, requiring a student to read an entire book to earn a reward would probably be too frustrating a task for a student with a reading problem. Instead, the student could be rewarded for each chapter (or even each chapter section or page) completed.

RESEARCH
N O T E

When schoolwide PBIS implemented were consistently, targeted schools showed significant improvement over comparison schools in terms of student achievement, the number of discipline referrals, and the social adjustment of students with serious behavior problems (Nelson, Martella, & Marchand-Martella, 2002).

FIGURE 12.5 Sample Student Contract

For _____Mia_____   Class _____U. S. History—Mr. Lee_____
　　　　　(Student name)

I agree to do these things (what, how much, how well, how often, how measured):

Every day when the bell rings, I will be in my seat with my book, notebook, and a

pen ready. During class, I will answer questions only when called on (2 warnings

per class for calling out).

For doing them I will receive (what, how much, how often, when):

1 point/day for being prepared, 1 point/day for appropriate class participation.

Every time I accumulate 8 points, I may earn 5 extra-credit points toward my

course grade.

Outstanding performance will be if I

Keep my contract 5 days in a row (10 points in a 5-day week)

_____

My bonus for outstanding performance is

The option of skipping 1 homework assignment during the week after the bonus

is earned

If I don't meet the terms of my contract, this is the consequence:

If fewer than 5 points are earned in a week, I forfeit participating in the History

Survivor competition the following Monday.

This contract will be renegotiated on

October 19, 2005

___Mia_____   ___Mr. Lee_____
Student signature   **Teacher signature**

___September 14, 2005_____   ___September 14, 2005_____
Date   **Date**

3. Rewards should be distributed frequently in small amounts. This approach has been proven a more effective method than using fewer, larger rewards.

4. A contract should call for and reward accomplishments rather than obedience; that is, reward the completion of assigned work or appropriate behavior rather than "teacher-pleasing" behaviors such as staying in one's seat.

5. Reward the performance only after it occurs. This rule seems obvious, but it is often overlooked. Students who are allowed privileges or rewards before or during assigned work are far less likely to complete the task successfully than those rewarded after it.

WWW
R E S O U R C E S

You can find 41 suggestions for discipline and classroom management on the Discipline and Classroom Management page of the Teacher Development Network, at http://members.tripod.com/~ozpk/disc.html. Each idea links to related information and resources.

6. The contract must be fair. The amount of work required of the student and the payoff for completing the work must be balanced.

7. The terms of the contract should be clear to the student. The contract should be put in writing and discussed with the student. Each component of the contract should be expressed in language the student understands. If the student is not able to understand a contract, this strategy is probably not the best one. The student and teacher should sign the contract.

8. The contract must be honest. The teacher should be willing to carry out the contract as written and to do so immediately. In practice, this means that you should be sure you can deliver on the promises you make.

9. The contract should be positive. It should specify student accomplishments and rewards rather than restrictions and punishments.

10. The contract should be used systematically. If the contract is enforced only occasionally, the result may be worse (or at least very confusing) for the student than not using one at all.

How Can You Help Students Manage Their Own Behavior?

The strategies just outlined for increasing positive and decreasing serious negative student behavior rely on the teacher providing rewards or consequences to the student. Another set of strategies, far less teacher-directed, involves having students take an active role in regulating their own behavior (Fox & Garrison, 2003; Paris & Winograd, 2003). These strategies are preferred because they promote student independence by giving students skills they can use in many school settings and outside school as well (Johnson & Johnson, 1999). They have been used with very young children; with students who have learning disabilities, emotional disabilities, autism, and intellectual disabilities, as well as other special needs; and with a wide range of academic and social behaviors.

Cognitive Behavior Management Strategies

In **cognitive behavior management (CBM),** students are taught to monitor their own behavior, to make judgments about its appropriateness, and to change it as needed

> In CBM, students are taught to monitor their own behavior, to make judgments about its appropriateness, and to change it as needed.

(for example, Gunter, Miller, Venn, Thomas, & House, 2002; Meichenbaum, 1977; Swaggart, 1998). Many elements of CBM have already been introduced in Chapter 10 as a means of increasing student independence in academic learning and organization. In this chapter they are applied to helping students manage their own classroom conduct and social behavior in a variety of situations. For example, Joseph, the student with a learning disability introduced at the beginning of this chapter, might be able to use CBM to manage his own classroom behavior. Two specific CBM strategies are commonly used to teach students how to manage their own behavior. These are self-monitoring and self-reinforcement.

SELF-MONITORING ● Students learn to monitor and record their own behavior in *self-monitoring*. For example, a student might keep a daily tally of the number of assignments completed or the number of times he waited until the teacher was between instructional groups to ask a question. A student might also use self-monitoring to monitor the rate at which she completes and turns in homework assignments, or any other behavior (Daly & Ranalli, 2003; Toney, Kelley, & Lanclos, 2003). Students with more advanced skills could even wear headphones to listen to an audiotape with pre-recorded signals and record whether they are on task at the sound of each tone. Students also can self-record their nonacademic behaviors. For instance, they can tally the number of times they leave their seat without permission or ask permission before leaving the classroom.

SELF-REINFORCEMENT ● Another CBM strategy, *self-reinforcement*, often is used in conjunction with self-monitoring. In this approach, students self-evaluate and then judge whether they have earned a reward. For example, Eric might award himself three points for a high self-monitoring score, two points for an average score, and no points for a low score. When he accumulates 20 points, he chooses a reward from his personal reinforcement menu. His favorite reward might be working on a timeline for critical events of the 20th century. The teacher periodically checks the accuracy of Eric's self-evaluation and self-reinforcement. He earns a bonus point for being accurate in his assessment of himself, even if that assessment is occasionally negative. If Eric has to give himself no points for a low score and his teacher checks his accuracy that day, he receives a bonus point because he accurately assessed his work.

Teaching Cognitive Behavior Management Strategies

Generally, teaching a CBM strategy to a student with special needs involves three main steps:

1. *Discuss the strategy with the student and present a rationale for its use.* If you cannot clarify for the student what the strategy is or how it works, the student might not be a good candidate for CBM. To check student understanding, ask the student to explain the approach back to you. You could even summarize the goal of the strategy and the rewards and consequences in a contract.

2. *Model for the student what you expect.* For example, you might use an old sample of the student's work and walk through the strategy you plan to use, such as, showing the amount of completed work that represents a high score or a low score. Alternatively, you might use a brief role-play to demonstrate to the student how to self-monitor behavior and record it.

3. *Provide practice and feedback.* For this step, the teacher rewards the student for correctly using the strategy until the student is confident enough to use it without such support. If you are teaching a student to use CBM, use reinforcers with the student until he or she has mastered the strategy. Even after mastery, it is helpful to reward the student periodically for successfully self-managing behavior. This step can be enhanced by helping the student develop a personal reinforcement menu so rewards are meaningful. Parents and colleagues sometimes can assist in implementing this step.

Although CBM is not appropriate for every student behavior problem, it has the advantage of teaching a student to monitor and take responsibility for his or her own behavior. Because of increased student responsibility, cognitive behavior management is a far more effective long-term strategy for some students than are more traditional classroom rewards. Students can transfer self-management strategies to other classrooms and teachers and even into adult life. By collaborating with special education teachers and other school professionals, you can design a CBM program that truly makes a difference in a student's life.

CONNECTIONS

CBM strategies are presented in an instructional context in Chapter 10.

CONNECTIONS

How can the steps in the INCLUDE process guide your responses to questions regarding classroom management and student behavior issues?

S U M M A R Y

Responding to student behavior begins with prevention: By setting clear expectations, fostering respect and communication, and establishing effective teaching methods, teachers can create a classroom learning environment that encourages appropriate behavior and discourages inappropriate behavior. Such basic techniques meet the needs of many students with disabilities. In addition, you can use simple group techniques, such as a token economy, to promote positive student behavior. One systematic approach for addressing prevention as well as the more intensive interventions needed by some students is called positive behavioral interventions and supports (PBIS).

For students needing additional behavior supports, using low-intrusion strategies such as Catch 'Em Being Good, grouping students, and managing surface behaviors can help prevent minor behavior problems from becoming serious ones. However, when such strategies are inadequate, you may find it necessary to participate in a functional behavior assessment with your team to prepare and follow a behavior intervention plan tailored to the student's needs. Such a plan may be part of the IEP if the need arises for any student with a disability. A behavior intervention plan may include one or many strategies for increasing desirable student behavior (for example, reinforcement) or decreasing undesirable student behavior (for example, extinction, removal punishment); it may also be presented to the student in the form of a behavior contract. For some students, cognitive behavior management strategies such as self-monitoring and self-reinforcement also can be employed.

Applications in **Teaching Practice**

Developing Strategies for Responding to Individual Student Behavior

Ms. Bind teaches eighth-grade English. One of her students is Russell, a student with learning and behavior problems. Russell tends to be a class clown. He makes flippant remarks that border on being disrespectful of other students and Ms. Bind. He is often reprimanded for chatting with other students instead of listening, and then he complains that he doesn't know how to do an assignment that was just explained. The other students generally like Russell, and they sometimes urge him to engage in more classroom antics. Ms. Bind is not alone in her concern about Russell's behavior. His other teachers report a similar pattern. All are concerned about his slipping grades and worry that in high school it will be difficult for him to get the adult supervision that has helped him be more successful in middle school. Ms. Bind's tally of classroom incidents from the last week suggests that Russell is reprimanded at least six times per class period. The reprimands tend to occur when the class is transitioning from one activity to another, for example, from a large-group lecture to an individual assignment. Ms. Bind also has noted that Russell brags about his friends in a gang and threatens to "get" other students with these friends.

Ms. Bind, special education teacher Mr. Clark, counselor Ms. Lassaux, and parent Ms. Pinelli have been meeting about Russell. The first step in their functional assessment was to think about whether any simple strategies have been effective and about the intent of Russell's behavior. They decide that the behaviors he has been displaying probably have to do with seeking attention from both peers and teachers, but they conclude that current interventions are inadequate. Using observational data from the classroom and interview information from other teachers, the lunchroom supervisor, and Russell himself, they spend considerable time discussing what sources of appropriate attention are available to Russell, and they weigh the pros and cons of various alternatives for responding to Russell's behavior. They also engage in a conversation about the impact the other students are having on maintaining Russell's behavior when they encourage him. Ms. Bind is convinced that if Russell's audience were not so attentive, many of his problems might take care of themselves.

QUESTIONS

1. What strategies could Ms. Bind and the other teachers use to address the group response to Russell's behavior? What cautions would you have for them in trying these strategies?
2. What simple strategies could Ms. Bind use to help Russell behave more appropriately in class? For each strategy, identify potential positive outcomes that could occur but also outline potential problems that could arise.
3. What information about Russell do you think the team gathered? How can this information help them create a behavior intervention plan?
4. What types of reinforcement might work for Russell? How could Ms. Bind ascertain which reinforcers to use if reinforcement is the strategy decided on? Which types of reinforcers would you avoid in this case?
5. How do you think Russell would respond to strategies designed to decrease his negative behavior? For example, how might Russell react if he received a detention each time he disrupted class? What type of negative consequence is detention?
6. Is Russell likely to be able to use cognitive behavior management? Why or why not? If you decided to try a CBM strategy, how would you go about it?
7. Draft a sample behavior intervention plan for Russell. Be prepared to defend the information you create for it and the interventions you plan to implement.
8. How should Russell and his mother be involved in the discussion about his behavior? What contributions could each one make?

WORKING THE **STANDARDS**

INTASC

INTASC PRINCIPLES REFLECTED IN THIS CHAPTER:

Principle #5 states that all teachers

- Help students with disabilities develop positive strategies for coping with frustrations in the learning situation that may be associated with their disabilities (Principle 5.02).

- Modify tasks and learning/social situations to optimize student success (Principle 5.02).

- Recognize factors and situations that are likely to promote (or diminish) intrinsic motivation, and create learning environments that encourage engagement and self-motivation of students with disabilities (Principle 5.04).

- Offer choices and options to students with disabilities so that they develop a sense of control (Principle 5.04).

- Tailor classroom management and grouping to individual needs using constructive behavior management strategies, a variety of grouping options, and positive behavioral support strategies to create a learning context in which students with disabilities can attend to learning and respond in appropriate ways (Principle 5.05).

Principle #9 states that all teachers

- Reflect on the potential interaction between a student's cultural experiences and his or her disability (Principle 9.04).

- Regularly question the extent to which they may be interpreting a student's responses on the basis of their own cultural values versus the cultural perspectives of the student or the student's family or community (Principle 9.04).

CEC CONTENT STANDARDS REFLECTED IN THIS CHAPTER:

Council for Exceptional Children

CEC Content Standard #5 states that special educators

- Shape environments to encourage the independence, self-motivation, self-direction, personal empowerment, and self-advocacy of individuals with exceptional learning needs.

- Use direct motivational and instructional interventions with individuals with exceptional learning needs to teach them to respond effectively to current expectations.

WORKING THE **STANDARDS** *(continued)*

CEC Content Standard #8 states that special educators conduct formal and informal assessments of behavior, learning, achievement, and environments to design learning experiences that support the growth and development of individuals with exceptional learning needs.

CEC Content Standard #9 states that special educators are aware of how their own and others' attitudes, behaviors, and ways of communicating can influence their practice.

BACK TO THE CASES

The standards and principles just listed relate to the cases described at the beginning of this chapter: Joseph, Katie, and David. The questions and activities that follow demonstrate how these standards and principles, along with other concepts that you have learned about in this chapter, connect to the everyday activities of all teachers.

Joseph

Mrs. Akers is sure that Joseph has the potential to be successful in her class. In addition, she is concerned that her attitude toward his behavior has limited her ability to support his needs. Based on her concern and desire to help him achieve, Mrs. Akers has spent several hours reading about behavior management techniques and discussing Joseph's individual needs with the special education teacher. She has decided that using a token economy will work best in her high school class, because she can reward all students who do well. She requests your help. (See INTASC Principles 5.04 and 5.05, and CEC Content Standards 5 and 9.) Her questions are these:

- What behaviors should I target with all students that would be most helpful with Joseph?
- What currency would be most appropriate for adolescents? (Make a list of those items that you think would be most motivational to adolescents.)
- How can I explain this to the students in a way that will motivate Joseph to participate?

Katie

Katie's behavior is hampering her successful inclusion in Mr. Lowell's sixth-grade class. Mr. Lowell will meet tomorrow with teachers from the sixth-grade team, the special education teacher, Katie's mother, her paraprofessional, and Katie. They will discuss a plan to use CBM in order to teach Katie more age-appropriate behaviors for school and to reinforce those behaviors at home. As a member of the team, you have been asked to come to the meeting with your written responses to the following concerns. (Of course, the team will want to hear your rationale for all of your answers.) (See INTASC Principles 5.02, 5.04, and 5.05; and CEC Content Standards 5 and 8.)

- What behavior(s) will you target first? If more than one behavior, list in order of priority.
- What schedule of reinforcement do you believe is most appropriate to begin this management plan?
- What reinforcer(s) do you suggest for Katie?
- How would you teach Katie to self-monitor this behavior?

David

Mr. Morgan has discovered that David's behavior is more difficult than he had imagined, but he cannot allow David's behavior to continue, and action must be taken. He is aware that there are five simple and effective responses to student behavior, but he is not sure which to use. He has asked you to list the pros and cons for using each of the five responses with David. (See INTASC Principles 5.04 and 5.05, and CEC Content Standards 5 and 9.) In addition, he is particularly interested in which of the techniques for managing surface behaviors you would recommend. Include the rationales for all of your decisions.

> Visit the companion website (http://www.ablongman. com/friend4e) for a complete correlation of this chapter to the INTASC Principles and CEC Standards.

Further **Readings**

Hinchey, P. H. (2003). Corporal punishment: Legalities, realities, and implications [Electronic version]. *Clearing House*, 76, 127–131.

This article includes a brief quiz to check your understanding of the use of corporal punishment in American schools. It also outlines legislation related to physical punishment and includes advice for teachers related to protecting the rights of their students.

Peck, A., & Scarpati, S. (Eds.). Using positive behavior support strategies [Special issue]. *Teaching Exceptional Children*, 37(1), 7–62.

This special issue of a journal designed for teachers includes eight articles related to using positive behavior supports. Topics range from evaluating school climate to decreasing acting out behavior to using peer mentoring with high school students. The articles describe specific cases and interventions and include checklists and forms that you can adapt for your own use.

Skiba, R. J., Michael, R. S., Nardo, A. B., & Peterson, R. L. (2002). The color of discipline: Sources of racial and gender disproportionality in school punishment [Electronic version]. *Urban Review, 34,* 317–342.

This article reports a large-scale study of the disciplinary records of middle school students in a large school district during a one-year period. The authors use the results to discuss how race and gender are related to teachers' responses in the classroom to student behaviors.

Sprick, R. S. (2002). *Discipline in the secondary classroom: A problem-by-problem survival guide* (2nd ed.). San Francisco: Jossey-Bass.

This book provides a wealth of practical information for secondary teachers for setting up an effective classroom management system, addressing everything from setting classroom expectations to establishing fair grading systems to specific strategies for responding to common student behavior problems. The book includes specific ideas for resolving 42 common student behavior issues.

Building Social Relationships

ERROL IS A FIFTH-GRADE student in Ms. Kim's class at Pleasant Springs Elementary School. He has a moderate intellectual disability. Ms. Kim has been working closely with Mr. Haring, the inclusion facilitator, to ensure that Errol is making friends. The two teachers have worked with Errol's parents to enroll Errol in a community recreation program that several other students in class attend, and Errol's mother and father have been very proactive in encouraging him to play with the other children. In school, the teachers have arranged for the social worker to work with the class once per week in group lessons on friendship and diversity, and class members have taken a pledge to make new friends among their classmates. ● *Why is it important for teachers to deliberately address the social interactions of their students with disabilities? What strategies can teachers use to foster friendships between students with and without disabilities? What is the role of parents and families in fostering the development of their children's social skills and relationships?*

KATHLEEN'S EIGHTH-GRADE social studies class is studying the effect of civil wars on the citizens and economies of developing countries. Mr. Geib announces at the beginning of class that the students should move into teams for a cooperative assignment that will take the entire class period. The 32 students shove desks into groups and gather their materials. After being reminded that this is not visiting time, the students settle into groups of 5 or 6. Kathleen's group has 5 members of varying abilities and skills. Behavior stemming from Kathleen's emotional disability usually is not evident in this group. Her peers do not respond to her teasing and inappropriate comments. They assist her to be a constructive group member to help the team get extra points and a possible "free pass" on a future assignment. The 2 other students in the class who have identified disabilities are in two other groups. Mr. Geib distributes materials to the students and gives directions. When everyone is working, he goes from group to group, answering questions and helping students stay focused on their assignment. ● *What is the impact of this type of grouping arrangement in a diverse classroom? Is it more or less effective than traditional instruction? How can Mr. Geib avoid the problem of some students doing all the work for their groups while other students contribute little? What is the social benefit of this classroom grouping arrangement?*

SEVERAL OF THE GOALS on Demetrius's IEP this year pertain to learning social skills, and his teachers and other service providers are committed to helping him interact more successfully with his peers and teachers. For example, as a junior with Asperger syndrome who academically is near grade level, Demetrius often forgets to take into account the expressions on people's faces when he is talking with them. The result is that he sometimes keeps talking about a topic long after his friends are showing through their expressions that they are bored or frustrated. The counselor is working with Demetrius on this skill so that he can effectively "read" nonverbal communication with his friends and in other situations. Demetrius also is planning to work in a local printing shop when he completes high school next year, so social skills for the work environment are being stressed, including speaking in an appropriate voice, asking for assistance when needed, listening politely to others, and greeting others appropriately. ● *Why do social skills need to be specifically taught to many students with disabilities? How can social skills instruction be integrated into inclusive classrooms? What is the role of the general education teacher in teaching social skills to students with disabilities?*

The current school reform movement, with its emphasis on academic accountability for all students, including those with disabilities and other special needs, clearly is influencing the current trends in inclusive education. However, another important reason for educating students with disabilities with their nondisabled peers is the social benefit (Copeland et al., 2004; Frederickson & Turner, 2003; Krajewski & Hyde, 2000). Many educators understand that students with disabilities and other exceptional needs learn appropriate social behaviors and develop friendships, collectively referred to as **social skills,** only when they have opportunities to interact with their nondisabled peers. At the same time, students without special needs learn that individuals with disabilities are people, and they develop sensitivity to people who may not be exactly like themselves and a sense of social responsibility to include individuals with special needs in the classroom community.

How do the social benefits of inclusive education occur? As you may guess, simply integrating students with disabilities into a classroom is not enough. Physically placing students together does not teach students with disabilities the skills they may need, nor does it prepare students without disabilities to be respectful of their classmates with special needs. As a teacher, you must be proactive to ensure that social benefits accrue to all students. Further, if challenges arise—for example, students tease their classmates or students continue to have difficulties in their social interactions with peers and adults—you have the responsibility to address these problems, enlisting the assistance of special educators, counselors, and others as necessary. This chapter provides several strategies that you can implement to build positive social relationships for all students in your classroom.

As you begin to think about the social dimension of inclusive education, keep in mind the following ideas. First, although your teacher preparation program emphasizes academics, your responsibilities as a teacher also include helping all students, whether or not they have special needs, learn social skills. The degree of success that any student can achieve in adulthood often is determined largely by that student's ability to effectively interact with others. Because social skills are so important, attention to them should begin at a very early age and continue throughout students' school years (Taylor, Peterson, McMurray-Schwarz, & Guillou, 2002). Second, you do not need to teach students social skills apart from the curriculum for which you will be responsible (Organ & Gonzalez-DeHass, 2004). As you read this chapter, you should realize that many skills related to developing positive social relationships can be incorporated into your daily instruction, as Mr. Geib was doing in Kathleen's class. Third, the issue of social relationships should be an integral part of your classroom expectations; that is, for some students the social component of their education is a primary classroom goal, whereas for others it is secondary. For example, Errol's IEP includes several goals related to peer interactions and the development of friendships; the purpose of his being in fifth grade has as much to do with learning important life social skills, such as talking to peers and participating in group activities, as it does with learning arithmetic skills. Kathleen is learning how to be a member of a group without being disruptive. For Demetrius, however, academic and social goals are equally important. One of your responsibilities as a teacher in an inclusive classroom is to clarify these expectations with special educators.

What Is Your Role in Promoting Positive Social Interactions among Students with and without Disabilities?

A beginning point for creating a classroom in which students understand, appreciate, support, and interact respectfully with each other is studying what we know about children's social interactions. This knowledge provides a basis for thinking about how to group students and supervise their interactions to accomplish the social goals of inclusion.

Research on social relationships and interactions among students with and without disabilities has been ongoing almost since special education programs began in public schools (Bennett, 1932). During the 1950s and 1960s, researchers studied the social adjustment and acceptance by peers of students with intellectual disabilities. Sometimes, they found that students in special education classes had better social adjustment than similar students in general education classes (Cassidy & Stanton, 1959). At other times, they found few differences (Blatt, 1958). More consistent were the findings on students' peer acceptance: Researchers found that students with intellectual disabilities were less often accepted and more often rejected by their peers than students without disabilities (Johnson & Kirk, 1950; Miller, 1956).

When mainstreaming became an important issue during the 1970s, additional studies were completed to help educators understand the social needs of students with disabilities in general education settings. What became clear was that placing students with disabilities, especially those with intellectual disabilities, in classrooms with nondisabled peers did not alone ensure that positive social relationships would develop. In fact, the opposite was true. Students in classes with mainstreamed peers generally disliked the students with disabilities, or did not accept them (Goodman, Gottlieb, & Harrison, 1972; Iano et al., 1974). In attempting to identify why these consistent negative findings occurred, many different characteristics of students with disabilities were examined, including academic potential, label, age, gender, behavior, and physical appearance. Also studied were the ways in which students received special education services, teachers' behaviors, the amount of time students spent in mainstream classrooms, and the types of interactions among students with and without disabilities. The picture that emerged was not clear. Many characteristics and other factors seemed to contribute to student social problems, but none was singularly important.

As students with disabilities in today's schools rightfully have come to spend more and more time in general education classrooms, attention has focused once again on the interactions between these students and their classmates without disabilities.

DIMENSIONS OF DIVERSITY

According to the U.S. Bureau of the Census, the overall rate of disability in the United States is 19.4 percent. However, the rate is highest for Native Americans, at 21.9 percent, followed closely by African Americans, at 20 percent. For Asian Americans, the rate of disability is 9.9 percent. Of what significance is this information when thinking about the social relationships of students with and without disabilities?

CONNECTIONS

This research is part of the efficacy studies that were mentioned in Chapter 1 in the section on the development of special education services.

DIMENSIONS
OF DIVERSITY

Some students experience social pressure related to school. For example, in a case study of a tenth-grade African American middle class student, Day-Vines, Patton, and Baytops (2003) reported that the student was chastised by her African American peers for succeeding academically, speaking standard English, and living in an affluent neighborhood while she simultaneously was teased by her white peers for her academic and social status. How could you as a teacher help in such a situation?

Although some studies continue to confirm earlier research suggesting that students with disabilities experience difficulty in being socially accepted by peers (for example, Doré, Dion, Wagner, & Brunet, 2002), other studies suggest a more positive outlook. For instance, although Freeman and Alkin (2000) found that the social acceptance ratings for students with intellectual disabilities in general education settings were not as high as those for typical learners, they were higher than those for students with intellectual disabilities in separate special education classrooms. Yet other research has found a mixed picture. When Pavri and Monda-Amaya (2001) interviewed elementary students with learning disabilities and their general and special education teachers about school social interactions, they found that students felt that they were part of the social network at school. However, the students also experienced loneliness at times. Further, the teachers tended to foster social interactions by using teacher-directed interventions such as arranging peer tutoring (discussed later in this chapter), even though students preferred to try to address social situations using their own skills. This complex picture of students' social relationships suggests that simply mixing students with and without disabilities in single classrooms may not result in an integrated social system for them (Copeland et al., 2004; Hall & McGregor, 2000). Especially for adolescents, social interactions in school—with peers as well as teachers—can be challenging. The Professional Edge on page 475 takes a look at this important topic.

It is essential to remember that the fact that student social relationships might not occur spontaneously does not mean that inclusive practices are unsuccessful. What it does mean is that teachers have a significant responsibility to ensure that peer relationships grow. Many professionals have been working to develop strategies to help you accomplish this. Generally, these strategies can be grouped into three categories: creating opportunities for students with and without disabilities to have meaningful face-to-face interactions, nurturing support and friendship between students with and without disabilities, and providing positive role models. Figure 13.1 illustrates these strategies.

Creating Opportunities for Social Interactions

The first component for promoting positive interactions among students with and without disabilities is providing opportunities for them to interact. In both elementary and secondary classrooms, this means structuring activities and assigning students to groups so that interactions become part of classroom instruction, as was accomplished in Mr. Geib's classroom described at the beginning of this chapter. Arranging service learning activities in which students with and without disabilities all participate is another way to encourage interactions (Kleinert et al., 2004). For instance, students might work together to pick up debris from a local park, to visit a senior citizen center, or to contact local government officials to support a new recycling initiative.

Special programs are another way to accomplish the goal of meaningful interactions. For example, in one high school, peer buddies were assigned to provide students with significant intellectual disabilities with more and better opportunities to participate in general education classes (Copeland et al., 2004). In this program, students without disabilities were partnered with students with disabilities to provide academic and social support. Data from group interviews of participating nondisabled students suggested that these students identified many ways that their classmates with disabilities were socially isolated in schools. They also learned that they could foster social interactions by advocating for their buddies, facilitating interactions with other students, and modeling appropriate social interactions.

> *Special programs are another way to accomplish the goal of meaningful interactions.*

Yet another way to encourage interactions among students concerns nonacademic activities. For example, Turnbull, Pereira, and Blue-Banning (2000) found that if

PROFESSIONAL EDGE

Understanding the Perspectives of High School Students

The relationships that adolescents have with their teachers are strong predictors of high school completion and academic effort and are an important dimension of their social competence. An obvious, but sometimes overlooked, way of understanding the academic and social experiences of high school students with disabilities is to ask them directly. Lovitt and his colleagues (Lovitt, Plavins, & Cushing, 1999) did just that, surveying more than 200 students and interviewing 54 of them. Students participating in this research offered the following suggestions for teachers:

- Explain more/better and provide more help.
- Give one-to-one assistance.
- Motivate and make learning more fun/interesting.
- Demonstrate how to do something.
- Be more patient.
- Go over content slowly.
- Teach without lectures.
- Keep the student on track.
- Talk to the students more.
- Quit treating the students like 5-year-olds.
- Provide a little more freedom.
- Speak the students' language.

When students were asked how they would improve their high school, they volunteered that they would fire teachers who treated high school like "a prison" and would require teachers to know multiple ways to reach their students. They expressed a preference for more meaningful instruction and less "busywork." Many of these high school students with disabilities also commented on their peer relationships, noting that they had been "made fun of" by typical peers throughout their school careers.

Recommendations

Based on the results of this study, the researchers recommend the following for teachers and others working with high school students who have disabilities:

1. Assist students to be more independent (for example, through self-evaluating and self-scheduling).

2. Make students more aware of what is being done for them (for example, the accommodations made and reasons for them).

3. Present students with a wider array of postschool options (for example, technical training programs, military, special college options, immediate employment opportunities).

4. Invest more time in teaching social skills to help student skills approach the levels of those of their typical peers.

5. Focus effort on strengths (for example, nurturing an area of pride for a student).

6. Continue working on basic skills, avoiding the tendency to abandon efforts to help students learn to read, write, and compute.

SOURCE: Adapted from "What Do Pupils with Disabilities Have to Say about Their Experience in High School?" by T. C. Lovitt, M. Plavins, and S. Cushing, 1999, *Remedial and Special Education, 20,* pp. 67–76, 83. Copyright © 1999 by PRO-ED, Inc. Reprinted with permission.

teachers encourage student participation in extracurricular activities that typical peers also enjoy, students with disabilities are likely to develop friendships. Similarly, when students with disabilities are included in team sports, all students are provided with opportunities to learn about and grow to value each other (Ohtake, 2004).

You may be able to identify many other strategies that you could use to foster interactions between students with and without disabilities, interactions that build positive social relationships. How could you do this in an elementary classroom? A middle school class? A high school class? In a nonacademic setting? Even a small amount of attention on your part to arrange such interactions can have a significant benefit for all of your students.

FIGURE 13.1 Creating Positive Peer Relationships

Providing opportunities for social interaction

Nurturing supportive behavior and friendships

Serving as a role model and providing access to other positive models

Nurturing Support and Friendship

Arranging student interactions is a start, but it is not enough. The second component in building social relationships is to nurture mutual support and friendship between students with and without disabilities. Here are several examples of programs and strategies for accomplishing this goal.

CIRCLE OF FRIENDS ● One specific program with demonstrated effectiveness in promoting friendships is **Circle of Friends** (Demchak, n.d.; Forest, Pierpoint, & O'Brien, 1996). When a new student, especially one with many special needs, joins a class group, the students in the group learn to build a circle of friends around that student. As part of this process, they review their own circle of friends by drawing four concentric circles around a figure representing themselves. The first circle contains closest friends, such as family members. The second circle contains others close to each student, such as neighbors and family friends. The third circle contains acquaintances, such as members of each student's soccer team. The outer circle contains people paid to help, such as teachers and camp counselors. The purpose of this step in the activity is to help students understand how many people are part of their lives.

Students then are shown the circles of a person with only a few names inserted, and they are asked how they would feel and act if their circles had so few entries. Next, a classmate with a disability is mentioned as possibly having few names in his circles. Students generate ideas of how they could become part of that classmate's circle of friends. Students who do become part of their classmate's circle meet regularly to discuss their friendship with that student. This structured friendship-building strategy has been demonstrated to be effective for fostering appropriate social interactions between students with and without disabilities, an effect that extends beyond the planned meetings to the entire school day (Miller, Cooke, Test, & White, 2003).

GENERAL FRIENDSHIP-BUILDING STRATEGIES ● Many general strategies can be used to nurture friendships among the students you teach. For example, teachers of elementary students might consider incorporating friendship skills into their instruction (Bovey & Strain, 2003). A teacher might discuss during morning circle time how to get a friend's attention or ask a friend for help. Enlisting the help of students who have these skills, the teacher can use role-playing to teach the skills to the class as a whole. As the day progresses, the teacher can point out students acting like friends in their interactions and reward the group for their positive behaviors. In particular, the teacher could direct Cami, a student with a learning disability, to ask Terri, a classmate with similar interests, for assistance with an assignment. This informal teaching and prompting can facilitate the development of positive interactions and friendships. By teaching students how to greet one another, how to express friendship, and how to resolve conflicts, teachers can foster positive peer relationships and provide students with a strong basis for lifelong interaction skills (Salend, 1999). You can learn more about teaching friendship skills to students in the Professional Edge on page 478.

Another general strategy for fostering support and friendships is making slight changes in activities to encourage the participation of students with disabilities (Turnbull, Percira, & Blue-Banning, 2000). In Ms. Kerner's civics class, students were asked to choose from among several civic organizations they might like to research. Instead of being asked to work independently, students who chose the same organizations were grouped and encouraged to use print, Internet, and other resources to complete the project. By intentionally placing students in groups, Ms. Kerner increased the participation of students with disabilities with classmates.

RESOLVING SUPPORT AND FRIENDSHIP PROBLEMS ● Sometimes you have to address problems related to student support and friendship, particularly for students whose IEPs contain significant accommodations and modifications. Some students (and some teachers, too) express concern about the fairness of making these adjustments for students with special needs, including changing the consequences for misbehavior, altering the amount or type of work expected, grading on a more generous scale, or using rewards to which other students may not have access. The Professional Edge on page 479 offers advice about responding to issues of fairness.

PARENTS AND FRIENDSHIP ● As you work with students to foster positive social interactions and friendships between students with and without disabilities, keep in mind that parents have a key role to play in this part of their children's lives. For example, parents of a student with disabilities can provide information about their child's communication strategies and make suggestions about including the student in classroom activities. Parents also can be very effective in exposing their children with special needs to a wide variety of individuals who may become friends (Geisthardt, Brotherson, & Cook, 2002). You also may find that parents of students without disabilities may take active steps to foster friendships with classmates with special needs because of the importance they place on helping their children understand the value of each person's abilities. Parents also may contribute in small but meaningful ways by providing transportation to recreational activities after school hours, arranging birthday parties and other social functions for students at their homes, and volunteering to lead school activities that bring students together for social interactions (for example, clubs) (Salend, 1999).

Keep in mind, though, that parents' perspectives on their children's friendships may be influenced by their cultures. For example, in one study of friendship between Hispanic children with disabilities and children without disabilities, the researchers

PROFESSIONAL EDGE

Teaching Students How to Make Friends

Although you can use many informal strategies to nurture friendships among students or you can access a formal instructional package designed for this purpose, another option, particularly with elementary students, is to directly teach friendship skills to students, teaching them these steps:

Step 1: Identify someone to whom you can introduce yourself.

Students should examine their surroundings and find someone with whom they would like to play or talk. Students should be given examples of how people look when they want to play or talk. To illustrate, the teacher can use pictures of students engaging in a variety of activities, for example, a student finishing a homework assignment, a student coloring alone, a student with a sad face, or a student with a happy face.

Step 2: Smile and approach the person.

The teacher should model walking up to someone with a smile on his or her face. Students should practice this while approaching a peer.

Step 3: Introduce yourself.

Students should say their names and ask the other person his or her name and should look at the person and smile. The teacher should continue modeling.

Step 4: Ask open-ended questions to get and give information.

Students can ask the other student what he or she is playing with, what's happening, and so forth. Students need to know what an open-ended question is: Open-ended questions have answers that have more than two or three words. Students should remember to look at the person and smile. The teacher now can ask two students to model for the class, or the teacher can continue modeling. A list of questions can be provided for the students if they are able to read, or the teacher can provide questioning prompts. This step will depend on the level of the students.

Step 5: Suggest something to play or do together.

Students should find some activity or game to play on the playground, during free time, or during passing period. The teacher can prompt pairs to engage in an activity and provide ideas for the students so that the interaction will continue.

Once students have learned these skills, you can provide them with simple reminder cards with words and/or pictures so that they can practice on their own. Teaching these steps can be even more effective if you use children's literature to illustrate how friends are made. Some books about making friends include these:

Books for Students Preschool through Middle School

- Aliki, *We Are Best Friends*
- Anglund, J. W., *A Friend Is Someone Who Likes You*
- Barkin, J. C., & James, E., *Are We Still Best Friends?*
- Berenstain, S., & Berenstain, J., *The Berenstain Bears and the Trouble with Friends*
- Cohen, M., *Will I Have a Friend?*
- Craig, H., *Angelina and Alice*
- Crary, E., *I Want to Play*
- De Regniers, B. S., *May I Bring a Friend?*
- Holabird, K., *Angelina and Alice*
- Iwasaki, C., *Will You Be My Friend?*
- Lystad, M., *That New Boy*
- Moncure, J. B., *A New Boy in Kindergarten*
- Prather, R., *New Neighbors*
- Robinson, N. K., *Wendy and the Bullies*
- Stevenson, J., *Fast Friends: Two Stories*
- Viorst, J., *Rosie and Michael*

Books for Students Middle School through High School

- Arrick, F., *What You Don't Know Can Kill You*
- Bauer, J., *Thwonk!*
- Creech, S., *Absolutely Normal Chaos*
- Draper, S., *Tears of a Tiger*
- Kindl, P., *Owl in Love*
- Lester, J., *Othello*
- Lowery, L., *The Giver*
- Mahy, M., *The Catalogue of the Universe*
- McDaniel, L., *Now I Lay me Down to Sleep*
- Myers, W. D., *Darnell Rock Reporting*
- Naylor, P. R., *Shiloh*
- Wiethorn, R. J., *Rock Finds a Friend*
- Wolff, V. E., *Make Lemonade*
- Woodson, J., *I Hadn't Meant To Tell You This*
- Zolotow, C., *The New Friend*

SOURCES: Adapted from "Friendship and Stories: Using Children's Literature to Teach Friendship Skills to Children with Learning Disabilities" (Electronic version), by K. L. DeGeorge, 1998, *Intervention in School and Clinic, 33*, pp. 157–162.

Madison Public Library. *Friends like these . . . Books for young teens about friendship.* Retrieved March 15, 2005, from http://www.madisonpubliclibrary.org/youth/booklists/friends.html.

PROFESSIONAL EDGE

On the Issue of Fairness

Many teachers struggle in deciding how to respond to students who claim that something in class is not fair—whether it is the fact that two students receive the same amount of credit for doing very different types of work; that several students take their tests in a small-group, separate setting with extra adult assistance available; or that one student's misbehavior results in a warning whereas another's results in a trip to the office. Although there are no easy answers to this dilemma, Welch (2000) suggests the following strategies:

- Reflect back a student's feelings, perhaps by asking the student to write you a note about his or her perspective on the issue.

- Listen for other meanings in students' comments because their complaints may be disguised requests for increased teacher attention.

- Offer something special to young children for hard work. If one student is receiving stickers, also offer them to a complaining student, but only for "extra hard" work.

- Respond to students' fairness complaints consistently and without explanation. Legally and ethically, you may not discuss one student's work with another student; your response should convey this unambiguously: "You know I won't talk to you about anyone's work but your own. How can I help you to do your work?"

- Teach students about three types of fairness: equality (everyone gets the same thing), equity (reward is based on contribution), and need (reward is greatest to those with the greatest need).

- Establish a procedure such as class meetings by which students can discuss their concerns about fairness.

- Develop a caring, cooperative classroom community using strategies suggested throughout this textbook and especially in this chapter.

- Provide and enforce schoolwide procedures related to fairness so that a consistent approach is used on the playground and in the cafeteria, gym, hallways, and other locations where fairness may become an issue.

- Clarify within yourself your legal and moral obligation to make accommodations for students with disabilities.

- Occasionally, a student has a legitimate concern about fairness. It is just as important to know when and how to push a student with a disability to do more as it is to know when to make accommodations.

SOURCE: Adapted from "Responding to Student Concerns about Fairness," by A. Welch, 2000, *Teaching Exceptional Children, 33*(2), pp. 36–40. Reprinted with permission.

found that although parents valued friendship development for their children with disabilities, the time parents spent facilitating those friendships sometimes was perceived as time taken away from highly valued extended-family interactions (Turnbull, Blue-Banning, & Pereira, 2000). Another finding was that children's friends often were their cousins or other relatives. You can review many of the suggestions presented throughout this textbook for working effectively with families in the Working Together feature on page 480.

Providing Positive Role Models

A third component of promoting positive peer relationships is offering positive role models. There are several ways to do this. First, as a teacher in an inclusive school, you might be the most influential model for students learning how to interact with a peer with a disability. If you are positive in your interactions and avoid responding to a student with a disability as a "guest" instead of a full classroom member, students will respond in kind. For example, if you talk to a student with a severe disability as though he or she were a very young child even though you are teaching an eighth-grade class, other students probably will treat the student as a young child. However, if you speak in an age-appropriate voice, so will your students. Similarly, if you expect a student with a learning disability to behave similarly to other students instead of making exceptions

WORKING **TOGETHER**

Collaborating with Families

Parents are your partners in fostering the development of students' social skills. Parents know their children in ways that educators cannot, and they have at heart their children's best interests. Here are some questions to think about as you prepare to interact with the parents of all your students, including those with disabilities.

- Do I use effective communication strategies in my interactions with families?
- Do I take into account families' preferences based on their cultures?
- Do I avoid using jargon?
- Do I define unfamiliar terms?
- Do I use good listening skills such as clarifying, paraphrasing, and summarizing?
- Do I attend to the nonverbal communication of parents and family members?
- Do I collaborate with families during IEP meetings?
- Do I seek verbal and written input from families regarding their children in my classroom?
- Do I inform families of students with disabilities about student progress at least as often as families of students without disabilities receive progress reports?
- Do I value the contributions of parents and family members?
- Do I base all interactions on the assumption that parents want what they believe is best for their children?
- Do I acknowledge the strengths and coping strategies a family has developed for working with a child with a disability?

- Do I recognize the contributions of members of extended families?
- Do I provide opportunities for families to be involved in the classroom and the school in ways that are meaningful?
- Do I seek to develop a collaborative relationship with families?
- Do I see the contributions of families as equal in value to the contributions of school staff?
- Do I seek to identify goals that are shared between the school and families?
- Do I recognize that the school and families share responsibility for student outcomes?
- Do I take the initiative to establish a collaborative relationship with families?
- Do I demonstrate caring and concern for students and their families?
- Do I get to know my students with disabilities in ways unrelated to their disabilities?
- Do I schedule meetings at times that are convenient for families?
- Do I help families access additional resources in the community when needed?
- Do I treat family members as I would want to be treated?

SOURCE: From *Collaborating with Families Checklist,* by the Training and Technical Assistance Center, College of William and Mary, 2002. Retrieved February 11, 2005, from http://www.wm.edu/ttac/articles/family/collab2.html.

FYI

A colleague or community member who has a disability might be a great resource as a positive role model for students.

(provided that this expectation is appropriate), peers in the class will have the same expectations. Interacting with students with disabilities in the same way that you interact with anyone else provides the modeling that helps shape all student interactions.

Students without disabilities also need to see that students with disabilities and other special needs have many contributions to make. Pointing out contributions made by a student with a disability, giving students with disabilities standard classroom responsibilities, and recognizing a student's best effort whether or not it fits within traditional curriculum standards—all these actions lead peers to recognize that students with special needs are valuable classroom community members. Family, community, and national support groups also can be resources for providing positive role models.

Promoting positive peer relationships needs to be part of your automatic teaching behavior throughout the school year. Evidence suggests that a long-term approach for fostering peer interactions is most effective and that when teachers stop attending to students' social relationships, these relationships tend to deteriorate (Freeman & Alkin, 2000; Salisbury & Palombaro, 1998).

How Can You Provide Education about Individuals with Disabilities?

Besides promoting positive social interactions between students with and without disabilities, teachers play an important role in educating their students about all types of differences among individuals, including disabilities. Even during years in which you have few or no students with disabilities in your class, you can positively affect student understanding and attitudes toward individuals with disabilities by incorporating information about them into your curriculum. This section describes three strategies for doing so: informing students through direct instruction, using video and print media, and demonstrating and using adaptive technology. The Case in Practice below suggests why there is a strong need for school-based disability awareness and sensitivity training to be embedded in a general program of fostering respect for diversity.

CONNECTIONS

In Chapter 6 you learned about students with autism. One technique for helping them learn to manage social interactions are social stories, simple tales that describe situations and tell students how to respond in a socially acceptable way.

Informing through Direct Instruction

One of the most straightforward strategies for teaching students about individuals with disabilities is to provide them with relevant information. For example, you might invite guest speakers to your class to discuss what it is like to have a disability and how people with disabilities lead successful lives. Alternatively, you might arrange to have

CASE IN PRACTICE

Intervening to Promote Positive Social Interactions

Ms. Giano is a middle school teacher, and she is in a quandary. This afternoon she received a phone call from Ms. Perez concerning Jesse, her son. Ms. Perez related that Jesse had come home from school looking disheveled and with torn books and papers. At first he wouldn't tell his mother what had happened, but he eventually related the story. Jesse has albinism; he has very little pigment in his skin, hair, and eyes. His skin is very pale and his hair seems almost white. In addition, Jesse has a serious vision problem related to his albinism, and he also has been identified as having a learning disability. He told his mother that several of his classmates had begun making fun of him on the walk to the

bus and then continued on the bus. They had been doing this almost since the beginning of the school year, but things had been getting worse lately. Today, Jesse explained, he couldn't stand it anymore and he lunged at the boys. The bus driver intervened, but all the boys now were to be brought back to school by their parents for fighting. Ms. Perez was upset. She also mentioned that Jesse had asked her not to call school, that he would deal with the situation and accept the discipline for fighting on the bus. He was afraid that his classmates' teasing would become even worse if it was made an issue. Ms. Perez is not satisfied; she wants something done to stop the teasing and protect her son.

REFLECTIONS

How does this story relate to the topic of bullying? If you were Ms. Giano, what would you say to Ms. Perez? What is the role of general education teachers in ensuring that their students are treated respectfully? How would you address this issue with Jesse? With the other boys? If you think they should have an additional consequence, what should it be? What might you try as an all-homeroom activity to foster better understanding among your diverse students? Do you think your response to the situation and interventions should be significantly different if you plan to teach elementary students? High school students?

professionals who provide services to individuals with disabilities talk about their careers. You can also find individuals to speak to your students through local disability advocacy groups or parent groups. A local college or university also might be a valuable resource.

You also can educate students about disabilities by incorporating relevant topics into the curriculum. As you teach, you can mention famous individuals with disabilities who contributed to various fields. For example, when studying the presidents, you can raise the fact that Franklin D. Roosevelt had polio and used a wheelchair. With older students you could explore the reasons why controversy arose about whether or not a statue of this president should depict him in a wheelchair. In science, you can explain Thomas Edison's hearing loss and Albert Einstein's alleged learning disability. In the fine arts, examples of individuals with disabilities include actor Christopher Reeve, singer Ray Charles, and composer Ludwig van Beethoven. Students' understanding of and respect for individuals with disabilities are fostered better through an ongoing education program than through occasional special events that highlight this topic. For example, if your school participates in an ongoing program to increase students' understanding of racial, cultural, religious, and other types of diversity, disability awareness is appropriately included as another type of diversity.

A third source of direct information about disabilities is special awareness programs. One program for use in inclusive classrooms in elementary schools that may be available through your school district or a community group that advocates for individuals with disabilities is Kids on the Block (Kids on the Block, 2004). Begun in 1977, this commercially available and internationally acclaimed program includes a set of puppets and supporting materials and books about disabilities. The first puppet developed and still used is Mark Riley, a young man in a wheelchair who has cerebral palsy. As Mark tells his story through the puppeteer, students are encouraged to ask him questions and thus they learn about this disability. Since its inception, Kids on the Block has expanded to include information on a wide range of disabilities including visual impairments, medical conditions such as AIDS, learning disabilities, and ADHD. For older students, your community may have a drama group that performs skits to educate students about individuals with disabilities, or a speaker's bureau that can help you connect with a person with a disability who can speak to your students. The special educators in your school should know what programs are available in your area and how you can access them.

Using Video and Print Media

Individuals with disabilities have been portrayed in print and other media for many years, but a shift gradually has occurred in the nature of that portrayal. Instead of being viewed as victims or objects of pity, people with disabilities now often are central characters and their disabilities are just one dimension of their roles. A trip to your local library or video store or a casual reading of television program guides or your newspaper can lead you to a wealth of information, as can a quick search of this topic on the Internet. You could identify media that relate to your instructional goals, find ways to incorporate them into your lessons, and arrange discussions so that your students feel free to ask questions and share their insights.

Your school or district might have educational videos about students with disabilities that are designed specifically for school-age children. Many award-winning movies also address disability and are appropriate for older students. These films include *Radio, My Left Foot, Rain Man, As Good as It Gets, Mr. Holland's Opus, Born on the*

> Students' understanding of and respect for individuals with disabilities are fostered better through an ongoing education program than through occasional "special events."

FYI

In addition to the puppet program related to students with disabilities, Kids on the Block includes puppets and programs to help students learn to address aggression, compassion, and perseverance.

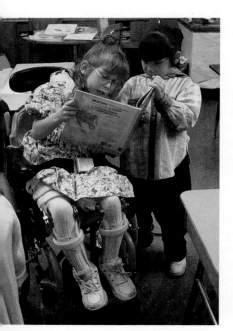

How do students without disabilities learn about their peers with disabilities? How can teachers promote friendships between students with and without exceptionalities?

Fourth of July, The Miracle Worker, If You Could See What I Hear, Mask, Children of a Lesser God, Forrest Gump, and *Shine* (Disability Films, 2004). Television shows and made-for-TV movies (for example, *Wit, Suddenly*) also address disability topics.

Books are written by and for children about virtually every type of disability and other special need. Reading or assigning an appropriate book to your class can be an excellent strategy for introducing a new student and his or her special needs or for promoting awareness. A reading assignment can also help open a discussion about interacting with and treating a classmate respectfully. Four criteria to consider in selecting children's literature that addresses disability include these (Smith-Arrezzo, 2003):

1. The structural elements of the book should be well developed.
2. The book should be appealing to children with the characters with disabilities portrayed in a realistic way.
3. The book should have a positive emotional tone.
4. The book should present information about special education accurately.

Newspapers carry stories about individuals with disabilities, requirements of the Americans with Disabilities Act, and trends toward inclusive education. National newspapers, such as *USA Today* and the *Wall Street Journal,* are good sources of this type of information, but local newspapers also carry stories you can use. For example, when a major league baseball player had a seizure during a ball game, a local newspaper ran a story on what to do when one sees someone having a seizure. The high-interest article became a valuable teaching tool for sports-minded middle school students.

ANALYZE AND REFLECT

What strategies can you use to effectively incorporate information about individuals with disabilities into your instructional program? How can individuals with disabilities take a leadership role in facilitating this type of instruction? What are the benefits of providing this information to students without disabilities?

Demonstrating and Using Adaptive Technology

Another means of educating students about individuals with disabilities is exploring technology resources (Behrmann & Jerome, 2002). For example, you can teach students about the powerful tools available to facilitate communication, including touch screens, talking word processors, customized computer keyboards, computer voice input, and word-prediction programs. You can demonstrate for students the capabilities of talking computers, calculators, and watches. You also can engage students in learning about low-tech devices such as talking watches and no-tech items such as pencil grips and study carrels. Some specific ideas for using technology to enhance communication among students with and without disabilities are included in the Technology Notes on page 484.

How Can You Develop and Support Peer Tutoring?

Students also learn about disabilities and other special needs through direct experience and structured interactions with classmates. **Peer tutoring** is a system of instruction in which pairs of students with relatively equal standing are given formal roles for promoting each other's achievement (Mathes & Babyak, 2001; Ryan, Reid, & Epstein, 2004). The tutor role is most often held by a peer in the same class, school, or school district as the tutee. Tutees are the students who receive the instruction from peer tutors. When peer tutoring is used with students with disabilities, the goal is often twofold: fostering social interactions and enhancing academic achievement (Fulk & King, 2001).

> " Peer tutoring is a system of instruction in which pairs of students with relatively equal standing are given formal roles for promoting each other's achievement. "

> TECHNOLOGY NOTES

Using Technology to Build Positive Peer Relationships

Technology can be a powerful tool for building positive social peer relationships in your classroom. Two examples of how to use technology with students with and without disabilities follow.

Dialogue Journals

Most teachers have learned that computers are important tools for motivating reluctant writers to share their thoughts and ideas. Using computers to create dialogue journals also can facilitate communication between students with and without disabilities. A dialogue journal is a realistic writing situation in which each student is encouraged to share thoughts and feelings with an age-mate while teachers simply manage and monitor the process. Dialogue journals focus on meanings rather than on formality, and they provide a nonthreatening climate for students' writing activities. A student is matched with either a known peer or a "mystery" peer from another class, and the two write to each other approximately once each week. Computer disks, CDs, or thumb drives make transferring journals from class to class a relatively simple task. At some point, teachers probably should arrange for partners to meet each other and discuss the journals face to face, but this is not as essential as the writing process itself.

By pairing students with and without disabilities, students can gain greater understanding of each other's perceptions. In a project in which hearing and deaf students participated (Kluwin, 1996), students responded very positively to the experience. However, teachers commented that some problems occurred when students were mismatched with regard to maturity or developmental levels, or when students in general did not have skills for personal writing. To maximize the effectiveness of dialogue journals, teachers should encourage students to use a conversational style in their writing; students without disabilities should not be overprepared for the experience, or else prejudice may occur; teachers should suggest topics as needed; students should be well matched; and teachers should monitor the writing, paying attention to issues of privacy.

Problem-Solving Videos

Teachers can use videotapes of popular television shows, movies, or other instructional video materials to work with

Students with disabilities sometimes communicate with peers and others by using adaptive technology.

students on social skills and problem solving. They can guide students to use the following steps in real-life interactions by applying them as they view a video:

1. Look for signs of different feelings.
2. Tell yourself what the problem is.
3. Decide on a goal.
4. Stop and think of as many solutions to the problem as you can.
5. For each solution, picture all the things that might happen.
6. Choose the best solution.
7. Plan it and make a final check.
8. Try it and rethink it.

This approach to addressing social skills and problem solving appears to have great value because it draws on television as a means of focusing student attention, enables even nonreaders to participate, promotes discussion, and presents opportunities for later role-playing. Younger students and those with attentional problems can be shown shorter videotapes, perhaps 15 minutes or less; older students and those with better attentional skills can view longer tapes. Teachers, of course, play a critical role in guiding student thinking and facilitating student discussion.

SOURCE: Adapted from "Building Social and Academic Skills via Problem Solving Videos," by M. J. Elias and M. E. Taylor, 1995, *Teaching Exceptional Children, 27*(3), pp. 14–17; and "Getting Hearing and Deaf Students to Write to Each Other through Dialogue Journals," by T. N. Kluwin, 1996, *Teaching Exceptional Children, 28*(2), pp. 50–53.

The effectiveness of peer tutoring for enhancing student social interactions and academic achievement has been established through more than two decades of research. For example, Mastropieri, Scruggs, Spencer, and Fontana (2003) compared two approaches to teaching history to students with mild disabilities. Some of the students were taught a structured note-taking process while others participated in a peer tutoring program. When achievement data for the two groups were compared, the students who had participated in the tutoring program outperformed the other students. The teachers reported that students in the tutoring program spent more time on task, and the students expressed interest in using peer tutoring in other academic classes. Socially, the students reported that peer tutoring made time in class go by quickly and that they enjoyed interacting with their classmates in order to learn.

In another study, first-grade teachers implemented a highly structured peer tutoring program called Peer-Assisted Learning Strategies (PALS) for their students with and without disabilities (Baker, Gersten, Dimino, & Griffiths, 2004). Several years after the initial successful research study, the teachers were still effectively using the peer tutoring program at least twice each week in math. Because the program includes a built-in data collection system, they also were able to report that the effect on student academic achievement was highly positive. The teachers also reported that PALS had a positive impact on student social development. Teachers noted that the program taught students to work effectively with many different peers instead of just their friends by helping them to learn how to say positive things to one another. This result carried far beyond the math instructional period.

Peer tutoring also has a positive impact on tutors, particularly when older tutors with marginal skills work with younger students. One study found that middle school students at very high risk for dropping out of school learned their academic content better and had more positive attitudes toward school and learning when they participated as tutors in a cross-age peer tutoring program (Nazzal, 2002). Jennifer, one of the tutors in the study, commented that tutoring made her want to try to learn harder because she realized that what she was doing was actually helping her younger tutee—that her efforts really made a difference.

Research on peer tutoring programs has addressed factors such as the age of the tutor and the tutee, the amount of time allocated for tutoring, the content selected for peer tutoring, students' characteristics, and the amount of program structure. All these factors can influence peer tutoring outcomes, but not in predictable ways. You may find that you need to experiment with several options for creating the most successful experiences for your students.

Developing Peer Tutoring Programs

Developing a peer tutoring program can be as simple or complex as you want it to be. You can create your own system within your classroom, partner some or all of your students with another group of students, or help coordinate a schoolwide tutoring program. Established and researched programs also exist, such as the **Classwide Peer Tutoring (CWPT)** program (for example, Burks, 2004; Fulk & King, 2001; Greenwood et al., 2001; Ryan et al., 2004) in which all the students in a class take on the roles of tutor and tutee in turn and follow a set of clear steps for helping each other to learn. CWPT is described in Figure 13.2. Steps for setting up a peer tutoring program of your own are described in the following sections.

SELECTING TUTORS ● To create a **same-age tutoring** program in your classroom, consider pairing students who are both high achievers rather than pairing a high achiever with a low achiever. Then pair other students whose understanding of the topic at hand is fairly similar. This arrangement reduces the problem of high achievers

ANALYZE AND REFLECT

How might peer tutoring benefit students with and without disabilities? How would you go about deciding which type of peer tutoring program to implement? How would you make a decision about its effectiveness?

FIGURE 13.2 Steps in Classwide Peer Tutoring

1. Assign all students to tutoring pairs that are changed weekly or biweekly.
2. Assign each tutoring pair to one of two classroom teams.
3. Teach all students a specific series of steps for presenting and practicing content.
4. Teach all students specific strategies for correcting tutees and rewarding correct responses.
5. Provide tutoring pairs with daily assignments.
6. Instruct tutors to keep score: When a tutee answers a question correctly, a point is scored for the team.
7. Announce the winning team and post points.
8. Reward the winning team with a privilege or class applause.
9. Reverse the tutor/tutee arrangement each session or have both students take the tutor role within each session.

RESEARCH
N O T E

In a review of the use of peer tutoring in specialized subjects such as art, music, horticulture, and physical education, Heron, Welsch, and Goddard (2003) found that although few empirical studies have been completed, they generally report positive academic and social results.

How can peer tutoring programs benefit students in your classroom? What combinations of tutors and tutees might work best for the grade level you plan to teach?

becoming impatient with low achievers and the concern about high-achieving students missing their own opportunities for learning. However, same-age tutoring done in this way has two drawbacks: High-achieving students do not learn the skills for interacting with students with special learning needs, and low-achieving students lose learning role models. Another approach is to pair students randomly and use a **reciprocal tutoring** approach in which both students alternate between the tutor and tutee roles.

In a **cross-age tutoring** approach, older students tutor younger ones. For example, if you teach in the primary grades, you might ask the fifth-grade teachers to provide tutors for your students. Teachers could collaborate to partner entire classes and institute regularly scheduled cross-class tutoring. If a middle school, junior high, or high school is located nearby, its students could also serve as tutors. If you teach in a middle school or high school, you might establish a peer tutoring program for the school a level below yours so that high school students tutor in the middle school and middle school students tutor in the elementary school. At the secondary level, older students might serve as tutors and mentors for younger students. Seniors might be paired with freshmen or sophomores in this way.

As you decide how to establish a tutoring program, keep in mind students with disabilities and other special needs. Sometimes, students with disabilities can serve as tutors to their classmates. An older student without a disability can be an ideal tutor for a younger student who has a disability. Also, an older student who has a learning or intellectual disability or who is at risk for school failure can be an effective tutor for a younger student with or without a disability. In other words, you can structure a tutoring program in many ways. What is important is making deliberate decisions about how to structure it, basing those decisions on the strengths and needs of the students.

Depending on your goals, you might try a variation of peer tutoring by turning to adult tutors. In some school districts, the best available pool of tutors is college students or adult volunteers such as students' parents or grandparents, recently retired teaching staff, or local business personnel. Adults can make better judgments about the content being taught and learned than student peers, and they might better be able to informally address student social skills. Tutees often look up to older tutors who provide a special type of individual attention. Adults also have the maturity that eliminates potential behavior problems that sometimes occur with peer partners. Of course, if your goals include helping students improve peer relations, some form of traditional peer tutoring is your best option.

DECIDING HOW MUCH TUTORING SHOULD OCCUR ● The specific time allocation for peer tutoring depends on the needs of the students and the structure of the program. Although no specific guidelines can be given, in many cases tutoring in elementary schools occurs two to four times each week for 20 or 30 minutes and as often as daily for one class period in high schools (Baker et al., 2004; Calhoun & Fuchs, 2003; Mortweet et al., 1999). This amount of tutoring ensures continuity yet does not detract significantly from the rest of students' educational programs.

PROVIDING TIME FOR PEER TUTORING ● Peer tutoring can occur as part of independent work time or as a periodic activity in which an entire class participates. Cross-age tutoring needs to occur on a schedule that accommodates both the tutor and the tutee. Optimal times can include the beginning of the school day as students arrive, the middle of the afternoon when both the tutor and the tutee need a change-of-pace activity, near the end of the school day, or after school. As much as possible, tutoring in a content area should occur within the content-area classes. In some middle schools and high schools, peer tutoring is a service learning activity that is an elective course. In such cases, tutoring occurs during the class period available for the tutor, and it might occur in the tutee's classroom, the library or media center, or a study hall or advisory classroom.

SELECTING CONTENT AND FORMAT FOR TUTORING ● Effective peer tutoring programs provide practice on skills already taught by the teacher and use standard formats that help tutors know how to do their job (Fulk & King, 2001). For example, many elementary peer tutoring programs have tutors and tutees working on basic math facts, spelling or vocabulary words, or comprehension questions on social studies or science materials already taught in class. In middle and high schools, peer tutoring may occur to review vocabulary, review concepts or skills, or to provide assistance to a student in a core academic class (for example, algebra or biology) that the tutor has already successfully completed.

Highly structured formats for tutoring sessions are best. For example, tutors might be instructed to begin a vocabulary session by reviewing all eight words from last time and then showing each new word, waiting for a response, and marking the response as correct or incorrect. The tutor praises correct responses, corrects errors, and asks the tutee to repeat corrected responses. If the students finish their list, they review it until the end of the tutoring session. This example illustrates the need for a clear set of procedures for tutors to follow, whatever format you use. Unambiguous procedures help keep participants in tutoring sessions on task.

CONNECTIONS

Chapters 2 and 3 included strategies for parent communication. These strategies could be part of your approach to communicating with parents about peer tutoring.

RESEARCH NOTE

Spencer and Balboni (2003) reviewed 35 studies of peer tutoring at the elementary level involving students with varying levels of mental retardation. The students successfully served as both tutors and tutees in teaching and learning academic, social, and daily living skills.

ANALYZE
AND**REFLECT**

How could you apply what you have learned about social skills and student social relationships to the students introduced in the stories at the beginning of this chapter—Errol, Kathleen, and Demetrius? How do the type and quality of social skills and student social relationships affect an individual's overall success in school? Throughout life?

TRAINING TUTORS ● Professionals generally agree that effective peer tutoring programs carefully prepare tutors for their teaching roles. Tutor training should accomplish five main purposes (Barron & Foot, 1991):

1. Training should provide tutors with structures and procedures for tutoring as described above.
2. Training should give tutors a systematic way of tracking the tutees' learning.
3. Training should help tutors develop positive interaction skills, including ways to praise tutees and ways to correct their errors.
4. Training should prepare tutors in problem-solving skills so that they can generate ideas about how to proceed when the procedures are not working, or when the tutees get confused or misbehave.
5. Training should add perceived value and credibility to the program and its participants.

Sample topics for a peer tutor training program are outlined in Figure 13.3.

Supporting Peer Tutoring Programs

A tutor training program includes follow-up and assessment. For example, in a cross-age tutoring program, it is important to bring tutors together periodically to discuss how they are doing and how they have resolved problems and to thank them for their work. When tutoring extends beyond your own class group, it is a nice touch to provide tutor appreciation certificates or other tokens of appreciation.

Several other factors go into the supports needed for a successful peer tutoring program. These factors are discussed in the sections that follow.

MANAGEMENT AND SUPERVISION ● Once your peer tutoring program is established, you should continue to supervise it. This ongoing supervision enables you to praise tutor pairs having constructive work sessions, to identify potential problems when they are small and easily resolved, and to monitor student learning. If you have the assistance of a paraprofessional in your classroom, this person can help with day-to-day supervision responsibilities. As your tutoring program progresses, you might

FIGURE 13.3 Topics for Training Peer Tutors

1. Sensitivity to others' feelings, needs for acceptance, and fears of rejection
2. Ways to develop positive relationships with tutees, including using respectful language, giving positive reinforcement, showing personal interest, and offering constructive feedback
3. Effective communication and interaction skills: giving clear directions, making teaching interesting to the tutee, acting interested and being interested, explaining things in another way, correcting the tutee without criticism, praising correct responses, and admitting mistakes
4. Tutoring procedures and guidelines: having all needed materials prepared, beginning a session without teacher assistance, breaking big steps into smaller ones, showing how to do something if the tutee does not understand, giving the tutee time to think before responding, helping but not doing the work for the tutee, monitoring time to finish on schedule, and reviewing what has been taught
5. Procedures for gathering data on the tutee's learning, such as using a checklist or helping the tutee chart progress
6. Problem solving about issues that could come up during peer tutoring
7. The tutoring schedule and the need for commitment

find it necessary to revise the format, regroup students, introduce "graduates," and devise new ways to thank the tutors for their work.

STAFF AND ADMINISTRATIVE SUPPORT ● Unless you plan a peer tutoring program that stays within the confines of your classroom, you will need the support of your colleagues and administrators. Other teachers might have ideas for how to pair students and arrange formats and opportunities for tutoring, and the special services staff might have creative ways of including students with special needs in the tutoring program. Administrators can provide support and assistance in arranging schedules, in communicating with parents, and in finding a small budget for the incidental supplies you might need.

> " Unless you plan a peer tutoring program that stays within the confines of your classroom, you will need the support of your colleagues and administrators. "

ASSISTANCE FROM VOLUNTEERS ● In addition to helping with tutoring, volunteers might also be willing to manage a peer tutoring program, thus relieving you from many of the details of operation. For example, volunteers could establish the procedures for recruiting peer tutors, offer the tutor training, match tutors with tutees, monitor the tutoring sessions, assess student learning, problem solve with tutors, and arrange a thank-you event for them. Education majors or other teacher trainees in local colleges or universities could assist in these tasks at the elementary or secondary school level, as could members of a parent or community organization familiar with peer tutoring.

COMMUNICATION ABOUT PEER TUTORING ● Support for peer tutoring programs often depends on communication with parents and other community members. If you plan a peer tutoring program for students, you should alert parents and explain your instructional approach and rationale. If you participate in a tutoring program that includes several classes, you might want to write a letter to parents announcing the availability of the program and providing its rationale. Although most parents will readily agree to permit their children to participate as tutors or tutees, a few might have questions about tutors losing instructional time teaching others and about the effectiveness of tutoring for students who have difficulty learning. Being prepared for questions such as these helps you answer them readily. Also, your administrator can provide support in this area. As your tutoring program progresses, you can keep parents apprised of student activities through periodic notes or class newsletters, or through updates provided by your home–school hotline or district newsletter. In middle schools and high schools where peer tutoring might be an elective course, information on the program can be added to the school website, possibly with a list of frequently asked questions and information for signing up as a tutor or tutee.

How Can You Use Cooperative Learning Strategies to Facilitate Social Inclusion?

Peer tutoring offers one structured alternative for promoting positive peer relationships while at the same time enhancing academic achievement. Another option for accomplishing these goals is **cooperative learning.** Cooperative learning has its roots in the U.S. civil rights and school desegregation movements. Very soon after the 1954 *Brown v. Board of Education* Supreme Court decision established that separate schools cannot be equal, Allport (1954) wrote that simply putting students of different races in the same schools would not accomplish integration. He went on to clarify that integration would

RESEARCH
NOTE

Stevens (2003) reported that when cooperative learning was used to re-structure reading and lan-guage arts instruction in middle schools, students were more actively engaged in and took more responsi-bility for their own learning.

require opportunities for students to interact with one another in situations in which they had equal status. Further, he stated that school administrators would have to en-dorse strongly the students' interactions. In practice, this meant that students needed opportunities to interact with one another in structured social situations not controlled by teachers but nevertheless strongly sanctioned by school authorities, situations free of unreasonable academic pressures that might inadvertently place some students in a lower status in terms of perceived competence. Cooperative learning was developed as a means of creating these conditions during traditional classroom instruction (Sharan et al., 1984). For nearly four decades, cooperative learning has been employed as a strat-egy for promoting positive student interactions in diverse classrooms. It has been used as a strategy for achieving racial and cultural integration, for assisting socially isolated learners, for fostering inclusive education for students with disabilities and other special needs, and for accommodating culture-based learning styles.

The Rationale for Cooperative Learning

As you can see from the history of cooperative learning, its primary purpose is to in-crease students' ability to interact with each other in appropriate ways. Many studies over the past 25 years have addressed this topic. For example, Gillies and Ashman (2000) found that after three school terms, students who had worked in cooperative learning groups were more involved in group activities and provided more direction and assistance to other group members than students who participated in loosely struc-tured groups. Students in cooperative classrooms also are more likely to show affection toward other class members, invite others to join a group activity, and thank or praise each other. Although fewer studies on secondary students are available, the same trend exists (McMaster & Fuchs, 2002).

For students with disabilities, the social benefits of cooperative learning appear to accrue in the same way that they do for other students. In one early review of nearly 100 studies of cooperative learning (Johnson, Johnson, & Maruyama, 1983), the posi-tive social impact existed for students with disabilities as well as for students with other special needs, especially when stu-dents were given specific instruction in collaborative skills. Other studies more recently have found similar results (Jenk-ins, Antil, Wayne, & Vadasy, 2003). In fact, cooperative learn-ing often is recommended as a fundamental component of inclusive classrooms (Piercy, Wilton, & Townsend, 2002; Rudd, 2002). Although the value of cooperative learning lies historically in its potential for creating positive peer interac-tions, it also can enhance learning and achievement (Maheady, Mitchell-Pendl, Mallette, & Harper, 2002; Ryan et al., 2004). For students without disabilities, cooperative learning has strongly and repeatedly been demonstrated to be an effective instructional approach for achievement in reading, math, science, physical education, and other areas (for example, Dyson, 2002; Emmer & Gerwels, 2002; Maheady et al., 2002; Jenkins et al., 2003).

> "Although the value of cooperative learning lies historically in its potential for creating positive peer interactions, it also can enhance learning and achievement."

The academic outcomes of cooperative learning for students with disabilities vary and cannot always be assumed to be strong (McMaster & Fuchs, 2002). However, some evidence suggests that for students with high-incidence disabilities, cooperative learn-ing is at least as effective as other instructional approaches (for example, Gillies & Ash-man, 2002; Ryan et al., 2004). Even stronger results have been noted for other students with special needs, including students who are English-language learners (Calderon, 1999; Slavin, 1999) and those at risk for school failure (Vaughan, 2002). For students with severe intellectual disabilities or multiple disabilities, the issue of academic achievement as traditionally measured is not usually a central concern.

Characteristics of Cooperative Learning Approaches

Cooperative learning generally has four fundamental and essential characteristics: positive interdependence, face-to-face interactions, individual accountability, and emphasis on interpersonal skills (Cross & Walker-Knight, 1997; Malmgren, 1998). First, the students in the groups have positive interdependence. Either they reach their goal together or no one is able to achieve it. For example, in Mr. Reilly's classroom, the students earn points when all the members in their cooperative groups get at least 70 percent on their weekly spelling test. Group members work very hard to help all members learn spelling words. Second, cooperative learning requires face-to-face interactions. In Mr. Sutter's class, students have opportunities to work directly with their group members to accomplish learning goals related to reviewing the use of advertising approaches in newspapers and magazines. Third, members of cooperative groups have individual accountability. On the weekly vocabulary test in Ms. Mather's chemistry class, students who have difficulty learning are not excused from taking the test, nor are high achievers permitted to answer for all group members. Each member is required to make a contribution. Finally, cooperative learning stresses student interpersonal skills, such as how to ask questions, how to praise classmates, and how to help another student learn. When Ms. Bolter notices positive interpersonal interactions among her seventh-grade English students, she gives them "Bolter Bucks" to spend on a variety of privileges and rewards.

These four characteristics of cooperative learning distinguish it from other approaches to learning common in schools. For example, much school learning is competitive, that is, based on winners and losers. Spelling matches or other instructional games in which only one student wins are competitive. Another example of school competition is found in many athletic programs. A second type of traditional learning approach is individualistic. In individualistic learning, student achievement is not dependent on how others achieve. For example, a teacher sets up a system in which all students who complete 90 percent of their homework, make at least a B average on unit tests, and complete two projects by meeting standards outlined in a rubric are assigned an A for the grading period. If all the students in the class meet the standard, all can earn that grade. If only one student meets the standard, only that student has earned an A. All students can be winners; one student's winning does not affect other students' chances of success. An individualistic approach is the basis for special education and most remedial programs.

All three approaches—cooperative, competitive, and individualistic—have a place in schools. However, the social and interactive components of cooperative learning are not possible in either of the other two approaches, so this approach especially needs to be incorporated into the school curriculum, particularly in inclusive schools striving to foster positive interactions between students with and without disabilities.

Developing Cooperative Learning Programs

Given the many positive effects of cooperative learning for all students, you probably will find it an effective instructional approach in your classroom. You might decide to use cooperative groups three times each week for language arts activities, for instance, or once each week for test review. Regardless of how you incorporate cooperative learning into your classroom, you can achieve the best results by following some basic guidelines.

FORM COOPERATIVE LEARNING GROUPS ● One of your first considerations in creating a cooperative learning program is deciding on the size and makeup of the groups. Regardless of the specific cooperative learning approach you choose, the age, abilities, and needs of your students help determine group size. For example, if you

WWW
R E S O U R C E S

The @ctivTeen website (http://www.disabilitycentral.com/activteen/about.htm) is managed by teenagers who have disabilities and is designed especially for them. The site includes an e-zine as well as message boards and activities pages.

WWW
R E S O U R C E S

Thousands of websites related to peer tutoring and cooperative learning can be found on the Internet. If you type either of those phrases into one of the major search engines (for example, Google), you'll find many resources to help you establish a successful program.

How can cooperative groups be used to teach both academic content and skills for working with peers? What skills do students need to work successfully?

teach second grade, you probably will use groups of three at the beginning of the school year and consider larger groups after students become accustomed to cooperative learning procedures. If you teach eighth grade, you might be able to begin the year with groups of five. Factors besides age should be considered, too. In a class with mature students, larger groups are possible; in a class with immature students, groups of three (or even teaming up in pairs) might be best. Students with very limited abilities might need a smaller group; more able students can succeed in a larger group. Notice that the range of group size is from two to five or six. Larger groups become difficult for students to participate in and for teachers to manage.

You should assign students to cooperative groups to create heterogeneous groupings; that is, if your class group includes four students with disabilities, you should distribute them among the cooperative groups. Likewise, high achievers and low achievers should be assigned across groups. The success of cooperative learning is based on students learning to value and respect each person's contributions. Although skill grouping sometimes is appropriate, deciding to place students together in groups according to ability generally undermines the purpose of cooperative learning.

> " You should assign students to cooperative groups to create heterogeneous groupings. "

Teachers sometimes ask how long cooperative groups should be kept intact. There is no single right answer to that question. If you change groups too frequently, students do not have enough opportunity to learn about each other and to reach a high level of cooperative functioning. However, if you keep the same groups for too long, students do not have the chance to work with other classmates. A general guideline is to keep cooperative groups for at least a 2- or 3-week period but to change them at least at the end of each grading period.

PREPARE STUDENTS FOR COOPERATIVE LEARNING ● A high school English teacher participated in a university class on cooperative learning and decided that she and the special educator could use this strategy in their inclusive class. They carefully planned a series of cooperative activities, assigned students to groups, and waited for positive results. They quickly learned why teaching students to cooperate is such an important component in developing cooperative learning programs! The students bickered with each other and were impatient with students who did not immediately answer questions. Some decided to try to complete their work alone, even though it required input from others. Before students work together, it is essential to teach them cooperative skills (Cooper, 2002).

The skills for cooperative group members have been recognized for many years (Johnson, Johnson, Holubec, & Roy, 1984) and can be categorized under the headings of forming, functioning, formulating, and fermenting.

1. *Forming.* Students need forming skills to move into cooperative groups and carry out basic tasks with politeness and respect. These skills are the most rudimentary.

2. *Functioning.* Functioning skills are procedural, including monitoring time limits, asking for help, and clarifying fellow group members' statements. These skills help groups interact constructively and productively.

3. *Formulating.* Formulating skills are more advanced procedural skills and include asking other students to elaborate on their comments so that everyone understands them better, devising strategies for remembering important information, and relating new information to information previously learned.

4. *Fermenting.* Fermenting skills are those students use to participate in their groups as critical thinkers and problem solvers. These skills include integrating members' ideas to form a new idea, questioning others about their ideas to analyze them further, attempting to provide multiple answers, and expressing or testing hypotheses.

Forming and functioning skills usually are introduced to students first and can be practiced in groups using games or simple instructional activities that have little academic demand. In addition to helping students learn how to get into their groups and how to speak to each other with respect, functioning skills also involve assigned student roles. All cooperative group members should have assigned roles that help the group function effectively. In some classrooms, group-member assignments include the encourager, the monitor, the leader, and the recorder, as shown in Figure 13.4. The *encourager* has the responsibility of making positive comments to other group members. The *monitor* helps keep the group on task and watches the time. The *leader* gets the

WWW
RESOURCES

The Arc, a nonprofit organization that advocates for individuals with developmental disabilities and other special needs, directly addresses the importance of friendships for individuals with and without disabilities. You can review this information and find additional pertinent references and resources at http://thearc.org/faqs/friend.html.

FIGURE 13.4 Student Roles in Cooperative Groups

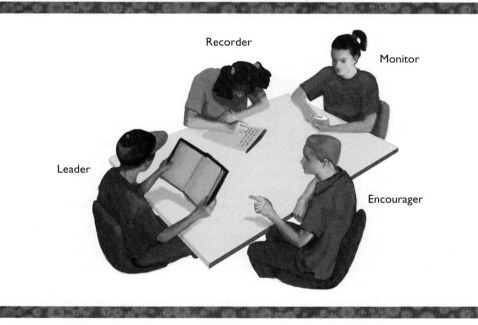

Recorder

Monitor

Leader

Encourager

group started on its task and facilitates its work. The *recorder* writes down any information the group is responsible for producing. Depending on students' ages and skills, additional responsibilities can be added. In some classrooms, group roles rotate so each student has an opportunity to try all roles. If a student with a disability cannot carry out a role (for example, that of recorder), a classmate might help out, or that student might not be assigned that role.

One other functioning skill is especially important: giving feedback. Students need to speak to each other respectfully and to assist each other with this skill, particularly when one student has made an error. Consider one student providing appropriate feedback to another student: "Cecily, today in the group you told Mel he was dumb because he didn't know the answer. That's against group rules." Notice how this very brief example helps the group interaction. The student speaking does not tell Cecily that she is the dumb one, nor does the student tell Cecily what she should have said. Instead, the speaker points out the group expectation for being respectful.

In general, preparing students for cooperative groups includes identifying the skills they need to learn, planning how you will teach them, teaching the skills and allowing students opportunities to practice them, and gradually increasing your expectations for students' cooperative behavior. More ideas for teaching cooperative skills are included in the Professional Edge on page 495.

SELECT CURRICULAR CONTENT ● Almost any subject matter you teach can be adapted for cooperative learning. In elementary schools, cooperative learning is used in language arts for reading and writing activities as well as in math, science, and social studies. In secondary schools, cooperative learning works well in English, math, science, social studies, fine arts, and other coursework. The key to selecting content is to be sure that you already have provided initial instruction to the students so that they are not expected to master new information without your guidance. Further, the content needs to be formatted clearly. It might be a chapter from a textbook, print materials you have duplicated, or a structure for preparing a report on the topic at hand. Students should be able to understand what the assignment is and how to go about completing it.

CHOOSE A COOPERATIVE LEARNING PROGRAM ● The number of approaches to cooperative learning seems to grow each year. For our discussion, three commonly used approaches are outlined: Jigsaw Classroom, Numbered Heads Together, and Cooperative Integrated Reading and Composition (CIRC).

In a **Jigsaw Classroom** (Aronson, 2005), students are assigned to heterogeneous work groups. Each member of the work group also is assigned to a separate expert group. Work groups meet and decide which member is to be assigned to which expert group. For example, in a unit on the Midwest, experts might be assigned for four topics: geography, economy, culture, and cities. All team members then read the material, with each member focusing on his or her expert topic. After reading, team members join their expert group, which is composed of all students in the room sharing the same expert topic. The expert groups review their portion of the instructional material, then return to teach it to their work-group members. Group members ask each expert questions to help clarify the information being presented. After all group members have taught their segments of the information and the groups have had an opportunity to review their learning, a quiz or other evaluation procedure is used, and each group member is graded individually on this assessment.

Since the original Jigsaw approach was created in the early 1970s, a number of variations of it have been published as Jigsaw II, Jigsaw III, and Jigsaw IV. The latter is the most recent (Holliday, 2002). In Jigsaw IV, students are given a clearer overview of the learning unit than in earlier versions and the expert groups are given a quiz to check their knowledge before members return to their work groups. Further, work

WWW RESOURCES

If you would like to learn more about types of cooperative learning, the Success For All Foundation has made available an extensive summary. You can find this information at http://www.successforall.com.

RESEARCH NOTE

Gut (2000) has identified several types of social behaviors that students learn by participating in cooperative learning groups, including conversation skills, listening skills, perspective taking, and predicting consequences.

PROFESSIONAL EDGE

Teaching Cooperative Skills

You can directly teach students the skills they need to succeed in cooperative learning. Here are five steps in the process (Johnson, Johnson, & Holubec, 1998):

Step 1. Make sure students understand the need for the teamwork skill.

- Ask students to develop a list of social skills needed to improve group work. From the skills they list, emphasize one or two.

- Present a case to students so they can see it is better to know the skill than not to know it. Compliment the students who use the skills in the classroom.

- Illustrate the need for the skill through a role-play that provides a counterexample in which the skill is obviously missing in a group.

Step 2. Make sure the students understand what the cooperative learning skill is and how and when to use the skill.

- Define the skill in terms of verbal and nonverbal behaviors and explain thoroughly what students have to do. After the skill is listed (for example, giving directions to the group's work), then ask the class: "What does this skill look like?" (nonverbal behaviors) and "What does this skill sound like?" (verbal behaviors).

- Demonstrate and model the skill in front of the students and explain it step-by-step so students have a concrete idea of what the skill entails in terms of verbal and nonverbal behaviors.

- Have the students practice the skill twice in their groups before the lesson starts.

Step 3. Set up practice situations and encourage skill mastery.

- Assign a social skill either as a specific role for certain students or as a general responsibility for all members of the group. Introduce skills gradually (for instance, one new skill every week), and at the same time repeat previously introduced skills until mastery occurs.

- Observe each group and record who uses the skill, how frequently, and how effectively. You can begin with a very simple observation form that measures only two or three skills. Student observers should be used as soon as possible.

- Cue the use of skills periodically during a lesson by having a student demonstrate the skill in front of the others.

- Intervene in the cooperative groups to explain the skills and show how to use them.

- Coach students on how to improve the use of the skill.

Step 4. Give students feedback on their use of the skill.

- Help students reflect on how to engage in the skill more effectively in the future.

- Have the observer in each group report to the group on the information gathered, and group members in turn report their impressions about their behavior.

- Have the observer provide positive feedback to all group members about their efforts to learn and help others learn. Provide your own feedback to the class as a whole.

Step 5. Make sure students practice the cooperative learning skill until it becomes automatic. There are four stages of skill development:

- awkward (the beginning stage, when there is awkwardness in engaging in the skill)

- phony (when students use the skill but feel inauthentic)

- mechanical

- integrated (when the skill occurs naturally)

SOURCE: From *Cooperation in the Classroom,* by D. Johnson, R. Johnson, and E. Holubec, 1998, Boston: Allyn & Bacon. Retrieved February 11, 2005, from http://www.intime.uni.edu/coop_learning/ch5/teaching.htm.

groups take a shared quiz as practice prior to being given an assessment in which each student is individually accountable.

In **Numbered Heads Together** (Kagan, 1990; Maheady et al., 2002), students are assigned to cooperative groups (usually four or five in a group) and count off by number. The teacher then poses a question to the group and students are asked to "put their heads together" to be sure that all group members know the answer. After a brief time, the teacher reassembles the whole class and calls out a number. All the students with that number stand and one student responds to the question, or they all write the answer on a slate and hold it up for the teacher to see. Students responding correctly score points for their teams. This simple cooperative learning approach can be used for questions with single correct answers as well as for those with many responses.

Cooperative Integrated Reading and Composition (CIRC) is a cooperative learning program designed to help students in elementary and middle schools work on reading, writing, and other language arts (Calderon, 1999; Education Commission of the States, 1999; Slavin, 1994). CIRC has three main components: activities related to the basal reading materials, direct instruction for reading comprehension, and integration of writing with language arts.

Although CIRC is a rather complex cooperative learning approach, generally it includes these activities: First, students are assigned to one of two or three reading groups based on their reading levels (alternatively, teachers may skip grouping and teach to the whole group). In addition, students are teamed with one or two other students within the reading group, and then two teams consisting of students with different reading groups (that is, four or six students) are created. These secondary teams foster heterogeneous grouping in the class and encourage students to help each other. The heterogeneous teams receive points based on each team member's performance on book reports, tests, and other class work. All teams that average 90% on assigned work are awarded Superteam status; those reaching an average of 80% are called Greatteams. Other key activities for CIRC include partner reading with the assigned homogeneous and heterogeneous teammate(s), direct instruction by the teacher on reading comprehension skills, story-related writing, word learning, story retelling, and spelling. Teammates also preassess each other and help each other practice skills not mastered before final testing occurs.

MONITOR PROGRAM EFFECTIVENESS ● Much of the work in developing a cooperative learning program is deciding which approach to use, preparing materials, and helping students learn cooperative skills. However, once students are established in cooperative groups, your role becomes one of monitoring and managing your class (Cooper, 2002). For example, if you notice that a student is having difficulty in a group, you might decide to join that group briefly to judge whether students can resolve the problem themselves or need your assistance. If a student seems to be struggling because of the complexity of the lesson content, you can make an on-the-spot adaptation to help the student and the group. If a student is being disruptive, your proximity might be sufficient to settle that student. As you monitor, you can also observe students' use of cooperative skills and check the progress of their learning. For example, you might observe whether students are using the learning strategies described in Chapter 10 to help them succeed in the lesson. By observing, you can plan your next lessons and address any issues concerning cooperative skills.

By applying the INCLUDE strategy, you quickly can see that many of the teaching strategies presented in this text can be incorporated into cooperative learning experiences. For example, a student in a cooperative group could have adapted materials. The group could use a learning strategy to practice problem solving. You can use an entire array of instructional interventions and strategies for independence as part of your cooperative learning activities. Cooperative groups provide a constructive classroom structure, one that provides opportunities for adapting instruction for individual needs, for building self-esteem and group spirit, for addressing students' own goals, and for promoting positive attitudes toward others. You have an almost limitless number of options for using this structure to accomplish your academic and social goals for students. One example of using assistive technology to facilitate cooperative learning activities for students with learning disabilities is presented in the Technology Notes on page 497.

ANALYZE AND **REFLECT**

Think about peer tutoring and cooperative learning programs. In what situations might each be most appropriate? To respond, take into account students' strengths and needs, your own teaching style, and the curricular content you would be addressing.

" Once students are established in cooperative groups, your role becomes one of monitoring and managing your class. "

INCLUDE

> TECHNOLOGY NOTES

Using Assistive Technology to Facilitate Cooperative Learning

Although cooperative learning has long been recognized as an effective education tool, one that enhances academic achievement as well as social interactions, students with disabilities often are at a disadvantage in cooperative learning groups when the groups rely heavily on reading skills or quick communication. Technology is helping students to overcome these barriers. For example, Xin (1999) found that using commercial math software packages with elementary students who worked in either cooperative groups or whole-group arrangements resulted in higher math achievement for the students who learned cooperatively. Furthermore, students with disabilities preferred the cooperative arrangement, because they felt accepted and supported. The following table describes many ways to use basic and sophisticated assistive technology to facilitate cooperative learning.

Adaptation	Compensatory Possibility
Tape recorder	Answers can be recorded.
Talking calculator with enlarged keys	Students with computational difficulties can use the calculator to check their answers; the visual display coupled with the auditory feedback provides corrective feedback; the enlarged keys make it easier for younger students to manipulate the symbols.
Electronic spelling devices	Students with spelling problems can use these devices to check and correct misspellings.
Voice recognition	Students with written communication problems and/or fine motor problems can generate printed text.
Alternative input devices	Students with fine motor problems can participate in the process of entering information into the computer.

SOURCE: Adapted from "Using Assistive Technology Adaptations to Include Students with Learning Disabilities in Cooperative Learning Activities," by D. P. Bryant and B. R. Bryant, 1998, *Journal of Learning Disabilities, 31,* pp. 41–54. Copyright © 1998 by PRO-ED, Inc. Reprinted with permission.

How Can You Help Students with Disabilities Improve Their Social Skills?

For many students with disabilities and other special needs, your efforts to create a classroom learning environment that fosters positive peer relationships will enable them to be class members who are liked and valued by their peers. For some students, though, you will need to go further. Research has shown that some students with disabilities have persistent problems in their social interactions (Gut & Safran, 2002; Lane, Pierson, & Givner, 2004; Olmeda & Trent, 2003) and that these students benefit from specific instruction to help them learn needed social skills (Gresham, Sugai, & Horner, 2001; Leffert, Siperstein, & Millikan, 2000).

Social skills can be thought of as the behaviors that help students interact successfully with their peers, teachers, and others and that help students win social acceptance. They include accurately recognizing and responding to emotions expressed by others; identifying and effectively solving social problems, such as disagreements about who can play with a toy or decisions about sneaking out of school with a group of peers; expressing preferences in socially acceptable ways; and initiating kind or helpful acts. Social skills range from very simple to complex. For example, for a young student or a student with a moderate intellectual disability, social skills might include learning how to greet others by saying hi instead of hugging, how to take turns during games or large-group activities, and how to ask to join a group. For adolescents with learning or behavior problems—students like Kathleen and Demetrius, whom you read about at the beginning of this chapter—social skills might include expressing emotions

RESEARCH NOTE

Social skills sometimes must be directly taught. For example, Carasea (2004) found that direct instruction, role-play, and peer modeling were successful strategies for teaching various social skills to a 13-year-old girl with mild autism.

appropriately, disagreeing with others (especially adults) in acceptable ways, and avoiding situations in which confrontation is likely to occur. Although special educators play an active role in teaching social skills to students with especially strong needs, you also can address these skills. Many of the ideas presented in this chapter assist students to learn social skills, but in this section additional specific strategies to bring social skills training to your classroom are outlined. These ways include informal instruction, behavioral interventions, and formal social skills training.

Using Informal Instruction

As illustrated throughout this chapter in examples of teachers actively nurturing the development of positive peer social relationships in their classrooms, you will have many informal opportunities to help students develop social skills needed throughout their lives. For example, if you are showing students an instructional video and appropriate student interactions occur as part of it, you might want to point out in a class discussion what made the interactions so positive. Then students could practice the same skills. Similarly, classrooms could include social skills as part of classwide or school themes. For example, in one middle school students illustrated stories that demonstrated how to respond when peers were pressuring them to make fun of other students. Finally, you can individually instruct students in social skills as appropriate situations occur. When Mr. Calles observed Charles, a sophomore with a mild intellectual disability, stick his tongue out at another student when the student laughed at him, he made it a point to speak with both boys about other ways to interact.

Even though you may consider your primary responsibility to be teaching specific curriculum competencies to your students, your awareness of the need to develop student social skills and your willingness to incorporate informal social skills instruction into your class activities can contribute significantly to a sense of classroom community. And forming a positive classroom community is essential for inclusive schools. The Special Emphasis On . . . feature on page 499 illustrates this approach to social skills training in a drama class.

Using Behavioral Interventions

A specific strategy for teaching social skills to students is to use behavioral interventions such as the ones you learned about in Chapter 12. For example, you can reward your entire class for treating a new class member with respect and friendship. If you have a student whose social problems include teasing class members or talking out of turn, you can reward your class for not responding to the inappropriate behaviors. To use these types of behavioral interventions, you need to identify clearly the behaviors you want to foster, choose an appropriate reward structure, create a simple record-keeping system, explain the intervention to students, and systematically implement your plan. For example, in a high school civics class serving sophomores and juniors, a student whose first language was Spanish and who also had learning disabilities enrolled in October. Rosana, a quiet individual very self-conscious about her English skills, seldom volunteered answers in class. When she did speak, several classmates mocked her accent and started calling her "Roseanna-danna," after the still-famous *Saturday Night Live* character. The teacher created a citizenship scorecard for the class that rewarded students for being respectful. Classmates soon pressured the name-callers to stop since their unkind words were penalizing the entire group.

Behavioral interventions also can be used to reinforce appropriate social skills. When teachers see a student with social skills needs interacting appropriately, they should make a positive comment to the student. In secondary schools, these comments usually are offered in private to avoid embarrassing the student. For example, a student

Special EMPHASIS On . . .

Fostering Social Skills in Drama Class

Although all teachers should recognize the importance of informally or formally teaching social skills to their students, teachers in related arts classes often have unique opportunities to address these essential life skills. One example is a drama class.

Think about Elliot, a twelfth-grade student with physical and intellectual disabilities who is attending Roosevelt High School. He is learning vocational skills, but he also spends three periods each day in the same classes his peers without disabilities enjoy. One of his classes this year is drama. This class was one that Elliot expressed an interest in taking, and the team responsible for his IEP agreed that it would provide a preferred context for addressing his social skills goals.

Here are some examples of the skills and activities that Mr. McKinnon, the drama teacher, is incorporating into the class for Elliot:

1. **Following directions**
   One important social skill is following directions given by another. In the drama class, students often are instructed to move their bodies in certain ways or to move to particular parts of the room.
2. **Expressing frustration**
   To express frustration, you can say that you are frustrated, show the emotion on your face, or let out your frustration by hitting a wall or throwing an object.

For Elliot, learning to express frustration verbally is important, and so Mr. McKinnon has ensured that several of the scenes related to emotions that students must act out include frustration.

3. **Interacting with peers**
   Elliot tends to sit by himself instead of initiating interactions with peers. In the drama class, he regularly is asked to initiate interactions and he is rewarded for doing so appropriately. He also works as the prop manager for the class. When classmates or the teacher ask for certain props, opportunities for interactions are created.
4. **Speaking in an appropriate tone of voice**
   When Elliot speaks, he often forgets whether to use an "inside" or an "outside" voice. In the drama class, students practice using their voices to convey meaning. As part of the exercises, Elliot learns to attend to this basic social skill.

What other social skills might students with disabilities be able to work on within the context of a drama class? What about other specialized classes such as art and music?

SOURCE: Based on "The High School Student" (pp. 143–167), by J. E. Downing, 2002, in *Including Students with Severe and Multiple Disabilities in Typical Classrooms: Practical Strategies for Teachers*, 2nd ed., Baltimore: Brookes.

advisor overheard a conversation between a chemistry teacher and a student with an explosive temper. The teacher was chiding the student for failing to turn in assignments on time. The student replied, "Yeah, I know I haven't been doing too well on the homework." Later, the advisor congratulated the student for acknowledging the teacher's feedback without becoming defensive or making a comment that might have led to detention. Think about the INCLUDE strategy that you have applied throughout this textbook. How could it be used to help you decide how to use behavioral approaches to teach and reinforce social skills?

Using Social Skills Training Programs

If you have several students who need social skills instruction, you might find useful one of the many prepackaged social skills training programs available to teachers. For example, Think Aloud (Camp & Bash, 1985; Wehmeyer, 2002) is a problem-solving package that can be used very effectively to teach social skills to elementary school students. Students are taught to ask themselves a series of questions whenever they are

CONNECTIONS

Chapter 12 addressed strategies for increasing desirable student behavior. These strategies also can be applied in teaching social skills.

faced with a problematic situation. The questions are What is the problem? What should I do? What is my plan? and Am I following the plan? Teachers rehearse these steps with students and provide opportunities for students to practice the steps in structured situations. Teachers also remind students to look for the steps when they observe students behaving appropriately.

An example of a social skills package for adolescents is *Skillstreaming the Adolescent* (Goldstein et al., 1980; Seferian, 1999). This package includes structured procedures for teaching nearly 50 different social skills using modeling, role-playing, and feedback. Teachers can select and use only the skill lessons most pertinent to their class groups. For example, if a high school class is having problems because several students are extremely aggressive, the module on that topic might be helpful.

However you decide to help students develop social skills, keep in mind that several other professionals are available in your school who may have advanced training in teaching social skills and who can assist you in this aspect of your curriculum. For example, if your school has a teacher for students with emotional disabilities, he or she might be able to co-teach social skills lessons with you. Similarly, a school counselor or social worker could help you build social skills lessons into your instructional program.

Final Thoughts about Inclusion and the INCLUDE Strategy

INCLUDE

With your understanding of strategies and approaches for building student social relationships, you now have the final ingredient for making your classroom a place where students want to come and want to learn. You know about the foundations of special education and the procedures followed for identifying students with disabilities. You have a strategy—INCLUDE—for guiding your decisions about student needs and interventions. You know how important the support and assistance of colleagues and parents are, whether for planning an instructional program for a student, teaching with you in the classroom, or problem solving when concerns arise. You also understand some of the most important characteristics and needs of students with disabilities and other special needs. You have learned many strategies for helping students succeed in your classroom, including creating a positive instructional environment, assessing student needs, making instructional interventions, helping students be independent, and evaluating their learning. You have learned, too, several approaches for responding to students' discipline and behavior needs and for fostering positive social relationships among students.

What is most important, however, is the statement that appeared in the first chapter of this text: Students with disabilities and other special needs are people first. If you keep that in mind and use the knowledge you have gained, you will positively touch the lives and learning of all the students who call you teacher.

SUMMARY

In addition to fostering the academic growth of students in inclusive schools, teachers also work to ensure that their students with and without disabilities and other special needs build positive social relationships. Learning social skills is especially important because research over the past four decades has demonstrated that students with disabilities are more likely than other students to have a negative status in their classrooms.

Teachers can help students develop positive peer relationships in inclusive classrooms by creating ways for students to have face-to-face interactions, nurturing the development of friendship and support among students, and providing positive role models. Another aspect of addressing the social curriculum in general education classrooms is educating students without special needs about individuals who have disabilities or other special needs. Direct presentation of information, the use of print and video media, and the demonstration of adaptive technology are approaches to introducing students to the characteristics and needs of students with disabilities.

One specific instructional approach that helps create positive student relationships is peer tutoring. Peer tutoring benefits both tutors and tutees, including students with disabilities. Teachers can create tutoring programs that are contained within their classrooms or that use several class groups or even an entire school. A second instructional approach recommended for inclusive classrooms is cooperative learning. To set up a cooperative learning program, teachers need to decide on the size and makeup of the groups, prepare students to work cooperatively, identify the instructional content to be used in the groups, select a cooperative learning approach, such as Jigsaw Classroom, Numbered Heads Together, or Cooperative Integrated Reading and Composition (CIRC), and monitor the effectiveness of the approach.

Sometimes, students with disabilities need additional intensive instruction to learn social skills. This instruction can involve informal social skills instruction as part of the classroom curriculum, behavioral interventions, and formal social skills training programs, often taught in partnership with special services providers such as special education teachers.

Applications in **Teaching Practice**

Planning for Promoting Positive Peer Relations

Mr. Barkley is reviewing his class roster and his plans for the upcoming school year. He knows that he will have four students with learning and behavior disabilities—Jay, Doug, Ray, and Jasmine—in his sixth-hour class. He will also have Theodore, a bright young man with cerebral palsy who uses a wheelchair and has a personal assistant. Theodore cannot write or type; he points to symbols on his communication board. Having talked to other teachers, Mr. Barkley is a little worried about this group because several of the other students in the class also have special needs, including Kusi, who has attention deficit–hyperactivity disorder, and Micki, who is gifted. Right now, the following items appear on his planning list:

1. Talk to Ms. M. [special education teacher]. What are reasonable expectations for the students with disabilities? Does Theodore need any extraordinary assistance? What is he going to be like in class? Do I need to know anything special about having the personal assistant in my classroom? How can I help Theodore connect with the other students in the class? How can I help Theodore participate in class discussion? What should my expectations be for Jay, Doug, Ray, and Jasmine? What should they be able to do in class—everything? 80 percent? What are the social goals for these students? Doug's IEP has several goals related to social skills—what is my responsibility for addressing these? Could we review the students' IEPs to clarify what I should stress with them?

2. Talk to the counselor. How feasible would it be to observe in the classroom and then perhaps facilitate some basic social skills lessons with the entire class during the first 9-week grading period? Twice each week for 20 minutes?

3. Set up cooperative learning groups for first grading period and get all materials ready. Goal: Two cooperative learning activities per week, with first 2 weeks spent on teaching social skills in groups. Group size? Maybe three, given class composition, with a move to four for the second quarter.

4. Check on availability of after-school tutoring program at elementary school this year. Reward for some of the students? Other peer tutoring options?

5. Request more information on Jasmine—see note about her participation in a social work group on Thursdays during advisory period.

Mr. Barkley's planning list goes on along these lines for another page.

QUESTIONS

1. Why is Mr. Barkley concerned about the social interactions of his students? Why is this a part of his responsibility as much as teaching his academic subject matter? How could Mr. Barkley balance the pressure he feels related to helping his students reach high standards and prepare for high-stakes testing with his understanding that students also need to learn effective strategies for working with each other and adults?

2. What strategies could Mr. Barkley use to sensitize his students to Theodore's needs? What might he do if Jay, Doug, Ray, or Jasmine becomes the object of student complaints about fairness during the school year?

3. What approach to peer tutoring is Mr. Barkley considering? What options might he try to arrange? Who in his class might be the best candidates for each of the peer tutoring approaches?

4. What questions might Mr. Barkley have concerning the social needs of Kusi and Micki?

5. Mr. Barkley notes that he needs to spend the first 2 weeks of cooperative learning sessions on social skills. What skills might he teach? How can he teach them? If you were Mr. Barkley, which type of cooperative learning would you implement?

6. It appears that Mr. Barkley has one student who will receive social skills instruction in a separate group, and he is requesting that the counselor help him teach social skills during the first grading period. How could a special education teacher also help Mr. Barkley address the social needs of all his students?

WORKING THE **STANDARDS**

INTASC **INTASC PRINCIPLES REFLECTED IN THIS CHAPTER:**

Principle #2 states that all teachers know the characteristics associated with specific disabilities and the potential impact that particular disabilities may have on learning and development (Principle 2.05).

Principle #5 states that all teachers

■ Modify tasks and learning/social situations to optimize student success (Principle 5.02).

■ Group students and construct learning tasks to help students with and without disabilities recognize the differential contributions that each student can make to the learning experience (Principle 5.03).

■ Tailor classroom management and grouping to individual needs using constructive behavior management strategies, a variety of grouping options, and positive behavioral support strategies to create a learning context in which students with disabilities can attend to learning and respond in appropriate ways (Principle 5.05).

WORKING THE **STANDARDS** *(continued)*

Principle #9 states that all teachers

- Reflect on how individual students with disabilities are functioning in the classroom and how alternative instructional decisions and interactions might influence the students' progress or behavior (Principle 9.01).

- Expect students with disabilities to participate in the activities of the learning community, and seek ways to alter the environment, curriculum, and teaching strategies as needed to facilitate student participation and promote positive learning outcomes (Principle 9.02).

CEC CONTENT STANDARDS REFLECTED IN THIS CHAPTER:

CEC Content Standard #2 states that special educators understand how exceptional conditions can interact with the domains of human development, and use this knowledge to respond to the varying abilities and behaviors of individuals with exceptional learning needs.

CEC Content Standard #5 states that special educators

- Foster environments in which diversity is valued and individuals are taught to live harmoniously and productively in a culturally diverse world.

- Shape environments to encourage the independence, self-motivation, self-direction, personal empowerment, and self-advocacy of individuals with exceptional learning needs.

- Use direct motivational and instructional interventions with individuals with exceptional learning needs to teach them to respond effectively to current expectations.

CEC Content Standard #9 states that special educators are aware of how their own and others' attitudes, behaviors, and ways of communicating can influence their practice.

BACK TO THE CASES

The standards and principles just listed relate to the cases described at the beginning of this chapter: Errol, Kathleen, and Demetrius. The questions and activities that follow demonstrate how these standards and principles, along with other concepts that you have learned about in this chapter, connect to the everyday activities of all teachers.

Errol

Since the social worker works with her students once each week on issues of friendship and diversity, Ms. Kim wants to support that work with additional activities. She has begun using commercial storybooks about students with exceptional needs, including those who are not in special education, such as students who are English-language learners or are from other cultures. One activity for helping nondisabled peers understand their peers with disabilities is to use age-appropriate literature or videos. Select five books and/or videos that you might use in your classroom (choose the grade level and content area). To find books, you might visit your local library, bookstore, or search an online bookstore such as Amazon.com. To find appropriate videos, you can visit a local video rental store or use Google.com to search the words *movies and disabilities* and find websites such as Bridges4Kids (http://www.bridges4kids.org/articles/1-03/iCAN1-03.html). Once you have found your materials, outline an activity to incorporate one of them into your curriculum. (See INTASC Principles 5.03 and 9.02, and CEC Content Standards 5 and 9.)

Kathleen

The case study describes a very positive inclusion situation for Kathleen. Her team members do not respond to her teasing or inappropriate remarks and expect her to contribute to their efforts. Such positive interactions may not occur without some training or support from the teacher. Explain how you believe Mr. Geib created a classroom environment where students with disabilities are expected to participate fully and successfully in cooperative learning groups. Be specific about activities or actions he used and why you believe these selected actions were successful. (See INTASC Principles 2.05, 5.03, 9.01, and 9.02; and CEC Content Standards 2, 5, and 9.)

Demetrius

Demetrius is making progress, with the counselor's help, in responding to nonverbal communications of others. However, he still has problems in the classroom. You think that he needs support from his peers for "real-life" experience in accepting feedback from others in social situations. Demetrius will need to be able to accept such responses from co-workers and customers at the print shop where he plans to work. As his classroom teacher, what would you do to teach his peers to provide positive, constructive feedback when Demetrius does not respond to nonverbal communication? (See INTASC Principles 2.05, 5.03, 9.01, and 9.02; and CEC Content Standards 2, 5, and 9.) For example, how should his peers respond if Demetrius continues to talk when others have lost interest or speaks too loudly during small-group work sessions? Naturally, you will

WORKING THE STANDARDS *(continued)*

need to help Demetrius learn to accept their prompts and suggestions. The chapter provides several suggestions for appropriate activities; select one and explain why you chose it.

 Visit the companion website (http://www.ablongman.com/friend4e) for a complete correlation of this chapter to the INTASC Principles and CEC Standards.

Further **Readings**

Gordon, E. E. (2005). *Peer tutoring: A teacher's resource guide.* New York: Scarecrow Education Press.

This handbook is designed to provide classroom teachers with all the information they need to develop and implement peer tutoring programs, from selecting a type of program to training tutors to judging program quality. Although not written specifically about students with special needs, it has a wealth of information.

Peck, A., & Scarpati, S. (Eds.). (2002). Social skills development [Special issue]. *Teaching Exceptional Children, 35*(1), 8–67.

This special journal issue provides several examples of social skills interventions that span a range from young children to adolescents. The editors place these interventions in the context of inclusive schools.

Snell, M. E., & Janney, R. (2000). *Social relationships and peer support.* Baltimore: Brookes.

This book, intended to help educators who are creating and sustaining inclusive practices in their schools, begins by ex-

ploring the importance of social relationships in such schools. It also outlines effective strategies for facilitating social relationships and provides ideas for teaching social skills to students. Finally, steps for starting and maintaining a social skills training program are included.

Utley, C. (Ed.). (2001). Peer-mediated instruction and interventions: Parts 1 and 2 [Special issues]. *Remedial and Special Education, 22*(1–2).

In these two consecutive issues of *RASE*, you can review an in-depth analysis of a variety of peer-mediated learning approaches including peer tutoring and cooperative learning and their application in general education settings. The articles address students with a variety of special needs as well as academic and behavior interventions.

Glossary

ABC analysis. Systematic recording of antecedents, behaviors, and consequences as a strategy for analyzing student behavior.

absence seizure. Seizure that is brief and often characterized by momentary lapses of attention. Also called a *petit mal seizure.*

academic learning time. The time students are meaningfully and successfully engaged in school.

academic survival skills. Skills needed to succeed in school, including regular and punctual attendance, organization, task completion, independence, motivation, and appropriate social skills.

acceleration. Approach for educating gifted and talented students based on allowing them to move through all or part of the curriculum at their own, accelerated pace.

accuracy. The extent to which a student's academic performance is without errors.

acquired immune deficiency syndrome (AIDS). Disease that results when students are infected with the human immunodeficiency virus (HIV) and their bodies lose the ability to fight infection.

activity reinforcer. Positive activity that causes a behavior to increase. An example of an activity reinforcer is a student being rewarded with extra time to work on the computer.

ADA. *See* Americans with Disabilities Act.

adaptive physical educator. Specialist with expertise in assessing students' motor needs and designing and delivering physical education programs that accommodate those needs.

ADD. *See* attention deficit disorder.

ADHD. *See* attention deficit–hyperactive disorder.

administrator. Professional responsible for managing some aspect of schools; includes principals, assistant principals, department chairpersons, team leaders, special services coordinators, district administrators, and others.

advance organizer. Information, often presented as organizational signals, that makes content more understandable by putting it within a more general framework.

advocate. Individual who works to ensure that parents understand their rights and that school professionals provide an appropriate education for parents' children with disabilities.

AIDS. *See* acquired immune deficiency syndrome.

alternate assessment. A form of functional assessment for students with severe disabilities who are unable to participate in the standard state and district-wide assessment programs.

alternative forms of questions. Testing adaptations that involve changing the construction of a test item or substituting one kind of test item for another. Examples of alternative forms of questions include reducing the choices on a multiple choice item from 4 to 2 or adding a word bank to fill-in-the-blank items.

alternative teaching. Co-teaching option in which students are divided into one large and one small group. The large group receives the planned instruction. The small group receives reteaching, preteaching, enrichment, or other special instruction.

alternatives to letter and number grades. Ways to evaluate student test performance using pass-fail grades and/or checklists of student skills.

alternative ways of administering tests. Testing adaptations that involve changing the ways students respond on tests and/or the ways teachers give tests. An example of changing the way students respond on tests is responding orally to written test items. An example of changing the way teachers give tests is giving a test orally.

American Sign Language (ASL). A sign language not based on the grammar or structures of English, used by some people with hearing impairments.

Americans with Disabilities Act. Civil rights law passed in 1990 that protects individuals with disabilities from discrimination and requires building and transportation accessibility and reasonable accommodations in the workplace.

anecdotal recording. Strategy for recording behavior in which incidents before and after a behavior are recorded along with a description of the behavior.

annual goal. Broad statement describing estimated yearly outcomes for a student with a disability. Annual goals address areas of identified needs.

annual review. Yearly process of convening a team that includes a parent, teacher, administrator, and others as needed to review and update a student's IEP.

ANOTES. Learning strategy for organizing lecture notes for test preparation. The steps are: ask yourself if you have a date and topic, name the main ideas and details, observe ideas also in text, try margin noting and use SAND strategy, examine for omissions or unclear ideas, and summarize key points.

anticipation guide. Series of statements, some of which may not be true, related to material that is about to be presented during instruction, given to students as a way of activating their knowledge by making predictions about the topic.

anxiety. Condition in which an individual experiences extraordinary worry in some situations or worries excessively about future situations.

articulation. Production of speech sounds.

Asperger's syndrome. Mild form of autism in which an individual develops speech but has gross motor problems, intense interests in a narrow range of topics, and chronic difficulty in forming and sustaining social relationships.

assessment. Process of gathering information to monitor progress and make educational decisions.

assistive technology. Any of a wide variety of technology applications designed to help students with disabilities learn, communicate, and otherwise function more independently by bypassing their disabilities.

asthma. Physical condition in which an individual experiences difficulty breathing, especially during physically or psychologically stressful activities.

at risk. Term used to describe students who have characteristics, live in conditions, or have experiences that make them more likely than others to experience failure in schools.

attention deficit disorder (ADD). Term sometimes used as a synonym for attention deficit–hyperactivity disorder.

attention deficit–hyperactivity disorder (ADHD). Medical condition in which students have significant inability to attend, excessive motor activity, and/or impulsivity.

attribution retraining. Teaching program that increases student task persistence and performance by convincing them that their failures are due to effort and can therefore be overcome.

augmentative and alternative communication (AAC). Ways other than speech to send a message to another individual, including nonaided communication such as using sign language or gestures and facial expressions and aided communication such as using computers or other simple or complex devices as communication tools.

authentic learning tasks. Tasks used in performance-based assessment that are based on real-world contexts and lead to real-world outcomes.

autism. Condition in which an individual lacks social responsiveness from a very early age, has a high need for structure and routines, and demonstrates significant language impairments. These characteristics interfere with learning.

autism spectrum disorder (ASD). Contemporary term used to convey the diversity of autism and related disorders, from classic autism that usually includes intellectual disabilities, to Asperger's syndrome in which individuals may be intellectually gifted.

balanced grading adaptation. A type of grading adaptation that considers effort and/or the performance of learning strategies along with products of performance when determining a student's grade.

basal textbook. A book used for instruction in basic-skills areas that contains all key components of the curriculum to be taught for that subject. Often called a *basal*.

basic-skills instruction. Instruction in the tool skills of reading, writing, and math.

behavior contract. Agreement between a teacher (or other adult) and student that clearly specifies student performance expectations, rewards for meeting expectations, consequences of not meeting expectations, and the time frame for which the agreement is valid.

behavior intervention plan (BIP). A detailed strategy, developed on the basis of a functional behavior assessment, to address significant behavior problems being experienced by a student with a disability. The plan typically includes detailed descriptions of interventions, persons responsible, a timeline, and methods for data collection. This plan is required by federal law when a student with a disability has significant behavior problems.

big ideas. Important principles that help learners understand the connections among facts and concepts they learn.

bilingual education program. Education approach in which students with limited English skills learn core subjects in a separate setting in their native language and spend the remainder of their school day with English-speaking peers.

bilingual special education program. Special education approach in which students with disabilities with limited English skills learn core subjects in a separate setting in their native language.

bilingual special education teacher. Teacher who works with students with disabilities whose native language is not English.

bilingual teacher. Teacher who teaches students whose native language is not English.

blind. Condition in which an individual has little or no vision and relies on auditory and other input for learning.

braille. Writing system, used by individuals who have vision impairments, that uses various combinations of six raised dots punched on paper read with the fingertips.

brainstorming. Strategy for generating solutions to problems in which participants call out ideas, building on one another's responses, deferring all evaluation.

Brown v. Board of Education. Supreme Court decision in 1954 that established that it is unlawful and discriminatory to create separate schools for African American students. This "separate cannot be equal" concept was later applied to students with disabilities.

bypass strategies. Ways of receiving or expressing information that allow students to gain access to or demonstrate mastery of the curriculum in alternate ways. For examples, a bypass strategy for a student with a reading disability would be a book on a CD-ROM.

CALL UP. Learning strategy for taking lecture notes. The steps are: copy from board or transparency, add details, listen and write the question, listen and write the answer, utilize the text, and put in your words.

CAPS. Four-step learning strategy for helping a student decide what is important in a story: ask who the characters are; identify the aim of the story; decide what problem happens; and determine how the problem is solved.

catch 'em being good. Behavior management strategy in which a teacher notices appropriate student behavior and positively comments on it, either privately to the student or publicly to the class.

CBA. *See* curriculum-based assessment.

CBM. *See* cognitive behavior management.

cerebral palsy. Most common type of orthopedic impairment among public school students, caused by brain injury before or during birth and resulting in poor motor coordination and abnormal motor patterns.

change letter or number grades. A way of clarifying letter and number grades by supplementing them with other ways of evaluating and reporting learner progress such as written or verbal comments, logs of student activities, and portfolios.

CHECK. Learning strategy for using spell-checkers more effectively. The steps are: check the beginning sound of the word; hunt for the correct consonants; examine the vowels; check changes in suggested word lists for hints; and keep repeating steps 1–4.

child abuse. Situation in which a parent or other caregiver inflicts or allows others to inflict injury on a child, or permits a substantial risk of injury to exist.

child neglect. Situation in which a parent or other caregiver fails to provide the necessary supports for a child's well-being.

CHROME. Mnemonic for remembering the six methods of scientific investigation: categorization, hypothesis, reasoning, observation, measurement, and experimentation.

chunking. Memorization strategy in which students are taught to remember five to seven key ideas at one time.

CIRC. *See* Cooperative Integrated Reading and Composition.

Circle of Friends. Program designed to help students without disabilities understand how important it is to have friends with disabilities and to encourage them to form friendships with classmates with disabilities.

classroom climate. The overall atmosphere of a classroom, including whether it is friendly and pleasant, based on the expectations of teachers and their interactions with students.

classroom grouping. Various grouping arrangements, such as teaching the whole class at once or in small groups, that modify the classroom environment. Classroom grouping may be teacher centered or peer mediated.

classroom instruction. Strategies through which a teacher presents curriculum content to students.

classroom organization. Strategies through which a teacher establishes and maintains order in a classroom.

classwide peer tutoring. Peer-mediated instruction in which all students in a class are partnered. Both students serve as the tutor and tutee following a clear procedure, and they are rewarded for demonstrating appropriate social behaviors.

cluster programs. Special education service delivery system in which students with similar needs from several schools or an entire district attend a single school to receive special education services.

cognitive behavior management (CBM). Behavior management strategy in which students learn to monitor and change their own behavior.

collaboration. A style of interaction professionals use in order to accomplish a goal they share, often stressed in inclusive schools.

community-based education. Approach to instruction in which what is learned in school is related to activities that occur in the community.

compensatory strategies. *See* bypass strategies.

competency checklist. Evaluation technique in which student learning is checked against a listing of key concepts or ideas being taught.

comprehension. Reading skill involving understanding the meaning of what has been read.

concept diagram. Specific type of graphic organizer used to present vocabulary words that includes definitions and characteristics.

concept map. Graphic organizer showing relationships among concepts of instruction as well as essential characteristics of the concepts.

constructivistic teaching. Type of teaching based on the belief that students are capable of constructing meaning on their own, in most cases, without explicit instruction.

consultant. Specialist who provides particular expertise to teachers and others when an extraordinary student need arises.

consultation. Specialized problem-solving process in which one professional with particular expertise assists another professional or parent who needs the benefit of that expertise; used as an instructional approach for some students with disabilities.

consulting teacher. Special education teacher who meets with general education teachers to problem solve and monitor student progress but who typically has little or no direct contact with students.

content-area textbook. A book used for instruction in science, social studies, or other content areas.

controlled materials. Instructional materials at the student's reading level, of high interest and free of complex vocabulary and concepts, often used while teaching students a learning strategy.

Cooperative Integrated Reading and Composition (CIRC). Cooperative learning program for teaching reading, writing, and other language arts to students in upper elementary grades.

cooperative learning. Student-centered instructional approach in which students work in small, mixed-ability groups with a shared learning goal.

COPS. Learning strategy for proofreading papers with these steps: Have I capitalized the first word and proper nouns? How is the overall appearance of my paper; have I made any handwriting, margin, or messy errors? Have I used end punctuation, commas, and semicolons carefully? Do words look like they are spelled right; can I sound them out or use a dictionary?

co-teaching. Instructional approach in which two or more teachers or other certified staff share instruction for a single group of students within a single classroom setting.

counselor. Specialist with expertise in meeting students' social and affective needs.

credit/no credit grading system. *See* pass/fail grading system.

cross-age tutoring. Peer tutoring approach in which older students tutor younger ones.

cross-categorical approach. Instructional approach in which the cognitive, learning, affective, and social and emotional needs of students, not their disability labels, form the basis for planning and delivering instruction.

cue words. Words that make patterns of information more conspicuous for students, such as the words "similar" and "different," signalling the presence of a compare/contrast pattern.

curriculum-based assessment (CBA). Method of measuring the level of achievement of students in terms of what they are taught in the classroom.

curriculum placement. Type of assessment decision concerning where to begin instruction for students.

cystic fibrosis. Genetically transmitted disease in which the body produces excessive mucus that eventually damages the lungs and causes heart failure.

daily activity log. Strategy for providing ongoing information for students and their parents about learning by noting daily observations of student work, effort, and outcomes.

DARE. A strategy for writing persuasive essays that stresses four key steps: develop a topic sentence, add supporting details, reject counter-arguments, and end with a conclusion.

deaf. Hearing impairment in which the individual cannot process linguistic information through hearing with or without the use of hearing aids and relies on visual and other input for learning.

deaf–blind. Condition in which an individual has both significant visual and hearing impairments that interfere with learning.

decibel (dB). Unit for measuring the loudness of sounds.

decoding. Reading skill involving accurately identifying words and fluently pronouncing them.

DEFENDS. Learning strategy for writing a defense of a position with these steps: decide on an exact position; examine the reasons for the position; form a list of points to explain each reason; expose the position in the first sentence; note each reason and supporting points; drive home the position in the last sentence; and search for errors and correct.

depression. Condition in which an individual is persistently and seriously unhappy, with a loss of interest or pleasure in all or almost all usual activities. Symptoms of depression include changes in appetite or weight, sleep disturbances, loss of energy, feelings of worthlessness, and thoughts of death or suicide.

developmental disability. A significant, chronic condition, typically physical, cognitive, or a combination of both, that results in the need for special education and related services. IDEA-97 permits the use of this term in lieu of a more specific disability label for children until age 9.

diabetes. Disease in which the body does not produce enough insulin to process the carbohydrates eaten.

diagnosis. Type of assessment decision concerning whether or not a student meets established federal guidelines for being classified as having a disability and, if so, the nature and extent of the disability.

diagnostic teaching. Sample lessons and other instructional activities carried out with students experiencing extreme academic or behavioral difficulty as part of screening.

differential reinforcement of incompatible behaviors. Reinforcing an appropriate behavior that is incompatible with another undesirable behavior in order to increase the positive behavior.

differentiated instruction. A form of instruction that meets students' diverse needs by providing materials and tasks of varied levels of difficulty, with varying degrees of support, through multiple instructional groups and time variations.

direct instruction. Research-based instructional approach in which the teacher presents subject matter using a review of previously taught information, presentation of new concepts or skills, guided practice, feedback and correction, independent student practice, and frequent review.

disability. Condition characterized by a physical, cognitive, psychological, or social difficulty so severe that it negatively affects student learning. In the Americans with Disabilities Act, a disability is defined as a condition that limits some major life activity.

discipline. Term to describe the set of classroom expectations, including rules for behavior, that serves as a means for facilitating student learning.

discovery learning. *See* inquiry learning.

Down syndrome. Most prevalent type of biologically caused cognitive disability, caused by the failure of one pair of chromosomes to separate at conception.

DRAW. Strategy for teaching multiplication facts that are not yet committed to memory, consisting of these steps: discover the sign; read the problem; answer, or draw and check; and write the answer.

drill and practice programs. A form of computer-assisted instruction in which students learn in small steps, are given systematic feedback, and engage in a lot of practice until mastery is attained.

due process. Procedures outlined in IDEA for ensuring that parents' and children's rights are protected and for resolving disputes between parents and school district personnel concerning any aspect of special education.

duration recording. Strategy for recording behavior in which the length of time a behavior occurs is recorded.

dyslexia. A word used to refer to the condition of a severe reading disability.

echolalic speech. Occurs when an individual communicates by repeating what others have said instead of producing original speech.

ED. *See* emotional disturbance.

Education for the Handicapped Act (EHA). *See* P.L. 94-142.

emotional disturbance (ED). Condition in which an individual has significant difficulty in the social and emotional domain, so much so that it interferes with learning.

English-language learner (ELL) Students whose native language is not English and who are developing their English skills while in school.

enrichment. Approach for educating gifted and talented students based on helping them elaborate on or extend concepts being presented to all students.

environmental inventory. Assessment procedure, often used for students with moderate or severe disabilities, designed to find out what adaptations or supports are needed to increase student participation in classroom and community environments.

epilepsy. Physical condition in which the brain experiences sudden but brief changes in its functioning leading to seizures.

evaluation. Procedures used to determine whether teaching is effective, to provide feedback to students and their parents about student learning, and to inform school boards and communities about school effectiveness.

event recording. Strategy for recording behavior in which each occurrence of the behavior is counted.

example selection. Teacher choice of examples during instruction. Example selection directly affects student understanding of instruction.

example sequence. Order of presentation of examples during instruction. Example sequence directly affects student understanding of instruction.

exemplar. A sample student performance designed to specify a level of achievement in authentic learning evaluation. For example, a writing sample of an "average" seventh grader is an exemplar against which other students' writing can be compared.

expressive language. An individual's ability to communicate meaning clearly through speech.

extinction. Strategy for decreasing negative behavior by no longer reinforcing it; most effective when the undesirable behavior has been inadvertently reinforced by the teacher.

facilitated communication. Method of assisting individuals with autism and other disabilities to communicate by gently supporting the wrist, arm, or shoulder on a typewriter or computer keyboard. This method is controversial.

fading out. Gradual process for decreasing the use of behavioral strategies to support appropriate student behavior.

FAE. *See* fetal alcohol effects.

family-centered practices. Approach for working with families based on the notion that outcomes are best for students when their families' perspectives are respected, family input is sincerely sought, and families gain information that can assist them to make the best decisions for their children.

FAS. *See* fetal alcohol syndrome.

FASTDRAW. Strategy for helping students make the transition from pictures to abstract numbers. The following steps are performed before beginning the DRAW strategy: find what you're solving for; ask yourself, "What are the parts of the problem?"; set up the numbers; and tie down the sign.

fetal alcohol effects (FAE). Mild form of fetal alcohol syndrome (FAS), often without physical characteristics. Students with FAE often experience a variety of learning and behavior problems in school.

fetal alcohol syndrome (FAS). Medical condition caused by prenatal maternal abuse of alcohol, often resulting in slight physical abnormalities and learning, cognitive, or emotional disabilities.

finger spelling. Communication system in which each alphabet letter is assigned a specific hand position. Finger spelling is often used to communicate proper names or technical words for which no other sign language signs exist.

five R's of note-taking. Learning strategy for note-taking with these steps: record the main ideas and important details; reduce to concise phrases; recite key information using your concise phrases as cues; reflect on your notes by adding your own ideas; and review all the key information.

fluency. The rate at which a student performs an academic task such as calculating math problems or reading.

FOIL. Four-step learning strategy for multiplying binomials in algebra: multiply the first terms; multiply the outermost terms; multiply the innermost terms; and multiply the last terms.

functional behavior assessment. The process of gathering detailed data on a student's behavior and the context in which it occurs for the purpose of determining the reasons for it and creating a behavior intervention plan. This process is required by federal law when a student with a disability has significant behavior problems.

functional curriculum. Instructional approach in which goals and objectives are based on real-life skills needed for adulthood. Examples of skills addressed in a functional curriculum include shopping and making purchases; reading common signs such as exit, stop, and sale; riding public transportation; and interacting with peers and adults.

general education teacher. Elementary, middle school, junior high, or high school teacher whose primary responsibility is teaching one or more class groups.

generalized tonic-clonic seizure. Seizure involving the entire body. Also called a *grand mal seizure*.

gifted and talented. Demonstrated ability far above average in one or several areas including overall intellectual ability, leadership, specific academic subjects, creativity, athletics, or the visual or performing arts.

GIVE ME FIVE. A learning strategy that focuses students' attention on five body parts to improve their listening skills: eyes on speaker, mouth quiet, body still, ears listening, and hands free.

Good Behavior Game. Strategy for reducing disruptive behavior and promoting positive behavior in the classroom in which students work on teams to earn points for appropriate behavior toward a reward.

grading adaptations. Changes made to student grades that involve basing all or part of a grade on progress on IEP objectives, improvement over past performances, performance on prioritized content, a balanced grade that includes learning strategy performance and effort, and modified weights and scales.

grading contract. Agreement between a teacher and student that specifies the quantity, quality, and timeliness of work required to receive a specific grade.

grading criteria. The standard on which a student's academic performance is evaluated and graded.

grand mal seizure. *See* generalized tonic-clonic seizure.

graphic organizer. Visual format that helps students to organize their understanding of information being presented or read and the relationships between various parts of the information.

group-administered standardized achievement test. Standardized achievement test given to large groups of students at one time, usually administered by general education teachers, useful as a screening measure.

group roles. Assigned roles for students in cooperative groups that help the group function effectively. Roles commonly assigned include encourager, monitor, leader, and recorder.

guided practice. A teaching technique where students are given verbal cues when first attempting a skill.

handicap. Term, generally no longer preferred, to describe disabilities.

hard of hearing. Hearing impairment in which an individual has some hearing through which to process linguistic information, possibly with the assistance of hearing aids or other assistive devices.

hearing impairment. Condition in which an individual has the inability or limited ability to receive information auditorily such that it interferes with learning.

hemophilia. Genetically transmitted disease in which blood does not properly coagulate.

hertz (Hz). Unit for measuring the pitch or tone of sounds.

heterogeneous grouping. *See* mixed-skill grouping.

high-incidence disability. Any of the most common disabilities outlined in P.L. 105-17, including learning disabilities, speech or language impairments, mild mental retardation, and serious emotional disturbance.

high-stakes tests. Assessments designed to measure whether students have obtained state learning standards.

HIV. *See* human immunodeficiency virus.

homework. The most common form of student practice.

homogeneous grouping. *See* same-skill grouping.

human immunodeficiency virus (HIV). Viral disease in which the body loses its ability to fight off infection. Individuals with HIV often become infected with AIDS.

hyperactive-impulsive disorder. Type of ADHD characterized by excessive movement and other motor activity including fidgeting, a need to move around a room even when others are seated, and rapid changes in activities.

Individuals with Disabilities Education Act (IDEA). *See* P.L. 101-476.

IEP. *See* individualized education program.

IFSP. *See* Individualized Family Service Plan.

improvement grade. Giving credit in evaluation of student performance for progress made, based on the student's level of learning prior to instruction.

impulsivity. The extent to which an individual acts before thinking, often a characteristic of students with high-incidence disabilities or ADHD.

INCLUDE. Strategy for accommodating students with special needs in the general education classroom.

inclusion. *See* inclusive practices.

inclusion specialist. Special education teacher responsible for providing a wide variety of supports to students with disabilities and general education teachers who teach them. Inclusion specialists most often work with students with low-incidence disabilities. Sometimes called a *support facilitator.*

inclusive practices. Term to describe a professional belief that students with disabilities should be integrated into general education classrooms whether or not they can meet traditional curricular standards and should be full members of those classrooms.

independent learning skills. Skills students need to manage their own learning, including note-taking, textbook reading, test-taking, written expression, and time management.

indirect instruction. A type of teaching based on the belief that children are natually active learners and that given the appropriate instructional environment, they actively construct knowledge and solve problems in developmentally appropriate ways.

individualized education program (IEP). Document prepared by the multidisciplinary team or annual review team that specifies a student's level of functioning and needs, the instructional goals and objectives for the student and how they will be evaluated, the nature and extent of special education and related services to be received, and the initiation date and duration of the services. Each student's IEP is updated annually.

individualized family service plan (IFSP). Education plan for children receiving services through P.L. 99-457. Similar to an IEP.

individualized instruction. Instruction designed to meet the specific needs of a student with a disability; a requirement of IDEA.

individually administered diagnostic test. Diagnostic achievement test given to one student at a time, often administered by a special education teacher or school psychologist, useful as a diagnostic measure. These tests provide more specific information than group-administered achievement tests do.

Individuals with Disabilities Education Act (IDEA). Federal education law that updates the 1975 Education of the Handicapped Act and ensures that students with disabilities receive special education and related services through prescribed policies and procedures.

inquiry learning. The most common method of nondirect instruction. *See also* nondirect instruction.

instructional accommodations. Services or supports provided to help students gain full access to class content and instruction, and to help them demonstrate accurately what they know.

instructional adaptation. Any strategy for adapting curriculum materials, teacher instruction, or student practice activities that increases the likelihood of success for students with special needs.

instructional assistance team (IAT). Team of teachers, specialists, and administrators that solves problems about students experiencing academic or behavior difficulty and decides whether students should be individually assessed for possible special education services.

instructional evaluation. Type of assessment decision concerning whether to continue or change instructional procedures that have been initiated with students.

instructional materials. The textbooks, manipulatives, models, and technology used as part of instruction.

instructional methods. The ways in which teachers present content or skills to students and evaluate whether learning has occurred.

instructional modifications. Changes in classroom instruction that involve altering student content expectations and performance outcomes.

integration. The physical, social, and instructional assimilation of students with disabilities in general education settings.

intellectual disability. Term sometimes used as a synonym for *mental retardation.*

intent. The purpose or goal of a student's behavior, not always clear from the behavior itself. An example of an intent occurs when a student repeatedly calls out in class to gain the teacher's attention; that is, the intent is teacher attention.

interval recording. Strategy for recording behavior in which observation occurs for brief segments of time and any occurrence of the behavior during the segment is noted.

intervention assisstance team. Group of professionals, including general education teachers, that analyzes the strengths and problems of referred students to identify strategies to address the problems. If not successful this team may recommend that a student be assessed to determine special education eligibility.

itinerant teacher. Special education teacher who provides services to students with disabilities and teaches in two or more schools.

Jigsaw classroom. Cooperative learning program in which work group team members are assigned to expert groups to master part of the assigned material to which no other group has access. In the work group, each team member has an opportunity to present his or her part of the material. Students are then assessed for mastery individually.

job coach. A special education professional who accompanies students with disabilities to job sites and helps them master the skills needed to perform the job.

keyword method. Mnemonic for remembering definitions and factual information in which visual imagery is used to enhance recall.

KWL Plus. Three-step learning strategy for reading comprehension: what you already know; what you want to know; and what you learned.

LAMPS. Learning strategy for remembering the steps for regrouping in addition with these steps: line up the numbers according to their decimal points; add the right column of numbers; if more than nine continue to the next step; put the 1s below the column; and send the 10s to the top of the next column.

LD. *See* learning disability.

learned helplessness. Characteristic of some students with disabilities in which they see little relationship between their own efforts and school or social success, often resulting in a belief that they cannot perform challenging tasks.

learning and behavior disabilities. Term used to describe collectively learning disabilities, serious emotional disturbance, and mild cognitive disabilities.

learning disability (LD). Condition in which a student has dysfunction in processing information typically found in language-based activities, resulting in interference with learning. Students with learning disabilities have average or above average intelligence but experience significant problems in learning how to read, write, and/or use a computer.

learning outcomes. Specific goals or outcomes students are expected to accomplish as a result of a unit of instruction.

learning strategies. Techniques, principles, or rules that enable a student to solve problems and complete tasks independently.

Learning Together. Cooperative learning program in which groups of two to six members learn specific skills for interacting with one another and then work together in various formal and informal group structures to learn material.

least restrictive environment (LRE). The setting as similar as possible to that for students without disabilities in which a student with a disability can be educated, with appropriate supports provided. For most students, the LRE is a general education classroom.

legal blindness. Visual impairment in which an individual's best eye, with correction, has vision of 20/200 or less, or the visual field is 20 percent or less.

lesson organizer routine. A teaching method that helps teachers convert content into understandable formats that meet the diverse needs of students. The method has three components: the lesson organizer device, linking steps, and cue-do-review sequence.

low demand request. Behavior management strategy in which the teacher helps a student transition from one activity to another by making a series of simple requests of the student that are unrelated to the targeted task.

low-incidence disability. Any of the less common disabilities outlined in P.L. 105-17, including multiple disabilities, hearing impairments, orthopedic impairments, other health impairments, visual impairments, deaf-blindness, autism, and traumatic brain injury.

LRE. *See* least restrictive environment.

mainstreaming. Term for placing students with disabilities in general education settings when they can meet traditional academic expectations with minimal assistance, or when those expectations are not relevant.

maintenance goal. Type of goal teams set that describes what the team wants to accomplish in terms of its own effectiveness.

manipulatives. Concrete objects or representational items used as part of instruction. Examples of commonly used manipulatives include blocks and counters.

MDT. *See* multidisciplinary team.

mediation. Process in which a neutral professional assists parents and school district personnel in resolving disputes concerning any aspect of a student's special education.

mental retardation. Condition in which an individual has significant limitations in cognitive ability and adaptive behaviors that interfere with learning. Also referred to as a *cognitive disability*.

mild intellectual disabilities. Condition in which students have some difficulty meeting the academic and social demands of general education classrooms due in large part to below average intellectual functioning (55–70 on an IQ test).

minimum intervention. Strategy for promoting positive behavior that is nonintrusive and often spontaneous instead of systematic and long term. Examples of minimum interventions include noticing positive student behavior and commenting on it and moving students from one activity to another by making unrelated but easily accomplished requests first.

mixed-skill grouping. Classroom grouping arrangement in which students are clustered for instruction without focusing on specific skill needs. Also referred to as *heterogeneous grouping*.

mnemonic. A device or code used to assist memory by imposing an order on the information to be remembered.

mobility specialist. Specialist who helps students with visual impairments learn to be familiar with their environments and able to travel from place to place independently and safely.

model. Concrete representation that can help students make connections between abstractions and real-life physical objects or processes.

modified test construction. Individualized changes made to tests to make them more accessible for students with disabilities. For example, triple spacing a test for a student with a learning disability who has difficulty reading tests that have lots of clutter.

modified weights and scales. A type of grading adaptation that involves changing the number of points or the percentages required to earn a specified grade or changing the weights assigned to different performance areas.

multicultural education. Approaches to education that reflect the diversity of society.

multidisciplinary team (MDT). Team including teachers, specialists, administrators, and parents who assess a student's individual needs, determine eligibility for special education, and develop the IEP.

multimedia software. Computer programs that combine written words, graphics, sound, and animation.

multiple disabilities. Condition in which individuals have two or more of the disabilities outlined in P.L. 101-476, although no one can be determined to be predominant.

multiple intelligences. Concept proposed by Howard Gardner (1993) that suggests there are seven types of intelligence, not just one.

multisensory approach. Instructional approach that emphasizes the use of more than one modality for teaching and learning. For example, having a student read a vocabulary word, spell it out loud, and then write it on paper is a multisensory approach to teaching vocabulary.

muscular dystrophy. Disease that weakens muscles, causing orthopedic impairments. This disease is progressive, often resulting in death during the late teenage years.

negative example. Instructional stimulus that does not illustrate the concept being taught, used with examples to ensure that students understand the instruction. Also called *nonexample*.

negative reinforcement. A potential negative consequence to a behavior that causes the behavior to increase.

No Child Left Behind Act of 2001. Re-authorization of the Elementary and Secondary Education Act of 1965; this law set high standards for student achievement, increased accountability for student learning, and criteria by which teachers are considered highly qualified.

novelty. Approach for educating gifted and talented students based on allowing students to learn traditional content using alternative or unusual strategies that might include working with an adult mentor, creating materials for other students to use, or using a problem-based learning approach.

Numbered Heads Together. Cooperative learning program in which students number off. The teacher poses a question; the students work together to ensure all members know the answer, and then the teacher calls a number. Students with the number stand, and one is called upon to respond to the question, with correct responses scoring points for the team.

nurse. Specialist who has expertise in understanding and responding to students' medical needs and who sometimes serves as a liaison between medical and school professionals.

occupational therapist. Specialist with expertise in meeting students' needs in the area of fine motor skills, including self-help skills such as feeding and dressing.

one-to-one instruction. Classroom grouping arrangement in which individual students work with either a teacher or computer in materials geared to their level and at their own pace.

organizational patterns. Ways in which content area texts are written to reflect main ideas such as compare-contrast, cause-effect, and problem solution.

orthopedic impairments. Physical conditions that seriously impair the ability to move about or to complete motor activities and interfere with learning.

other health impairments. Medical or health conditions such as AIDS, seizure disorders, cancer, juvenile diabetes, and asthma that are serious enough that they negatively affect a student's educational performance.

overcorrection. Type of presentation punishment in which a student makes restitution for misbehavior. An example of overcorrection is a student cleaning all the desks in a room as a consequence for writing on one desk.

parallel teaching. Co-teaching option in which students are divided into small groups and each group receives the same instruction from one of the teachers in the room.

paraprofessional. Noncertified staff member employed to assist certified staff in carrying out education programs and otherwise help in the instruction of students with disabilities.

PARS. Learning strategy for reading textbooks with these steps: preview the material, ask questions, read the chapter, and summarize the main ideas.

partially sighted. Condition in which an individual has a significant visual impairment but is able to capitalize on residual sight using magnification devices and other adaptive materials.

passive learner. Learner who does not believe in his or her own ability, has limited knowledge of problem-solving strategies, and is unable to determine when to use a strategy.

pattern guide. A graphic organizer designed to help students organize their written papers.

peer comparison. A component of curriculum-based assessment in which a student's performance is compared to that of classmates as a means of determining whether a learning problem exists.

peer editing. Component of student writing in which students review, evaluate, and provide feedback to each other about their written work.

peer tutoring. Student-centered instructional approach in which pairs of students help one another and learn by teaching.

performance-based assessment. Method of evaluation that measures what students can do with knowledge rather than measuring specific bits of knowledge the student possesses.

permanent product recording. Strategy for recording behavior in which samples of student work and other permanent evidence of student behavior are collected and evaluated.

personal assistant. Paraprofessional specially trained to monitor and assist a particular student with a disability.

personal role. One of the roles individuals bring to a team, consisting of characteristics, knowledge, skills, and perceptions based on life experiences broader than those in the professional area.

petit mal seizure. *See* absence seizure.

physical punishment. Type of presentation punishment, not recommended for use by teachers, that involves a negative physical consequence for misbehavior.

physical therapist. Specialist with expertise in meeting students' needs in the area of gross motor skills.

placement. Location in which education will occur for a student with a disability.

planning think sheet. Set of questions to which students respond as a strategy for assisting them to activate background knowledge in preparation for writing.

portfolio assessment. Method of evaluation in which a purposeful collection of student work is used to determine student effort, progress, and achievement in one or more areas.

positive behavioral interventions and supports (PBIS) Strategies for preventing behavior challenges as well as techniques for addressing common and intensive behavior problems; PBIS is based on clearly defined outcomes, behavioral and biomedical science, research-validated practices, and systematic approaches.

positive reinforcement. A consequence to a behavior that causes it to increase. Also called a *reward.*

POSSE. Learning strategy for reading comprehension with these steps: predict ideas, organize the ideas, search for the structure, summarize the main ideas, and evaluate your understanding.

POWER. Learning strategy for writing with these steps: planning, organizing, writing, editing, and revising.

practice test. An adaptation used before students take tests. Students are given a test with the same format and content but different questions. Practice tests clarify test expectations and familiarize students with test content.

PReP strategy. Strategy for determining how much background information students have about a topic.

prereferral assistance team. *See* instructional assistance team.

present level of functioning. Information about a student's current level of academic achievement, social skills, behavior, communication skills, and other areas that is included on an IEP.

presentation punishment. Presenting negative consequences as a strategy for decreasing behavior.

preskill. Basic skill necessary for performing a more complex skill.

primary reinforcer. Food or other items related to human needs that cause a behavior to increase, used only occasion-

ally in schools. An example of a primary reinforcer is a piece of licorice earned for appropriate behavior.

prioritization of curriculum. A type of grading adaptation in which a student's grade is based on specific content determined to be most important by the teacher.

probe. Quick and easy measure of student performance (accuracy and fluency) in the basic-skill areas of reading, math, and written expression consisting of timed samples of academic behaviors.

probe of basic academic skills. *See* probe.

probe of prerequisite skills. Specific type of probe designed to assess whether a student has the prerequisite skills needed to succeed in the planned instruction.

professional role. One of the roles individuals bring to a team, including knowledge, skills, and perceptions based on professional training and experience.

program evaluation. Type of assessment decision concerning whether a special education program should be terminated, continued as is, or modified.

program placement. Type of assessment decision concerning where a student's special education services will take place.

progress on IEP objectives. A type of grading adaptation in which a student's grade is based on the measurable goals and objectives and progress monitoring components of the IEP.

psychological test. Test designed to measure how efficiently students learn in an instructional situation; often used to assess intelligence and to determine whether learning disabilities exist.

psychologist. *See* school psychologist.

psychometrist. Specialist with expertise in assessment who in some states completes much of the individual assessment required to determine eligibility for special education services.

pullout model. Instructional approach in which students with disabilities leave the general education classroom once or more each day to receive special education services.

punishment. Any response of consequence that has the effect of decreasing a behavior.

rate of skill introduction. The pace at which new skills are introduced during instruction.

RAP. Reading comprehension strategy consisting of three steps: read the paragraph; ask yourself "What was the main idea and what were two details?"; put the main idea and details in your own words.

READS. Textbook-reading strategy consisting of five steps: review headings and subheadings; examine boldfaced words; ask, "What do I expect to learn?"; do it—read!; summarize in your own words.

reasoning. A range of important learning skills, including comprehension, generalization, induction, and sequencing.

receptive language. An individual's ability to understand what people mean when they speak.

reciprocal teaching. Teaching students to comprehend reading material by providing them with teacher and peer models of thinking behavior and then allowing them to practice these thinking behaviors with their peers.

reciprocal tutoring. Same-age tutoring approach in which students in the same class are randomly assigned and take turns teaching each other. *See also* reciprocal teaching.

regular class. One placement for students with disabilities. Also referred to as a *general education class.*

rehearsal strategy. Test-taking strategy that involves saying information out loud, repeating it, checking it for accuracy, and repeating it again as part of studying.

reinforcement. Any response or consequence that causes a behavior to increase.

reinforcement menu. List of rewards from which students may choose, often most effective if students participate in its development.

related services. Services students with disabilities need to benefit from their educational experience. Examples of related services include transportation, speech therapy, physical therapy, and counseling.

removal punishment. Taking away from a student something that is desired as a strategy for decreasing inappropriate behavior.

residential facility. Placement for students with disabilities when their needs cannot be met at a school. Students attend school and live at a residential facility.

resource room. Classroom to which students come for less than 50 percent of the school day to receive special education.

resource teacher. Special education teacher who provides direct services to students with disabilities either in a special education or general education classroom and who also meets to solve problems with teachers. Resource teachers most often work with students with high-incidence disabilities.

response cost. Type of removal punishment in which a student loses privileges or other rewards as a consequence of inappropriate behavior.

response format. The way in which a student is expected to respond to test items. Examples of response formats include writing true or false, circling a correct answer from a list of four, drawing a line to match items, or writing an essay.

retention. Ability to remember information after time has passed.

RICE. Strategy for involving students in the portfolio process. Steps include: rationale—why are you keeping a portfolio?; identify goals—what do you want to improve?; contents—what will you include in your portfolio?; evaluation—how, and when, will you assess your portfolio?

Ritalin. Psychostimulant medication commonly prescribed for individuals with ADHD.

RUDPC. Learning strategy to help students derive important information from a web page. The steps are read the title and headings, use the cursor to skim the page, decide whether you need the page, print the page, and copy the bibliographic information.

same-age tutoring. Peer tutoring approach in which students in the same class or grade level tutor one another, typically with higher-achieving students assisting lower-achieving students.

same-skill grouping. Classroom grouping arrangement in which all students needing instruction on a particular skill are clustered for that instruction. Also referred to as *homogeneous grouping.*

SAND. Learning strategy to visually organize lecture notes. The steps are: state important ideas; arrange arrows to connect ideas; number key points in order; and devise abbreviations.

satiation. Situation in which a positive reinforcer, used repeatedly, loses its effectiveness.

scaffolding. Instructional approach for teaching higher-order thinking skills in which the teacher supports student learning by reviewing the cognitive strategy to be addressed, regulating difficulty during practice, providing varying contexts for student practice, providing feedback, increasing student responsibility for learning, and creating opportunities for independent student practice.

school psychologist. Specialist with expertise to give individual assessments of students in cognitive, academic, social, emotional, and behavioral domains. This professional also designs strategies to address students' academic and social behavior problems.

SCAN. Self-questioning strategy for proofreading sentences. The questions are: Does it make sense?; Is it connected to my belief?; Can I add more?; and Are there any errors to note?

screening. Type of assessment decision concerning whether or not a student's academic or behavior performance is different enough from that of his or her peers to merit further, more in-depth assessment.

SCROL. Learning strategy for teaching students to use text headings to aid their comprehension with these steps: survey the headings, connect, read the text, outline, and look back.

Section 504. The section of the Vocational Rehabilitation Act of 1973 that prohibits discrimination against all individuals with disabilities in programs that receive federal funds.

self-advocacy. Extent to which a student can identify supports needed to succeed and communicate that information effectively to others, including teachers and employers.

self-awareness. Extent to which a student has an accurate perception of his or her learning strengths, learning needs, and ability to use strategies to learn independently.

self-control training. A strategy in which students who lack self-control are taught to redirect their actions by talking to themselves.

self-determination. Providing meaningful opportunities for students with disabilities to express their needs and goals so that their wishes guide decision-making.

self-image. Individual's perception of his or her own abilities, appearance, and competence.

self-instruction. Strategy in which students are taught to talk themselves through tasks.

self-monitoring. Strategy in which students are taught to check whether they have performed targeted behaviors.

self-questioning. Strategy in which students are taught to guide their performance by asking themselves relevant questions.

self-reinforcement. Strategy in which students reward themselves for behaving appropriately or achieving success in learning tasks.

sensory impairment. Disability related to vision or hearing.

separate class. Classroom in which students with disabilities spend 50 percent or more of the school day.

separate school. School serving only students with disabilities.

shared problem solving. Process used by groups of professionals, sometimes including parents, for identifying problems, generating potential solutions, selecting and implementing solutions, and evaluating the effectiveness of solutions.

short-term objective. Description of a step followed in order to achieve an annual goal.

sickle-cell anemia. Inherited disorder occurring most often in African Americans in which red blood cells are abnormally shaped and weakened.

sign language interpreter. Specialist who listens to instruction and other communication and relays it to students with hearing impairments through sign language.

simulation. Activity in which students experience what it might be like to have a disability; in a technology context, simulations are computer programs that teach problem solving, decision making, and risk taking by having students react to real-life and imaginary situations.

SLANT. Learning strategy to help student stay engaged while the teacher is talking. The steps are: sit up straight, lean forward, ask questions, nod your head, and track the teacher with your eyes.

SLICK. A learning strategy for helping students comprehend textbooks recorded on CD-ROM. The steps in using a text on CD-ROM include: set it up, look ahead through the chapter, comprehend, and keep it together.

SLOBS. Learning strategy to help students with regrouping in subtraction with these steps: if smaller, follow the steps; if larger, leap to subtract; cross off the number in the next column; borrow by taking one 10 and adding to the next column; subtract.

slow learner. Student whose educational progress is below average, but not so severe as to be considered a cognitive disability, and is consistent with the student's abilities.

social cues. Verbal or nonverbal signals people give that communicate a social message.

social reinforcer. Positive interpersonal interaction that causes a behavior to increase. An example of a social reinforcer is a teacher praising a student's appropriate behavior.

social skills. Behaviors that help students interact successfully with their peers, teachers, and others and that help them win social acceptance.

social worker. Specialist with expertise in meeting students' social needs and fostering working relationships with families.

sophistication. Approach for educating gifted and talented students based on helping students learn complex principles about subject matter being presented to the entire class.

SPACE. A strategy for writing stories that emphasizes five key story elements: setting, problem, actions, consequence, and emotions.

special education. Specially designed instruction provided by the school district or other local education agency that meets the unique needs of students identified as disabled.

special education teacher. Teacher whose primary responsibility is delivering and managing the delivery of special education services to students with disabilities.

Special Friends. Program designed to promote friendships between students with disabilities and those without disabilities.

special services coordinator. Administrator responsible for interpreting guidelines related to educating students with disabilities and assisting other school district personnel in carrying out those guidelines.

speech articulation. The ability to produce sounds correctly at the age where they would normally be expected to develop.

speech or language impairment. Condition in which student has extraordinary difficulties in communicating with others due to causes other than maturation and that interferes with learning.

speech reading. Strategy used by individuals with hearing impairments to gain information by watching a person's lips, mouth, and expression. Only a small proportion of a spoken message can typically be discerned through speech reading.

speech/language therapist. Specialist with expertise in meeting students' communication needs, including articulation and language development.

spina bifida. Birth defect in which there is an abnormal opening in the spinal column, often leading to partial paralysis.

spinal cord injury. Condition in which the spinal cord is damaged or severed because of accident or injury, leading to orthopedic impairments.

STAD. *See* Student Teams–Achievement Divisions.

standardized achievement test. Norm-referenced test designed to measure academic progress, or what students have retained in the curriculum.

standards-based education. Education that is based on meeting state expectations of what students should know or be able to do as a result of public education.

STAR. Learning strategy that helps older students solve math problems, including algebra. The steps are: search the word problem, translate the word problem, answer the problem, and review the solution.

station teaching. Co-teaching option in which students are divided into small groups and each group receives part of its instruction from each teacher.

stereotypic behavior. An action or motion repeated over and over again. Examples of stereotypic behaviors include spinning an object, rocking the body, and twirling.

story grammar. Description of the typical elements of stories, including theme, setting, character, initiating events, attempts at resolution, resolution, and reactions.

story map. Graphic organizer for narrative material.

student evaluation. Determination of the extent to which students have mastered academic skills or other instructional content, frequently communicated through grades.

student self-evaluation. Assessment approach in which students are asked to perform a task, are given a checklist of strategy steps for the task, and then are asked to tell which of these steps they did or did not use.

study guide. General term for outlines, abstracts, or questions that emphasize important information in texts.

stuttering. Speech impairment in which an individual involuntarily repeats a sound or word, resulting in a loss of speech fluency.

support facilitator. *See* inclusion specialist.

surface behavior. Initial student behaviors that teachers could interpret as misbehavior. Responding appropriately to surface behaviors can prevent them from escalating into more serious discipline problems.

TAG. Learning strategy for peer editing with these steps: tell what you like, ask questions, and give suggestions.

TALS. A listening strategy that helps students prepare for the material to come and sift through all they hear for the most important information. The steps are: think, ask why, listen for what?, and say to self.

tangible reinforcer. Prizes or other objects students want and can earn through appropriate behavior and that cause that behavior to increase. An example of a tangible reinforcer is a school pencil earned for appropriate behavior.

task analysis. Six-step strategy for managing time: decide exactly what you must do; decide how many steps are needed to complete the task; decide how much time each step will take; set up a schedule; get started; finish the task.

task goal. Type of goal teams set that describes the business the team was formed to accomplish.

TASSEL. A learning strategy that helps students sustain their attention during longer lectures. The steps include: try not to doodle, arrive at class prepared, sit near the front, sit away from friends, end day dreaming, and look at the teacher.

TBI. *See* traumatic brain injury.

teacher-centered instruction. Classroom instructional arrangement in which the pattern of interaction is between teacher and student, with the teacher as the central figure.

team. Formal work group that has clear goals, active and committed members, leaders, clear procedures followed in order to accomplish goals, and strategies for monitoring effectiveness.

team role. One of the formal or informal roles individuals bring to a team, consisting of contributions made to help ensure effective team functioning. Examples of formal team roles include team facilitator, recorder, and timekeeper. Examples of informal team roles include compromiser, information seeker, and reality checker.

team teaching. Co-teaching option in which students remain in one large group and teachers share leadership in the instructional activity of the classroom.

test administration. The conditions under which a test is given to students.

test construction. The way in which test items are worded, ordered on the test, and formatted.

test site. The location in which a test is given.

test-taking skills. Learning strategies taught to students to help them succeed in studying for and taking tests.

thinking reader. An enhanced electronic version of a textbook designed to offer support for students in word identification, comprehension, and study skills.

three-year reevaluation. Triannual process of reassessing the needs of a student with a disability, carried out by a multidisciplinary team.

time-out. Type of removal punishment in which a student is removed from opportunities for reward. An example of time out is a "penalty box" for misbehavior on the playground.

time sampling. Strategy for recording behavior in which a behavior is periodically observed and measured during a specified time period.

token economy. Group behavior management procedure in which students earn a representative or token currency for appropriate behavior that can later be exchanged for rewards.

tracking. Educational practice of grouping students for instruction by their perceived ability level.

transition plan. Document for students with disabilities who are as young as 14 years old that describes strategies for assisting them prepare to leave school for adult life.

transition specialist. Special educator who helps prepare students with disabilities for postschool activities, including employment, vocational training, or higher education.

transition time. The time it takes a group of students to change from one classroom activity to another.

traumatic brain injury (TBI). Condition in which an individual experiences a significant trauma to the head from accident, illness, or injury and that affects learning.

tutorial. Computer program designed to present new material to students in small sequential steps and/or to review concepts.

unison responding. All students responding at once to teacher questions or other instruction.

universal design. The design of instructional materials, methods, and assessments that are compatible with a diverse range of student needs and minimize the need for labor-intensive adaptations.

video self modeling. A form of instruction in which students learn by watching themselves successfully perform a behavior.

visual impairment. Condition in which an individual has an inability or limited ability to receive information visually, so much so that it interferes with learning.

wait time. Amount of time a teacher gives a student to respond to a question.

written language difficulties. Problems that students with learning and behavior disabilities have with skills related to handwriting, spelling, and written expression.

References

Abedi, J., Hofstetter, C. H., & Lord, C. (2004). Assessment accommodations for English language learners: Implications for policy-based empirical research. *Review of Educational Research, 74*(1), 1–28.

Affleck, J. Q., Lowenbraun, S., & Archer, A. (1980). *Teaching the mildly handicapped in the regular classroom.* Columbus, OH: Merrill.

Agran, M., Blanchard, C., Wehmeyer, M., & Hughes, C. (2002). Increasing the problem-solving skills of students with developmental disabilities participating in general education. *Remedial and Special Education, 23,* 279–288.

Ahearn, E. (2001). Public charter schools and students with disabilities (ERIC Digest No. E609). Arlington, VA: ERIC Clearinghouse on Disabilities and Gifted Education. (ERIC Document Reproduction Service No. ED455656)

Akins, K. P., Parkinson, K. M., & Reeder, P. H. (2002). *The perceptions of third through fifth grade classroom teachers and special service teachers toward their involvement in collaborative instruction.* (ERIC Document Reproduction Service No. ED465722)

Alberto, P. A., & Troutman, A. C. (2002). *Applied behavior analysis for teachers* (6th ed). Upper Saddle River, NJ: Prentice Hall.

Aleksander, E., & Ryan, A. (2003). Race and cognitive ability test performance: The mediating effects of test preparation, test-taking strategy use and self efficacy. *Journal of Social Psychology, 33,* 2607–2629.

Algozzine, B., Audette, B., Ellis, E., Marr, M. B., & White, R. (2000). Supporting teachers, principals—and students— through unified discipline. *Teaching Exceptional Children, 33*(2), 42–47.

Algozzine, B., Ysseldyke, J. E., & Campbell, P. (1994). Strategies and tactics for effective instruction. *Teaching Exceptional Children, 26*(3), 34–36.

Al-Hassan, S., & Gardner, R. (2002). Involving immigrant parents of students with disabilities in the educational process. *Teaching Exceptional Children, 34*(5), 52–59.

Alley, G. R. (1988). Effects of generalization instruction on the written language performance of adolescents with learning disabilities in the mainstream classroom. *Reading, Writing, and Learning Disabilities, 4,* 291–309.

Allinder, R. M., Bolling, R. M., Oats, R. G., & Gagnon, W. A. (2000). Effects of teacher self-monitoring on implementation of curriculum-based measurement and mathematics computation achievement of students with disabilities. *Remedial and Special Education, 21,* 219–226.

Allport, G. (1954). *The nature of prejudice.* Cambridge, MA: Addison-Wesley.

Altwerger, B., & Ivener, B. L. (1996). Self-esteem: Access to literacy in multicultural and multilingual classrooms. In R. Pritchard & K. Spangenberg-Urbschat (Eds.), *Kids come in all languages: Reading instruction for ESL students* (pp. 65–81). Newark, DE: International Reading Association.

Ambrose, R. (2002). Are we overemphasizing manipulatives in the primary grades to the detriment of girls? *Teaching Children Mathematics, 9*(1), 16–22.

American Academy of Pediatrics. (1998). Learning disabilities, dyslexia, and vision. *Pediatrics, 102*(5), 1217–1219.

American Academy of Pediatrics. (2000). Clinical practice guideline: Diagnosis and evaluation of the child with attention-deficit/hyperactivity disorder. *Pediatrics, 105,* 1158–1170.

American Association on Mental Retardation. (2002). *Mental retardation: Definition, classification, and systems of supports* (10th ed.). Washington, DC: Author.

American Institutes for Research. (1999, February). *Voluntary national tests in reading and math: Background paper reviewing laws and regulations, current practice, and research relevant to inclusion and accommodation for students with limited English proficiency.* Palo Alto, CA: Author.

American Psychiatric Association. (2000). *Diagnostic and statistical manual of mental disorders* (4th ed., text rev.). Washington, DC: Author.

American Speech-Language-Hearing Association. (1993). Definitions of communication disorders and variations. *ASHA, 35*(Suppl. 10), 40–41.

Anderson, J. A., Kutash, K., & Duchnowski, A. J. (2001). A comparison of the academic progress of students with EBD and students with LD. *Journal of Emotional and Behavioral Disorders, 9,* 106–115.

Archer, A. L., Gleason, M. M., & Vachon, V. L. (2003). Decoding and fluency: Foundation skills for struggling older readers. *Learning Disability Quarterly, 26,* 89–101.

Archer, A. (1977). *Instructional materials for the mildly handicapped: Selection, utilization, and modification.* Eugene, Oregon: University of Oregon, Northwest Learning Resources System.

Archer, A., & Gleason, M. (2004). Direct instruction in content-area reading. In D. W. Carnine, J. Silbert, E. J. Kameíenui, & S. G. Tarver (Eds.), *Direct instruction reading* (4th ed, pp. 260–306). Upper Saddle River, NJ: Merrill/Prentice Hall.

Arends, R. I. (2004). *Learning to teach* (6th ed). New York, NY: McGraw-Hill.

Armbruster, B. B. (1984). The problem of "inconsiderate text." In G. G. Duffy, L. R. Roehler, & J. Mason (Eds.), *Comprehensive instruction: Perspectives and suggestions* (pp. 202–217). New York: Longman.

Armbruster, B. B., & Anderson, T. H. (1988). On selecting "considerate" content area textbooks. *Remedial and Special Education, 9*(1), 47–52.

Armbruster, B., Lehr, F., & Osborn, J. (2001). *Put reading first: The research building blocks for teaching children to read.* Washington, DC: Partnership for Reading.

Aronson, E. (2005). *Jigsaw in 10 easy steps.* Middletown, CT: Social Psychology Network. Retrieved February 8, 2005, from http://www.jigsaw.org/index.html

Artiles, A. J., Harry, B., Reschly, D. J., & Chinn, P. C. (1994). Overrepresentation of students of color in special education: A critical overview. *Multicultural Perspectives, 4*(1), 3–10.

Ashton, T. M. (1999). Spell checking: Making writing meaningful in the inclusive classroom. *Teaching Exceptional Children, 32*(2), 24–27.

Asmus, J. M., Vollmer, T. R., & Borrero, J. C. (2002). Functional behavioral assessment: A school based model [Electronic version]. *Education and Treatment of Children, 25*, 67–90.

Austin, V. L. (2001). Teachers' beliefs about co-teaching. *Remedial and Special Education, 22*, 245–255.

Austin, V. L. (2003). Fear and loathing in the classroom: A candid look at school violence and the policies and practices that address it. *Journal of Disability Policy Studies, 14*, 17–22.

Bagwell, C. L., Molina, B. S., Pelham, W. E., & Hoza, B. (2001). Attention-deficit hyperactivity disorder and problems in peer relations: Predications from childhood to adolescence. *Journal of the American Academy of Child and Adolescent Psychiatry, 40*, 1285–1293.

Bahamonde, C., & Friend, M. (1999). Bilingual education: An alternative approach for collaborative service delivery. *Journal of Educational and Psychological Consultation, 10*, 1–24.

Bahr, M. W., Whitten, E., Dieker, L., Kocarek, C. E., & Manson, D. (1999). A comparison of school-based intervention teams: Implications for educational and legal reform. *Exceptional Children, 66*, 67–84.

Bailey, J., & McTighe, H. (1996). Reporting achievement at the secondary level: What and how. In T. Guskey (Ed.), *Communicating student learning* (pp. 199–240). Alexandria, VA: Association for Supervision and Curriculum Development.

Baker, J. M., & Zigmond, N. (1995). The meaning and practices of inclusion for students with learning disabilities: Implications from the five cases. *The Journal of Special Education, 29*, 163–180.

Baker, S., Gersten, R., Dimino, J. A., & Griffiths, R. (2004). The sustained use of research-based instructional practice: A case study of peer-assisted learning strategies in mathematics. *Remedial and Special Education, 25*, 5–24.

Banks, J. A. (2001). *Cultural diversity in education: Foundations, curriculum and teaching.* Boston: Allyn and Bacon.

Barkley, R. (1995). *Taking charge of ADHD: The complete authoritative guide for parents.* New York: Guilford Press.

Barkley, R. A. (1998a). *ADHD and the nature of self-control.* New York: Guilford.

Barkley, R. A. (1998b). Attention-deficit hyperactivity disorder. *Scientific American, 279*(3), 66–71.

Barkley, R. A. (2004). Adolescents with attention-deficit/hyperactivity disorder: An overview of empirically based treatments [Electronic version]. *Journal of Psychiatric Practice, 10*, 39–56.

Barkley, R. A., et al. (2002). International consensus statement on ADHD. *Clinical Child and Family Psychology Review, 5*, 89–111.

Barnhill, G., Hagiwara, T., Myles, B. S., & Simpson, R. L. (2000). Asperger syndrome: A study of the cognitive profiles of 37 children and adolescents. *Focus on Autism and Other Developmental Disabilities, 15*, 146–153.

Barootchi, N., & Keshavarz, M. H. (2002). Assessment of achievement through portfolios and teacher-made tests. *Educational Research, 44*, 279–288.

Barrie, W., & McDonald, J. (2002). Administrative support for student-led individualized education programs. *Remedial and Special Education, 23*, 116–121.

Barron, A. M., & Foot, H. (1991). Peer tutoring and tutor training. *Educational Research, 33*, 174–185.

Bartelt, L., Marchio, T., & Reynolds, D. (1994). *The READS strategy.* Unpublished manuscript, Northern Illinois University.

Bateman, D., & Bateman, C. F. (2002). What does a principal need to know about inclusion (ERIC Digest E635). Arlington, VA: ERIC Clearinghouse on Disabilities and Gifted Education. (ERIC Document Reproduction Service No. ED473828)

Baxendell, B. W. (2003). Consistent, coherent, creative: The 3 C's graphic organizers. *Teaching Exceptional Children, 35*(3), 46–53.

Bear, G. G., Quinn, M. M., & Burkholder, S. (2001). *Interim alternative educational settings for children with disabilities.* Bethesda, MD: National Association of School Psychologists. Retrieved October 3, 2004, from http://www.eric .ed.gov/contentdelivery/servlet/ ERICServlet?accno=ED458747

Beck, I. L., & McKeown, M. G. (2002). *Bringing words to life.* NY: Guilford.

Behrmann, M., & Jerome, M. K. (2002). Assistive technology for students with mild disabilities: Update 2002 (ERIC Digest No. E623). Arlington, VA: ERIC Clearinghouse on Disabilities and Gifted Education. (Eric Docu-

ment Reproduction Service No. ED463595)

Beigel, A. R. (2000). Assistive technology assessment: More than the device. *Intervention in School and Clinic, 35*, 237–245.

Benner, S. M. (1998). *Special education issues within the context of American society.* Belmont, CA: Wadsworth.

Bennett, A. (1932). *Subnormal children in elementary grades.* New York: Columbia University, Teacher's College, Bureau of Publications.

Bennett, C. I. (2003). *Comprehensive multicultural education: Theory and practice* (5th ed.). Boston: Allyn and Bacon.

Bergan, J. R., & Tombari, M. L. (1975). The analysis of verbal interactions occurring during consultation. *Journal of School Psychology, 13*, 209–226.

Berliner, D. C. (1984). The half-full glass: A review of research on teaching. In P. L. Hosford (Ed.), *Using what we know about teaching (1984 yearbook)* (pp. 69–83). Alexandria, VA: Association for Supervision and Curriculum Development.

Biederman, J. (2003). Pharmacotherapy for attention-deficit/hyperactivity disorder (ADHD) decreases the risk for substance abuse: Findings from a longitudinal follow-up of youths with and without ADHD. *Journal of Clinical Psychiatry, 64*, 3–8.

Blatt, B. (1958). The physical, personality, and academic status of children who are mentally retarded attending special classes as compared with children who are mentally retarded attending regular class. *American Journal of Mental Deficiency, 62*, 810–818.

Blatt, B. (1987). *The conquest of mental retardation.* Austin, TX: PRO-ED.

Bloom, L. A., Perlmutter, J., & Burrell, L. (1999). The general educator: Applying constructivism to inclusive classrooms. *Intervention in School and Clinic, 34*, 132–138.

Blue-Banning, M., Summers, J. A., Frankland, H. C., Nelson, L. L., & Beegle, G. (2004). Dimensions of family and professional partnerships: Constructive guidelines for collaboration. *Exceptional Children, 70*, 167–184.

Blue-Banning, M., Turnbull, A. P., & Pereira, L. (2002). Hispanic youth/ young adults with disabilities: Parents' visions for the future. *Journal of the Association for Persons with Severe Handicaps (JASH), 27*, 204–219.

Bock, R. (1999). Research from NICHD's in learning disabilities. *National Insti-*

tute of Child Health and Human Development. Retrieved October 7, 1999, from http://www.nichd.nih.gov/publications/pubs/readbro.htm

Boethel, M. (2003). *Diversity: School, family, and community connections.* Austin, TX: National Center for Family and Community Connections with Schools, Southwest Educational Development Lab. Retrieved December 4, 2004, from http://www.sedl.org/connections/resources/diversity-synthesis.pdf

Bondy, A., & Frost, L. (2002). *A picture's worth: PECS and other visual communication strategies in autism.* Bethseda, MD: Woodbine House.

Bonner, F. A. (2003). To be young, gifted, African American, and male [electronic version]. *Gifted Child Today, 26*(2), 26–34.

Bos, C. S., & Vaughn, S. (2004). *Strategies for teaching students with learning and behavior problems* (3rd ed.). Boston: Allyn and Bacon.

Bovey, T., & Strain, P. (2003). *Promoting positive peer social interactions. What works briefs.* Champaign: Center on the Social and Emotional Foundations for Early Learning, University of Illinois. (Eric Document Reproduction Service No. ED481996)

Bowen, S. (n.d.). *Daily story problem.* Retrieved November 23, 2004, from http://www.pacificnet.net/~mandel/math.html

Boyle, E. A., Washburn, S. G., Rosenberg, M. S., Connelly, V. J., Brinckerhoff, L. C., & Banerjee, M. (2002). Reading's SLiCK with new audio texts and strategies. *Teaching Exceptional Children, 35*(2), 50–55.

Boyle, J. R., & Weishaar, M. (2001). The effects of strategic notetaking on the recall and comprehension of lecture information for high school students with learning disabilities. *Learning Disabilities: Research and Practice, 16,* 133–141.

Bradley, D. F., & Calvin, M. B. (1998). Grading modified assignments: Equity or compromise? *Teaching Exceptional Children, 31*(2), 24–29.

Brain Injury Association of America. (2004). *Causes of brain injury.* McLean, VA: Author. Retrieved March 13, 2004, from http://www.biausa.org/Pages/causes_of_brain_injury.html

Brandwein, P. F., & Bauer, N. W. (1980). *The United States, living in our world: Research, evaluation, and writing.* Barton R. Clark et al., consulting social scientists. San Francisco and New York: Center for the Study of Instruction/Harcourt Brace Jovanovich.

Brinckerhoff, L. (1994). Developing effective self-advocacy skills in college-bound students with learning disabilities. *Intervention in School and Clinic, 29*(4), 229–237.

Browder, M. D., Spooner, F., Algozzine, R., Ahlgrim-Delzell, L., Flowers, C., Karvonen, M. (2003). What we know and need to know about alternative assessment. *Exceptional Children, 70*(1), 45–61.

Brown, G. M., Kerr, M. M., Zigmond, N., & Harris, A. L. (1984). What's important for student success in high school? "Successful" and "unsuccessful" students discuss school survival skills. *High School Journal, 68,* 10–17.

Brown, M. (2000). Access, instruction, and barriers. *Remedial and Special Education, 21,* 182–192.

Bryan, T. (1997). Assessing the personal and social status of students with learning disabilities. *Learning Disabilities Research and Practice, 12*(1), 63–76.

Bryan, T. H., & Bryan, J. H. (1986). *Understanding learning disabilities* (3rd ed.). Palo Alto, CA: Mayfield.

Bryant, B. R., Bryant, D. P., & Kethley, C. I. (2004). Reading assessment: Introduction to the special series. *Assessment for Effective Intervention, 29*(4), 3–12.

Buck, G. H., Polloway, E. A., Smith-Thomas, A., & Cook, K. W. (2003). Prereferral intervention processes: A survey of state practices. *Exceptional Children, 69,* 349–360.

Bulgren, J. A., Schumaker, J. B., & Deshler, D. (1988). Effectiveness of a concept teaching routine in enhancing the performance of LD students in secondary-level mainstream classes. *Learning Disability Quarterly, 11,* 3–17.

Bullara, D. T. (1993). Classroom management strategies to reduce racially-biased treatment of students. *Journal of Educational and Psychological Consultation, 4*(4), 357–368.

Burcroff, T. L., Radogna, D. M., & Wright, E. H. (2003). Community forays: Addressing students' functional skills in inclusive settings. *Teaching Exceptional Children, 35*(5), 52–57.

Burks, M. (2004). Effects of classwide peer tutoring on the number of words spelled correctly by students with LD. *Intervention in School and Clinic, 39,* 301–304.

Burns, M. K. (2004). Empirical analysis of drill ratio research: Refining the instructional level for drill tasks. *Remedial and special education, 25*(3), 167–173.

Burns, P. C., Roe, B. D., & Ross, E. P. (2001). *Teaching reading in today's elementary schools* (8th ed.). Boston: Houghton Mifflin.

Burstein, N., Sears, S., Wilcoxen, A., Cabello, B., & Spagna, M. (2004). Moving toward inclusive practices. *Remedial and Special Education, 25,* 104–116.

Bursuck, B., Damer, M. & Dickson, S. (2005, May). Translating reading research to practice in three urban schools: An account of successful school-wide change. Presented at Annual Convention of the Association for Behavioral Analysis, Chicago, IL.

Bursuck, W. D., & Damer, M. (2006). *Literacy instruction for special education/at risk students.* Boston: Allyn and Bacon.

Bursuck, W. D., & Lessen, E. (1987). A classroom-based model for assessing students with learning disabilities. *Learning Disabilities Focus, 3*(1), 17–29.

Bursuck, W. D., Harniss, M. K., Epstein, M. H., Polloway, E. A., Jayanthi, M., & Wissinger, L. M. (1999). Solving communication problems about homework: Recommendations of special education teachers. *Learning Disabilities Research and Practice, 14,* 149–158.

Bursuck, W. D., Munk, D., & Olson, D. (1999). The fairness of report card grading adaptations: What do students with and without learning disabilities think? *Remedial and Special Education, 20,* 84–92.

Bursuck, W. D., Polloway, E. A., Plante, L., Epstein, M. H., Jayanthi, M., & McConeghy, J. (1996). Report card grading and adaptations: A national survey of classroom practices. *Exceptional Children, 62,* 301–318.

Bursuck, W. D., Smith, T., Munk, D., Damer, M., Mehlig, L., & Perry, J. (2004). Evaluating the impact of a prevention-based model of reading on children who are at risk. *Remedial and Special Education, 25,* 303–313.

Calderon, M. E. (1999). *Promoting language proficiency and academic achievement through cooperation.* Washington, DC: ERIC Clearinghouse on Languages and Linguistics. (ERIC Document Reproduction Service No. ED436983)

Calhoon, M. B., & Fuchs, L. S. (2003). The effects of peer-assisted learning strategies and curriculum-based measurement on the mathematics performance of secondary students with disabilities. *Remedial and Special Education, 24,* 235–245.

Camp, B. W., & Bash, M. A. (1985). *Think aloud.* Champaign, IL: Research Press.

Carlo, M. S., August, D., Mclaughlin, B., Snow, C. E., Dressler, C., Lippman, D. N., Lively, T. J., & White, C. E. (2004). Closing the gap: Addressing the vocabulary needs of English-language learners in bilingual and mainstream classrooms. *Reading Research quarterly, 39,* 188–215.

Carlson, C., & Henning, M. (1993). *The TAG peer editing procedure.* Unpublished manuscript, Northern Illinois University.

Carlson, E., Liwan, C., Schroll, K., & Klein, S. (2002). *SPeNSE study of personnel needs in special education: Final report of the paperwork substudy.* Rockville, MD: Westat. Retrieved August 15, 2004, from http://www.eric.ed.gov/contentdelivery/servlet/ERICServlet?accno=ED479674

Carney, R. N., Levin, M. E., & Levin, J. R. (1993). Mnemonic strategies: Instructional techniques worth remembering. *Teaching Exceptional Children, 25*(4), 24–30.

Carnine, D. W. (1981). High and low implementation of direct instruction teaching techniques. *Education and Treatment of Children, 4,* 42–51.

Carnine, D. W., Crawford, D., Harniss, M., & Hollenbeck, K. (1995). *Understanding U.S. history: Volume 1. Through the Civil War.* Eugene, OR: Considerate Publishing.

Carnine, D. W., Silbert, J., Kame'enui, E. J., & Tarver, S. G. (2004). *Direct instruction reading* (4th ed.). Upper Saddle River, NJ: Pearson/Merrill Prentice Hall.

Carr, M., & Jessup, D. L. (1997). Gender differences in first grade mathematics strategy use: Social and metacognitive influences. *Journal of Educational Psychology, 89,* 318–328.

Carroll, D. (2001). Considering paraeducator training, roles, and responsibilities. *Teaching Exceptional Children, 34*(2), 60–65.

Carter, E. W., & Wehby, J. H. (2003). Job performance of transition-age youth with emotional and behavioral disorders. *Exceptional Children, 69,* 449–465.

Casella, R. (2003). Zero tolerance policy in schools: Rationale, consequences, and alternatives [Electronic version]. *Teachers College Record, 105,* 872–892.

Casey, J. (2003, July). *Adult ADHD: A difficult diagnosis.* Retrieved September 1, 2003, from http://my.webmd.com/content/Article/66/79905.htm?pagenumber=2

Cass, M., Cates, D., Smith, M., & Jackson, C. (2003). Effects of manipulative instruction on solving area and perimeter problems by students with learning disabilities. *Learning Disabilities Research & Practice, 18*(2), 112–120.

Cassidy, V. M., & Stanton, J. E. (1959). *An investigation of factors involved in the educational placement of mentally retarded children: A study of differences between children in special and regular classes in Ohio.* (U.S. Office of Education Cooperative Research Program, Project No. 43) Columbus: Ohio State University. (ERIC Document Reproduction Service No. ED002752)

Cawley, J. F., Miller, J., & School, B. (1987). A brief inquiry of arithmetic word problem solving among learning disabled secondary students. *Learning Disabilities Focus, 2*(2), 87–93.

Cawley, J., Hayden, S., Cade, E., & Baker-Kroczynski, S. (2002). Including students with disabilities into the general education science classroom. *Exceptional Children, 68,* 423–436.

Cawley, J., Parmar, R., Foley, T. E., Salmon, S., Roy, S. (2001). Arithmetic performance of students: Implications for standards and programming. *Exceptional Children, 67,* 311–328.

Center for the Study of Reading. (1988). *A guide to selecting basal reading programs: Workbooks.* Cambridge, MA: Bolt, Beraneck, and Newman.

Centers for Disease Control and Prevention. (2002). *AIDS in the United States.* Retrieved November 15, 2004, from http://www.cchs.net/health/health-info/docs/1100/1171.asp?index=5905

Centers for Disease Control and Prevention. (2004). *Tourette syndrome.* Retrieved November 20, 2004, from http://www.cdc.gov/ncbddd/tourette/default.htm

Cermak, L. S. (1976). *Improving your memory.* New York: Norton.

Cesaroni, L., & Garber, M. (1991). Exploring the experience of autism through firsthand accounts. *Journal of Autism and Developmental Disorders, 21,* 303–313.

Chaffin, J. (1975). Will the real "mainstreaming" program please stand up! (Or . . . should Dunn have done it?). In E. L. Meyen, G. A. Vergason, & R. J. Whelan (Eds.), *Alternatives for teaching exceptional children.* Denver: Love.

Chard, D., & Dickson, S. V. (1999). Phonological awareness: Instructional and assessment guidelines. *Intervention in School and Clinic, 5,* 261–270.

Cheek, E. H., Jr., & Cheek, M. C. (1983). *Reading instruction through content teaching.* Columbus, OH: Merrill.

Child abuse characteristics. (2000). Retrieved September 13, 2000, from http://www.angelfire.com/fl2/ChildAbuse/Characteristics.html

Children's Defense Fund. (2003). *2002 facts on child poverty in America.* Washington, DC: Author. Retrieved December 4, 2004, from http://www.childrensdefense.org/familyincome/childpoverty/basicfacts.asp

Choate, J. S., Enright, B. E., Miller, L. J., Poteet, J. A., & Rakes, T. A. (1995). *Curriculum-based assessment and programming.* Boston: Allyn and Bacon.

Chopra, R. V., Sandoval-Lucero, E., Aragon, L., Bernal, C., De Balderas, H. B., & Carroll, D. (2004). The paraprofessional role of connector. *Remedial and Special Education, 25,* 219–232.

Christopolos, F., & Renz, P. (1969). A critical examination of special education programs. *Journal of Special Education, 3,* 371–379.

Clark, E., Russman, S., & Orme, S. F. (1999). Traumatic brain injury: Effects on school functioning and intervention strategies. *School Psychology Review, 28,* 242–250.

Closs, A. (Ed.). (2000). *The education of children with medical conditions.* London: David Fulton.

Cohen, M., & Riel, M. M. (1989). The effect of distant audiences on students' writing. *American Educational Research Journal, 26,* 143–159.

Cohen, S. B. (1983). Assigning report card grades to the mainstreamed child. *Teaching Exceptional Children, 15,* 186–189.

Colangelo, N. (2002, Fall). Counseling gifted and talented students. *National Research Center on the Gifted and Talented Newsletter.* Storrs, CT: National Research Center on the Gifted and Talented. (ERIC Document Reproduction Service No. ED447662)

Colangelo, N., & Davis, G. A. (Eds.). (2003). *Handbook on gifted education* (3rd edition). Boston: Allyn and Bacon.

Cole, C. M., Waldron, N., & Majd, M. (2004). Academic progress of students across inclusive and traditional settings [Electronic version]. *Mental Retardation, 42,* 136–144.

Coleman, M. C., & Webber, J. (2002). *Emotional and behavioral disorders: The-*

ory and practice (4th ed.). Boston: Allyn and Bacon.

Colson, S. E., & Brandt, M. D. (2000). Working with families of children with attention-deficit/hyperactivity disorder. In M. J. Fine & R. L. Simpson (Eds.), *Collaboration with parents and families of children and youth with exceptionalities* (2nd ed.), (pp. 347–367) Austin, TX: PRO-ED.

Connors, C. K., & Blouin, A. G. (1982/1983). Nutritional effects on the behavior of children. *Journal of Psychiatric Research, 17,* 193–201.

Conroy, M., Clark, D., Gable, R. A., & Fox, J. J. (1999). A look at IDEA 1997 discipline provisions: Implications for change in the roles and responsibilities of school personnel. *Preventing School Failure, 43,* 64–70.

Consortium for Appropriate Dispute Resolution in Special Education. (2001). *Special education mediation: A guide for parents.* Eugene, OR: Author. (ERIC Document Reproduction Service No. ED456583)

Conyers, C., Miltenberger, R., Romaniuk, C., Kopp, B., & Himle, M. (2003). Evaluation of DRO schedules to reduce disruptive behavior in a preschool classroom [Electronic version]. *Child and Family Behavior Therapy, 25,* 1–6.

Cook, B. G. (2001). A comparison of teachers' attitudes toward their included students with mild and severe disabilities. *Journal of Special Education, 34,* 203–213.

Cook, B. G. (2002). Special educators' views of community-based job training and inclusion as indicators of job competencies for students with mild and moderate disabilities. *Career Development for Exceptional Individuals, 25,* 7–24.

Cook, B. G., Semmel, M. I., & Gerber, M. M. (1999). Attitudes of principals and special education teachers toward the inclusion of students with mild disabilities. *Remedial and Special Education, 20,* 199–207, 243.

Cooper, H. (1989). Synthesis of research on homework. *Educational Leadership, 47*(3), 85–91.

Cooper, H., & Valentine, J. C. (2001). Using research to answer practical questions about homework. *Educational Psychologist, 36,* 143–153.

Cooper, S. M. A. (2002). Classroom choices for enabling peer learning [Electronic version]. *Theory into Practice, 41*(1), 53–57.

Copeland, S. R., Hughes, C., Carter, E. W., Guth, C., Presley, J. A.,

Williams, C. R., & Fowler, S. E. (2004). Increasing access to general education: Perspectives of participants in a high school peer support program. *Remedial and Special Education, 25,* 342–352.

Cott, A. (1977). *The orthomolecular approach to learning disabilities.* New York: Huxley Institute.

Cott, A. (1985). *Help for your learning disabled child: The orthomolecular treatment.* New York: Time Books.

Council of State Directors of Programs for the Gifted. (2001). *The 1999–2000 state of the states gifted and talented education report.* Longmont, CO: Author.

Cowen, E. L., Pederson, A., Babijian, H., Izzo, L. D., & Trost, M. A. (1973). Long-term follow-up of early detected vulnerable children. *Journal of Consulting and Clinical Psychology, 41,* 438–446.

Coyne, P., Pisha, B., Dalton, B., Deysher, S., & Eagleton, M. (2004). Manuscript in preparation.

Crawford, C. G. (1980). *Math without fear.* New York: New Viewpoints/Vision Books.

Cross, L., & Walker-Knight, D. (1997). Inclusion: Developing collaborative and cooperative school communities. *Educational Forum, 61,* 269–277.

Cullinan, D., Epstein, M. H., & Lloyd, J. (1983). *Behavior disorders of children and adolescents.* Englewood Cliffs, NJ: Prentice-Hall.

Cullinan, D., Evans, C., Epstein, M. H., & Ryser, G. (2003). Characteristics of emotional disturbance of elementary school students. *Behavioral Disorders, 28,* 94–110.

Curry, C. (2003). Universal design: Accessibility for all learners. *Educational Leadership, 61*(2), 55–60.

Cushner, K., McClelland, A., & Safford, P. (2000). *Human diversity in education: An integrative approach.* New York: McGraw-Hill.

Czarnecki, E., Rosko, D., & Fine, F. (1998). How to CALL UP notetaking skills. *Teaching Exceptional Children, 30*(6), 14–19.

D'Angelo, A., Lutz, J. G., & Zirkel, P. A. (2004). Are published IDEA hearing officer decisions representative? *Journal of Disability Policy Studies, 14,* 241–252.

da Costa, J. L., Marshall, J. L., & Riordan, G. (1998, April). *Case study of the development of a collaborative teaching culture in an inner city elementary school.* Paper presented at the Annual Meeting of the American Educational Research Association, San Diego. (ERIC Documentation Reproduction Service No. ED420630)

Dabkowski, D. M. (2004). Encouraging active parent participation in IEP team meetings. *Teaching Exceptional Children, 36*(3), 34–39.

Dalton, B., & Pisha, B. (2001). Developing strategic readers: A comparison of computer-suggested versus traditional strategy instruction on struggling readers' comprehension of quality children's literature. Paper presented at the 51st annual meeting of the National Reading Conference, San Antonio, TX.

Daly, P. M., & Ranalli, P. (2003). Using countoons to teach self-monitoring skills. *Teaching Exceptional Children, 35*(5), 30–35.

Daniels, V. I. (1998). How to manage disruptive behavior in inclusive classrooms. *Teaching Exceptional Children, 30*(4), 26–31.

Darch, C., & Gersten, R. (1985). The effects of teaching presentation and praise on LD students' oral reading performance. *British Journal of Educational Psychology, 55,* 295–303.

Darch, C., Carnine, D., & Gersten, R. (1984). Explicit instruction in mathematics problem solving. *Journal of Educational Research, 77,* 351–358.

Davern, L. (2004). School-to-home notebooks. *Teaching Exceptional Children 36*(5), 22–28.

Davies, D. M., Stock, S., & Wehmeyer, M. L. (2002). Enhancing independent time management and personal scheduling for individuals with mental retardation through use of a palmtop visual and audio prompting system. *Mental Retardation, 40,* 358–365.

Day-Vines, N. L., Patton, J. M., & Baytops, J. L. (2003). Counseling African American adolescents: The impact of face, culture, and middle class status [Electronic version]. *Professional School Counseling, 7,* 40–51.

Dean, A. V., Salend, S. J., & Taylor, L. (1994). Multicultural education: A challenge for special educators. *Teaching Exceptional Children, 26*(1), 40–43.

DeBettencourt, L. U. (1999). General educators' attitudes toward students with mild disabilities and their use of instructional strategies: Implications for training. *Remedial and Special Education, 20,* 27–35.

DeBettencourt, L. U. (2002). Understanding the differences between IDEA and Section 504. *Teaching Exceptional Children, 34*(3), 16–23.

Deitz, D. E. D., & Ormsby, D. (1992). A comparison of verbal social behavior of adolescents with behavioral disorders and regular class peers. *Behavioral Modification, 16,* 504–524.

DeLaPaz, S. (1999). Composing via dictation and speech recognition systems: Compensatory technology for students with learning disabilities. *Learning Disabilities Quarterly, 22,* 173–182.

Demchak, M. A. (n.d.). *Fact Sheet: Circles of friends.* Reno: Nevada Dual Sensory Impairment Project, University of Nevada, Reno. Retrieved February 9, 2005, from http://www.unr.edu/educ/ndsip/factsheets/circle.friends.pdf

Denham, A., & Lahm, E. A. (2001). Using technology to construct alternate portfolios of students with moderate and severe disabilities. *Teaching Exceptional Children, 33*(5), 10–17.

Deno, S. L. (1985). Curriculum-based measurement: The emerging alternative. *Exceptional Children, 52,* 219–232.

Deno, S. L. (1989). Curriculum-based measurement and special education services: A fundamental and direct relationship. In M. Shinn (Ed.), *Curriculum-based measurement: Assessing special children* (pp. 1–17). New York: Guilford Press.

Deno, S. L. (2003). Developments in curriculum-based measurement. *Journal of Special Education, 37,* 184–192.

Deno, S. L., Reschly-Anderson, A., Lembke, E., Zorka, H., & Callender, S. (2002). *A model for school wide implementation: A case example.* Paper presented at the annual meeting of the National Association of School Psychology, Chicago, IL.

Denton, C. A., Hasbrouch, J. E., & Sekaquaptewa, S. (2003). The consulting teacher: A descriptive case study in responsive systems consultation. *Journal of Educational and Psychological Consultation, 14,* 41–73.

DePaepe, P., Garrison-Kane, L., & Doelling, J. (2002). Supporting students with health needs in schools: An overview of selected health conditions. *Focus on Exceptional Children, 35*(1), 1–24.

Dettmer, P., Thurston, L. P., & Dyck, N. J. (2005). *Consultation, collaboration, and teamwork for students with special needs* (5th ed.). Englewood Cliffs, NJ: Prentice-Hall.

Dickson, S. V., & Bursuck, W. D. (1999). Implementing a model for preventing reading failure. *Learning Disabilities Research and Practice, 14*(4), 191–202.

Dickson, S. V., & Bursuck, W. D. (2003). Implementing an outcomes-based collaborative partnership fro preventing reading failure. In D. L. Wiseman & S. L. Knight (Eds.), *Linking school-university collaboration and K–12 student outcomes* (pp. 131–146). Washington, DC: AACTE.

Dickson, S. V., Collins, V., Simmons, D. C., & Kame'enui, E. J. (1998). Metacognition: Curricular and instructional implications for diverse learners. In D. C. Simmons & E. J. Kame'enui (Eds.), *What reading research tells us about children with diverse learning needs* (pp. 361–380). Hillsdale, NJ: Lawrence Erlbaum.

Dickson, S., Chard, D., & Simmons, D. (1993). An integrated reading/writing curriculum: A focus on scaffolding. *LD Forum, 18*(4), 12–16.

Dieker, L. A. (2001). What are the characterisics of "effective" middle and high school co-taught teams for students with disabilities? *Preventing School Failure, 46*(1), 14–23.

Dieterich, C. A., Villani, C. J., & Bennett, P. T. (2003). Functional behavioral assessments: Beyond student behavior [Electronic version]. *Journal of Law and Education, 32,* 357–368.

DiPaola, M. F., & Walther-Thomas, C. (2003). *Principals and special education: The critical role of school leaders.* Arlington, VA: National Clearinghouse on Professions in Special Education. (ERIC Document Reproduction Service No. ED477115)

Disability Films. (2004). *Recommended film list by title.* Retrieved February 8, 2005, from http://www.disabilityfilms.co.uk//rec1/rec1dex.htm

Dole, R. L. (2004). Collaborating successfully with your school's physical therapist. *Teaching Exceptional Children, 36*(5), 28–35.

Doman, G., & Delacato, D. (1968). Doman–Delacato philosophy. *Human Potential, 1,* 113–116.

Donovan, M. S., & Cross, C. T. (Eds.). (2002). *Minority students in special and gifted education.* Washington, DC: National Academy Press. Retrieved February 26, 2004, from http://www.edrs.com/members/sp.cfm?AN=ED469543

Doré, R., Dion, E., Wagner, S., & Brunet, J. P. (2002). High school inclusion of adolescents with mental retardation: A multiple case study. *Education and Training in Mental Retardation and Developmental Disabilities, 37,* 253–261.

Downing, J. E. (2002). *Including students with severe and multiple disabilities in typical classrooms: Practical strategies for teachers* (2nd ed.). Baltimore: Brookes.

Downing, J. E., & Eichinger, J. (2003). Creating learning opportunities for students with severe disabilities in inclusive classrooms. *Teaching Exceptional Children, 36*(1), 26–31.

Doyle, W. (1986). Classroom organization and management. In M. Wittrock (Ed.), *Handbook of research on teaching* (pp. 392–431). New York: Macmillan.

Doyle, W. (1990). Classroom management techniques. In O. C. Moles (Ed.), *Student discipline strategies* (pp. 83–105). Albany: State University of New York Press.

Drasgow, E., & Yell, M. L. (2001). Functional behavioral assessments: Legal requirements and challenges [Electronic version]. *School Psychology Review, 30,* 239–251.

Drasgow, E., Yell, M. L., & Robinson, T. R. (2001). Developing legally correct and educationally appropriate IEPs. *Remedial and Special Education, 22,* 359–373.

Duke, N. K. (2000). 36 minutes per day: The scarcity of informational texts in first grade. *Reading Research Quarterly, 35,* 202–224.

Dunn, C., Chambers, D., & Rabren, K. (2004). Variables affecting students' decisions to drop out of school. *Remedial and Special Education, 25,* 314–323.

Dunn, L. M. (1968). Special education for the mildly handicapped—Is much of it justifiable? *Exceptional Children, 35,* 5–22.

Dunst, C. J. (2002). Family-centered practices: Birth through high school. *Journal of Special Education, 36,* 139–147.

Durand, V. M., & Merges, E. (2001). Functional communication training: A contemporary behavior analytic intervention for problem behaviors. *Focus on Autism and Other Developmental Disabilities, 16,* 110–119.

Dyson, B. (2002). The implementation of cooperative learning in an elementary physical education program [Electronic version]. *Journal of Teaching in Physical Education, 22,* 69–85.

Easterbrooks, S. (1999). Improving practices for students with hearing impairments. *Exceptional Children, 65,* 537–554.

Echevarria, J. C. (1998). Preparing text and classroom materials for English-language learners: Curriculum adaptations in secondary school settings. In R. Gersten & R. Jimenez (Eds.), *Pro-*

moting learning for culturally and linguistically diverse students: Classroom applications from contemporary research. Belmont, CA: Wadsworth.

Edelson, M. G. (1995). *Social stories.* Salem, OR: Center for the Study of Autism. Retrieved November 22, 2004, from http://www.autism.org/stories.html

Edelson, S. M. (n.d.). *Treatment tips: A brief overview of common problems and fixes.* Salem, OR: Center for the Study of Autism. Retrieved November 22, 2004, from http://www.autism.org/quickfix.html

Education Commission of the States. (1999). *Cooperative Integrated Reading and Composition (CIRC).* Denver, CO: Author. (ERIC Document Reproduction Service No. ED447423)

Ehri, L. C. (2004). Teaching phonemic awareness and phonics: An explanation of the National Reading Panel meta-analyses. In P. McCardle & V. Chhabra (Eds.), *The voice of evidence in reading research* (pp. 153–186). Baltimore: Brookes.

Eigenbrood, R. (2004). IDEA requirements for children with disabilities in faith-based schools: Implications for practice. *Journal of Disability Policy Studies, 15,* 2–8.

Eisenman, L. T. (2001). Conceptualizing the contribution of career-oriented schooling to self-determination [Electronic version]. *Career Development for Exceptional Individuals, 24*(1), 3–17.

Elbaum, B., Moody, S. W., & Schumm, J. S. (1999). Mixed-ability grouping for reading: What students think. *Learning Disabilities Research and Practice, 14,* 61–66.

Eli Lilly. (2003). *The history of ADHD.* Retrieved June 28, 2003, from http://www.strattera.com/1_3_childhood_adhd/1_3_1_1_2_history.jsp

Elliott, S. N. (1998). Performance assessment of students' achievement: Research and practice. *Learning Disabilities Research and Practice, 13,* 233–241.

Ellis, E. (1996). Reading strategy instruction. In D. Deshler, E. Ellis, & K. Lenz (Eds.), *Teaching adolescents with learning disabilities: Strategies and methods* (2nd ed., pp. 61–125). Denver: Love.

Ellis, E. S., & Colvert, G. (1996). Writing strategy instruction. In D. Deshler, E. Ellis, and B. Lenz (Eds.), *Teaching adolescents with learning disabilities: Strategies and methods* (2nd ed., pp. 127–207). Denver: Love.

Ellis, E. S., & Sabornie, E. S. (1990). Strategy-based adaptive instruction in content-area classes: Social validity of six options. *Teacher Education and Special Education, 13,* 133–144.

Ellis, E., & Lenz, B. K. (1996). Perspectives on instruction in learning strategies. In D. Deshler, E. Ellis, & B. K. Lenz (Eds.), *Teaching adolescents with learning disabilities: Strategies and methods* (2nd ed., pp. 9–60). Denver: Love.

Ellis, E., & Lenz, K. (1987). A component analysis of effective learning strategies for LD students. *Learning Disabilities Focus, 2,* 94–107.

Ellis, E., Lenz, B. K., & Sabornie, E. (1987a). Generalization and adaptation of learning strategies to natural environments: Part 1: Critical agents. *Remedial and Special Education, 8*(2), 6–24.

Ellis, E., Lenz, B. K., & Sabornie, E. (1987b). Generalization and adaptation of learning strategies to natural environments: Part 2: Research into practice. *Remedial and Special Education, 8*(2), 6–23.

Emmer, E. T., & Gerwels, M. C. (2002). Cooperative learning in elementary classrooms: Teaching practices and lesson characteristics [Electronic version]. *Elementary School Journal, 103,* 76–91.

Emmer, E. T., Evertson, C. M., Sanford, J. P., Clements, B. S., & Worsham, M. E. (1983). *Organizing and managing the junior high classroom.* Austin: Research and Development Center for Teacher Education, University of Texas.

Engelmann, S., & Bruner, E. C. (2003). *Reading mastery classic.* Columbus, OH: SRA/McGraw-Hill.

Engelmann, S., & Grossen, B. (2001). *Reasoning and writing: A direct instruction program.* Columbus, Ohio: SRA.

Engleman, D., Griffin, H. C., Griffin, L. W., & Maddox, J. I. (1999). A teacher's guide to communicating with students with deaf-blindness. *Teaching Exceptional Children, 31*(5), 64–71.

Engleman, M. D., Griffin, H. C., & Wheeler, L. (1998). Deaf-blindness and communication: Practical knowledge and strategies. *Journal of Visual Impairment and Blindness, 92,* 783–798.

Englert, C. S., Raphael, T. E., Anderson, L. M., Anthony, H. M., Fear, K. L., & Gregg, S. L. (1988). A case for writing intervention: Strategies for writing informational text. *Learning Disabilities Focus, 3*(2), 98–113.

Englert, C., & Mariage, T. (1991). Making students partners in the compre-

hension process: Organizing the reading "POSSE." *Learning Disability Quarterly, 14,* 123–138.

Epstein, M. H. (2004). *Behavioral and emotional rating scale* (2nd ed.). Austin, TX: PRO-ED.

Epstein, M. H., Kinder, D., & Bursuck, W. D. (1989). The academic status of adolescents with behavior disorders. *Behavioral Disorders, 4,* 157–165.

Epstein, M. H., Polloway, E. A., Buck, G. H., Bursuck, W. D., Wissinger, L., Whitehouse, F., & Jayanthi, M. (1997). Homework-related communication problems: Perspectives of general education teachers. *Learning Disabilities Research and Practices, 12,* 221–227.

Epstein, M. H., Rudolph, S., & Epstein, A. (2000). Using strength-based assessment in transition planning. *Teaching Exceptional Children, 32*(6), 50–55.

Etscheidt, S. (2002). Discipline provisions of IDEA: Misguided policy or tacit reform initiatives? *Behavioral Disorders, 27,* 408–422.

Evertson, C. M., Emmer, E. T., Clements, B. S., Sanford, J. P., Worsham, M. E., & Williams, E. L. (1983). *Organizing and managing the elementary school classroom.* Austin: Research and Development Center for Teacher Education, University of Texas.

Farmer, T. W., Goforth, J. B., Clemmer, J. T., & Thompson, J. H. (2004). School discipline problems in rural African American early adolescents: Characteristics of students with major, minor, and no offenses. *Behavioral Disorders, 29,* 317–336.

Feingold, B. F. (1975). *Why your child is hyperactive.* New York: Random House.

Fennema, E., Carpenter, T. P., Jacobs, V. R., Franke, M. L., & Levi, L. (1998). A longitudinal study of gender differences in young children's mathematical thinking. *Educational Researcher, 27*(5), 6–11.

Ferguson, P. M. (2002). A place in the family: An historical interpretation of research on parental reactions to having a child with a disability. *Journal of Special Education, 36,* 124–130.

Field, S., Sarver, M. D., & Shaw, S. F. (2003). Self-determination: A key to success in postsecondary education for students with learning disabilities. *Remedial and Special Education, 24,* 339–349.

Fisher, C. W., Berliner, D., Filby, N., Marliare, R., Cahan, L., & Dishaw, M.

(1980). Teaching behavior, academic learning time, and student achievement: An overview. In C. Denham & A. Lieberman (Eds.), *Time to learn* (pp. 7–32). Washington, DC: National Institute of Education, Department of Education.

Fitch, F. (2003). Inclusion, exclusion, and ideology: Special education students' changing sense of self [Electronic version]. *Urban Review, 35,* 233–252.

Fleischer, D. Z., & Zames, F. (2001). *The disability rights movement: From charity to confrontation.* Philadelphia: Temple University Press.

Fleming, J. L., & Monda-Amaya, L. E. (2001). Process variables critical for team effectiveness: A Delphi study of wraparound team members. *Remedial and Special Education, 22,* 158–171.

Fletcher, J., & Martinez, G. (1994). An eye-movement analysis of the effects of scotopic sensitivity correction on parsing and comprehension. *Journal of Learning Disabilities, 27,* 67–70.

Fombonne, E. (2003). The prevalence of autism. *Journal of the American Medical Association, 289,* 87–89.

Foorman, B. R. (Ed.). (2003). *Preventing and remediating reading difficulties: Bringing science to scale.* Baltimore: York.

Foorman, B. R., Goldenberg, C., Carlson, C. D., Saunders, W. M., & Pollard-Durodola, S. D. (2004). How teachers allocate time during literacy instruction in primary-grade English language learner classrooms. In P. McCardle & V. Chhabra (Eds.), *The voice of evidence in reading research* (pp. 289–322). Baltimore: Paul H. Brookes.

Forest, M., Pierpoint, J., & O'Brien, J. (1996). MAPS, Circles of Friends, and PATH: Powerful tools to help build caring communities. In S. Stainback & W. Stainback (Eds.), *Inclusion: A guide for educators.* Baltimore: Paul H. Brookes.

Forness, S. R., & Kavale, K. A. (2001). ADHD and a return to the medical model of special education. *Education and Treatment of Children, 24,* 224–247.

Forness, S. R., Kavale, K. A., Blum, I. M., & Lloyd, J. W. (1997). Mega-analysis of meta-analyses: What works in special education. *Teaching Exceptional Children, 29*(6), 4–9.

Foster, M. (1997). *Black teachers on teaching.* New York: New press.

Foster, M.(1995) African American teachers and culturally-relevant pedagogy.

In J. A. Banks & C. A. M. Banks (Eds.). *Handbook of research on multicultural education* (pp. 570–581). New York: Macmillan.

Fox, L., & Garrison, S. (2003). *Helping children learn to manage their own behavior. What works briefs.* Champaign, IL: Center on the Social and Emotional Foundations for Early Learning. (ERIC Document Reproduction Service No. ED481995)

Frederickson, N., & Turner, J. (2003). Utilizing the classroom peer group to address children's social needs: An evaluation of the Circle of Friends intervention approach. *Journal of Special Education, 36,* 234–245.

Freeman, J. (2000). Teaching for talent: Lessons from the research. In C. M. F. van Lieshout & P. G. Heymans (Eds.), *Developing talent across the life span* (pp. 231–248). Philadelphia: Psychology Press.

Freeman, S. F. N., & Alkin, M. C. (2000). Academic and social attainments of children with mental retardation in general education and special education settings. *Remedial and Special Education, 21*(1), 3–18.

French, N. (1999). Paraeducators: Who are they and what do they do? *Teaching Exceptional Children, 32*(1), 65–69.

French, N. K. (2003). *Managing paraeducators in your school: How to hire, train, and supervise non-certified staff.* Thousand Oaks, CA: Corwin.

Friend, M. (2000). Perspective: Myths and misunderstandings about professional collaboration. *Remedial and Special Education, 21,* 130–132, 160.

Friend, M. (2005). *Special education: Contemporary perspectives for school professionals.* Boston: Allyn and Bacon.

Friend, M., & Cook, L. (2003). *Interactions: Collaboration skills for school professionals* (4th ed.). Boston: Allyn and Bacon.

Friend, M., & Cook, L. (2004). Collaborating with professionals and parents without being overwhelmed: Building partnerships and teams. In J. Burnette, & C. Peters-Johnson (Eds.), *Thriving as a special educator: Balancing your practices and ideals* (pp. 29–39). Arlington, VA: Council for Exceptional Children.

Fuchs, L. S., & Fuchs, D. (2001). Helping teachers formulate sound test accommodation decisions for students with learning disabilities. *Learning Disabilities Research and Practice, 16,* 174–181.

Fuchs, L. S., Fuchs, D., Hamlett, C. L., & Stecker, P. M. (1991). Effects of cur-

riculum-based measurement and consultation on teacher planning and student achievement in mathematics operations. *American Educational Research Journal, 28,* 617–641.

Fuchs, L. S., Fuchs, D., Hamlett, C., Philips, N., & Bentz, J. (1994). Classwide curriculum-based measurement: Helping general educators meet the challenge of student diversity. *Exceptional Children, 60,* 518–537.

Fuchs, L. S., Fuchs, D., Kazdan, S., Karns, K., Calhoon, M. B., Hamlett, C. L., & Hewlett, S. (2000). Effects of workgroup structure and size on student productivity during collaborative work on complex tasks. *Elementary School Journal, 100,* 201–210.

Fujiura, G. T., & Yamaki, K. (2000). Trends in demography of childhood poverty and disability. *Exceptional Children, 66,* 187–199.

Fulk, B. M., & King, K. (2001). Classwide peer tutoring at work. *Teaching Exceptional Children, 34*(2), 48–53.

Furlong, M., & Morrison, G. (2000). The *school* in school violence: Definitions and facts. *Journal of Emotional and Behavioral Disorders, 8,* 71–82.

Gabe, J., Bury, M., & Ramsay, R. (2002). Living with asthma: The experiences of young people at home and at school [Electronic version]. *Social Science and Medicine, 55,* 1619–1633.

Gagnon, E. (2001). *The Power Card Strategy: Using special interests to motivate children and youth with Asperger syndrome.* Shawnee Mission, KS: Autism Asperger Publishing.

Gagnon, J. C., & Maccini, P. (2001). Preparing students with disabilities for algebra. *Teaching Exceptional Children, 34*(1), 8–15.

Gallagher, J. J. (2002). *Society's role in educating gifted students: The role of public policy* (Senior Scholar Series). Storrs: University of Connecticut, National Research Center on the Gifted and Talented. Retrieved February 27, 2004, from http://www.edrs.com/members/sp.cfm?AN=ED476370

Gallimore, L., & Woodruff, S. (1996). The bilingual-bicultural (bi-bi) approach: A professional point of view. In S. Schwartz (Ed.), *Choices in deafness* (pp. 89–95). Bethesda, MD: Woodbine House.

Gans, A. M., Kenny, M. C., & Ghany, D. L. (2003). Comparing the self-concept of students with and without learning disabilities. *Journal of Learning Disabilities, 36*(3), 287–295.

Gardner, H. (1993). *Multiple intelligences: The theory in practice.* New York: Basic Books.

Gardner, R., Sainato, D. M., Cooper, J. O., Heron, T. E., Heward, W. L., Eshelman, J. W., & Grossi, T. A. (1994). *Behavior analysis in education: Focus on measurably superior instruction.* Pacific Grove, CA: Brooks/Cole.

Garnes, L., & Menlove, R. (2003, March). School-wide discipline practices: A look at the effectiveness of common practices. In R. Menlove (Ed.), *Rural survival: Proceedings of the annual conference of the American Council on Rural Special Education (ACRES)*, Salt Lake City, Utah.

Gavin, M. K., & Reis, S. M. (2003). Helping teachers to encourage talented girls in mathematics [Electronic version]. *Gifted Child Today, 26,* 32–44.

Gay, G. (2002). Culturally responsive teaching in special education for ethnically diverse students: Setting the stage. *Qualitative studies in education,* 15(6), 613–629.

Geisthardt, C. L., Brotherson, M. J., & Cook, C. C. (2002). Friendships of children with disabilities in the home environment. *Education and Training in Mental Retardation and Developmental Disabilities, 37,* 235–252.

Germinario, V., Cervalli, J., & Ogden, E. H. (1992). *All children successful: Real answers for helping at risk elementary students.* Lancaster, PA: Technomic.

Gersten, R., Baker, S. K., & Marks, S. U. (1998). *Teaching English language learners with learning difficulties.* Eugene, OR: Eugene Research Institute.

Gersten, R., Fuchs, L. S., Williams, J. P., & Baker, S. (2001). Teaching reading comprehension strategies to students with learning disabilities: A review of research. *Review of Educational Research, 71,* 279–320.

Gersten, R., Vaughn, S., & Brengelman, S. U. (1996). Grading and academic feedback for special education students and students with learning difficulties. In T. R. Guskey (Ed.), *Communicating student learning.* Alexandria, VA: Association for Supervision and Curriculum Development.

Getch, Y. Q., & Neuharth-Pritchett, S. (1999). Children with asthma: Strategies for educators. *Teaching Exceptional Children, 31*(3), 30–36.

Getty, L. A., & Summy, S. E. (2004). The course of due process. *Teaching Exceptional Children, 36*(3), 40–43.

Ghaziuddin, M. (2000). Autism in mental retardation [Electronic version]. *Current Opinion in Psychiatry, 13,* 481–484.

Giangreco, M. F., & Doyle, M. B. (2002). Students with disabilities and paraprofessional supports: Benefits, balance, and band-aids [Electronic version]. *Focus on Exceptional Children, 34*(7), 1–12.

Giangreco, M. F., Edelman, S. W., & Broer, S. M. (2003). Schoolwide planning to improve paraeducator supports. *Exceptional Children, 70,* 63–80.

Giangreco, M. F., Edelman, S. W., Luiselli, T. E., & MacFarland, S. Z. C. (1997). Helping or hovering? Effects of instructional assistant proximity on students with disabilities. *Exceptional Children, 64,* 7–18.

Giangreco, M. F., Edelman, S. W., MacFarland, S., & Luiselli, T. E. (1997). Attitudes about educational and related service provision for students with deaf-blindness and multiple disabilities. *Exceptional Children, 63,* 329–342.

Giangreco, M. F., Prelock, P. A., Reid, R. R., Dennis, R. E., & Edelman, S. W. (2000). Role of related services personnel in inclusive schools. In R. A. Villa & J. S. Thousand (Eds.), *Restructuring for caring and effective education: Piecing the puzzle together* (pp. 360–388). Baltimore: Paul H. Brookes.

Gillberg, C. (1999). Prevalence of disorders in the autism spectrum. *Infants and Young Children, 12,* 64–89.

Gillies, R. M., & Ashman, A. F. (2000). The effects of cooperative learning on students with learning difficulties in the lower elementary school. *Journal of Special Education, 34,* 19–27.

Glassberg, L. A., Hooper, S. R., & Mattison, R. E. (1999). Prevalence of learning disabilities at enrollment in special education students with behavioral disorders. *Behavioral Disorders, 25,* 9–21.

Goetz, L., & O'Farrell, N. (1999). Connections: Facilitating social supports for students with deaf-blindness in general education classrooms. *Journal of Visual Impairment and Blindness, 92,* 704–715.

Goldstein, A. P., Sprafkin, R. P., Gershaw, N. J., & Klein, P. (1980). *Skillstreaming the adolescent.* Champaign, IL: Research Press.

Goldstein, H., Moss, J. W., & Jordan, L. J. (1965). *The efficacy of special class training on the development of mentally retarded children* (U.S. Office of Education Cooperative Research Program Project No. 619). Urbana: University of Illinois Institute for Research on Exceptional Children. (ERIC Document Reproduction Service No. ED002907)

Good, R. (2002, April). *Catching kids before they fall: What schools can do.* Presentation at the Illinois branch of the International Dyslexia Association, Lincolnwood, IL.

Good, R. H., Gruba, J., & Kaminki, R. A. (2002). Best practices in using dynamic indicators of basic early literacy skills (DIBELS) in an outcomes-driven model. In A. Thomas & J. Grimes (Eds.), *Best practices in school psychology IV* (pp. 699–720). Bethesda, MD: National Association of School Psychologists.

Good, T. L., & Brophy, I. E. (1986). School effects. In M. C. Wittrock (Ed.), *Handbook of research on teaching* (3rd ed., pp. 570–602). Upper Saddle River, NJ: Prentice Hall.

Goodman, H., Gottlieb, J., & Harrison, R. H. (1972). Social acceptance of EMR children integrated into a nongraded elementary school. *American Journal of Mental Deficiency, 76,* 412–417.

Gordon, R., Piana, L. D., & Keleher, T. (2002). *Facing the consequences: An examination of racial discrimination in U.S. public schools.* Oakland, CA: Applied Research Center. Retrieved December 4, 2004, from http://www.arc.org/erase/FTC1intro.html

Graham, S. (1999). Handwriting and spelling instruction for students with learning disabilities: A review. *Learning Disability Quarterly, 22,* 77–98.

Graham, S., & Freeman, S. (1986). Strategy training and teacher- vs. student-controlled study conditions: Effects on LD students' spelling performance. *Learning Disability Quarterly, 9,* 15–22.

Graham, S., & Harris, K. R. (1987). Improving composition skills of inefficient learners with self-instructional strategy training. *Topics in Language Disorders, 7*(4), 66–77.

Grandin, T. (2002). *Teaching tips for children and adults with autism.* Salem, OR: Center for the Study of Autism. Retrieved November 22, 2004, from http://www.autism.org/temple/tips.html

Grant, R. (1993). Strategic training for using text headings to improve students' processing of content. *Journal of Reading, 36*, 482–488.

Gravois, T. A., Knotek, S., & Babinski, L. (2002). Educating practitioners as consultants: Development and implementation of the instructional consultation team consortium. *Journal of Educational and Psychological Consultation, 13*, 113–132.

Gray, C. A., & Garand, J. D. (1993). Social stories: Improving responses of students with autism with accurate social information. *Focus on Autistic Behavior, 8*, 1–10.

Greenwood, C. R., Arreaga-Mayer, C., Utley, C. A., Gavin, K. M., & Terry, B. J. (2001). Classwide peer tutoring learning management system: Applications with elementary-level English language learners. *Remedial and Special Education, 22*, 34–47.

Gresham, F. M., Sugai, G., & Horner, R. H. (2001). Outcomes of social skills training for students with high-incidence disabilities. *Exceptional Children, 67*, 331–344.

Gringel, M., Neubert, D. A., Moon, M. S., & Graham, S. (2003). Self-determination for students with disabilities: Views of parents and teachers. *Exceptional Children, 70*, 97–111.

Grossen, B. J. (2002). The BIG accommodation model: The direct instruction model for secondary schools. *Journal of Education for Students Placed At Risk, 7*, 241–263.

Grossman, H. (1995). *Special education in a diverse society.* Boston: Allyn and Bacon.

Gubbins, E. J. (Ed.). (2002, Fall). *National Research Center on the Gifted and Talented Newsletter.* Storrs: University of Connecticut, National Research Center on the Gifted and Talented. (ERIC Document Reproduction Service No. ED477662)

Guetzloe, E. (2000). Teacher preparation in the age of violence: What do educators need to know? *Teacher Educator, 35*(3), 19–27.

Gunter, P. L., & Denny, R. K. (1998). Trends and issues in research regarding academic instruction of students with emotional and behavioral disorders. *Behavioral Disorders, 24*, 44–50.

Gunter, P. L., Miller, K. A., Venn, M. L., Thomas, K., & House, S. (2002). Self-graphing to success. *Teaching Exceptional Children, 35*(2), 30–35.

Guskey, T. R., & Bailey, J. M. (2001). *Developing grading and reporting systems for*

student learning. Thousand Oaks, CA: Corwin.

Gut, D. M. (2000). We are social beings: Learning how to learn cooperatively. *Teaching Exceptional Children, 32* (5), 46–52.

Gut, D. M., & Safran, S. P. (2002). Cooperative learning and social stories: Effective social skills strategies for reading teachers [Electronic version]. *Reading and Writing Quarterly: Overcoming Learning Difficulties, 18*, 87–91.

Haager, D., & Klinger, J. K. (2004). *Differentiating instruction in inclusive classrooms: The special educator's guide.* Boston: Allyn & Bacon.

Hail, J. M. (2000). Take a break: A token economy in the fifth grade [Electronic version]. *Social Education, 64*(4), 5–7.

Hall, J. P. (2002). Narrowing the breach: Can disability culture and full educational inclusion be reconciled? *Journal of Disability Policy Studies, 13*, 144–152.

Hall, L. J., & McGregor, J. A. (2000). A follow-up study of the peer relationships of children with disabilities in an inclusive school. *Journal of Special Education, 34*, 114–126.

Hallahan, D. P., Lloyd, J. W., Kauffman, J. M., Weiss, M. P. & Martinez, E. A. (2005). *Learning disabilities: Foundations, characteristics, and effective teaching* (3rd ed). Boston, MA: Allyn and Bacon.

Hammer, M. R. (2004). Using the self-advocacy strategy to increase student participation in IEP conferences. *Intervention in School and Clinic, 39*, 295–300.

Handler, B. R. (2003, April). *Special education practices: An evaluation of educational environmental placement trends since the regular education initiative.* Paper presentation at the Annual meeting of the American Educational Research Association, Chicago. Retrieved October 4, 2004, from http://www.eric.ed.gov/contentdelivery/servlet/ERICServlet?accno=ED480184

Hanline, M. F., & Daley, S. (2002). "Mom, will Kaelie always have possibilities?" The realities of early childhood inclusion. *Phi Delta Kappan, 84*, 73–76.

Hardman, M. L., Drew, C. J., & Egan, M. W. (2004). *Human exceptionality: School, community, and family* (8th ed). Boston, MA: Allyn and Bacon.

Harley, D. A., Nowak, T. M., Gassway, L. J., & Savage, T. A. (2002). Lesbian, gay, bisexual, and transgender college students with disabilities: A look at

multiple cultural minorities. *Psychology in the Schools, 39*, 525–538.

Harniss, M. K., Epstein, M. H., Bursuck, W. D., Nelson, J., & Jayanthi, M. (2001). Resolving homework-related communication problems: Recommendations of parents of children with and without disabilities. *Reading and Writing Quarterly, 17*, 205–225.

Harris, C. A., Miller, S. P., & Mercer, C. D. (1995). Teaching initial multiplication skills to students with disabilities in general education classrooms. *Learning Disabilities Research and Practice, 10*, 180–195.

Harry, B. (2002). Trends and issues in serving culturally diverse families of children with disabilities. *Journal of Special Education, 36*, 131–138.

Hartwig, E. P., & Ruesch, G. M. (2000). Disciplining students in special education. *Journal of Special Education, 33*, 240–247.

Hasbrouck, J. E., & Tindal, G. (1992). Curriculum-based oral reading fluency norms for students in grades 2–5. *Teaching Exceptional Children, 24*(3), 41–44.

Head, G., Robison, L. M., Sclar, D. A., Skaer, T. L., & Galin, R. S. (1999). National trends in the prevalence of attention-deficit/hyperactivity disorder and the prescribing of methylphenidate among school-age children: 1990–1995. *Clinical Pediatrics, 38*, 209–217.

Heath, D. (1993). Using portfolio assessment with secondary LED students yields a cross-cultural advantage for all. *BeOutreach, 4*(1), 27.

Heath, N. L., & Ross, S. (2000). Prevalence and expression of depressive symptomatology in students with and without learning disabilities. *Learning Disability Quarterly, 23*, 24–36.

Heller, K. W., Fredrick, L. D., Best, S., Dykes, M. K., & Cohen, E. T. (2000). Specialized health care procedures in the school: Training and service delivery. *Exceptional Children 66*, 173–186.

Helmstetter, E., Curry, C. A., Brennan, M., & Sampson-Saul, M. (1998). Comparison of general and special education classrooms of students with severe disabilities. *Education and Training in Mental Retardation and Developmental Disabilities, 33*, 216–227.

Henderson, K. (2001). Overview of ADA, IDEA, and Section 504: Update 2001. (ERIC Digest No. E606). Arlington, VA: ERIC Clearinghouse on Disabilities and Gifted Education. (ERIC Document Reproduction Service No. ED452627)

Henderson, N., & Milstein, M. M. (1996). *Resiliency in schools: Making it happen for students and educators.* Thousand Oaks, CA: Corwin.

Heron, T. E., Welsch, R. G., & Goddard, Y. L. (2003). Applications of tutoring systems in specialized subject areas. *Remedial and Special Education, 24,* 288–300.

Hetzroni, O. E., & Shrieber, B. (2004). Word processing as an assistive technology tool for enhancing academic outcomes of students with writing disabilities in the general classroom. *Journal of Learning Disabilities, 37,* 143–154.

Hickson, L., Blackman, L. S., & Reis, E. M. (1995). *Mental retardation: Foundations of educational programming.* Boston: Allyn and Bacon.

Hinchey, P. H. (2003). Corporal punishment: Legalities, realities, and implications [Electronic version]. *Clearing House, 76,* 127–131.

Hinson, J. M., & Fossey, R. (2000). Child abuse: What teachers in the 90s know, think,and do. *Journal of Education for Students Placed at Risk, 5,* 251–266.

Hinton, C. A. (2003). The perceptions of people with disabilities as to the effectiveness of the Americans with Disabilities Act. *Journal of Disability Policy Studies, 13,* 210–220.

Hitchcock, C. H., Dowrick, P. W., & Prater, M. A. (2003). Video self-modeling intervention in school-based settings. *Remedial and Special Education, 24,* 36–45.

Hitchcock, C., Meyer, A., Rose, D., & Jackson, R. (2002). Providing new access to the general curriculum: Universal Design for Learning. *Teaching Exceptional Children, 35*(2), 8–17.

Hobbs, N. (1975). *The futures of children.* San Francisco: Jossey-Bass.

Hodgkinson, H. (2000/2001). Educational demographics: What teachers should know. *Educational Leadership, 58*(4), 6–11.

Holliday, D. C. (2002). *Jigsaw IV: Using student/teacher concerns to improve Jigsaw III.* (ERIC Document Reproduction Service No. ED465687)

Hollingsworth, H. L. (2001). We need to talk: Communication strategies for effective collaboration. *Teaching Exceptional Children, 33*(5), 6–9.

Hollowood, T. M., Salisbury, C. L., Rainforth, B., & Palombaro, M. M. (1995). Use of instructional time in classrooms serving students with and without severe disabilities. *Exceptional Children, 61,* 242–253.

Homes for the Homeless. (2001). *Back to the future: The Brownstone and Futurelink after-school programs for homeless children.* New York: Author. Retrieved December 4, 2004, from http://www.homesforthehomeless.com/PDF/reports/foster.pdf?Submit1=Free+Download

Homes for the Homeless. (2004). *Reports and statistics.* Retrieved December 4, 2004, from http://www.homesforthehomeless.com/index.asp?CID=3&PID=18

Homme, L. (1970). *How to use contingency contracting in the classroom.* Champaign, IL: Research Press.

Horton, S. V. (1987). *Study guides: A paper on curriculum modification.* Unpublished manuscript, University of Washington.

Hosp, J. L., & Reschly, D. J. (2002). Predictors of restrictiveness of placement for African-American and Caucasian students. *Exceptional Children, 68,* 225–238.

Hosp, J. L., & Reschly, D. J. (2003). Referral rates for intervention or assessment: A meta-analysis of racial differences. *Journal of Special Education, 37,* 67–80.

Hosp, J. L., & Reschly, D. J. (2004). Disproportionate representation of minority students in special education: Academic, demographic, and economic indicators. *Exceptional Children, 70,* 185–200.

Howell, K. M., & Morehead, M. K. (1993). *Curriculum-based evaluation for special and remedial education* (2nd ed.). Columbus, OH: Merrill.

Howell, K. W., & Wolford, B. I. (2002). Corrections and juvenile justice: current education practices for youth with learning and other disabilities (monograph series on education, disability and juvenile justice). Washington, DC: American Institutes for Research. Retrieved October 3, 2003, from http://www.eric.ed.gov/contentdelivery/servlet/ERICServlet?accno=ED471211

Huefner, D. S. (2000). The risks and opportunities of the IEP requirements under IDEA '97. *Journal of Special Education, 33,* 195–204.

Hunt, P., Soto, G., Maier, J., & Doering, K. (2003). Collaborative teaming to support students at risk and students with severe disabilities in general education classrooms. *Exceptional Children, 69,* 315–332.

Hyman, I. A., & Snook, P. A. (2000). Dangerous schools and what you can do about them. *Phi Delta Kappan, 81,* 489–501.

Iano, R. P., Ayers, D., Heller, H. B., McGettigan, J. F., & Walker, V. S. (1974). Sociometric status of retarded children in an integrative program. *Exceptional Children, 40,* 267–271.

IDEA: Focusing on improving results for children with disabilities: Hearing before the Subcommittee on Education Reform of the Committee on Education and the Workforce, House of Representatives, 108th Cong., 1(2003).

Ira, V. B. (2000). Safe and secure on the web: Pointers on determining a web site's credibility. *Exceptional Parent, 30*(1), 148.

Irlen, H. (1991). *Reading by the colors: Overcoming dyslexia and other reading disabilities through the Irlen method.* Garden City Park, NY: Avery.

Isaacson, S. (2001). Written language. In P. J. Schloss, M. A. Smith, & C. N. Schloss (Eds.), *Instructional methods for secondary students with learning and behavior problems* (3rd ed., pp. 222–245). Boston: Allyn and Bacon.

Ishii-Jordan, S. R. (2000). Behavioral interventions used with diverse students. *Behavioral Disorders, 25,* 299–309.

Ives, B., & Hoy, C. (2003). Graphic organizers applied to higher-level secondary mathematics. *Learning Disabilities: Research and Practice, 18,* 36–51.

Jackson, C. W., & Larkin, M. J. (2002). RUBRIC: Teaching students to use grading rubrics. *Teaching Exceptional Children, 35*(1), 40–45.

Janiga, S. J., & Costenbader, V. (2002). The transition from high school to postsecondary education for students with learning disabilities: A survey of college service coordinators. *Journal of Learning Disabilities, 35,* 462–468.

Janisch, C., & Johnson, M. (2003). Effective literacy practices and challenging curriculum for at-risk learners: Great expectations [Electronic version]. *Journal of Education for Students Placed at Risk, 8,* 295–308.

Jarolimek, J., Foster, C. D., & Kellough, R. D. (2004). *Teaching and learning in the elementary school* (8th ed.) Upper Saddle River, NJ: Prentice Hall.

Jenkins, J. R., Antil, L. R., Wayne, S. K., & Vadasy, P. F. (2003). How cooperative learning works for special education and remedial students. *Exceptional Children, 69,* 279–292.

Jensen, R. J. (2004). Discipline preferences and styles among Latino families: Implications for special educators. *Multiple Voices, 7*(1), 60–73.

Jenson, W. R., Sheridan, S. M., Olympia, D., & Andrews, D. (1994). Homework and students with learning disabilities and behavior disorders: A practical, parent-based approach. *Journal of Learning Disabilities, 27,* 538–549.

Johnson, D. W., Johnson, R. T., & Maruyama, G. (1983). Interdependence and interpersonal attraction among heterogeneous and homogeneous individuals: A theoretical formulation and a meta-analysis of the research. *Review of Educational Research, 53,* 5–54.

Johnson, D. W., Johnson, R. T., Holubec, E. J., & Roy, P. (1984). *Circles of learning.* Alexandria, VA: Association for Supervision and Curriculum Development.

Johnson, D., Johnson, R., & Holubec, E. (1998). *Cooperation in the classroom.* Boston: Allyn and Bacon. Retrieved February 11, 2005, from http://www.intime.uni.edu/coop_learning/ch5/teaching.htm

Johnson, E. S. (2000). The effects of accommodations on performance assessments. *Remedial and Special Education, 21,* 261–267.

Johnson, E., & Arnold, N. (2004). Validating an alternate assessment. *Remedial and Special Education, 25,* 266–275.

Johnson, G. O., & Kirk, S. A. (1950). Are mentally handicapped children segregated in the regular grades? *Exceptional Children, 17,* 65–68, 87–88.

Johnson, J., & Duffett, A. (2002). *When it's your own child: A report on special education from the families who use it.* New York: Public Agenda Foundation. (ERIC Document Reproduction Service No. ED471033)

Johnson, L. R., & Johnson, C. E. (1999). Teaching students to regulate their own behavior. *Teaching Exceptional Children, 31*(4), 6–10.

Johnston, S. S., & O'Neill, R. E. (2001). Searching for effectiveness and efficiency in conducting functional assessments: A review and proposed process for teachers and other practitioners [Electronic version]. *Focus on Autism and Other Developmental Disabilities, 16,* 205–214.

Jones, V. F., & Jones, L. S. (1990). *Comprehensive classroom management.* Boston: Allyn and Bacon.

Jones, V. F., & Jones, L. S. (2001). *Comprehensive classroom management: Creating communities of support and solving problems* (6th ed.). Boston: Allyn and Bacon.

Joseph, J. (2000). Not in their genes: A critical view of the genetics of attention-deficit hyperactivity disorder. *Developmental Review, 20,* 539–567.

Juel, C. (1988). Learning to read and write: A longitudinal study of 54 children from first through fourth grades. *Journal of Educational Psychology, 80*(4), 437–447.

Kagan, S. (1990). A structural approach to cooperative learning. *Educational Leadership, 47*(4), 12–15.

Kalyanpur, M., & Harry, B. (1999). Legal and epistemological underpinnings of the construction of disability. In *Culture in special education: Building reciprocal family-professional relationships* (pp. 15–46). Baltimore: Paul H. Brookes.

Kalyanpur, M., Harry, B., & Skrtic, T. (2000). Equity and advocacy expectations of culturally diverse families' participation in special education [Electronic version]. *International Journal of Disability, Development and Education, 47,* 119–136.

Kame'enui, E. J., & Darch, C. (1995). *Instructional classroom management: A proactive approach to behavior management.* White Plains, NY: Longmont.

Kame'enui, E. J., Carnine, D. W., Dixon, R. C., Simmons, D. C., & Coyne, M. D. (2002). *Effective teaching strategies that accommodate diverse learners* (2nd ed.). Upper Saddle River, NJ: Merrill/Prentice Hall.

Kaminski, R. A., & Good, R. H. (1996). Toward a technology for assessing basic early literacy skills. *School Psychology Review, 25,* 215–227.

Kampfer, S. H., Horvath, L. S., Kleinert, H. L., & Kearns, J. F. (2001). Teachers' perceptions of one state's alternative assessment implications for practice and preparation. *Exceptional Children, 67,* 361–374.

Kamps, M. D., Tankersley, M., & Ellis, C. (2000). Social skills interventions for young at-risk students: A two-year follow-up study. *Behavioral Disorders, 25,* 310–324.

Kampwirth, T. J. (2002). *Collaborative consultation in the schools: Effective practices for students with learning and behavior problems* (2nd edition). Upper Saddle River, NJ: Merrill/Prentice Hall.

Karger, J. (2004). *Access to the general curriculum for students with disabilities: The role of the IEP.* Washington, DC: National Center on Accessing the General Curriculum. Retrieved August 15, 2004, from http://www.cast.org/ncac/index.cfm?i=5312

Kauffman, J. M. (2005). *Cases in emotional and behavioral disorders of children and youth.* Upper Saddle River, NJ: Merrill/Prentice Hall.

Kauffman, J. M. (2005). *Characteristics of emotional and behavioral disorders of children and youth* (8th ed.) Upper Saddle River, NJ: Merrill/Prentice Hall.

Kauffman, J. M., Mostert, M. P., Trent, S. C., & Hallahan, D. P. (2002). *Managing classroom behavior: A reflective, case-based approach* (3rd ed.). Boston: Allyn and Bacon.

Kavale, K. (2002). Mainstreaming to full inclusion: From orthogenesis to pathogenesis of an idea [Electronic version]. *International Journal of Disability, Development, and Education, 49,* 201–214.

Kavale, K. A., & Forness, S. R. (1987). Substance over style: Assessing the efficacy of modality testing and teaching. *Exceptional Children, 54,* 228–239.

Kavale, K. A., & Forness, S. R. (2000). History, rhetoric, and reality: Analysis of inclusion debate. *Remedial and Special education, 21,* 279–296.

Kazdin, A. E. (1977). *The token economy: A review and evaluation.* New York: Plenum.

Kearns, J., Kleinert, H., Clayton, J., Burdge, M., & Williams, R. (1998). Inclusive educational assessments at the elementary school level: Perspectives from Kentucky. *Teaching Exceptional Children, 31*(2), 16–23.

Keefe, E. B., Moore, V., & Duff, F. (2004). The four "knows" of collaborative teaching. *Teaching Exceptional Children, 36*(5), 36–43.

Kehle, T. J., Bray, M. A., & Theodore, L. A. (2000). A multi-component intervention designed to reduce disruptive classroom behavior [Electronic version]. *Psychology in the Schools, 37,* 475–481.

Kennedy, K. Y., Higgins, K., & Pierce, T. (2002). Collaborative partnerships among teachers of students who are gifted and have learning disabilities. *Intervention in School and Clinic, 38,* 36–39.

Kern, L., Delaney, B., Clarke, S., Dunlap, G., & Childs, K. (2001). Improving the classroom behavior of students with emotional and behavioral disorders using individualized curricular modifications. *Journal of Emotional and Behavioral Disorders, 9,* 239–247.

Kerr, M. M., & Nelson, C. M.(1998). *Strategies for managing behavior problems in the classroom* (3rd ed.). Columbus, Ohio: Merrill/Prentice Hall.

Kerschner, J. R. (1990). Self-concept and IQ as predictors of remedial success in children with learning disabilities. *Journal of Learning Disabilities, 23,* 368–374.

Keyser-Marcus, L, Briel, L., Sherron-Targett, P., Yasuda, S., Johnson, S., & Wehman, P. (2002). Enhancing the schooling of students with traumatic brain injury. *Teaching Exceptional Children, 34*(4), 62–67.

Khisty, L. L. (2002). Mathematics learning and the Latino student: Suggestions from research for classroom practice. *Teaching Children Mathematics, 9*(1), 32–36.

Kids on the Block. (2004). *History of Kids on the Block puppets.* Retrieved February 9, 2005, from http://www.kotb.com

Kilgore, K., Griffin, C. C., Sindelar, P. T., & Webb, R. B. (2002). Restructuring for inclusion: Changing teaching practices (Part II) [Electronic version]. *Middle School Journal, 33*(3), 7–13.

Kinch, C., Lewis-Palmer, T., Hagan-Burke, S., & Sugai, G. (2001). A comparison of teacher and student functional behavior assessment interview information from low-risk and high-risk classrooms [Electronic version]. *Education and Treatment of Children, 24,* 480–494.

King, M. B., & Youngs, P. (2003). *Classroom teachers' views on inclusion (Riser Brief No. 7).* Madison: University of Wisconsin-Madison, Research Institute on Secondary Education Reform for Youth with Disabilities (RISER). (ERIC Document Reproduction Service No. ED477878)

King-Sears, M. E. (2001). Three steps for gaining access to the general education curriculum for learners with disabilities. *Intervention in School and Clinic, 37,* 67–76.

King-Sears, M. E., Burgess, M., & Lawson, T. L. (1999). Applying curriculum-based assessment in inclusive settings. *Teaching Exceptional Children, 32*(1), 30–38.

Kleinert, H., Green, P., Hurte, M., Clayton, J., & Oetinger, C. (2002). Creating and using meaningful alternates. *Teaching Exceptional Children, 34*(4), 40–48.

Kleinert, H., Kearns, J., & Kennedy, S. (1997). Accountability for all students: Kentucky's alternate portfolio system for students with moderate and severe cognitive disabilities. *Journal of the Association for Persons with Severe Handicaps* (JASH), *22,* 88–101.

Kleinert, H., McGregor, V., Durbin, M., Blandford, T., Jones, K., Owens, J., Harrison, B., & Miracle, S. (2004). Service-learning opportunities that include students with moderate and severe disabilities. *Teaching Exceptional Children, 37*(2), 28–35.

Klinger, J. K., & Vaughn, S. (2002). The changing roles and responsibilities of an LD specialist [Electronic version]. *Learning Disability Quarterly, 25,* 19–31.

Kluwin, T. N. (1996). Getting hearing and deaf students to write to each other through dialogue journals. *Teaching Exceptional Children, 28*(2), 50–53.

Knight, Jim. (2002). Crossing boundaries: what constructivists can teach intensive-explicit instructors and vice versa. *Focus on Exceptional Children, 35*(4), 1–15.

Knotek, S. (2003). Bias in problem solving and the social process of student study teams: A qualitative investigation of two SSTs. *Journal of Special Education, 37,* 2–14.

Kode, K. (2002). *Elizabeth Farrell and the history of special education.* Arlington, VA: Council for Exceptional Children.

Kohn, A. (2003). Almost there, but not quite. *Educational Leadership, 60*(6), 26–29.

Kohn, A. (2004). Challenging students . . . and how to have more of them. *Phi Delta Kappan, 86,* 184–193.

Kolb, S. M., & Hanley-Maxwell, C. (2003). Critical social skills for adolescents with high incidence disabilities: Parental perspectives. *Exceptional Children, 69,* 163–180.

Kollins, S. H., Barkley, R. A., & DuPaul, G. J. (2001). Use and management of medications for children diagnosed with attention deficit disorder. *Focus on Exceptional Children, 33*(5), 1–24.

Kovaleski, J. F., Gickling, E. E., Morrow, H., & Swank, P. R. (1999). High versus low implementation of instructional support teams: A case for maintaining program fidelity. *Remedial and Special Education, 20,* 170–183.

Krajewski, J. J., & Hyde, M. S. (2000). Comparison of teen attitudes toward individuals with mental retardation between 1987 and 1998: Has inclusion made a difference? *Education and Training in Mental Retardation and Developmental Disabilities, 35,* 284–293.

Kroesbergen, E. H., Van Luit, J. E. H., & Maas, C. J. M. (2004). Effectiveness of explicit and constructivist mathematics instruction for low-achieving students in the Netherlands. *The elementary School Journal, 104*(3), 233–251.

Ladner, M., & Hammons, C. (2001). Special but unequal: Race and special education. In C. Finn, A. J. Rotherham, & C. R. Hokanson (Eds.), *Rethinking special education for a new century* (pp. 85–110). Thomas B. Fordham Foundation; Washington, DC: Progressive Policy Institute.

Ladson-Billings, G. J. (1999). Preparing teachers for diverse student populations: A critical race theory perspective. In A. Iran-Nejad & P. D. Pearson (Eds.), *Review of research in education* (Vol. 24, pp. 211–247). Washington, DC: American Educational Research Association.

Ladson-Billings, G. (1994). *The dreamkeepers: Successful teachers for African American children.* San Francisco: Jossey-Bass.

Lane, K. L., Givner, C. C., & Pierson, M. R. (2004). Teacher expectations of student behavior: Social skills necessary in elementary school classrooms. *Journal of Special Education, 38,* 104–110.

Lane, K. L., Mahdavi, J. N., & Borthwick-Duffy, S. (2003). Teacher perceptions of the prereferral intervention process: A call for assistance with school-based interventions. *Preventing School Failure, 47,* 148–155.

Lane, K. L., Pierson, M. R., & Givner, C. C. (2004). Secondary teachers' views on social competence: Skills essential for success. *Journal of Special Education, 38,* 174–187.

Lane, S., Parke, C. S., & Stone, C. A. (2002). The impact of a state performance-based assessment and accountability program on mathematics instruction and student learning: Evidence from survey data and school performance. *Educational Assessment, 8,* 279–316.

Langer, J. (1984). Examining background knowledge and text comprehension. *Reading Research Quarterly, 19,* 468–481.

Larkin, M. J. (2001). Providing support for student independence through scaffolded instruction. *Teaching Exceptional Children, 34*(1), 30–34.

Lassman, K. A., Jolivette, K., & Wehby, J. H. (1999). "My teacher said I did good work today!" Using collaborative behavioral contracting. *Teaching Exceptional Children, 31*(4), 12–18.

Lavoie, R. (1991). *How difficult can this be? Understanding learning disabilities* [videotape]. Portland, OR: Educational Productions.

Lavoie, R. D. (1989). *Mainstreaming: A collection of field-tested strategies to help make the mainstreaming classroom more successful for learning disabled children, their classmates . . . and their teachers.* Norwalk: Connecticut Association for Children with Learning Disabilities.

Lawton, M. (1995, Nov. 8). Students post dismal results on history test. *Education Week, 1,* 12.

Lee, S. W., & Jamison, T. R. (2003). Including the FBA process in student assistance teams: An exploratory study of team communications and intervention selection. *Journal of Educational and Psychological Consultation, 14,* 209–239.

Leedy, A., Bates, P., & Safran, S. P. (2004). Bridging the research-to-practice gap: Improving hallway behavior using positive behavior supports. *Behavioral Disorders, 29,* 130–139.

LeFever, G. B., Villers, M. S., Morrow, A. L., & Vaughn, E. S. (2002). Parental perceptions of adverse educational outcomes among children diagnosed and treated for ADHD: A call for improved school/provider collaboration. *Psychology in the Schools, 39,* 63–71.

Leffert, J. S., Siperstein, G. N., & Millikan, E. (2000). Understanding social adaptation in children with mental retardation: A social-cognitive perspective. *Exceptional Children, 66,* 530–545.

Leinhardt, G., & Zigmond, N. (1988). The effects of self-questioning and story structure training on the reading comprehension of poor readers. *Learning Disabilities Research, 4*(1), 41–51.

Lemanek, K. L. (2004). Adherence. In R. T. Brown (Ed.)., *Handbook of pediatric psychology in school settings* (pp. 129–148). Mahwah, NJ: Erlbaum.

Lenz, B. K. (1983). Using the advance organizer. *Pointer, 27,* 11–13.

Lenz, B. K., Ellis, E. S., & Scanlon, D. (1996). *Teaching learning strategies to adolescents and adults with learning disabilities.* Austin, TX: PRO-ED.

Lerner, J. (2006). *Learning disabilities: Theories, diagnosis, and teaching strategies* (10th ed.). Boston: Houghton Mifflin.

Lerner, J. (2003). *Learning disabilities: Theories, diagnosis, and teaching strategies* (9th ed). Boston, MA: Houghton Mifflin

Lesesne, C., Abramowitz, A., Perou, R., & Brann, E. (2000, March 15). *Attention deficit/hyperactivity disorder: A public health research agenda.* Retrieved April 22, 2004, from the National Center on Birth Defects and Developmental Disabilities, Centers for Disease Control and Prevention, website, http://www.cdc.gov/ncbddd/adhd/dadphra.htm

Lessen, E., Sommers, M., & Bursuck, W. (1987). *Curriculum-based assessment and instructional design.* DeKalb, IL: DeKalb County Special Education Association.

Licht, B. G., Kistner, J. A., Ozkaragoz, T., Shapiro, S., & Clausen, L. (1985). Causal attributions of learning disabled children: Individual differences and their implications for persistence. *Journal of Educational Psychology, 77,* 208–216.

Lignugaris-Kraft, B., Marchand-Martella, N., & Martella, R. C. (2001). Strategies for writing better goals and short-term objectives or benchmarks. *Teaching Exceptional Children, 34*(1), 52–58.

Lilly, M. S. (1971). A training model for special education. *Exceptional Children, 37,* 740–749.

Lindamood, P., & Lindamood, P. (1998). *LiPS: The Lindamood phoneme sequencing program for reading, spelling, and speech: LiPS teacher's manual for the classroom and clinic* (3rd ed.). Austin, TX: PRO-ED.

Lindquist, T. (1995). *Seeing the whole through social studies.* Portsmouth, NH: Heinemann.

Little, J. W. (1993). Teachers' professional development in a climate of educational reform. *Educational Evaluation and Policy Analysis, 15,* 129–151.

Lonergan, G. J. (2000). Some facts and figures about child abuse. *Child Abuse Referral and Education Network.* Bethesda, MD: Uniformed Services University of the Health Sciences. Retrieved September 14, 2000, from http://rad.usuhs.mil/rad/home/peds/pedindex.html

Long, N. J., & Newman, R. G. (1971). Managing surface behavior of children in school. In N. J. Long, W. C. Morse, & R. G. Newman (Eds.), *Conflict in the classroom: The education of children with problems* (2nd ed., pp. 442–452). Belmont, CA: Wadsworth.

Lorenzi, D. G., Horvat, M., & Pellegrini, A. D. (2000). Physical activity of children with and without mental retardation in inclusive recess settings. *Education and Training in Mental Retardation and Developmental Disabilities, 35,* 160–167.

Lortie, D. C. (1975). *Schoolteacher: A sociological study.* Chicago: University of Chicago Press.

Lott, B. (2003). Recognizing and welcoming the standpoint of low-income parents in the public schools. *Journal of Educational and Psychological Consultation, 14,* 91–104.

Lovitt, T. C., Plavins, M., & Cushing, S. (1999). What do pupils with disabilities have to say about their experience in high school? *Remedial and Special Education, 20,* 67–76, 83.

Lovitt, T. C., Rudsit, J., Jenkins, J., Pious, C., & Benedetti, D. (1985). Two methods of adapting science materials for learning disabled and regular seventh graders. *Learning Disability Quarterly, 8,* 275–285.

Lowell-York, J., Doyle, M. E., & Kronberg, R. (1995). *Module 3. Curriculum as everything students learn in school: Individualizing learning opportunities.* Baltimore: Paul H. Brookes.

LRP Publications (1997). *Grading individuals with disabilities education law report, 25(4),* 381–391.

Luckner, J. L., & Muir, S. (2001). Successful students who are deaf in general education settings. *American Annals of the Deaf, 146,* 450–461.

Luster, J. N., & Durrett, J. (2003, November). *Does educational placement matter in the performance of students with disabilities?* Paper presented at the annual meeting of the Mid-South Educational Research Association, Biloxi, MS. (ERIC Document Reproduction Service No. ED482518)

Lyon, G. R. (1998). *Overview of reading and literacy initiatives.* Statement presented to National Institute of Child Health and Human Development. Retrieved October 7, 1999, from http://www.nichd.nih.gov/publications/pubs/jeffords.htm

Lytle, R. K., & Bordin, J. (2001). Enhancing the IEP team: Strategies for parents and professionals. *Teaching Exceptional Children, 33*(5), 40–45.

Maag, J. (2004). *Behavior management: From theoretical implications to practical applications* (2nd ed.). Belmont, CA: Wadsworth.

Maag, J. W. (2001). Management of surface behavior: A new look at an old approach. *Counseling and Human Development, 33*(9), 1–10.

MacArthur, C. (1998). From illegible to understandable: How word recognition and speech synthesis can help. *Teaching Exceptional Children, 30*(6), 66–71.

MacArthur, C. A., & Stoddard, B. (1990, April). *Teaching learning disabled students to revise: A peer editor strategy.* Paper presented at the Annual Meeting of the American Education Research Association, Boston.

Madden, J. A. (2000). Managing asthma at school. *Educational Leadership, 57*(6), 50–52.

Magiati, I., & Howland, P. (2003). A pilot evaluation study of the picture exchange communication system [Electronic version]. *Autism: The International Journal of Research and Practice, 7,* 297–320.

Maheady, L., Harper, G. F., & Mallette, B. (2001). Peer-mediated instruction and interventions and students with mild disabilities. *Remedial and Special Education, 22,* 4–14.

Malmgren, K. W. (1998). Cooperative learning as an academic intervention for students with mild disabilities. *Focus on Exceptional Children, 31*(4), 1–6.

Mandlebaum, L. H., & Wilson, R. (1989). Teaching listening skills. *LD Forum, 15*(1), 7–9.

Marchand-Martella, N. E., Slocum, T. A., & Martella, R. C. (2004). *Introduction to direct instruction.* Boston, MA: Allyn and Bacon.

Marchant, G. J. (2002). Professional development schools and indicators of student achievement [Electronic version]. *Teacher Educator, 38,* 112–125.

Marks, S. U., Schrader, C., & Levine, M. (1999). Paraeducator experiences in inclusive settings: Helping, hovering, or holding their own? *Exceptional Children, 65,* 315–328.

Maroney, S. A., Finson, K. D., Beaver, J. B., & Jensen, M. M. (2003). Preparing for successful inquiry in inclusive science classrooms. *Teaching Exceptional Children, 36*(1), 18–25.

Marschart, M. (1997). *Raising and educating a deaf child.* New York: Oxford University Press.

Marsh, L. G., & Cooke, N. L. (1996). The effects of using manipulatives in teaching math problem solving to students with learning disabilities. *Learning Disabilities Research and Practice, 11,* 58–65.

Marston, D. B. (1989). A curriculum-based measurement approach to asesssing academic performance: What it is and why do it. In M. R. Shinn (Ed.), *Curriculum-based measurement: Assessing special children* (pp. 18–78). New York: Guilford Press.

Marston, D. B. (1996). A comparison of inclusion only, pull-out only, and combined service models for students with mild disabilities. *Journal of Special Education, 30*(2), 121–132.

Marston, D. B., Tindal, G., & Deno, S. (1984). Eligibility for learning disability services: A direct and repeated measurement approach. *Exceptional Children, 50,* 554–556.

Marston, D., Muyskens, P., Lau, M., & Canter, A. (2003). Problem-solving model for decision making with high-incidence disabilities: The Minneapolis experience. *Learning Disabilities Research and Practice, 18*(3), 187–200.

Martin, B. N., Johnson, J. A., Ireland, H., & Claxton, K. (2003). Perceptions of teachers on inclusion in four rural Midwest school districts [Electronic version]. *Rural Educator, 24*(3), 3–10.

Martin, J. E., Marshall, L. H., & Sale, P. (2004). A 3-year study of middle, junior high, and high school IEP meetings. *Exceptional Children, 70,* 285–298.

Marzola, E. S. (1987). Using manipulatives in math instruction. *Reading, Writing, and Learning Disabilities, 3,* 9–20.

Mason, C. Y., McGahee-Kovac, M., & Johnson, L. (2004). How to help students lead their IEP meetings. *Teaching Exceptional Children, 36*(3), 18–25.

Mason, C., Field, S., & Sawilowsky, S. (2004). Implementation of self-determination activities and student participation in IEPs. *Exceptional Children, 70,* 441–452.

Mason, S., O'Sullivan, A., O'Sullivan, T., & Cullen, M. A. (2000). Parents' expectations and experiences of their children's education. In A. Closs (Ed.), *The education of children with medical conditions* (pp. 51–64). London: Fulton.

Mastropieri, M. A. (1988). Using the keyword method. *Teaching Exceptional Children, 20*(4), 4–8.

Mastropieri, M. A., Scruggs, T. E., Spencer, V., & Fontana, J. (2003). Promoting success in high school world history: Peer tutoring versus guided notes. *Learning Disabilities: Research and Practice, 18,* 52–65.

Mathes, P. G., & Babyak, A. E. (2001). The effects of peer-assisted literacy strategies for first-grade readers with and

without additional mini-skills lessons [Electronic version]. *Learning Disabilities: Research and Practice, 16,* 28–44.

McCardle, P., & Chhabra, V. (Eds.). (2004). *The voice of evidence in reading research.* Baltimore: Brookes.

McCleary, L. (2002). Parenting adolescents with attention deficit hyperactivity disorder: Analysis of the literature for social work practice [Electronic version]. *Health and Social Work, 27,* 285–292.

McDonnell, J., Thorson, N., Disher, S., Mathot-Buckner, C., Mendel, J., & Ray, L. (2003). The achievement of students with developmental disabilities and their peers without disabilities in inclusive settings: An exploratory study [Electronic version]. *Education and Treatment of Children, 26,* 224–236.

McDougall, D., & Brady, M. P. (1998). Initiating and fading self-management interventions to increase math fluency in general education classes. *Exceptional Children, 64,* 151–166.

McGrath, M. Z., Johns, B. H., & Mathur, S. R. (2004). Is history repeating itself? Services for children with disabilities endangered. *Teaching Exceptional Children, 37*(1), 70–71.

McLaughlin, M. J. (2002). Examining special and general education collaborative practices in exemplary schools. *Journal of Educational and Psychological Consultation, 13,* 279–284.

McLeskey, J., Henry, D., & Axelrod, M. I. (1999). Inclusion of students with learning disabilities: An examination of data from reports to Congress. *Exceptional Children, 66,* 55–66.

McLeskey, J., Waldron, N. L., So, T. H., Swanson, K., & Loveland, T. (2001). Perspectives of teachers toward inclusive school programs. *Teacher Education and Special Education, 24,* 108–115.

McMaster, K. N., & Fuchs, D. (2002). Effects of cooperative learning on the academic achievement of students with learning disabilities: An update of Tateyama-Sniezek's review. *Learning Disabilities: Research and Practice, 17,* 107–117.

Meichenbaum, D. (1977). *Cognitive behavior modification: An integrative approach.* New York: Plenum.

Mercer, C. D., & Mercer, A. R. (2001). *Teaching students with learning problems* (6th ed.). Upper Saddle River, OH: Merrill/Prentice Hall.

Mercer, C. D., & Pullen, P. C. (2005). *Students with learning disabilities* (6th ed.). Upper Saddle River, NJ: Pearson.

Miles-Bonart, S. (2002, March). A look at variables affecting parent satisfaction with IEP meetings. In *No Child Left Behind: The vital role of rural schools. Annual national conference proceedings of the American Council on Rural Special Education (ACRES) (22nd, Reno, Nevada, March 7–9, 2002)* (pp. 180–187). Logan, UT: ACRES. (ERIC Document Reproduction Service No. ED463119)

Miller, J., Bieker, R., & Copenhaver, J. (2002). *Section 504/ADA: Guidelines for educators in Kansas.* Topeka: Kansas Department of Education. (ERIC Document Reproduction Service No. ED 481290)

Miller, M. C., Cooke, N. L., Test, D. W., & White, R. (2003). Effects of friendship circles on the social interactions of elementary age students with mild disabilities [Electronic version]. *Journal of Behavioral Education, 12,* 167–184.

Miller, R. V. (1956). Social status of socioempathic differences. *Exceptional Children, 23,* 114–119.

Miller, S. P. (1996), Perspectives on mathematics instruction. In D. D. Deshler, E. S. Ellis, & B. K. Lenz (Eds.), *Teaching adolescents with learning disabilities: Strategies and methods* (2nd ed., pp. 313–367). Denver, CO: Love Publishing Company.

Mills, G. E., & Duff-Mallams, K. (2000). Special education mediation. *Teaching Exceptional Children, 32*(4), 72–78.

Minskoff, E., & Allsopp, D. (2003). *Academic success strategies for adolescents with learning disabilities and ADHD.* Baltimore: Paul H. Brookes.

Miranda, A., & Guerrero, M. (1986). The funny farola. In *Adventures* (pp. 42–53). Boston: Houghton Mifflin.

Mitchell, A. (1997). Teacher identity: A key to increased collaboration. *Action in Teacher Education, 19*(3), 1–14.

Mitchell, A., & Arnold, M. (2004). Behavior management skills as predictors of retention among south Texas special educators [Electronic version]. *Journal of Instructional Psychology, 31,* 214–219.

Mock, D. R., & Kauffman, J. M. (2002). Preparing teachers for full inclusion: Is it possible? [Electronic version]. *Teacher Educator, 37,* 202–215.

Montgomery, K. (2001). *Authentic assessment: A guide for elementary teachers.* New York: Longman.

Moody, J. D., & Gifford, V. D. (1990). *The effect of grouping by formal reasoning ability, formal reasoning ability levels, group size, and gender on achievement in laboratory chemistry.* (ERIC Document Reproduction Service No. ED326443)

Moreno, S. J. (2000). *Tips for teaching high-functioning people with autism.* Crown Point, IN: MAAP Services for Autism and Asperger Spectrum. Retrieved November 16, 2004, from http://maapservices.org/MAP_Sub_Find_It_-_Tips_For_Teaching.htm

Morocco, C. C., & Aguilar, C. M. (2002). Co-teaching for content understanding: A schoolwide model. *Journal of Educational and Psychological Consultation, 13,* 315–348.

Morse, W. C. (1987). Introduction to the special issue. *Teaching Exceptional Children, 19*(4), 4–6.

Mortweet, S. L., Utley, C. A., Walker, D., Dawson, H. L., Delquadri, J. C., Reddy, S. S., Greenwood, C. R., Hamilton, S., & Ledford, D. (1999). Classwide peer tutoring: Teaching students with mild mental retardation in inclusive classrooms. *Exceptional Children, 65,* 524–536.

Mosteller, F., Light, R., & Sachs, J. (1996). Sustained inquiry in education: Lessons from skill grouping and class size. *Harvard Educational Review, 66,* 797–828.

Mostert, M. P. (2001). Facilitated communication since 1995: A review of published studies [Electronic version]. *Journal of Autism and Developmental Disorders, 31,* 287–313.

MTA Cooperative Group. (2004). National Institute of Mental Health multimodal treatment study of ADHD follow-up: 24-month outcomes of treatment strategies for attention-deficit/hyperactivity disorder [Electronic version]. *Pediatrics, 113,* 754–761.

Munk, D. D. (2003). *Solving the grading puzzle for students with disabilities.* Whitefish Bay, WI: Knowledge by Design.

Munk, D. D., & Bursuck, W. D. (2001). Personalized grading plans: A systematic approach to making the grades of included students more accurate and meaningful. In L. Denti & P. Tefft-Cousin (Eds.), *Looking at learning disabilities in new ways: Connections to classroom practice* (pp. 111–127). Denver, CO: Love.

Munk, D. D., & Bursuck, W. D. (2003). Grading students with disabilities. *Educational Leadership, 61*(2), 38–43.

Munk, D. D., & Bursuck, W. D. (2005). *Personalized grading plans for students with disabilities. Manuscript in preparation.*

Munk, D. D., Bursuck, W. D., Epstein, M. H., Jayanthi, M., Nelson, J., & Polloway, E. A. (2001). Homework communication problems: Perspectives of special and general education parents. *Reading and Writing Quarterly, 17*(3), 189–203.

Munoz, M. A., Dossett, D., & Judy-Gullans, K. (2003). *Educating students placed at risk: Evaluating the impact of Success for All in urban settings.* (ERIC Document Reproduction Service No. ED480178)

Murawski, W. W., & Dieker, L. A. (2004). Tips and strategies for co-teaching at the secondary level. *Teaching Exceptional Children, 36*(5), 52–59.

Muyskens, P., & Ysseldyke, J. E. (1998). Student academic responding time as a function of classroom ecology and time of day. *Journal of Special Education, 31,* 411–424.

Myles, B. S., & Adreon, D. (2001). *Asperger syndrome and adolescence: Practical solutions for school success.* Shawnee Mission, KS: Autism Asperger Publishing.

Myles, B. S., & Southwick, J. (1999). *Asperger syndrome and difficult moments: Practical solutions for tantrums, rage, and meltdowns.* Lawrence, KS: Autism Asperger Publishing.

Nansel, T., Overpeck, M., Pilla, R., Ruan, W., Simons-Morton, B., & Scheidt, P. (2001). Bullying behaviors among US youth: Prevalence and association with psychosocial adjustment. *Journal of the American Medical Association, 285,* 2094–2100.

Nash, J. M., & Bonesteel, A. (2002, May 6). The geek syndrome. *Time 159* (18), 50–51.

National Alliance of Black School Educators. (2002). *Addressing over-representation of African American students in special education: The prereferral intervention process.* Arlington, VA: Council for Exceptional Education.

National Association of School Psychologists. (2002). *Position statement on inclusive programs for students with disabilities.* Retrieved September 5, 2004, from http://www.nasponline.org/information/pospaper_ipsd.html

National Cancer Institute. (2002). *National Cancer Institute research on childhood cancers.* Washington, DC: Author. Retrieved November 8, 2004, from http://cis.nci.nih.gov/fact/6_40.htm

National Center for Children in Poverty. (2004). *Low-income children in the United States.* New York: Columbia University. Retrieved December 4, 2004, from http://www.nccp.org/pub_cpf04.html

National Center for Education Statistics. (2002). *The condition of education.* Washington, DC: U.S. Department of Education.

National Center for Education Statistics. (2004). *Crime and safety in America's public schools: Selected findings from the school survey on crime and safety.* The school survey on crime and safety website: Retrieved December 30, 2004, from http://nces.ed.gov/surveys/ssocs

National Center for Education Statistics. (2004). *Issue brief: Educational attainment of high school dropouts 8 years later.* Washington, DC: U.S. Department of Education. Retrieved December 4, 2004, from http://nces.ed.gov/pubs2005/2005026.pdf

National Center on Birth Defects and Developmental Disabilities, Centers for Disease Control. (2003). *What is attention-deficit/hyperactivity disorder (ADHD)?* Retrieved June 12, 2003, from http://www.cdc.gov/ncbddd/adhd/what.htm

National Center on Secondary Education and Transition. (2002). *Age of majority: Preparing your child for making good choices.* Minneapolis, MN: Author. (ERIC Document Reproduction Service No. ED467248)

National Clearinghouse for Professions in Special Education. (2003). *School counselor: Making a difference in the lives of students with special needs* [brochure]. Arlington, VA: Author. Retrieved April 19, 2003, from http://www.special-ed-careers.org/pdf/schcoun.pdf.

National Clearinghouse for Professions in Special Education. (2003). *Interpreter for students who are deaf or hard of hearing.* Arlington, VA: Author. Retrieved April 19, 2003, from http://www.specialedcareers.org/career_choices/profiles/professions/int_deaf.html

National Council of Teachers of Mathematics (2000). *Principles and standards for school mathematics.* Reston, VA: Author.

National Dissemination Center for Children with Disabilities. (2004a, January). *Epilepsy* (Fact Sheet No. 6). Washington, DC: Author. Retrieved November 20, 2004, from http://www.nichcy.org/pubs/factshe/fs6txt.htm

National Dissemination Center for Children with Disabilities. (2004b, January). *Traumatic brain injury* (Fact Sheet No. 18). Washington, DC: Author. Retrieved November 20, 2004, from http://www.nichcy.org/pubs/factshe/fs18txt.htm

National Institute of Mental Health. (2003). *Attention deficit hyperactivity disorder.* Bethesda, MD: Author. Retrieved December 3, 2004, from http://www.nimh.nih.gov/publicat/adhd.cfm

National Institute of Neurological Disorders and Stroke. (2001). *NINDS muscular dystrophy (MD) information page.* Bethesda, MD: Author. Retrieved March 9, 2004, from http://www.ninds.nih.gov/health_and_medical/disorders/md.htm#What_is_Muscular_Dystrophy__(MD)

National Institute on Drug Abuse. (2004). *NIDA infofacts: High school and youth trends.* Washington, DC: Department of Health and Human Services. Retrieved December 4, 2004, from http://www.drugabuse.gov/Infofax/HSYouth trends.html

National Institutes of Health. (2000). *Depression in children and adolescents.* Washington, DC: Department of Health and Human Services. Retrieved July 10, 2004, from http://www.nimh.nih.gov/publicat/depchildresfact.cfm. 2000

National Organization on Fetal Alcohol Syndrome. (2004). *What are the statistics and facts about FAS and FASD?* Washington, DC: Author. Retrieved December 4, 2004, from http://www.nofas.org/faqs.aspx?ID=1

National Reading Panel (2000). *Teaching children to read: An evidence-based assessment of the scientific research literature on reading and its implications for reading instruction.* Washington, DC: National Institute of Child Health and Human Development.

National Spinal Cord Injury Association. (2004). *Factsheet on spinal cord injury.* Bethesda, MD: Author. Retrieved March 9, 2004, from http://www.spinalcord.org/html/factsheets/spinstat.php

Nazzal, A. (2002). Peer tutoring and at-risk students: An exploratory study. *Action in Teacher Education, 24,* 68–80.

Neace, W. P., Munoz, M. A., Weber, J., & Johnson, K. (2002, November). *Evaluating a safety net for at-risk students: Impact of research-based interventions on non-cognitive and cognitive measures.* Paper presented at the Annual Meeting of the American Evaluation Association, Washington, DC. (ERIC Document Reproduction Service No. Ed476379)

Neal, L. V. I., McCray, A. D., Webb-Johnson, G., & Bridgest, S. T. (2003). The effects of African American movement styles on teachers' perceptions and reactions. *Journal of Special Education, 37,* 49–57.

Nelson, J. R. (1996). Designing schools to meet the needs of students who exhibit disruptive behavior. *Journal of Emotional and Behavioral Disorders, 4,* 147–161.

Nelson, J. R., Martella, R. M., & Marchand-Martella, N. (2002). Maximizing student learning: The effects of a comprehensive school-based program for preventing problem behaviors. *Journal of Emotional and Behavioral Disorders, 10,* 136–148.

Nelson, J. S., Epstein, M. H., Bursuck, W. D., Jayanthi, M., & Sawyer, V. (1998). The preferences of middle school students for homework adaptations made by general education teachers. *Learning Disabilities: Research and Practice, 13,* 109–117.

Nelson, J. S., Jayanthi, M., Epstein, M. H., & Bursuck, W. D. (2000). Student preferences for adaptations in classroom testing. *Remedial and Special Education, 21,* 41–52.

Nelson, L. G. L., Summers, J. A., & Turnbull, A. P. (2004). Boundaries in family-professional relationships: Implications for special education. *Remedial and Special Education, 25,* 153–166.

Newcomer, L. L., & Lewis, T. J. (2004). Functional behavioral assessment: An investigation of assessment reliability and effectiveness of function-based interventions. *Journal of Emotional and Behavioral Disorders, 12,* 168–181.

Newcorn, J. H., (2001). Symptom profiles in children with ADHD: Effects of co-morbidity and gender. *Journal of the American Academy of Child and Adolescent Psychiatry, 40,* 137–146.

Nieto, S. M. (2002/2003). Profoundly multicultural questions. *Educational Leadership, 60*(4), 6–10.

Noguera, P. A. (2002). Beyond size: The challenge of high school reform. *Educational Leadership, 59*(5), 60–63.

Nolet, V., & McLaughlin, M. J. (2000). *Accessing the general curriculum: Including students with disabilities in standards-based reform.* Thousand Oaks, CA: Corwin.

O'Connor, R. (2000). Increasing the intensity of intervention in kindergarten and first grade. *Learning Disabilities: Research and Practice, 15*: 43–54.

Oakes, J., & Lipton, M. (2003). *Teaching to change the world.* Boston: McGraw-Hill.

Oakland, T., Black, J. L., Stanford, G., Nussbaum, N. L., & Balise, R. R. (1998). An evaluation of the dyslexia training program: A multisensory method for promoting reading in students with reading disabilities. *Journal of Learning Disabilities, 31,* 140–147.

Obiakor, F. E., Utley, C. A., Smith, R., & Harris-Obiakor, P. (2002). The comprehensive support model for culturally diverse exceptional learners: Intervention in an age of change. *Intervention in School and Clinic, 38,* 14–27.

Ogle, D. M. (1986). K. W. L.: A teaching model that develops active reading of expository text. *Reading Teacher, 39,* 565.

Ohtake, T. (2004). Meaningful inclusion of all students in team sports. *Teaching Exceptional Children, 37*(2), 22–27.

Okolo, C. M. (1993). Computers and individuals with mild disabilities. In J. Lindsey (Ed.), *Computers and exceptional individuals* (pp. 111–141). Austin, TX: PRO-ED.

Okolo, C. M. (2000). Features of effective instructional software. In J. Lindsey (Ed.), *Technology and exceptional individuals* (3rd ed.). Austin, TX: PRO-ED.

Olmeda, R. E., & Trent, S. C. (2003). Social skills training research with minority students with learning disabilities [Electronic version]. *Learning Disabilities, 12*(1), 23–33.

Olson, J. L., & Platt, J. C. (2004). *Teaching children and adolescents with special needs* (4th ed). Upper Saddle River, NJ: Merrill/Prentice Hall.

Operation Sickle Cell. (2001). *Sickle cell disease.* Retrieved November 4, 2004, from http://www.sicklecellnc.org/disease.php

Orfield, G., & Lee, C. (2004). *Brown at 50: King's dream or Plessy's nightmare?* Cambridge, MA: Harvard Civil Rights Project. Retrieved December 5, 2004, from http://www.civilrightsproject.harvard.edu/research/reseg04/brown50.pdf

Organ, J., & Gonzalez-DeHass, A. (2004). How to infuse social skills training into literacy instruction. *Teaching Exceptional Children, 36*(6), 24–31.

Ormsbee, C. K. (2001). Effective pre-assessment team procedures: Making the process work for teachers and students. *Intervention in School and Clinic, 36,* 146–153.

Ornstein, A. C., & Lasley, T. J. II. (2004). *Strategies for effective teaching* (4th ed). New York, NY: McGraw-Hill.

Overton, T. (2003). *Assessing learners with special needs: An applied approach* (4th ed.). Upper Saddle River, NJ: Merrill/Prentice Hall.

Overton, T., Fielding, C., & Simonsson, M. (2004). Decision making in determining eligibility of culturally and linguistically diverse learners: Reasons given by assessment personnel. *Journal of Learning Disabilities, 37,* 319–330.

Paese, P. C. (2003). Impact of professional development schools: Preservice through induction. *Action in Teacher Education, 25,* 83–88.

Pagliaro, C. (2001). Addressing deaf culture in the classroom. *Kappa Delta Pi Record, 37,* 173–178.

Paine, S. C., Radicchi, J., Rosellini, L. C., Deutchman, L., & Darch, C. B. (1983). *Structuring your classroom for academic success.* Champaign, IL: Research Press.

Palincsar, A., & Brown, A. (1988). Teaching and practicing thinking skills to promote comprehension in the context of group problem solving. *Remedial and Special Education, 9*(1), 53–59.

Panacek, L. J., & Dunlap, G. (2003). The social lives of children with emotional and behavioral disorders in self-contained classrooms: A descriptive analysis. *Exceptional Children, 69,* 333–348.

Parette, H. P., Hourcade, J. J., & Huer, M. B. (2003). Using assistive technology focus groups with families across cultures. *Education and Training in Developmental Disabilities, 38,* 429–440.

Paris, S. G., & Winograd, P. (2003). *The role of self-regulated learning in contextual teaching: Principles and practices for teacher preparation.* Washington, DC: Office of Educational Research and Improvement. (ERIC Document Reproduction Service No. ED479905)

Parrish, T. (2000). *Disparities in the identification, funding, and provision of special education.* Paper presented at the conference of the Civil Rights Project on Minority Issues in Special Education, Cambridge, MA.

Patton, J. R. (1994). Practical recommendations for using homework with students with disabilities. *Journal of Learning Disabilities, 27,* 570–578.

Patton, J. R., Payne, J. S., & Beirne-Smith, M. (1986). *Mental retardation* (2nd ed.). Columbus, OH: Merrill.

Pavri, S., & Monda-Amaya, L. (2001). Social support in inclusive schools: Student and teacher perspectives. *Exceptional Children, 67,* 391–411.

Pearson, P. D., & Fielding, L. (1991). Comprehension instruction. In R. Barr, M. L. Kamil, P. Mosenthal, & P. D. Pearson (Eds.), *Handbook of reading research* (Vol. 2, pp. 815–860). White Plains, NY: Longman.

Peck-Peterson, S. M., Derby, K. M., Berg, W. K., & Horner, R. H. (2002). Collaboration with families in the functional behavior assessment of and intervention for severe behavior problems [Electronic version]. *Education and Treatment of Children, 25,* 5–25.

Pedrotty-Bryant, D., Bryant, B. R., & Raskind, M. H. (1998). Using assistive technology to enhance the skills of students with learning disabilities. *Intervention in School and Clinic, 34,* 53–58.

Péladeau N., Forget, J., & Gagné, F. (2003). Effect of paced and unpaced practice on skill application and retention: how much is enough? *American Educational Research Journal, 40*(3), 769–801.

Penfriend. [Computer software]. (2003). Moulton Park, Northampton, UK: Crick Software.

Pertsch, C. F. (1936). *A comparative study of the progress of subnormal pupils in the grades and in special classes.* New York: Teacher's College, Columbia University, Bureau of Publications.

Peterson, R. L., & Ishii-Jordan, S. (Eds.). (1994). *Multicultural issues in the education of students with behavior disorders.* Cambridge, MA: Brookline Books.

Piercy, M., Wilton, K., & Townsend, M. (2002). Promoting social acceptance of young children with moderate-severe intellectual disabilities using cooperative-learning techniques [Electronic version]. *American Journal on Mental Retardation, 107,* 352–360.

Pisha, B., & Coyne, P. (2001). Smart from the start: The promise of universal design for learning. *Remedial and special education, 22*(4), 197–203.

Pivik, J., McComas, J., & Laflamme, M. (2002). Barriers and facilitators to inclusive education. *Exceptional Children, 69,* 97–108.

Pogrund, R. L., & Fazzi, D. L. (Eds.). (2002). *Early focus: Working with young blind and visually impaired children and their families* (2nd ed.). New York: American Foundation for the Blind.

Pollard-Durodola, S. (2003). Wesley Elementary: A beacon of hope for at-risk students [Electronic version]. *Education and Urban Society, 36,* 94–117.

Polloway, E. A., Bursuck, W. D., & Epstein, M. H. (2001). Homework for students with learning disabilities: The challenge of home-school communication. *Reading and Writing Quarterly, 17*(3), 181–187.

Polloway, E. A., Bursuck, W. D., Jayanthi, M., Epstein, M. H., & Nelson, J. S. (1996). Treatment acceptability: Determining appropriate interventions within inclusive classrooms. *Intervention in School and Clinic, 31,* 133–144.

Polloway, E. A., Epstein, M. H., Bursuck, W. D., Jayanthi, M., & Cumblad, C. (1994). Homework practices of general education teachers. *Journal of Learning Disabilities, 27,* 100–109.

Popham, W. J. (2004). "Teaching to the test": An expression to eliminate. *Educational Leadership, 62*(3), 82–83.

Popham, W. J. (2004). A game without winners. *Educational Leadership, 62*(3), 46–50.

Popp, P. A., Stronge, J. H., & Hindman, J. L. (2003). *Students on the move: Reaching and teaching highly mobile children and youth* (Urban Diversity Series). Washington, DC: National Center for Homeless Education and ERIC Clearinghouse on Urban Education. (ERIC Document Reproduction Service No. ED482661)

Poston, D., & Turnbull, A. (2004). Role of spirituality and religion in family quality of life for families of children with disabilities. *Education and Training in Developmental Disabilities, 39,* 95–108.

Poteet, J. A., Choate, J. S., & Stewart, S. C. (1993). Performance assessment and special education: Practices and prospects. *Focus on Exceptional Children, 26*(1), 1–20.

Praisner, C. L. (2003). Attitudes of elementary school principals toward the inclusion of students with disabilities. *Exceptional Children, 69,* 135–145.

Pressley, M. (2000). What should comprehension instruction be the instruction of? In M. Kamil, P. B. Mosenthal, P. D. Pearson, & R. Barr (Eds.), *Handbook of Reading Research* (Vol. 3). Mahwah, NJ: Erlbaum.

Pugach, M. C., & Johnson, L. J. (2002). *Collaborative practitioners, collaborative schools* (2nd ed.). Denver, CO: Love.

Rafferty, Y., Piscitelli, V., & Beottcher, C. (2003). The impact of inclusion on language development and social competence among preschoolers with disabilities. *Exceptional Children, 69,* 467–480.

Ramsey, W. L., Gabriel, L. A., McGuirk, J. F., Phillips, C. R., & Watenpaugh, T. R. (1983). *General science.* New York: Holt, Rinehart, and Winston.

Raphael, T. E., Kirschner, B. W., & Englert, C. S. (1986). *Text structure instruction within process writing classrooms: A manual for instruction* (Occasional Paper No. 104). East Lansing: Michigan State University, Institute for Research on Teaching.

Rappaport, J. (1982/1983). Effects of dietary substances in children. *Journal of Psychiatric Research, 17,* 187–191.

Rea, P. J., McLaughlin, V. L., & Walther-Thomas, C. (2002). Outcomes for students with learning disabilities in inclusive and pullout programs. *Exceptional Children, 68,* 203–224.

Readence, J. E., Moore, D. W., & Rickelman, R. (2000). *Prereading activities for content-area reading and learning* (3rd ed.). Newark, DE: International Reading Association.

Reetz, L., & Rasmussen, T. (1988). Arithmetic mind joggers. *Academic Therapy, 24*(1), 79–82.

Reid, R. (1996). Research in self-monitoring with students with learning disabilities: The present, the prospects, the pitfalls. *Journal of Learning Disabilities, 29,* 317–331.

Reid, R. (1999), Attention deficit hyperactivity disorder: Effective methods for the classroom. *Focus on Exceptional Children, 32,* 1-19.

Reid, R., & Nelson, J. R. (2002). The utility, acceptability, and practicality of functional behavioral assessment for students with high-incidence problem behaviors. *Remedial and Special Education, 23,* 15–23.

Reimers, T. M., Wacker, D. P., & Koeppl, G. (1987). Acceptability of behavioral interventions: A review of the literature. *School Psychology Review, 16,* 212–227.

Reis, S. M., & Renzulli, J. S. (2004). Curriculum compacting: A systematic procedure for modifying the curriculum for above average ability students. Storrs, CT: National Research Center on the Gifted and Talented. Retrieved April 1, 2004 from http://www.sp.uconn.edu/~nrcgt/sem/semart08.html.

Renzaglia, A., Karvonen, M., Drasgow, E., & Stoxen, C. C. (2003). Promoting a lifetime of inclusion [Electronic version]. *Focus on Autism and Other Developmental Disabilities, 18,* 140–149.

Renzulli, J. S., & Park, S. (2002). *Giftedness and high school dropouts: Personal, family, and school-related factors* (Research Monograph Series). Storrs, CT: National Research Center on the Gifted and Talented. (ERIC Document Reproduction Service No. 480177)

Renzulli, J. S., & Reis, S. M. (2002). What is schoolwide enrichment? How gifted programs relate to total school improvement [electronic version]. *Gifted Child Today, 25,* 18-25, 64.

Reyes, M. L., & Molner, L. A. (1991). Instructional strategies for second-language learners in the content areas. *Journal of Reading, 35,* 96–103.

Richardson, B. G., & Shupe, M. J. (2003). The importance of teacher self-awareness in working with students with emotional and behavioral disorders. *Teaching Exceptional Children, 36*(2), 8–13.

Richardson, L., & Hines, M. T. (Eds.). (2002). *Equity in education: A balancing act.* Orangeburg: South Carolina State University. (ERIC Document Reproduction Service No. ED476548)

Riggs, C. G. (2004). To teachers: What paraeducators want you to know. *Teaching Exceptional Children, 36*(5), 8–13.

Robinson, B. L., & Lieberman, L. J. (2004). Effects of visual impairment, gender, and age on self-determination. *Journal of Visual Impairment and Blindness, 98,* 315–366.

Robinson, D. H., Katayama, A. D., DuBois, N. F., & DeVaney, T. (1998). Interactive effects of graphic organizers and delayed review in concept acquisition. *Journal of Experimental Education, 67,* 17–31.

Roblyer, M. D. (2004). *2004 Update: Integrating education technology into teaching* (3rd ed). Upper Saddle River, NJ: Merrill/Prentice-Hall.

Rodgers-Rhyme, A., & Volpiansky, P. (1991). *PARTNERS in problem solving staff development program: Participant guide.* Madison: Wisconsin Department of Public Instruction.

Roeber, E. D. (2002, November). *Appropriate inclusion of students with disabilities in state accountability systems.* Retrieved August 3, 2004, from Education Commission of the States website: http://www.ecs.org/clearinghouse/40/11/4011.htm

Rogers-Adkinson, D. L., Ochoa, T. A., & Delgado, B. (2003). Developing cross-cultural competence: Serving families of children with significant developmental needs [Electronic version]. *Focus on Autism and Other Developmental Disabilities, 19,* 4–8.

Rose, L. C., & Gallup, A. M. (2004). The 36th annual Phi Delta Kappa/Gallup Poll of the public's attitudes toward the public schools. *Phi Delta Kappan, 86,* 41–56.

Rose, R. (2001). Primary school teacher perceptions of the conditions required to include pupils with special educational needs [Electronic version]. *Educational Review, 53,* 147–156.

Rosenshine, B., & Meister, C. (1992). The use of scaffolds for teaching higher-level cognitive strategies. *Educational Leadership, 49,* 26–33.

Rosenshine, B., & Stevens, R. (1986). Teaching functions. In M. C. Wittrock (Ed.), *Handbook of research on teaching* (pp. 376–391). New York: Macmillan.

Ross, R., & Kurtz, R. (1993). Making manipulatives work: A strategy for success. *Arithmetic Teacher, 40*(5), 254–257.

Rothstein, L. L. F. (1995). *Special education law* (2nd ed.). New York: Longman.

Rowland, A. S., Umbach, D. M., Stallone, L., Naftel, A. J., Bohlig, E. M., & Sandler, D. P. (2002). Prevalence of medication treatment for attention deficit-hyperactivity disorder among elementary school children in Johnston County, North Carolina [Electronic version]. *American Journal of Public Health, 92,* 231-234.

Rubinson, F. (2002). Lessons learned from implementing problem-solving teams in urban high schools. *Journal of Educational and Psychological Consultation, 13,* 185–217.

Rudd, F. (2002). *Grasping the promise of inclusion.* (ERIC Document Reproduction Service No. ED471855)

Ruddell, R. B. (2006). *Teaching children to read and write: Becoming an effective literacy teacher* (4th ed.). Boston: Allyn and Bacon.

Ryan, A. L., Halsey, H. N., & Matthews, W. J. (2003). Using functional assessment to promote desirable student behavior in schools. *Teaching Exceptional Children, 35*(5), 8–15.

Ryan, J. B., Reid, R., & Epstein, M. H. (2004). Peer-mediated intervention studies on academic achievement for students with EBD: A review. *Remedial and Special Education, 25,* 330–341.

Ryndak, D. L., & Alper, S. (2003). *Curriculum and instruction for students with significant disabilities in inclusive settings* (2nd ed.). Boston: Allyn and Bacon.

Sabornie, E. J., & deBettencourt, L. U. (2004). *Teaching students with mild and high-incidence disabilities at the secondary level* (2nd ed.). Upper Saddle River, NJ: Pearson/Merrill Prentice Hall.

Sacks, S. Z., & Silberman, R. K. (2000). Social skills. In A. J. Koenig & M. C. Holbrook (Eds.), *Foundations of education: Vol. 2. Instructional strategies for teaching children and youths with visual impairments* (2nd ed., pp. 616–652). New York: AFB Press.

Safran, S. P., & Oswald, K. (2003). Positive behavior supports: Can schools reshape disciplinary practices? *Exceptional Children, 69,* 361–373.

Sale, P., & Carey, D. M. (1995). The sociometric status of students with disabilities in a full-inclusion school. *Exceptional Children, 62,* 6–19.

Salend, S. J. (1999). Facilitating friendships among diverse students. *Intervention in School and Clinic, 35,* 9–15.

Salend, S. J., & Duhaney, L. M. G. (2002). What do families have to say about inclusion? How to pay attention and get results. *Teaching Exceptional Children, 35*(1), 62–66.

Salend, S. J., & Duhaney, L. M. G., (2002). Grading students in inclusive settings. *Teaching Exceptional Children, 34*(3), 8–15.

Salend, S. J., & Rohena, E. (2003). Students with attention deficit disorders: an overview. *Intervention in School and Clinic, 38,* 259-266.

Salend, S. J., & Taylor, L. S. (2002). Cultural perspectives: Missing pieces in the functional assessment process. *Intervention in School and Clinic, 38,* 104–112.

Salend, S. J., Dorney, J. A., & Mazo, M. (1997). The roles of bilingual special educators in creating inclusive classrooms. *Remedial and Special Education, 18,* 54–64.

Salend, S. J., Duhaney, D., Anderson, D. J., & Gottschalk, C. (2004). Using the internet to improve homework communication and completion. *Teaching Exceptional Children, 36*(3), 64–74.

Salend, S. J., Gordon, J., & Lopez-Vona, K. (2002). Evaluating cooperative teaching teams [Electronic version]. *Intervention in School and Clinic, 37,* 195–200.

Salisbury, C. L., & McGregor, G. (2002). The administrative climate and context of inclusive elementary schools. *Exceptional Children, 68,* 259–274.

Salisbury, C. L., & Palombaro, M. M. (1998). Friends and acquaintances: Evolving relationships in an inclusive elementary school. In L. H. Meyer, H. S. Park, M. Grenot-Scheyer, I. S. Schwartz, & B. Harry (Eds.), *Making friends: The influences of culture and development* (pp. 81–104). Baltimore: Paul H. Brookes.

Sall, N., & Mar, H. H. (1999). In the community of a classroom: Inclusive education of a student with deaf-blindness [Electronic version]. *Journal of Visual Impairment and Blindness, 93,* 197–210.

Salvia, J., & Ysseldyke, J. E.. (2004). *Assessment in special and inclusive education.* (9th ed.). Boston: Houghton Mifflin.

Sánchez, S. Y. (1999). Learning from the stories of culturally and linguistically diverse families and communities. *Remedial and Special Education, 20,* 351–359.

Sanders, M. F., & Harvey, A. (2002). Beyond the school walls: A case study of principal leadership for school-community collaboration [Electronic version]. *Teachers College Record, 104,* 1345–1368.

Sands, S., & Buchholz, E. S. (1997). The underutilization of computers to assist in the remediation of dyslexia. *International Journal of Instructional Media, 24,* 153–175.

Scanlon, D., & Mellard, D. F. (2002). Academic and participation profiles of school-age dropouts with and without disabilities. *Exceptional Children, 68,* 239–258.

Scheerenberger, R. C. (1983). *A history of mental retardation.* Baltimore: Paul H. Brookes.

Scheuermann, B., & Webber, J. (2002). *Autism: Teaching does make a difference.* Stamford, CT: Wadsworth.

Schifini, A. (1994). Language, literacy, and content instruction: Strategies for teachers. In K. Spangenberg-Unbschat & R. Pritchard (Eds.), *Kids come in all languages: Reading instruction for ESL students* (pp. 158–179). Newark, DE: International Reading Association.

Schloss, P. J., & Smith, M. A. (1994). *Applied behavior analysis in the classroom.* Boston: Allyn and Bacon.

Schmitz, M. F., & Velez, M. (2003). Latino cultural differences in maternal assessments of attention deficit/hyperactivity symptoms in children [Electronic version]. *Hispanic Journal of Behavior Sciences, 25*(1), 110–122.

Schoen, S. F., & Nolen, J. (2004). Action research: Decreasing acting-out behavior and increasing learning. *Teaching Exceptional Children, 37*(1), 26–31.

Schuler, P. (2002). Gifted kids at risk: Who's listening? New York: Advocacy for Gifted and Talented Education in New York. Retrieved March 3, 2004 from http://washougalhicap.virtualave.net/gifted.htm.

Schulte, A. C. (2002). Moving from abstract to concrete descriptions of good schools for children with disabilities. *Journal of Educational & Psychological Consultation, 13*, 393–402.

Schulte, A. C., & Osborne, S. S. (2003). When assumptive worlds collide: A review of definitions of collaboration in consultation. *Journal of Educational and Psychological Consultation, 14*, 109–137.

Schumaker, J. B., Deshler, D. D., & Denton, P. (1984). *The learning strategies curriculum: The paraphrasing strategy.* Lawrence: University of Kansas.

Schunk, D. (1989). Self-efficacy and cognitive achievement: Implications for students with learning disabilities. *Journal of Learning Disabilities, 22*, 14–22.

Schwartz, W. (Ed.). (2001). School practices for equitable discipline of African American students (ERIC Digest No. 166). New York: ERIC Clearinghouse on Urban Education. (ERIC Document Reproduction Service No. ED455343)

Scott, P. B., & Raborn, D. T. (1996). Realizing the gifts of diversity among students with learning disabilities. *LD Forum, 21*(2), 10–18.

Scott, T. M., McIntyre, J., Liaupsin, C., Nelson, C. M., & Conroy, M. (2004). An examination of functional behavior assessment in public school settings: Collaborative teams, experts, and methodology. *Behavioral Disorders, 29*, 384–395.

Scott, T. M., Nelson, C. M., & Liaupsin, C. J. (2001). Effective instruction: The forgotten component in preventing school violence. *Education and Treatment of children, 24*, 309–322.

Seferian, R. (1999). *Design and implementation of a social-skills program for middle school students with learning and behavioral disabilities.* (ERIC Document Reproduction Service No. ED436863)

Shapiro, D. R., & Sayers, L. K. (2003). Who does what on the interdisciplinary team regarding physical education for students with disabilities? *Teaching Exceptional Children, 35*(6), 32–38.

Sharan, S., Kussell, P., Hertz-Lazarowitz, R., Bejarano, Y., Raviv, S., & Sharan, Y. (1984). *Cooperative learning in the classroom: Research in desegregated schools.* Hillsdale, NJ: Lawrence Erlbaum.

Shaywitz, S. (2003). *Overcoming dyslexia: A new and complete science-based program for reading problems at any level.* NY: Knopf.

Sheets, R. H. (2002). "You're just a kid that's there"—Chicano perception of disciplinary events [Electronic version]. *Journal of Latinos and Education, 1*, 105–122.

Shepard, M. P., & Mahon, M. M. (2002). Family considerations. In L. L. Hayman, M. M. Mahon, & J. R. Turner (Eds.), *Chronic illness in children: An evidence-based approach* (pp. 143–170). New York: Springer.

Shin, J., Deno, S. L., & Espin, C. (2000). Technical adequacy of the maze task for curriculum-based measurement of reading growth. *Journal of Special Education, 34*, 164–172.

Shinn, M. R., Collins, V. L., & Gallagher, S. (1998). Curriculum-based measurement and problem solving assessment. In M. R. Shinn (Ed.), *Advanced applications of curriculum-based measurement* (pp. 143–174). New York: Guilford Press.

Shinn, M. R.., Bamonoto, S., Cornachione, C., Parker, C., Peterson, K., Thurber, R., & Whalen, A. (1997). *Curriculum-based measurement and problem-solving assessment: Training modules* (5th ed.). Eugene: University of Oregon.

Shippen, M. E., Simpson, R. G., & Crites, S. A. (2003). A practical guide to functional behavioral assessment. *Teaching Exceptional Children, 35*(5), 36–44.

Short, D., & Echevarria, J. (2004/2005). Teacher skills to support English language learners. *Educational Leadership, 62*(4), 8–13.

Siegal, L. S. (1989). IQ is irrelevant to the definition of learning disabilities. *Journal of Learning Disabilities, 22*, 469–486.

Sigafoos, J., & Littlewood, R. (1999). Communication intervention on the playground: A case study on teaching requesting to a young child with autism. *International Journal of Disability, Development, and Education, 46*, 421–429.

Silva, M., Munk, D. D., & Bursuck, W. D. (in press). Grading adaptation for students with disabilities. *Intervention in School and Clinic.*

Silver, L. (1998). *The misunderstood child: Understanding and coping with your child's learning disabilities* (3rd ed.). New York: Times Books.

Simpson, R. L., & Myles, B. S. (1998). Aggression among children and youth who have Asperger's syndrome: A different population requiring different strategies [Electronic version]. *Preventing School Failure, 42*, 149–1153.

Skiba, R. J., Michael, R. S., Nardo, A. B., & Peterson, R. L. (2002). The color of discipline: Sources of racial and gender disproportionality in school punishment [Electronic version]. *Urban Review, 34*, 317–342.

Skiba, R., & Peterson, R. (2003). Teaching the social curriculum: School discipline as instruction. *Preventing School Failure, 47*(2), 66–73.

Slavin, R. E. (1994). *Cooperative learning* (2nd ed.). Boston: Allyn and Bacon.

Slavin, R. E. (1999). Comprehensive approaches to cooperative learning [Electronic version]. *Theory into Practice, 38*, 74–79.

Slonski-Fowler, K. E., & Truscott, S. D. (2004). General education teachers' perceptions of the prereferral intervention team process. *Journal of Educational and Psychological Consultation, 15*, 1–39.

Smalley, S. Y., & Reyes-Blanes, M. E. (2001, March). *Lessons learned: Effective strategies for partnering with rural African-American parents.* Paper presented at Growing Partnerships for Rural Special Education conference, San Diego, CA. (ERIC Document Reproduction Service No. ED453029)

Smith, C. R. (2004). *Learning disabilities: The interaction of students and their environments* (5th ed). Boston, MA: Allyn and Bacon.

Smith, K., & Weitz, M. (2003). Problem solving and gifted education: A differentiated fifth-grade fantasy unit [Electronic version]. *Gifted Child Today, 26*(3), 56–60.

Smith, S., Boone, R., & Higgins, K. (1998). Expanding the writing process to the web. *Teaching Exceptional Children, 30*(5), 22–26.

Smith, T. E. C. (2001). Section 504, the ADA, and public schools: What educators need to know. *Remedial and Special Education, 22,* 335–343.

Smith, T. E. C. (2002). Section 504: What teachers need to know. *Intervention in School and Clinic, 37,* 259–266.

Smith-Arrezzo, W. M. (2003). Diversity in children's literature: Not just a black and white issue [Electronic version]. *Children's Literature in Education, 34,* 75–94.

Snider, V. E. (1997). Transfer of decoding skills to a literature basal. *Learning Disabilities Research and Practice, 12*(1), 54–62.

Snow, C. E., & Biancarosa, G. (2003). *Adolescent literacy and the achievement gap: What do we know about where do we go from here.* New York: Carnegie Corporation of New York.

Snow, C. E., Burns, M. S., & Griffin, P. C. (1998). *Preventing reading difficulties in young children.* Washington, DC: National Academy Press.

Sparks, D., & Sparks, G. M. (1984). Effective teaching for higher achievement. *Educational Leadership, 49*(7).

Sparks, S. (2000). Classroom and curriculum accommodations for Native American students. *Intervention in School and Clinic, 35,* 259–263.

Speigel, G. L., Cutler, S. K., & Yetter, C. E. (1996). What every teacher should know about epilepsy. *Intervention in School and Clinic, 32,* 34–38.

Spencer, V. G., & Balboni, G. (2003). Can students with mental retardation teach their peers? *Education and Training in Mental Retardation and Developmental Disabilities, 38,* 32–61.

Sprague, J. R., & Horner, R. H. (1990). Easy does it: Preventing challenging behaviors. *Teaching Exceptional Children, 23*(1), 13–15.

Stainback, S., & Stainback, W. (1988). Educating students with severe disabilities in regular classes. *Teaching Exceptional Children, 21*(1), 16–19.

Stanovich, K., & Siegel, L. S. (1994). Phenotypic performance profile of children with reading disabilities: A regression-based test of the phonological-core variable-difference model. *Journal of Educational Psychology, 86,* 24–53.

Stanovich, P. J., & Jordan, A. (2002). Preparing general educators to teach in inclusive classrooms: Some food for thought [Electronic version]. *Teacher Education, 37,* 173–185.

Staton, J., Shuy, R. W., Kreeft-Peyton, J. K., & Reed, L. (1988). *Dialogue jour-nal communication: Classroom, linguistic, social, and cognitive views.* Norwood, NJ: Ablex.

Stein, M., Silbert, J., & Carnine, D. (1997). *Designing effective mathematics instruction: A direct instruction approach* (3rd ed.). Columbus, OH: Merrill.

Stevens, R. J. (2003). Student team reading and writing: A cooperative learning approach to middle school literacy instruction [Electronic version]. *Educational Research and Evaluation: An International Journal on Theory and Practice, 9,* 137–160.

Strang, J. D., & Rourke, B. P. (1985). Arithmetic disability subtypes: The neuropsychological significance of specific arithmetical impairment in childhood. In B. P. Rourke (Ed.), *Neuropsychology of learning disabilities* (pp. 167–182). New York: Guilford Press.

Straus, M. A. (2001). New evidence for the benefits of never spanking [Electronic version]. *Society, 38*(6), 52–60.

Stronge, J. H. (2002). *Qualities of effective teachers.* Alexandria, VA: Association of Supervision and Curriculum Development.

Substance Abuse and Mental Health Services Administration. (1999). *1998 national household survey on drug abuse.* Washington, DC: U.S. Department of Health and Human Services. Retrieved August 18, 1999, from http://www.samhsa.gov/NHSDA.htm

Sugai, G., Lewis-Palmer, T., & Hagan, S. (1998). Using functional assessments to develop behavior support plans. *Preventing School Failure, 43,* 6–13.

Sutherland, K. S., Wehby, J. H., & Copeland, S. R. (2000). Effect of varying rates of behavior-specific praise on the on-task behavior of students with EBD. *Journal of Emotional and Behavioral Disorders, 8,* 2–8.

Swaggart, B. L. (1998). Implementing a cognitive behavior management program [Electronic version]. *Intervention in School and Clinic, 33,* 235–238.

Swain, K. D., Friehe, M. M., & Harrington, J. M. (2004). Teaching listening strategies in the inclusive classroom. *Intervention in School and Clinic, 40,* 48–54.

Swanson, H. L. (2000). What instruction words for students with learning disabilities? Summarizing the results from a meta-analysis of intervention studies. In R. Gersten, E. Schiller, & S. Vaughn (Eds.), *Contemporary special education research: Syntheses of the knowledge based on critical instructional issues.* Mahwah, NJ: Lawrence Erlbaum Associates.

Swanson, H. L., & Deshler, D. (2003). Instructing adolescents with learning disabilities: Converting a meta-analysis to practice. *Journal of Learning Disabilities, 36,* 124–135.

Swanson, M. (2002). National survey on the state governance of K-12 gifted and talented education: Summary report. Retrieved February 27, 2004 from http://www.edrs.com/members/sp.cfm?AN=ED471886.

Taber, T. A., Alberto, P. A., Hughes, M., & Seltzer, A. (2002). A strategy for students with moderate disabilities when lost in the community [Electronic version]. *Journal of the Association for Persons with Severe Handicaps (JASH), 27,* 141–152.

Taunt, H. M., & Hastings, R. P. (2002). Positive impact of children with developmental disabilities on their families: A preliminary study. *Education and Training in Mental Retardation and Developmental Disabilities, 37,* 410–420.

Taylor, A. S., Peterson, C. A., McMurray-Schwartz, P., & Guillou, T. S. (2002). Social skills interventions: Not just for children with special needs [Electronic version]. *Young Exceptional Children, 5*(4), 19–26.

Taylor, R. L., Richards, S. B., Goldstein, P. A., & Schilit, J. (1997). Teacher perceptions of inclusive settings. *Teaching Exceptional Children, 29*(3), 50–54.

Terman, L. (1925). *Genetic studies of genius: Vol. 1. Mental and physical traits of 1000 gifted children.* Stanford, CA: Stanford University Press.

Terrill, M. C., Scruggs, T. E., & Mastropieri, M. A. (2004). SAT vocabulary instruction for high school students with learning disabilities. *Intervention in School and Clinic, 39,* 288–294.

Test, D. W., Mason, C., Hughes, C., Konrad, M., Neale, M., & Wood, W. M. (2004). Student involvement in individualized education program meetings. *Exceptional Children, 70,* 391–412.

Thompson, S., & Thurlow, M. (2003). *2003 state special education outcomes: Marching on.* Minneapolis, MN: University of Minnesota, National Center on Educational Outcomes. Retrieved January 31, 2005, from http://education.umn.edu/NCEO/OnlinePubs/2003StateReport.htm./

Thurlow, M. L., Elliott, J. L., & Ysseldyke, J. F. (1998). *Testing students with disabilities: Practical strategies for complying with district and state require-*

ments. Thousand Oaks, CA: Corwin Press.

Tindal, G. A., & Marston, D. B. (1990). *Classroom-based assessment: Evaluating instructional outcomes.* Columbus, OH: Merrill.

Tindal, G., Mcdonald, M., Tedesco, M., Glasgow, A., Almond, P., Crawford, L., & Hollenbeck, K. (2003). Alternate assessments in reading and math: Development and validation for students with significant disabilities. *Exceptional Children, 69,* 481–494.

Todd, L. P., & Curti, M. (1982). *Rise of the American nation.* Orlando, FL: Harcourt Brace Jovanovich.

Tomlinson, C. A. (2000). Reconcilable differences? Standards-based teaching and differentiation. *Educational Leadership, 58*(1), 6–11.

Tomlinson, C. A. (2001). *How to differentiate instruction in mixed-ability classrooms* (2nd ed.). Alexandria, VA: Association for Supervision and Curriculum Development.

Toney, L. P., Kelley, M. L., & Lanclos, N. F. (2003). Self- and parental monitoring of homework in adolescents: Comparative effects on parents' perceptions of homework behavior problems [Electronic version]. *Child and Family Behavior Therapy, 25,* 35–51.

Torgesen, J. (1991). Learning disabilities: Historical and conceptual issues. In B. Wong (Ed.), *Learning about learning disabilities* (pp. 3–39). San Diego, CA: Academic Press.

Torgesen, J. K. (2000). Increasing the intensity of interventions in reading: The lingering problem of treatment resisters. *Learning Disabilities: Research and Practice, 15*(1), 55–64.

Tournaki, N. (2003). The differential effects of teaching addition through strategy instruction versus drill and practice to students with and without learning disabilities. *Journal of Learning Disabilities, 36,* 449–458.

Tournaki, N., & Criscitiello, E. (2003). Using peer tutoring as a successful part of behavior management. *Teaching Exceptional Children, 36*(2), 22–29.

Townsend, B. L. (2000). The disproportionate discipline of African American learners: Reducing school suspensions and expulsions. *Exceptional Children, 66,* 381–391.

Trautman, M. L. (2004). Preparing and managing paraprofessionals. *Intervention in School and Clinic, 39,* 131–138.

Troia, G. A., Graham, S., & Harris, K. R. (1999). Teaching students with learning disabilities to mindfully plan with writing. *Exceptional Children, 65,* 235–252.

Tucker, J. A. (1985). Curriculum-based assessment: An introduction. *Exceptional Children, 52,* 199–204.

Turnbull, A. P., & Turnbull, H. R. (1997). *Families, professionals and exceptionality: A special partnership* (3rd ed.). Upper Saddle River, NJ: Merrill.

Turnbull, A. P., Blue-Banning, M., & Pereira, L. (2000). Successful friendships of Hispanic children and youth with disabilities: An exploratory study. *Mental Retardation, 38,* 138–153.

Turnbull, A. P., Pereira, L., & Blue-Banning, M. J. (2000). Teachers as friendship facilitators. *Teaching Exceptional Children, 32*(5), 66–70.

Turnbull, H. R., Turnbull, A. P., Wehmeyer, M. L., & Park, J. (2003). A quality of life framework for special education outcomes. *Remedial and Special Education, 24,* 67–74.

U.S. Department of Education. (1999). *21st annual report to Congress on the implementation of the Individual with Disabilities Education Act.* Washington, DC: Author.

U.S. Department of Education. (2004). PBIS goals. Retrieved December 19, 2004, from The U.S. Office of Special Education Programs, National Technical Assistance Center on Positive Behavioral Interventions and Supports (PBIS) website: http://www.pbis.org.

U.S. Department of Health and Human Services. (2000). *Youth violence: A report of the surgeon general.* Washington, DC: Author. Retrieved December 20, 2004, from http://www.surgeongeneral.gov/library/youthviolence/report.html

Uberti, H. Z., Mastropieri, M. A., & Scruggs, T. E. (2004). Check it off: Individualizing a math algorithm for students with disabilities via self-monitoring checklists. *Intervention in School and Clinic, 39,* 269–275.

Uberti, H. Z., Scruggs, T. E., & Mastropieri, M. A. (2003). Keywords make the difference! Mnemonic instruction in inclusive classrooms. *Teaching Exceptional Children, 35*(3), 56–61.

Ulrich, M. E., & Bauer, A. M. (2003). Levels of awareness: A closer look at communication between parents and professionals. *Teaching Exceptional Children, 35*(6), 20–25.

United Cerebral Palsy (n.d.). *Cerebral palsy—facts and figures.* Retrieved November 26, 2004 from http://www.ucp.org/ucp_generaldoc.cfm/1/9/37/37-37/447

Vacca, R. T., & Vacca, J. L. (2004). *Content area reading: Literacy and learning across the curriculum* (8th ed.). Boston: Little, Brown.

Vallecorsa, A. L., deBettencourt, L. U., & Zigmond, N. (2000). *Students with mild disabilities in general education settings: A guide for special educators.* Upper Saddle River, NJ: Prentice-Hall.

Vandercook, T., York, J., & Forest, M. (1989). The McGill Action Planning System (MAPS): A strategy for building the vision. *Journal of the Association for Persons with Severe Handicaps (JASH), 14*(3), 205–218.

VanTassel-Baska, J. (2003). *Curriculum planning and instructional design for gifted learners.* Denver, CO: Love.

Vaughan, W. (2002). Effects of cooperative learning on achievement and attitudes among students of color. *Journal of Educational Research, 95,* 359–364.

Vaughn, S., Gersten, R., & Chard, D. J. (2000). The underlying message in LD intervention research: Findings from research syntheses. *Exceptional Children, 67,* 99–114.

Vaughn, S., Linan-Thompson, S., & Hickman, P. (2003). Response to instruction as a means of identifying students with reading/learning disabilities. *Exceptional Children, 69,* 391–409.

Vaughn, S., Linan-Thompson, S., Kouzekanani, K., Bryant, D. P., Dickson, S., & Blozis, S. A. (2003). Reading instruction grouping for students with reading difficulties. *Remedial and Special education, 24,* 301–315.

Voix, R. G. (1968). *Evaluating reading and study skills in the secondary classroom: A guide for content teachers.* Newark, DE: International Reading Association.

Wagner, M., Cadwallader, T. W., Garza, N., & Cameto, R. (2004, March). *Social activities of youth with disabilities* (NLTS2 Data Brief). Retrieved November 20, 2004, from http://www.ncset.org

Walker, J. E., Shea, T. M., & Bauer, A. M. (2003). *Behavior management: A practical approach for educators* (8th ed.). Columbus, OH: Merrill/Prentice Hall.

Wallace, T., Anderson, A. R., & Bartholomay, T. (2002). Collaboration: An element associated with the success of four inclusive high schools. *Journal of Educational and Psychological Consultation, 13,* 349–382.

Wang, M. C., Reynolds, M. C., & Walberg, H. J. (1988). Integrating the children of the second system. *Phi Delta Kappan, 70,* 248–251.

Ward, M. J., Montague, N., & Linton, T. H. (2003). *Including students with disabilities and achieving accountability: Educators' emerging challenge.* (ERIC Document Reproduction Service No. ED481111)

Watson, S. (2004). Open the science doorway: Strategies and suggestions for incorporating English language learners in the science classroom. *Science Teacher, 71*(2), 32–35.

Wehmeyer, M. (2002). *Self-determination and the education of students with disabilities* (ERIC Digest). Reston, VA: ERIC Clearinghouse on Disabilities and Gifted Education. (ERIC Documentation Reproduction Service No. ED470036)

Wehmeyer, M. L., Lattin, D. L., Lapp-Rincker, G., & Agran, M. (2003). Access to the general curriculum of middle school students with mental retardation: An observational study. *Remedial and Special Education, 24,* 262–272.

Wehmeyer, M. L., Yeager, D., Bolding, N., Agran, M., & Hughes, C. (2003). The effects of self-regulation strategies on goal attainment for students with developmental disabilities in general education classrooms. *Journal of Developmental and Physical Disabilities, 15,* 79–91.

Weiss, M. P., & Lloyd, J. (2003). Conditions for co-teaching: Lessons from a case study. *Teacher Education and Special Education, 26,* 27–41.

Weiss, M. P., & Lloyd, J. W. (2002). Congruence between roles and actions of secondary special educators in co-taught and special education settings. *Journal of Special Education, 36,* 58–68.

Welch, A. B. (2000). Responding to student concerns about fairness. *Teaching Exceptional Children, 33*(2), 36–40.

Welch, M., Brownell, K., & Sheridan, S. M. (1999). What's the score and game plan on teaming in schools? A review of the literature on team teaching and school based problem solving. *Remedial and Special Education, 20,* 36–49.

Wells, K. C. et al., (2000). Psychosocial treatment strategies in the MTA study: Rationale, methods, and critical issues in design and implementation. *Journal of Abnormal Child Psychology, 28,* 483–505.

Welton, E., Vakil, S., & Carasea, C. (2004). Strategies for increasing positive social interactions in children with autism: A case study. *Teaching Exceptional Children, 37*(1), 40–46.

Wenz-Gross, M., & Siperstein, G. N. (1998). Students with learning problems at risk in middle school: Stress, social support, and adjustment. *Exceptional Children, 65,* 91–100.

Whalen, C. K., Jamner, L. D., Henker, B., Delfino, R. J., & Lozano, J. (2002). The ADHD spectrum and everyday life: Experience sampling of moods, activities, smoking, and drinking. *Child Development, 73,* 209–227.

Wheeler, J. J., & Richey, D. D. (2005). *Behavior management: Principles and practices of positive behavior supports.* Upper Saddle River, NJ: Merrill/Prentice Hall.

Wilen, W. W., Ishler, M., Hutchinson, J., & Kindsvatter, R. (1999). *Dynamics of effective teaching* (4th ed.). Boston: Allyn and Bacon.

Williams, G. J., & Reisberg, L. (2003). Successful inclusion: Teaching social skills through curriculum integration. *Intervention in School and Clinic, 38,* 205–210.

Wilson, L. M., & Corpus, D. A. (2001). What research says: The effects of reward systems on academic performance [Electronic version]. *Middle School Journal, 33*(1), 56–60.

Winzer, M. A. (1993). *The history of special education: From isolation to integration.* Washington, DC: Gallaudet University Press.

Witzel, B. S., & Mercer, C. D. (2003). Using rewards to teach students with disabilities: Implications for motivation. *Remedial and Special Education, 24,* 88–96.

Woerz, M., & Maples, W. C. (1997). Test-retest reliability of colored filter testing. *Journal of Learning Disabilities, 30*(2), 214–221.

Wolf, P. S., & Hall, T. E. (2003). Making inclusion a reality for students with severe disabilities. *Teaching Exceptional Children, 35*(4), 56–61.

Wolfgang, C. H. (2001). The many views of "time-out": Teaching strategies [Electronic version]. *Journal of Early Education and Family Review, 8*(5), 18–28.

Wood, J. W., Miederhoff, J. W., & Ulschmid, B. (1989). Adapting test construction for mainstreamed social studies students. *Social Education, 53*(1), 46–49.

Wood, M. (1998). Whose job is it anyway? Educational roles in inclusion. *Exceptional Children, 64,* 181–196.

Yarger, C. C. (2001). Educational interpreting: Understanding the rural experience. *American Annals of the Deaf, 146,* 16–30.

Yates, G. C. R. (1999). Applying learning style research in the classroom: Some cautions and the way ahead. In R. Riding & S. Rayner (Eds.), *New directions in learning and cognitive style* (pp. 347–364). Stamford, CT: JAI Press.

Yell, M. L. (1990). The use of corporal punishment, suspension, expulsion, and timeout with behaviorally disordered students in public schools: Legal considerations. *Behavioral Disorders, 15,* 100–109.

Yell, M. L. (1998). *The law and special education.* Upper Saddle River, NJ: Merrill/Prentice Hall.

Yell, M. L., & Shriner, J. G. (1997). The IDEA amendments of 1997: Implications for special and general education teachers, administrators, and teacher trainers. *Focus on Exceptional Children, 30*(1), 1–19.

Yell, M. L., Rogers, D., & Rogers, E. L. (1998). The legal history of special education: What a long, strange trip it's been! *Remedial and Special Education, 19,* 219–228.

Yell, M., Clyde, K., & Puyallup, S. K. (1995). School district: The courts, inclusion, and students with behavioral disorders. *Behavioral Disorders, 20,* 179–189.

Youse, K. M., Le, K. N., Cannizzaro, M. S., & Coelho, C. A. (2002, June). Traumatic brain injury: A primer for professionals. *ASHA Leader Online.* Retrieved February 20, 2005, from http://www.asha.org/about/publications/leader-online/archives/2002/q2/020625a.htm

Ysseldyke, J., Algozzine, B., & Thurlow, M. L. (2000). *Critical issues in special education* (3rd ed.). Boston: Houghton Mifflin.

Zhang, C., & Bennett, T. (2003). Facilitating the meaningful participation of culturally and linguistically diverse families in the IFSP and IEP process [Electronic version]. *Focus on Autism and Other Developmental Disabilities, 18,* 51–59.

Zhang, D., & Katsiyannis, A. (2002). Minority representation in special education: A persistent challenge. *Remedial and Special Education, 23,* 180–187.

Zigmond, M. (2003). Where should students with disabilities receive special education services? Is one place better than another? *Journal of Special Education, 37,* 193–199.

Zimmerman, J. A., & Grier, H. (2003). *School restructuring: Fitting the pieces together.* (ERIC Document Reproduction Service No. ED482351)

Name Index

Subject Index

Photo Credits